M000288153

Oxford Socio-Legal Studies

Law as a Social System

OXFORD SOCIO-LEGAL STUDIES

Oxford Socio-Legal Studies is a series of books exploring the role of law in society for both an academic and a wider readership. The series publishes theoretical and empirically informed work, from the United Kingdom and elsewhere, by social scientists and lawyers which advances understanding of the social reality of law and legal processes.

LAW AS A SOCIAL SYSTEM

NIKLAS LUHMANN

Translated by Klaus A. Ziegert

Edited by Fatima Kastner, Richard Nobles,
David Schiff, and Rosamund Ziegert

With an Introduction by:
Richard Nobles and David Schiff

OXFORD
UNIVERSITY PRESS

OXFORD

UNIVERSITY PRESS

Great Clarendon Street, Oxford OX2 6DP

Oxford University Press is a department of the University of Oxford.
It furthers the University's objective of excellence in research, scholarship,
and education by publishing worldwide in

Oxford New York

Auckland   Cape Town Dar es Salaam   Hong Kong   Karachi
Kuala Lumpur Madrid Melbourne Mexico City   Nairobi
New Delhi Shanghai Taipei Toronto
With offices in
Argentina Austria Brazil Chile Czech Republic France Greece
Guatemala Hungary Italy Japan South Korea Poland Portugal
Singapore Switzerland Thailand Turkey Ukraine Vietnam

ISBN 978-0-19-954612-1

Printed in the United Kingdom by
Lightning Source UK Ltd., Milton Keynes

General Editor's Introduction

The late Niklas Luhmann is widely regarded as one of the most significant social theorists of recent years. Luhmann's work is concerned with the development of a general theory of modern society treated as a communication system, comprising a number of functionally specialized, self-referential, and self-reproducing sub-systems. Law is one such sub-system, and each chapter in *Law as a Social System* applies the theory to themes relating to law and the legal system, many of which have long been among the central concerns of legal philosophers.

A great deal of care has been lavished on the preparation of this English-language version of Luhmann's book. With few exceptions, Luhmann's writings have not been well served by his translators. The present volume, however, benefits from a translation by one of his former pupils. Professor Klaus Ziegert of the University of Sydney, not only studied with Luhmann but is also a distinguished sociologist of law in his own right, as well as an accomplished linguist. Ziegert's translation of *Law as a Social System* has been carefully edited, and two of the editors, Richard Nobles and David Schiff of the London School of Economics, have added an extremely helpful introduction.

Keith Hawkins
Oxford, January 2004

Preface

The following text can be read, as far as its subject matter is concerned, as a text in the sociology of law—in both a broader and a narrower sense. Its context is a theory of society rather than of any particular special sociology, one that provides a marker for the characterization of sociological associations or of individual academic disciplines. Nobody would deny the importance of law in society. Thus, a theory of society needs to occupy itself with society's law. This applies to the most intricate refinements of judicial semantics as well as to each decision made in law—even when they refer only to the diameter of apples or the ingredients of different kinds of beer which can be sold—because even the most detailed legal propositions happen to emerge in society and society alone. Nothing can be too esoteric or too strange to be excluded from consideration within the domain of sociological relevance. Only sociological theory can decide what is included and what excluded.

Of course, this may mean different things to different people. Since what follows refers to society as a comprehensive system, which includes everything social, this also implies a certain limitation when compared to the approach of a theory of institutions, of social action, or of the sociology of professions. Such a limitation does not necessarily mean that concepts derived from other sources are not relevant; however, how they are relevant, how allocated, is the task of a theory of society. Concepts (such as operative closure, function, coding/programming, functional differentiation, structural coupling, self-concept, evolution, etc.) have been chosen in such a way as to be just as applicable in other functional areas of modern society, not only law. (How successful this approach will be remains to be seen.) If such a holistic attempt to apply abstract terms to widely different subject areas such as politics, religion, science, education, economy, and, of course, law were to succeed, then there would be reason to assume that the consistency demonstrated is not purely coincidental, but indicative of specific characteristics of modern society. This would show precisely that such findings (consistent characteristics) could not be deduced from any particular functional area, from the 'spirit of law' or any other 'spirit', but from society itself.

With this approach to the evidence, the ensuing observations in this book try to understand legal communication as a part of society in operation. It always assumes, even when not explicitly stated, that there are two systems to be referred to: the legal system and the social system (society). With this approach, this study follows in the footsteps of my studies on the economy and on science, which have already been published.[1] Other publications of this kind are planned.

---

[1] See Niklas Luhmann, *Die Wirtschaft der Gesellschaft* (Frankfurt, 1990); *Die Wissenschaft der Gesellschaft* (Frankfurt, 1990).

My work on the subject of the legal system has a long history. Originally this study was designed as a parallel publication to my book on the sociology of law with its evolutionary theory approach, which had assumed certain systems theory aspects, without being able to include them fully.[2] Since then, my visits to the Northwestern University Law School in Chicago and the Yeshiva University, Cardozo Law School have provided me with the opportunity to familiarize myself with common law reasoning. I am grateful to my American colleagues for their support. I have benefited from their critiques offered at conferences and seminars. The arguments presented in this study have also been influenced by other critical writings on the as yet incomplete concept of an 'autopoiesis' of law.[3] I hope that here I have managed to resolve the misunderstandings of this concept, which have occurred far too hastily. It goes without saying that every theory with a distinct approach invites well-reasoned rejections. However, in considering these one should recall a distinctive feature of Jewish legal interpretation: that it is important to adjust dissent to an appropriate level, and to preserve it as tradition.

Niklas Luhmann
Bielefeld, June 1993

[2] See Niklas Luhmann, *Rechtssoziologie*, 1972, 2nd edn. (Opladen, 1983); English translation: *A Sociological Theory of Law* (London, 1985).

[3] See, above all, Gunther Teubner (ed.), *Autopoietic Law: A New Approach to Law and Society* (Berlin, 1988), and 13 *Cardozo Law Review* 5 (1992).

Acknowledgements

The publication of this English translation of Niklas Luhmann's *Das Recht der Gesellschaft* (first published in Germany by Suhrkamp Verlag Frankfurt am Main, 1993) would not have been possible without generous financial support from Inter Nationes, the Modern Law Review, and the Holcombe Academic Translation Trust.

The following individuals have given considerable help to this project: Taslima Ahmed, David Goldman, Michael King, Tim Murphy, and Gunther Teubner.

Contents

Introduction

Richard Nobles and David Schiff

Introducing the introduction

This book needs to be accessible to an English-speaking audience. It is a profound work of increasing significance in the twenty-first century. It presents what is probably the most important, original, and complete statement made about law in the second half of the twentieth century by a social theorist, a statement about the autopoiesis of law. It may well be the most complete statement since the one made at the beginning of that century by one of the founders of modern sociology, Weber, or perhaps the gradual reinterpretation during the twentieth century of Marx's socio-economic analysis and its application to law by Pashukanis, Renner, Althusser, and Poulantzas.

The key question in this book is central to legal theory: what differentiates law from other parts of society? However, unlike conventional legal theory this book seeks to provide an answer in terms of a general social theory, that of modern systems theory, which provides a methodology that answers this question in a manner that is applicable not only to law, but to all other subsystems (Luhmann principally refers to these as function systems) in society, such as politics, the economy, religion, media, and education. This is a truly sociological approach, and one that offers a rigorous application to law of a theory that can be used to describe and analyse all of the complex and highly differentiated systems within contemporary societies. In modern systems theory, society performs through its communications. These are its empirical reality, what can be observed and studied. Such observation and study requires a theory appropriate to the task. Systems theory identifies how communications operate within a physical world and how different subsystems of communication operate alongside each other. Utilizing systems theory Luhmann is able to offer an authoritative statement of sociology of law (but by no means a final statement of the autopoiesis of law).

Luhmann's offering is not an easy read. To achieve its aims it needs to clarify its own terminology and concepts with precision and deal with the many variables that sometimes cloud and sometimes refine our understanding of the phenomena that are the focus of the description. Further, in doing this Luhmann engages in responding to a number of the critics of his theory, which requires further elaboration and exposition. But, once the ingredients of the analysis are understood, it is possible to engage in its refinements and find in them an extraordinary depth of meaning, as well as detailed and wide-ranging historical and comparative references.

This book needs to be available to be read in English by academics and future academics who wish to pursue research into law in modern societies, or more particularly for Luhmann, law as a social system. Our current understanding of law as it operates in society is, according to the analysis presented in this book, seriously deficient. Using the tools of analysis presented here a wealth of opportunities arise for the researcher to improve that understanding and advance our current knowledge about our contemporary world and the role played by law in it.

The introduction that you are about to read has as its primary aim the task of introducing what Luhmann has written in this landmark book (which, with the series of books starting with 'Social System' in 1984, can be described as Luhamnn's magnum opus[1]), but does so by breaking out from what Luhmann has written in order to allow the reader to enter into it. The text of the book is a thorough analysis in its own terms, but the uninitiated reader needs considerable help with those terms, in a number of ways. The help that is being offered here is in the form of road maps to each of the chapters that develop Luhmann's description of law, his sociology of law, his account of law's autopoiesis. Each chapter is part of his description. Some chapters are more complex than others, some more controversial. All are developed using the tools of analysis that Luhmann sets out in the early chapters, and in particular in Chapter 2. Some of the road maps are longer than others, as we feel is necessary to enable the reader to go on and engage with what Luhmann has actually written. As the road maps develop the arguments they gradually introduce Luhmann's systems theory, the terms in which he develops that theory, and the subject matter to which, with a focus on law, it can be applied. So, the later road maps are able to take more for granted; in other words, they can use more of Luhmann's discourse, his communications as representing his description. We hope that, by the end of reading the road maps, the reader will have become sufficiently acquainted with not only the rubrics of the theory but also the terms in which the theory can be developed and applied.

Before beginning this road map exercise, however, two words of warning are necessary. A first and simple warning refers to the current use of the language of road maps and its association with an idea of progress (e.g. road maps to peace), an idea thoroughly refuted in the course of Luhmann's analysis. Equally, these road maps do not lead anywhere, they are not

---

[1] The introduction to this series appeared in 1984 entitled *Soziale Systeme*. Since then, the following studies have appeared: *Die Wirtschaft der Gesellschaft* (1988, The Economy as a Social System); *Die Wissenschaft der Gesellschaft* (1990, Science as a Social System); *Das Recht der Gesellschaft* (1993, Law as a Social System); *Die Kunst der Gesellschaft* (1995, Art as a Social System); *Die Gesellschaft der Gesellschaft* (1997, Society as a Social System); *Die Politik der Gesellschaft* (2000, Politics as a Social System). Suhrkamp Verlag, Frankfurt am Main, published all the books in this series.

progressive, but rather represent the discontinuities between Luhmann's text and its translation. That is the beginning of the second, more complicated warning. This book is a translation of Luhmann's *Das Recht der Gesellschaft*, published in 1993. It cannot do justice to the original work, by definition, according to the theory it presents. Luhmann's description is already one step removed from its subject, law, it represents his external observations on that subject, trying to use the communications available in general social communication, but more particularly having selected those communications that operate as scientific, or at least, as part of sociological observation of the empirical reality of its subject. There is no adequate meta-language, a language of all languages, to translate all the nuances of individual languages, to allow for this translation to be a straightforward replication of what Luhmann wrote. Furthermore, communications do not stand still, which makes some of the projections described by Luhmann, particularly in the last chapter, beyond simple translation. We can only observe what he has written and, not with his scientific task in mind, but an alternative function, that of enabling understanding, an educational function, re-present his ideas. That is what we attempt in these road maps, as, in its different form, is what is being attempted in the translation written by Klaus Ziegert, as edited by Fatima Kastner, Rosamund Ziegert, and ourselves.

We repeat: this book needs to be translated in order that it will be accessible to an English-speaking audience. But the overall task involved may be, according to the theory Luhmann presents, contingent and involve the invisibilization of a paradox, which make both the translation and our introduction to it both his text and not his text at the same time, both one form of his text and its other form. To translate, or introduce, is to attempt do what the text itself is doing and can only do, namely carry out its performance. Nevertheless our considered view is that it is worth re-performing. On the other hand, we must admit that nothing in the theory itself would permit such an evaluative judgement (that this exercise is worthwhile) to be made.

Chapter 1. The Location of Legal Theory

In the first chapter Luhmann identifies how systems theory, which in a modern version Luhmann develops, relates to pre-existing forms of legal theory. The latter take two forms. The earliest kinds of legal theory seek to make sense of legal practice. Theories about legal doctrine, principles, etc., are a response to the necessity for consistency in the processing (retrieval and re-use) of legal decisions. These theories serve both legal practice and legal education. In the latter sphere, there can be greater abstraction (legal philosophy), but the focus on legal practice, and the need to make statements that can be used in legal practice (if only to reform it) restricts the ability of legal theory, even within education, to develop far beyond the self-understandings of practising lawyers. Within the last three decades, there have been attempts, using a variety of perspectives, to take things 'further'. This second kind of legal theory has adopted a wide range of approaches, including hermeneutics, theories of institutions, systems theory, and theories of rhetoric and argumentation.

These two kinds of legal theory are not completely separate from each other. Despite attempts by the second kind of legal theory to be more scientific, the distinctions used in this legal theory are different from those of science. Science distinguishes between facts and concepts, the latter being used to organize and understand the former. Legal theory maintains its contact with law using the distinction between fact and norm. This ties legal theory to law's understanding of itself, as there is no source for the normative character of laws outside of law itself: 'everything, which is available using the title of legal theory, has been produced in conjunction with self-descriptions of the legal system' (page 60).

For Luhmann, a *strictly* scientific form of legal theory would take as its function that of constituting its object. The question that best serves this function is: 'what are the boundaries of law?' Existing legal theories adopt different approaches to this task, often talking past each other. Subjective approaches to the problem lead to a situation in which every observer identifies their own object. To avoid this, Luhmann starts from the assumption that the object (law) and not the observer define the boundaries of law. Starting with this assumption, the next question is: 'how does law proceed in determining its own boundaries?' Luhmann argues that systems theory is the theory best placed to answer this question.

Luhmann makes a number of claims for the superiority of systems theory in this context. First, the central distinction and concepts of the theory goes directly to the question. The theory's central distinction is system and environment, and one of its central concepts is that of the observing system: observing how systems use self-produced observations. Secondly, no other currently available theory can deal as adequately with the issue of complexity. Attempts to define law's environment as 'society' both ignore law's existence within society, and provide inadequate means to analyse the numerous and highly differentiated contexts in which law has to establish its borders. (In the chapter the most developed example given of an inadequate rival theory is economic analysis of law, which not only seeks to reduce all legal decisions to calculations of utility, but also assumes that all of the activity surrounding the law is economic in nature.) Only a theory that can analyse how all systems construct their own borders from their own self-observations (rather than a theory that only has regard to the manner in which one system such as law or the economy undertakes this task) can hope to integrate the 'poly-contextual contexts' that need to be organized. Thirdly, alternative sociological theories of law seek to distance themselves from the juristic views that constitute conventional legal theory, and adopt an external view of law. In seeking a more scientific basis for the observation of law, such as empirical research, such theories lose sight of the question that establishes law as an object: how does law establish its own boundaries? The self-descriptions of lawyers, how lawyers understand their own activity, are an essential part of what needs to be described.

The superiority of systems theory is linked to developments within society. Law has responded to society's increasing complexity. Luhmann gives the particular example of legal evidence, which has changed from formal proofs to assessments of internal states: intentions, motives, etc. These changes threaten to undermine the function of law (see Chapter 3), which is to produce expectations. Expectations here are not a matter of causality (what will happen) but the ability to make consistent and meaningful communications about what ought to happen. Lawyers have responded to such changes in society by developing their own form of legal theory: doctrine and principles. This form of theorizing insulates law from the corruption of outside influences (like cases can be treated alike), and produces material that is both chaotic and rational. While such theories reduce the element of surprise, allowing what can be expected (what ought to happen) to remain calculable, they are incapable of developing a theory of law as a unity.

Natural law, positivism, and sociological theories have attempted to theorize law's unity. Natural law started by theorizing law as a hierarchy of laws (divine, natural, human) within a society organized through a hierarchy of ranks. With the breakdown of the *ancien régime*, and the emergence of welfare as the basis of political legitimacy, natural law theories were organized around ideas of progress. The central idea became that of civilization, and law was theorized through the concept of the social contract as a mechanism for the domestication of violence. The creation of new knowledge, with the birth of social science, undermined the ability to conceive of society as simply a contract. Positivist theories of law abandoned substantive bases for the unity of law in favour of procedural ones. Ultimately these conceive the unity of law in terms of the rules of legal argumentation, and the distinction between facts and (legal) values: which (rules, principles, standards) are appropriate to determine expectations about any particular constellation of facts?

Each of these theories provides an inadequate basis for understanding the boundaries of law. They offer no appropriate distinction between what is law, and what is not. Natural law conflates injustice with all that is not law. Economic analysis of law (which Luhmann sees as an extension of the welfare focus of social contract theories) reduces all that is not law in society to calculations of costs and benefits. Positivist theories, with their focus on the basis for legal decisions, treat legal decisions as if they decided what constituted the unity of law. This is an error. The unity of law is produced through legal decisions, but legal decisions do not decide the basis of law's unity (its boundaries).

Luhmann claims that the difficulties of distinguishing law can be solved if one succeeds in describing law as an autopoietic, self-distinguishing system. This implies that law produces by itself all the distinctions and concepts that it uses, and the unity of law is nothing but the fact of this self-production. This is law's operative closure. And the development of such closure is a necessary reaction to society's increasing complexity. Law cannot achieve its unity through values located outside it. Its borders cannot be established through ethics, or economics. In order to continue to produce calculable expectations law has to simplify its relationship with its environment to something distinctly less complicated than that environment. At the same time, it has to respond to the complexity of that environment (so, for example, it cannot treat all of its environment as an economic phenomenon). Law achieves this, as do other functional systems, by reproducing its environment internally, through the manipulation of its own concepts and distinctions.

Within systems theory, law's operations, through which it reproduces itself (producing its own structures and boundaries), are meaningful communications. Law has to differentiate itself within society by identifying which communications are legal communications. Although lawyers use some specialist terms, they do not have a separate language. As such, the boundaries of law cannot be studied through the use of linguistic theory. Instead, one needs a theory based on communications theory. Legal communications, like all other communications, have a circular relationship between their structures and operations. Structures can only be established and varied by operations that, in turn, are specified by structures. In studying these communications, one has to use a complex series of distinctions. Within communications theory, these are information/message/understanding. To understand the dynamic relationship between operations and structures, one also needs to utilize distinctions taken from evolutionary theory: variation/selection/restabilization.

Luhmann acknowledges that his theory is complex, but claims that a complex theory is necessary to understand complex matters. He also acknowledges that, whilst his theory seeks to observe and describe the self-understandings of law, it requires a level of interdisciplinary knowledge and abstraction that prevents any claim that it could be used to guide legal practice (except incidentally).

Chapter 2. The Operative Closure of the Legal System

Here Luhmann provides an exposition of some of the most troubling concepts of systems theory and uses them to explain the nature of law's autonomy or autopoiesis. The central concept is operative closure. This is a concept common to all systems, not just law. Law's particular form of operative closure is that of normative closure.

It is helpful to start with what is not operative closure. It does not mean causal independence, which in the case of law would require a legal system that is unaffected by everything from politics to global destruction. The legal system has a causal relationship to geography, morality, money, class, etc. But causal accounts of legal systems have to be secondary to the enterprise undertaken by systems theory: accounting for the boundaries of law. Before we can describe the development of law in terms of, say, politics, we have to establish the separate existence of politics and law: how these systems differentiate themselves from each other. This also applies to action theories. In order to account for events in terms of the orientations of individuals towards law, we presuppose a recognizable object, the law, towards which those individuals can exhibit orientations.

Operative closure is not a concept about causal relationships, but about identity: how systems reproduce themselves. However, certain aspects of causality within modern societies provide a starting point from which to understand the concept. Modern society is complex. All sorts of things are having causal effects on each other, all of the time. While some of this causality can be located in our physical environment, a great deal of it (to say the least) occurs within society. The complexity of such interactions does not allow for different areas of social life to have stable and simple (mechanical) relationships with each other. Responses to what occurs under conditions of complexity inevitably involve a wide range of possibilities, which points in turn to the need to make selections. The question is on what basis can those selections be made? To this complexity we must add the problem of time. Whilst we construct histories, and predict futures, everything exists only in the present. This means that law, politics, and everything else that exists in society exists (reproduces itself) only from moment to moment, from one communication to the next. Put this all together, and we can see that modern society exists as complex differentiated sub-systems, with communications linking each to each other and selections being made from moment to moment. How can this be achieved?

Operational closure is an answer to this question that derives from theories of evolution. To deal with complex causality, organisms have to become closed to their environment. Instead of simple and direct relationships to their environment, organisms develop a limited range of responses and an internal basis for selection. This internal basis for selection provides them with their autonomy, which in turn allows them to develop more complex internal responses to their environment. (A paradigm example is human consciousness, but this was only possible because earlier more simple organisms developed internal complexity.) Applied within systems theory this becomes operational closure. Systems cannot develop complexity without autonomy. And autonomy is achieved when the basis of selection (most importantly the selection of communications that belong to the system) is internal to the system.

All autopoietic systems exhibit operational closure. Their individual operations, which are communications, are identified as such by themselves. Politics may influence the development of law, but it cannot be law (see Chapter 9). Politics operates alongside law, but so do religion, science, and the physical environment. Law may respond to these (its environment), but it can only do so by altering its selections. And the possibilities of selection (what communications can take place within the legal system) are established by the legal system itself.

All systems are operationally closed, but cognitively open. This statement follows quite logically. The operations of any system are those communications recognized by the system as belonging to it. A social system only exists through its communications, and can only respond to its environment by making communications. Because its operations are identified as such by itself, and not by other systems or the physical environment, it can be described as operationally closed. At the same time it is cognitively open. This latter phrase means that the system is capable of responding to its environment. This does not mean that it always responds, but that it is capable of responding. Its openness to its environment may be described as cognitive, for two reasons. First, because it is capable of making limited responses to its environment. The selections internally open to a system will be far less complicated than the infinity of social and physical events that operate in the real world. This limited response, an inevitable simplification of the real world, operates as a form of cognition. Secondly, the openness can be described as cognitive because the system can learn. This means that it may respond to its environment by making communications that alter the possibilities of what will, in future, constitute a communication within that system.

The alternative to operational closure would be operational openness. For example, if one treated political communications, the operations of the political system, simultaneously and identically, as constituting legal communications. The difficulties of this can be seen through the example of legislation. Legislation forms part of the political process: our political system identifies legislation as part of itself. It also forms part of our legal system. But what each recognizes as a communication belonging to itself can only be achieved internally, by each system, for itself. Law will recognize a statute, and will conceptualize the meaning of that statute by reference to interpretative practices which it calls 'the intention of parliament'. These interpretative practices (attributing a holistic meaning to a text, and locating that text alongside other legal texts) are not political communications. By contrast the political system can connect a statute to its own communications in quite different ways. It can be described as the 'will of the people', or the outcome of negotiations between interest groups, or the carrying out of an election promise. These political communications do not dictate, or replicate, the legal communications generated by the statute. In time, law may 'learn'. For example, the intention of parliament may be interpreted to allow courts to entertain arguments based on election manifestos. But this learning only occurs if law alters its communications in such a way as to recognize the manifestos. Only operations of law can provide the necessary act of recognition. And if this recognition occurs, it will still not connect the legal system to all the communications that an election manifesto can connect to within the political system.

Operational closure is common to all systems. What differentiates systems is the different ways in which they achieve operational closure. This is a consequence of their different codes and functions. The codes and function peculiar to law result in a form of operative closure that can be described as normative. The function of law is to maintain normative expectations in the face of disappointment. Law's communications about what ought to occur must, if they are to continue as expectations, remain meaningful despite the inevitability that what ought to occur will not always occur. Law is not alone in making communications about what ought to occur. Morality and religion will contain such communications. Thus function alone is not sufficient to differentiate law. But what is sufficient is that law achieves this function by coding events in its environment using a binary code that is unique to itself: legal/illegal. All its communications make, or are linked to communications that make, this distinction. It can also code its own earlier communications as legal or illegal. It is the combination of function and code, maintaining communications that utilize the binary distinction legal/illegal, which allows law to differentiate itself (maintain its boundaries).

The reason why law's operative closure can be described as normative closure can be seen from the way in which law responds to its environment. Law's environment is both the physical environment, and all other communications (i.e. general social communication, and the communications of all other sub-systems). Law's operations are structured through a norm/fact distinction. Law compares facts with its norms (pre-existing law) and responds to those facts that are identified (selected) by legal norms. Operative closure is achieved because no norms (custom, morals, religion) can in themselves be legal norms. Legal norms can recognize the norms of other systems as facts and respond to them, but only where its own norms have the capacity to recognize those norms as facts. Law can also develop (learn) by developing new legal norms in response to its environment, which environment includes norms from other systems. But this process does not mean that moral norms simply become, or enter into, the legal system, any more than the recognition of election manifestos within statutory interpretation means that political communications have simply become legal ones.

Law's normative closure achieves a form of cognition (cognitive openness) because it simplifies the complexity of its environment. Law does not respond to its entire environment. It responds only to that part of its environment that is selected by its norms. It is therefore possible to say that law identifies its environment, internally, by reference to its existing communications (existing law). It is also possible to say that law recognizes itself, as a system of norms, as something separate from the environment (facts) that it has recognized through its norms. Thus its operative closure not only allows it to maintain its boundaries, but to construct those boundaries internally, by making communications that use a distinction (norm/fact) which constructs both itself as self-reference, and its environment as external reference. The ability to do all this work through internally linked communications (operational closure) is what gives legal systems, within modern society, their autonomy.

All systems code their environment, and all systems stabilize this coding by developing programmes (structures) for the application of the code. But while the code is essential to the continued existence of the system (indeed the present, not the past or the future, momentary operations of coding *are* the system), the content of these programmes is contingent. This claim is the basis of Luhmann's criticism of positivist legal theories. Positivist theories accept the contingency of law's programming in respect to substantive law. Indeed, the rejection of moral constraints on what may constitute a valid law is how legal positivism defines itself in contrast to natural law theories. But positivist legal theories attempt to identify structures which stabilize what can become valid law, e.g. Austin's sovereign, Hart's rule of recognition, and Kelsen's historically first constitution validated by a presupposed basic norm. These theories can be seen as attempts to break out of a paradox generated by the contingency of law's normative programmes. Once we accept that the law can have any substantive content, what establishes what can be law? Do we have to conclude that the law decides what can be law? If we reach this conclusion, we are involved in paradox. How can something decide law, which is at the same time law? How can such a thing be inside (law) and outside (deciding what can be law) at the same time? Positivists look to structures outside law to establish the content of law. Particular kinds of communications are identified as legal because they have some kind of meaningful (logical, rational, semantic, etc.) relationship with a pre-existing structure. Austin relies on the consistent (non-arbitrary) application of political force (by the sovereign). Hart's rule of recognition is a structure that is subtly external to valid law: the rule that establishes what can be a rule of law cannot itself be a rule of law. Hart's rule of recognition is not a rule of the system at all, but an attitude expressed by officials towards what could constitute a rule of the system. Kelsen's source of validity, the basic norm, is outside the legal system in terms of fact, but at the same time also linked to each norm of the system as a presupposed fiction. The stability offered by these structures has been subject to sustained criticism pointing to their circularity: the circularity that Austin's sovereign is identified by law, as are Hart's and Kelsen's pre-existing structures.

Luhmann offers the concept of operational closure as a more scientific basis to positivist (structural) accounts of identity under conditions of contingency. The law does indeed identify the law. Luhmann does not deny the existence of structures, or their stabilizing influences. Normative programmes are structures. However, they are also operations: legal communications. Normative programmes are a particular kind of legal operation: an observation based upon a distinction. The law codes, through its operations, in terms of its binary code, legal/illegal. In turn (never at the same moment) it observes its own coding. This observation, which Luhmann argues is structured by the need to identify what is connected (equal or unequal) with earlier coding, produces normative programmes. The law understands its own earlier coding in terms of its normative programmes. But while these programmes stabilize, their own existence is contingent on their ability to connect legal communications about coding. Thus, unlike positivist theories, there is nothing outside the legal system to produce its validity. Law's conditional programmes (existing law) are produced by itself through self-observation on its previous coding. And there is no hierarchy. Structures do not pre-exist and determine what can be a legal communication, but are stabilizing elements that are formed by, and can be changed by, what is coded legal/illegal. Thus structures, while they stabilize, are also dynamic and capable of change. Structures are constituted by what they stabilize: legal communications coding as legal/illegal. As such, they can be changed by those communications.

While this theory offers an account of the legal system that is dynamic, it is not anarchic. The premiss of operational closure is not that each communication that can be recognized as legal is known with absolute certainty from moment to moment. The theory is premised upon the reduction of complexity: that the range of communications that can be connected to other legal communications at any moment is limited by the need to establish that connection. However, the degree of constraint can be better understood if one concentrates on the need for such connections to be made in the present. Law only exists, throughout society, from moment to moment (i.e. in the present) if the connections between its communications can be established in that moment. Thus, for a highly complex system like law to exist, millions of communications have to be recognized as legal in a moment. From this basis, while the content of all normative programmes is contingent, they cannot all be treated, all of the time, as contingent. Most of the existing law is treated, most of the time, as a structure stabilizing what can connect to it. From this perspective, law's self-observations (its normative programmes) are both stable and contingent. This focus on the enormity of what has to be accomplished for a legal system to exist is also Luhmann's explanation for why systems have binary codes. If every coding involved third values, and communications could only exist in degrees (half legal, etc.), the task of connecting legal communications in order to generate further legal communications would break down.

To stabilize itself, law not only generates self-observation, but self-description. The law can make communications about itself as a unity. Such descriptions can be legal communications, and as such they are real, and not merely ideological. However, what may cause them to be taken as ideological is their inability to account for all of what they attempt to describe: every communication in the legal system. For example, alongside tort doctrine (a normative programme stabilizing the application of legal/illegal within an internally identified area of legal communications) one finds communications about the constitution. Constitutional law doctrine is a self-observation about a hierarchical structure (unchanging law), which stabilizes the process of changing law. Observing these various self-observations leads to the generation of descriptions of the legal system as a system: its values, role, functions, and limitations. These self-descriptions do not provide a way of knowing what can be legal. The possibilities of connection within the legal system only exist through the evolution of that system, and while that system is stabilized by self-observation and self-description, its evolution is determined by the communications made at any moment. Its communications constantly change its structures, which alter the possibilities of what can be connected to it. We can only find the possibilities of connection by looking at how the communications that interest us are made: locally. Focusing on law's operations (legal communications) *in situ* not only gives us a different view of law's self-descriptions, but also widens our understanding of sites of production of legal communications. These are not limited to courts, or even lawyers. They occur whenever communications are made that connect to existing legal communications, i.e. whenever law reproduces operative closure (through applying legal norms to facts—including facts about its own earlier operations).

If law is not held stable by any fundamental idea, or master rule, what is the status of the values that are found within self-descriptions of the law: justice, equality and the rule of law? Within systems theory, values do not enter law from the outside, to stabilize its operations. Rather, they exist internally, generated by the operations of law. The first of these values is validity. Legal validity is not law that has political or moral legitimacy, as would be the case within natural law theory, and in the practices of less differentiated societies where systems have not achieved operational closure. Legal validity is simply the connection of legal communications to other legal communications. Communications that are recognized as legal by the legal system are valid. Those that are not so recognized are not. There is no value or test for validity outside the system itself. And the validity of the system as a whole is nothing more than its existence as a system: the connection of all new legal communications to the system itself.

Equality as a value of the legal system also exists solely through the operations of law. But whereas validity is a value exhibited by every operation of law, every communication of the legal system, equality is a value generated only by self-observation within law. Every coding can be observed to see if the drawing of the distinction legal/illegal has taken place on a basis that is equal or unequal. Equal distinctions have to be justified. Unequal ones do not. The basis for assessing equality is the existing law: the conditional programmes that steer the applications of the binary code. An illustrative question would be: does the application of the code treat the relevant parties equally? The necessity for this to be an internal assessment is contained in the world 'relevant'. The law itself has to construct the basis of comparison. For example, much of the law of labour relations has been generated through reflection upon the rights and duties of employers and employees. But in identifying what is appropriate to a contract of employment, law does not simply accept, from the outside, what political or other systems identify as equality between the parties as they construct them. Thus, whatever politics or ethical systems identify as employers and employees (do family firms and single-employee companies count?), the law identifies these terms within contracts of employment as the parties to the legal contract. And whatever politics or ethics has to say about the appropriate basis for equality, the basis of equality within law is an assessment of legal rights and duties, which is inevitably situated within, and compared with, other existing allocations of rights and duties.

Chapter 3. The Function of Law

Luhmann argues that, from a system differentiation perspective, one has to see what the specific function of law could be. Earlier systems theories that stressed integration (Parsons) are challenged by conflict theories (the critical legal theorists and Marxists). Attempts to articulate function in terms like dispute resolution are not function-specific to law; there are functional equivalents in other systems. One must also be wary of theories that attempt to attribute general functions to law that exceed its performance, only to claim that the distance between these functions and their performance represents some failure of function. Lastly, there is little explanatory power in calling every effect of law one of its functions: is it a function of law to provide lawyers with income?

Luhmann constructs a distinction between function and performance. The function of law is specific, even though its performance in terms of its contribution to such matters as dispute resolution is not. For Luhmann, the sole function for the legal system is the maintenance (stabilization) of expectations despite disappointments (counterfactual examples). It is a normativity of normative expectations. No other system can rival law in this function, which function is not simply a consequence of coercion and the level of enforcement. Luhmann describes this in terms of time binding. This is developed at some length. It is not just the time taken to communicate, or even the fact that all communications are linked between past (communications) and future ones. It is the fact that expectations are generated as communications that link the present with the future—they are future-oriented communications. Expectation here is not a psychological event, but a communication. It is a communication about what is approved, and as time-binding, what will be approved. Such communication covers not only prohibitions, such as criminal law, but also 'artificial freedoms' like contract and property.

The time binding nature of legal communications shares features common to all language. Repeated use of language within society creates meanings that cannot easily be rejected. Such established meanings have social costs (they have effects, including winners and losers). There is also the possibility of dissent (rejecting common meanings), but in the absence of conflict, and even in its presence depending on the difficulties of challenging existing meaning, fixed meanings operate, even if the only sanction is an individual's tendency to perceive different usage as a mistake, and self-correct. Similarly with law. Law's normative form involves expectations as to what will be approved in future. There can be dissent, but in the absence of rival norms, those asserting law's norms have an advantage. Even in the presence of rival norms, the expectations of law are stabilized by forming part of a dense and complex network of expectations that has internal relationships as well as stable relationships between itself and other (function) systems. While norms can be asserted which conflict with legal norms, there is no system of norms that can rival law in its function of stabilizing expectations. This is not because legal norms have a closer relationship to 'human nature' than other norms, but the reverse. Because of law's operative closure, it has developed autonomy from the rest of society, which allows its norms to be more consistent, and therefore stable, than a system of norms based on whatever has been perceived as 'normal', 'natural', or 'ethical'. This has led, through evolution, to complex and stable norms that support the operations of other systems. For example, the corporation is a legal form that supports operations within the economy and politics. Indeed, such is the superiority of contemporary law's ability to maintain consistent and stable norms, that where one desires to stabilize ethical norms, one inserts them into this system, i.e. one jurifidies them.

Luhmann does not claim that law is capable of maintaining stable expectations under any circumstances. He explores the conditions, both internal and external, which allow law to carry out this function. Internally, the ability of law to develop complex and consistent norms requires the system to develop a sub-system for decisions as to what law is (which includes when law is changed). This sub-system is staffed by persons, identified by their membership (the legal profession and the judiciary), whose particular task is to provide consistency to legal expectations (see Chapter 7). As a sub-system it represents one of the important structures that law can generate through its communications. (Though unlike certain legal theories, this structure does not represent all of law, or even exhaust the possibilities of law, both of which reside in the current state of all legal communications.) External factors include the need to manage dissent. Luhmann calls this the social dimension of law, contrasting it with its temporal dimension (the maintenance of meaningful communications of normative expectations). Law's autopoiesis increases the stability of its expectations, but the very autonomy that creates certainty as to what can constitute a legal communication also reduces law's sensitivity to what will provoke dissent. In addition, law's success in meeting expectations is not a legally relevant consideration in deciding what expectations are legal. If it were such, the law could not carry out its function of maintaining expectations in the face of disappointment. Luhmann argues that the management of dissent is largely externalized to the political system. Politics, and sometimes ethics, have to manage dissent created by law.

Luhmann accepts that the ability of law to maintain expectations in the face of disappointment makes enforcement important. However, the complexity and density of legal communications, and the networks that they support, allow law to maintain expectations in the face of considerable degrees of disappointment. For example, the presence of theft will not lead people to learn that they cannot expect to own property. Punishment reaffirms this expectation. And it is not even necessary for punishment to occur in response to each theft. The presence of expectations that captured and convicted thieves will be punished stabilizes expectations represented by the law of theft even if only a few criminals are punished relative to the amount of crime. The minimal situation is that a person must not be a fool for having expectations based on law. When does it become meaningless to say: 'If you take that, you commit theft'? This minimal situation is linked to law's symbolic level. Alongside the specific expectations of law, there is the general expectation that the expectations of law will be met.

This is in turn part of a general understanding that law motivates human behaviour: motivating people to obey law, or to learn from punishment, or to carry out their official duties to punish. These understandings are symbolic, in that there is no clear referent. At what level of disobedience and disappointment would one have to conclude that law's expectations were not being met, and that legal norms could not be understood in some general way to bind time? Law fails to carry out its function only when its expectations cease to be normative. The normativity of expectations lies in the distinction between normative and cognitive. Cognitive expectations are ones where one learns from disappointment: 'it will never rain in July'. Normative expectations are where one does not: 'it is illegal to park on double yellow lines'.

Law's function allows it to contribute to dispute resolution, and regulation, but these are examples of law's performance, and should not be confused with its function. In the case of regulation, there are simply too many equivalent systems for steering human behaviour for it to be claimed that this is law's differentiated function within society. All kinds of activities steer human behaviour, e.g. the design of aisles in supermarkets. Describing law's function as regulation conflates it with all other such activities, and loses its specific contribution based on its function: the production and stabilization of normative expectations. Similarly with dispute resolution. Law's function as a system of normative expectations, and its operative closure whereby it generates those expectations from its current communications, allows us to see how law's performance as dispute resolution differs from the performance of other systems. For example, whereas small groups may undertake dispute resolution as an informed exploration of the possibilities of continuing ongoing relationships, dispute resolution through law takes the form of enforcing or compromising expectations that may bear little relation to those relationships.

Law is not alone in trying to maintain expectations (time binding) in the face of social dimensions generating dissent. The economic system has a function of creating expectations of access to scarce resources in the future by reference to the payment of money. Both law and the economy can be expected to have varying degrees of success in balancing their temporal and social dimensions. Internally, reconciliation can only be an indirect consequence of each system's operations. Reaction will be incremental, in the sense that no single response ends the possibilities of further responses. It will also be crude in that reconfigurations of reflexive communications will not be reproductions or even always be equally compatible with what stimulates them. In the case of law, learning (by changing law's normative expectations) or not learning (by not changing) can be likened to a form of immunization. What law resists by stabilizing expectations is the proliferation of disorganized and inconsistent norms. However, Luhmann questions whether society is about to face problems which cannot be solved through autopoietic systems, problems for which there is no possibility of immunization, where the operations of a system cannot block developments that could destroy them. In particular, he is concerned with the nature of risk under modern conditions, where a 'wrong' decision cannot be corrected by later decisions of the system, and where there may be no system in place at all. Some possibilities arising from this issue are examined more fully in Chapter 12.

Chapter 4. Coding and Programming

Function is not an adequate description of law. Alone it cannot clarify what the legal system uses when it reproduces itself and draws boundaries between itself and its environment. For this, we need the distinction between coding and programming: 'codes enable us to distinguish between belonging to the system and not belonging to the system, while programmes, which attribute the values legal/illegal, are the objects of judgements of valid/invalid' (page 209).

Law codes facts as legal and illegal. Legal is the positive side of the code, and illegal is the negative side. Unlike natural law theories, this does not mean that legal is good, and illegal is bad, or that legal is just and illegal is unjust. Law operates a binary code whose meaning at the moment of coding is solely a distinction: something that is coded illegal has not been coded legal; and something that has been coded legal has not been coded illegal. Coding is essential to any system's reproduction. Binary codes produce bi-stability. The coding produces just two states to which future communications can be linked, in the case of law, that the facts were legal, or illegal. Introducing third values undermines the ability to code, and in turn to link communications to each other in a system.

The application of a system's code is regulated through that system's programming: the conditions, which that system establishes, for when it is appropriate to apply the negative or the positive side of the code. In legal theories these might simply be called the 'rules' of law. As the programmes determine which side of the code is applied, lawyers tend to concentrate on the programmes alone and neglect the code. Yet the link (or distinction) between code and programming is essential. While there are aspects of law's programming that are peculiar to law, the system would not be able to maintain its boundaries without its distinct code. In addition, while the content of law's programming is completely changeable (even those 'constitutional' laws presumed to be unchangeable at particular times have been amended when conditions have changed), its code does not change. As such, it is the code, or rather the continual coding, that reproduces law as a separate sub-system of society.

In order to describe the relationship between programmes and code, Luhmann first explores the logic of binary codes. This is a form from which there can be no appeal to a higher (or meta) value. In isolation, knowing that something has been coded legal tells us nothing except that it has not been coded illegal, and vice versa. (If I told you that an unspecified event, known only as 'X', had been coded legal, what would this tell you?) This situation involves paradox, tautology, and contradiction. The tautology comes from the nature of operative closure: only the law can code events as legal or illegal. The legal is legal. Paradox arises because what is legal is also illegal. This is because legal and illegal exist in unavoidable conjunction. Luhmann gives the example of a dispute between two parties. The state of affairs which gives rise to a dispute is a single state. If we decide that one party wins the dispute (acted legally) and another party loses (acted illegally) we are not applying the code to two different situations but to one: the two sides of the code are always applied simultaneously to the same situation. This paradox leads in turn to contradiction. As there is nothing within the code itself that determines what, within any situation, is assigned to each side of the code, then there is nothing 'to distinguish' what is assigned a positive as opposed to a negative value (and vice versa). As nothing distinguishes that which is coded legal from that which is coded illegal, one is left with a paradox that is also a contradiction: the legal is at the same time illegal, and vice versa.

This description of the logic of law's form as a code sets out the challenge facing law's programmes. These are analysed as mechanisms to unfold and avoid the paradox and contradictions that arise from using a code that has no meaning in itself other than assigning facts to one side or other of a distinction. Remember, there is no value involved in this assignment. Legal is not for the common good, or for health, or for the stabilization of expectations (law's function), or for anything else. And there is nothing that law within a modern functionally differentiated society can do which will inject a third value into the code to enable law to decide what should be coded legal, as opposed to illegal. (Any such third value would undermine the legal system's ability to link its communications, reproduce itself, and establish its boundaries.) And not only can one not resort to a third value to say whether something has been coded legal or illegal appropriately, the logic of a binary code (that it is an opposition without any content beyond that opposition) means that there is no *logical* way of telling that the code has been applied *legally* or not.

Law develops structures (conditional programmes) for application of the code. This involves second-order observation. Secondary observation here is the operation of observing coding. The code can be applied to itself, to say whether the previous coding was valid or invalid. As an operation of coding this has no greater meaning, in itself, than the original coding (so all the elements of paradox, tautology, and contradiction remain within this observation). But the observation offers rationality. Why was the earlier coding appropriate (valid or invalid)? Answers to this question create conditional programmes: 'In the presence of fact X, code Y legal. In the presence of fact Z, code Y illegal.' These programmes also constitute norms: those facts that comply with the system's norms are labelled legal; those facts that violate the system's norms are labelled illegal.

These second-order observations cannot answer the question: what is the distinction between legal and illegal? They cannot address the question of whether the distinction between legal and illegal is itself legal. They can only produce relatively stable applications of the code, allowing law to carry out its function of maintaining stable expectations. These stable applications of the code allow the legal system, in its operations, to avoid paradox and contradiction. Law's programmes determine the application of the distinction legal/illegal. This allows for meaningful communications that something is illegal or legal. Something that law (through its conditional programmes) has identified as legal is not at the same time illegal. At a latter time the conditional programmes may change, or the individual coding may simply be revisited and the coding altered. As such, validity (the appropriateness of a coding) can only be temporary. Nevertheless, the ability of the legal system to code, in the present, what is legal and illegal, by reference to its conditional programmes (which are structures produced by its own operations), gives law its social dimension. Autopoiesis (the legal system's reproduction of itself through its operations) overcomes the lack of any logical (or epistemological) basis for its distinctions.

Law's conditional programmes allow law to be an open system. When observing coding, and articulating programmes that account for it, law can utilize values communicated within any of society's sub-systems (function systems), or within general societal communication. Indeed, because the values form part of programmes working towards a single code, one can have relationships between values that would otherwise be incompatible. While conditional programmes may be constructed by reference to every kind of value communicated within society, they never impose a value that determines, for the system as a whole, what is legal and illegal (not even the value of legality). There are two reasons for this. First, the conditional programmes of law utilize too many values for law to be reduced to any single value. Second, and this is more fundamental, to assume that the values utilized within conditional programming could determine the value of the code is to misunderstand the distinction between programmes and code. No value utilized within a conditional programme to structure coding is applied in the same manner as it exists in the system from which it originates. An example will assist here. Criminal law often uses forensic science. This is necessary to get at the 'truth', which is important to coding behaviour as legal or illegal. But law only wants to use 'truth' to reach the conclusion whether something is legal or illegal. So forensic science will be used within a process constructed by rules of procedure rather than an experimental situation, in order to decide whether an individual committed a particular act, with a view to finding him/her guilty of a crime. This process inevitably means that finding an individual guilty of a crime (so that punishment is legal) does not mean that it is 'true' (according to the meaning of that value within science as a system). And this is not just because the conditions under which science is applied within law are different from science. It is because the code applied by law (this punishment is legal/illegal) is not the code applied by science (this communication is true/false). Another way of putting this is to say that law can borrow the values of other systems, but not their codes. If legal proceedings ended with the coding that something was 'true', rather than 'legal', then its subjects will have ceased to participate within the legal system.

The distinction between coding and programming also has implications for the ability of the legal system to continue reproducing itself through its operations. Coding ('this punishment is legal') provides conditions for further coding ('a parole board may consider releasing this prisoner after X years'). The programme (and the values utilized) to make one coding is not necessary to the next coding (although it may be relevant if *this* coding needs to be reassessed/reobserved). This ability of coding to provide the basis for further coding (and thus link legal communications) is enhanced by the logic of 're-entry' or the application of a form to itself. In the case of a binary code, the re-entry is 'doubled' as the code can be reapplied to either side of the distinction created by an earlier coding. For example, if an ongoing situation is identified as a robbery, the actions of the participants are illegal. This distinction has divided the world into two: what is legal, and what is illegal. But the distinction can be applied again, and to both sides of what was previously distinguished. We can ask whether the arrests of those who acted illegally were legal, or whether the reactions of bystanders were illegal. This means that the coding does not simply result in the linking of communications that code facts as legal. Coding something as illegal is also a basis for making further distinctions as to what is legal and illegal. If one could only attach further legal communications to one side of the code (what is legal) the application of the code would gradually shut down what could be coded. But as we can recode both what is legal and illegal, the whole world remains accessible to the legal system, and vice versa.

Luhmann calls the requirement of an effective coding its *technicalization*. This means that the application of the code to the pre-existing state of facts (including earlier coding) depends on only a few conditions and not on either the sense that the world (other sub-systems and general societal communication) makes of it, nor on the particular characteristics of the subject applying the code. This is not a condition that excludes uncertainty in the application of the code. Technicalization exists when, even without being particularly knowledgeable, one can know and anticipate the conditions under which something being legal or illegal depends in a particular case. (It could be explained to one, even if one would not have known without explanation.) It also allows error-checking. Within a blurred margin of acceptance, it can be established whether an error has been made in the application of the code. And while one has a hierarchy to check errors, the ability for there to be errors, rather than simply different points of view, assumes that, except in particular circumstances, it will not matter which court applies the code.

Luhmann's analysis of conditional programmes as structures that unfold the paradox of law's code leads him to particular insights into law's operations that differ from those reached through other theories.

- While the distinction between legal and illegal can be maintained for individual coding, the system as a unity can never decide the basis of what is legal or illegal. It can never apply the code to itself as a system. There is no foundational value establishing what is legal or illegal, only operations.
- The rigidity and costs of coding legal/illegal can be reduced by delay. Law can delay coding through proceedings. Proceedings allow participation in the system prior to a coding decision. Here delay (the decision cannot be made until the proceedings are completed) is justice. Theories that seek certainty without proceedings ignore the advantages to law that arise from delay.
- Law's programmes are conditional rather than purposive. The need to develop programmes that decide what is legal/illegal, and the need to make further coding based upon earlier coding, restricts the ability to use programmes based on a continuous assessment of the present. Law has to reduce any assessment of circumstances by reference to achieving some future state into its judgment as to whether that assessment was legal or illegal at the time it was made. And the latest when law's judgment can be made is when the code is applied. This considerably reduces the ability to use goal-based instructions as legal programmes.
- Law develops programmes to achieve what in prior periods amounted to a rejection of law. Luhmann uses the example of non-prosecution in situations where prosecution would threaten general law and order. Emergency powers, derogation from constitutional law, theories of abuse of law, all represent the application of law's coding, through its own conditional programmes, to what previously would have represented the suspension of law. The only true rejection of law is a refusal to code, which is actually the application of the code of another system in place of coding through law.

Chapter 5. Justice, a Formula for Contingency

The unfolding of the paradox of law through the operation of law's conditional programmes leads one to a situation in which there is apparently no role for justice. Justice cannot be a third value alongside legal/illegal, for this would prevent the code from being binary, and undermine validity (the connection between legal communications). Nor is justice a conditional programme in itself, for there is no law of justice in the same way in which there is a law of the sea, law for road traffic, etc. Moral imperatives can become incorporated into law, juridified, but this is no different from having conditional programmes that refer to accountancy standards. Does this mean, as legal positivism would lead us to believe, that justice is exiled from law to become a sub-system of ethics or politics?

While justice may form the subject of communications in ethics and politics, it also forms the basis of legal communications. Justice operates at a level above the secondary observation that produces and sustains conditional programmes. It is a self-description, or representation, of the unity of the system to itself. Internally, to the legal system, justice is understood as a value with which the legal system identifies, and is 'canonized'. But while law represents itself as connected to justice, how can it do this, without defining some of its own operations (by reason of their being unjust) as not law? This brings us back to natural law, which cannot operate as the basis for law under modern conditions.

Luhmann argues that we can understand how justice is able to operate within the whole of the legal system without the natural law phenomena of defining part of the legal system as not-law, if justice is treated as a formula for the contingency of the legal system. Contingency here is not the possible facts that may confront a system, but the possible ways of reacting to those facts. In the case of law, all the rules, principles, and doctrines that exist are contingent, in the sense that they could all be different. All structures are operations, and operations can lead to new structures. However, in general, systems manage their operations through structures that stabilize their operations. (Contingency does not make change inevitable on all occasions, since one possibility is always to repeat what was done before.) The legal system, being operationally closed, loses direct contact with the rest of the social system. In order to maintain a responsiveness (irritability) to the rest of the social system, autopoietic systems have to develop internal mechanisms to trigger change in themselves; these include formulae for contingency and, in the case of the legal system, the formula is justice.

As stated above, justice is not a conditional programme. Rather it is a norm directed at all of law's conditional programmes: 'Be just'. As a norm, it gives rise to expectations despite the inevitability of disappointment. As a norm directed to all of law's programmes, it is able to represent (as a self-description) the unity of the legal system. Justice as a formula for contingency is a scheme for the search for reasons or values, which can only become legally valid in the form of programmes.

Most of the chapter is devoted to justice as equality, which is the application of the distinction equal/unequal. This is a form of equality peculiar to law, as it consists not of equal wealth or opportunity (communications about justice that might be expected in the systems of ethics or politics) but of the equal (consistent) treatment of legal cases. At the level of individual programmes the requirement, to treat like cases alike, is synonymous with the operation of the programme: 'in facts X, Y is legal'. This can be applied throughout the system, but it leads to justice being simply the routine operations of the legal system. Justice can be more than the application of the existing law because equality operates not only within the programmes, but between them: 'equality is given by the form in which conditioned relations are related to each other, by the similarities or differences of the 'ifs' in conditional programmes' (page 224). A second order observation (an observation of earlier applications of the distinction legal/illegal) applying the distinction equal/unequal provides a scheme for earlier observations to be revisited, and different decisions to be made. In this way the scheme allows the observers to cross the boundary between determinacy (repeating coding based on existing programmes) and indeterminacy (changing the programmes). It also (see the road map to Chapter 3) provides a scheme for the initial development of conditional programmes from earlier applications of the code.

Justice does not guide the development of the legal system in the manner that advocates of reform might expect. It does not become more just, or realize ever greater levels of equality. The application of the distinction equal/unequal has, like the binary code legal/illegal, no third quality or value that determines what lies on either side. And, like the relationship of the conditional programmes to the code legal/illegal, the content of each side is established by the repeated application of the distinction. The application of the distinction equal/unequal remains closed to the communications about equality within ethics because what lies either side of the distinction is legal decisions. The secondary observation of legal coding (legal/illegal) which both develops and compares legal programmes is first and foremost a search for meaning based on consistency. Law's normative closure will have selected the facts and generated the cases that have to be observed using a scheme of equal/unequal. As such, the applications of the distinction equal/unequal within law will be unique to law. Ethics as a system would not select the same facts for the application of the distinction, and would thus not put the same things on either side of the distinction. This means both that equality within law is not the same thing as equality within ethics and politics, and that law can never 'achieve' justice as equality because there will always be meanings of equality circulating within the systems of politics and ethics that are different from those within law.

Luhmann argues that legislation has resulted in temporal change being accepted (new law can be unequal) and a greater tendency to see justice as a principle with merely an emotional appeal. Another tendency affecting the operation of justice within law is the tendency for social welfare programmes to create purpose-specific programmes in which individual desert (those individuals who bear the particular costs of such programmes) remains problematic. Here, if law attempts to apply justice as equality, one arbitrary decision is likely to be replaced by another. Instead, justice operates its supplementary role, not deciding desert, or trying to reapply the purpose specifications, but stipulating which facts are required to be considered, and which are not suitable as legal measures. Alongside these challenges to justice, there is also the increase in the sheer complexity of law, which increases the difficulties of treating like cases alike.

Justice does not operate only as a scheme based on the distinction equal/unequal. It also operates as the distinction freedom/limitation. (These two distinctions allow human rights to operate as justice inside the legal system.) As with equality and the code legal/illegal, the distinction cannot establish through logic what lies on either side. Only the repeated application of the distinction gives it content. Also, the application of the distinction, as a formula for contingency to the programmes of law, produces a content to the meaning of freedom, as justice, in law, that does not replicate its meaning in other systems.

Chapter 6. The Evolution of Law

Luhmann does not present a new history of law, but seeks to evaluate law's history using evolutionary theory. In so doing, he also wishes to show the connections between law's history, as analysed as through evolutionary theory, and the legal system as an operationally closed system, reproducing itself through its own elements. This requires him to show how law has evolved into a closed system, and the contribution which law, as a closed system, has made to its own evolution. This is not an analysis organized around concepts of progress, with autopoietic systems as an inevitable result of evolutionary development. Rather, evolution here takes the form of shifts, or accidents, which have unintended effects but which, if stabilized, provide the basis for further evolution.

The closure of law, and the contribution which this allows law to make to its own and society's evolution, is considered 'improbable' if one starts from earlier historical periods, when dispute resolution was closely tied to social relations. And the closure of a system from its environment is difficult to reconcile with a theory that is commonly understood to explain developments as the reaction of organisms and social systems to events within their environments. Luhmann shows how closure, once achieved, allows the evolution of law to continue in a manner that cannot be measured but, nevertheless, can be generally understood, alongside other aspects of modern society, as exhibiting ever-increased levels of complexity and adaptability.

Evolutionary theory provides a schema of variation, selection, and stabilization. Mapping these onto autopoietic theory we can say that evolution occurs when there is:

1. variation of one autopoietic element compared with a previous pattern of reproduction;
2. selection of a structure, which is now possible as a condition of reproduction;
3. maintenance of the stability of the system, in the sense of dynamic stability, that is, the continuation of the autopoietic, structurally determined reproduction in this changed form.

Luhmann starts from the premiss that society as a system of communication is both autopoietic and evolutionary; that society exists through its communications, uses communications to establish structures, and stabilizes those structures to form the basis for communications that establish new structures (evolution); and that it communicates to itself about its environment, and thus establishes its physical environment for itself within its communications and itself as separate from that environment (autopoiesis). The question that remains is whether history can be understood as further evolution within an evolving society, in particular, the evolution of the legal system as an autopoietic system that affects its own evolution.

There is no suggestion that the legal system emerged suddenly as a separate system. Pre-adaptive advances precede new formations. In the case of the legal system the important advance was the establishment of a level of secondary self-observation on the basis of long experience in arbitrating normative conflicts with the code legal/illegal. Long before this coding starts to act in a strict binary manner, there is a wealth of conditional programmes. These conditional programmes take on the function of allocating the code legal/illegal, and mature with that function. A further evolutionary step is taken when law is obliged to defend its autonomy in the new context of a functionally differentiated society.

Luhmann's analysis of law's history as the evolution of structures starts with the importance of writing. This did not allow legal rules to be recorded (a later development). The most immediate connection between law and writing was transactional: writing recorded transactions that were worth recording such as marriages, wills, purchases, etc. Writing was also utilized within formal divination practices which, applying the binary code favourable/unfavourable, developed a form which would be adapted to the law's conditional programmes: 'if the cock crows three times before dawn, then . . . '. Writing also allows for the differentiation of texts. The uncertainty of recall is replaced by the uncertainty of interpretation. While there may be disagreements over the meaning of particular texts, the act of disagreeing or agreeing on the meaning of particular texts reinforces the identity and independence of those texts. It also allows for the possibility of legal texts to be distinguished from other kinds of texts. (These last two developments allow for the possibility of future controversies such as that of the correct interpretation of constitutions.)

The threshold for the autonomy of the evolution of the legal system is the operative closure of the legal system. This is an outcome of structures that evolve from the communication of unexpected normative expectations. Expectations arise from the rejection of behaviour, an experience that is, with the benefit of hindsight, one of disappointment. This does not initially involve the application of rules. Undifferentiated societies solve such disputes without distinguishing between variation and selection (without a change of structure). What is eventually passed on as an expectation depends on social conditions, and the procedures for resolution may be a direct expression of these (as with resolution through oath-taking which depends on the ability to arouse support). Case-by-case conflicts require no stable norms. Further development depends on the differentiation of systems, allowing for the negotiation of solutions to conflicts of norms (with the possibility of norm and solution being distinguished). This then becomes more than conflict resolution, allowing for procedures leading to the application of the distinction legal/illegal. Further evolution also depends on the development of norms of competence, and proceedings that allow a few people (judges, legislators) to take the validity of norms as binding for all of the people.

The decisive variation in these specialized proceedings occurred when arguments were no longer *ad hoc and ad hominem*. The defences of troublemakers create the possibility of second-order observation, and the prohibition of kinds of argumentation leads to the evolution of law-specific arguments. In turn, this marks the beginning of the removal of legal proceedings from the direct influence of class and family on the administration of justice. When *ad hoc* arguments are not allowed, demands for justification must move in the direction of the identification of binding norms and the development of concepts and rules for decision-making, which can be assumed to apply to other cases as well. This allows equal cases to be decided equally, and unequal ones unequally. The long-term effect is a base of concepts, which allow a judge to reject *ad hoc* arguments: 'The specification of the way in which arguments refer to legal materials in the legal system is the true carrier of the evolution of the legal system and the breakthrough to an autonomous legal culture, which can then even be differentiated from morals, common sense, and the everyday use of words' (page 248).

Luhmann locates much of this evolutionary development within the Roman system for the administration of justice. The decisive change here was the creation of a Roman civil law, which arose in turn from the appointment of judges who were given instructions, edicts, on how to act. Attempts to order what was happening led to classifications and abstractions, and made a law-centred evolution possible. Complexity necessitated expertise, and in conjunction there emerged special roles for lawyers, at first restricted to the Roman aristocracy. This marks the beginning of the legal profession, only completed much later with the canon and common law of the Middle Ages (and the separation of clerical roles from family status). Initially law develops by analogies and the pressure of case development, and without self-descriptions of itself as a separate system, or without the need for changing law (working instead with the ever more abstract conceptual development of traditional law). This marks the beginnings of what Luhmann terms legal dogmatics. The Roman tendency to condense law in legal propositions was further developed in the Middle Ages. Dogmatics (a secondary observation of law as doctrine) guarantees that the legal system approves its changes as a system, and not as a direct response to its environment. The evolution of legislation and the concept of changing law became possible when innovations were no longer justified by reference to the reworking of classificatory schemes, but directly by reference to norms of competence.

The above is a brief summary of a large number of observations that the reader will need to read for him or herself. In the context of this introduction, which aims to assist (not to remove the necessity for) reading, it is more appropriate to move the focus from what Luhmann describes, to what he seeks to show by his analysis of that description.

With the exception of the discussion of the importance of physical sanctions (see below), the description of the legal system's evolution is internal. It is not a history of social or political movements, wars, scientific developments, religious schisms, or any of the various changes that might be expected to have formed part of the environment of any legal system. But this is Luhmann's point. While at a very general level changes within society (including the evolution of other systems) have effects on the legal system, much of what can be shown to influence the evolution of the legal system represents only a very superficial level of analysis. Luhmann gives the particular example here of the spread of literacy (which opened up the possibility of the written dissemination of laws), conceding that this ran parallel to society's move from a segmented to a stratified society, with the resource of literacy concentrated in the upper classes. Luhmann calls this parallel development a superficial level of analysis: 'For it goes almost without saying that all forms of communication are tightly linked to the forms of differentiation in their respective societies' (page 240). Luhmann's history shows how law's evolution has been both more particular and more law-centred than a history of the societies in which law has developed might suggest. The role played by Roman civil law is crucial, and the point is that this occurred in Rome because of particular developments within Rome's system for the administration of justice, not because Rome was a distinct or superior empire to those that preceded it.

Luhmann's history is able to ignore the content of wider social histories, because there is no point-to-point contact between the evolution of the legal system and other social developments. Taking again the example of Roman civil law, Luhmann does not deny that these developments had links with other aspects of Roman society. However, the linkages which he identifies are not direct influences of dominant classes, leading families, or important individuals (can such interventions ever produce variations, selections, and stabilization of the system as a basis for further evolution?) but the loose connections between the Roman economy and the legal forms which Roman civil law developed: contract and property. The development of these legal forms was in part a response to developments in the economy that could no longer operate on the basis of physical possession and immediate exchange. The juridification of property and contract, the creation of concepts that could be developed through conceptual schemes driven by a desire for consistency, and reasoned out by reference to analogies, is both an internal development of the legal system and functional for the development of the economy. These kinds of relationships, which Luhmann calls 'structural coupling' (see Chapter 9), are not a point-to-point correspondence between law and economy. Rather, the law provides structures that can be utilized by other systems of society while those systems provide cases, which further stimulate (irritate) the legal system, provoking further evolution. And what irritates the legal system is not determined by the importance or meaning of the dispute within the system where the dispute arises. Irritations are where the legal system formulates that there is a problem, and solutions are constructions within the reach of law.

If law's evolution is not driven by a point-to-point correspondence with events in the rest of society, neither is it 'planned' (externally or internally). The legal system cannot control the factors that lead to a dispute. And while judges may, within legal proceedings, find new rules or render some aspect of legal practice redundant, this incremental transformation is not the outcome of a plan, or even the 'result' of a purpose (as the secondary observation of legal communications by reference to the distinction equal/unequal is not a purpose or goal-based activity). To express this in terms of evolutionary theory, the development of changes in the law through legal dogmatics is the 'result of the ongoing reproduction of the difference between variation and selection and is a residue of effective evolutionary difference' (page 252).

Luhmann sees this process as an increase in complexity. We can understand how this is so, even within systems working only with traditional law (without a norm of competence allowing for legislation) if we think about the distinction so important to the development of legal doctrines: rule and exception. Cases can be organized into rules. New cases that do not fit easily within those rules can give rise to exceptions. Cases that come within the exception but do not fit easily within it can become an exception to the (rule about) exceptions (the application of the distinction again); and so on.

With the development of norms of competence (particularly legislation) law has become more dynamic. This is not just because new rules issue from the legislature, but also because law can now create its own conflicts. New statutes can create conflicts that would not otherwise have occurred. There is no longer the same need to wait for disputes within the social system to be litigated. And these statutes have to be integrated into the legal system, applied consistently, even though they allow for degrees of temporal inconsistency far in excess of what was possible through the development of the classificatory schemes of traditional law. That said, the level of consistency required (even allowing for the application of the distinction 'new/old law') has decreased, with the legal system developing a high tolerance of ambiguity, the use of indeterminate legal concepts, and *ad hoc* solutions which cannot establish a thoroughly consistent legal practice. Luhmann is nevertheless adamant that the legal system remains an autopoietic system because, whatever the increased indeterminacy introduced by these developments, it continues to reproduce itself from its own elements (legal communications remain legal communications identified as such by their links to other legal communications). It increases its variety, but at the cost of a decrease in redundancy (less ability to reuse information such as precedents).

The law has evolved by itself, with society as its environment providing accidental impulses, which have caused variations and occasional innovative selections, and which when stabilized have provided the platform for further evolution. But there are conditions crucial to the ability of a legal system to become operationally closed. In particular, it depends on a decisive development within the political system: the withdrawal of physical force from the society and its consolidation within the political system. Although law has to deal with conflicts that might need to be resolved violently, and needs to maintain expectations which require some ability for enforcement (see the comments on Chapter 3 above), the symptomatic incorporation of violence into law is a barrier to law's autonomy. Where the form of legal statements is consistently varied by reference to the likelihood of a violent reaction, law cannot maintain operational closure. It remains tied to social conditions of kinship and clan. Autonomy depends upon a condition of peace, which became possible only when politics took control of physical force. Then the problem of violence is not present in all legal communications, but is restricted to the relationship between politics and law. This relationship allows both systems to maintain their operative closure, which prevents their communications being reducible to each other. This is another example of structural coupling. Structural coupling (stabilization of the elements of adjoining systems) is a condition that allows for further evolution within each system.

The capacity of a legal system to adapt to its environment depends on its variability. One key structural change that has given law considerable variability is the concept of subjective legal rights. This is not a concept that is dictated to law by its environment, but is an internal development within law. This has allowed the 'personalization' of the law, and facilitated a number of important developments. These rights have unfolded the paradox of freedom (the necessity of limiting freedom as a condition of freedom). Legal capacity independent of status and birth has been achieved through this legal form, and with this the general access of law to all of the population. It has also removed individuals from their kinship and clan relationships, as they can only encounter the law through their juristic personality. But while this form facilitates certain relationships between law and its environment, it 'blocks' others. In particular, it is not suited to certain political and ecological problems.

Chapter 7. The Position of Courts in the Legal System

The courts operate within the legal system as a sub-system. Sub-systems have to differentiate themselves from each other (internal differentiation). But what form does this differentiation take?

Some sociological and legal theories have associated access to the courts with access to law, which gives legal communications outside the courts an inferior status. Such theories not only demote the activities of non-judicial officials (policemen, lawyers, etc.) and non-lawyers (citizens' knowledge and use of legal rules), they also challenge hierarchies that serve to legitimize the role of courts. Supposedly, parliament (and private parties through contracts, wills, etc.) makes the laws, while the courts merely apply them. At its most extreme, focusing on courts can remove internal differentiation, replacing it with a vicious circle: law is what the court/judges say it is.

Luhmann argues that under modern conditions, the internal differentiation of the legal system does not take the form of a hierarchy, a segmented arrangement (the courts or lawyers as a separate tribe) or one of equality. Instead, the appropriate differentiation is centre and periphery, with the courts occupying the centre, and other structures (parliament, lawyers, clients, etc.) forming the periphery. This distinction is not offered simply as a metaphorical antidote to overly court-focused theories. Within a theory that seeks to explain the evolution of law, it is necessary to identify the structure or structures whose evolution has made it more appropriate to describe the internal differentiation of the legal system using this distinction, rather than others. The structure, which has generated changes that justify the use of this distinction, is the requirement, placed uniquely upon the courts, to decide cases even when there are no (good) reasons for deciding them: the prohibition of the denial of justice.

Luhmann traces this prohibition within the evolution of the distinction between legislation and jurisdiction. The increased role played by legislation from the second half of the sixteenth century leads to an understanding of legislation as a fusion of political and legal sovereignty. The internal differentiation of the legal system at this period is hierarchical, with the courts, which merely find and apply law, being seen to be inferior to the legislature, which can make and change it. However, the evolution of constitutions places the courts in a position that necessarily subverts that hierarchy. They have to decide on the constitutionality of legislative procedure and output. As such, they cannot be understood simply to obey the legislature. 'And only this conception of the judicial task makes it possible to create norms about the prohibition of denial of justice and to demand that courts must decide all cases brought to them by themselves' (page 279).

Constitutions require interpretation, and only bodies identified by norms of competence to undertake this can do this: namely the courts. They have to decide what is legal and illegal. There is no position between legal and illegal, occupied by what is neither legal nor illegal. There are all sorts of (legal) ways to delay making and avoid making particular decisions (time limits, legal standing, etc.), but these result in other decisions on what is legal and illegal. A world in which the courts operated merely as agents of a political sovereignty might maintain the hierarchy of legislation and jurisdiction, by the courts refusing to decide whenever the output of the legislature was unclear. But constitutions do not allow the courts to act in this way. They are not the agents of the sovereign. Responsibility for deciding what is legal or illegal lies with the courts. This responsibility carries with it a presumption: that it is possible to decide what is legal and illegal. And this responsibility forces the courts to confront the central paradox of the legal system: that there is no inherent value or logical operation that decides what is legal or illegal. There is only the existing law, its earlier distinctions. And while these may indicate what constitutes a consistent application of the distinction legal/illegal in many cases, existing law cannot determine the outcome in all cases. There will be cases in which the courts have no (good) reason for choosing one alternative rather than another.

This means that the courts have to make law. But this does not result in a reverse hierarchy: that the courts command parliament. Rather, what results is a kind of 'cybernetic circle'. In making law, the legislator has to anticipate the forms in which cases are brought to court and decided (including the fact that they *will* be decided). Likewise, in interpreting statute law, a judge must attempt to observe the intentions of the legislator, and a methodology for the interpretation of intention develops. This circular, mutually limited relationship is not how the legal system explains its internal differentiation to itself (self-description). Within such description, the relationship remains hierarchical, with the legislator in the superior position. The courts apply, find, or even develop the law (with a restricted methodology and by reference to approved reasons), but they cannot make law in the manner of a legislator. If they did, how could the judge be said to be bound by law? Within legal theory, the subordinate relationship of the courts to the legislator and the existing law has been maintained by the development of the doctrine of sources of law.

The need to present a circle as an asymmetrical relationship is not the direct result of political or ethical concerns, for example, a reaction to the judiciary's lack of a democratic mandate. It is attributable to the prohibition against the denial of justice, and the paradox of the code legal/illegal (that there is no basis for the distinction between legal and illegal other than the earlier application of this distinction, and its speculative application in future cases, and an internal scheme which attempts to establish consistency in these applications). There is no source of law outside of law's own decisions, and there is no possibility that a scheme of observation based on consistency (equal/unequal) can determine, or even provide particularly good reasons, for *every* decision that will need to be made. Outside the sub-system of the courts, this paradox can be avoided. Legislators, and those who enter into private law arrangements, do not have to decide every matter put to them. They can decide that they do not know what the law requires in particular circumstances, and respond to this uncertainty by not deciding. Contracts and statutes can be drafted (or avoided) on the assumption that the legality of a particular matter cannot be known prior to the matter being decided. For example, a contract or statute may exclude a kind of liability whose parameters are uncertain. But this avoidance is not open to the courts. They receive concrete cases, which raise particular issues framed by existing law, and inevitably, and regularly, have to decide what is undecidable.

This places the courts at the centre of the legal system because they occupy a site where the paradox of autopoietic law cannot be avoided. The paradox can be unfolded, and rendered invisible, by the development of conditional programmes. Without these programmes the paradox would become obvious—there would be no basis for distinguishing what is legal from what is illegal. As such, there is no way in which legal communications could continue in the absence of these programmes. And these programmes will include modes of interpretation (such as, under appropriate conditions, the construction of the intention of the legislator). But they cannot hope to determine all the issues that come before the courts, and in these circumstances, the courts will still have to decide. 'Only courts have to transform indeterminacy into determinacy where necessary, only courts have to construct fictitiously the availability or unavailability of principles, where necessary' (page 292).

'The overall order of the comprehensive system (for present purposes the legal system) is expressed by limiting the system/environment relation of sub-systems through an ordering design for system-to-system relations' (page 274). In the legal system, this means that the relationship between the centre and periphery allows each to have different degrees of contact with law's environment. On the periphery, where decisions as to legality do not have to be made, the legal system can be more open to its environment (it can apply more norms, more of the time, in the construction of its environment). This allows for greater irritation. At the centre, where there is, ultimately, no freedom (not to decide), the environment which the legal system creates for itself must be kept at greater distance. Courts work under a higher degree of cognitive self-isolation. This is facilitated by their construction as institutional systems. Organizations are structures that produce their identity (organize their boundaries) through membership. In the case of courts, this allows for the conduct of judges to be limited. They have to work and operate within the time frame established by the legal system. There are standards of conduct. Rebellion is structured within a framework of acceptable arguments, which includes recognition of the hierarchical order established at the centre (a judge cannot keep repeating the same argument despite repeated rejections from a higher court). All this means that decisions are reached subject to applicable methodological and substantive standards. At the same time, the organization filters out the consequences of decision-making for an individual judge. Income and status can be assured by meeting acceptable (internal) standards, rather than by responding immediately to class or social pressures (should the latter occur this is understood as corruption, and not reflexive law). The ability of courts to decide is further assisted by the existence of the legal profession as an organizational system. This operates as a buffer for the centre, screening out the arguments that will be put to the court, turning the uncertainty of legal decisions into settlement, failing to share the motivations of clients, and engaging in preventative practice.

The requirement to decide also influences the manner in which court decisions are reached. They have to develop rules of decision-making that may remain contested, and cannot guarantee that any reasons will do more than decide the current case. There is a commitment to consistency, which not only requires past decisions to be assessed for consistency, but also requires rules to be announced that will decide future cases. (This allows the decisions of courts, acting in the present, to link the past of the legal system with its future.) But these decisions do not actually decide the future, as what they decide (other than in the case in question) is displaced onto the concept of a *ratio decidendi.*

This form of decision-making, secondary observation (the observation of the making of distinctions) as practised by the courts, cannot result in law as a logical application of rules, or the uniform application of principles. Nevertheless, the decisions of courts will carry the symbol of validity, since validity is only the connection of communications applying the code legal/illegal within the system. These decisions without reasons, or applying inconsistent reasons, are therefore part of the system. This means in turn that, whatever reasons or formal methods are utilized by the courts, the unity of the system as a system cannot be reduced to those reasons, methods, etc. This also means that the prohibition against the denial of justice assists in the execution of the autopoiesis of the system. Law cannot be the expression of morals, or ethics. The need to decide, and the requirement to observe what has been decided in terms of formal schemes of justice, will never be a direct expression of morality or ethics as those values are reproduced within communications outside the legal system.

Chapter 8. Legal Argumentation

Arguments are operations of the legal system, but unlike decisions, they do not assign the symbol of validity (apply the code legal/illegal). Their role is preparative: clarifying, without determining, how and when the code will be applied. They operate at the second-order level of observation. At the first-order level of observation, the code legal/illegal is applied without regard to legal arguments. Here, the existing law is reason enough. It excludes enough for it to be meaningful for the first-order observer to understand what is meant by errors. Here legal texts (statutes, contracts, wills, codes, established recursively as legal texts by the system) are given literal, technical, and routine meanings. Argumentation occurs at the second-order level of observation, in response to the question, 'what was a text intended to mean?' Within the legal system, the primary distinctions used to observe arguments are twofold. First, there is the distinction of errors in reading texts that represent valid law (error/non-error). This distinction would allow, for example, a successful appeal from a decision arising from an erroneous first-order observation. Secondly, there is the distinction between good and less good reasons for particular interpretations.

The fact that second-order observation involves distinguishing between good and less good reasons, leads to theories of argumentation (a third-order level of observation, from outside the system) that seek to find reasons for reasons. This is a process of analysis that offers challenges to the concept of operative closure. Looking for reasons why legal reasons might be arranged in a hierarchy, even if one can no longer order such a ranking by reference to ideas of God or nature, nevertheless points to links between the legal system and things within its environment, such as morality. While such theories are not utilized within legal practice, the proponents of such theories can nevertheless point to features of legal argumentation, such as references to principles, or the use of terms familiar to morality (fault, good faith, etc.) which support the claim that legal reasons are linked to, and ordered by, matters which lie outside the legal system.

These theories of argumentation apply concepts that are themselves arguments: justifications for the use of particular reasons. Luhmann offers a third-order level of observation of the nature of legal argumentation that is not itself a justification. Instead, legal argumentation can be observed using the distinctions redundancy/information, and redundancy/variety. Redundancy is what is not new in communication. One cannot have information without redundancy. Information is that which makes a difference within communication. It cannot be established except by reference to redundancy (what stays the same). Redundancy also helps to stabilize the process of passing information. For example, it is easier to detect the presence and significance of a variation (information) within a stream of accompanying redundancy (routine, repetitive communications) than without this. Thus, something like the weather forecast is easy to follow, because it comes within a routine format, terminology, etc., which makes it easy to extract what is different: the information. Redundancy can also help us to identify errors (when the weather man mistakenly uses centigrade instead of Fahrenheit, predicting temperatures of 100 degrees). Redundancies operate as 'local attractors'. It is possible to communicate information by reference to particular redundancies, without having to trace them to a meaningful beginning, or referring to the whole of the system of which they are a part (no knowledge of meteorology is required).

Redundancy and information operate as a distinction within all communications. To understand the development of the legal system, and the function of legal argumentation within that development, we need to apply the distinction redundancy/variety. Variety is the number and diversity of operations that a system can identify as its own and execute. It represents the possibilities for adding new information. The existence of such possibilities, within a system open to evolution, includes the selection of new structures, and their stabilization as a basis for further evolution. But variety is never completely open. What can be communicated as information at any time depends on a system's condition in terms of redundancy.

These distinctions form some of the conditions for the possibility of legal reasoning, and help us to understand why specific legal reasons, within any particular context, can present themselves as compelling. Legal concepts, rules, and principles are formulas for redundancy within the legal system. They are reusable. They are also local in their application. To understand how they operate it is useful to think of how barristers might put arguments to a court. Barristers need to identify whatever rules, principles, concepts, and cases support their client's case. Essentially, they will be arguing that a consistent application of this material allows their client to succeed. Where a principle or case works against them, they will seek to distinguish it. Why distinguish? Why not, for example, urge the High Court simply to overrule or ignore a long-standing High Court decision which, applied consistently (an internal standard) would require their client to lose? The answer lies in the same understandings of consistency. What are the implications for making legal decisions (applying the code) if High Court decisions could be ignored whenever a later High Court judge dislikes the outcome? The result would be that concepts, principles, and rules based on High Court decisions (of which there are a great deal in the United Kingdom's legal system) would no longer represent part of the system's redundancy. Enormous numbers of routine, first-order observations would no longer be able to be made. Clients who urged their barrister to run this strategy as a legal argument would be told that it was not possible. By contrast, a case that can succeed through a distinction of an earlier authority (creating a limited exception) faces a far less challenging task. And, if the distinction is accepted (is reused), then not only has the redundancy of most of the legal system been left intact, but also the system has exhibited variety, and moved to a higher state of complexity.

Thinking about legal argumentation in terms of the distinction redundancy/variety reveals a lot about its nature. It takes place in a concrete context (a case) in which argument requires one to reason from formulas that are accepted (redundant). It therefore takes place within an existing web of argumentation. That web is more than the logical application of single rules. The dominant tool for examining the argument being offered is consistency: what implications will this argument, if accepted, have for other concrete situations (how will they be coded legal/illegal)? Rules are built up from a process of considering the implications for coding along the lines of the following statement: 'a consistent treatment of this case and all others that are equal to it can be stated in the form of the following rule . . . '. Variety includes the possibilities of altering what was formerly redundant, but to succeed requires us to understand what is now redundant (what difference has occurred). Variety in legal argumentation therefore requires those who expound it to explain its implications for the legal system's redundancy. This encourages those who seek variety to keep their dispute, in terms of the system's redundancy, local.

This form of argumentation does not fit into the description offered by other theories of argumentation. There are no meta-reasons ranking reasons across the system. The compelling nature of a legal reason is always in context, arguing from the redundancy formulas that surround the case, and examining the implications for all cases that would need to be treated consistently. Formulas that appear to come from outside the system (such as principles of good faith, and fault) provide bridging concepts within the system. They allow for analogies to be drawn across local boundaries of doctrine, but they take their concrete meaning from their prior application in each area. Thus they represent a comparison of internal analogies, and not the use of a differently contextualized value from outside the system. Better reasons are always assessed as such from inside the system (what are the implications for coding?). Reasoning takes place by reasoning forward from what, within the system, cannot be questioned.

The distinction variety/redundancy is not used by those engaged in second-order observation from within the system. It is not a juridical argument. Internally, the commitment to redundancy and variety is articulated by reference to the distinctions concept/interest and formal/substantive. In each case, the first part of the distinction refers to the system's commitment to consistency as redundancy. In each case the second part of the distinction refers to the system's assessment, in terms of consequences, for its environment. This environment is not an objective reality, but the version of reality that the legal system creates for itself through its own programmes and coding (the world as seen entirely, and only, through law). These partial glimpses of other systems, social communication, and the physical universe, assessed, in the moment of a case, by reference to the anticipated consequences of legal coding, can be described as 'imagination with a legal effect'. Nevertheless, these elements of consequential reasoning provide an alternative commitment to that of redundancy, allowing for variety and self-development.

Chapter 9. Politics and Law

The obviously close relationship between law and politics offers a major challenge to systems theory, which treats these as separate sub-systems of society. In the social conditions of medieval Europe, with a pope claiming authority over principalities, the separation of politics and law was central to natural law reasoning. But with the creation of nation-states, and the development of an increased competence to enact law through legislation, the unity of law and politics has been assumed. This assumed unity exists on many levels. From the sixteenth century, particularly in the writings of Hobbes, political and legal authority is united in the figure of the sovereign, and it is only through the existence of this body that individuals are constituted as legal and political subjects. The state is seen as both a political and legal entity. Law is subordinate to politics, with no legal right of resistance to the sovereign's actions. Law is viewed as an instrument of politics, with much political activity being devoted to the creation of statutes. The passing of legislation is a unitary event, which belongs to both politics and law. The funding of the legal system is a political decision. Politicians commonly decide appointments to the judiciary. Law legitimizes itself by legalizing parliamentary democracy. Many politicians are trained lawyers. Some separation of law and politics is suggested by the notion of the rule of law (*Rechtsstaat*): that politics is held legally accountable. But from the point of view of law, the rule of law adds nothing to positive law. It is a tautology: the rule of law consists of the rules of law. In light of the interpenetration of law and politics on so many levels (theoretical, operational, historical) what is the case for treating law and politics as separate autopoietic sub-systems of society?

Luhmann does not deny the causal links between law and politics (or law and money), but insists that an adequate description of such links requires us to accept that law and politics are two separate systems. He makes many arguments in support of this separation, but a useful starting point to understand them is to unpack the idea of law as an instrument of politics. The function of politics is to make collectively binding decisions. Politics can be understood as a generalized power to secure obedience to commands, but this, by itself, would never allow politics to evolve in to a complex system involving political parties, campaigns, media briefings, and a vast machinery for public administration (the state). In order to develop complexity, politics has to unpack its own paradoxes. It legitimates itself in terms of democracy, and claims authority to decide, for itself, the scope of the political. But in order to evolve into a complex system, able to use instruments like law and money, it must not be able to determine, politically, what constitutes law or money. It has to interact (structurally couple) with systems that create their own forms of communication for themselves. Take the example of the passage through parliament of a statute. If the political talk that led to the passing of the statute continued to determine the legal meaning of the statute (rather than the legal fiction whereby this kind of text is interpreted as an intention of a single legislator), what is the effect on the ability of politics to produce collectively binding decisions? What structures would politics develop if these were only maintained by its own ability (always in the present) to apply force, or achieve consensus? Law is a medium for politics to achieve goals through forms different from itself.

There is no doubt that politics and law have supported their respective developments. Law benefits from peace and the possibility of enforcement provided by the political system. Moreover, just as politics can achieve more by existing alongside (rather than as a unity with) law, law benefits from the separate operational existence of politics. Law does not have to secure the peace and enforcement necessary for its own operations, to the extent that it does not even have to refer to these in its routine operations. For example, rights and duties can be the subject of meaningful communications without reference to the local constellation of political power. But the argument is not that politics and law benefit from respecting each other's autonomy. It is that they are different systems of communication, with different conditional programmes, and different codes, and that this prevents the dissolution of each into the other, and that this inevitable separation has allowed for an increase in the complexity of both.

Politics is not the ongoing interpretation of a legally fixed constitution. And no adequate theory of the legal system can be constructed if its factual operations are defined as the implementation of political programmes. All attempts to steer the courts politically founder on their internal workings—their mode of argumentation. The conservatism (redundancy) vs. activism (variety) that operates within legal argumentation cannot be reduced to the ongoing politics of the political system. Questions that are meaningful within politics (what institutions can be taken as expressions of democracy) cannot be decided by the law, which codes things legal/illegal. Problems have to be justiciable to be decided by law, and typically involve the alleged violation of a subjective right.

Politics is not limited to what is justiciable. In the political system, the code is government/opposition. As with the code legal/illegal, communications connect from both sides of this distinction. Politics observes itself in relation to its function of producing collectively binding decisions, assigning alternatives to each side of its code. The inner side of the form (government) is only there because of the outer side (opposition). There is no inherent value that decides what will be government and what will constitute opposition. There are only the conditional programmes, developed within the political system, that establish the structures (parliament, parties, forums, etc.) that stabilize the operations that apply this distinction. From this perspective, the legal system can be seen to handle its alternatives quite differently. It is not coding government/opposition but legal/illegal. It is not applying the conditional programmes of politics but its own. The manner of its argumentation is (see Chapter 8) quite different from that of politics. While the arguments, which are coded opposition, can condense and link to each other, the rejected alternatives of law remain scattered and dependent on individual cases and rules, and they cannot form a consolidated opposition.

The passing of legislation may be a unitary event, in the sense that it can be observed as a unity by an observer, but as soon as one considers the recursive network of the communications within the two systems, the unity of the individual act disappears. The communications with which it connects within the political system are not the same as those within the legal system. The negotiations, compromises, and public declarations that culminate in the symbolic act of legislation are not the interpretative practices identified within the legal system as finding the intention of the legislature. And post-legislation, the two systems will communicate about the statute quite differently. Law has no equivalent of the political assessment of a piece of legislation as a success or failure. The connection between law and its enforcement within the legal system requires only operations relating to evidence and interpretation. Within the political system, administrative officers are aware that law enforcement can have wide-reaching political implications if directed at groups that can be represented politically (farmers, local industry, etc.). Law enforcement within the political system operates politically, with prosecutions as a last resort, reached only after negotiations that are unlikely to be justiciable. Even illegality by officials of state is understood politically as a risk that can be exploited as opposition.

The incorporation of legislation within law's conditional programmes ('If a statute is passed by both Houses and the sovereign it is law') has had major implications for the development of both systems. Traditional law, subjected to conceptual reworking, has quite a slow rate of change, when compared to the volatility of the demands processed within the political system. While both carry out their operations in (and only in) the present, the staging of their operations is quite different. While politics benefits from inducing operations within the legal system that have different sequences from itself (what if every political operation stimulated an immediate legal response?), more responsiveness is required for a complex political system than would be possible with traditional law. Legislation balances the different time frames of the two systems. Law can become more responsive to its environment by developing structures (of which legislation is one) that allow it to structurally couple with other systems.

Chapter 10. Structural Couplings

The theory of autopoiesis does not deny the existence of a reality that lies outside communications. The physical universe forms society's environment. This environment not only includes material conditions external to individuals (geography, etc.) but those internal to individuals (neurology, psychology, etc.). At the level of society, the claim that the social system cannot communicate with the physical environment using its own operations is uncontroversial. To be affected by its environment, society (as a system of communication) depends upon stable relationships with systems of consciousness. Only through the involvement of consciousness can society carry out its operations (communications) in response to the physical environment. This is not a direct relationship of cause and effect. We cannot know in advance, with 'scientific precision', exactly what communications will result from each and every event within the physical universe. In the case of individuals, this inability is often described as 'subjectivity'. This form of response, which is not a casual relationship, can be described as 'irritation'. The physical environment can irritate society, and in certain circumstances this process of irritation will form extremely stable patterns of communication. These stable patterns of responses to irritations can be described as 'structural coupling'.

Starting from this position, one can turn to the relationship between different sub-systems of society. Operational closure results in the autopoietic sub-systems of society being closed not only to the physical environment (in common with society) but also to each other. As with the relationship between society and the physical environment, this is not to deny that systems have effects upon each other and that, in defined circumstances, these effects can be observed using the distinctions appropriate to the communications of causality. But they cannot communicate with each other. Nor are the communications of one system 'inputs' to another, causing that second system to generate determined 'outputs'. The operations of each system can only connect with other communications from the same system. Just as society must construct its environment for itself, through communications (while the actual physical environment remains outside of communications) so too each system must construct its environment for itself, with the physical environment and other systems outside each system. In Chapter 9, Luhmann gives the example of politics and law as two systems whose communications connect recursively to themselves, applying separate codes and developing different conditional programmes, and thus remaining (productively) closed to each other. But understanding systems as closed, communicating about each other (and the physical universe) but not directly to each other, or having simple cause-and-effect relationships with each other, appears to open up the vision of a world of chaos, with no possibilities of coordination between different areas of social life. As with the relationship between society, consciousness, and the physical environment, Luhmann offers the same distinctions to enable us to understand the interaction between separate systems: irritation and structural coupling.

Luhmann begins by distinguishing operative coupling from structural coupling. Operative coupling is the coupling of operations with operations. This can take two forms. First, there is the coupling of operations within an autopoietic system. This is just the production of operations by the system's operations: their recursive connections. Secondly, there is a coupling of operations from different systems. This is not a connection of inter-communication, or a casual relationship. It is simply a consequence of the fact that all operations take place in (and only in) the present. This allows a system to couple with an operation that it attributes to its environment. Thus when the legal system identifies something as being outside itself but relevant to itself (which it does through its norms) that something occurs at the same moment as the operation (selection) by law. And if that happens again, it will also happen at the same moment both in law and outside. This creates the possibility of coordination between any system and events outside itself. But while a common present is necessary, it is not sufficient. For systems to coordinate with each other, without communicating with each other, each system's communications must represent a stable pattern of events for the other system, in order to trigger (irritate) stable communications within the other system. 'Coupling mechanisms are called structural couplings if a system presupposes certain features of its environment on an ongoing basis and relies on them structurally (page 382).'

Co-ordinated patterns of communication are not the same thing as synchronization. Law and politics are not synchronized. The time frame of operations is decided separately in each system, making synchronization impossible. Law has its time frames (procedural time limits, limitation periods, appeals, exchanges of legal correspondence, etc.) that do not copy those of politics (parliamentary sessions, consultation periods, public announcements, etc.). The operations which structure time within politics are simply not the same as those which structure time within law. For example, the enactment of legislation is an event in both the legal and political systems. This does not mean that the passing (consultation, bill, debate, vote, etc.) of legislation is synchronized with operations of the legal system. Indeed, the political communications surrounding legislation generally do not even register as an event within the legal system, but are only retrospectively constructed as such if the bill is eventually passed. Synchronization needs to be contrasted with synchronicity. The latter occurs when an operation in one system triggers (irritates) an operation in another. To give a negative example, a bill (as opposed to a statute) is neither synchronized, nor does it exhibit synchronicity. The lack of synchronicity is because, although the procedures surrounding a bill take place in the same moment as operations in the legal system, they are not selected and reconstructed by the legal system (in that same moment—operative coupling) as events in law's environment.

The selection of an event by a system through its own operations (operational closure) does not necessarily offer very much co-ordination between systems. Selection by one system will be ordered through the structures of that system, but this selection may not trigger any response in another system (the example of the bill in the legal system). Structural coupling occurs when the operations of one system are expected to trigger responses in the other (and vice versa). Again, a statute provides a good example. While the meaning of a statute for the political system is not the same as its meaning within the legal system, the political system expects to provoke a response from the legal system (irritation) through the enactment of a statute.

For systems to irritate each other, an operation of one must be treated as an event by the other system, and vice versa. Logically therefore, this is a coupling of structures. Without structures in each system (expectations) there would be no selection or recognition (cognition) of the other's operations as an event. Such moments represent an opportunity for each system to develop further structures, which increase the mutual triggering of operations, i.e. increase synchronicity. Luhmann describes such *ongoing* mutual couplings as structural couplings: 'Coupling mechanisms are called structural couplings if a system presupposes certain features of its environment on an ongoing basis . . . ' There is always an ambiguity of identity involved in coupling between systems, whether this occurs on an occasional or ongoing basis. This is because the event is selected (identified) only through the separate recursive operations of each system. Thus even where the same language is involved, this will not mean the same thing in each system: contract in the economic system is a transaction involving exchange, while in the legal system it is a (re)configuration of legal relationships.

Structural coupling replaces the direct influence of an environment upon a system. In the case of social systems, it might be more accurate to say that structural coupling has replaced undifferentiated communications. Societies in which family structures are also political and economic structures do not have any environment for their communications except those of the physical universe. By the process of operative closure, systems become available to each other only as environment. If social systems could determine each other's communications through their own communications, this can either be described as an environment dictating to a system, or as undifferentiated communication. By replacing direct influence or undifferentiated forms of communication with separate systems and structural coupling, systems may be said to both reduce and facilitate their influences upon each other. We can talk about reduction, because a system that determines through its own operations what aspects of other systems it will recognize may be said to have reduced its sensitivity to those other systems. We can talk about facilitation, if the inability of one system to determine whether and how it will register within another system enables both systems to increase their variety (complexity).

An example, one of those discussed by Luhmann in this chapter, should assist. Property within early agrarian societies was synonymous with family relationships, which were also political relationships, and all of these were organized in relation to land. There was relatively little trade in land, and it could be said that the economy was relatively undeveloped within such societies. Property has evolved into a mechanism for structural coupling between systems, rather than a common communication and experience across society. Within law it can be distinguished from contract, or distinguished as a right *in rem* rather than a right *in personam*, or distinguished from obligations. The distinction drawn is always within the network of law's operations, depending on the legal question one is trying to answer, and the real and hypothetical cases one is trying to compare. (Such is the nature of legal argumentation.) These distinctions, which can be traced within legal histories (legal evolution) by reference to, among other things, changes to the causes of action (writs), are not the same distinctions by which property is understood and communicated about within the economic system. Economics has its own understanding of property. The economic system requires owners to be identified in order to know whose consents must be obtained in which circumstances, and to whom one must offer payment. This is a different network of communications using a common term within a different set of distinctions. The development of this understanding is part of the development of a market economy: a separate economic system. Each system does things that facilitate the operations of the other. Property, in law, can establish ownership of things, but it cannot give them value. Economics can establish the value of things, but it cannot determine ownership. Each system needs events to occur within its environment that it cannot achieve through its own operations, and it needs to achieve this without reversing its closure (and losing control of its environment). And this need is mutual. If economics attempted to dictate the legal meaning of property (e.g. to allocate rights to whoever could pay most for them), it would not only interfere with the legal system's ability to reproduce its own operations, it would also undermine its own. For, without stable patterns of ownership (established for economics by law), on what basis does anybody know what they can afford to pay for anything? In the language of the theory we can therefore also say that one of the paradoxes of economics (that it distinguishes the world in terms of value but has no basis, within itself, to establish value) is externalized through structural coupling with the legal system.

Chapter 11. The Self-description of the Legal System

In this chapter Luhmann analyses jurisprudence (which he calls legal philosophy, as jurisprudence is the continental term for legal doctrine) as a form of self-description. He contrasts jurisprudence, as self-description, with sociological approaches, which are external descriptions. Lastly, he offers systems theory as a form of structural coupling between self-description and scientific theory.

Systems can be described from the inside, or the outside. An internal self-description is the presentation of the unity of the system *in the system*. This is when the system makes a topic of itself. It represents a third level of observation. Second level self-observation is the co-ordination of individual operations with the structures and operations of the system. This is carried out within the centre of the system, by courts (see Chapter 7). It involves the implication or explication of the application of the code legal/illegal to a given set of facts. Self-description is an attempt to account for the whole of the system by reference to what has already been identified by the system as belonging to itself.

Self-descriptions create texts that are reusable within the system itself. As such, they can be described as autological texts—they include themselves in what they mean. They also, by being an operation of the system they describe, change what they describe (different self-descriptions are descriptions of different objects). They are not utopian statements but concrete operations. They depend upon the state of the system they describe. Thus while they alter what they describe, what can constitute a self-description is dependent upon the operations then occurring within the system being described. But while not being utopian, they have a limitation that may make them appear so, when compared with external (sociological) descriptions: they cannot deny that the system is entitled to distinguish between valid and invalid, and that one has to adhere to valid norms. Thus a self-description will not describe legal norms as facts, but treat them as statements of appropriate conduct, and seek to account (provide reasons) for the identity of the norms of the system. Given that the norms of the legal system operationalize its operative closure (see Chapter 2), the distinction between norms and facts is crucial to the system's abilities to identify its own boundaries. Thus self-descriptions cannot abandon this distinction and treat norms as facts.

Maintaining the distinction between facts and norms (treating norms as statements of what one ought to do) self-descriptions seek to account for the conditional programmes of law, but fail to account for its binary coding. Thus they do not accept the paradox of the code: that it is a distinction with no basis for distinguishing (other than earlier distinctions). As such, they also fail to have regard to the nature of compulsory decision-making (the prohibition of the denial of justice) and the consequences of this for legal argumentation (see Chapter 8). A self-description must presuppose that controversial communications are being dealt with in and by the system, and are not the result of any unavoidable defect. The communications in the system are styled as leading to decisions, which decisions can be claimed to be based on good (substantive, source-based, or methodologically acceptable) reasons. A self-description may lead to the criticism of some of the system's norms but it must always offer a substitute solution.

The real problem for self-description is dealing with what is implied when a system promises to give an answer to every question and forces the operations of the system to presuppose that there is such an answer. Self-descriptions look for a way to externalize this problem, and find a principled basis for (legal) validity outside of the system itself: in religion, ethics or economics: 'unable to explain its status of being without contradictions (as a symbol of unity) by reference to itself and must find the conditions for that outside and apart from itself' (page 429). From a systems theory perspective, the environment of the legal system is constructed through the application of legal norms and, as such, is a construction of the legal system. Hence a self-description, which locates the unity of the system 'inside' or 'outside', is still trying to make a part of the system represent it as a whole. In addition, the operations of the system cannot be reduced to its self-observations. Operations will include decisions that are not observed, including, inevitably, operations of self-observation (which cannot be both made and observed at the same time). And of course, operations produce new (local) points of departure for new observations, further undermining any attempt to capture them as a unity from within the system.

Luhmann presents a historical description of the evolution of the legal system's self-descriptions. Here he notes how those descriptions, which attempt to show that law is more than positive law, have ceased to refer to religious and ethical values in society at large, and now point to expectations generated within the legal system itself. Modern society is not capable of generating reflexive values as a source of consensus. Natural law has lost its connection to nature and the natural sciences. Knowledge of the nature of reason has, after law achieved operative closure, been replaced by the discussion of reasonable principles of legal reason:

'After the erosion of their cosmological foundations, the advocates of reason today distil the self-description of the legal system from the arguments produced within the system and maintain, on the basis of those arguments and supported within the system, that there are indeed things like good reasons (and less good reasons), reasonable principles, or ultimate values as the nominal values of the system' (page 442).

The difficulties with this self-description have been signalled at length in Chapter 8. Positivists see the difficulties of attempting to abstract principles from the operations of the legal system, and the further difficulties then of reasoning forward from such principles to distinguish between valid and invalid applications of the code legal/illegal. Instead, they seek to avoid this by identifying valid law using a theory of sources of law. This strategy founders after the acceptance of binding precedent as a source, since then the sources of law can no longer be claimed to lie outside of the legal system. Positivism ends up trying to accept that (legal) principles are a source of law, without accepting that the legal system decides for itself what is valid law.

Meanwhile, in the everyday operations of the system, the metaphor of the sources of law operates as a formula for contingency (see Chapter 5). The tautology that the legal system decides what is law is unfolded inside the system by a sequence of arguments on the recognition of law (statutory interpretation, status of custom, interpretation of cases, etc). At the same time, observation of the courts (observation of secondary observation) can lead to the identification of principles. But these principles are what remain stable during such secondary observation. Luhmann calls these eigenvalues. They are entirely internal to the system. They are the values expressed through the repetition of the system's operations. For example, justice as equality is the eigenvalue expressed by the endless attempt to distinguish cases, which is simply sorting them endlessly into what is equal and unequal.

Neither positivism nor approaches based on reason can account for the unity of the system in the system. The unity of the system cannot be accounted for in the system, but only externally. Externally it is possible for an observer to observe that there is no meta-value that establishes what is valid within the system. Validity is simply the connection of operations within the system, and its unity is no more than the totality of those connections, and the system's own observation of them.

External (sociological) descriptions have not treated the self-description of the legal system as an object of research. Instead, applying scientific methods, such as statistical analysis, sociology has developed its own classifications, in order to generate empirical findings. For example: a study might show that '70 per cent of rape case offenders receive sentences below 6 months', and then utilize that statistic to make recommendations for reform (statutory minimum sentences), without seeking to identify how the legal system 'sees' rape cases, or how the legal system is likely to react to the 'irritation' of reforms. A systems theory observation of the legal system would not be limited to self-description (which is limited to law's understanding of its environment), but would be able to look at the relationships between the legal system and other social systems. In particular, through the concept of structural coupling, the theory would be able to examine the social conditions of law's autonomy: the ecological dependencies of the system. Thus, for example, such a theory would examine the conditions which allow structural coupling between the legal system's concept of property and the economic system's concept of value, or the separate but compatible construction of the subject in the legal, political, and economic systems (described as a unity as 'individualism', see Chapter 10).

Luhmann does not rule out the possibility that self-descriptions could come to include autopoietic closure. This does not mean that lawyers would seek to employ the theory in legal practice (a task which he admitted in Chapter 1 was too complex). Self-descriptions are not located in the niches of the legal system: the fifteenth-century magistrate's ignorance of Aquinas' *Summa Theologica* did not prevent this forming part of contemporary self-description. The reasons why such a development is unlikely lie in the difficulties that the legal system would have in unfolding its paradoxes self-consciously. (What happens to the redundancy and variety produced by the constant reasons for decisions, if the system forms an acceptance that there are no good reasons for decisions?) Nevertheless, Luhmann believes that there could be a sociological theory that would allow science to take self-describing systems as its object, and thus legal systems that equip their self-reflection with the conceptual achievements provided by a theory of self-referential systems. Such theories would not represent a direct input of sociology or science into law or vice versa (which would contradict the premises of systems theory). Rather, they would have to take the form of structural coupling between the science system and the reflexive theories of society's functioning sub-systems.

Chapter 12. Society and its Law

A theory that sees society as an autopoietic system, internally differentiated by functional differentiating sub-systems, cannot be used to develop precise (or necessarily optimistic) speculations on society's future. Unlike theories of 'open' systems, which are premised on society's adaptation to its environment, closed systems are only open to what they construct for themselves, and adapt only in response to what they perceive, internally, to be problems. There is no guarantee that a system's reproduction can continue. Nevertheless, autopoietic systems theory can make a contribution to our understanding of the futures facing society, and the possible evolution of the legal system within those futures.

The function of law, as a system for the stabilization of normative expectations, allows it to operate as an 'immune system'. Cognitive expectations involve learning from disappointment. Normative expectations are premised on not learning. This allows the legal system to couple structurally with other systems by offering relatively stable structures. Luhmann insists that this reference to immune systems is not a metaphor. The legal system reacts to the conflicts that it identifies through its norms by producing generalized solutions: rules. Rules represent structures, which will process other conflicts (they have a surplus value). They are also time-binding, in that they support expectations about what, in future, will be coded legal/illegal. As such, law does not have to provide a 'point to point' defence to every potential conflict. This serves to reduce the systemic 'risk' operating within contemporary society. Law has general responses to (and will stabilize expectations relating to) conflicts that have not yet occurred.

If law offers an immune system, can it continue to do so within a global society? Global society is not here the assimilation of cultures, or the equalization of access to resources, but the functional differentiation of society at a global level. This is seen most clearly with the economic system, which has a system of credits and payments that transcends nation-states. Science too acknowledges no national boundaries. The political system is less developed, and continues to operate predominantly through and between nation-states, although regional structures are beginning to evolve. In this context, can the legal system evolve to continue to offer a productive resource through structural coupling to these other globally differentiated systems? 'If there are ever to be legal concepts which are socially adequate, they will have to be found through a testing and re-testing of solutions to establish potential eigenvalues of the legal system in modern society (page 473).'

Luhmann identifies structural features that might incline one towards pessimism. The ability of law to stabilize normative expectations (bind time) may be declining. The dynamic production of legal norms leads to the temporalization of law: law is only valid until further notice (or as academic lawyers now routinely put in their prefaces, 'this was the law when I stopped writing X months ago'). Temporalization is increased when legal norms come equipped with assumptions of reality that are subject to internal or external errors. For example, internally law may construct versions of science that allow it to convict criminals with great certainty, only to have to revisit enormous numbers of such convictions, years later, when that certainty is challenged by the legal system's current constructions of science. Externally, the political system passes legislation by reference to its construction of a social problem, only to pass new legislation when that problem is reformulated. Temporalization takes us beyond discussions of the legal system's ability to respond to risks generated within other sub-systems, to an awareness that the legal system is itself a source of risk: who can be certain that any law will not be changed? How can the legal system stabilize expectations (bind time) when its norms are so sensitive to time?

In his answer to this problem, Luhmann offers a concrete example of structural coupling between science and the self-descriptions of the legal system. Systems theory might 'irritate' the legal system, leading it to evolve in ways that make it more responsive to the risks that it is generating. This is not a recommendation for unchanging law (which might lead to revolution). It is rather that the legal system could experiment with structures that impose partial limitations on its ability to change the law, particularly in areas where it is aware that there are high social costs imposed on persons who cannot adjust their positions in response to legal changes (no retrospective changes in pension law for persons aged 64!).

Another source of pessimism for the legal system's ability to evolve is the decline in the normativity of normative expectations. Standing up for your rights is, Luhmann suggests, a less common occurrence, which severely impairs the ability of the system to develop. Without expectations of normativity, the legal system loses its connections to systems of consciousness that produce conflicts, which in turn irritate the legal system and produce evolution. While this decline is linked to temporalization, there are other reasons. The dynamic production of legal norms produces a situation in which it is not only impossible to obey the law, but obedience to the law may have catastrophic consequences for other functioning systems. For example, the sudden loss of the worldwide 'black economy' could cause a meltdown in the global economic system. At the level of the individual, obedience to all laws, all of the time, would paralyse self-determination.

The most important reason for a decline in the ability of the legal system to generate the conflicts necessary to its evolution is exclusion. By exclusion Luhmann does not mean the stratification of class, although his concept recognizes conditions that have been described in this way. The functional systems can fail to couple structurally with systems of consciousness. They do not couple evenly with all persons. For example, the political system will couple structurally with the consciousness of politicians and state bureaucrats (inclusion) but not with those who do not perceive politics to have any relevance to their lives. Luhmann suggests that what is commonly termed 'social exclusion' is the exclusion of the same individuals from numerous points of structural coupling with social sub-systems. This exclusion has cumulative effects: the illiterate do not register to vote, acquire passports, or engage in litigation. While the process of exclusion can be understood only through identifying the points of exclusion from structural coupling, the distinction exclusion/inclusion can be seen as a meta-structure, common to all systems.

Against the background of a widespread decoupling of individuals' consciousness and the legal system, what can generate law within global society? Luhmann identifies human rights. Human rights have become a 'catch-up' term. Through their extension into social welfare rights, intended to equalize disparate access to the economic and political systems, they lose the ability to generate a global law. They have no resonance in the face of national legal systems that routinely allocate political and economic liberties contrary to the egalitarian ideals of human (social welfare) rights. However, Luhmann identifies a residual normativity of normative expectations, exhibited in response to gross violations of human rights. There are some treatments of human beings (and asymmetrical allocations of roles, e.g. racism), which remain as counterfactual expectations in the face of disappointment. There are 'wrongs' which, despite the disparities of the conditional programmes of the legal systems of nation-states, are still perceived as 'wrongs' (although more likely in cases associated with the treatment of particular individuals than groups). This represents a continued connection between consciousness and legal systems, which may stimulate the evolution of a global legal system.

There is no certainty about any of this. Accepting that law evolves through the development of its structures, in response to its operations, closes out the possibility of it being an intended consequence of human action. Redundancy/variety, positive feedback/negative feedback—these are alternatives that are always present. Evolution is not only the consequence of the selections made, but also the order of their choosing (they are historically path-specific). In response to this Luhmann ends with a possibility which cannot be excluded. The functional differentiation of law, which commenced in Europe, may not evolve into a global system: 'it may well be that the current prominence of the legal system and the dependence of society itself and of most of its functional systems on a functioning legal coding are nothing but a European anomaly, which might well level off with the evolution of global society' (page 490).

Concluding the Introduction

The analysis offered by Luhmann in this book, although written at the end of the twentieth century, is a paradigm for twenty-first-century observation on the nature of society as a system, and its law as a system. It has the potential to generate new forms of analysis on the interface between the legal system and society's other systems, and general social communication. This introduction cannot do justice to the wealth of knowledge that Luhmann brought to this task, using social and legal history, as well as concepts from mathematics, biology, social theory, logic, communications, and evolutionary theory. This work does not use biology as a metaphor (systems as organisms), nor is it a pastiche of interdisciplinary methodologies. It is an acutely logical description of law's autopoiesis. We hope that this introduction (as an introduction) has done justice to the rigour of Luhmann's reasoning, and made the reader aware of the richness of his insights.

Luhmann presents this work first and foremost as a contribution to science, offering concepts for the understanding of its object (self-referential social systems) that are superior to the available sociological theories of law. The latter, by rejecting self-description and self-observation, could not describe the operation of such systems *as* systems. Any assessment of the contribution of this theory to jurisprudence must, necessarily, be more circumspect. Luhmann shows how jurisprudence evolves with the evolution of the legal system. He demonstrates how it performs within the legal system, changing as the system changes. His analysis is not one of deconstruction. Self-observation and self-description are part of the reproduction of the legal system. The absence of any ontology does not make self-description and self-observation any less of a reality. They are operations within the legal system that manage, despite the absence of foundational values, to achieve socially productive stability. A theory that demonstrates how this can be achieved can claim to be scientifically superior to one that simply points to the gap between a system's operations and its espoused values. However, a theory that shows how jurisprudence performs operations within the legal system does not necessarily provide a better basis for the performance of those operations.

In his final chapter Luhmann tries to approach the future, through law and the contemporary society in which it currently performs. To do so he needed to address the question of what this contemporary society is, and how the future, or our perception of that future, permeates what it is. However, his theory shows us that there is no future beyond the self-referential selections made as communications within society and its various functioning sub-systems. The future is out there, but for society it can only be grasped through communications.

1 The Location of Legal Theory

I

Theoretical exercises are nothing unusual in the world of law. Legal theories of the most diverse kind have been developed in both the traditions of Roman civil law and the common law.[1] This has been due in part to the needs of legal education and in part to those of legal practice, with the latter ultimately becoming more important. Initially it was the arguments used by the parties in legal proceedings that were focused on, but later the major concern came to be the reasons for judicial decisions and, in this context, their consistent usage in courts. Experience of cases and concepts had to be processed and stored for further use. This need for processing and arranging has a double structure, as we shall analyse in detail below. On the one hand, concepts and theories have had to be condensed in such a way as to keep their identity while being processed. On the other hand, this processing happens in different situations and is occasioned by new cases. Nevertheless, the unvarying meaning structures have had to be confirmed. So, in one way, the outcome is a reduction and in another an enrichment of meaning. And the one necessitates the other.

Legal theories that are produced in response to legal practice do not, however, match up to the expectations raised by the notion of theory in the scientific field. Such theories are, rather, a by-product of the need to arrive at binding decisions. Without wanting to take this point too far, with legal theories one could rank methodological concerns higher than theoretical ones. Theories classify the subject matter, they organize the opaque material with which legal practice is faced and turn it into problem-related and case-related constellations, which from then on can restrict and guide the process of decision-making. For instance, when it is necessary to regulate a conflict of interests as a conflict of *legally* accepted interests (in areas of law such as the law of restitution, emergency powers, or product liability) it is sensible to develop rules for 'balancing interests' which do not in principle classify one party's interest as unlawful. And when an 'unjust enrichment' has to be transferred to the disadvantaged party, legal practice soon finds itself in troubled waters, unable to steer a course that conforms to its own principles; yet rules have to be developed which can be applied, and points of view have to be expressed which can be generalized.[2]

---

[1] As far as the common law is concerned, the relevant concepts are more likely to be found under the (perhaps more precise) category of 'rules'.

[2] See, in relation to this example, Charles Fried, '*The Artificial Reason of the Law, or: What Lawyers Know*', Texas Law Review 60 (1981), 35–58.

A second fundamental basis for organizing conceptual abstractions and the systematization of theories is legal education. The relevance of legal theory in legal education can be evaluated rather differently from its relevance to legal practice.[3] This is so even though it is the education system's training that prepares people to work as legal professionals. Legal education can afford to provide more abstraction, more generalization of decisions, and even more 'philosophy' than will ever be applied in practical work. Developing theory for educational purposes has often led to a failure to recognize fully the dependency of legal arguments on legal texts and cases, that is to an underestimation of the 'local' (intrinsic) character of legal rationality.[4] Nevertheless, to some extent, any kind of developing legal theory will be attentive to its acceptance in the operating system. The American Law Schools are closely associated with the American Bar Association. In Germany, law school examinations are 'state' examinations. What is produced in universities, be it people or texts, can have the effect of advising the practice of the legal system to make changes, but if the textbooks and monographs occasionally referred to in legal decisions suggest a change, it needs to be a change which can be applied within the system; and it must be a change of something which was already there. Obviously, scientific research has had to respect similar constraints—but in an entirely different context.

'Legal theories' which are produced by legal practice and legal education are, together with applied law texts, the form in which law presents itself as the result of its self-interpretation. They are, in this sense, products of the legal system observing itself. But this does not mean that they are fully reflexive theories that define the unity of the system, the meaning of law, the function of law, etc., in order to draw conclusions and arouse expectations.

Further than this, work on legal theories, legal doctrine, legal principles, and legal notions which goes on inside the legal system should not be seen as the work of a profession defending itself against criticism and justifying its own actions, or as a symbolic process of legitimizing functions.[5] Rather, it is an endeavour to establish a consistency of terms, a probing into how far

---

[3] In referring to England, Cotterrell even goes so far as to say: 'Jurisprudence derives such unity as it possesses, from its place within legal education' (R. Cotterrell, 'Jurisprudence and Sociology of Law', in William M. Evan (ed.), *The Sociology of Law: A Social-Structural Perspective* (New York, 1980), 21–9, at p. 23.

[4] A parallel example in economics would be the dependency of the rationality of economic decisions on accounts and budgets.

[5] The Critical Legal Studies movement in the United States was motivated by such conceptions for a long time. However, they are increasingly replaced by an interest in the social relevance of legal forms, which is not exclusively concerned with 'ideology critique', see e.g. Alan Hunt, 'The Ideology of Law: Advances and Problems in Recent Applications of the Concepts of Ideology to the Analysis of Law', *Law and Society Review* 19 (1985), 11–37; Stewart Field, 'Without the Law? Professor Arthurs and the Early Factory Inspectorate', *Journal of Law and Society* 17 (1990), 445–68.

principles, notions, and rules for decision-making can be generalized, that is, 'amplification'[6] and correction when generalizations have gone too far, especially when applying the operating scheme of rules and exceptions. Seen from inside the system, it is precisely this process that can be understood as doing work on justice and can thus be related to a value concept, which enables lawyers to see meaning in what they are doing. The problem of legitimation arises only from the indispensable need for selecting decisions (from the range of possible decisions); that is, it is a reflection of the visible contingency that results from this work.

It is only during the last three decades or so that there have been attempts to take things further. These theoretical enterprises have not wanted themselves to be restricted to either dogmatic theories or 'legal philosophy'. They have advertised their projects under the heading of 'legal theory' (note the singular),[7] in an attempt to combine logical and hermeneutical offerings with those of (late positivist) theories of institutions and systems theory, rhetoric, and theories of argumentation (or at least contributions based on such approaches). Up until now, a clear profile cannot be made out, even though the distinction between legal doctrinal theories and legal theory in a general sense has at least become fairly well established.[8] The lack of a clear profile does not, however, mean that relating legal theory to perspectives from within the legal system has been given up. In all respects, the legal theory concept of the norm is also seen in legal doctrine as an indispensable *basic concept*.[9] Basic concept here means a concept that is defined in itself, that is, as a short-circuited way to describe its self-reference. The norm prescribes what ought to be. That is why one needs a supplementary distinction, between norms and facts, as a main distinction, where a fact is considered as such (or assumed to be) that which is capable of conforming with or deviating from the norm. This assumption alone shows that legal theory subordinates itself to the legal system.[10] We are

---

[6] So, for example, Christian Atias, *Épistémologie juridique* (Paris, 1985), 86.

[7] See above all the journal *Rechtstheorie* (Legal Theory) and many publications by its chief editor, Werner Krawietz, which explore this ground, such as: *Juristische Entscheidung und wissenschaftliche Erkenntnis—eine Untersuchung zum Verhältnis von dogmatischer Rechtswissenschaft und rechtswissenschaftlicher Grundlagenforschung* (Vienna, 1978); id., *Recht als Regelsystem* (Wiesbaden, 1984). In France there was an earlier recognition of a *théorie générale du droit*, understood as a clarification of the basic concepts and terms of law, which was supposed to live up to the demands of positive science in Comte's terms.

[8] See only Krawietz, *Juristische Entscheidung*, 210.

[9] See especially on this point Werner Krawietz, 'Staatliches oder gesellschaftliches Recht? Systemabhängigkeiten normativer Strukturbildung im Funktionssystem Recht', in id. and Michael Welker (eds.), *Kritik der Theorie sozialer Systeme: Auseinandersetzungen mit Luhmanns Hauptwerk* (Frankfurt, 1992), 247–301. I shall revisit this issue when dealing with the concept of norm in Ch. 3.

[10] Even if this is vehemently denied by Krawietz, 'Staatliches des gesellschaftliches Recht'.

consistently faced with a reflexive theory of the legal system, and one that is driven toward abstractions. It is a theory which tries to make interdisciplinary contacts but which still follows the basic fundamental thesis that norms cannot be 'deduced' from facts or described by facts wherever one wants to understand their intrinsic value, their meaning as 'ought', their sense of obligation. Indeed that is always the case when one focuses on the meaning of normativity. However, the fact that this is done unveils legal theory as a reflexive attempt that seeks to find out what the law is all about, in its own terms.

Philosophers at all times have been concerned with questions which were so abstract that no one thought that lawyers, or lay people who were involved in legal questions, would be interested in them. There is, for example, the question of obedience to law.[11] This is definitely a question that one would expect the legal system to answer positively (that there is an obligation to obey law), because otherwise 'law' would collapse into itself. On the other hand, there are borderline cases and exceptions (the right of resistance!). In these situations, a theoretical clarification of the question of obligation may be helpful, even if legal practice will not address this issue unless triggered by a concrete case (which is, after all, an accurate response to any such issue).

This tendency towards abstraction within legal theory is pushed further by efforts to compare different legal orders or families of legal orders, as for instance those of common law compared with those legal orders where important sections of the law have been codified. As far as comparative law is concerned, it is important to gain a distance from the specific values itemized within given legal orders and yet to reinforce the general self-affirmation of law, for instance, by not questioning that law has to be enforced, that a statute has to be made concrete case by case, and that there are better and less good reasons for interpreting legal texts in particular ways.[12] In relation to comparative law one can observe a rudimentary

---

[11] 'Who cares?' asks, for instance, Philip Soper, *A Theory of Law* (Cambridge, Mass., 1984), in his introduction to research on this issue. His answer: philosophy is not very satisfying because it leads to the next question of how philosophy can know the relevance of this question, and why it cannot simply (as one would hope) answer the question in the negative.

[12] See for such a commitment to residual values in law (as compared to ideological or merely personal views) the section 'Rational Reconstruction' (as a concern of methodology) in D. Neil McCormick and Robert Summers (eds.), *Interpreting Statutes: A Comparative Study* (Aldershot, 1992), 18. For example, there is no doubt here that 'justifications' are necessary and that they can be judged as to their use of arguments: 'for rational reconstruction has also a normative element in so far as the rationally reconstructed underlying structure presupposes a model of good or acceptable justification for the decisions of rational beings' (p. 22); and a statement such as 'interpretation is through and through a matter implicating fundamental values of the law' (at 538) is obviously also approved by those who conclude their research with such a finding (and who would find otherwise when such formulations are used).

development of a global legal culture that allows for a wide range of differences but which is nevertheless committed to its own (legal) standards and which rejects any interference from outside.

Here, and in so many different ways, the term 'legal theory' is used. However, a strictly scientific analysis provides this term with a vastly different function, namely the function of constituting its object. Any scientific endeavour needs to be confident, from the outset, about its object. It has to define, and that means to distinguish, its object. Whenever one is operating with questions of epistemology, that is, whether one is more committed to a realist, an idealist, or a constructivist theory, the rule about definitions (and distinctions) will apply. Defining the object in the pluralist context of science involves the possibility, in fact the very real probability, that different theories and to an even greater extent different disciplines will define their objects differently and so fail to communicate with each other. They talk about different things even if they use the same terms, as in our case the term 'law'. This makes it easy to fill page upon page with 'debates', but these debates have no resolution, or at best only serve to sharpen the weaponry of each side. In effect, each side misses the other's point.

This problem is particularly acute in the case of the relationship between legal knowledge and sociology. Legal knowledge is concerned with a normative order. Sociology is concerned with, depending on its theoretical orientation, social behaviour, institutions, social systems—that is, with something that is what it is, and which, at best, calls for a prognosis or an explanation. One can leave it at that, simply stating this difference, but then in so doing one would have to concede that disciplines, and the different theoretical strands within disciplines, have nothing to say to each other. A general theory of law, or rather what is taught in introductory courses, has to be restricted to listing what theories are around: legal realism in its American and Scandinavian variants, analytical jurisprudence, sociological jurisprudence, sociology of law, rationalist and positivist strands of legal theory with their varying mellowings in later phases, law and economics, systems theory. A common denominator cannot be found, or can it be?

Perhaps one can agree, at least, on the point that there is nothing to be gained from arguing over a 'nature' or 'essence' of law,[13] and that the worthwhile question that should be asked is: what are the boundaries of law?[14] This question points to the well-known issue as to whether these boundaries are analytical or concrete, that is, whether they are defined by the observer or by the object itself. If the answer is 'analytical' (and there

---

[13] For a recent overview of such attempts with the finding that their results were ambiguous see Manuel Atienza, *Introducción al Derecho* (Barcelona, 1985), 5.

[14] See André-Jean Arnaud, 'Droit et société: Un carrefour interdisciplinaire', *Revue interdisciplinaire d'études juridiques* 10 (1988), 7–32 (at p. 8). See also id., 'Essai d'une définition stipulative du droit', *Droits* 10 (1989), 11–14.

are some who feel, wrongly, that they are bound by the theory of science to answer in this way), one allows each observer to decide his own objectivity and so ends up where one started from, that is, stating that interdisciplinary communication is impossible. It is for these reasons that our answer is 'the boundaries are defined by the object'. This means, in fact, that the law itself defines what the boundaries of law are, and what belongs to law and what does not. Answering the controversy this way shifts to the question: *how* does the law proceed in determining its boundaries?

If efforts to arrive at a common starting point of interdisciplinary and international approaches to legal theory can be pushed this far, then theories that have anything meaningful to say become rare. This position can be summarized through stating the following four points:

1. The theory that describes how something creates its own boundaries in relation to its environment is, currently, systems theory. There may be other theories on offer; however, if they exist they have kept themselves well hidden.[15] As such, it is not possible to decide (at this time) whether one should search for a variation on the repertory of systems theory or a competing alternative.

2. Even if a 'purely analytical' definition of the boundaries of law is rejected, this does not invalidate the statement that everything that is said is said by an observer.[16] Moreover, a theory that leaves the definition of the boundaries of the object to the object itself is, nevertheless, a theory advanced by an observer. This observer, however, has to organize their own observations on a second-order level if she/he wants to do justice to an object that defines its own boundaries; and even if she/he only wants to raise the object as a topic for discussion. The observer must observe its own objects as an observer, and that means, observe them as objects that are oriented in this observation around the distinction between system and environment.

---

[15] Nonetheless, Ranulph Glanville attempts a cybernetic theory of second-order observations, which exceeds the claims of systems theory by far (*Objekte* (Berlin, 1988)). There are quite a number of theoretical approaches under this heading of 'the observer' which seem to be independent of systems theory formulations. See e.g. Niklas Luhmann et al., *Beobachter: Konvergenz der Erkenntnistheorien?* (Munich 1990). Game theories are also relevant here; however, whether or not they can keep themselves apart from a constructivist systems theory in the long run, cannot be reliably assessed today. See in this respect the special issue Droit et société 17–18, 1991; further François Ost, 'Pour une théorie ludique du droit', *Droit et société* 20–21 (1992), 89–98, and Michel van der Kerchove and François Ost, *Le Droit ou les paradoxes du jeu* (Paris, 1992), including references to the recent discussion.

[16] This formulation is used by Humberto R. Maturana, 'Biologie der Kognition', quoted in id., *Erkennen: Die Organisation und Verkörperung von Wirklichkeit: Ausgewählte Arbeiten zur biologischen Epistemologie* (Brunswick, 1982), 34.

3. In proposing the concept of an observing system, systems theory opens the way to a fairly general constructivist epistemology. This allows not only for assessing systems that specialize in cognition,[17] but also for observing systems of all sorts that use self-produced observations. Such self-produced observations manage a system's relationship with its environment, which cannot be accessed directly in any operative way—which includes systems such as religion, art, economy, politics, and, of course, law.[18] The integration of such diverse, multi-contextual constructs has to be organized through a theory of second-order observations.

4. Having come this far, we can make out two alternatives and can accordingly distinguish two ways of observing law (whereby law is always as a system which observes itself)—a juristic and a sociological way. Sociologists observe the law from outside and lawyers observe the law from inside.[19] Sociologists are only bound by their own system that, for instance, might demand that they conduct 'empirical research'.[20] Lawyers, likewise, are only bound by their system; the system here, however, is the legal system itself. A sociological theory of law would, therefore, lead to an external description of the legal system. However, such a theory would only be an adequate theory if it described the system as a system that describes itself (and this has, as yet, rarely been tried in the sociology of law). A legal theory would lead to a self-description of the legal system, which had to account for the circumstance that self-observation and self-descriptions can only conceptualize their object in comparison with something else. They have to identify, that is, to distinguish, their object, in order to be able to assign themselves to it. So far, however, in this exercise, only problematic formulae have been advanced, such as 'law and society', which formulae promote the misconception that the law could exist outside society.[21] This

---

[17] See Niklas Luhmann, *Die Wissenschaft der Gesellschaft* (Frankfurt 1990).

[18] Concerning the possibilities of securing the interdisciplinary orientation of legal theory in a constructivist epistemology see André-Jean Arnaud, 'Droit et société: du constat à la construction d'un champs commun', *Droit et société* 20–21 (1992), 17–37, and Gunther Teubner, 'How the Law Thinks: Towards a Constructivist Epistemology of Law', *Law and Society Review* 23 (1989), 727–57.

[19] This distinction between internal and external is so well established since Hart as to be used in dictionaries; see the contribution in *Dictionnaire encyclopédique de théorie et de sociologie du droit* (Paris, 1988), 197, and François Ost and Michel van der Kerchove, 'De la scène au balcon: d'ou vient la science de droit', in François Chazel and Jacques Commaille (eds.), *Normes juridiques et régulation sociale* (Paris, 1991), 67–80. However, this discussion lacks the context of elaborate systems theory.

[20] Whether this happens or not, and there are proponents clamouring vehemently for it (e.g. Hubert Rottleuthner, *Rechtstheorie und Rechtssoziologie* (Freiburg 1981)), all depends on how narrowly the canon of methods is designed and on how many topics that are relevant in relation to the reality of law, are excluded from socio-legal research.

[21] See also the arguments of Csaba Varga against this 'fallacy of distinction' in 'Macrosociological Theories of Law: From the 'Lawyers' World Concept' to a Social Science Conception of

is precisely why the title of this book has been deliberately chosen to be 'society's law'.

These few remarks on the implications of an interdisciplinary dialogue already lead us straight into questions which theory has not yet solved. However, we have to stop at this point with the comment that an adequate sociological theory of law, on the one hand, can take full advantage of its being an external description, which is not bound to respect the norms, conventions, and premises of the understanding of its object. Such a description can, and necessarily has, to use incongruent perspectives. On the other hand, such a sociological theory should not lose sight of its object. This means that it has to describe its object in a way in which lawyers will understand it. The sociological object (just as much as the legal one) is one that observes and describes itself. To acknowledge the fact that there are self-observations and self-descriptions of the object is the condition for a scientifically appropriate, realistic, and I venture to say, empirically adequate description. Otherwise one would simply and inappropriately deny that there are self-observations and self-descriptions in the legal system.

II

The considerations set out above necessitate the statement that everything, which is available using the title of legal theory, has been produced in conjunction with self-descriptions of the legal system. These are attempts at theory that—despite their often critical approaches—respect the character of law, and are committed to its corresponding normative references. This view applies to legal theories in the narrow sense in which they grow out of case law and relate their rules to more generalized points of view, for example, to the principle of trust. It applies, too, to reflexive theories of the legal system that reflect on the production of an intrinsic value in law and the meaning of the autonomy of the legal system itself. If one formulates such tendencies in normative terms, which arise 'naturally', as it were, from legal practice, they lead one to the need for *consistent* decision-making. This can be represented as deflecting external influences ('without fear or favour') or as reflecting an internal legal norm of justice, that is, the requirement to treat like cases alike. Obviously such criteria demand further specification, namely further distinctions, such as distinctions between relevant and

Law', in Eugene Kamenka, Robert S. Summers, and William L. Twining (eds.), *Soziologische Jurisprudenz and realistische Theorien des Rechts*, Special Issue of *Rechtstheorie* 9 (Berlin, 1986), 197–215, at p. 198. This should not mean, however, that one has to relinquish the distinction between 'internal' and 'external'; all that is required is the adequate theoretical foundation of the distinction.

irrelevant personal characteristics or between cases that are and those that are not alike. This is done with the help of concepts and theories, such as those used to decide the conditions for attributing causes, or for spelling out the subjective components of acts (premeditation, negligence), or for distinguishing various formal errors which can occur when contracts are made or performed. However, the overall material, which results from producing theory in this way, appears to outsiders as rational and as chaotic at the same time.

As far as lawyers themselves are concerned, they tend to keep their distance from such theory and concept construction. They assess legal constructions in relation to their effects, that is, by asking the question 'What is the result?' But lawyers have, of course, no way of telling what the empirical outcomes of their theory and concept construction will be. In this sense, any consequentialist orientation is for them nothing more than an indicator of the positivity of law, that is, an indicator of the competence to make decisions using their own estimations. In any event, such a consequentialist orientation does not itself generate theory.

Problems of consistency are principally nothing but problems that result from the *redundancy of information*. Logical consistency, or what might be seen as a self-imposed guarantee for the provision of propositions which are free from internal contradiction, is not required. There is, however, the requirement of providing information and thereby reducing demand for further information, in order to minimize the surprise effect of decisions, to compact information and thereby to make those decisions that can be expected. Law needs to be as predictable as possible or an instrument whose effects should be capable of being calculated in advance. Ideally a key concept reflects any legal decision—just as a precise analysis following the finding of a bone leads to the definition of the species to which that bone belongs.

But redundancy collides with the variety of the facts of life and of legal cases. The more multifaceted are the facts of life that appear under the gaze of the legal system, the more difficult it becomes to maintain consistency. That is why so much old law was guided mainly by formalities. As soon as there are 'internal states of affairs', 'motives', and 'intentions' to be reckoned with, a revision of the guiding concepts is called for. The same applies to the extension of legal proceedings towards a more demanding, indirect handling of evidence. In a historical perspective, it was by no means self-evident that law itself should provide the evidence in relation to questions regarding both facts and law; indeed, upon reflection, this is a rather surprising demand to make of law. For what we are concerned with here is, in essence, the issue of dissolving a paradox through self-organization and the implementation of societal autonomy. Apparently the breakthrough happened in the twelfth century.[22] This development was driven forward with great success in medieval times but with a corresponding loss of certainty; a special jurisprudence then had to be developed which responded to this loss of certainty in order to pre-empt problems for decision-making.

All of this is only of marginal interest at the outset of our study, but we will have to revisit these issues later. All that matters for the moment is a summary of the consequences that flow from this way of developing theories. It produced a number of legal theories, but not a theory of law. It led to a reflection of its case-method in problem-specific theories, but did not result in an adequate understanding of law as a unity, which produces itself. The result was a plurality of theories but not a self-conceptualization of law as law. This approach managed to account for the demands for consistency (redundancy of information) raised by legal practice; its premisses, however, had to be introduced or assumed 'doctrinally', that is, with the help of abstractions, which themselves remained unanalysed.

These considerations are not meant to be a critique of the development of such theories, or an assessment of the level of their rationality. On the contrary: one can even claim that there is a deficiency today in the processing of information in this professional-rational sense.[23] So we are not concerned with a redefinition and re-articulation of the characteristics of this rationality. The issue with which we are concerned here is the question of how law can be conceptualized as a unity; in response to it, we shall apply the apparatus of systems theory in order to analyse what it means to define the unity of law as a system.

This is not a new issue, of course. There are a number of typical approaches which, however—and this should be a warning—never achieved any particular impact on legal practice.[24] Possibly the most influential, or certainly the most respected, approach to a construction of the unity of law used a hierarchy of sources of law or legal types: eternal law, natural law, and positive law. This approach relied on a stratified social system and, correspondingly, on a hierarchical architecture of the world; it postulated, however, the necessity for such a hierarchical order dogmatically, and thus obscured the paradox of unity from multitude. Unity, then, could only be the *difference* between the social ranks.

---

[22] See Harold J. Berman, *Recht und Revolution: Die Bildung der westlichen Rechtstradition* (Frankfurt, 1991), 252 (orig. *Law and Revolution. The Formation of the Western Legal Tradition*, 1983) for a view on the development of the methods of evidence and the introduction of assumptions (which had to be refuted). As to the problem of a paradox in this context see Roberta Kevelson, *Peirce, Paradox, Praxis: The Image, the Conflict, and the Law* (Berlin, 1990), 35.

[23] See Niklas Luhmann, *Rechtssystem und Rechtsdogmatik* (Stuttgart, 1974).

[24] There are notable exceptions, though. The arguments of the natural law approaches of Grotius or Pufendorf have found their way into jurisprudential literature while those of Hobbes or Locke have not.

This changed in the eighteenth century when the unifying difference between ranks was reorganized on the basis of the concept of progress, in the belief that the traditional order had broken down, with the increasing secularization and historical conception of descriptions of structure.[25] According to Hume, Rousseau, Linguet, Kant, and others, law is the historical domestication of violence. Darwin, however, already categorically rejected any attempt to mention 'higher' and 'lower'—and so sabotaged the idea of progress. This progressive reasoning was also undermined by evidence that came from Hegel's metaphysics of the spirit.

Another unexpected source of competition for legal theories also arose in the eighteenth and nineteenth centuries—at first in the form of social statistics, later as various social sciences that rapidly became differentiated. Up until then, law teachers were led to believe they were in charge of the concepts of society.[26] This induced them to treat 'societas' as a legal term and to regard the origins of society as if they followed the pattern of a contract. Their sociological competitors, however, very soon demonstrated how much law teachers were tied to their legal concepts. Their presentation of society as a legal institution could be undermined and rejected. The jurists had to seek refuge in theories of positive law, which ran into the problems of legitimation. Since the middle of the nineteenth century, therefore, legal theories retreated to a *validity of values*, which remained uncontested even if (or perhaps precisely because) it had no consequences for concrete cases.[27] The guiding difference was now between facts and legal validity, and in order to find the law only procedural conditions were acceptable and no longer material ones. This seemed to make it possible to conceptualize the unity of law as encapsulated in the rules for legal argumentation, or to put it more simply, in a balance of interests that had to be negotiated. Remarkably, all these efforts were afflicted by a peculiar sense of distance from the law. However, such a conceptualization seemed plausible and presumably unavoidable. For legal decision-making does not make decisions on the unity of law as such, rather it is produced and reproduced by deciding on issues of law as such. The approach of the economic analysis of law seems to manage to avoid this discrepancy between theories relating to problems, which are jurisprudentially productive, and, for the first time,

---

[25] See Wolf Lepenies, *Das Ende der Naturgeschichte: Wandel kultureller Selbstverständlichkeiten in den Wissenschaften des 18. und 19. Jahrhunderts* (Munich, 1976).

[26] As far as the common law is concerned, see W. T. Murphy, 'The Oldest Social Science? The Epistemic Properties of the Common Law Tradition', *Modern Law Review* 54 (1991), 182–215.

[27] This rough time frame does not deny that the idea of progress and with it the scheme of violence/civilization still have their protagonists. See' for instance, Walter Bagehot who assumes a development towards an 'age of discussion' in Physics and Politics: Thoughts on the Application of the Principles of 'Natural Selection' and Inheritance to Political Society 1869, quoted in *Works*, vol. IV (Hartford, 1895), pp. 427–592.

descriptions of the unity of law.[28] It offers a calculation of utility that is rational in a specific sense, and at the same time that is easy to apply. This has led to a surprising convergence of theory and jurisprudence, especially in the United States. However, this convergence comes at the price of simplification, without which the application of this approach to the various fields of practice would not be possible, but which largely restricts its impact to use in courts. After long experience with a kind of utilitarianism that is interpreted strictly and with regard to each individual, with the problems of aggregating individual preferences as social preferences, and with the distinction between the utility of actions and the utility of rules, sufficient opportunities are available for decision-making. The hypothesis that circumvents the known problems of aggregation is that it is possible, taking the individual as the starting point, to calculate a solution that is more or less beneficial for the common good (but, of course, is not the common good itself). Nevertheless, many problems remain. Possibly the most important one follows: the future cannot be calculated. Accordingly, the legal validity of the results of such calculations of utility cannot depend on their turning out to be right or wrong in the end. Like all attempts at introducing the unity of law in whatever form (and, that is, through a relevant distinction) into law, this attempt also rests on the dissolution (unfolding, making invisible, civilizing, making asymmetrical) of a paradox. And this indifference to right or wrong in relation to the future realization of expectations is a typical feature of risky actions. In this sense, the approach of the economic analysis of law justifies legal decision-making as a form of risk-taking.

These considerations encourage us to look for other approaches, but without going into detailed polemics.[29] We use as our guiding difference the distinction of system and environment, which is the basis for all more recent variants of systems theory. This has the important advantage, as can easily be seen, that society (and its entire environment) can be envisaged as the environment of the legal system. The approach of the economic analysis of law can account for society only as a general system for the balance of advantages, however indirectly achieved.[30] Systems theory can elaborate on

---

[28] This approach has now found its way into legal textbooks even in Germany. See for instance Hans-Bernd Schäfer and Claus Ott, *Lehrbuch der ökonomischen Analyse des Zivilrechts* (Berlin, 1986).

[29] See, for example, Karl-Heinz Fezer, 'Aspekte einer Rechtskritik an der economic analysis of law und am property rights approach', *Juristen-Zeitung* 41 (1986), 817–24; id., 'Nochmals: Kritik an der ökonomischen Analyse des Rechts', *Juristen-Zeitung* 43 (1988), 223–8. Also in the American law schools scholars are highly and unforgivingly divided on this issue. For a view on the other side see, for instance, Bruce A. Ackerman, *Reconstructing American Law* (Cambridge, Mass., 1984).

[30] This means also that delays have to be accounted for and exposes the approach of the economic analysis of law at its most vulnerable point: the impossibility of accounting for the future.

a much richer, more concrete description of society, and this not least in relation to *other* functional systems of society. In this way, the environment of law as internal to society appears as highly complex, with the consequence that law is referred back to itself: to its autonomy, its self-determined boundaries, its own code, and its highly selective filters which, when widened, could threaten the existence of the system or could even dissolve the structures which determine that system. Systems theory, like the approach of the economic analysis of law, has its disadvantages. In contrast to the legal theories outlined earlier, both are of a new kind, but they work in quite specific and different ways. The disadvantage of systems theory (if this is a disadvantage) lies in its high intrinsic complexity and the related abstractness of its concepts. Its cognitive base is interdisciplinary and it can only be accessed in segments when approached with the conventional means of scientific disciplines (even if they are hyper-disciplines such as physics, biology, psychology, or sociology). Jurists would be hard pressed to be informed sufficiently about these related disciplines, let alone to keep themselves informed of the rapid developments within these fields. This is not to say that practical applications would be impossible, but they will happen rather sporadically and incidentally, rather more at random and in the form of irritations than in the form of logical conclusions. Therefore, we do not attempt to present a theory that is supposed to guide practice. Instead, we describe the legal system as a system that observes itself and describes itself. Our description is of a system which develops its own theories and which, in doing so, has to proceed in a 'constructivist' mode, and that means without any attempt to represent the outside world in the system.

In addition, systems theory manifestly uses its own guiding difference, the difference between system and environment. It always has to define the reference to the system in relation to which something else appears as environment. If one considers the ability of systems to describe themselves, one inevitably arrives at the difference between the self-description of the legal system and its external description. Of course, one can propose an integration of both perspectives under the heading of 'legal theory'; however, one must expect, seen from the perspective of systems theory, that these approaches will then separate from each other again as soon as one spells out what is specifically required from a theory.

The purpose of this kind of description in the setting of systems theory is, above all, to establish a connection between legal theory and social theory, that is, a reflection of law in social theory. European society has developed, when compared internationally and interculturally, an unusual density and intensity of legal regulations since medieval times, even going as far as defining society itself as a legal institution. Here one has to note that a number of official positions were staffed in medieval times with clerics who had not studied theology at all but canon law. Further, one has to note the directly related significance of law for the development of the modern state and the significance of proprietorship for the development of the modern economy—that is, legal institutions which we will examine below under the heading of structural couplings of law with other functional systems in society. The transformation of medieval society into modern society has been achieved with the help of law (and revolutions, seen as breaking the law, are included in this view of legal forms). There is nothing that justifies the assumption that this type of legal culture, which invades, permeates, and regulates the everyday life of a modern society, is here to stay. Already a quick glimpse at developing societies (and even those with modern industries, etc.) suffices to raise doubts.[31] Phenomena of overloading within existing legal systems are widely discussed. They may be a transitional problem that results from old claims for a density of legal regulation and new conditions for their application. But one only needs to mention the difficulty of shaping problems of risk or ecological problems into legal forms. How can one assess these issues, which type of theory can assist if the question is to determine the position of law in modern society, and to account for the changes that are beginning to reveal themselves? Definitely not by returning to a natural law of the Aristotelian or post-Aristotelian kind (i.e. legal rationalism); nor by trying to use the various 'ethics' approaches that lack conceptual clarity;[32] nor by resorting to the economic analysis of law, which informs us too little about the society to which it is supposed to apply.

Systems theory analysis today, if understood in broad terms, is the only candidate with a ready-made concept for the task.[33] It requires, first of all, that one replace the explanation through a principle (justice, calculation of utility, violence) with an explanation through a difference, in this instance, as outlined above, the difference between system and environment. However, there is mounting evidence that this is not enough and that a whole galaxy of distinctions is required, distinctions adjusted to each other. These are, alongside the difference between system and environment, above all the differences of variation/selection/restabilization, derived from evolution theory; the differences of information/message/understanding, derived

---

[31] See, for example, Volkmar Gessner, *Recht und Konflikt: Eine soziologische Untersuchung privatrechtlicher Konflikte in Mexiko* (Tübingen, 1976); Marcelo Neves, *Verfassung und Positivität des Rechts in der peripheren Moderne: Eine theoretische Betrachtung und eine Interpretation des Falls Brasilien* (Berlin, 1992).

[32] On the contrary, today such 'ethics analyses' or 'ethics commissions' serve the political preparation of agreed foundations for legal regulation and owe to the law their confidence that everything could be changed if new information came to hand or the situation were to be assessed differently in the future.

[33] It is important to note the historical character of this statement, which does not exclude other possibilities.

from communication theory; and, far more fundamentally, the difference between operation and observation. The resulting terminological apparatus will be used only selectively and appropriately. For the moment it is only important to point out the particular type of theory. A complex society cannot be described other than by a complex theory, even if one cannot achieve a strictly corresponding complexity (requisite variety). Nor can society's law be assessed in any other way.

III

We assume, on the basis of a general theory of knowledge, that each observation and description is founded on a distinction.[34] In order to describe (mean, thematize) something, an observation must be able to distinguish that thing. In so far as the observation distinguishes one thing from another it describes *objects*. However, when it distinguishes something from certain counter-concepts, it describes *concepts*. It follows that concepts can only be constructed when one can distinguish distinctions. A theoretical understanding of law requires a construction of concepts at least in the sense that has been roughly sketched out so far in this chapter.[35]

Let us review the approaches to legal theory one more time. It is evident that different legal theories apply different distinctions, and so provide different 'forms',[36] and thus construct different objects.

The old European Natural Law worked with a static architecture of the world, and so used a distinction between top and bottom, understood as a difference between ranks and quality. A general cosmological hierarchy of the essence of things supports this hierarchy of levels (of sources and of qualities) and law comes to be distinguished as a special essence within this hierarchy. This means that Natural Law does not rely only on knowledge of nature (such as physics today) but is supported—together with the hierarchy through which it is supported—by an ontological understanding of the world that is expressed in a binary logic. As a result, it is unclear what could possibly be seen as the other side. Illegality is not law. Theory cannot distinguish between injustice and non-law (although not every action results in a legal problem) and this non-distinction promotes, in turn, the impression that a legal order is inevitable.

[34] For an account which develops this idea see George Spencer Brown, *Laws of Form* (reprint, New York, 1979); as for the implications of the relationship between distinction and self-reference, see also Louis Kauffman, 'Self-reference and Recursive Forms', *Journal of Social and Biological Structures* 10 (1987), 53–72.

[35] It goes without saying that the elaboration of *theories* must satisfy further demands and that requires the construction of concepts only under specific conditions. One example here would be the requirement of consistency (redundancy) with increasing complexity.

[36] 'Forms', used in the sense of George Spencer Brown, as markers for boundaries that separate two sides.

The rationalist philosophy of law of the seventeenth and eighteenth centuries assumed to a higher degree a perspective of utility (of welfare) that moderates the relevance of stratification. Here the guiding distinction was useful/useless or harmful, and the postulate of freedom was put forward on the premiss that there was a large realm of human activity in which individuals could promote their own benefit without harm to others. Today's economic analysis of law can be seen as a continuation of this concept in response to concerns that have been expressed since the seventeenth and eighteenth centuries. *The postulate of generalization formulated by transcendental philosophy refers to this assumption as a principle.*

Running alongside these movements we find the temporal distinction between violence and civilization, a distinction that entitles the Enlightenment to claim that it is promoting progress. From its inception, this distinction has, in the concept 'violence' (*vis*, not *potestas*), a law-specific approach. Hence Natural Law has been seen, since the writings of the German jurist Thomasius, merely as law which is enforceable and which can be distinguished from morality, by relying on the distinction between inside and outside. In this form, the distinction between violence and civilization already had a tendency to accept only positive law. The term 'civilization', however, (created in the eighteenth century)[37] related to society's total development (including education and the advantages associated with an increased division of labour) and so made legal theory dependent upon an assumption of civilization's progress. In contrast to the older Natural Law with its waning significance over time, and the tendency to restrict the meaning of law to positive law only (however rationally thought through and guided by arguments), from the eighteenth century one sees a clear reorientation as representative of the conditions of modern society.

The distinction violence/civilization was already under attack in the eighteenth century, although initially without having any particular impact.[38] It disintegrated—not so much as a distinction but as a fundamental theory of law—as confidence in progress dwindled, and it was replaced by the distinction between facts and validity, or of facts and the validity of values. This distinction allows law to go on its own way, separately from the facts of social life; to ascertain its own 'intellectual' existence and to claim its autonomy as a separate part of culture. This led to doctrinal controversies within legal theory, for example the controversy between a jurisprudence of concepts ('Begriffsjurisprudenz') and a jurisprudence of interests

[37] According to Werner Kraus (*Zur Anthropologie des 18. Jahrhunderts: Die Frühgeschichte der Menschheit im Blickpunkt der Aufklärung* (Munich, 1979), 65) the term 'civilisation' is used for the first time by Nicolas-Antoine Boulanger, *L'Antiquité devoilée par ces usages* (Amsterdam, 1766). The term 'civiliser' is already used in the seventeenth century.

[38] See, for example, Simon-Nicolas-Henri Linguet, *Théorie des loix civiles, ou Principes fondamentaux de la société*, 2 vols. (London, 1767), especially the 'discours préliminaire'.

('Interessenjurisprudenz') and to a further distinction between legality and legitimacy where the latter is defined by reference to values.

Against this background it is not difficult to understand how the distinction between norms and facts supported early writings on the sociology of law and, at the same time, kept those writings at a distance from other legal theory.[39] Legal practitioners have always taken it for granted that they also have to assess facts and the relations between facts, all the more so when they are supposedly involved in 'social engineering'. In this sense the reduction of jurisprudence to a science of norms led to the complementary postulate that sociology of law should be an ancillary science of jurisdiction and legislation—in the form of what some have called, right up until today, 'research into legal facts'.[40] This did not have much impact on sociology. Sociology was more concerned with establishing a claim for the autonomy of its discipline, thereby presenting society as a fact which generated norms and yet which had to rely on other's normative orientations (such as those of religion, morals, law).[41] In any event, it was and is impossible for sociology, including sociology of law, to define the objectives of its research with the help of a distinction between norms and facts.

After such a long history, in the course of which a considerable number of distinctions have been used, demonstrating in each case not only their special virtues but also their limitations, one is faced with the question of how one can retain the knowledge that has been achieved and yet come up with a new formulation of legal theory. One could think of some attempt to mediate between the distinctions that have been applied so far. However, the next question would be: which distinction could have such transcending qualities as to be able to achieve this? Of course, lawyers are aware of the consequences of their decisions and may judge them differently depending on whose interests are at stake. And, of course, law is aware of the distinctions between norms and facts, and between facts and validity. However, apparently none of these distinctions provides a handle for using

---

[39] For a classical formulation see Hans Kelsen, 'Zur Soziologie des Rechts: Kritische Betrachtungen', *Archiv für Sozialwissenschaft und Sozialpolitik* 34 (1912), 601–14; id., *Der soziologische und der juristische Staatsbegriff: Kritische Untersuchung des Verhältnisses zwischen Staat und Recht* (Tübingen, 1922).

[40] See, for example, the monograph series under this title ('Rechtstatsachenforschung'), edited by the Federal Ministry of Justice in Germany. For an overview from the perspective of the user see Dietrich Strempel, 'Empirische Rechtsforschung als Ressortforschung im Bundesministerium der Justiz', *Zeitschrift für Rechtssoziologie* 9 (1988), 190–201.

[41] Some links between sociology and legal theory were made with the help of the concept of 'institution' (which is experiencing a revival at present). See above all Santi Roman, *L'ordinamento giuiridico*. Reprint of the 2nd edition (Florence, 1962); Maurice Hauriou, *Die Theorie der Institution und zwei andere Aufsätze*, German translation, ed. Roman Schnur (Berlin, 1965). These approaches may have provided sociological concepts for the sources of law but have not precipitated much further legal development.

those distinctions in a way that one side of them designates the law and the other side something else. Equally, it becomes apparent that none of these distinctions defines the form of law in terms of an object of observation and description. Rather, one has to assume that the law produces these distinctions by itself in order to gain guidance for its operations and to equip them with a capacity for observation. Tradition does not yield distinctions that constitute law but rather distinctions which are produced by legal practice and which are used in legal practice with varying degrees of success.

Having arrived at the question of how law can be distinguished, we can now lay our cards on the table. The question can be solved if one succeeds in describing law as an autopoietic, self-distinguishing system. A theory design of this kind implies that the law produces by itself all the distinctions and concepts which it uses, and that the unity of law is nothing but the fact of this self-production, this 'autopoiesis'. Society, then, must be seen as the environment that makes such a self-production of law possible and, moreover, tolerates it. One can use the term 'encourages' for 'tolerates' if one wishes. Although one typical objection to this theory design is that it advocates the total isolation of law from society, a kind of juridical solipsism, in fact the contrary applies. However, this can only be shown if one presents a complete account of some of the more recent developments of systems theory. Unfortunately, such a presentation, in turn, burdens the suggested approach with a heavy load of complex and highly abstract preliminary concepts which, by comparison, make all other legal theories appear endowed with an almost classic simplicity. If, however, it has precisely been the reliance on an inadequately constructed distinction that has been the problem with other theories, and thus the way in which they have distinguished law has proved to be inadequate, we cannot see any other approach to take but to develop theories with a superior ordering power and with a higher structural complexity. These do not necessarily have to follow along the lines that will be sketched out below; however, once the problem is defined in this way every acceptable theory must somehow be able to deal with the problem as defined.

IV

The sociology of law is addressed to science and not to the legal system. This contrasts with jurisprudential, philosophical, or other legal theories, which have as their goal their use in the legal system or which at least pick up and digest what makes sense in the legal system. This difference has to be kept in mind, however close the theoretical terms used are to those used in legal theory (after all, the object in each instance is law). This means, above all, that the following analyses strictly avoid normative implications. Their propositions remain throughout on the level of facts as they can be ascertained by sociology. In this sense, all concepts that are used here have an empirical reference. However, this does not mean that the propositions will be restricted to only those that are supported or could be supported by empirical research relying on ordinary research methods. The scope of these ordinary methods is far too small for that.[42]

This makes it all the more important to choose carefully those terms which define the facts that can be observed, even if they do not comply with the proposed restriction to rely only on those propositions that can be ascertained by an empirical test. In other words, we avoid propositions in a world of ideas, that particular 'higher' level of values, norms, or 'ought', in Kelsen's sense, without an empirical reference. There is no 'idea of the law' above the law (for sociologists). Likewise there is no concept of a 'supra-legal law' (for sociologists) at a special level above legal operation from which an assessment could be made as to whether or not law is actually law.[43] Rather, law makes this assessment of itself by itself, and if this does not happen it (such an assessment) does not happen. This is why law formulates what could be seen as 'supra-legal law' in the positive norms of constitutional law. Without doing it in this way such law could not be recognized as law. The term 'norm' refers to a certain form of factual expectation, which has to be observable either psychologically or as the intended and understandable meaning of communication. Such expectations either exist or they do not exist. And if one wants to formulate an argument that expectations should exist, one does not have to refer to a separate level of normative 'ought' but, in turn, to further expectations—that is, expectations which normatively expect that there are normative expectations.

Similarly, the concept of validity is not understood here in a normative sense as if it had the implication that what is valid should be valid. We sever any recourse to a 'higher level' on which a value is allocated to 'ought'. Law is valid if it is signed with the symbol of validity—and if this does not happen, it is not valid.

Finally, the meaning of the concept of function does not contain any normative or even teleological connotations. All that is involved is a point of view representing a limiting effect, and seen from the point of view of society, a problem, the solution of which (with the one or other variant of law) is a precondition for the evolution of higher degrees of system complexity.

---

[42] This, in turn, is frequently seen as a deficiency of the theory of an autopoietic legal system that follows. See, for example, William M. Evan, *Social Structure and Law: Theoretical and Empirical Perspectives* (Newbury Park, 1990). However, with regard to how the ideas of this author proceed to such exaggerated claims, which exceed by far what empirical research can actually provide, it would be better not to make certain claims in the first place.

[43] For an example from the juridical side see Otto Bachof, *Verfassungswidrige Verfassungsnormen?* (Tübingen, 1951), reprinted in O. Bachof, *Wege zum Rechtsstaat, Ausgewählte Studien zum öffentlichen Recht* (Königstein, 1979), 1–48.

Legal theory, too, has at times come close to such a decidedly fact-oriented self-description of law, for instance under the influence of behaviourism in the first half of the twentieth century or of the 'unity of science' movement. However, a closer analysis can fairly quickly show the weaknesses in the argumentation, or at least ambiguities that can be found in the actual positions where such legal theory is expected to provide an understanding of a normative proposition. So, for instance, Karl Olivecrona introduced his programmatic monograph *Law as Fact*[44] with the topic 'The Binding Force of Law' and attempted to filter out all mystical notions of natural law or of positivist theory associated with the will of the state. But if one observed strictly the facticity of law as it happens, one would not even formulate the problem in this way. Law has no binding force. It consists purely of communication and of structural deposits of communication, which convey such meanings. We will also use the term '*Zeitbindung*' (time-binding)—but only in the sense in which one could also say that language is binding time by determining the meaning of words for the further use of words with that meaning.

To insist that the distinction between norms and facts is only made by the legal system internally is simply another version of distancing us from a 'law-friendly' legal theory. Merely by elaborating on this distinction legal theory defers to the legal system and is subsumed by it. For science this distinction has no relevance—as a distinction. In other words: when we are talking in the following chapters about the distinction between norms and facts then this refers to a fact, namely the fact that the legal system (understandably) uses this distinction. The system of science, however, deals only with facts and distinguishes between facts and concepts such as external reference and self-reference. That is why it is ultimately of such little importance to point out the non-normative character of the concepts and propositions in the text that follows.

V

Our starting point is the proposition that the legal system is a sub-system of the social system.[45] This differs from other approaches to the sociology of law that, usually, demonstrates their relationship with sociology by their use of empirical methods and then go on to apply sociological theories to law. Even though the analyses that will be presented here are also, primarily, a contribution to social theory, they are not principally interested in how

---

[44] Karl Olivecrona, *Law as Fact* (Copenhagen and London, 1939).

[45] For a similar view see Adam Podgórecki, Christopher J. Whelan, and Dinesh Koshla (eds.), *Legal Systems and Social Systems* (London, 1985).

society influences law (also in contrast to other sociological analyses of law). The formulation of the objectives of research, as is usually found in 'law and society' studies, assumes that the law is already constituted as something that is more or less susceptible to the influences of society. However, the more fundamental question as to how law is at all possible in society is then neither questioned nor answered.

The rest of this chapter and the one following will elaborate further on this question. We assume that the unity of the system can only be produced and reproduced by the system itself and not by any factors in its environment. This applies both to society and to its legal system. Even if we consistently state throughout in the following analyses that the system to which we refer is the 'legal system', it is necessary to clarify at the outset that the relationship of this system with the all-embracing social system is ambivalent. On the one hand society is the environment for its legal system; on the other hand, all operations of the legal system are always also operations in society, that is, operations of the society. The legal system performs in society by differentiating itself within the society. In other words, the legal system creates its own territory by its own operations (which are at the same time social operations). Only when doing so does it develop a social environment of law within society. This, then, allows the question to be asked as to how the influences of this environment can be brought to bear on law, without the consequence being that law and society cannot be distinguished from one another.

The problematic concept of the ambivalent relationship between law and society stands out, when we apply a strictly operative approach. The unity of a system (and this includes the structures and boundaries of the system) is produced and reproduced by the operations of the system. Thus, we will need to use the term 'operative closure' of the system. This applies both to the social system and the legal system. The mode of operation, which produces and reproduces the social system, is meaningful communication.[46] This statement enables us to say that the legal system is a subsystem of the social system in so far as it uses the mode of operation of communication, that is, that it cannot do anything else but frame forms (sentences) in the medium of meaning with the help of communication. It is an achievement of the social system that this has become possible, and that a long socio-cultural evolution has made this self-evident. This achievement, for instance, provides the legal system with the guarantee that neither paper nor ink, neither people nor other organisms, neither courthouses and their rooms nor telephones or computers are part of the

---

[46] See also Niklas Luhmann and Raffaele De Giorgi, *Teoria della società* (Milan, 1992), and for social systems in general: Niklas Luhmann, *Soziale Systeme: Grundriß einer allgemeinen Theorie* (Frankfurt, 1984); English-language version: *Social Systems* (Stanford, 1995).

system.[47] The social system has already constituted this frontier. Those who try to communicate with their telephones ('stop ringing, phone!') misunderstand systems; one can communicate not to but only with the help of a telephone.

Consequently, the legal system operates in the form of communication under the protection of boundaries that are drawn by society. This means, however, that the legal system must distinguish in a special way all that has to be treated as legal communication in the social system. This topic will be dealt with extensively. All that matters for now is how a position can be reached through the theory of operatively closed systems which goes beyond the debate which has kept semiotics and linguistic analysis busy for a long time, including their applications to law.[48] As far as signs or language are concerned, the French tradition founded on the writings of Ferdinand de Saussure accentuated more the structural aspects, while the American tradition based on Peirce stressed the pragmatic aspects. In the one tradition, the weight is on the structural constraints on which the use of linguistic signs depends (whatever philosophers claim to be their domain, for instance, under the concept of the autonomy of thought[49]). In the other tradition, the accent is on the intention of the speaker, on 'speech acts' in the sense of Austin and Searle.

So far neither the structuralist thesis nor analysis following the theory of the speech act have turned out to be particularly fruitful.[50] Obviously, lawyers use ordinary language as regards phonology, syntax, etc. (which represent the main interests of linguistics), interspersed only with some special terms or words which assume a meaning in juridical discourse which differs from the meaning they have in everyday speech. The idea of an 'autonomous' legal discourse or of an operatively closed system would be inconceivable when considered purely in relation to language since, of course, this language and its discourse takes place in society. However, the

---

[47] Objections to such an externalization not so much of houses as of people are legion. See, for instance, in relation to the sociology of law: Walter Kargl, 'Kommunikation kommuniziert? Kritik des rechtssoziologischen Autopoiesisbegriffs', *Rechtstheorie* 21 (1990), 352–73. However, even the most cursory of readings of these assessments reveals that they use terms like 'human being', 'subject', and 'individual' in the singular and so avoid reflection on who is actually implied. If one were to take account empirically of the states of affairs that are meant by these terms, there is no substance to the assertion that the reference to any individual (please give me: name, age, address, gender, etc.) would be suitable to explain social phenomena. To those who polemicize in this way we counter with the objection that they do not take the human being seriously as an individual.

[48] See, for instance, Bernard S. Jackson, *Semiotics and Legal Theory* (London, 1985), esp. 25.

[49] This also includes Jacques Derrida, 'Le supplément de copule', in Jacques Derrida, *Marges de la philosophie* (Paris, 1972), 209–46, who 'deconstructs' this distinction in his own way.

[50] See, in relation to linguistics, philosophy of language, etc., the presentation of a symposium, 'Le langage du droit', in *Archives de philosophie du droit* 19 (1974).

problem is that one often cannot understand legal discourse unless one is specially trained. This includes not only the understanding of meanings but also and, to an even greater extent, the understanding of the intentions and consequences of certain statements.

Only the switch from an analysis based on linguistic theory to an analysis based on communication theory opens the way for legal theory and sociology of law, and then to the problems associated with their intersection. This switch puts the relevance of the controversy between structuralists and speech act theorists in perspective. Both parties to this controversy only cover one part of the phenomenon. Communication cannot happen without either structures or speech acts. However, communication cannot be reduced to speech acts. It includes information and understanding as well. Further, there is a circular relationship between structure and operation, which means that structures can only be established and varied by operations that, in turn, are specified by structures. In both those respects the theory of society as an operatively closed communication system is the more comprehensive theoretical approach; and by defining the legal system as a sub-system of the social system any pretensions as to the dominance of either pragmatist or structuralist perspectives can be excluded from consideration.

There is not much point in deciding whether a theory of this kind should be called sociology or sociology of law, when it includes controversial issues of legal theory, linguistic theory, and semiotic theory. With sociology of this kind, which is so clearly bound by its interdisciplinary obligations, categorizing it in terms of a discipline makes little sense. All that matters is that the venture moves ahead at a level of abstraction which is rarely encouraged in current sociology.

2 The Operative Closure of the Legal System

I

The topic of this chapter proceeds under the heading of the 'positivity' of law in legal theory and its ancillary literature. Since Bentham's polemics on the absurd theories of reason in the common law and since the philosophical polemics on the impractical attempts to build the principles of law on the basis of transcendental theories (Feuerbach, Hugo), modern law has described itself as positive law.[1] The remaining disputed question is: whether law in the way in which it is valid needs a further reason or 'legitimacy'. The status of such a further reason as it relates to law internally is unclear. Of course, one can talk about a political and moral assessment of valid law. However, a legal system that acknowledges another law that does not need to be grounded in positive law, alongside positive law, provides a reason for resistance to positive law. Understandably, most refrain from such a proposition—with the exception of some extreme theories.

Theoretical discussions may take up such questions, and we shall return to them in Chapter 11, in which self-descriptions of the legal system will be elaborated on further. However, the essential problems of 'legal positivism' are not related to the problem of legitimacy, and even less to the distinction between natural law and legal rationalism. Rather, the essential problem is that the concept of positivity is theoretically inadequate. It may be appropriate when applied in the context of reflexive theories of the legal system; however, when applied in a scientific context it lacks connection to other theoretical concepts.

The concept of positivity suggests that it can be understood through the concept of decision. Positive law is supposed to be validated through decisions. This leads to the charge of 'decisionism' in the sense of a possibility to decide in an arbitrary fashion, dependent only on the coercive force behind such decisions. Thus, this leads in fact to a dead-end; after all, everybody knows that in law decisions are never simply made arbitrarily. Something went awry with this line of reasoning, and we must assume that the mistake is related to the insufficiency of the concept of positivity.

Positive law has, indeed, been characterized as 'arbitrary' in the context of natural law.[2] However, this characterization has to be seen in relation to the

---

[1] See especially: Gustav Hugo, *Lehrbuch des Naturrechts als einer Philosophie des positiven Rechts, besonders des Privatrechts* (1798; reprint Vaduz 1971). See also Jürgen Blühdorn, '"Kantianer" und Kant: Die Wende von der Rechtsmetaphysik zur Wissenschaft vom positiven Recht', *Kant-Studien* 64 (1973), 363–94.

[2] See, for instance, Jean Domat, *Les Loix civiles dans leur ordre naturel*, 2nd edn. (Paris, 1697), vol. 1, LVI.

guiding distinction between unchangeable and changeable law. If changeable law is characterized as 'arbitrary' this means only that it cannot be deduced from unchangeable (divine, natural) law but has to be adjusted to the circumstances of time and situation; and it is precisely this requirement that excludes the possibility that decisions could ever be made arbitrarily.[3] The distinction between unchangeable and changeable preserved the old priority of natural law, though in a fashion that essentially, as time passed, was no longer justified. Once the distinction between natural law and positive law had been discarded and the unchangeability of law had to be mandated in positive law by 'constitutions', the guarantee for the unchangeability of an unchangeable law, which is founded on 'nature', could be dispensed with. Nevertheless, this did not mean that arbitrariness became acceptable but only that law made its own changeability available for the tasks of regulation.

One can ask what is supposed to be excluded by the concept of positivity. This refers back to the medieval notion of a cosmologically founded, hierarchical architecture, which provided for natural and divine law, alongside positive law for regulating whatever happened. However, once one relinquishes this concept, any counter-concept to the concept of positivity fails, and what remains is only a certain dissatisfaction with the state of affairs, a dissatisfaction that is hard to articulate.

Since the eighteenth century the distinction that has been used instead is the distinction between law and morals, depending, as it does, on whether one is concerned with external or internal constraints.[4] One may accept this distinction but it does nothing for legal theory—apart from, of course, providing confirmation that law is positive law and that it can also be assessed morally (without immediate legal effects). However, the (theoretical) insufficiency of the distinction is related to the concept of positivity itself; this (undeniably reasonable) distinction between law and morals does not lead anywhere but to debates which have to accept the distinction between law and morals, but at the same time are unable to accept it.[5]

---

[3] David Hume, *A Treatise of Human Nature*, book III, part II, sect. I, quoted from the edition of Everyman's Library (London, 1956), vol 2, p. 190: 'Though the rules of justice be *artificial* [in contrast to natural (N.L.)] they are not *arbitrary*.'

[4] Apparently this version of the problem was motivated by the late reception of Western European natural and rationalist law in Germany, and, in the process, it made natural law side with a law which was founded on an external coercive force of sanctions while ethics specialized in a theory of the justification of moral judgements. See, for instance, Fritz von Hippel, *Zum Aufbau und Sinnwandel unseres Privatrechts* (Tübingen, 1957), 42; Werner Schneiders, *Naturrecht und Liebesethik: Zur Geschichte der praktischen Philosophie im Hinblick auf Christian Thomasius* (Hildesheim, 1971). Only if law is 'hardened' in this way can it appear as the guarantor for subjective freedom, including the freedom to choose one's own morals as long as this is not against the law.

[5] For current discussion of this topic see for instance David Lyons, *Ethics and the Rule of Law* (Cambridge, 1984); Ottfried Höffe, *Kategorische Rechtsprinzipien: Ein Kontrapunkt der Moderne*

As one looks at attempts to deal with the problem of the contextualization of the positivity of law, they leave the option of formulating the problem—which is only insufficiently defined as 'positivity'—in conceptually different ways. We will do this in the following chapter with the help of systems theory. But we do not use 'system' like some lawyers who mean by it a context of coordinated rules.[6] We mean by 'system' a context of factually enacted operations, which have to be communicated because they are social operations, whatever defines them—and in addition to that—have to be communicated as legal communication. This means, however, that the basic distinction is not to be found in a typology of norms or of values but in a distinction between system and environment.

The transition to a system/environment theory requires a further distinction, which needs to be clarified in advance. Usually legal theories refer to structures (rules, norms, texts) that can be classified as law. This applies especially to theories of positive law, as, for instance, explicitly to the 'rules of recognition' of Hart's legal theory.[7] In this way, the question as to what is law and what it is not is relevant only in relation to the specificity of certain rules. If one, in contrast, wants to follow suggestions which have been formulated by more recent systems theory, one has to switch from structures to operations.[8] The basic question is then how operations produce the difference between system and environment and—because this requires recursivity—how *operations* recognize which *operations* belong to the system and which do not. Structures are necessary for the highly selective interlacing of operations, but the identity of law is not given by any stable ideal but exclusively by those operations that produce and reproduce a specific legal meaning. In addition we assume that these operations always have to be the operations of the legal system itself (which can, of course, be observed from outside). This and this alone is implied by the thesis of operative closure.

(Frankfurt, 1990). One solution, which does not involve much conceptual effort, is the reduction of the problem to specific legal questions such as interpretations of constitutional law and human rights. This means, however, forgoing the question as to the unity of law in relation to morals.

[6] See here (but arguing against a reduction to the linguistic form of the rules without concern for their effects on behaviour) W. Krawietz, *Recht als Regelsystem* (Wiesbaden, 1984). One should also keep in mind that the law contains countless texts which appear linguistically neither as rules nor as 'ought'—for example: *pater est quem nuptiae demonstrant.* (This is also an example of the closure of the legal system as there is obviously no mention of the sire of a child who is normally called father.)

[7] See H. L. A. Hart, *The Concept of Law* (Oxford, 1961). Even if this reference is clear, nevertheless Hart cannot avoid having to refer to something like institutional practices when it comes to applying rules.

[8] This is not altogether surprising for legal theory. For instance, Melvin Aaron Eisenberg, *The Nature of Common Law* (Cambridge, Mass., 1988), distinguishes text-based theories from generative theories, from opts for the latter (as against the theories of Hart and Raz).

In adopting the terminology of a theory of knowledge one could also speak of 'operative constructivism'.

II

Research on systems is divided on the issue as to what is meant by system as opposed to environment. All statements by systems theory have to be formulated as statements that relate to the difference between system and environment or at least need to start from the form of this distinction if the pitfall of the thermodynamic law of entropy is to be avoided. Older systems theory suggested in response a form of 'open systems'. The point of attack of this thesis was the second law of entropy which offered the insight that systems which are closed in relation to their environments adapt to their environment by and large, that is, they dissolve because they lose energy and so irreversibly encounter their death by warming up. Therefore a continuous exchange with the environment is necessary—either in the form of energy, or in the form of information—in order to grow in complexity and to establish and maintain 'negentropy'. Put more formally, such systems transform inputs to outputs according to a transformation function that enables them to retain a surplus for their maintenance on a plateau of complexity achieved through evolution.

This thesis is not rejected by the theory of operatively closed systems, even if it often adopts different emphases[9] (for instance, in relation to 'information'). The input/output models allowed for systems to use their output as input.[10] The later development of the theory 'internalized' this feedback loop and declares it to be a necessary condition of its operation.

---

[9] Francesco Varela goes so far as to juxtapose input-type descriptions and closure-type descriptions as two different 'complementary modes of descriptions'; see Hans Ulrich and Gilbert J. B. Probst (eds.), *Self-Organization and Management of Social Systems: Insights, Promises, Doubts, and Questions* (Berlin, 1984), 25–32. See also id., 'L'auto-organisation: De l'apparence au mécanisme', in Paul Dumouchel and Jean-Pierre Dupuy (eds.), *L'auto-organisation: De la physique au politique* (Paris, 1983) 147–64. This distinction is too poorly elaborated in these texts to allow for a critique. We assume that both these types of description are not equivalent but require the prerequisite input/output descriptions of operative closure because otherwise there would not be a carrier for the transformation function; further, they are rarely adequate, and in any event not for the legal system because they have to assume a high specification of interdependencies with the environment.

[10] Including applications for legal systems. See above all Jay A. Sigler, 'A Cybernetic Model of the Judicial System', *Temple Law Quarterly* 41 (1968), 398–428. See also, in the form of an introductory text, id., *An Introduction to the Legal System* (Homewood, Ill., 1968), and Charles D. Raab, 'Suggestions for a Cybernetic Approach to Sociological Jurisprudence', *Journal of Legal Education* 17 (1965), 397–411; Ottmar Ballweg, *Rechtswissenschaft und Jurisprudenz* (Basel, 1970), esp. at 76; William J. Chambliss and Robert B. Seidman, *Law, Order, and Power* (Reading, Mass., 1971), and under the aspect of a sub-system of the political system Glendon Schubert, *Judicial Policy Making*, 2nd edn. (Glenview, Ill., 1974), 138.

This progression of the theory comes from the insight that the accumulation of internal complexity is possible only through operative closure—frequently formulated as a condition of 'order from noise'.[11] This is usually demonstrated by reference to the operative closure of the brain as a paradigm example. A rather more theoretical argument could show that exceeding a minimum level of number and diversity in elements is possible only if one does not strive for a complete linkage of one element with any other element at any given moment. However, this presupposes a selection of the actually executed linkages[12] and thus, in turn, an internal conditioning of this selection. Only the selective linkage 'qualifies' the elements, and only this makes it meaningful to talk about elements *that belong to* the system, and about the boundaries of the system or about its differentiation.

The theory of operatively closed systems is, in addition, a theory of the distinction between system and environment. Closure must not be misunderstood as isolation. The theory does not object to, and indeed highlights in its own way, the intensive causal links between systems and their environments, and that interdependencies of a causal kind are structurally necessary for the system. Take, for instance, the complex and highly selective physical conditions for life on earth. Here it would be truly absurd to ignore common sense. Thus, systems theory has long since accepted that the openness (dependence of the system on its environment) on the basis of matter or energy does not conflict with the thesis of informational or semantic closure.[13] Therefore, we distinguish between causal closure (isolation) and operative closure. The theory of operative closure separates itself from the causal relations between system and environment when it defines its object.

First of all it is necessary to clarify what there is to observe (even if one wants to examine interdependencies between system and environment). We call those systems operatively closed that rely on their own network of operations for the production of their own operations and which, in this

[11] According to Heinz von Foerster, 'On Self-Organizing Systems and their Environments', in Marshall C. Yovits and Scott Cameron (eds.), *Self-Organizing Systems: Proceedings of an Interdisciplinary Conference 5 and 6 May 1959* (Oxford, 1960), 31–50.

[12] Through this, the options which have not been considered become *potentialized*, to use the formulation of Yves Barel, *Le paradoxe et le système: Essai sur le fantastique social*, 2nd edn. (Grenoble, 1989), 71. This means that they are given the status of mere options for other combinations which require the system to provide the conditions for their being options; this status can eventually be transferred from non-actuality to actuality by operations of the system—as a precondition for evolutionary structural change. In other words: the system also recalls what it has discarded.

[13] See, for example, Gerhard Roth, 'Die Konstitution von Bedeutung im Gehirn', in Siegfried J. Schmidt (ed.), *Gedächtnis: Probleme und Perspektiven der interdisziplinären Gedächtnisforschung* (Frankfurt, 1991), 360–70.

sense, reproduce themselves.[14] Using a somewhat less rigid formulation it could be said that the system has to assume its own existence in order to engage in its own reproduction through further operations over time, or in other words, the system produces its operations by going back to and anticipating its other operations and it can only determine in this way what belongs to the system and what belongs to the environment.

The innovation achieved by introducing the concept of autopoiesis shifts the idea of a self-referential make-up to the level of the elementary operations of the system (i.e. those which cannot be reduced further by the system) and, in doing so, to everything that constitutes unity for the system. What is involved here is no longer only a self-organization in the sense of a control and change of structures by the system itself, and so no longer only autonomy in the old sense of self-regulation. This innovation casts new light on an old problem, and that is the relationship between structure and operation (process), or norm and action, or rule and decision.

What is irritating about the concept of autopoiesis, which leads to extensive critical discussion, is that the revolutionary effect of the concept is inversely related to its explanatory value. The concept merely states that the elements and structures of a system exist only as long as it manages to maintain its autopoiesis. The concept does not say anything about the kind of structures that are developed in cooperation with the structural couplings between system and environment. Accordingly, autopoiesis is introduced as an 'invariant'. It is always the same with all kinds of life and with all kinds of communication. And if the legal system is an autopoietic system *sui generis*, then this applies to all legal regimes equally, only referring to the code that attributes the operations of these systems to the system. However, this does not explain which normative programmes are developed by the system.[15]

---

[14] It is important to note that the concept of production *never* requires that there is control over *all* the causes of the product. For instance, the most important cause of the production of a photograph of—say, the Eiffel Tower—is the Eiffel Tower itself. It alone is indispensable—the camera and even the photographer are exchangeable. It follows that the most important cause is outside the production process. The concept of production only designates what is necessary for the establishment and maintenance of a *deviation*—that is, a deviation from what would be the case otherwise. A further typical criterion is that of the *disposition in the system*. Only if there is an additional provision for producing the disposition in the system by the system itself, can one talk of an *auto*poietic system in the strict sense. However, these are additional, i.e., restrictive, requirements which in no way change the fact that no system can control all causes which could not be dropped without also dropping the autopoiesis itself. *Therefore* autopoietic reproduction always involves also the reproduction of the boundaries of the system which separate the internal and external causes.

[15] Accordingly I agree with all the critics who point out that the concept of autopoiesis does not explain anything empirically. However, this applies to *all* concepts, including, for instance, the concept of action. The pressure for adaptation, which new concepts exert on theory contexts, gives the meaning of incisive changes in terminology. And only theories can be assessed for their grasp on reality.

If one assumes that operations are self-produced, it follows that everything that is happening is happening in the present. This also means that everything that is happening is happening at the same time. Also past and future are always, and only, relevant at the same time, and are discernible as such only in the present. Their recursive linkages are established in their actual operations. Therefore, the requisite structures are also only presently in use—or they are not in use. The system oscillates from operation to operation with the help of these structures—and it does that, *at the same time*, with an extremely varied array of performances.

The same applies to every observation on this state of affairs and to observations that are both external and internal to the system. Observations are also operations. An observer also can only observe when he does so, not when he does not do so. He can distinguish between constant structures and eventual operations as if they were still objects in motion, but *only if* he does this can he register structural changes. An observer is thus caught in the system that is tied to the conditions of time in its own right, that is, tied to the time which he respectively constructs as his horizon through its own distinctions in his own present time.

There are no exceptions—either for the science system, or for the legal system. Questions as to the stability of norms, the duration of the validity of norms, and the change of norms relate to a secondary phenomenon. This applies, *a fortiori*, to the further question as to how and how far the legal system is independent in its autopoiesis—and, therefore, its dynamic stability— from ongoing changes in its structure; in other words, whether the system can 'survive' structural changes or can even utilize those changes to perform its autopoiesis. Furthermore, this question is decided from moment to moment (and never, by structural change, once and for all), and typically without doubting that life goes on. If there are any uncertainties left—which have to be kept at manageable low levels—they concern the question *how?*

Structures are only really real when they are used for linking communicative events; norms only when they are quoted explicitly or implicitly; expectations only when they are expressed through communication. Therefore, the system has an immense capacity for adaptation by simply forgetting, by not reusing expectations with their structuring effects—so much so that the invention of writing becomes a nuisance. As soon as writing becomes available and textual fixtures become possible, the system is confronted with its memory. Forgetting is not so easy now; one must guard against an accidental quoting of norms at any given moment. A certain animosity against written forms develops.[16] This can be clearly found as late as

---

[16] See Peter Goodrich, 'Literacy and the Language of the Early Common Law', *Journal of Law and Society* 13 (1987), 422–44. Also, in more detail, id., *Languages of Law: From Logics of Memory to Nomadic Masks* (London, 1990).

the Middle Ages and in early modern times, and at the same time there are compensatory developments which react to this new problem as a functionally equivalent device for forgetting, namely (1) the development of jurisprudence and professional skills for the *possible* handling of texts—just in case, if there is a problem; and (2) the acceptance of norm changes which are performed with the help of procedures which the system provides for this case, as a functional equivalent for forgetting.

However, none of this changes the basic state of affairs that the system is only actualized through its operations; that only what happens happens; that everything that happens—in the system and in its environment—happens at the same time.

If one wants to conduct research applying systems theory on these terms, sufficient accuracy is required in defining the operation that executes the autopoietic reproduction. In the case of biology one can assume some form of consensus on the basis of biochemical research—including the view of many biologists that the concept of autopoiesis is trivial because it only offers a word for something which can be described much more accurately through defining the form of the operation.[17] A theory of social systems cannot count on such a consensus; this is even more so the case if one wants to describe the legal system as an autopoietic, operatively closed social system. Legal science as a text-based science has no need of explanations in this respect. Sociology of law is usually restricted to a vague notion of social action or behaviour, and makes up for the contents that are specifically legal by assumptions about the ideas and intentions of the actor and the 'intended meaning' (Max Weber) of acting. This will not suffice here. We do not reject the suggestion that psychological equivalents of legally

[17] In view of the unrelenting criticisms of the 'reception' of the concept, one can only point out again that the use of the concept of autopoiesis does not propose an analogy and neither is it meant metaphorically. This is the misunderstanding of Hubert Rottleuthner, 'Biological Metaphors in Legal Thoughts', in Gunther Teubner (ed.), *Autopoietic Law: A New Approach to Law and Society* (Berlin, 1988), 92–127. See also Klaus von Beyme, 'Ein Paradigmawechsel aus dem Geist der Naturwissenschaften: Die Theorien der Selbststeuerung von Systemen (Autopoiesis)', *Journal für Sozialforschung* 31 (1991), 3–24. For a counter-criticism see Walter Kargl, 'Kritik der rechtssoziologischen Autopoiese-Kritik', *Zeitschrift für Rechtssoziologie* 12 (1991), 120–41. However, there is no point in arguing whether or not the concept can be applied to living systems. Therefore it is equally invalid to argue that the application of the concept to social systems represented a falsification of the meaning given to it by Manturana and Varela (see, for example, Ulrich Druwe, 'Recht als autopoietisches System: Zur Kritik des reflexiven Rechtskonstrukts', *Jahresschrift für Rechtspolitologie* 4 (1990), 120–41). We should be allowed to ask critics that they distinguish between the abstract meaning of a term and its materialization in biochemical or communicative operations. All that matters in the sociological context is whether or not the concept of autopoiesis leads to the formulation of hypotheses, which are fruitful science (and this includes empirically fruitful). Incidentally, this view of the problem is also shared by Richard Lempert, 'The Autonomy of Law: Two Visions Compared', in Teubner, *Autopoietic Law*, 152–90, at 155.

relevant operations are formed and that they can be measured empirically (but with a well-understood degree of unreliability). However, someone who is consciously oriented to law must already know what he has in mind. This individual must be able to refer to a social system, law, which is already constituted, or to the textual sediments of such a system. The answer to the question as to which operations reproduce law must be presumed. Psychological systems observe the law but they do not produce it, otherwise law would be locked away deep in what Hegel once called 'the innermost dark thoughts of the mind'.[18] Therefore, it is impossible to take psychological systems, consciousness, or even the whole human individual as a part or as an internal component of the legal system.[19] The autopoiesis of law can only be realized through social operations.

Autopoietic systems are, in this way, tied to the type of operations that they perform, and this applies to both the creation of further operations and the formation of structures. In other words, there is no 'difference in essence' or any 'material difference' between operation and structure. In the biological life process of cells, enzymes are at the same time data, factors for production, and programs. The same applies to language in the social system. Therefore, a description of the legal system cannot start from the assumption that norms (here we shall distinguish further between codes and programmes) are made up of a different substance or quality than communications. Law-related communications have, as operations of the legal system, always a double function as factors for production and as

---

[18] Cf. *Vorlesungen über die Ästhetik*, vol 1, quoted from *Works*, vol. 13 (Frankfurt, 1973), 18.

[19] Nevertheless, this is a controversial point. See, for instance, Christopher Grzegorczyk, 'Système juridique et réalité: Discussion de la théorie autopoiétique du droit', in Paul Amselek and Christopher Grzegorczyk (eds.), *Controverse autour de l'ontologie du droit* (Paris, 1989), 179–209; Arthur J. Jacobson, 'Autopoietic Law: The New Science of Niklas Luhmann', *Michigan Law Review* 87 (1989), 1647–1689; Alan Wolfe, 'Sociological Theory in the Absence of People: The Limits of Luhmann's System Theory', *Cardozo Law Review* 13 (1992), 1729–1743; David E. Van Zand, 'The Breath of Life in the Law', *Cardozo Law Review* 13 (1992), 1745–1761. Unfortunately, the opponents of the consequences of the concept of autopoietic closure restrict themselves to the trivial remark that nothing works without people. However, this does not allow us to decide whether concrete human individuals are, as parts of the legal system, components of its autopoiesis—an assumption that is hard to envisage—or whether they are indispensable as conditions in its environment. Incidentally, Jacobson, *Autopoietic Law*, admits that 'human individual' does not mean the living and conscious system human being: 'Individuals figure in the common law only in the character they display through inter-action oriented toward the values expressed in prior applications of norms. The individuals applying norms may have hosts of attitudes (personality, emotion) toward the application. The attitudes do not matter: only the *display* of the character in interaction matters' (p. 1684). We can only agree. However, such a shrunk concept of individuality is nothing else but the concept of person, that is, a selection of criteria that is produced by communication, and not something which could explain the action. It is precisely the theory of autopoietic systems that takes human individuals seriously in contrast to humanist theories. Indeed it could have the headline 'taking individuals seriously'.

preservers of structure. In this sense autopoietic systems are always historical systems, which start from the state in which they have put themselves. They do whatever they do always for the first and for the last time. All repetitions are a matter of the artificial fixation of structure. And they are historical in the further sense that they owe their structures to the sequence of their operations and from there evolve in a direction of bifurcation and diversification.[20] As an observer, one can distinguish between the functions of the determination or production of their conditions and of the selection of structures, but operatively these cannot be held apart. The operation provides its unity as an autopoietic element precisely by serving both.

The concept of operation deserves more attention than is usually given to it. In a temporal sense, operations are events, that is, they are realizations of meaningful possibilities that—as soon as they are realized—disappear again. Operations as events have no duration, even if there is a minimal duration in which they can be observed (for instance: the time it takes to pronounce a legal judgment). Hence, as they have no duration, they cannot be changed. All duration, all changeability, each structure—have yet to be produced in the system, through operations that are provided by the system as its own operations. There is, in other words, no external determination of structures. Only the law itself can say what law is. This process of the production of structures is designed in a circular fashion because the operations require structures in order to define themselves by referring recursively to other operations. The performance of autopoiesis is not only the production of one operation by another operation but also, and even more so, the condensation and confirmation of structures through operations which are oriented by those structures. It is in this sense that we shall define the legal system also as a system with a (self-)determined structure.

Factually, operations can be understood as creating a difference. Something has changed after the operation and has been made different by the operation. Here one could think of filing a legal action or simply of referring to a question of law in everyday life. It is this discriminating effect of the operation which, given a sufficient duration of the operation and the opportunity to weave its outcomes into a recursive network of further operations, creates a difference between system and environment; or, as we put it,

---

[20] Determination is, of course, found in the system and not in the concept of autopoiesis. Critics who concentrate on the concept of autopoiesis and who accuse the theory of autopoietic systems for having poor explanatory power overlook this; see, for instance, Walter L. Bühl, *Sozialer Wandel im Ungleichgewicht: Zyklen, Fluktuationen, Katastrophen* (Stuttgart, 1990), 189; id., 'Politische Grenzen der Autopoiesis sozialer Systeme', in Hans Rudi Fischer (ed.), *Autopoiesis: Eine Theorie im Brennpunkt der Kritik* (Heidelberg, 1991), 201–25. The point is precisely that one cannot infer, as Hegel did, the movement from the concept. The theory of autopoiesis holds that self-determination would not be possible without operative closure—not more, but not less either.

differentiates a system. This has to be understood as a factual happening—independent of the question of who is observing it and by which distinctions it is observed and described. An operation can be observed and described in many different ways. The filing of a legal action, for instance, can be described as the suffering of an indignity, or as providing a welcome ground for the final breaking off of social relations, as permitted by law, or as an item in a statistical count, or as a reason for the registration and recording of a file number, etc. If one wants to know how an operation is observed, one has to observe the observers.

In view of such a plurality of possibilities for both distinction and observation, we have to distinguish terminologically between operation and observation. At the same time, the observation is itself an operation, and therefore everything applies to it that has been shown to apply to operations.[21] The observation creates, as an operation, a new condition of the system. The observation contributes to autopoiesis and with that to the differentiation of the observing system. Further, we have to think of situations in which the basic operation of the system implies an observation; this means that the operation cannot succeed without concurrent self-observation. In such a case the scheme for observation cannot be chosen arbitrarily but is defined through the type of operation. In this way communication can only be achieved if one can distinguish between information, message, and understanding in the performance of the operation, and if the communication process itself controls which of the three components it will refer to on its further course.[22] If operations that are specific for law are concerned, we shall find that the self-observation oriented by the distinction between law and injustice is indispensable.

Taking these ideas further, a closed system can be defined as a self-referential system. In this terminology, 'referring' has to be understood as designating, namely as a designation in the context of a distinction which has an alternative other side at its disposal (which is also enabled to refer to something). In this sense, self-reference always implies external reference, and vice versa. The system that has emerged by operational discrimination (and through that has become visible for observers) designates itself in contrast to its environment and so, through observation, catches up with what has already happened. The observation is still an operation of the system (otherwise it would be an external observation), which in the moment of its

---

[21] Therefore a theory which uses the distinction between operation and observation is always an 'autological' theory. This means: it produces a description which fits for itself both as an operation and as an observation, and so can also test the description on itself or at least must not be refuted by assumptions about itself.

[22] Of course, this does not exclude other observations, for instance, regarding the accent with which a person talks. However, these observations are not indispensable for the autopoiesis of the system and are options that are only realized occasionally.

execution discriminates only by using a specific (and no other) distinction. As an operation, observations—including the observation based on the distinction between self-reference and external reference—are 'blind' because they cannot distinguish and designate, while executing the distinction and designation, the used distinction from other distinctions.

The concepts of observation and self-reference imply each other. For, on the one hand, observers can only observe when they can distinguish between themselves and their observation instruments, their distinctions and designations, and so manage not to keep confusing themselves with their objects. On the other hand, this is precisely what self-reference is needed for. Louis Kauffman rightly says:

At least one distinction is involved in the presence of self-reference. The self appears, and an indication of that self can be seen as separate from the self. Any distinction involves the self-reference of the one who distinguishes. Therefore, self-reference and the idea of distinction are inseparable (hence conceptually identical).[23]

Nevertheless the concepts of self-reference and observation adopt different forms because a distinction is made between them and respective counter-concepts. The circle of the definition of concepts is broken up. Observation differs from designation (distinction from indication), and self-reference differs from external reference. After the execution of the operation of distinguishing between different sides, the derived concepts also differ, and we can designate different things with 'observation' and 'self-reference', respectively. The legal system is able—as a system with its operations tied to self-observation—to reintroduce the difference between system and environment, which is reproduced by these operations, into the system and to observe itself by using the distinction between system (self-reference) and environment (external reference). Every external observation and description of this system must be aware that the system itself controls the distinction between self-reference and external reference.

Further, it must be maintained that self-referring always designates the system as an *object* not as a *concept*. This is only to say that the system is distinguished from *everything else*, and not from a *certain other*. This corresponds to its indeterminate relationship with its environment (which can only be determined by the system's own reduction of complexity). So the system not only designates itself as a system, as a social system, or as a legal system in contrast to other entities, but also as something which is performing the self-designation whatever else may happen.

Finally it is important to note in this framework of preparatory discussion that self-reference can be realized in different forms. Even the most basic operations of the system require, if they depend on and to the degree

[23] Louis Kauffman, 'Self-reference and Recursive Forms', *Journal of Social and Biological Structures* 10 (1987), 53–72, at 53.

to which they depend on self-observation, the involvement of self-reference. A system that confronts itself with a number of options as to how to proceed (we call this meaningful processing) must be able to distinguish between its own operations and other situations when deciding on its next operation. A social system must run a parallel procedure of recognition while performing its autopoiesis, which determines which earlier and later events have to be counted as communication (and especially as communication within its own system) *and which not*. In relation to these instances, the distinction between self-reference and other-reference is already a requirement of its autopoiesis. This means that the system operates with a sideways look at the *simultaneously* existing environment, and that it does not simply orient by the effects of its own operations in the system as a kind of cybernetic feedback control.

We have to distinguish between these and more demanding forms of self-reference, especially those of the *self-description* of the system. By that we mean the identification of the system as a unit and the description of its properties (its meaning, its function, etc.) in the system. *Self*-description is an operation of the system, and can as such only happen as an operation of the system and as one among many operations. We will call such designs of models or texts of the system, in the system, reflection [reflexion]. It is easy to admit, based on the design of this theory, that self-descriptions of this kind may have only a marginal relevance and one that will vary with the degree of the system's differentiation and the forms of differentiation that society allows.

Given all this, we can talk of autopoiesis and operative closure only if the operations that reproduce each other—and in this way reproduce the system—show certain characteristics. They form *emergent units* that can come about only through the operative closure of the system; and as such they achieve an *independent reduction of complexity*—both of the environment of the system and of the system itself. The fact of the performance alone requires that not everything that exists can be considered. Instead, the selective but operative coupling and the recursive network of the autopoietic reproduction step in as the substitutes for such a complete match between the system and its environment.

III

If one wants to determine the special characteristics of the legal system's self-referential mode of operation in the terms set out so far, a whole hierarchy of concepts comes to the fore.[24] An operative approach cannot

---

[24] Accordingly readers must sort out their objections, depending on the level they are addressing: objections against the theory of autopoietic systems as such, or against the concept of the social system being defined by communication, or only against the presentation of the legal system as one of many of the autopoietic systems in society.

conceive of the unity of the legal system as the unity of a text or the consistent linking of a sum of texts,[25] but only as a particular social system. The basic operation, which defines social systems in their environment, can be understood as communication.[26] This basic operation defines the concept of society as a comprehensive system of all communication in an environment in which there are no communications but only events of different types.

This array of concepts has far-reaching consequences. If one accepts it, all social systems must be understood as part of the performance of society. Accordingly, the legal system also is a system which is a part of society and which performs in society. Headings such as 'law and society',[27] then, do not refer to two independent objects that are opposed to each other but to objects that have to be reformulated in the terms of a theory of differentiation. To repeat this important point: the legal system is a sub-system of the social system.[28] Accordingly, society is not simply the environment of the legal system. Partly, society is more—in so far as it includes the operations of the legal system itself. Partly, it is less—in so far as the legal system deals with the environment of the social system as well as with the mental and physical states of human beings, but also with other physical, chemical, and biological states, depending on which aspects the legal system deems legally relevant.

In the way in which the operations of the legal system are those of a social system and perform as part of society, they have characteristics that are realized not only in the legal system.[29] This applies to all characteristics that relate to a communication as such, for instance the realization of

---

[25] This is the traditional juridical concept of system with a tradition that goes back to the beginning of the seventeenth century. See, for instance, Claus-Wilhelm Canaris, *Systemdenken und Systembegriff in der Jurisprudenz am Beispiel des deutschen Privatrechts* (Berlin, 1969); and Franz-Josef Peine, *Das Recht als System* (Berlin, 1983), who accentuates values as the basis for the formation of a system. Mediating between these positions and therefore ambiguous is Torstein Eckhoff and Nils Kristian Sundby, *Rechtssysteme: Eine systemtheoretische Einführung in die Rechtstheorie* (Berlin, 1988). They state that the legal system consists of 'norms and activities' (p. 41).

[26] See for more details Niklas Luhmann, *Soziale Systeme: Grundriß einer allgemeinen Theorie* (Frankfurt, 1984), 191 (trans., *Social Systems* (Stanford, 1995), 137).

[27] See, for example, Stig Jørgensen, *Recht und Gesellschaft* (Göttingen, 1971).

[28] See Ch. 1.V above.

[29] To make this quite clear, one must point out that it is different in the case of the social system. Communication exists only as a performance of society, only by a recursive reference to the other communications of the social system, and there is nothing that corresponds to this in the environment of the system (provided one understands communication among animals differently, namely as a realization of meaning and not as a link with other social operations). Gunther Teubner rightly insists that there is an essential difference between the operative closure of the social system and that of the sub-systems, see: 'L'ouvert s'appuye sur le fermé: Questioni aperte intorno all'apertura dei sistemi chiusi', *Iride* 6 (1991), 248–52. I would not, however, go as far as he does in respect of the consequences that follow from this difference.

meaning and the possibility to distinguish between an act of notification and one of information. It applies above all to the mechanisms of structural coupling of communication and consciousness in order to catch attention, that is, it applies to language.[30] In so far as it uses language to communicate, the legal system always requires the link with operations outside the legal system. The press can report on new laws and judgments. Legal issues can become the topic of daily conversations. Even if the legal system cannot talk with society as a system, its boundaries are porous as far as communication is concerned. Therefore, the legal system can understand, pick up, and process internally what has been said in society without any concern for law. The legal system simply requires communication to work and to be understood or misunderstood, to suggest acceptance or provoke rejection.

Set against this background, the question of the specific characteristics of legal operations becomes all the more urgent. We recall the need to be accurate in this respect as required by the theory. The theory of an operatively closed autopoietic legal system depends on a satisfactory answer to this question of the specific characteristics of legal operations.

Directly or indirectly all the following analyses will be concerned with this question. We shall merely sketch rough outlines here and put them in context, and come back to a more thorough discussion of them later. The starting point is a purely tautological, formal, hollow answer which holds only that all the following analyses will appear as an 'unfolding' of a tautology (and not as the logical deduction from axioms). Following Tarski and Löfgren, 'unfolding' means to break up an identity (law is law) with the help of distinctions that replace that identity with the unity of the distinction (as compared with the distinction of what has been distinguished).[31] So to start with, we maintain only that the differentiation of an operatively closed legal system is taking place through a recursive reference of legal operations to legal operations. The system operates, like any other autopoietic system, in constant contact with itself. In order to be able to specify its operations as legal, it has to ascertain what it has done so far or what it will also do in future in order to specify its own operations as legal ones.

This version, which appears to be tautological in the way in which it is formulated (that is, for an observer), presents no problem at all for legal practice. Legal practice can use existing law for its orientation. Even and

---

[30] See also Niklas Luhmann, 'Wie ist Bewußtsein an Kommunikation beteiligt?', in Hans Ulrich Gumbrecht and K. Ludwig Pfeiffer (eds.), *Materialität der Kommunikation* (Frankfurt, 1988), 884–905; id., *Die Wissenschaft der Gesellschaft* (Frankfurt, 1990), 11.

[31] See Lars Löfgren, 'Unfoldement of Self-reference in Logic and Computer Science', in Finn V. Jensen, Brien H. Mayoh, and Karen K. Møller (eds.), *Proceedings of the 5th Scandinvavian Logic Symposium* (Aalborg, 1979), 205–29. Usually this term is taken to designate a distinction of hierarchical or linguistic 'levels'. Our text will follow other ideas which are more firmly grounded in systems theory.

especially when changes to law are concerned, what will be changed can be assumed to be known or to be determinable. The answer to the question as to what will be changed will never be: 'Everything!' Not even in revolutions. And it never matters where it all began and where the reference to the historical origin can be found. The origin of law may play a role in the context of myths of legitimacy, that is, in self-descriptions of a certain kind, as a kind of disruption of the circle—the divine gift of the Decalogue as a collective guidance for a tribal society or the divine institution of the *areopagus* as a disruption of the vicious circle of vengeance which transforms right into wrong. Legal practice always operates with a law that has historically always been there because it could not otherwise entertain the notion of distinguishing itself as legal practice. When seen in a historical perspective, there is no origin to law but only situations in which it was sufficiently plausible to assume that earlier peoples also followed legal norms. Therefore, understanding the evolution of law as an autopoietic system is not a problem. The time that is necessary for this evolution is always a construction in the middle of time, in the respective present; all that one can do with the objectifying perspective of an historian is to find out the conditions under which such a construction can be made plausible. For instance, there must always have been conflicts in which the winners could present their victories as law and thus as binding for the future. Or, to quote the famous beginning of the second part of the *Discours sur l'origine et les fondements de l'inégalité parmi les hommes*: 'Le premier qui ayant enclos sur un terrain, s'avisa de dire, *ceci est à moi*, et trouva des gens assés simple pour le croire, fut le vrai fondateur de la société civile.'[32]

Law is also a historical machine in the sense that each autopoietic operation changes the system, changes the state of the machine, and so creates changed conditions for all further operations. According to the terminology of Heinz von Foerster, this is not a trivial machine that always transforms inputs to outputs in the same repetitive way (if it works properly and/or is not broken). It is a machine that involves its own condition in each operation and so constructs a new machine with each operation.[33] Only against this background can one understand the meaning of the postulate that the legal system should function predictably and like a trivial machine, and should be set up accordingly (for instance, by disengaging itself from time).

---

[32] 'The first person who, having fenced off his land, took it into his hands to say "This is mine" and found people simple enough to believe him was the true founder of civil society' (Jean-Jacques Rousseau, *Œuvres complètes* vol. 3, éd. de la Pléiade (Paris 1964), 164.

[33] See Heinz von Foerster, 'Principles of Self-Organization—In a Socio-Managerial Context', in Hans Ulrich and Gilbert J. B. Probst (eds.), *Self-Organization and Management of Social Systems: Insights, Promises, Doubts, and Questions* (Berlin, 1984), 2–24, at 8.

The possibility of recognizing law as law suffices to get the administration of justice started as social autopoiesis. However, it does not suffice to close the legal system, that is, to refer exclusively to contacts with itself. The law remains embedded in general social arrangements, remains dependent on structures that also serve other functions (for instance, the family or a religiously founded morality). Above all, law is co-determined by social stratification and the decisive differences between urban and country settings. The artefacts which have been left to us by older high cultures allow us to see not only these correlations but also a kind of counter-movement. The king or the local court in town was supposed to protect the poor against the wealthy when the former were in the right. However, in the villages people mistrusted the town courts and they preferred their own criminal expertise, their knowledge of persons and local pressures. And in the towns, there was hardly anybody who would litigate against a master or who would stand witness against him while he was in a dependent relationship. Even the reason for a division between legislation and jurisdiction as provided by Aristotle reflected the continuing existence of these social conditions and at the same time the desire to neutralize them. According to Aristotle, jurisdiction on its own would be exposed to social pressures, the friendships and hostilities of judges and their families. Such particulars would be difficult to counter at the level of jurisdiction because it would be hard to predict how the law would be applied in the future. Therefore there had to be legislation and a commitment on the part of the judge towards that legislation.[34] The embedding of law in socially given structures can be neutralized only with the help of a *legally specific* distinction, and not by the powerful claims of a ruler or through religious conditioning concerning the chances for salvation. Such critical impulses and early semantic developments demonstrate that the administration of justice itself had to replace solidarity with society. But how can that be achieved?

It can be achieved, first and foremost, when the law itself recognizes the dominant social structures and replicates them in the forms of distinctions that are relevant to law. Not only, for instance, did the aristocracy in the Europe of old have a different legal position and different rights, especially with regard to procedures. There was also a general rule that in a case between a member of the aristocracy and a member of the bourgeoisie, the aristocrat would prevail if unclear factors left any doubt.[35] With the change

---

[34] See *Rhetorics* 1354^{a}32–1354^{b}15. On the reception of this concept at the height of the Middle Ages see Aegidius Columnae Romanus (Egidio Colonna), *De regimine principum*, part II, book III (Rome, 1607; reprint Aalen 1967), 507. For more detail see below at Ch. 7.II.

[35] Estienne Pasquier, *Les Recherches de la France* (Paris, 1665), 557, reports a case in which the emperor elevated a bourgeois to the ranks of the nobility during a trial in order to give him legal rights against a noble adversary. But how often does it happen that one has an emperor at hand?

of social structures, the forms also change in which law *on its own initiative* accounts for the change of those social structures.[36] As complexity increases isomorphic (corresponding) similarities and semantic congruencies decrease; the social reference of norms becomes abstract and can generally no longer be identified by what they are supposed to regulate. However, the form of the solution remains the same: the legal system becomes differentiated in order to be able to account for the changing social structures on its own initiative, together with all the problems which follow from a complete reconstruction of social relations through the provisions available within the legal system.

Two further achievements appear to be necessary for the differentiation of the legal system and its operative closure, achievements which stimulate each other. They are:

1. a functional specification of law, that is, a focus on a specific problem of society; and
2. a binary coding of the system through a scheme that provides a positive value (legal) and a negative value (illegal).

Contrary to the assumption of an earlier version of the theory of functional differentiation and specification, which was oriented around the advantages of the division of labour, orientation by function alone is not sufficient. This follows from the simple fact that the reference to a function is always an invitation to look for functionally equivalent alternatives, that is, to cross system boundaries. However, it is also evident that the 'function of law' does not play a role in legal practice as a reference that is used for the purposes of legal argument. At best, the civil law term '*causa*' comes close to this reference; however, '*nomen et causa*' were merely requirements for the entitlement to a claim under the old law and, as a consequence, today *causa* is only a reference to the interpretation of individual legal institutions. Law itself does not need a *causa*. If lawyers want to find out whether or not a communication belongs to the legal system, they must always examine whether or not there is an attribution to law, that is, whether or not the domain of legal coding is concerned. Only with both achievements, function and coding, taken together, does it follow that operations which are specific to law can be distinguished clearly from other communications and can reproduce themselves through themselves with only a marginal blurring of distinctions.

We shall discuss both of these achievements in greater detail below and restrict ourselves here to a rough characterization. Functional specification

---

[36] See my attempt to interpret human rights with reference to the functional differentiation of the social system in: Niklas Luhmann, *Grundrechte als Institution: Ein Beitrag zur politischen Soziologie* (Berlin, 1965).

restricts what can be considered as an operation of the system. It refers to the operations of the system and can be recognized by its orientation to operations by norms. The binary coding refers to the observation of operations of the system and can be recognized by its attribution of the values legal/illegal to those operations. This distinction appears to be artificial, but it is an artificial arrangement that is produced within the system itself (NB the circularity of the arguments). Normativity only determines that certain expectations can be maintained, even when faced with disappointment. This in itself formulates a directive for making distinctions of this type according to the scheme expectation/disappointment. In this sense, each operation of the legal system consists of observations which are oriented around forms and which are guided by distinctions. Such an operation does not simply accept what happens. However, only an observation of this observing, only the evaluation guided by the scheme legal/illegal attributes to law the intention of obstinately maintaining expectations counterfactually. In other words one could say: the differentiation of an operatively closed legal system requires the system to operate on the level of observations of the second order, and that this is not only occasional but continuously the case. All operations of the legal system are controlled on this level, including those of discriminating in the first instance and thus of merely communicating disappointments in relation to expectations.[37] Everything that cannot be brought under this controlling scheme of legal/illegal does not belong to the legal system but to its internal or external social environment.

The legal system establishes itself as an autopoietic system as soon as the conditions mentioned above have been met. It constructs and reproduces *emergent units* (including itself) that would not exist without operative closure. In this way it provides an autonomous *reduction of complexity*, a selective approach to operating in the light of a wide scope of possibilities, which— whether they are ignored or rejected—remain disregarded in any event *without an adverse effect on the autopoiesis of the legal system.*

Using a number of documents, Harold Berman established that this reorganization of the legal system towards autonomy had already taken place in the eleventh and twelfth centuries in the form of a 'revolution' of the complete legal culture.[38] This would explain both the 'deviance' of Europe, when seen in global comparison, in giving law an extraordinary level of significance in everyday life, and much of the social development of Europe.

---

[37] See for an account of the genesis of the second-order mode of observing and of its relationship with the genesis of logic and scientific procedures of evidence, see Yehuda Elkana, 'Das Experiment als Begriff zweiter Ordnung', *Rechtshistorisches Journal* 7 (1988), 244–71.

[38] See Harold J. Berman, *Recht und Revolution: Die Bildung der westlichen Rechtstradition* (Frankfurt, 1991).

IV

Francisco Varela has suggested that the operative closure of a system should be called its 'autonomy'.[39] Gordon Pask states: 'Computing systems owe their autonomy to computing their own boundaries.'[40] As far as the social sciences are concerned, the use of the term 'autonomy' has caused confusion.[41] If we nevertheless insist on using the concept of autonomy here, it is precisely because this confusion stimulates reflection.

If one wants to retain the traditional formulation of the concept which is associated with '*nómos*',[42] the assistance of knowledge is required (others would say an assertion is made) through applying the thesis that the structures of the system can be produced only by the operations of the system and can either be used, case by case, or not used, ignored or forgotten. So autonomy means verbally: self-limitation. Seen from this perspective, autonomy is not synonymous with but a consequence of operative closure.[43]

In contrast, traditional legal doctrine proceeds on the basis of assuming persons rather than operations. The autonomy of the legal system is thus preserved by the independence of judges and possibly by the independence

[39] See Francisco Varela, *Principles of Biological Autonomy* (New York, 1979); or, id., 'On Being Autonomous: The Lessons of Natural History for Systems Theory', in George J. Klir (ed.), *Applied General Systems Research: Recent Developments and Trends* (New York, 1978), 77–84.

[40] See his 'Developments in Conversation Theory: Actual and Potential Applications', in George E. Lasker (ed.), *Applied Systems and Cybernetics III* (New York, 1981), 1326–1338, at 1327.

[41] See for the following discussion: Richard Lempert, 'The Autonomy of Law: Two Visions Compared', in Gunther Teubner (ed.), *Autopoietic Law: A New Approach to Law and Society* (Berlin, 1988), 152–90; Gunther Teubner, *Recht als autopoietisches System* (Frankfurt, 1989) 42 and 87; see also Richard Lempert and Joseph Sanders, *An Invitation to Law and Social Science* (New York, 1986), 401. Even among the protagonists of the concept of autopoiesis the *choice of the word* is often criticized. See, for instance, Wolfram K. Köck, 'Autopoiese, Kognition und Kommunikation: Einige kritische Bemerkungen zu Humberto R. Maturanas Bio-Estimologie und ihre Konsequenzen', in Volker Riegas and Christian Vetter (eds.), *Zur Biologie der Kognition* (Frankfurt, 1990), 159–88, at 179. However, it corresponds strictly to the original meaning of '*nómos*' as a consequence of drawing boundaries, a distinction which only needs to be kept free from causal implications.

[42] This is, by the way, a tradition, which until Kant's times (and Kant's predilections for juridical metaphors are well known) was dominated by juridical and political interpretations of the concept. See the references in the article of R. Pohlmann, 'Autonomie', *Historisches Wörterbuch der Philosophie*, vol. 1. (Basel, 1971), 701–19.

[43] This is also at variance with Varela who defines autonomy as 'the assertion of the system's identity through its internal functioning and self-regulation ('On being Autonomous', 77). This transfer of the concept to the level of self-observation and self-description (instead of only to the level of the production of structures) causes Jacques Miermont, 'Les conditions formelles de l'état autonome', *Revue internationale de systémique* 3 (1989), 295–314, to understand autonomy as a product of the imagination of the system: it only exists as a meta-reference for self-reference and other-reference (but wouldn't it suffice to call this identity?). In contrast, we insist on the distinction between operation and observation (as an operation of a special kind) throughout this text.

of lawyers,[44] and independence is defined by the absence of external pressures which can be fended off, if not by transcendental means, at least by tenure and by not being bound by any instructions from their own organization.[45] Nobody would contest the institutional and political importance of such safeguards; after all, there have been bad experiences not only in Germany after 1933 but also everywhere else in the world. As far as the autonomy of the legal system is concerned, politics can become destructive when attacking the law at these points. However, this is not a concern for the concept. (After all, it is not the coffee that tastes bad if one puts salt in it instead of sugar.) The question remains as to what exactly autonomy is, so that measures may be put in place to protect it from dangers. Indeed it must be protected. (We protect the coffee, in our example, by keeping sugar and salt in clearly marked containers.)

As a sociologist, one tends first to treat the concept of autonomy of individuals, relative to how they might be seduced by or accede to pressures from their social environment, as a 'myth' or as an ideology.[46] However, when this denial of the concept does not lead to its clarification, one tends to retreat from this discomfiture to the useless concept of 'relative autonomy'.[47] Some shaded concept of autonomy is conventional generally in sociology,[48] but it does not provide empirical research with any clues (apart from the one to avoid absurdities). This is equivalent to the response found

[44] For the relationship between lawyer and client see, for example, John P. Heinz, 'The Power of Lawyers', *Georgia Law Review* 17 (1983), 891–911.

[45] See on this point Joachim Rückert, *Autonomie des Rechts in rechtshistorischer Perspektive* (Hanover, 1988), who provides rich material even if he does not keep strictly to the topic. See also, for approval, Klaus Luig, 'Autonomie und Heteronomie des Rechts im 19. Jahrhundert', *Zeitschrift der Savigny-Stiftung für Rechtsgeschichte, romanistische Abteilung* 107 (1990), 387–95. Rückert is of the opinion that autonomy involves 'the concrete ability and readiness [of persons in an institutional context, N.L.] to conduct oneself critically or uncritically toward a given law' (ibid. 35). Can law, accordingly, reject itself in order to be autonomous? Or isn't it rather the case that under the heading of the autonomy of law it is not the autonomy of law which is involved but the critical engagement of lawyers who use the law for their purposes?

[46] For instance, Magali Sarfatti Larson, *The Rise of Professionalism: A Sociological Analysis* (Berkeley, 1977), talks of a 'receding bourgeois ideology of independence' as far as lawyers and medical doctors are concerned (p. 177). See also ch. 12 (p. 208) on 'Monopolies of Competence and Bourgeois Ideology'.

[47] Here I also refute formulations that I used earlier and which were not sufficiently thought through. See now, above all, Lempert, 'The Autonomy of Law', with the surprising statement that the concept of relative autonomy, which does not exclude anything, is particularly well suited for empirical research. However, based on this concept empirical research is superfluous, since this variable will always be confirmed. See also Lawrence M. Friedman on 'relative autonomy' (as self-evident), *Total Justice* (New York, 1985), 27, who, however, insists that there is clearly a problem with a definition that relates to the boundaries of the system.

[48] See only Alvin W. Gouldner, 'Reciprocity and Autonomy in Functional Theory', in Llewellyn Gross (ed.), *Symposium on Sociological Theory* (Evanston Ill, 1959), 241–70; Fred E. Katz, *Autonomy and Organizations: The Limits of Social Control* (New York, 1968).

in the more recent socio-legal literature in relation to the disappointment with 'state and law' or similar radical Marxist approaches.[49] This holds that the law would simply become relatively more autonomous by becoming more complex in the course of the development of its decisions.[50] However, this approach has not contributed anything to the clarification of the *concept* of autonomy: the question as to the degree of dependence or independence remains open. Causal relations can hardly be the decisive factor for the concept of autonomy because—if one adopts a sufficiently broad view—there are always external reasons to be found for all internal operations and this contingency explodes this version of the concept of autonomy. One could not even talk about 'relative autonomy' any more, since everything would depend on the selective attribution of causes and effects made by an observer. For all these reasons, we prefer a concept of autonomy which is backed up by the concept of autopoiesis; that is, one which spells out that autonomy is either given or not and which does not allow for any grey areas. One should add preventively that statements such as 'more or less' are not excluded by this concept. However, these statements have to be introduced conceptually in a different way, for instance with regard to the complexity of the system which operates autopoietically, in an operatively closed way, and autonomously.

When we look more closely at what could possibly be meant by 'relative autonomy', a formulation by Lempert lends a helping hand. According to Lempert, the relative autonomy of law is 'the degree to which the legal system looks to itself rather than to the standards of some external social, political or ethical system for guidance in making or applying law'.[51] Even this statement can be interpreted in different ways. But in any event it represents a concept of autonomy in the sense in which it is used here because 'looking' is an internal operation of the legal system. The question, then, is only how the legal system can balance the self-reference and the external reference, which are always both implied at the same time. In this respect, however, our assumption is that the legal system needs an internal legitimization for finding the environment worth considering, not only as a realm of facts but also with regard to the 'standards' which can be found there. We shall return to this point in section VI.

[49] See Marc V. Tushnett, *The American Law of Slavery, 1810–1860: Considerations of Humanity and Interest* (Princeton, 1981); id., 'American Law of Slavery 1810–1860: A Study in the Persistence of Legal Autonomy', *Law and Society Review* 10 (1985), 119–84; Isaac D. Balbus, 'Commodity Form and Legal Form: An Essay on the 'Relative Autonomy' of the Law, *Law and Society Review* 11 (1977), 571–88 (here only autonomy in relation to the preferences of individual actors and not in relation to the conditions of capitalist society); Alan Stone, 'The Place of Law in the Marxian Structure-Superstructure Archetype', *Law and Society Review* 19 (1985), 39–67.

[50] See Tushnett, 'The American Law of Slavery', for the presentation of a related transition from an analogical use of arguments to a conceptual use of arguments.

[51] Lempert, 'The Autonomy of Law', 159.

V

If one describes operative closure, autopoietic self-reproduction, and the autonomy of the legal system in the way described above, which communications are included and where does the system draw its own boundaries?

The sociological literature which employs the term 'legal system' usually assumes that this refers only to organized legal practice, that is, mainly practice in courts and parliaments, but also occasionally in administrations which make law based on delegated norms or in legal organizations and associations which channel access to the courts. In this sense, it is principally only lawyers who operate in the legal system.[52] Difficulties arise if one is thinking through the concept of the system of people as members of the system, or at least of people as certain 'role-actors'. To be run over by a car is not a role in the legal system. It is not even an event in the legal system, even if it is obviously legally relevant. After all, it may have happened because someone insisted on their (assumed) right to cross the road at a marked pedestrian crossing and thereby to make cars stop. Is this an event in the legal system or not? Are contracts internal operations of the legal system? Are contracts legal system operations, if those involved do not even realize that they are concluding a contract because they falsely believed that this requires some written form? Is it a legal system operation if a criminal hides while being sought by the police? Is an invention a legal act because one could register it as a patent? Questions such as these arise because of the universality of legal relevance. All conduct is either permitted or prohibited, but that does not mean that all conduct is an internal operation of the legal system.

We reach firmer ground only when we recall that social systems are made up of communications which refer recursively to other communications and which construct their own meaning, their own connectivity to the system in this way. Consequently, a communication must be found in order to deduce that a legal system operation has taken place, and this cannot be just any conduct, for example, merely the dangerous condition of a building forcing police to intervene, or the presence of sheep on the road (which is treated differently by laws in England and in Scotland). Apparently not just any communication qualifies, for if this were the case, again the legal system would be congruent with (and indistinguishable from) society; nor does just any use of a legal term or a word with a legal meaning qualify— take for instance 'The bill, please!' in a restaurant. In such uses the law is only one aspect of the connections made within everyday life or in other functioning systems. Only code-oriented communication belongs to the

---

[52] Often the vague term of legal institutions also serves as a placeholder. Or one deems that to which one refers to be known. Or one discusses the problem, as Lawrence Friedman does, only to reject any definition, see: *The Legal System: A Social Science Perspective* (New York, 1975), 1.

legal system proper, only such communication that assumes an attribution of the values 'legal' and 'illegal'; for only a communication of this type looks for and assumes a recursive networking in the legal system; only a communication of this type employs coding as a form for its autopoietic openness and as a requirement for further communications in the legal system. This may happen for a variety of reasons in everyday life. The director of a public agency may say to an employee's spouse who has come to enquire about promotion for her husband because she sees how much he is suffering from not being promoted: 'I have no right to talk to you about official matters'. He may say that in order to get rid of her; but this is only his motive. The communication itself is, according to the definition above, a communication in the legal system. Further, any suggestion for changing the law becomes, as soon as a reference to the norm which one wants to change is stated, a communication in the legal system—even if this suggestion is promoted by a political group, a pressure group, or a social movement. Examples here would include, for example, attempts to change the law on abortion, or to introduce an article on the protection of the environment into the Constitution, or the activities of the civil rights movement in the United States.

Such a widening of the margins of what should be included in the concept of the legal system[53] has considerable consequences for research practices. Put in merely quantitative terms, the legal system operates largely outside the organizational-professional inner core. Accordingly, law in everyday life is governed by completely different conditions from those that lawyers see and imagine. The strict order of coding is fully implemented: either it is that it is legal or that it is illegal—in any other way law would not be recognized as law, and this includes a basic willingness to get along well together, which is founded on law. One must also note that legal knowledge is not systematized in paragraphs but can only be learned and recalled contextually. One has experience of what is legal in a limited milieu, and possibly mainly with 'trouble cases' which have to be avoided. Anyone who has owned a house is familiar with workmen moonlighting, be it in connection with avoiding tax law or social security payments or simply cutting red tape. Moreover, law in everyday life is, as a consequence of the binarity of its coding, uncertain and definitely not as certain as lawyers

[53] See (here correctly) Kargl, 'Kritik', 134. On the other hand, I cannot follow Kargl (in: Walter Kargl, 'Kommunikation kommuniziert? Kritik des rechtssoziologischen Autopoiesebegriffs', *Rechtstheorie* 21 (1990), 352–73), when he considers that the concept of the political system would be watered down by this widening of the concept of the legal system. Irrespective of the fact that there are also legal issues involved in party politics, as everybody knows who has experience in these matters, acting in parliament, the top echelons of bureaucracies, and even in local councils would be altogether impossible if one could not distinguish between political issues and legal issues.

would like to assume or would wish. Every communication about law leads quite quickly to uncertainty and even seeing a lawyer or going to court provides certainty only in a conditional and not in a definitively expressed form. Therefore, even court proceedings are experienced as a processing of uncertainty—and everything is done to underline this experience (the juridical counterstatement says: the judge acts even-handedly and without prejudice). Thus one cannot find any correlation between rule and case in the extra-juridical everyday life of the legal system but only the experience gained from dealing with law and, above all, avoiding trouble.

However, this also has to be understood in terms of an internal state of affairs because both uncertainty and dependence on specific contacts with law are consequences of binary coding, and they only arise if the question of law arises. The operative closure of the legal system is confirmed by the existence of different perspectives within the legal system and, therefore, by the fact that there is an observing of observers which itself has been organized within that system. The legal system is and remains thoroughly but always only internally irritated by countless incidents. The legal system is, in the words of Heinz von Foerster, 'coded undifferentiatedly' with regard to those incidents that imitate it, or perhaps it would be better to say: it is 'coded indifferently'.[54] Consequently, there is no input of legal communication into the legal system because there is no legal communication whatsoever outside the legal system. This is a consequence of the transition from input-type descriptions to closure-type descriptions of systems (Varela).[55] And this is a result of the consequence that only the legal system itself can effect its closure, reproduce its operations, and define its boundaries, *and that there is no other authority in society which can proclaim: this is legal and this is illegal.*

Thus, any reference to the negative value of coding (illegal) has the same effect of attribution as the positive value (legal). The important point is that communication defers to its regulation through coding. Of course, it is not the words which matter but the understanding of their intended meaning.

The guarantee of the self-attribution of operations to the system, and as a result the closure of the system, requires one single code as its binary scheme. It excludes other codes. And it excludes third, fourth, or fifth values.[56] But

[54] See 'Erkenntnistheorien und Selbstorganisation', in Siegfried J. Schmidt (ed.), *Der Diskurs des Radikalen Konstruktivismus* (Frankfurt, 1987), 133–58, at 137.

[55] See above Ch. 2, section II, n. 1.

[56] I maintain this in spite of the objections of Hubert Rottleuthner, 'A Purified Theory of Law: Niklas Luhmann on the Autonomy of the Legal System', *Law and Society Review* 23 (1989), 779–97, at 792. Because each addition of further distinctions at the level of coding (for instance, permitted/prohibited, valid law/invalid law) would exclude an unequivocal drawing of boundaries by each operation and so would create ambiguities. Parsons, incidentally, referred to the advantage of the speediness which binary schemes have in establishing complex systems for similar reasons; he, however, suggested a four-field table that only permits advantages for classification (formulation of types).

that does not hinder the use of further distinctions in each instance. There is no supreme norm which guarantees that coding represents the unity of the system within the system—that would result in an infinite regress, or as will be shown below, in a paradox. Coding itself is not a norm. It is merely a structure for a procedure of recognition and attribution of social autopoiesis. Whenever there is a reference to law or injustice, such a communication attributes itself to the legal system. It cannot be recognized as belonging to the legal system in any other way and it cannot be linked to the legal system in any other way. The law of society is realized through the reference to its binary coding—and not by any generative rule (however hypothetical or categorical, reasonable or factual).

Coding legal/illegal can only be managed on the level of second-order observations, that is, only by observing observers. Such coding is indifferent as to whether or not first-order observers, that is, the perpetrators of acts and their victims, classify their references to the world with law and injustice in mind, or not. If first-order observers assume that they are right or have been wronged and report that, the observer who is observing them may assess the same situation quite differently. If the former did not even think of law or injustice but had something else in mind, the second-order observer nevertheless can apply the code legal/illegal. In contrast to the normativity of expectations (which is clearly indispensable for operations) and in contrast to the reference to historically given structures which can be interpreted as law, coding has two peculiar properties: it can be applied universally no matter what is being communicated, and it makes the closure of the system possible by reformulating its unity as a difference.

Expectations can also, on occasions, be normatively processed. Such a normative process attempts to achieve a consensus in the face of congruent descriptions of facts. This is possible and necessary even at the level of second-order observations. A system can, for instance, observe that another system relates normatively to certain matters, say algae in the sea, and that such a system concludes from the proliferation of algae that a perpetrator must be sought and found. Observers of this observer may draw their own conclusions and may, for instance, consider the increase of such modes of observation (by, for example, ecological groups) as politically questionable (or, on the other hand, remarkable). They are free to do so in accordance with the contexts of their own systems. They are, in this way, linked to the networks of being observed by further observers (including those whom they observe themselves). However, this in itself leads only to the continuing autopoiesis of society and not to the closure of the legal system in society. The operative closure of the legal system *in* society is achieved *only* at the level of the second order and *only by a scheme that can be operated at this level alone.*[57]

---

[57] The same applies to science and its coding with the values true and false.

Only if the products of such a form of distinction (law's coding), namely second-order observations, refer recursively to each other (and can pretend that this has always been the case) can the legal system tighten and become operatively closed.[58] This must have been the case in the Mediterranean city cultures of antiquity, and certainly not by chance only in those cities. This does not exclude 'feral' norm constructing (some would say, natural norm constructing)—just as the development of a level of second-order observation in science has done little to eradicate magic.[59] In this sense, the functional specificity of law in processing normative expectations is, in itself, not a sufficient explanation for the evolutionary differentiation of the legal system,[60] even though the latter is also not possible without engagement with a specific legal problem. Only coding provides a correlate for the universality of law,[61] that is, for its ability to be applicable to all matters and to be capable of being irritated by every communication, quite independent of the motives of the first-order observers.

Coding legal/illegal cannot be applied to itself without running into a paradox that blocks further observations. But coding can be distinguished and designated. One can disregard the application of the code and try to achieve an agreement outside the system. The unity of a conflict as an interaction system, which involves persons or organizations, can provide a basis for the decision to opt out of the legal system. However, the legal system even regulates this decision by protecting its concerns. For instance, there is no way of avoiding participation in the legal system altogether (we are enslaved to it); an agreement outside the courts also has to satisfy certain legal requirements if it is to be valid. Persons, interactions, and organizations are venues for the introduction of a communication to the legal system and for its removal from the system. The legal system is indifferent in relation to such operations. It does not pursue imperialist interests to attract as much communication as possible and to retain it in the system. It is not an attracting system. It only predicates: *if* law is to be used, that is, if

---

[58] This is an attempt to find a different answer from Gunther Teubner, to the question as to how the evolution of autopoietic (operatively closed!) systems is thinkable. Teubner's concept of a hypercycle seems only to transfer the problem onto the question of how the closure of such a hypercycle can evolve. See Gunther Teubner, *Recht als autopoietisches System* (Frankfurt, 1989), 61, and on this point see also William M. Evan, *Social Structure and Law: Theoretical and Empirical Perspectives* (Newbury Park, 1990), 44.

[59] See the convincing arguments put forward by G. E. R. Lloyd, *Magic, Reason and Experience: Studies in the Origin and Development of Greek Science* (Cambridge, 1979).

[60] This is above all the argument of theories that depend on economic doctrines of the division of labour and which claim that differentiation at large is an achievement in welfare terms which has been obtained well-nigh blindly by evolution.

[61] Here I have to correct my own findings set out in the book *Rechtssoziologie* (1972), which did not consider the coding of law sufficiently and where I worked primarily with a complementary relationship of differentiation (specialization) and generalization.

there is a question as to law and injustice, it can be used only *on the terms set by the legal system*. Exactly in this sense the legal system is an operatively closed and structurally determined system.

Finally one has to note that not every mention of the code-values legal/illegal turns a communication into a legal operation. For instance, one can discuss cases in legal education or report court proceedings and judgments in the press without involving a disposition to the code-values. Rather, that disposition can clearly belong to a different functional context, and this applies in cases such as where a law teacher or journalist puts forward a personal opinion. The difference becomes immediately clear when law teachers or journalists make comments in a 'personal note' or commentary (in which their dispositions may operate in relation to the functional codes of education or the media).

Contrary to what logicians require and differently from what Kelsen assumed, the *unity* of the legal system is not an operative assumption of the legal system. Such a unity cannot be understood as either a principle or a norm. No judgment needs to refer to it, let alone demonstrate it. No legislative act refers to it as a component of its regulations. This unity is reproduced with each operation, if successful, just as the unity of a living system is reproduced by the exchange of cells. However, it cannot itself *be* an operation of the system, because the performance of such an operation itself would immediately change everything that pertained to the unity of the system. Therefore, law does not need a hierarchical structure for its operations, which would have the function of guaranteeing the unity of the law by referring to a supreme norm (the basic norm), a supreme law (the constitution), or a supreme instance. Such accounts may make sense as a description of the system in the system, and we shall revisit this issue later. However, they are not prerequisites for a successful communication in the legal system, that is, that communications are understood and followed. The unity of the system cannot be reintroduced to the system.

This does not mean, on the other hand, that there is no self-reference. The reference to unity is replaced by, 'represented' by, the reference to the binary code, to the distinction between legal and illegal and an assumption of the normative validity of all those expectations which need to be put into place to make such coding explicit. The direct reference is substituted by an indirect one that, however, ensures that operations of the system can be linked to other operations in the system. In other words, there are indicators of unity which can be employed; thus the social differentiation of an operatively closed legal system can be measured by changes to the semantics of those indicators, above all in the transition from ontological and natural law arguments for the validity of law to a fully developed positivist approach to law.

We can, of course, often dispense with words such as 'law', 'injustice', and 'norm'. We are no longer in the era of a formalistic, quasi-magical working of law. However, we have to make it known and understood, at least implicitly, that a communication is involved which makes a claim on counterfactual, law-based validity and which requires, at the same time, that law and injustice exclude each other. This can be done, however, through everyday communication, for in a modern society there are no slaves and everybody has the right to be included in the law and also the right to use legal symbols. Even if a binding decision on legal issues can only be achieved by its association with the political function, that is, as a collectively binding decision, which guarantees its enforcement, this does not mean that massive amounts of communication are not taking place outside the narrow ambit of courts and parliaments. Indeed, it does not mean that massive amounts of positive law are not being produced without involving courts and parliaments, and accordingly without any political control—namely through contracts.

Even if the unity of the system cannot be a component of the operations of the system (or has to be represented for this purpose by *specific* distinctions), it can be observed and it can be described. Only an observer who, in turn, has to be an observer within an autopoietic system, can do this. Such an observer may be an external observer (for instance, from the perspective of science) or the observer may be internal, even the legal system itself. Accordingly, we can distinguish between self-observation and external observation. This is an issue we shall deal with in a later chapter.[62] But, the relationship between self-observation/self-description and the operative closure of the system needs to be clarified at this point.

If the unity of law (that is, law as a totality of its operations and structures) needs to be observed, that observation has to be distinguished from something else. In addition to it, a determination of unity cannot consist of an enumeration of all elements and their relations but can only be achieved by abbreviation and simplification. Both criteria apply to external and internal observations at the same time. Both the distinction, which is selected to this effect, and the simplification are performances that are executed by the observing system. It is also often said that observation (and *a fortiori* operations which are determined by it such as planning, control, and theoretical reflections) requires a 'model' of the legal system.[63] In any case, what is described is not the complete reality of the system. In order to mark the reduction which is required we are going to call the unity which is an object of both observation and description *identity*.

---

[62] See Ch. 11.

[63] See Jean-Louis Le Moigne, *La théorie du système général: Théorie de la modélisation* (Paris, 1977). One of the examples used by Le Moigne is gross national product as a self-description of a system (p. 56). The example shows at the same time how complex (and misleading!) can be the prerequisites which are required by such a kind of modelling.

External observers—such as Heinrich von Kleist, Franz Kafka, or Walter Benjamin—can identify the legal system in rather different ways. If one wants to find out in which ways, one has to observe the observer. The legal system is less free in the ways in which it observes itself and describes itself, but in turn, as if to make up for this, it is more secure and it is better informed. The legal system has to perform such observations and also descriptions through the operations of its closed system, and that means: it has to provide these operations with their normative status and by reference to the code legal/illegal. It has to insist, for instance, that it is right to distinguish between legal and illegal whereas external observers may see this precisely as an injustice. In this respect, the theory of operatively closed self-referential systems is not only a theory of objects but also includes the reflexive performances of the described system. It describes the system as a system that describes itself.

VI

The description of systems as operatively closed portrays a rather one-sided picture that we are now going to put into perspective. A system constitutes its unity and its environment in a certain domain through operative closure. Neither the existence nor the relevance of the environment is denied. Quite the contrary: the distinction between system and environment is precisely the form that makes it possible to designate a system or an environment by a distinction relative to each other. Consequently, we are by no means making the absurd claim that law exists without society, without people, without the special physical and chemical conditions on our planet. However, relations with such an environment can only be established on the basis of the internal activity of the system, through executing its own operations, which become available only through all those recursive links which we have called closure. Or, to put it briefly: openness is only possible through closure.

The earlier doctrine of open systems interpreted this openness causally and required an independent observer to detect regular patterns in the relationship between systems and their environments. We do not doubt that approach. As a matter of course an observer can detect causal relations and probabilities in the relationship between systems and their environments based on his own criteria and on his own preferences for attributions, and he can find, for instance, that law provides members of the upper class with preferential treatment. However, our starting point is prior to that approach. It is the question as to how the law can operate at all and how it can observe its own operations and their effects. This shifts the problem to the question of the forms of 'internalization' of the distinction between system and environment through the system itself, or expressed more formally: the question of the re-entrance of the distinction into what the distinction has distinguished[64] and the virtual space of possibilities which the system opens up through this operation.

In order to demonstrate the internal use of this distinction clearly, we shall distinguish between *self-reference* and external reference and say that a system which is equipped with observation skills of this kind can distinguish between self-reference and external reference. Using this terminology places us at the level of second-order observation (and this is different from the earlier doctrine of open systems). We observe how the system observes and how it, in so doing, operationalizes the distinction between self-reference and external reference.

In contrast to the usual understanding of autonomy, we distinguish strictly between questions that relate to a causal dependence or independence (which can be answered by observers in any way they like depending on their selection of causes and effects) and questions as to references that always require that the system is the observer. Therefore, external reference is not an indication for us that the autonomy of a system is limited because the operation of referring remains an operation of the system, which is made possible by the internal links within the system, and that means, which needs to be reflected in norms.[65] That is precisely why the operation of observing based on the distinction between self-reference and external reference in the first instance simply characterizes the system itself, and does so in exactly the way in which it manages its autonomy.

Depending on whether we direct our attention to the function that is preserved in the normative style of expectations, or to the coding legal/illegal, we find different forms used by the legal system in order to disentangle self-reference and external reference. In relation to that function we can note that the legal system operates in a normatively closed and, at the same time, cognitively open way.[66] This concise formula has met with considerable

---

[64] Re-entry in the sense used by George Spencer Brown, *Laws of Form*, 56 and 69.

[65] See in contrast Lempert, 'The Autonomy of Law', 159 with the definition quoted above (see n. 51), which already defines through the concept of autonomy whether the system refers to itself (formalisms, procedures, concepts) or to its environment. The definition in our text simply expresses a greater distance in relation to causal statements which ultimately only provide conclusions about and for those who make them.

[66] Arthur J. Jacobson, 'Autopoietic Law: The New Science of Niklas Luhmann', *Michigan Law Review* 87 (1989), 1647–1689, at 1650, 1685, assumes that there is no empirical evidence that this distinction is indeed used in legal systems. This objection is difficult to understand. Evidently the use of the words 'normatively' and 'cognitively' is not what is meant here. The hypothesis could easily be tested (and refuted) if one were to collect cases in which a form from an extra-juridical area became relevant in law without being legally authorized; or in a case in which the mere infringement of a norm set aside that norm because the judge was forced to learn from the infringement. The empirical test must account for its power of resolution of a theory, namely if it is to be verified or refuted. So it is not enough to state that everyday life does not use such distinctions.

difficulties of understanding, especially in the context of a discussion on autonomy and causal dependencies on the environment.[67] Therefore, a thorough comment is in order.

The thesis on normative closure above all opposes the idea that morality could immediately or intrinsically be understood as valid in the legal system. This intrinsic validity has been excluded in many older legal orders through formalism—but was then compensated for by the distinction between justice and equity. In modern society, any understanding of an immediate validity of morals in the legal system is even less possible, and for obvious reasons. The legal system must provide sufficiently reliable consistency in its decisions and, in this respect, in its function as a unity. Moral assessments, by contrast, are typically pluralist, and there is always the possibility—when consensus cannot be reached—of recurring to each assessment's fragmented support, that is, to group support.[68] However, this only applies if the moralists cannot provide themselves with the force of law and equally it only applies within the framework of territorial peace. More precisely, the legal system must account for the fact that even though the moral *code* applies to the whole society as a binary scheme, the moral *programmes*, that is, the criteria for a distinction between good and bad or good and evil, are no longer consensual. Although a moral critique of law is possible, it is highly unlikely that morals require obedience to the law in every case.[69] It does not follow, however, that the arguments used by such a critique are legally compelling ones. Above all it cannot be assumed that morals, which oppose law, are universally accepted. Rather this would be a case of contested morality.[70]

It is this refinement on issues of moral sensitivity that requires that moral judgements do not lead to immediate legal consequences. Otherwise all moral controversies would have to be followed through in the legal system. This state of affairs has been well known in principle since the eighteenth century. However, it has been clouded by the use of anthropological formulations (for instance, by a distinction between internal and external coercion) so that its relevance for society has often been overlooked. Moreover,

---

[67] See, above all, the very careful arguments of Lempert, 'The Autonomy of Law', 178.

[68] Robert M. Cover has pointed out, against the dominant opinion on constitutional law in the United States, that minorities are entitled to have their beliefs respected as morals and that, therefore, judges cannot simply claim the majority opinion to be *the morals*. See The Supreme Court, '1982 Term. Foreword: Nomos and Narrative', *Harvard Law Review* 97 (1983), 4–68; also id., 'The Folktales of Justice: Tales of Jurisdiction', *The Capital University Law Review* 14 (1985), 179–203. This opinion is based on the tradition of a religious recognition of minority opinions in the Judaic law of the Talmud.

[69] See on this issue Luc J. Wintgens, 'Law and Morality: A Critical Relation', *Ratio Juris* 4 (1991), 177–201.

[70] Also on this issue, see Niklas Luhmann, 'The Code of the Moral', *Cardozo Law Review* 14 (1993), 995–1009.

it cannot be denied that ethical and legal reasoning can converge. However, the practical relevance of such convergence (and of arguments that support them in general) should not be overestimated. In the vast sum of legal decisions and in the even greater sum of references to law in everyday life convergence between ethical and legal reasoning does not matter.[71]

Only when law is differentiated from the ever-changing tidal flow of moral communication, and only when distinctions based on law's own criteria for validity can be made, is it possible to specify the facts which are legally relevant and separate them from general appraisal made by persons. Openness to cognitive issues depends directly on normative closure of the system and it can only become more differentiated and more specific if the criteria for assessing the relevance of all these various facts are determined in the system itself.

If one wants to analyse the combinations of normative and cognitive expectation including the combinations of self-reference and external reference, one has to step back to a level of second-order observations, and ask the question: how are expectations expected?[72] Even if, at the level of primary-order observation, expectations are held normatively in response to emerging legal problems (and if they were not held in this way, such an operation would not attribute itself to the legal system), an observer of this kind of expecting can see things differently. He can expect normative expectations either normatively or cognitively as long as the various levels of observation can be differentiated, which means: as long as events can be specialized differently. Then one can expect normatively, on the one hand, that normative expectations ought to be maintained and implemented, and the support for the legal system in society as a whole depends largely on this mode of expecting. On the other hand, one can just as well expect that, in a cognitive context, normative expectations can also be changed through learning (for instance, by having regard to the eventual outcomes of legal decision-making), or even that they should be changed (when looked upon from a tertiary level of observation). Like all the functioning systems in modern society the legal system can only achieve adequate complexity at the level of second-order observations. But that does not change the fact that the basic operative level of autopoietic reproduction is achieved by the normative mode of expecting.

---

[71] Many controversies in legal theory on this issue seem to be caused by limiting the problematic relationship between law and morals to this issue. Of course, nobody would deny that there is always a minimum of convergent reasoning (an 'ethical minimum' of law). However, this insight does not provide assistance for the specific reasoning in order to reach decisions in hard cases, and it cannot change the fact that law *always* has to prove by reference to legal texts that it is law.

[72] Otherwise, as critics have stated again and again, glaring contradictions arise if it is said that cognitive and normative expectations exclude each other while being practised at the same time.

Normative closure, therefore, not only means operative closure—although, of course, it means this as well—but also means that norms have to be resistant to disappointments. The breaking of norms alone does not lead to any adaptive learning that could change norms. However, this does lead to the question as to how such a counterfactual resistance to disappointment, how this stubbornness, can be attained and secured within the system. The answer is given by the recursive networking of the system's autopoiesis. The norm is maintained by previous and subsequent practice, by sequences of operations that always make the norm turn out the same way (whatever the discretionary ambit that interpretations may provide). As a matter of fact, this does not exclude either unlawful behaviour within the legal system or unlawful decisions made by courts. One can declare, then, something as unlawful, which nevertheless has consequences for the further operations of the system—maybe in the reversing of a decision that is not yet final, or by setting it aside for a further consideration of precedents. Accordingly, normative closure is the context for ongoing self-observations by the system within the scheme of lawful/unlawful. Learning and changing norms also remain an option, either internally induced by the legal consequences that can no longer be accepted, or externally induced by changes in society's estimation of what specific norms mean. Nevertheless, the task facing the system is not to achieve a framework of references to *knowledge* and to be cognitively closed but to achieve a framework of references to *norms*. Cognitive opening is always premised on the autopoietic condition of having to incorporate the individual case or a changed norm in the concurrent and ongoing practice of the decision-making of the system. An arbitrary act, as a response to the powerful demands of the political system, could be recognized in the legal system as a breach of law—even if this recognition remained without consequences owing to the lack of power to support it.

A legal system which is frequently exposed to such interference over a wide range of issues—and who could deny that this does happen?—is operating in a state of corruption.[73] Having regard to its norms it recognizes that it cannot withstand political pressure. It maintains the dummy of legality. It also maintains, and does not renounce, norms at large. However, it mediates the binary code legal/illegal through a prior distinction, namely a rejection, or a value of rejection, as Gotthard Günther would say, which allows for its opportunist adaptation to powerful elites. This leads, then, to a preliminary examination of the question, in cases which are selected for this purpose, as to whether law is to be applied or not. In the most extreme borderline situations law is left to function merely occasionally

---

[73] See for ample evidence Marcelo Neves, *Verfassung und Positivität des Rechts in der peripheren Moderne: Eine theoretische Betrachtung und eine Darstellung des Falls Brasilien* (Berlin, 1992).

and inconsistently as a system that is oriented to itself but is experienced, internally and externally, as a sheer instrument of power. It is difficult to say in abstract terms where these borderline situations are to be found because generalized mechanisms of trust or mistrust are involved here. In the most extreme cases, there is no autopoietic closure to be found, and not even any cognitive learning in relation to norms.

Even in these extreme cases, or in cases that are seen as extreme in our legal culture, there is a normal state of dependency on the regular admin-istration of justice. The National Socialists in Germany did not revoke paragraph 1 of the Judicature Act that guaranteed the independence of the courts despite all their politically resounding rhetoric about the unity of state and law and their orientation to the principle of leadership. They changed the substance of law by adding to the binding force of the law the binding force of the new political maxims, removed undesirable judges from office, and established special courts. But this was enough to render the political will valid under the law. Everything depended on prevailing politically in every conceivable conflict. Even though the courts were seen as forms for the implementation of the will of the 'Führer' and the spheres of jurisdiction were formed accordingly—including the option of institut-ing proceedings in the special courts—still this did not permit political interference in much of the ongoing proceedings. A leading doctrinal text-book at the time states: 'There is no jurisdiction, either by definition or in essence, without independent judges. All respect for the court, all confid-ence of the people in their judges and in their law will be destroyed if the independence of the courts is removed or set aside.'[74] There was no point in terminating the functioning of law. And even if *we* hold that there was no independent administration of justice at the time, the understanding *at the time* was different; it was based on a change of orientation of the legal system and assumed the possibility of an autopoietic execution of this change.[75] Autopoiesis is neither a political nor an ethical criterion for the acceptability of law.[76]

These analyses show that self-reference and external reference need to cooperate in the form of normative closure and cognitive opening, based on normative closure. The system can leave learning to chance, that is, to external stimuli for which there is no provision in the system, if it has the capacity to practise changes as changes of valid law and to weave them into the recursive network of the interdependent interpretations of its norms.

---

[74] Ernst Rudolf Huber, *Verfassungsrecht des Großdeutschen Reiches* (Hamburg, 1939), 279.

[75] See on this issue Dieter Simon, 'Waren die NS-Richter "unabhängige Richter"?' *Rechtshistorisches Journal* 4 (1985), 102–16.

[76] This remark is aimed at attempts, which are quite common, to express the ethical and political rejection of this regime by corrections to legal theory. The message here is that what matters is political vigilance and not vigilance by legal theory.

Pressures can be absorbed and adjusted—for instance, dropping the prosecution of serious crimes on the discretion given to the prosecutor's department, or the stay of execution of a judgment with reference to the higher legal value of avoiding civil unrest. The autopoiesis of the system is a rather robust principle—in law as in society and in life—precisely because it can either go on or stop. However, this does not mean that destruction is not possible, and there are alarm signals that can be read from the way in which the system is forced to learn. This is why the liberal state, with a legal culture which has never again been attained in this form, disseminated, and not by accident, the myth that the absolute state had been ruled by the fiat of the monarch—only to implement an opposing principle, that of the division of powers.[77]

Even reflecting on momentous historical changes and threats, in relation to the specific problems of regions where the principle of the differentiation of a legal system did not succeed either partially or fully, one should not lose sight of the normal content which is compatible with a wide range of different structures; that is, different norm contents. The typical form in which normative closure and cognitive openness are combined is that of a conditional programme.[78] This form requires that normative rules for decision-making (which can be sustained only *within the system*) are phrased in such a way that a deduction of the decision from the facts (which have to be established cognitively) is possible: if fact a is given, decision x is legal.[79] Prescribing the forms of facts that have this trigger-effect is achieved by formulating norms, that is, by operations in the system. Already in Roman civil law such operations applied largely juridical terminology, which was different from the everyday use of language.[80] Even formulations that appeared to call for an acceptance of moral judgments, for instance 'bona fides', were used in law to give a specific juridical meaning.[81] However, the norm

---

[77] See on this issue Regina Ogorek, 'Das Machtspruchmysterium', *Rechtshistorisches Journal* 3 (1984), 82–107.   [78] See for detail Ch. 4.IV.

[79] It should be self-evident, and mentioned here only preventively, that deduction in this frame of reference does not mean a *method for interpretation*. The requirements for the combination of self-reference and external reference mentioned above do not infer anything about the use of logic in the interpretation of law.

[80] See for detail the analyses by Antonio Carcaterra, *Struttura del Linguaggio giuridico-precettivo romano: Contributi* (Bari, 1968); id., *Dolus bonus/dolus malus: Esegesi di D.4.3.1.2–3* (Naples, 1979); id., *Semantica degli enunciati normativo-giuridici romani: Interpretatio iuris* (Bari, 1972). In contrast to a usual finding of the peculiarities of legal *terminology*, Carcaterra holds that there is a different *language* that also constructs reality differently: 'realtà quale è vista e disciplinata dal diritto' (*Struttura*, 210).

[81] Remarkably, juridification can be demonstrated precisely in the transition from *fides* to *bona fides*. See Aldo Schiavone, *Nascita della giurisprudenza: Cultura aristocatica e pensiero giuridico nella Roma tardo-repubblicano* (Bari, 1976), 147, with reference to the differentiation of jurisprudence from the older *ragione signorile*. See also Antonio Carcaterra, *Intorno ai bonae fides iudicia* (Naples, 1964).

does not prejudge whether or not the *facts* are given which put a conditional programme in place; this can only be established cognitively.

Accordingly, the legal system can take note of external facts but only as internally produced information, that is, only as a 'difference that makes a difference' (Bateson), and the difference in the state of the system has to relate to the application of law, and eventually to its coding. In other words, the legal system can relate knowledge, but not norms, to the environment. But even such a statement of knowledge occasioned initially from a perturbation in its environment is merely an internal operation and not an operation of 'transfer' of information. (This is exactly what Bateson means with his combined concept of information—'a difference that makes a difference'. It makes clear that it is information that makes a system change *its* state with reference to a difference.)[82] 'Cognitively open', therefore, means only that the system produces relevant information in a condition of external reference, and then relates that information to its differences from its environment.

The distinction between normatively closed and cognitively open is practised *within* the system only (and definitely not as an objectively given state of affairs). Through it, the legal system makes itself a law unto itself. In this way, morality as such has no legal relevance—neither as a code (good/bad, good/evil), nor in its individual values. Long ago Paulus knew that *non omne quod licet honestum est*,[83] more recently Oliver Wendell Holmes knew that too.[84] The law can accept directly normative premises from morals or from other social sources, but can only do so through an explicit transformation.[85] The contrary applies to everything that has to be treated

[82] Of course, this goes against older concepts of information as treatable and transferable 'data'. Therefore, there are frequent complaints that the theory of autopoietic systems is unclear on this point and that it does not demonstrate how information passes through from outside to inside. (See, for example, William M. Evan, *Social Structure and Law: Theoretical and Empirical Perspectives* (Newbury Park, 1990), 38, 42.) The theory is not unclear in this respect; it only excludes the possibility that, conceptually, such a transfer process can take place.

[83] See D 50.17.144. The more famous 'iuris praecepta sunt haec: honeste vivere ...' (D 1.1.10.1, Ulpian) has to be understood in the sense of this restriction, if not simply taken as a rhetorical exaggeration.

[84] See his analyses of the difference of law and morals in his famous speech 'The Path of the Law', *Harvard Law Review* 10 (1897), 457–78, which started the 'Legal Realism' movement.

[85] Following from this one could discuss which requirements have to be met by an 'explicit' transformation. David Lyons holds a comparatively radical position; see David Lyons, 'Justification and Judicial Responsibility', *California Law Review* 72 (1984), 172–99. According to Lyons, the fact that the legal system forces courts to make decisions in 'hard cases', even if no unequivocal, deductively applicable rule for decision-making can be found, means that *all* legal decisions need a moral justification. Therefore the prohibition of the denial of justice would *implicitly* contain a reference to morals. One can object to that. Even if Lyons was right, it would still apply that there is a *legal* (and not a moral) justification for the relevance of morals for the law, namely the prohibition of the denial of justice. See further Ch. 6.III.

as knowledge. So, for example, the legal system is oriented by scientific findings when it comes to ecological problems. This may even mean that it has to work out differences between various statistical calculations and approaches to empirical methodology. However, errors in the assessment of the state of the art of scientific research are relevant in the legal system only as legal errors. If it appears that research findings are uncertain (which scientists can freely admit), the legal system is at liberty to resort to policy decisions, shifts in the burden of proof, etc., that is, 'home-made' devices.[86] The system cannot treat facts as non-facts if they are legally relevant. But the facts cannot change the norms. In other words: from the mere fact that law is breached it does not follow that law is not law. It is precisely because of its normative closure that law is open to countless states of environmental influence, to countless events in its environment from which it derives valuable information, but only through that information and those systems that operate within its system. The legal system can, and under certain conditions has to, learn that behavioural disorders point to a psychopathology that involves, as far as law is concerned, mental incapacity, lack of culpability, etc.

So the distinction between norms and facts in the legal system gains an importance which cannot be found in any other functioning system.[87] Thus it does not matter that norms, reflecting and respecting facts as such, play a role, as this applies to more or less all areas of society; what matters is that the *distinction* between facts and norms is more important in the legal system than in any other sphere, and this includes the attention and care with which both sides of the distinction are distinguished and how the blending of the two is avoided. It is this distinction which represents the difference between self-reference and external reference in the system, that is, the way in which each operation of the system reflects the difference between system and environment. This alone would have to preclude logic, if it existed, from being allowed to deduce norms from facts (even if these were facts of the rational mind) or vice versa, facts from norms.

If one takes into account the fact that the distinction between self-reference and external reference involves the unity of a form which needs to provide connectivity for both sides, the conclusion is inescapable that a reflection of the increasing complexity of society is taking place on both sides. On the one hand, the legal system is growing in the complexity of its body of norms.

[86] For a wealth of material on this see R. Bruce Dickson, 'Risk Assessment and the Law: Evolving Criteria by which Carcinogenicity Risk Assessments Are Evaluated in the Legal Community', in Vincent T. Covello et al. (eds.), *Uncertainty in Risk Assessment and Decision Making* (New York, 1987), 145–57.

[87] See also Vilhelm Aubert, 'The Structure of Legal Thinking', in *Legal Essays. Festskrift til Frede Castberg* (Copenhagen, 1963), 41–63, and Christian Atia, *Epistémologie juridique* (Paris, 1985), 123, for a typical reflection of legal theory on this distinction.

Some writers assume that they are able to detect a shift from factual generalizations to procedural regulations (proceduralization).[88] But the cognitive side, and in this respect the reference to criteria external to the law, is also increasing in importance. In essence there is no difference whether the reference is to external norms (ethical criteria, conventions, local customs of certain professions, etc.) or to areas of knowledge (state of the art, state of scientific knowledge).[89] Whether such a reference is to be found or not needs careful consideration from case to case, since it does not follow directly from the mere use of terminologies (*bona fides*, loyalty and good faith, reasonable practice), which are current outside law where they take on more moral significance.[90] One must assume that the contrary is the case. The same applies to the reference to areas of knowledge (state of the art, state of scientific knowledge). Here too it is not enough if only words are used (such as 'risk') which are also used in the sciences. If, however, law encounters a scientific reference it is forced by internal legal conditions to pay attention to research findings or to a scientific presentation of data. This can also be the case without a specific reference. If there are actuarial statistics on mortality a judge can no longer rely exclusively on his discretion in assessing life expectancies. 'Customary law' is also just a matter of legal, that is, internal, acceptance and reference, as legal procedures exist to enable the making of legal decisions. Today customary law is only valid in so far as judges base their decisions on it. In each case we find a general mention of matters relating to the environment, which are related to internal legal conditions in highly complex ways. The effect of using such matters is that the opinions of experts or organizations are taken seriously in legal proceedings and frequently give them a decisive turn.[91]

---

[88] See for example Reiner Frey, *Vom Subjekt zur Selbstreferenz: Rechtstheoretische Überlegungen zur Rekonstruktion der Rechtskategorie* (Berlin, 1989), esp. at 100 in support of Wiethölter.

[89] See for example Peter Marburger, *Die Regeln der Technik im Recht* (Berlin, 1979); Rainer Wolf, *Der Stand der Technik: Geschichte, Strukturelemente und Funktion der Verrechtlichung technischer Risiken am Beispiel des Immissionsschutzes* (Opladen, 1986). As far as I can see, the structural similarity of the reference to technology and to public morals has not been noted anywhere. In any event, the normative prerequisites for an assessment of the juridical relevance of external rules and of the assessments of facts and circumstances are not constants. They are themselves subject to a judicial and legislative development of law. See, for example, Gerd Winter, 'Die Angst des Richters bei der Technikbewertung', *Zeitschrift für Rechtspolitik* (1987), 425–31, who calls for such a development.

[90] In respect of Roman law see Yan Thomas, 'Le langagage du droit romain: Problèmes et méthodes', *Archives de Philosophie du Droit* 19 (1974), 103–25, who speaks out against one widely held (but not properly thought through) opinion. See also the remarks on 'The Autonomy of the Legal Lexicon', in Bernard S. Jackson, *Semiotics and Legal Theory* (London, 1985), 46. For one particularly important case see Carcaterra, *Intorno ai bonae fidei iudicia.*

[91] Helmut Schelsky has repeatedly addressed the issue of the consequences of involving experts either as expert witnesses or as participants in proceedings as provided for by statutes. See, for instance, *Die Soziologen und das Recht: Abhandlungen und Vorträge zur Soziologie von Recht,*

There is considerable discussion whether law needs a moral 'reason' or not. Especially in the common law of the United States it is often assumed that this it does. Here judges, when in doubt, are supposed to resort to what they see as the 'moral aspirations' of the community.[92] We pointed out earlier how this stance is fraught with problems.[93] Of course, the method of empirical research by survey is not used, so it is only a case of judges asking *themselves* what they take to be the moral position of *others*. A test case would be (and this can only be put in the form of a paradox) whether the law respects a moral restriction to obey the law, a restriction which cannot itself be deduced from the law. However, if law respects such restrictions, this follows from law's operation. If law does not respect them, it does not accept them either. This paradox can only be avoided if one applies what is characteristically called re-entry, namely that one accepts the external references to morals as part of the operations of the legal system itself.

So far we have discussed external criteria, standards and norms to which the law on occasion recurrently refers for internal reasons. The same argument applies to recourse to external reasons for legal norms such as subliminal interests, intentions and secondary intentions, and motives, especially in the area of legislation. Here, there is also an internal filtering of what is appropriate for the interpretation of norms under the circumstances, and of what is not. Not all 'motives' of the legislator can be turned into law. One will never find written in the reasons of a judgment the statement that a legislative act was due to the manoeuvring of a political party or to the circumstance that it is now politically correct to take an anti-big-business position. Even in the famous discussion about 'original intent', as a dictum in constitutional interpretation in the United States, nobody has seriously considered conducting historical research. There has only been one key issue and that has been how to restrict the active interpretation of moral zealots.

It follows that neither recourse to external rules nor reference to empirically discovered motives for legislation are qualified to refute the thesis of the operative closure and the autonomy of the legal system. The same

---

Institution und Planung (Opladen, 1980) 39. See also, Julian L. Woodward, 'A Scientific Attempt to provide Evidence for a Decision on Change of Venue', *American Sociological Review* 17 (1952), 447–52 for problems of evidence in relation to a purely scientific investigation and evaluation of facts. (Woodward, however, is concerned with an untypical juridical and more politically 'sensational' investigation of prejudices in a case where blacks were given a death sentence for the rape of a white woman.)

[92] See David Lyons, *Ethics and the Rule of Law* (Cambridge, 1984), or (less radical) Melvon Aron Eisenber, *The Nature of the Common Law* (Cambridge, Mass., 1988), 14. As a European one is tempted to ask how Americans are able to know what they mean when they talk about morals.

[93] See above in this section.

can be said when courts refer to ordinary language when they interpret statutes.[94] In all these cases the point is that they are evidence neither for the thesis of de-differentiation nor for that of a loss of the importance of law in society, but that they are examples of interpenetration. This means that the law presupposes that its environment has already structured and reduced its complexity and simply uses the result without, in turn, engaging in an analysis of how this came about (or only relying on purely legal perspectives for such an analysis).[95] This does not lead to a blurring of system boundaries or to an overlap of systems or to a shift from the centre of gravity of law to that of other functioning systems, as far as all of society is concerned. This is the quite ordinary process of absorbing insecurity in the exchange between systems (just like the brain uses the chemical ordering of neurons without assigning them as its own operations). The autonomy remains intact and this can be seen in the fact that decisions are normally involved which are *specific* to law and yet require recourse to something outside law. This recourse is accounted for in the legal system with quite a narrow value, which represents the link. Further, this can be seen in the fact that the authority of law also takes in errors, for instance in relation to the technical feasibility of imposing conditions on calculated costs, whereas technical mechanisms with direct input would simply not function in a similar way. In all cognitive legal operations the legal system assumes that it can err lawfully and then decide afterwards whether or not something should be done about the error if it is discovered.[96]

The bare fact that law needs to legitimize legal decisions when they refer to non-law shows that such cognitively established external references reflect aspects of internal legal operations. However, sociological research on how knowledge is used in the legal system leads even further than that fact.[97] Such research shows that expert knowledge loses essential elements of its scientific quality in juridical and political-administrative decision-making proceedings, and is tailored in such a way that it can lead to results under the conditions of necessary simplification and the time pressures of those proceedings. This means above all for the legal system that knowledge is declared to be knowledge of facts with which one can arrive directly at decisions with the help of legal norms. In other words, knowledge is pressed into the form

---

[94] D. Neil McCormick and Robert S. Summers, 'Interpretation and Justification', in id., *Interpreting Statutes: A Comparative Study* (Aldershot, 1992), 511–44, at 517, remark: 'in this sense ordinary meaning is as much a construct of the law as is legal principle'.

[95] For this concept of interpenetration as a general link to external complexity see more detail in Luhmann, *Soziale Systeme*, 286 (*Social Systems*, 210).

[96] Today such discoveries increasingly lead to constitutional courts imposing conditions on the legislator. However, this involves only the errors of legislators and not the errors of judges.

[97] See above all Roger Smith and Brian Wynne (eds.), *Expert Evidence: Interpreting Science in the Law* (London, 1989).

that law has provided for it.[98] Law supports the pretension of the validity of law through a presentation in which a decision, given the rules, *follows from the facts*. Of course, one can also find such pretentious presentations of findings by individual researchers in the sciences.[99] However, there is a clear difference between their form and context—for instance, in the way in which a science-internal presentation uses the precise declaration of the validity of its results but also the admission of the degrees of remaining uncertainty as a strategy to protect those research results from criticism. In contrast, the legal system focuses primarily on the tenability of its own decisions and can avoid presenting a general uncertainty as to the foundations of knowledge and their dependence on theoretical frameworks, etc., because only the legally relevant details are of any interest. And typically one finds that there is a higher demand on the certainty/uncertainty of scientific findings if questions of legal responsibility, punishability, liability and compensation for damages depend on them. This means that the level of how exacting the demands are is regulated up-front by the expected legal consequences. Accordingly, the context of application distinguishes a scientific and a legal use of knowledge and leads to different forms of presentation, which depend on the recursive network in which this knowledge is recognized as useful.

Finally it should be noted, as clarification, that the distinction between normative/cognitive is not identical with a distinction between system and environment. For instance, the law can acknowledge the simple existence of norms in the environment as facts (for example norms of religious fundamentalists). Additionally law can also learn, that is, it can process information cognitively, above all in the area of interpretative argumentation (scientific dispute about facts) or in the area of legislative self-correction. But that does not affect a state of affairs in which such self-references are stabilized by a recursive reference to not being allowed to learn, by a contrafactual stability of norms, however open for learning the law may be, based as it is on such a normative stability. Only because there is the norm that contracts are to be kept, are there extremely high demands for learning the contents of contracts, a genuine wish of parties to come to an agreement, the possibility of identifying errors, etc.[100]

---

[98] Smith and Wynne, *Expert Evidence*, 3 observe: 'It follows that the many areas of legal decision making which draw on scientific or technical expertise value a firm structuring and classification of problems, clear distinctions between what is and is not an issue, precise decision rules (leading as far as possible to decisions following automatically from the facts of a problem) and efficiency in presentation and procedure.'

[99] See, for example, Susan Leigh Star, 'Scientific Work and Uncertainty', *Social Studies of Science* 15 (1985), 391–427; Brian L. Campbell, 'Uncertainty as Symbolic Action in Disputes among Experts', *Social Studies of Science* 14 (1985), 429–53.

[100] This example also shows how essential it is to take historical developments into consideration. Law did not accept the high risk involved with learning in relation to the will of contracting parties until the nineteenth century.

In addition, system and environment always coexist and one side of the form of the system is never without the other side of its environment. However, by internalizing this distinction in the form of the distinction between self-reference and external reference, the system gains the freedom to change 'leadership' in what it refers to for guiding its own (and always only its own!) operations. It can shift from self-reference to external reference and back. The problem of a specific decision can be seen either as a matter of the investigation of facts or as a matter of the interpretation of norms. In proceeding from operation to operation, the system can oscillate between internal reference and external reference without ever having to step outside its boundaries. This also allows it to resolve (but never to remove) the inevitable synchronicity of world and operation through an observation scheme along a time-dimension. Past and future facts can be attributed with the meaning arrived at in the present time. Thus, the system gains a capacity for synchronization.

The autopoiesis of law recognizes itself by the unavoidably normative style of expectations which are the foundation for its processing of legal communications. In practice, this happens by reference to existing law that orients both the attitudes to what can be claimed and the authorized decisions that can be made. A second safety line is the reference to the binary scheme of legal and illegal. One must ask, however, how the difference between self-reference and external reference, between closure and openness, can be expressed if each explicit or implicit reference to the values which are expressed by coding symbolizes the closure of the system.

My answer is: through the difference between coding and programming.

As far as coding is concerned, the openness of the system consists only of its short-circuited self-references, that is, the fact that each operation controls the value of *both* legal and illegal at any given moment. This reflects openness as to the dimension of time, in contrast to all sorts of teleology that insist on a good (natural, perfect, etc.) end. There is no termination, only connection. This, however, necessarily leaves open the question as to how the values 'legal' and 'illegal' are allocated and what is right or wrong with respect to them. We will call the rules for this allocation (with whatever margin for interpretation) programmes. We are thinking of legislative acts here but also of other premises for decisions in the legal system, such as a commitment to precedents in court practice. The operative closure of the legal system is secured by coding. But at the level of programming it can be determined on which grounds and in which respects the system has to process cognitions. In societies that are becoming more complex, this can lead to highly open states as to the appropriate conditions in the environment, conditions which cannot be determined in advance. This never leads, however, to the dissolution of the unity of law as long as this unity is present in the system through one, and only one, binary code, which cannot be used in the same way anywhere else in society.

Finally, it could be asked whether or not there are cases in which the legal system is forced by society to change.[101] One could think here of the effects of the civil rights movement in the United States or of the increasing awareness of risks associated with occupational safety and consumer protection.[102] Would one not have to concede that the legal system is bound to yield to these enormous social pressures out of concern for its 'legitimacy' (to put this point in the style of 'Critical Legal Studies')?[103] If this were a question of power and not merely a question of (cognitive) learning, such a statement of fact would be incompatible with what is understood by the notion of 'rule of law', and it would no longer make it possible to understand communications of this kind as legal system communications. Appropriately, no social movement and no media campaign can change the law. Change is not possible except through the legal system itself choosing the forms with which it accounts for the changes in public opinion, for instance by the prohibition of racial discrimination in public institutions or by the introduction of product liability. Under the current conditions of mass print media and TV such changes of orientation happen much faster than in a time when the adjustment of law to the conditions of a capitalist economy was involved.[104] Therefore the oscillations of legal change can be more erratic and more quickly prone to a review which, in turn, makes the causal relation between change of opinion and legal change appear more plausible. Without doubt this situation can be described as a causal relation. However, this still requires that a transformation of themes take place, and it does not exclude the case that adjustments in the legal system are too difficult (for instance, the filing of a general, populist suit concerning environment law) to be made as a concession to suggestions from outside. Law itself is the organ of society that is used for turning a change in public opinion into a legal form. The autopoiesis of law does not hinder this. However, it must be achieved in one way or the other if the instrument itself—with which society achieves legal change—is not to be destroyed in the process.

[101] See Joel Handler, *Social Movements and Legal Systems: A Theory of Law Reform and Social Change* (New York, 1978). However, Handler's study focuses on the social movement and with reference to that system the legal system appears as only one of the variables, which explain the success or lack of success of social movements, in relation to a legal change.

[102] George L. Priest, 'The New Legal Structure of Risk Control', *Daedalus* 119/4 (1990), 207–27, talks of an outright revolution in American civil (private) law.

[103] Majorie Schaafsma voiced this objection in the paper she presented at my course in autumn 1989 at Northwestern University Law School.

[104] See James W. Hurst, *Law and the Conditions of Freedom in the Nineteenth-Century United States* (Madison, 1956), and id., *Law and Social Process in United States History* (Ann Arbor, 1960); Morton J. Horwitz, *The Transformation of American Law, 1780–1860* (Cambridge, Mass., 1977).

Seen from the position of the legal system, there must be a filter that allows it to perceive a change of public opinion as a reason to learn—that is, cognitively—and not as a direct imposition of new norms.

VII

There is no exception to the principle of the operative closure of the legal system. It is not a normative principle. There is no provision for the violation of this principle in the legal system. A communication is not unlawful, rather it is an impossible one, if it does not fit into the coding legal/illegal. The communication is simply not attributed to the legal system but is seen as a fact in its environment. (Whether or not it is attributed to any other functioning system has to be decided according to the coding of the respective sub-systems.) In other words, the 'sanction' is only given by the difference between system and environment. There is no exception even where the legal system is differentiating constitutional law and other law. Consequently, constitutional law is included—how could it be law otherwise? This applies then to the situation when constitutional law supplements legal coding with the additional coding constitutional/unconstitutional.[105] Constitutional law requires a high degree of interpretation, including interpretation that goes further than that which is laid down in many legal texts. Interpreters of constitutions are continuously faced with the question as to how the meaning inferred by the constitution can be determined. There is reason to doubt whether the ordinary methods of interpretation apply as well here, or whether the difference between constitutional law and ordinary law also implies a differentiation of the points of view on interpretation. In this sense, there is often an assumption of higher standards applying, for instance moral or ethical ones, as if one could not reach a decision any other way (for example, by doctrinal analysis).[106] It is as if the interpreters of constitutional law, who are already dealing with higher law, have to refer to something even higher in order to cope with their insecurities.

In apparent contrast to that position (and some people argue that this is an ideological contrast), one finds the principle that the constitution is not identical with religious, moral, and ideological concepts of society.[107]

[105] See further below Ch. 10.IV.

[106] Michael Perry, *Morality, Politics and Law* (London, 1988), talks about a shift to the moral aspirations of the people. Ronald Dworkin, *Taking Rights Seriously* (London, 1978), sounds more cautious in referring to constitutional morality, as does Neil MacCormick in referring to institutional morality ('Institutional Morality and the Constitution', in Neil MacCormick and Ota Weinberger, *An Institutional Theory of Law: New Approaches to Legal Positivism* (Dordrecht, 1986), 171–88).

[107] See Herbert Krüger, Staatslehre, 2nd edn. (Stuttgart, 1966), 178; Alexander Hollerbach, 'Ideologie und Verfassung', in Werner Maihofer (ed.), *Ideologie und Recht* (Frankfurt, 1969), 37–61, at 52; Reinhold Zippelius, *Allgemeine Staatslehre*, 3rd edn. (Munich, 1971), 112.

In Germany, the attractiveness of this principle stems above all from the experience of National Socialism, which principally rejected such a distance between law and ideology as representing a leftover from the liberal *Rechtsstaat.*[108] A more thorough analysis can easily show that the presumed contradiction between non-identity with ideological concepts and the reference to values can be resolved. Non-identity is also represented under the label of pluralism. Such a representation indicates merely that the constitution accepts ideological and political differences as within the domain of politics, but that it does not represent a legal text *per se* as favouring one side of the political divide rather than the other. One also finds a number of different values in constitutional texts and *no radical rules for conflicts between them.* Just think here of freedom and equality. We can take it, then, that the constitution requires a functioning legal system for the treatment of such conflicts and so refers to the inside of the legal system and not to its outside. This confirms indirectly, but in practice unavoidably, that the law refers in everything it says to itself, and that all references to values, whether ordinary ones or 'higher' ones, are used only as formulations in decision-making. They are launched from law and return to law.

These features are especially apparent in the Federal Republic of Germany. Here, the Constitutional Court avoids presenting its own opinion as the opinion of the German people. But it has transformed the basic laws of classical liberal provenance into general value programmes in order not to lose juridical control over the development of a welfare state and that state's utilitarian programmes. Whereas value concepts have gone out of fashion everywhere else (above all, of course, in philosophy), they can still be found in the decision-making of the Constitutional Court—and in the commitments of the programmes of political parties. Both situations tap the potential provided by value concepts to obtain legitimacy whilst, at the same time, keeping options open where decisions over conflicts of values are concerned—and this means: all decisions! Is this an indication of a de-differentiation in the relationship between the legal system and the political system?

Not at all! The division is certainly maintained at the organizational level, and the recursively applied, self-referential networks that lay down meaning within those two systems also differ. The legal system is controlled by requirements of consistency to a higher degree than the political system. Party programmes are tuned to opposition, even if only superficially. It is precisely this system differentiation that explains the problems arising from the fact that both the legal system and the political system continuously have to make decisions when conflicts of values occur. Such problems are

[108] See principally Ernst Rudolf Huber, *Verfassungsrecht des Großdeutschen Reiches* (Hamburg, 1939).

evident, for instance, in the question of the 'democratic legitimacy' of the Constitutional Court. On this level, the legal system moves away from clear dogmatic concepts and replaces them with a commitment of the court to its own decisions, which is only cautiously modified. In the political system similar effects of inertia are evident—such as a commitment to well-tried formulae for absorbing uncertainty, well-established battlefields for conflicts, risks that have previously been recognized.[109] When assessed on a global scale, such arrangements might merit the appraisal 'just satisfactory'. One can hardly say, however, that they exhaust the full potential of internal rationality provided by the functional differentiation of systems.

VIII

The legal system provides itself with a symbol that marks the unity of the system in the interactive sequence of its operations, just like other functional sub-systems. In contrast to reflexive theories, which will be discussed in greater detail in Chapter 11, such a symbol is not a description of the system but an operative function. So the symbol does not link observations but operations—even if all operations can be observed and described in the system, including the symbol for the system itself. This operative symbolization goes deeper than observations do; it is indispensable for proceeding from operation to operation, that is, for the production of recursive references and for the finding of subsequent operations—independently from how an observer may distinguish and determine this. We have chosen the concept 'symbol', because we are concerned with how the *unity* of the system can be preserved and reproduced through its diverse array of operations. In the legal system this is achieved through the symbol of *legal validity*.[110] This can be abbreviated to validity as long as it does not lead to misunderstanding.

Validity is, like money, a symbol without intrinsic value. It does not refer to the quality of a statute, judgment, or contract in any way. It evades any qualitative assessment, which would lead to a 'better or worse' validity. The third amendment of a European Union decree about the procedures permitted to determine the gender of privately kept reptiles could be valid or not, even if it is not fully clear whether or not there are any cases to which this decree applies and whether or not reptiles kept in zoos fall within the terms of the decree. Once again like money, 'validity' symbolizes only the acceptance of communication, that is, only the autopoiesis of the

[109] See on this issue also Niklas Luhmann, 'Die Unbeliebtheit der politischen Parteien', in Siegfried Unseld (ed.), *Politik ohne Projekt? Nachdenken über Deutschland* (Frankfurt, 1993), 43–53.

[110] For example, according to Alf Ross, 'Validity is a quality ascribed to the system as a whole' (*On Law and Justice*, London, 1958) at 36.

communications of the legal system. This does not exclude the possibility for the validity of immoral contracts or of unconstitutional laws to be disallowed[111]—but once again not because of any intrinsic quality of the norm, but on the basis of valid law that prescribes the conditions for legal validity.

It is on this point that a debate with Habermas is called for.[112] Habermas insists on the normative qualification of legal validity (perhaps one should say: he insists on the validity of legal validity) with the argument that only in this way could both the legal system and the political system be provided with legitimacy. At first sight, this appears highly plausible. However, how can this claim be supported? Habermas employs a 'discourse ethics' which is rich in detail. Its basic premiss holds that 'valid forms of action are precisely those which have been consented to in a participatory rational discourse by all those who could possibly be affected by these actions'.[113] However, such a criterion for the distinction between validity/invalidity cannot be tested in a court. It is not justiciable, and thus it cannot be practised in the legal system itself. Any superficial glance at the 'ecologically' mediated involvement of participants in legal proceedings should suffice to clarify this point.[114] Thus, this criterion can only work as a legal fiction.[115] One could assume that its requirements have been met when all the usual rules of due process have been adhered to. On this basis, certain procedural reforms could be established/non-established—but then obviously without any effect on the validity of law. A system-wide universal test of validity/invalidity for *each* legal norm apparently is not convertible into practical programmes. Validity is founded on some kind of idealization of something that is absent.

The unalterable fact that legitimacy is based on a legal fiction confirms that a concept of validity, which is free from norms and which can then be conditioned, is more appropriate for dealing with the discrepancy between the complexity of the system and the actual decisions it achieves. Seen from the perspective of a history of theories, this concept of validity as a symbol of the unity of law replaces that of the sources of law and thus replaces the

---

[111] This happens in a juridical setting applying juridical reasoning. If one held that contravention of the constitution equalled the invalidity of a law this would decisively paralyse the resolve of the Constitutional Court to exercise its judicial review of legislation as predictive of the impact of legislation—and this can be seen as desirable or as a disadvantage.

[112] See Jürgen Habermas, *Fakitizität und Geltung: Beiträge zur Diskurstheorie des Rechts und des demokratischen Rechtsstaats* (Frankfurt, 1992) (*Between Norms and Facts* (Oxford, 1996)).

[113] Ibid. 138.

[114] Basically, Habermas simply generalizes the old liberal rule that each individual can enjoy his or her freedom (that is, make a claim on validity) as long as this does not involve harm to others (that is, individuals who are involved have no reasonable grounds to object). However, it is difficult to think, under current conditions (key terms: democracy, redistributive state, ecological sensibilities) of even one case in which this rule could be applied.

[115] Habermas calls this 'the assumption of rational acceptability' (ibid. 188).

starting point for all 'positivist' legal theories.[116] The concept of the sources of law approached the problem too ambitiously. The metaphor of the sources of law, for example, led Savigny to reject emphatically the suggestion that a contract was a 'source of law'.[117] In addition, the concept of a source of law implies an external reference (for Savigny 'the people'; for others the politically implemented 'authority', that is, the authority of office; for the early sociology of law something like 'folkways', 'living law', given regimes of expectations which the written law could not change or, at best, could only reinstitutionalize).[118] However, in relation to a symbol of validity one can imagine very well a meaningful element that circulates exclusively inside the system. Finally, the concept of sources of law serves as an instrument for reasoning. It is used as a criterion in situations of legal decision-making in which there is doubt whether or not the law to which someone refers is really valid law. The operative symbol, in contrast, refers to changes in the state of law; for a change, be it through legislation, or contract, can only be achieved if it is assumed that a certain form of law was *not* valid until then.

It is an empirical question whether or not the legal system uses the instrument of sources of law in order to exclude doubt. One can find out how the instrument is actually used. However, the significance of the semantics of validity does not stop there. One has to ask further which function validity, that is, the distinction between validity and non-validity, has? The transition to a theory of self-referential operatively closed systems demands such a revision of theory. Validity is an eigenvalue of the legal

---

[116] However, this does not apply to the normal discourse of legal theory on the concept and criteria of legal validity, which reflects nearly all controversies which take place in legal theory and which is void of any delineation of the phenomenon from other approaches to determine law. See François Ost and Michel van de Kerchove, *Jalons pour une théorie critique du droit* (Brussels, 1987), 257, and the literature which the authors evaluate there.

[117] See Friedrich Carl von Savigny, *System des heutigen Römischen Rechts*, vol. 1 (Berlin, 1840), 12. However, this is inconsistent with Roman civil law. The Romans especially talked of *lex contractus* and meant by that a substantial definition of validity through contract (I am grateful to Dieter Simon for pointing this out to me). And in the reconstructions of a broader concept of contract on the basis of natural law one can still read, for instance: 'Les conventions tiennent lieu des loix' (Jean Domat, *Les Loix civiles dan leur ordre natural*, 2nd edn. (Paris, 1697), vol. 1, p. 72). It seems that only the later prevalence of legislative positivism has led to a situation in which the tight connection between legal and contractual disposition has been lost from view, and this has not changed since, even though—and this applies above all to labour law—a contrary view is discussed today. See Klaus Adomeit, *Rechtsquellenfragen im Arbeitsrecht* (Munich, 1969), esp. 77.

[118] See William Graham Sumner, *Folkways: A Study of the Importance of Usages, Manners, Customs. Mores and Morals* (1906; new edn. New York, 1960); Eugen Ehrlich, *Grundlegung der Soziologie des Rechts* (1913; reprint Berlin, 1967). On a modification of the theory of double institutionalization see Paul Bohannan, 'Law and Legal Institutions', *International Encyclopedia of the Social Sciences*, vol. 9 (Chicago, 1968), 73–8.

system; namely a value that is constituted by the recursive performance of the system's own operations and one that *cannot be used anywhere else.*[119]

Even if the concept of sources of law is still used by lawyers, in legal theory it has long since been overtaken by instruments, which could be called the resolution of paradoxes (or unfolding of tautologies), with the tendency to externalize references. Following developments in logic and linguistics, this is the launch of a meta-level at which rules regulate the validity of rules. Kelsen's 'Grundnorm' (basic norm) offers a theory of this kind; Hart's 'secondary rule of recognition' is another. However, the most convincing solution of the problem posed in this way is by reference to the language that is in practice used by lawyers.[120] The starting point for this line of thought is the following: all law is valid law. Law which is not valid is not law. It follows that the rule that makes validity recognizable cannot be one of the valid rules. There cannot be any rule in the system that regulates the applicability/non-applicability of all the rules of the system. The problem has to be 'gödelized'[121] by a reference to an external foundation. And in this situation language, that is, society at large, is a convincing way out because law is after all a part of society's language, as are all scientific languages, embedded as they are in common language. The unfolding of the tautology 'law is valid law' by a distinction of several levels of regulation is grounded on the fact of social differentiation, that is, the differentiation of the legal system from within the social system.

Unfortunately, the concept of several levels is in itself not logically appropriate because the distinction of several levels of language or of regulation easily becomes paradoxical as soon as the question of the unity of the plurality of levels is raised. However, this is only a problem for an observer who has to use distinctions to define something (here: as valid law) and who cannot observe the unity of the distinction while using the distinction. Therefore we transfer the problem onto the operative level and see in the symbol of the validity of law only the performance of the transition from one state of law to another, that is, only the unity of the difference between states of law that were valid before and those which are valid after the transition.[122]

---

[119] See, in relation to the more general points of view of social theory, Robert Platt, 'Reflexivity, Recursion and Social Life: Elements for a Postmodern Sociology', *Sociological Review* 37 (1989), 636–67.

[120] So Alexander Peczenik, *The Concept of 'Valid Law'* (Stockholm, 1972), also in *Scandinavian Studies in Law* (1972).

[121] [Luhmann refers here to Gödel's theorem (1931), which states that it is impossible to prove the consistency of a formal system of the arithmetic of natural numbers within the system itself (Translator's note).]

[122] Obviously the problem of the observer is not solved in this way. However, if the self-transformation of law, that is, its autopoiesis, has become operative and the methods to ascertain this are assured, observers are free to entertain divergent theories.

The symbol of the validity of law as a symbol for the unity of law goes further than the distinction between cognitive and normative questions. In relation to this difference its status is ambivalent. Validity in this sense is not an a priori condition for knowledge (even though without validity there would not be any object in legal knowledge, that is, law). Validity does not come in the form of a cognitive statement about law.[123] Neither is validity the result of the impact of an external cause such as a transcending, transcendental, or immanently authoritative ('state') reason for validity. Validity is only the form in which operations refer to their relationship with the system and relate to the context of other operations in the same system while reproducing it. Validity is the form for participating in the unity of the system.

In the same sense, validity is not a norm,[124] and it is neither a basic norm nor a meta-norm.[125] Validity is not an expectation which has been designed to cope with disappointment and which needs to be protected against disappointment.[126] What is valid in the legal system is not what ought to be valid—it is valid or it is not. This is why the legal system can change what is valid without breaking its own norms. In any event, a change of law is not barred by the assumption of validity alone but possibly by procedural norms that specify, and through that restrict, the ways in which validity can be produced, that is, in which law can be changed. Constitutional law even lays down norms that stipulate that certain norms, including themselves, are not to be changed. This leads to a much-discussed paradox.[127] The prohibition on changing the law could be changed by law in turn—and so on *ad infinitum*. This problem cannot be contained normatively. It has to be 'gödelized' in the direction of politics. That is, political vigilance is called for. Or, in other words, the paradox of changing the law can be resolved by distinguishing between normativity and validity and by taking into account

[123] Many legal theories of validity operate on this premiss and then have difficulty in distinguishing the difference between validity and non-validity from the difference between true and untrue statements about law.

[124] The theory of institutions arrives at the same conclusion albeit with different terminology. See, above all, Santi Romano, *L'ordinamento giuridico* (1918; reprint of the second edition Florence, 1962).

[125] If one follows Kelsen the question is most often asked the other way around: what is the special status of a basic norm in relation to validity—extra-legal, hypothetical, moral? See for instance Julius Stone, *Legal System and Lawyers' Reasonings* (Stanford, 1964), 203.

[126] See Ch. 3.II for a discussion of the concept of norm, which is here assumed.

[127] See, for example, David R. Dow, 'When Words Mean What We Believe They Say: The Case of Article V', *Iowa Law Review* 76 (1990), 1–66. Dow finds, in referring to the Torah, a religiously grounded paradox that cannot be resolved, that is, accepted cognitively. See also Peter Suber, *The Paradox of Self-Amendment* (New York, 1990), who presents the thesis of a participatory (that is: political!) solution. We argue against that solution in the text above, that each paradox can be resolved by adding distinctions, even if not in a logically controlled and hence cogent way.

politically that changing the prohibition on changing constitutional law is creating valid law (all the while the character of this event as a violation of norms is paradoxical and therefore without any consequence).

In this way, validity is not a norm but a form. As such the symbol of validity marks two sides of a difference: on the one hand, what is valid and on the other hand, what is not valid. In the words of George Spencer Brown, what is valid is the internal side of the form and what is not valid is the external side of the form. The system needs time to cross over from one side of the form to the other—be it in order to turn norms with the status valid into norms with the status non-valid, or vice versa. Alternatively, in observing and describing norms, it may cross over from a statement that they are valid to a statement that they are not valid, or vice versa. In each case, the form exists only as a two-sided form, and one side cannot exist without the other. And in each case, both descriptions—the positive as well as the negative—are the result of the internal operations of the system and are related to its internal states. Even invalidity, for instance a void contract or an invalid statute, is a state of the legal system and not that of its environment. As happens with all symbols, a devilish counter-indication is induced. It can happen that operations start with an assumption of validity, which later turns out to have been made in error. Or it may happen that decisions lead to long-term commitments (for instance, investment of capital) under the assumption of validity, but the law has changed in the meantime and what was valid before is no longer valid.

One should also note that the symbol of validity reacts to the *intrinsic dynamics* of the legal system and is called upon only when the legal system is differentiated to such a degree *that it can change itself.* Even up to the Middle Ages the lawfulness of law (if one can say this) was accepted as given and seen as a question of knowledge—even in the case of legislation.[128] Accordingly, the source of law lay in the conviction that something was lawful and part of a necessary order of human communality (*opinio iuris, opinio necessitatis*). The important imperial, principality, and municipal regulatory practice which already existed then, could be understood as one of these necessities of order, and was thus not an exception to the principle, let alone a reason for relating the concept of validity (or source of law) to law-making.[129] Only the theological voluntarism of the late Middle Ages (above all influenced by Ockham) paved the way for a different approach to the problem by referring to the human will and *auctoritas.* The symbol of validity as it is used today is, actually, an achievement of modernity.

---

[128] See, for example, Juan B. Vallet de Goytisolo, 'Del legislar como "legere" al legislar como "facere" ', in id., *Estudios sobre fuentes del derecho y metodo juridico* (Madrid, 1982), 939–88.

[129] This is not always clear even to legal historians who refer simply to the fact of existing legislation. (See, for instance, Joachim Rückert, *Autonomie des Rechts in rechtshistorischer Perspektive* (Hanover, 1988).)

The symbol of validity is attached to the normative expectations of the system. It qualifies norms as valid or not valid. However, this applies only if a legal position is changed. Any observer can freely state, at any point of time, which law is valid and which is not. In this respect, he *understands* validity as *duration* (which is limited in time and can be revoked). So, *theories* of validity, such as the ones that relate validity to a beginning, a reason, the will of god, or other authoritative criteria, are theories of observers. Moreover, the legal system can observe itself, for instance in judicial reviews or legal reforms. In this manner, however, the unity of the legal system could never be 'identified'. Each act of observation needs to reduce the complexity already produced, that is, it needs to proceed selectively. The real process of a permanent revalidation of what is valid is removed from observation; it takes a considerable effort of theory building to argue plausibly that the roots for validity are to be found here.

Validity is nothing but the symbol for the nexus that is part and parcel of all legal operations. It cannot be validated point by point but only recursively, that is, by recourse to valid law.[130] Validity achieves connectivity in the system. It alone provides a sanction, which is, however, the prerequisite for all other sanctions if they are to be communicated as legally valid sanctions. Invalid norms mean nothing to the system. This is most clearly demonstrated by the fact that nobody would even try to apply invalid norms; nobody would argue that certain legal norms are invalid but they help to win the case nevertheless. Such inputs are automatically translated into an argument about the validity of law or about changing the currently valid law. The negative value, that is, invalidity, is only useful as a reflexive value for clarifying the conditions under which validity operates, but it does not produce possibilities of further connections. This distinguishes the form validity/invalidity from the code legal/illegal which, even though it is also structured in the form of a positive versus a negative value, can provide that injustice has certain legal consequences, such as penalties, liability, or rendering void the legal effects of certain acts. Prisoners also have rights, which they can enforce as the case may be,[131] and everyone has a right to have the law confirm that they acted outside the law when they acted outside the law. So the symbol of validity is necessary, especially for crossing the boundary between legal/illegal. In order to produce opportunities for further connections, a reference to valid law is required, and this applies both

---

[130] See similarly Ost and van der Kerchove, *Jalons*, 225: 'A l'idée d'une validité conçue come obligatoriété nécessaire et a priori nous opposons l'idée d'une prétention à la validité qui demande à être confirmée et évaluée.' See also pp. 228 and 283 with respect to recursivity; with respect to 'validation' see also Michel van der Kerchove and François Ost, *Le système juridique entre ordre et désordre* (Paris, 1988), 142.

[131] But this is not without problems, as practice shows. See Jim Thomas, *Prisoner Litigation: The Paradox of the Jailhouse Lawyer* (Totowa, NJ, 1988).

to the case of declaring certain expectations or actions as lawful and to the contrary case of unlawfulness.

Therefore, according to Talcott Parsons, validity can also be called a circulating symbol handed on to further operations with each use—just like solvency in the economy or collective binding in politics. The symbol is transferred from operation to operation and exists only in this permanent reproduction. It is not a symbol for continuance alongside which the flow of factual legal events passes. It is a symbol for the dynamic stability of the system, which is expressed in backward and forward references to the past and the future. Tomorrow's validity will be a different validity because a decision has been made today, although the symbolic function always remains the same. As we have stated before, law is a historical machine that turns into a different machine with each of its operations.

The linguistic term 'shift' describes something similar. It means that symbols can only be used by reference to the process that is using them, and they therefore change their references from moment to moment.[132] This requires that stable external references be relinquished, but rather it provides some kind of existential anchorage in a system that uses these shifts to equip itself with controlled dynamics in order to keep itself apart from its environment.

However, not all legal communication carries validity in this way. A simple example of this is the legal claim. It is imperative that there be legally binding decisions. These are not only the decisions of legislators and courts but they are also found to a large extent in the establishment of corporations or exchange of contracts, affecting the legal situation and changing it.[133] Unilaterally binding statements are sufficient (for example, wills), but facts, which simply have legal consequences, are not sufficient—for instance, the death of a testator or a criminal act. Just as the transfer of money does not equate with the overall number of operations in the economic system, the transfer of validity in the legal system is not identical with the overall number of operations in the legal system. Transfer operations, however, are those that execute the autopoiesis of the system and without which the differentiation of an operatively closed legal system is not possible.

---

[132] See, for example, Roman Jakobson, 'Verschieber, Verbkategorien, und das russische Verb', in id., *Form und Sinn: Sprachwissenschaftliche Betrachtungen* (Munich, 1974), 35–54.

[133] Legal theory should bear in mind that since the eighteenth century, and as a reaction to a differentiating monetary economy, private individuals have also had access to the use of a symbol of validity without its effectiveness being curbed—further evidence for the differentiation of legal systems and political systems. See Arthur J. Jacobson, 'The Private Use of Public Authority: Sovereignty and Associations in the Common Law', *Buffalo Law Review* 29 (1980), 599–665; Morton Horwitz, *The Transformation of American Law 1780–1860* (Cambridge, Mass., 1977), 160. See Ch. 10 for more details.

Legal theories conceived in the legal system for the legal system have tried over and over again to find an asymmetrical form for the validity of law, but this form can only be described as a circle. So, although the authors of the constitution of the United States, for example, were courageous enough to come up with a new concept and text, they insisted that the constitution only 'constituted' the unity of the people and the instrument of government but not the individual rights, which were the reason for the whole exercise in the first place.[134] Individual rights were only *acknowledged* and within the legal system *specified*. In characterizing this description it is easy to see that it is again only validity as a formula which renders validity in the system disposable.

Hart tries a different approach. He reveals hierarchies (theories of stages) imminent in law as insufficient and indeterminable but he also rejects the externalization of the problem of validity by relating it to extra-legal reasons of validity or natural law. His suggestion for a substitute is the well-known distinction between two kinds of rules: rules of obligation and those of power conferment, especially recognition. This solution, however, has to be paid for by the renunciation of any claim to validity by the rules of recognition (for this would require further rules of recognition). A rule of recognition 'can neither be valid or invalid but is simply accepted as appropriate for use in this way'.[135] This has all the advantages and disadvantages of a solution which has risen to prominence in the history of theory under the critique of David Hume, and which, above all, leaves open the definition of the unity of a system made up by obligations and habits, by valid rules and invalid (but not void) rules (Hart's concept of a 'union of primary and secondary rules'). It is this point precisely that is the target of the concept of autopoiesis. What we are talking about here are the internally connected operations of the system, which could be called 'practices of recognition', and even when the system externalizes reasons of validity such an externalization would still remain an internal operation of the system. On the level of a second-order observation a circular definition is

---

[134] Therefore it was consistent to distinguish editorially between the Bill of Rights and the Constitution—so in the Constitution of Virginia of 1776 the famous 'Bill of Rights' and following it the 'Constitution or Form of Government'. For the text see Francis N. Thorpe (ed.), *The Federal and State Constitutions, Colonial Charters and Other Organic Laws*, vol. 7 (Washington, 1909), 3812–19. Even the Constitution of Virginia of 1830 only quotes the Bill of Rights and states that it 'shall be prefixed to this constitution and have the same relation thereto as it had to the former constitution of this commonwealth' (ibid. 3820). At the same time, a constitutional concept which emphatically includes human rights gives reason to suspect that these rights are inferior and only positive law, which can be changed through constitutional law. So the constitution has to be understood as founded on itself. See also the strong arguments for this in Dworkin, *Taking Rights Seriously*. It should be added that this problem could not come up in English common law because the 'constitutional' limits on governmental power are interpreted as incorporated in the *result* of the long historical development of the protection of individual rights.   [135] Hart, *The Concept of Law*, 105.

unavoidable, and all that can be permitted are asymmetrical operations in a time dimension. At each moment the legal that was previously illegal, and which is now valid, is that which was made valid before.

The classic hierarchical theories of legal validity always assume a scale that persists, namely one that can be used over and over again. It can be viewed from top to bottom and bottom to top in order to find reasons for validity and to articulate them. The theory of temporal validity proposed here does away with this premiss. Validity is a product of the system, which has to be created anew from moment to moment. Therefore, it can only be secured by connecting operations recursively with a minimum expenditure of information (redundancy). This also means that the system reproduces its own individuality. For time is an individualizing factor through the selectivity that it requires: one can only move from 1 to 2 once.

The switch from hierarchy to time allows us to dispense with a normative reason for validity in the form of a 'supreme' norm. Any normative reason for validity would lose its way in an infinite regress; or, in other words, it would require itself as premiss, which would require its own premiss, and so on. The only inalienable basis for validity is therefore given by *time*. More precisely it is given by the *synchronicity* of all the factual operations of the social system and its environment. For everything that happens, is happening *now*—and not in the past or in the future. Time horizons are empty horizons in relation to what is actually happening, and the only purpose they serve is to orient the present and move along with it. However, synchronicity means that it is *impossible to know and to affect what is happening at the same time* and it means that one is reduced to making assumptions, suppositions, and fictions. The validity of the symbol of validity is based on this *incapacity*. Without convincing evidence one cannot but presuppose that at any given moment other operations in the legal system and its social and psychological environments activate the symbol of validity as well. Thus the only available test is the success of the ongoing change of the status of the system's validity, of the ongoing connecting of one operation to the next, of the autopoiesis of the system. A side-product of the system's ongoing process of self-reassurance is what an observer describes as complexity. There is no other final reason for this but the mode of and the limitation of the mode of its production.

IX

In addition to the formal symbol of validity the legal system is provided with a second possibility for expressing its operative closure, namely the *principle of equality*.[136] Since antiquity this principle has been part of the fundamental

[136] See, further Raffaele De Giorgi, 'Modelli giuridici dell'uguaglianza e dell'equità', *Sociologia del diritto* 18 (1991), 19–31.

reasoning of every legal culture. It is accepted as if it were self-evident. Equality is the most abstract preference of the system, the final criterion for the attribution of conflicts as legal and illegal. With this function the legal system adopts the name of 'justice'.[137] One cannot question this further, and as such this is a reliable indicator that we have a principle here with a high level of theoretical relevance. However, what has it got to do with operative closure?

First, it is notable that it is not asserted that everything is equal or that everything should be made equal. Rather, equality in its form in the legal system is a concept based on the notion that there is another side: inequality. Equality does not make sense without inequality, and vice versa. If equal is to be treated as alike, unequal has be treated as unalike; otherwise it would be impossible to treat something which appears to be unalike in certain respects as equal from case to case. If one abandons a normative concept of equality one arrives at the Aristotelian rule that equality is that which must be treated equally and that inequality is that which must be treated unequally. So, what we have here is a scheme for observation that merely encourages the development of certain norms and preferences but does not predetermine a preference for equality itself. (It would not be very plausible to demand that all criminals should be subjected to the same punishment.) The form of equality, therefore, serves to highlight inequalities, which in turn deserve to be treated alike in the framework of established differences until this equal treatment also leads to observations and definitions of other inequalities. Like all comparisons this one also fulfils the purpose of finding out what is not alike and leads to the further question as to whether or not these dissimilarities prevent equal treatment. This question is the only one that makes any practical sense in the development of law.

From this position, equality can be transformed from a form into a norm. Equal treatment serves, then, as the rule from which there can be exceptions if the dissimilarity between cases under consideration is clear. Equal treatment is a reason in itself, but unequal treatment requires a justification. The symmetry of the two sides of a form is turned into asymmetry through the scheme of rule/exception to the rule.

However, it is the form and not the norm that closes off the operations of the system: 'Distinction is perfect contingence'.[138] The distinction equal/unequal contains everything, even itself, for the principle of equality also has to be applied equally to all cases. On closer inspection, one can identify a programme for solving a paradox. The universality (contingence) of the principle of equality provides that whenever *it* is applied there are only similar cases and no dissimilar ones. In this respect, the principle of

---

[137] See, for a more detailed discussion, Ch. 5.
[138] George Spencer Brown, *Laws of Form*, 1.

equality represents the system in the system. It does not need any further reasons because it simply describes the autopoiesis of the system. The logical trick (or the logical jump from a paradox to the asymmetry of a practical rule) is to interpret the form as a norm.[139]

The form of equality is so formal that it can readily be adapted to the ever-changing forms of differentiation of the social system. In stratified societies different social status is the reason that justifies unequal treatment. *Unde oportet quod etiam leges imponantur hominibus secundum eorum conditionem.*[140] In functionally differentiated societies it is only the point of reference that is changed. 'Unequal' now refers to what has to be treated differently in the internal operations of the functional systems in order for them to fulfil their functions. Now 'the form of equality', however, means no longer the need to recognize phenomena according to their similarities and differences, but to make the whole system more dynamic by frequent repetition of the question as to whether something is equal or unequal.[141]

However, today one also has to distinguish the use of the principle of equality in politics on the one hand from law on the other. Politics requires people to be treated as equals. The law requires cases to be treated as equal. The principle of equality in a constitution, seen as a legal norm, may lead to situations in which political equality is interpreted legally as equality/inequality; politically, however, this is never completely successful because politics takes up new initiatives for equality and transforms them into law (and only through this process into cases).

The scheme equal/unequal creates a demand for criteria. However, it does not determine which criteria are required. Equality is not a criterion for equality (just as little as truth is a criterion for truth). While natural law has emphasized the principles of rationality, the common law has accentuated the historical continuity of the practice of making distinctions, at least since the sixteenth century. The premiss was (and is here) that the tradition

---

[139] This suggests a theological reverse in the order of Doomsday: God too uses the principle of equality as a programme to solve paradoxes, but in reverse order. He treats all sinners (but not, one would hope, all sins) unequally, namely as individuals. For his application of the principle of equality the case of equality does not apply.

[140] See Thomas Aquinas, *Summa Theologiae* Ia IIae.q.96, art. 2 (Turin edn., 1952), 435.

[141] See, for example, Guido Calabresi, *A Common Law for the Age of Statutes* (Cambridge, Mass., 1982), 13, in relation to the jurisdiction on the equal protection clause: 'The most powerful engine of change in the common law was, strangely enough, the great principles that like cases should be treated alike'. And similarly—*justitia semper reformanda*—Reinhold Zippelius, 'Der Gleichheitssatz', *Veröffentlichungen der Vereinigung der Deutschen Staatsrechtslehrer* 57 (1991), 7–32, at 31. However, generally this effect of increased dynamics is so self-evident that there is more interest in the causes (both legal and social) of the difficulties of legal reform. See, for many such difficulties, Leon H. Mayhew, *Law and Equal Opportunity: A Study of the Massachusetts Commission against Discrimination* (Cambridge, Mass., 1968); Dinesh Khosla, 'Untouchability—a Case Study of Law in Life', in Adam Podgórecki et al. (eds.), *Legal Systems and Social Systems* (London, 1985), 126–73.

of legal decision-making could always be taken for granted as it has distinguished between cases that can be treated equally or must be treated unequally. Following this tradition, a judge can always find the scheme equal/unequal in a concrete form. He has to keep within that tradition, if there is to be a legal decision at all.[142] On the other hand, it is precisely this tradition that allows the judge to make his own distinctions and to set aside cases for unlike treatment, if he discovers an inequality that lends itself to equal treatment and that can be supported with convincing arguments. The 'reason' behind this practice lies in the handling of the two-sided form equal/unequal and this has provided it, as experience has shown, with a continuous renewing link between continuity and innovation.[143] Natural law (as rational law) on the other hand, being based on principles, runs into the difficulties of the deductive inconsistency and interpretative indeterminacy of those principles and is therefore inclined to burden the legislator, assisted by academics, with the task of codification and innovation.[144] However, no matter which route the evolution of law takes, its results are observed and refined with the help of the scheme equal/unequal. This scheme is a scheme of evolutionary differentiation, and that means, last but not least: a scheme that produces more equalities and inequalities. When new cases are recognized as different, they must be subsumed under a rule that lets them be turned into a series of equal cases. The scheme equal/unequal is reproduced in itself. It serves as a principle for bifurcation within the system. Bifurcation always means the establishment of a historically irreversible order. The concept of justice is an expression of how the system describes this process. This makes it possible for tradition to admonish, commend, and disapprove.

Seen from the perspective of systems theory, several quite different aspects come to light. From this one can understand that an autopoiesis of the legal system is put into effect by coordinating and reflecting on matters through conflicts, resolutions of arguments in individual cases, rejected and also confirmed claims as premises for further practice and not only as a recall for historical events. Since new cases can be seen as equal as well as unequal, tradition alone cannot specify the decisions that follow. What one can see, however, is the recursive connecting of earlier with later decisions within the same system, that is, what we call operative closure. To say what is legal and what is illegal can only be found out in contrast with earlier

---

[142] See on this point Gerald J. Postema, *Bentham and the Common Law Tradition* (Oxford, 1986), 3; W. T. Murphy, 'The Oldest Social Science? The Epistemic Properties of the Common Law Tradition', *The Modern Law Review* 54 (1991), 182–215.

[143] See the typology of lawyers in R. C. van Caenegem, *Judges, Legislators and Professors: Chapters in European Legal History* (Cambridge, 1987).

[144] For a more detailed account see Niklas Luhmann, 'Am Anfang war kein Unrecht', in id., *Gesellschaftsstruktur und Semantik*, vol. 3 (Frankfurt, 1989), 11–64.

decisions and, but to a lesser degree, with a view to future decisions, and the guideline for this is provided by the two-sided form of equality. This means that only internally produced distinctions can be used when a decision has to be made whether different cases are to be treated as equal or as unequal.

In this sense equality is interesting precisely because there are differences, and therefore inequality is a different thing from dissimilarity. Dissimilarity must already have existed in paradise or in the mythological primary group. According to an old saying dissimilarity is a moment in the perfecting of the creation. Inequality only happened through the fall from grace or, according to natural law theories, through the differential use of property.[145] The observation scheme equal/unequal is, in contrast to a mere recognition of dissimilarities, a universal and at the same time highly specific scheme. It brings into play the history of a system and so leads to the establishment (and change) of criteria that only apply to that system. The system then articulates its decisions according to these criteria. Hence we can see again what is found in operatively closed systems generally: systems cannot import their structures from outside—they have to establish, vary, or forget about them through their own operations.

Finally, based on this analysis, we can relate the right to equality to the area of general norms of human rights, or even take it as a paradigm example for human rights. In doing so, we disassociate ourselves from a juridical interpretation which is intended for the purposes of legal practice. Human rights deal with the difficulties of coping with a complex world, that is, essentially also with the effects of functional differentiation. Human rights correspond exactly to the structurally induced open-ended character of modern society. If individuals are to attain access to all functional systems in their respectively different ways and if, at the same time, their inclusion is internally controlled in these functional systems by deciding what is seen as equal and what is not, with the help of functional criteria—if all this is part and parcel of the structural imperatives of modern society, *it is impossible to say in advance who has to say what or who has to contribute what.* Under these circumstances, assumptions about what constitutes human 'nature', and about which rights logically accrue according to that nature, are at best picturesque details in judicial reasoning. Functionally, human rights are designed to keep the future open for the diverse autopoietic reproductions of respective systems. No distribution, no classification, and above all no political sorting of people can limit the future. For people belong to the environment of the system and the future at any given point develops

---

[145] For a different approach, which starts from the premiss of a causal concept of autonomy, see Richard Lempert, 'The Autonomy of Law: Two Visions', in Gunther Teubner (ed.), *Autopoietic Law: A New Approach to Law and Society* (Berlin, 1988), 152–90, at 166.

unpredictably and only through the autopoiesis and structural drift of society.

So far we have dealt only with one segment of the problem of equality, the semantics of the form of equality as it were, which forces the system to produce its own equality criteria. However, there is a second problem, independent of the first: the equality of the competence to act in the system. This is not a problem of autonomy but a problem of inclusion.[146] Obviously chances for inclusion vary in court proceedings, but chances to influence legislation also vary in relation to socio-economic status. This is because differences in financial resources, language skills, interactive competence, and also stereotypes of alleged civility co-vary with socio-economic status.[147] Neither in relation to the function of law nor in relation to the autonomy of the legal system do differences in the access to law and in the competence to act in the legal system have any function. Whether or not and how they influence the evolution of law is difficult to establish unless one is concerned with individual cases or specific problem areas.[148] Internal efforts in the legal system to balance equal opportunities (for example with the use of the instrument of legal aid with respect to costs) are limited by the fact that socio-economic differentiation has not ceased to exist in modern societies. Moreover, lower-class interests are primarily interests whose justification does not follow from lower-class status or interests as such. A legal case cannot be decided differently only because the participants belong to a disadvantaged class, unless the law provides otherwise.

X

We have taken some time over discussing the description of the operative closure of the legal system. This was unavoidable as one cannot start on empirical work, let alone causal explanations, if one does not know precisely what one is dealing with. First and foremost, systems theory increases demands on the exactness and detail of descriptions. But that does not mean that its potential is limited to this and that its inquiries end

---

[146] For a theoretical outline, see Marc Galanter, 'Why the "Haves" Come out Ahead: Speculations on the Limits of Legal Change', *Law and Society Review* 9 (1974), 95–160. Here one can find a number of references.

[147] See, for example, Marvin E. Wolfgang and Marc Riedel, 'Race, Judicial Discretion and the Death Penalty', *Annals of the American Academy of Political and Social Sciences* 407 (1973), 119–33.

[148] The frequently voiced demand for an empirical application of systems theory analyses is fully justified; however, it is obviously not appropriate in relation to the *concept* of autopoiesis and largely remains so unclear that one is led to believe that the call for empirical research is always raised like a reflex when people are lured onto unknown territory. This applies to an even greater degree to the complaint about the degree of abstractness of systems theory. Obviously the so-called empirical studies operate on a much higher level of abstractness for methodological reasons but are just not aware of this.

here.[149] Our next step is to explore the structural conditions for operative closure. The starting point is the assumption that there must be structural arrangements that raise the probability of fulfilling normative expectations because otherwise the significance of operative closure would be trivial and would represent only the most elementary structures of human interactive practice.[150]

We shall restrict this discussion to outlining two different conditions that interlock in the course of the evolution of law with highly varied, historically and culturally variable, forms of combinations. First, what law requires needs to be sufficiently specific, so that it is possible to return to it and repeat, condense, or expand on it. Secondly, law must have a sufficient chance of implementation because otherwise one would resign oneself to accepting the facts and learn from them. Law cannot rely only on reassuring those who have been disappointed in their expectations of law that their expectations were right.[151] Something has to be done to achieve either a real or at least some compensatory enforcement of the law.

The distilling of specific legal expectations is, above all, a matter for the memory of society, which then increasingly becomes a matter of restricting what needs to be achieved as the basis for future case law. This requires first the memory of the living, some recollection, and then written annotations. Memory is not simply a repertoire of past facts but above all the organization of access to information. This organization—and not what really happened in the past—is what leads to its use in concrete operations, which can only be executed in the present. The temporal reconstruction made by distinguishing between present and past is only an auxiliary tool and remains a construction of the memory. Memory then legitimizes its own product, if need be by reference to origin, duration, success; but, of course, it can simply function factually (just as one does not need to recall the first time one learned that a door could be opened by a door handle, and, when

---

[149] As far as little differentiated (and not yet colonized) tribal societies are concerned, there is scepticism today as to the degree of fulfilling expectations. See for example, Leopold Pospisil, *Kapauku Papuans and their Law* (New Haven, 1958; reprint 1964), esp. 250; Ronald M. Berndt, *Excess and Restraint: Social Control among a New Guinea Mountain People* (Chicago, 1962).

[150] This function of mere reassurance is, in many respects, fulfilled by religion, which, in turn, is stuck with the problem of having to explain suffering, injustice and bad luck. Religion appears to crystallize in this point the deficiency of law enforcement by stimulating, in combination with new kinds of moral concepts, expectations that have to remain without legal sanctions. This can be seen in the distinguishing of new motivational claims from legal reasons headed by the principle of *lex talionis*, especially in the Old Testament.

[151] In the sense found in Heinz von Foerster, 'Gegenstände: greifbare Symbole für (Eigen)-Verhalten', in id., *Sicht und Einsicht: Versuche zu einer operativen Erkenntnistheorie* (Braunschweig, 1985), 207–16. See also: 'Gedächtnis ohne Aufzeichnung', ibid. 133–71, and id., 'What is Memory that it May Have Hindsight and Foresight as Well?', in Samuel Bogoch (ed.), *The Future of the Brain Sciences* (New York, 1969), 19–64.

this did not work, was locked; it is as simple as that). Therefore, one can also say that memory keeps the eigen values of the mode of production of the system at its disposal.[152]

Societies, which can only communicate orally, have to resort to psychological systems, both to recall their capacities and their skills, and to communicate plausibly all that has been memorized for others who did not witness or have forgotten. In such societies old age often assumes authority. It is well known that this leads to fluctuations in norm concepts and to their adjustment to new situations. Nevertheless, the insecurity that can be expected to result from these arrangements is not very high because the range, which is covered by norms, is not very wide.

As soon as writing was available, the system's memory lost its ease of forgetting, of not returning to an issue, or of remoulding a suitable past. Now the memory became hardened through writing and at the same time psychologically de-conditioned. Probably the most impressive treatment of this original problem with writing can be found in Jewish law, which takes the form of distinctions that point to precisely this problem.[153] The law of the Torah was revealed at Mount Sinai as a text that is qualified by religion. It was revealed to Moses who could *hear* it and to the people who could *see* what was happening. The law is revealed for *written* and *oral* tradition, thereby securing both the authenticity of the text and, at the same time, the continuous adjustment and the softening of any initial strictness.[154] Moreover, tradition has to pass on both *consent* and *dissent*, and both the majority opinion, which leads to a binding decision, and the opinions rejected by it that are also recorded in the revealed text, which demonstrates its religious characteristics, in its very ambiguity.[155] Evidently, these are the distinctions of a later period, especially the period after the destruction of the Second Temple. They exhibit impressively the unfolding of the

---

[152] See generally Arthur J. Jacobson, 'The Idolatry of Rules: Writing Law according to Moses, with Reference to Other Jurisprudences', *Cardozo Law Review* 11 (1990), 1079–132.

[153] See Georg Horowitz, *The Spirit of Jewish Law* (1953; reprint New York, 1873); Louis Ginzberg, *On Jewish Law and Lore* (1955; reprint New York, 1977); Geza Vermes, *Scripture and Tradition in Judaism—Haggadic Studies*, 2nd edn. (Leiden, 1973) (largely exegetical); id., 'Scripture and Tradition in Judaism and Oral Torah', in Gerd Baumann (ed.), *The Written Word: Literacy in Transition* (Oxford, 1986), 79–95; Eliezer Berkowitz, *Not in Heaven: The Nature and Function of the Halakha* (New York, 1983), esp. 50; José Faur, *Golden Doves with Silver Dots: Semiotics and Textuality in Rabbinic Tradition* (Bloomington, 1986), esp. 84; see also: Ishak Englard, 'Majority Decision vs. Individual Truth: The Interpretation of the "Oven of Achnai" Aggadah', *Tradition: A Journal of Orthodox Jewish Thought* 15 (1975), 137–52.

[154] See Jeffrey I. Roth, 'Responding to Dissent in Jewish Law: Suppression Versus Self-Restraint', *Rutgers Law Review* 40 (1987), 31–99; id., 'The Justification for Controversy under Jewish Law', *California Law Review* 76 (1988), 338–87; Suzanne Last Stone, 'In Pursuit of the Countertext: The Reclaiming of Jewish Sources in Contemporary American Legal Scholarship', MS 1992.

[155] See principally Benjamin N. Cardozo, *The Paradoxes of Legal Science* (New York, 1928).

original paradox of law by using distinctions that focus precisely on this paradox; and if one takes as empirical evidence the tradition of thousands of years, which survived without a state, it demonstrates that a solution has been found that remained stable under those particular circumstances. However, each attempt to adjust it and orient to it entangles one further in the paradox and in the freedom given to problem solving—with consent and/or dissent. Under these circumstances it is not surprising that Jewish authors find it easier than others to accept the paradox that constitutes the law.[156]

Hence, literacy appears to be the reason why the unity of the system was recorded through distinctions whose unity could only be formulated paradoxically. Even when this is not explicit, one can clearly see how the legal system responds to being fixed in writing with its potential correctives— either by allowing freedom of interpretation, or by the institutionalization of proceedings to change the law, or by expansion to areas which were previously undocumented legally.[157] The material substratum of the memory of the system has obvious effects on the development of law, but evidently only if legal norms are already sufficiently specific.[158] Only that which is proven, and not that which assumed to be law, has to be remembered; and only the normative aspects of a case and not any successful arguments about contested facts. That is, the memory of the system remembers only those things which sustain the autopoiesis of law as factually operating and which can be used again for this purpose. This has constituted such a remarkable effort of selectivity, in view of the vagaries of all the acts of remembering and forgetting, that a role-specific safeguard has proved successful, one which could be institutionalized and has prevailed, where it has developed in the evolution of law. This selective stabilization became an

---

[156] In this sense it appears no coincidence that the concept of police in early modernity was introduced at a period at which printing began to spread, that is *c.* 1500. Police simply means the power to regulate in areas which (then) had not yet been fully subjected to jurisdiction and its fixed texts.

[157] Independent of this formal relationship there are also semantic relationships which concern legal concepts; see for example in relation to the development of alphabetical writing Eric A. Havelock, *The Greek Concept of Justice: From its Shadows in Honour to its Substance in Plato* (Cambridge, Mass., 1978).

[158] Here it is less important whether and since when and under which special circumstances judicial office can provide binding decisions for the resolution of legal disputes or only effective influence for their resolution. Rank societies usually manage to cope without a binding instrumentality which is backed up legally (that is, circularly). On rank societies, see for example, Morton H. Fried, *The Evolution of Political Societies: An Essay in Political Anthropology* (New York, 1967). This issue cannot easily be decided for a society such as the one described by Homer either. In this respect, it is not possible to decide without doubt whether judicial office has produced the function of selective stabilization or, conversely, the function has produced the office. In all these cases, the establishment of an achievement depends on evolution and evolution means: the circularly produced reinforcement of a deviation from a previous state, that is, deviation amplification.

indirect and long-term function of the judicial office alongside the function of direct dispute resolution.[159] Once this had been achieved, the step to legislation, that is, to a binding programming for the decisions of a judge, was not far away.

For the most part, the greater the specification of those norms which are worth recording the lesser the likelihood of their enforcement in case of a disappointment. For where would the interest and readiness come from to support someone who has been disappointed, when his expectations are defined so precisely that nobody can understand how it feels to be in a similar situation or nobody expects to be in a similar situation? Thus, support has to be based on generalized participation, has to be extended to a duty to support those who provide support by making the relations of smaller associations with larger ones hierarchical, and has to be brought, finally, to the form of a differentiated stabilization through the political system.[160] This requires a functional specialization of politics for decision-making, which is collectively binding (even on issues in extra-legal areas, like those of war and peace), and its stabilization through control over the use of physical force.

This does not mean, as one might suspect at first glance, that the legal system and the political system form one system together. But they do resort to special forms of structural coupling and are linked to each other through that coupling. One of the most significant and momentous inventions in this area was the Roman office of the praetor. The praetor had to formulate the conditions under which he would accept an action, that is, commission a court with the dispute-resolution role and provide it with a guarantee of execution. The system of the *leges actiones* of Roman law developed on the basis of recycling these formulae through doctrinal analysis and interpretation of case law into what is known as Roman law today. A functionally equivalent mechanism is provided by modern constitutions, as will be shown in more detail below.

In the end, this branch of evolution has honoured the promise that was bestowed on it, as it has led to a highly complex system of normative expectations equipped with a political guarantee that they will be implemented and backed up by law. Of course, this does not mean that the level of

---

[159] This has been thoroughly researched for segmental societies. See, for example, Max Gluckman, *Custom and Conflict in Africa* (Oxford, 1955); P. H. Gulliver, 'Structural Dichotomy and Jural Processes among the Arusha of Northern Tanganyika', *Africa* 31 (1961), 19–35.

[160] For to the perception of this as an oddity from the perspective of modern law, see Franz Wieacker, *Vom römischen Recht* (Leipzig, 1944), 86. On the development of the office, the practice of edicts and the *des agere per formulas* see also Mario Bretone, *Storia del diritto romano* (Bari, 1987), 139. On the comparison with rather similar conditions for the development of the (English) common law see Hans Peter, *Actio und Writ: Eine vergleichende Darstellung römischer und englischer Rechtsbehelfe* (Tübingen, 1957).

happiness of social life generally has been raised effectively, let alone that law reflects correctly the factual state of a given society. The counterfactual structure of norms indicates otherwise, and even the political guarantee of law cannot ensure that every expectation will be fulfilled. One has to resort to compensation for non-fulfilment, and above all to punishment and penalties. However, what has undoubtedly been achieved is the creation of an internal complexity built on the foundation of differentiating the legal system through operative closure.

3 The Function of Law

I

What is the function of law? This question is asked here in relation to the social system. In other words, we are concerned with the question of which of the problems of the social system are solved by differentiating specialized legal norms and arriving eventually at the differentiation of a specialized legal system. Asking the question in this way excludes asking, in particular, psychological and anthropological questions.[1] Rejecting them does not mean that they are wrong. Their problem, however, is that, empirically, people exist only as individuals and that general statements about humankind, consciousness, and person are difficult to test. In contrast, 'society' means here a concrete, even if highly complex, single system which exists through ongoing communications and which can be observed empirically. Therefore we do not have to make and verify statements that could be generalized by an immense number of different systems.

As far as the system of society is concerned, one can debate if and in what sense 'reference problems' and therefore functions can exist independently of a differentiation of respective operations and functional systems. There is an obvious risk of an answer that is merely tautological (but this applies equally to utilitarian and needs-oriented approaches). We escape this risk by abstraction. We describe the reference problem of the function of law in different, more abstract terms than law itself does. Logicians may call this the 'unfolding' of a tautology, that is, the dissolution of a self-referential cycle into distinctive identities. The hypothesis, which we will set out in detail here, holds that law solves a problem in relation to time. This problem always occurs when one communicates in society and when the ongoing communication is not sufficient in itself—whether as an expression or as 'praxis'—but is guided by expectations in a temporal extension of its meaning and expresses those expectations. The function of law deals with expectations that are directed at society and not at individuals.[2] It deals with the possibility of communicating expectations and having them accepted in

[1] For a contrary position with reference to Malinowski cf. Helmut Schelsky, 'Systemfunktionaler, anthropologischer und personfunktionaler Ansatz der Rechtssoziologie', in id., *Die Soziologen und das Recht: Abhandlungen und Vorträge zur Soziologie von Recht, Institution und Planung* (Opladen, 1980), 95–146. See also Norberto Bobbio, 'L'analisi funzionale del diritto: tendenze e problemi', in id., *Dalla struttura alla funzione: Nuovi studi di teoria del diritto* (Milan, 1977), 89–121, at 111, for a distinction between social and individual functional relations.

[2] For the individual (and then utilitarian) perspective, see Jeremy Bentham as a prominent author. Cf. in relation to the topic of security of expectations, Gerald J. Postema, *Bentham and the Common Law Tradition* (Oxford, 1986), 159.

communication. 'Expectation', then, does not refer to an actual state of consciousness of a given individual human being but to the temporal aspect of the meaning of communications.

In stressing the *temporal* dimension as the basis of the function of law we disagree with an older doctrine in sociology of law that stressed the *social* function of law using concepts like 'social control' or 'integration'.[3] With the choice of such concepts, which are central for the understanding of social systems at large, one runs the risk of misunderstanding the peculiar characteristics of law.[4] Any advantage of the older doctrine, focusing on only one (or at least, one primary) function comes at the price of having to account for too many functional equivalents. As a result the differentiation of law can be understood only at the level of professions or organizations.

The social relevance of law is indisputable. However, its integrative function is very much in doubt. This has been pointed out time and again by, above all, the critical legal studies movement and by other critics inspired by Marx. We can avoid this controversy by moving the problem to the temporal dimension. We see the social meaning of law in the fact that there are social consequences if expectations can be secured as stable expectations over time.

Obviously, social operations take time. Even if a single communication lasts only for a short moment, or not even that, when it moves from the moment at which it is invoked, it still needs to define itself in relation to time

[3] See principally Roscoe Pound, *Social Control through Law* (New Haven, 1942); Talcott Parsons, 'The Law and Social Control', in William M. Evan (ed.), *Law and Sociology* (New York, 1962), 56–72, and with a retrospective on the history of theory in relation to a sociology of law which did not acknowledge sufficiently the social function of law, id., 'Law as an Intellectual Stepchild', in Harry M. Johnson (ed.), *Social System and Legal Process* (San Francisco, 1978), 11–58. Further, see also Harry C. Bredemeier, 'Law as an Integrative Mechanism', in Evan, *Law and Sociology*, 73–90; F. James Davis et al., *Society and the Law: New Meanings of an Old Profession* (New York, 1962), 39; Manuel Atienza, *Introduccion al Derecho* (Barcelona, 1985), 61; Donald Black, *The Social Structure of Right and Wrong* (San Diego, 1993). At present, the most prominent protagonist of a social integrative function of law is Jürgen Habermas, see: *Faktizität und Geltung. Beiträge zur Diskurstheorie des Rechts und des demokratischen Rechtsstaats* (Frankfurt, 1992). His systematic treatment of this concept exhibits paradigmatically the difficulties that result from having to define the operations which effectively achieve integration. Is it merely an exchange of assumptions about how a communicative understanding *could* be reached? Or is it only 'the circulation of communications of fora and quasi-organizations without a subject' (p. 170)? Or is it the eloquent empathy of those who utter on every occasion their concern about their being concerned? Or, how is it possible, to take a concrete case, to find a regulation of the problems of immigration which are 'of equal interest for the actual and the aspiring members of the community' (p. 158) if one first of all has to find out which regulation is acceptable to all concerned?

[4] The concept of 'double institutionalization' coined by Paul Bohannan, 'Law and Legal Institutions', *International Encyclopedia of the Social Sciences*, vol. 9 (Chicago, 1968), 73–8, hints at these peculiarities of law but seems rather to state the problem than to solve it.

by recursive networking, that is, by relating both to past, already completed communications and to possible connections in the future. In this sense, each communication is binding time in so far as it determines the state of the system that the next communication has to assume.[5] One has to distinguish between this and the maintenance of a fixed meaning for repeated use, for instance the attribution of meaning to words, concepts, and true statements.[6] We call such a self-binding of a communication system semantics. Only the sedimentary deposit of semantics for further repository use leads to 'time binding' in the narrow sense, which will be discussed as follows.[7]

The repeated use of communicated meaning fulfils a double requirement: the results are, finally, a meaning that is fixed by language and a differentiated societal communication. On the one hand, such repeated uses of meaning must condense the used description in order to make sure that the meaning is recognized as the same, even in a new context. This leads to invariance, which can be identified again. On the other hand, such repeated uses of meaning must confirm the reused meaning and demonstrate that the meaning can also apply in a different context. This leads to the surplus of references, which can be shown in direct experience, and which render any concrete fixed definition of meaning impossible; all future use of those references, then, comes under the pressure to be selected for such use.[8] In a highly abstract form, this is a description of the genesis of meaning.[9] Only those who participate in this logic of condensation and confirmation of meaning can participate in communication by language and can thus couple their consciousnesses with social operations.

---

[5] One can boycott such a time binding explicitly by responding, by interrupting; however, this only draws attention to what would have been if the communication had it not been interrupted.

[6] The assumption here is that this attribution of meaning is an achievement of the system's communication and not an achievement of consciousness, even less a representation of external states in that consciousness. For criticism of such (quite widespread) ideas see Dean MacCannell and Juliet F. MacCannel, *The Time of the Sign: A Semiotic Interpretation of Modern Culture* (Bloomington, 1982), esp. 152; Benny Shanon, 'Metaphors for Language and Communication', *Revue internationale de systémique* 3 (1989), 43–59. The assumed position also compels one to abandon the idea that communication is a 'transfer' of preconceived meaning to another system.

[7] Cf. in this sense Alfred Korzybski, *Science and Sanity: An Introduction to non-Aristotelian Systems and General Semantics* (1933; 4th edn. Lakeville, 1958), where he talks about time binding as a function of language.

[8] This thesis of a double requirement follows George Spencer Brown, *Laws and Forms* (New York, 1979), 10, but not in the interpretation as presented here.

[9] For more detail see Niklas Luhmann, 'Identität—was oder wie?' in id., *Soziologische Aufklärung*, vol. 5 (Opladen, 1990), 14–30.

This phenomenon has been denounced in highly vague terminology as the power or the violence of language.[10] However, to put it this way is to leave the most important question unanswered: how can the ubiquity of power be explained in a highly complex system? We avoid such strong words and the prejudices inherent in them. But we maintain that even at this level time binding cannot be achieved without social consequences. This is all the more the case when we approach the domain of normative expectations and, with it, the function of law.

The condensation and confirmation of meaning, which enable and accompany repetitions, reduce the leeway that would normally exist given the arbitrariness of the relationship between the signifier and the signified. This leads to norms of correct speech and moreover to norms for the correct use of language which are accepted and adhered to, *even where one could do something else.* As shown by 'ethnomethodological' research, sanctions exist originally only as attempts at self-correction of communication.[11] Norms reduce variation in the reduction of contingency, namely the stabilization of an approved reduction of the arbitrary use of signs. The only alternative to such a fundamental normativeness is, as has been pointed out principally by Durkheim, anomie. The design of schemes such as right/wrong, acceptable/unacceptable, normal/deviant or eventually legal/illegal already lies *within* the social order containing *both sides* of the distinction. Also, the side of the distinction that is deemed to be negative remains in the realm of what is understandable; it is this side in particular about which one can and will communicate. The negative assessment of an option to disagree—which is only given by having a norm—defines the social costs of *time binding* and also who has to bear them in a given case. These costs are defined *within* the system; they are not left to the environment and then ignored.

Obviously the legal system is not only concerned with a communicative assessment of communication but—on this basis—with communication about all forms of behavioural patterns which are registered by law and referred by law to norms. This too is based, however, on the condition that definitions will not revert to arbitrariness, and, here too, time binding has to be paid for in the form of establishing what is 'illegal' and then allocating it.

---

[10] See, for example, Pierre Bourdieu, who talks about *pouvoir symbolique, rapports de force, domination* before discussing any alternative to freedom and coercion: id., *Ce que parler veut dire: l'économie des échange linguistiques* (Paris, 1982). For an application to the political use of language see Wolfgang Bergsdorf, *Herrschaft und Sprache: Studien zur politischen Terminologie der Bundesrepublik Deutschland* (Pfullingen, 1983), with clear reservations as to manipulation merely based on language. Also, the vociferous complaints about the 'speechlessness' of women and their disadvantaged treatment by the differentiation of gender by language belong in this context.

[11] See Harold Garfinkel, *Studies in Ethnomethodology* (Englewood Cliffs, 1967).

Social problems rise dramatically if and in so far as, in order to stabilize time binding, one also has to support expectations which do not correspond to reality but which are geared to coping with possible disappointments. Those who confess to having expectations of this kind must decide conflicts in advance without knowing who will be involved in them and how. Time binding prejudices social partiality. Freedom of conduct becomes restricted in advance, if not factually, then at least at the level of expectations. Those who, for whatever personal, situational, or factual reasons, want to violate expectations are at a disadvantage right from the start. Law discriminates. It decides for someone and against someone else—and all this with regard to a future that is unknown.

Usually, these problems of time binding are hidden by the fact that the law credits itself with a motivational function. This is also part of the symbolism of 'ought' expressed in the expectations of law. Those whose privileges are taken away by law, say murderers and thieves, are supposed to learn, are supposed to adjust, *even though it is not their own lives and not their own property which are at stake but other people's.*[12] However, this is so only because one wants to be certain about the future, which is inherently uncertain.

This reference of the function of law to the future explains the need for the symbolization of all legal order. Legal norms are a structure of *symbolically* generalized expectations. In this way, not only are generalized instructions issued which are independent of given situations but also symbols always represent something which is invisible and cannot become visible— here that something is the future. Using symbolization society produces specific stabilities and specific sensibilities, as is well known from the field of religion. One relies on the symbol precisely because one cannot see what the meaning of the symbol refers to. The sign becomes reflexive as a sign, is signified as a sign, and this defines the concept of a symbol. Nevertheless this cannot effectively exclude a reality that takes a different course and prevails, and in which one is left disappointed in the end. In most cases, however, the effect outlasts by far the initial occasion of disappointment.

Law's relation to time, therefore, is neither given by the duration of the validity of those norms that can be distinguished as changeable/unchangeable, nor by the immanent historicity of law.[13] Nor does this reference to

---

[12] Openness and the need to restrict it, which becomes visible in this way, have been recognized and discussed by Thomas Hobbes above all. As is well known, he had no impact on the jurisprudential practice of his time. As we want to show here, there is hardly any need for the concept of 'subjective rights' (which, after all, is still close to law) in order to formulate the problem. With this step forward in abstraction, the perspective widens from a political theory, which in its core is still formulated in the context of a 'civil society', to a theory of society in which the political system and the legal system have the functions of sub-systems.

[13] See especially Mario Bertone, 'Le norme e il tempo: Fra tradizione classica e coscienza moderna', *Materiali per una storia della cultura giuridica* 19 (1989), 7–26.

time lie in the 'material' of law, which is any given human conduct in space and time. Law's relation to time lies rather in the function of norms, that is, in the attempt to anticipate, at least on the level of expectations, a still unknown, genuinely uncertain future. This is also why the extent to which society produces an uncertain future varies with its norms.

Obviously, an increase of time binding, based on using counterfactually stabilized expectations, militates against what could be taken as free discretion in the framework of social conventions. A more extensive and intensive use of normative time binding produces new occasions for consensus/dissent in the social dimension. It produces its own circumstances for decision-making by defining situations in such a way that one has to take a position for or against the expectation. It produces deviance, as proponents of the labelling approach would call it. Of course, it also produces conformity. The result is indeed the two-sided form of consensus/dissent and all the social tensions stirred up by it. The result is a division, a bifurcation with the typical consequences of bifurcations: a story that evolves depends on which path was taken, and what at the outset may have been minor factors can have major effects through the amplification of deviation.

In general terms, this analysis shows that time binding is not to be achieved without social costs. Or, expressed even more generally, that the temporal and the social dimensions of meaning can be distinguished analytically; they are implied by each meaningful experience but they cannot be isolated empirically from each other. Here we conceive of law as a form which is related to the tensions between the temporal and the social dimensions and which makes it possible to cope with them even under the conditions of an evolutionary rise of social complexity. So far this does not say anything about the limits of this process or how much further it can go. However, the form of law is found in the combination of two distinctions, that is, the modes of cognitive/normative expecting, and the code legal/illegal. All social adjustments of law operate within this framework; they vary the factual meaning, the 'contents' of the legal norms and programmes which regulate a 'correct' coordination of the values legal and illegal, in order to maintain time binding and the character of consensus/dissent in a realm of reciprocal compatibility. *And it is precisely because it is the factual dimension that administers this balancing function that there is no factual definition of law.* The factual definition of law is replaced by the system reference 'legal system'.

II

In view of the analysis conducted above, the question of the function of law is shunted onto two different tracks depending on how the problem to which the question refers is defined. Abstractly, law deals with the social costs of the time binding of expectations. Concretely, law deals with the function of the stabilization of normative expectations by regulating how they are generalized in relation to their temporal, factual, and social dimensions.[14] Law makes it possible to know which expectations will meet with social approval and which not. Given this certainty of expectations, one can take on the disappointments of everyday life with a higher degree of composure; at least one knows that one will not be discredited for one's expectations. One can afford a higher degree of uncertain confidence or even of mistrust as long as one has confidence in law.[15] Last but not least, this means that one can live in a more complex society, in which personal or interaction mechanisms to secure trust no longer suffice.[16] However, it also means that law is susceptible to symbolically conveyed crises of trust. Where law is no longer respected, or is no longer enforced as far as it is possible so to do, the consequences extend much further than what amounts to breach of law, and the system has to retreat to much more basic forms of securing confidence.

At any rate, we assume that law fulfils *only one* function that, of course, can be specified in more detail by reference to further problems, and hence in further sub-functions.[17] Analytically, one can identify numerous problems and thus numerous functions to which they refer depending on what one wants to compare and what functional equivalents one wants to

---

[14] See Niklas Luhmann, *Rechtssoziologie*, 2nd edn. (Opladen, 1983), 40. See also id., 'Die Funktion des Rechts: Erwartungssicherung oder Verhaltenssteuerung?', in id., *Ausdifferenzierung des Rechts: Beiträge zur Rechtssoziologie und Rechtstheorie* (Frankfurt, 1981), 73–91.

[15] See Bernard Barber, *The Logic and Limits of Trust* (New Brunswick, 1983), 22 and *passim.*

[16] See also Niklas Luhmann, *Vertrauen: Ein Mechanismus der Reduktion sozialer Komplexität*, 3rd edn. (Stuttgart, 1989), 50; id., 'Familiarity, Confidence, Trust: Problems and Alternatives', in Diego Gambetta (ed.), *Trust: Making and Breaking Cooperative Relations* (Oxford, 1988), 94–107.

[17] See Joseph Raz, 'On the Functions of Law', in A. W. B. Simpson (ed.), *Oxford Essays in Jurisprudence* (2nd Series) (Oxford, 1973), 278–304, for a complex table of legal functions. However, his leading distinction between normative and social functions fudges the very problem that is considered important here: the social function of the normative form of expectations. Vincenzo Ferrari, *Funzioni del diritto: Saggio critico-ricostruttivo* (Rome, 1987), 87, discusses three different functions of law which partly go much further than law ('orientamento sociale'!), but rejects a concentration on a unitary formula with the argument that this would militate against the conceptual requirements of the term 'function'. Apart from Ferrari the assumption is frequently made that law has to fulfil a plurality of functions—typically in giving such a listing, see, for example, Davis et al., *Society and the Law*, 65; Michel van de Kerchove and François Ost, *Le système juridique entre ordre et désordre* (Paris, 1988), 161, following R. Summers and C. Howard, *Law, its Nature, Functions and Limits*, 2nd edn. (Englewood Cliffs, 1975). (There is, of course, no doubt that observers who are not concerned with the problem of the unity of law can analyse the law referring to a great number of functional points of view, as obviously each norm has its own function.) William Chambliss and Robert B. Seidman, *Law, Order, and Power* (Reading, 1971), 9, assume that law 'performs a myriad of functions, both manifest and latent', and then (understandably) declare themselves incapable of picking the most important one. In this way a clarification of the concept of a legal system is shelved.

talk about. In this sense, ultimately law also has the function of providing lawyers with income. However, if one is solely concerned with the differentiation of a functioning system the assumption that a system has one function only can lead to clear results. A multiplicity of functions would result in problems of incomplete overlap and in an unclear demarcation of law.

Our functional definition of law leads to certain consequences concerning the concept norm (or more pedantically: the concept of the normative mode of expectations). In contrast to a large body of literature in legal theory, the concept norm is not defined by special attributes of the character of a norm but by a distinction; this distinction refers to the possibilities of responding in the case of disappointment.[18]

Expectations are either given up when they have been disappointed or they are retained. If one anticipates such a bifurcation and opts in advance for one of its strands, one predetermines one's expectations as cognitive in the first case and as normative in the second.[19] In this way, the concept norm defines the one side of a form, which form also has another side. The concept does not exist without that other side; it must be pitched against it while keeping options open for transition from the one side to the other. The concept norm is the result of an option that an observer has, and it occurs empirically only when this form is used for making distinctions.

The functional concept of the norm as a counterfactually stabilized expectation does not require a pre-emptive decision to be made as to why norms are followed or not. On the contrary, it is precisely this decision that has to be ignored if the norm is to fulfil its function. For instance, a norm

---

[18] See for a different view Werner Krawietz, 'Zur Einführung: Neue Sequenzierung der Theoriebildung und Kritik der allgemeinen Theorie sozialer System', and id., 'Staatliches und gesellschaftliches Recht? Systemabhängigkeiten normativer Strukturbildung im Funktionssystem Recht', in Werner Krawietz and Michael Welker (eds.), *Kritik der Theorie sozialer Systeme: Auseinandersetzungen mit Luhmanns Hauptwerk* (Frankfurt, 1992), 14–42 and 247–301. Krawietz holds that this 'behaviourist' version of the concept norm does not do justice to the characteristics of norms. Regardless of what is meant by 'behaviourist', as a sociologist one would not like to be left without the idea that norms exist *factually* in social reality as structures for meaning. Alternatively one would be forced to say: there are no norms, a mistake has been made. Neither lawyers nor sociologists would go that far. And even the idea that norms have a fictional or illusionary reality could not work without having its basis in some form of factual experience and communication. Even the position that Krawietz seems to take and which holds that the normative quality of norms could only be obtained from norms (p. 30) needs to demonstrate where this mental operation fits into the real world.

It is an altogether different question which *concept opposite* to the concept norm can be used. If not cognition which is ready to learn, what else? The critique does not make any other suggestions for solving the problem. At any rate, it should be possible, and this is the difficulty, to agree that norm conflict, breech of norms, etc. require a norm concept (one can only negate what is held as identical) and therefore does not solve *this* problem.

[19] See Johan Galtung, 'Expectation and Interaction Processes', *Inquiry* 2 (1959), 213–34, who was the first to suggest such a distinction.

may not be obeyed because it is unknown (once known motives to resist or circumvent the norm may arise). Or, the norm may not be obeyed where it provides information—for instance, information about risks in traffic law or environmental law—but one relies more heavily on one's own information than on that provided by the norm. There may be an issue whether one takes the norm as adequately reasoned (legitimate, etc.), even if such cases are rare; or an issue whether the norm is seen as not being in line with moral values or as neutral, or even as being in conflict with other moral positions. Requested conduct can even occur without normative regulation, for example where it is brought about by the constraints of interaction. If one wants to influence the course of action, not only norms but also other devices such as positive incentives or specific uncertainties are the obvious choice.

And, of course, the expectation of sanctions has an effect. Today, there is general consensus that the concept norm cannot be defined solely by reference to the threat of sanctions, let alone by reference to imposing sanctions. Nevertheless, the prospect of sanctions is part of the symbolic apparatus that allows one to identify whether or not one's expectations are in line with the law. So, if sanctions do not occur as one was entitled to expect, drastic consequences may follow that go further than the individual case, and which often arise when symbols for something invisible—here the future—are violated.

Many legal theories suggest motives for obeying norms of one sort or another,[20] but they end up on a slippery slope. Without wanting to contest the empirical relevance of these questions and their significance for policies pertaining to individual norms, one has to realize that the function of the norm is not aimed at guiding motives (if this were the case, there would be too many accidents and too many functional equivalents involved) but at a counterfactual stabilization which specifically guards against an oversupply of motives. Norms do not promise conduct that conforms to norms but they protect all those who are expecting such conduct. In this way they provide advantages in interaction, especially when there are no conflicts or, especially, norm conflicts. Norms promote their own enforcement in a number of ways. Whether or not norms can be maintained when they are pitted against a reality that differs from their expectations on a massive scale is a question that only the theory of operatively closed systems can address meaningfully. The history of human rights, which was launched in a society engaged in the slave trade with its considerable suppression of political opposition and drastic restrictions on the freedom of religion, in short, in the American society of 1776, is proof that norms can still prevail.

---

[20] See, as a particularly clear example, Karl Olivecrona, *Law as Fact* (Copenhagen and London, 1939).

The issue of norm enforcement, which is raised here, can accordingly be treated as a precondition for the stable projection of norms. If norms are not followed at all, they are difficult to maintain. But, if one goes a step further and assumes that the steering of behaviour is a second function of law,[21] many more (and quite different) functional equivalents come into view than those associated merely with the contra-factual stabilization of expectations. And it is difficult to see how an autopoietic system could achieve operative closure in fulfilling such a second function.

Further, the assumption of the function of law as establishing and stabilizing normative expectations does not impose limitations in relation to another aspect of law, which also refers to behaviour. Law is often understood as a *restriction* on behavioural choices. Equally well, however, law can be understood as *support* for behaviour, support which would not be possible without law. Here one can refer to the opportunities which are given in private law by the concepts of property, contract, or juristic persons with limited liability. Administrative law also, regardless of how it is related to state law, cannot properly be understood if it is seen as residing in the capriciousness of a sovereign. Administrative law is today—more so than ever—a law which provides the power of attorney (under given conditions) which would not exist without the law. Both scenarios, the prohibitive and the supportive (and reality is made up of a mixture of them), assume a normative structure of expectations. The common factor is the certainty of being able to form appropriate expectations at a given distance from what will factually happen from case to case.

There is a further point in which our approach deviates from traditional approaches in legal theory. We do not define law by attributing a special status to legal norms, for example, as having a given essence, which can then perhaps be subdivided into genus and species. We understand norms as the form of a general stabilizing function, which derives its specific legal quality only from being differentiated as and in the legal system. This is a consequence of the theory of autopoietic systems, which postulates that systems of this type produce their own elements and through them their own structures.[22] Of course, there are countless normative expectations without legal quality—just as there are countless truths without scientific quality, or countless goods (for instance, clean air) without economic quality, and just as there is a whole lot of power without political quality. The formation of functioning systems extracts from everyday life only those expectations that are somehow problematic; it reacts only to the improbability of the success

[21] So Luhmann, *Rechtssoziologie.*

[22] This position, that the starting point for distinguishing legal from other norms is not found in the norm concept but in the system concept, is also shared by other systems theory approaches. See explicitly Torstein Eckhoff and Nils Kristian Sundby, *Rechtssysteme: Eine systemtheoretische Einführung in die Rechtstheorie* (Berlin, 1988), 43 and 121.

of communications, which increases as evolution moves on. In this way, autopoietic systems take shape by reference to the potential for increasing communication, which can be read off from the structures that already exist. Differentiating such systems in an evolutionary way requires the ground to be prepared, as we shall see below. To put this precisely, auto-poietic systems differentiate themselves from and against the truisms of everyday life.

If law has the function of stabilizing normative expectations in the face of an unorganized growth of normative expectations (in the form of con-ventions, as merely moral approval, or as customs which could not be vio-lated without being noticed), this can be achieved only by a selection of those expectations that are worth protecting. This also appears to be the position adopted in dominant legal theories. There is a further conse-quence, however, which has a deeper impact. It is the consequence that morality (or, in a reflected form, ethics) is unsuitable as a reason for the validity of legal norms.[23] There may be an argumentational advantage in certain situations, when problems of interpretation occur and one can refer to allegedly uncontested moral values, and morality always has signific-ant rhetorical benefits. One cannot, however, refer to it if one wants to equip normative expectations with greater prospects of success and stabil-ity. In this case the norm, which is to be brought into this safety zone, has to be juridified. And if this is not done in spite of an opportunity to do so, then one should anticipate the question: why not?

Whether a norm is a legal one or not can only be ascertained through observation of the recursive network that produces legal norms; that is, through an observation of the context of production which becomes a dif-ferentiated system through its operations. Normative expectations gain a certain degree of certainty—in contrast to mere projections, intentions, and attempts to communicate—only through such a use of the normative side of the normative/cognitive scheme (which is repeated in the system). This alone enables expectations to crystallize as expectations which are stable and give guidance in situations that neither furnish sufficient control over a reasonably certain future nor allow for the possibility of a gradual learning of alternatives. We know that expectations in the mode of normal-ity and expectations in the mode of normativity are closely related to each other and that even those expectations which are not established as partic-ularly certain are not easily discarded when occasionally disturbed. The odd shower does not bring about a change of the image of regions that are well known for their fine weather. In other words, there are also non-normative forms of refusing to learn. As soon, however, as the conduct of oth-ers appears to be their own choice—and this is a necessary consequence of

---

[23] See, for the same finding, Habermas, *Faktizität und Geltung.*

increasing complexity—one can no longer be satisfied with a mix of normality and normativity. Then norms have to be differentiated and set against the alternative conduct that one observes in others. Thresholds of development in the evolution of societies hinge on this possibility of an arbitrary norm creation—initially that happens, probably always in conjunction with making this factor of arbitrariness of norm creation invisible, or at least by legitimating it away, as it were. Because the mixed form normality/normativity (distinguished from the unfamiliar, the unexpected, the surprising) always precedes this development, law can read the past from these developmental thresholds as if it had always existed. Law never has to 'begin'. It can always join traditions as they are found. Law can, if society enables its differentiation, close its system's operations self-referentially, and work with a body of norms that has always been there.

The function of law as the stabilization of normative expectations goes much further than what is understood by the concept of conflict resolution. The fact that expectations conflict with each other, that is, that they contradict each other in communication, is in itself a special situation, and one which is dealt with to a large extent outside law.[24] It is equally disappointing when someone who does not dispute that another has the law on his or her side acts regardless. Examples can be found in instances of deviation from the criminal law or of non-fulfilment of contracts owing to incompetent performance. In these situations, too, expectations have to be confirmed for those who have the law on their side—perhaps by transformation to a different form, for example, to that of punishment. The concept of conflict would have to be unduly widened if it were also to be applied to these situations. The distinction between contentious and non-contentious disappointments has great significance for the evolution of law, because law develops its special instruments out of controversies about law. As a result law not only regulates conflicts but it also creates them. By referring to law one can reject unreasonable demands and resist social pressures.[25] Nevertheless, law assumes that deviant behaviour must be envisaged as a possible form of conduct, regardless of what the motives for it are, and that such conduct is rejected because of the possible consequences for the maintenance of expectations. If one dismisses this specifically normative element

[24] If one sees the problem in this way, the result is a highly problematic discussion on 'alternatives to law' which no longer examines what the function of law could be, in relation to which functional equivalents can be found. See, for example, *Jahrbuch für Rechtssoziologie u. Rechtstheorie*, 6 (1980), with regard to the topic 'alternative forms of law and alternatives for law'; also typical, see Donald Black, *Sociological Justice* (New York and Oxford, 1989), 74.

[25] On such a 'heteronomous' nature of law see Julien Freund, 'Le droit comme motif et solution des conflits', in Luis Legaz y Lacambra (ed.), *Die Funktionen des Rechts*, Special Issue 8 of *Archiv für Rechts- und Sozialphilosophie* 74 (1974), 47–62; id., *Sociologie du conflit* (Paris, 1983), 22 and 327.

and describes the function of law generally as a regulation of networks of relations—including regulation with non-normative means—one loses sight of the specificity of law.[26] One might as well take the design of the aisles in supermarkets or of a computerized air traffic system, or even language itself, to be a part of the legal order.

With the variety of issues under analysis, other possibilities and further functional equivalents come into view. We have talked above about the inevitable social costs of any form of time binding, or, even more abstractly, about problems of compatibility between arrangements in the temporal dimension and those in the social dimension. This formulation allows us to see that law is not alone in dealing with these difficult issues. One may reasonably assume that there also existed, in older societies, some mixed temporal and social forms which can be disentangled into clearly differentiated forms only in the course of evolution and with the increase of complexity. Here are just two examples of what is meant by this.

One functional equivalent is organized around the concept of scarcity. If one envisages that the provision of goods and services is limited to a certain constant sum, each access of a scarce item runs counter to the interests of others. Those who provide themselves with scarce items do so at the expense of others. This may have been relatively harmless in the archaic societies of abundance, and some expanding societies (such as societies in medieval Europe or in the colonized Americas) that would have had the option of modifying the problem of constant sums by expanding their territories. However, as the economy changed to the use of money and, through this, differentiated itself as an operatively closed system, conditions changed. On the one hand, the opportunities for the accumulation of economic values in the form of money were seen to be limitless, as has been noted even as far back as Aristotle. This meant that one could render highly differentiated and long-term economic interests secure by money without having to be concerned with the needs of others, in the present. The future could then be tied down in the present in an undetermined form, but this was a different resource from property in the form of real estate. The politico-economic morality, which was based on real estate, collapsed. On the other hand, money created new forms of constant sums and sanctioned them through inflations and deflations. The social concern for others became limited to one form only—which, however, had

---

[26] See Karl-Heinz Ladeur, 'Computerkultur und Evolution der Methodendiskussion in der Rechtswissenschaft: Zur Theorie rechtlichen Entscheidens in komplexen Handlungsfeldern', *Archiv für Rechts- und Sozialphilosophie* 74 (1988), 218–38, at 233, for observations on developments which appear to go in that direction. Perhaps Ladeur would deny that he has given up the norm concept; then, however, he would have to explain what he means by the norm concept if not the stabilization of contra-factual expectations.

its own stringency—namely that one had to pay for everything that one wanted.[27]

Problems associated with the social conditioning for dealing with scarcity were seen as legal problems well into modern times. Property, which is the parcelling of chances for access while acknowledging the corresponding chances of others, was seen as a legal institution and society was seen as a society of property owners who could coexist with each other on the basis of contractual agreements.[28] Labour for wages never fitted easily into this scheme because there was no right to work that was compatible with the money economy—no matter how much has been said about this. The economic function of property also lies outside legal regulation even though it can become the object of legal reasoning like any other form of conduct. Scarcity and the normative creation of expectations are different forms of the collision between time binding and social issues; they are different problems altogether. These problems are differentiated when societies grow in complexity. It follows that the legal system and the economic system are operatively closed functioning systems in their own right, becoming such if and when societies can manage their differentiation.

Our second example is almost premature. It has only been under discussion for a few years and the semantics of it are still at a pre-conceptual stage. We will discuss this example under the heading of 'risk'. Risk refers to decisions which accept the chance of possible negative consequences; these consequences are not anticipated in the form of costs which can be accounted for and which can be justified, but in the form of more or less improbable harm which, if it materialized, would let the decision be branded as the causal factor and expose it to the effect of retrospective regret.

The problem arises because the harm caused does not affect only those who have made a risky decision or only those who have profited from the positive effects of that decision. Again we are faced with a form of time binding resulting in social costs, but a form here of quite a different type. While the norm produces a bifurcation along the lines of the formula conforming/deviant and while the access to scarce goods discriminates along the lines of the formula advantaged/disadvantaged, the bifurcation with which we are concerned here is between decision-makers and involved parties. The perception of how much risk is acceptable and the acceptance of risk differ depending on whether one sees oneself as a decision-maker or as an involved party. The more the perception of the future forms a part of

---

[27] See, for detail, Niklas Luhmann, *Die Wirtschaft der Gesellschaft* (Frankfurt, 1988).

[28] For the disappearance of this tradition see Niklas Luhmann, 'Am Anfang war kein Unrecht', in id., *Gesellschaftsstruktur und Semantik*, vol. 3 (Frankfurt, 1989), 11–64.

decision-making in a modern society, the more acute the divide between decision-makers and involved parties will become; and the more one is forced to see that the legal and financial instruments of regulation which have been designed to deal with quite different problems will no longer serve here.[29]

In all cases, but especially here, the respective conflicts are pulled into the present. One does not wait for the future to happen; one assumes now that one has a legal title, or that one is perceived as acting legally or illegally, that one is rich or poor, right now. One already has a different perception of risk now depending on whether one is faced with situations in which one has to make decisions and cannot avoid risk-taking whichever way the decision goes, or one lives in fear of 'normal accidents'[30] which decision-makers create in the form of sudden or creeping catastrophes and which are more or less unavoidable, or so it appears. Therefore, what is defined here as a tension between the social and the temporal perspectives is really always a phenomenon in the present. The social costs arise together with time binding, even if the way in which these costs are evaluated may change later and with hindsight.

The more acute the distinctions associated with these problems, the more they lead to distinctions in the assessment of the future. As far as law is concerned, one can feel relatively sure that—short of revolution and political coup—all previously accrued rights will be respected when the law changes. In the economy, there is mobility from poor to rich and vice versa with the maintenance, diminution, or accentuation of the gap being conditioned by the economy. In terms of risks, however, the future is seen as a totally different entity—on the one hand for its uncertainty, and on the other hand for the potentially pervasive catastrophes which leave everything unrecognizable in their wake. These distinctions could mean that the differentiation of separately coded, operatively closed systems, which have been achieved successfully in law and in the economy, becomes difficult to envisage: how can one respond to the social consequences of risky conduct with similar, system-generating forms?

III

Who can project something so that it keeps its validity even though it is not realized? And what has to be presupposed if the matter is to produce, maintain, and validate increasingly complex counterfactual expectations? These questions lead us from the definition of the function to the realization of

---

[29] See for a more detailed account Niklas Luhmann, *Soziologie des Risikos* (Berlin, 1991).

[30] In the sense in which Perrow introduced the concept, cf. Charles Perrow, *Normal Accidents: Living with High Risk Technologies* (New York, 1984).

that function in systems and to two system references which are contained within each other: society and its legal system.

To answer these questions one has to assume that the system has established the distinction between system and environment. A system that turns expectations into norms confirms *itself* by entering a difference *into its environment*, which exists only in this deliberate form and would not be there without the system. Establishing norms in relation to which one can deviate, more or less, attains this. It makes *a difference to the system*, then, whether norms are followed on the terms on which they were designed *in the system* or not. But the system remains stable within the limits of its possibilities, no matter what happens in its environment.

Being an autopoietic, operatively closed system, law has to guarantee its function by itself. Evidently this cannot mean that all empirical conditions for a reproduction of the operation of the system are produced in the system itself; this would amount to including the world in the system. Nevertheless, law must remain operative as a functioning system which is determined by its structure, and it must project the continuity of serving its own function internally. 'Internally', however, means with its own type of operations.

To describe this process as an observer (either external or internal) is really only to formulate tautologies: law is what law deems to be law. However, this tautology can be 'unfolded', that is, distributed to different expectations. If one is concerned with the structural effect of the operations (i.e. stabilizing expectations), reflexive relations come into play: it is normatively expected that one must expect normatively. Law is, in other words, not indifferent towards itself. Neither does it merely demand that it be obeyed. It transforms the distinction between cognitive and normative expectations into an object of normative expectations in its own right. It operates reflexively. The mode of expecting is not random, nor is it left to simple social convenience. It is provided for in the legal system itself. In this way the system controls itself at the level of second-order observations, which is a typical condition for differentiation and operative closure, and which can also be found in other functioning systems.[31] Law is not something

---

[31] See, in relation to the economic system, Dirk Baecker, *Information und Risiko in der Marktwirtschaft* (Frankfurt, 1988), with the example of the second-order observation of markets on the basis of prices; in relation to the science system, see Niklas Luhmann, *Die Wissenschaft der Gesellschaft* (Frankfurt, 1990), with regard to the observation of scientific statements with the help of the code true/false in relation to their publication; in relation to the system of fine arts, see Niklas Luhmann, 'Weltkunst', in Niklas Luhmann, Frederick D. Bunsen, and Dirk Baecker, *Unbeobachtbare Welt: Über Kunst und Architektur* (Bielefeld, 1990), 7–45; in relation to the political system, see Niklas Luhmann, 'Gesellschaftliche Komplexität und öffentliche Meinung', in id., *Soziologische Aufklärung*, vol. 5 (Opladen, 1990), 170–82; id., 'Die Beobachtung der Beobachter im politischen System: Zur Theorie der öffentlichen Meinung', in Jürgen Willke (ed.), *Öffentliche Meinung* (Freiburg, 1992), 77–86.

that is simply maintained with the help of powerful political support and then, more or less, enforced. Law is only law if there is reason to expect that normative expectations can be expected normatively. Also, in this respect, law is not determined hierarchically from the top down but hetero-archically or collaterally, that is, in neighbourhood networks.

This, then, is the most general formulation of circular self-assertion. However, does this description hold true empirically? And what would follow if this description were valid only with considerable restrictions?

The answer to this question is given with another distinction. In order to make a consistent observation of observing possible, that is, a universal and reliably expected coding in relation to the formula legal/illegal, a more confined area of legally binding decision-making is developed in the legal system—either to identify the law, or to change it. This is an organized subsystem, that is, a system which is differentiated through the distinction between members/non-members and which commits the members to their membership roles in order to produce decisions which are guided by the programmes of the system (which can be changed within the organization), namely by legal norms.[32] There are terms for this decision-making system in the legal system, which refer to the even further differentiated systems such as courts and parliaments (respectively, in terms of the doctrine of the division of powers: jurisdiction and legislation), but there is no description for the system's unity. Therefore we will call it the organized decision-making system of the legal system.

This system organizes its own area of circularly linked operations. It changes law in the light of future decisions in courts and is guided by existing valid law that, in turn, may lead to events and opportunities for observations to change the law.[33] In order to differentiate the conditions for this framework for decision-making (and only for this purpose!), the system describes itself as a hierarchy—be it of organs, be it of norms. At any rate, the circular and recursive reproduction of legal decisions is the primary process.

Well-established forms of reflexivity have developed for this area of decision-making within the legal system. They utilize the form of a double modality. They apply norms to the application of norms, but they restrict the use of

---

[32] Similar structures of a universally operating functional system with an organized core area can also be found—for instance, in the political system and the organization of the state, or in the educational system in the form of schools.

[33] See here for the cybernetical concept of feedback, Torstein Eckhoff and Nils Kristian Sundby, *Rechtssysteme: Eine systemtheoretische Einführung in die Rechtstheorie* (Berlin, 1988). See also id., 'The Notion of Basic Norm(s) in Jurisprudence', *Scandinavian Studies in Law* 19 (1975), 123–51. For the circular relationship between rule and decision see also Josef Esser, *Grundsatz und Norm in der richterlichen Fortbildung des Privatrechts* (Tübingen, 1956); id., *Vorverständnis und Methodenwahl in der Rechtsfindung* (Frankfurt, 1970).

this possibility to the applications that are required in the system. Best known are the rules of procedure, which lead, when observed, to the result that the decision made has its own binding force. The borderline case is a mere norm of competence as the embodiment of the principle of legal sovereignty: regardless of what the person who is installed as the decision-maker decides, it becomes law. The other side of the coin is the indispensability of this norm: no matter how the decision-making is restricted by legal provisions, a residual uncertainty (either resulting from interpretation or in the course of substantiation in facts) can be eliminated only by a norm of competence. *In this sense the whole system of legal decision-making is based on the reflexivity of the application of norms.* This is not just one thing, which exists alongside many others. This is a specific presentation of the unity of the system in the system (embodied in specific norms) and it correlates in this respect with the universality of law, in its competence as a functioning system.

The functioning of this structure is evident; it is made visible in persons, buildings, documents, and addresses. Non-sociological theory of law has focused on this and elaborated on the positivity of the process of producing all of these concepts (norms of procedure and competence). However, a sociologist may find that only a sub-system of law is discussed in this way, with the only topic treated being the decision-making system of the legal system, and that other areas of the double modality of reflexive norms remain out of sight—with the same phenomena existing in arenas outside the decision-making system. Normative expectations regarding normative expectations are equally maintained in the everyday life of the non-members of legal organizations. So, for instance, someone whose rights have supposedly been violated will expect normatively that others will support his cause. At the very least, a claimant will not be deterred by the indifference of others who really 'should' support law and discourage injustice. It may also be the case that third parties expect that there is support for the claimant, and that a violation of rights is not just tacitly accepted.[34] The legal system as a whole operates on normative expectations of normative expectations as its secure base. It differentiates itself on the basis of the reflexivity of its own operations. Only in this way is the competence to make decisions in the legal system socially understandable and acceptable. Only in

---

[34] If the modern family is a social system, in which *everything* that family members do or experience can be talked about (see Niklas Luhmann, 'Sozialsystem Familie', in id., *Soziologische Aufklärung*, vol. 5 (Opladen, 1990), 196–217), this is an area in which the relevance and the demise of this kind of normatively expecting normative expectation could be tested empirically. Does one accept the shoplifting of one's own children, does one treat them merely cognitively (don't get caught!), does one also accept leniency towards the violation of law by others, for instance, one's neighbours? What effects does insurance have in this area? And so on.

this way are instances of legal decision-making more than what they were in most of the high cultures: alien elements of a corporative kind in a society ordered by families (houses), with the consequence that communication among neighbours or the community-based justice of the village or guild was always preferable to going to court. Only in this way can confidence in formal law and a differentiated use of law develop to give structure to the problems of everyday life, and achieve this in competition with local structures which are the more probable ones as far as evolution is concerned.

However, what can one say about an empirical assessment of this foundation to law? And what are the conditions on which an answer to this question can be given?

We assume the existence of a double effect. On the one hand, the organizational and professional streamlining of valid law curbs and domesticates the unorganized growth of normative presentations. One can ascertain what is officially legal/illegal, or one can have someone find this out. The more societies differentiate—and in the Old World this meant the process of the development of cities—the more they depend on such reductions. On the other hand, the differentiation of a special system for decision-making in the legal system can have a negative effect and can make the expectation of normative expectations normatively difficult to accept; the specialized decision-making system can even lead to the erosion of the very foundation of this reflexivity and can ultimately survive only as an organization supported by politics. This isolation of the centres of decision-making, which were indispensable and could clearly be observed in the older high cultures, coincides here with the form of differentiation of centre and periphery. In a modern society, however, the unity of the system can no longer be achieved by a comprehensive reflexivity of normatively expecting normative expectations, even though an orientation to and by law in everyday life is practised to a high degree. The decision-making system cannot turn the condition that everybody in a given society is to expect normative expectations normatively into norms for binding decisions. The decision-making system can provide individuals with individually devised rights and obligations but it cannot guarantee everybody else's collective expectations (hardly ever, securing expectations concerning everybody else's collective expectations). It cannot see this condition for mutual confirmation through normative expectations (and we are not concerned with 'consensus' here, but with claims!), and it cannot treat this condition as a legal matter. The decision-making system remains indifferent in relation to this institutionalization of normative expectations. Juridically this condition is irrelevant. Nobody can use the strength (or the lack of it) with which others insist that normative expectations are to be maintained as an argument, or even construct a claim on the basis of them. The boundaries of the system do not allow for this information and filter it out. In this way, this element is absent in the official presentation of 'valid law'. The decision-making organizations of the legal system have no control over the fact that they are embedded in a motivational legal culture; and therefore decision-making organizations have no sensors to alert them when they begin to expose their social foundations, upon which their own activities depend, to a process of erosion.

Indeed, the decision-making system builds up its complexity without concern for its double modality. If decisions do not depend on it, the relevant facts are not registered and cannot be recalled. Even legal theory, reflecting legal practice, did not and does not notice them. At best, they are accounted for by such diffuse terms as 'legal consciousness' or by vague definitions such as written law/living law. Empirical research in the area of legal knowledge and legal consciousness in society at large does not provide a theoretical conceptualization that is adequate for our discussion.[35] Also in a logical sense, that is, in relation to research techniques, problems of normative expectations receive insufficient coverage because, normally, binary logic has great difficulties with second-order observations which it can hardly solve and which it can, at best, only represent by constructions along the lines of modal logic (which have not been developed very far). On all these grounds the problem of the double modality of law eludes communication—except as a dispute between different opinions about conduct in everyday life.

After all, the reflexivity which has been developed in the organized decision-making system has been built up precisely in order to relieve itself from the task of coping with everyday life. One cannot and one does not have to rely on the normative expectations of others in order to know whether one acts legally or illegally. It all depends on how the judge is going to decide. One can respond to the pressure exerted by others by referring to the possible outcomes of a court case or to problems with evidence— just as lawyers do in relation to their clients. Here pragmatic attitudes win the day and they do indeed control whether a communication with reference to law is expressed at all. The boundaries of what is operated by the organized decision-making system function as forward-operating boundaries in relation to the external boundaries of the legal system overall and in relation to an internal communication about what is legal and what is illegal. Law puts itself at the disposal of the individual users in this way,

[35] See for instance Adam Podgórecki, *Knowledge and Opinion about Law* (London, 1973). For older Polish and Scandinavian research see Klaus A. Ziegert, *Zur Effektivität der Rechtssoziologie: Die Rekonstruktion der Gesellschaft durch Recht* (Stuttgart, 1975), 189. The discussion on how much theory is involved in KOL-research (knowledge and opinion about law) also belongs to this area, see *Zeitschrift für Rechtssoziologie*, 2–4 (1981–3); for contemporary research on a particular problem, see Jacek Kurczewski, 'Carnal Sins and the Privatization of the Body: Research Notes', *Zeitschrift für Rechtssoziologie* 11 (1990), 51–70.

abstracting from the social context of their motives, from the pressures to which they are exposed or, conversely, from their separate motivations.

In this manner society has to pay for cutting the legal system loose from its social moorings and for declaring individual human beings to be individuals. A compensatory effect for this exists in the development of strong normative expectations that, while being based on the normative expecting of normative expectations, cannot take the form of law. They take the form of political demands and, in some other cases, the form of social movements. Their semantics use the concept of value and sometimes, as if to make a point of distancing themselves from law, the title 'ethics'. Everything that can be mobilized as contra-factual defiance finds a channel here that leads directly to the centres of political decision-making. The legal system is left with the classification of such phenomena as legal/illegal; it can respond to its own irritations internally and can use a flexible armoury of interests and concepts adapted externally to each other's functioning operations, as will be set out in greater detail below. This may happen more or less professionally or be accomplished politically. However, the true resources for the formation of law, the normative expectations that are directed at normative expectations, are circumnavigated juridically and reflexively.

IV

One of the most important consequences of understanding norms as a form, which fulfils the function of law, is the differentiation between law and politics that is constituted by this form.[36] Obviously, both systems are dependent on each other, and this makes it difficult to discover their functional differentiation. In order for law to be enforced it needs politics, and without the prospect of enforcement there is no stability to norms that are credible to (or which are expected by) everybody. Conversely, politics use law to diversify access to politically concentrated power. But, to put it simply, because of this cooperation between the systems, it is necessary that they be differentiated.

A straightforward line of thought is sufficient to discover the point of departure for such a differentiation. Politics use the medium of power, and political power is articulated as superior authority coupled with the threat of force. As soon as political tendencies are integrated into a collectively binding decision via a kind of transformer, which translates the struggles about projects into enforceable decisions, compliance with them can be brought about coercively.[37] Normative 'ought', in contrast, does not require superior power or indeed any superiority at all on the part of someone who

---

[36] See Ch. 9 for more detail.

[37] A separate issue is that this can be prevented, or at least made more difficult, with the help of a politically motivated legal technique. *And even then the political motive does not appear as*

formulates respective expectations.[38] At the time of the ancient high cultures, and even more so in Athens at the time of Pericles and Euripides, protecting the poor against the rich and the powerful was seen as a major function of law, or at least that claim could be made. Occasionally, in medieval times, a distinction was constructed between governmental authority (*gubernaculum*) and the administration of justice (*iurisdictio*) of the sovereign. However futile it may seem to pit law against power and however advisable it may be to say nothing and lift one's eyes to heaven, law and power are different forms of the communication of expectations in relation to the conduct of others.

Since Hobbes this difference between law and politics has been formulated as the opposition between (sovereign) state and individual rights (which emanate from 'nature' and pre-date the state). This does not, however, suffice. From the perspective of a history of doctrinal thought, the idiom of 'natural' rights was used only as transitional semantics, expressing the spirit of the age; it was only a symbol of *a politically uncontrolled genesis of law*; this symbol became dispensable as soon as sufficient forms of positive law were developed. This happened with the recognition of the freedom of contract, of freely disposable property, and, from the beginning of the eighteenth century, with the recognition of the legal capacity of corporations that were not based on a decree made by the political sovereign. Once all of this had been secured, 'subjective rights' could be denaturalized and reconstructed as merely reflexes of the objective law (including the constitution). However, this became possible only because normative expectations do not depend on positions of superiority for their validation. Indeed, lawyers may have a professional interest in retaining the possibility of pleading for the underdog.

The autonomy of law's function, its order, lies in the importance of knowing what one is entitled to expect from others (and from oneself!); or, to put it more colloquially, to know which expectations won't end up making one look a fool. Uncertainty of expectation is far harder to bear than surprises or disappointments. Anomie, in the sense in which Durkheim uses it, refers to uncertainty of expectation, not to facts demonstrating the behaviour of others. Of course, expectations and behaviour stabilize each other but norms produce a higher degree of certainty of expectation than is warranted by behaviour, and that is their specific contribution to the autopoiesis of societal communication.

a legal argument. See for an illuminating case study Leon H. Mayhew, *Law and Equal Opportunity: A Study of the Massachusetts Commission Against Discrimination* (Cambridge, Mass, 1968).

[38] This is D. Neil MacCormick's argument against the legal theory of John Austin who insisted on the 'command' as a source of norms. See MacCormick, 'Legal Obligations and the Imperative Fallacy', in A. W. B. Simpson (ed.), *Oxford Essays in Jurisprudence* (2nd Series) (Oxford, 1973), 100–30.

This observation casts significant light on the problem that is often discussed of the *enforcement of law*. Seen from a political perspective, the issue is whether or not a prescribed action or a failure to act can be enforced by the use of power. Similarly in the sociology of law, reference to the sanctioning power of law and distinguishing between law as an external force and morals as an internal force, following a formula that derives from the eighteenth century, has a primarily political perspective.[39] The same applies if, like Jeremy Bentham, one sees certainty of expectation evidenced by the fact that people act according to expectations. On further thought, however, oddities become apparent. If the function of law were defined by the enforcement of a prescribed action or a failure to act through coercive power and sanctions, the actual administration of justice would be constantly, even predominantly, concerned with its own inefficiency. In essence law would be the management of its own defects, or to put it differently, law would be concerned with the deficiencies of the realization of political projects. Why would one need a coding legal/illegal? Why would one leave the enforcement of law, apart from criminal law, to the initiative of a private plaintiff? And why the considerable realm of free action, which leaves the legal form up to the will of private parties and facilitates only the prospect of the eventual outcome being relevant to law?

Facts like these make it pertinent to shift the centre of gravity of the problem of law enforcement from behaviour to expectations and, in line with that, to elaborate on the difference between law and politics in the direction of an efficient implementation of collectively binding decisions. The function of law is solely to bring about certainty of expectation, especially in anticipation of unavoidable disappointment. But this change of direction goes only part of the way to solving the problem. Certainty of expectation is also at risk when conduct, which conforms to expectations supported by law, cannot be assured and when there is not even the slightest chance that expectations can be fulfilled. Law cannot always say: you are right, but unfortunately we cannot help you. Law must at least be able to offer substitutes (punishment, damages, etc.) and to enforce them. And even then law cannot guarantee that the guilty party is solvent;[40] and the

---

[39] This applies particularly, even if with important distinctions, to the sociology of law of Theodor Geiger; see especially: *Vorstudien zu einer Soziologie des Rechts* (Aarhus, 1947; reprint Neuwied, 1964), and on Geiger recently: Heinz Mohnhaupt, 'Anfänge einer "Soziologie der Rechts-Durchsetzung" und die Justiz in der Rechtssoziologie Theodor Geigers', *Ius Commune* 16 (1989), 149–77.

[40] See on this point Klaus A. Ziegert, 'Gerichte auf der Flucht in die Zukunft: Die Bedeutungslosigkeit der gerichtlichen Entscheidung bei der Durchsetzung von Geldforderungen', in Erhard Blankenburg and Rüdiger Voigt (eds.), *Implementation von Gerichtsentscheidungen* (Opladen, 1987), 110–20. See also Volkmar Gessner, Barbara Rhode, Gerhard Strate, and Klaus A. Ziegert, *Die Praxis der Konkursabwicklung in der Bundesrepublik Deutschland. Eine rechtssoziologische Untersuchung* (Cologne, 1978), and, in a more strategic

political system will not assume that it is its task to step in and pay in lieu of the guilty party just in order to lead law to victory.

A certain synthesis of political and legal functions is indispensable—but on the particular basis of their different functions.[41] If politics actually achieved its goal of enforcing binding decisions collectively, the legal system would find itself in a paradoxical situation. Law would not have a problem left to deal with because there would no longer be any disappointment of expectation. Presumably the legal system would, however, be disappointed in its own expectations of the political system. In other words, there are good reasons for limiting law enforcement to what is necessary to make expectations resistant to disappointment and for otherwise letting it remain the functional difference between the political system and the legal system.

V

In this section we will use law as an example for discussing a general problem with understanding function in the context of functional differentiation and, indirectly, in the context of a description of modern society. In this connection people often refer to a 'loss of function'—for instance, the loss of function of the family or the loss of function of religion. This could, however, be merely an optical illusion. One projects a broad concept of function, which includes everything that one can attribute to the societal areas in question, onto the past, and finds a loss. This approach to historical comparison ignores the growth of function-specific performances deriving from the differentiation of the respective systems.

Leon Mayhew proposes such an approach in relation to law, which is derived in turn from Parsons's theoretical concepts.[42] The function of law is ranked high in the hierarchy—following the general position of normative regulation in Parsons's theory. Law is supposed to guarantee social control and the inclusion of individuals in society (especially via the norm of equality). The same approach resurfaces today when people try to salvage the assumption that there is a social steering through law no matter how limited it is (instead of the self-steering only of the legal system);[43] or when people believe that one can observe legal change in relation to the

sense, Knut Holzschek et al., *Die Praxis des Konsumentkredits: Eine empirische Untersuchung zur Rechtssoziologie und Ökonomie des Konsumentenkredits* (Cologne, 1982).

[41] See also Niklas Luhmann, 'Rechtszwang und politische Gewalt', in id., *Ausdifferenzierung des Rechts*, 154–72.

[42] See above all Leon H. Mayhew, 'Stability and Change in Legal Systems', in Bernard Barber and Alex Inkeles (eds.), *Stability and Social Change* (Boston, 1971), 187–210; Talcott Parsons, 'The Law and Social Control', in William M. Evans (ed.), *Law and Sociology* (New York, 1962), 56–72.

[43] See above all Gunther Teubner and Helmut Willke, 'Kontext und Autonomie: Gesellschaftliche Selbststeuerung durch Recht', *Zeitschrift für Rechtssoziologie* 5 (1984), 4–35;

function of the legal system and not merely in relation to its programmes and doctrines.[44]

Depending on which concept of function is used explicitly or implicitly, the modern differentiation of the legal system appears to be a problem. In contrast to traditional expectations, which see an integration of society through law, this differentiation is observed as a loss of function, as a 'lack of sufficient articulation between and with the other differentiated systems of society'.[45] From this perspective, for example, law is no longer able to enforce the positions of the civil rights movement in spite of unequivocal support from jurists, especially in the context of racial equality, against the opposition from economic, but also family, neighbourhood and other interests.[46] This may be so, but the question nonetheless remains as to whether one can see this finding as a loss of function or whether it would not be more correct (especially from the point of view of empirical research) to test the definition of function regardless of whether it is traditional or modern. Embracing a definition of function that is broad and accentuates positive aspects obviously leads to given facts that have to be disapproved of. One might wish for that, or even might like to see that outcome as the mission of sociology (in contrast to jurisprudence, which is then criticized for its conformism within society, conformism which really

---

Helmut Willke, 'Kontextsteuerung durch Recht? Zur Steuerungsfunktion des Rechts in polyzentrischer Gesellschaft', in Manfred Glagow and Helmut Willke (eds.), *Dezentrale Gesellschaftssteuerung: Probleme der Integration polyzentrischer Gesellschaft* (Pfaffenweiler, 1987), 3–26; Gunther Teubner, *Recht als autopoietisches System* (Frankfurt, 1989), 81 ff. These assumptions have been received with great interest and critical comment. It is apparent that, from a more historical perspective, the discussion does not refer to the function of law any more—as if it was self-evident that this function is given by the 'steering of society'.

[44] This is suggested by Karl-Heinz Ladeur in several of his publications, combining prognosis and recommendation. See especially: *'Abwägung'—Ein neues Paradigma des Verwaltungsrechts: Von der Einheit der Rechtsordnung zum Rechtspluralismus* (Frankfurt, 1984); id., 'Die Akzeptanz von Ungwißheit—Ein Schritt auf dem Weg zu einem "ökologischen" Rechtskonzept', in Rüdiger Voigt (ed.), *Recht als Instrument der Politik* (Opladen, 1986), 60–85; id., 'Computerkultur und Evolution der Methodendiskussion in der Rechtswissenschaft: Zur Theorie rechtlichen Entscheidens in komplexen Handlungsfeldern', *Archiv für Rechts- und Sozialphilosophie* 74 (1988), 218–38; id., 'Lernfähigkeit durch Recht (Erwiderung auf J. Nocke)', in *Jahresschrift für Rechtspolitologie* 4 (1990), 141–7. According to Ladeur the function of law is now the 'maintenance of the ability to learn and the flexibility of the social sub-systems and organized networks of relations' ('Lernfähigkeit', 142). If one assumes a change in the function of law everything that others diagnose as decay can be shown in a friendlier light, and Ladeur has earned, at least, the merit to have drawn attention to this development. On the other hand, his formula for the change of the function of law includes so much—for instance, liquidity in business firms, language skills, basic research—that one can no longer speak of any differentiated legal system. See also the objections of Joachim Nocke, 'Alles fließt—Zur Kritik des "strategischen Rechts"', *Jahresschrift für Rechtspolitologie* 4 (1990), 125–40.

[45] Mayhew, *Law and Equal Opportunity*, 188.

[46] See, for more detail, Mayhew, *Law and Equal Opportunity*.

has to be rejected). However, such strategic manoeuvring with terminology is too superficial and the results cannot show more than bias in the research design. If the discussion is to remain on this level, counter-positions cannot be much more than articulations of counter-prejudice.[47]

It is not easy to go beyond superficial polemics of this type. One possibility is to be painstakingly accurate in the definition of function and the use of concepts within an overall context that supports this approach. This would mean that concepts such as social control or inclusion, ought, values, equality, consensus, coercion, time, contra-factual stabilization, which could contribute to a definition of the function of law, could not simply be accepted without more analysis but would have to be further clarified and fitted into a more complex web of concepts. Of course, this would not stop anybody from assuming that this was another (only more complex) ideological masking exercise and from reducing the theory (of their counterpart in debate) to just such an exercise. At least such preconceptions might become more tolerable in so far as they could, as a side effect, assist the development of scientific theory.

VI

The discussion about 'steering through law' could benefit from the introduction of a further distinction. One must distinguish between the *function* and the *performance* that law achieves in relation to its environment within society and above all in relation to the other functioning systems of society. The function of law is given by reference to society as a whole. The legal system is differentiated in order to fulfil a certain function and, as discussed above, what matters here is that one can rely on certain expectations as expectations (and not as predictions of behaviour). Expectations of certain performances, which can be more important or less important for the environment of the legal system, within society, or which can be replaced more easily or less easily, are linked to this function. These two aspects, function and performance, can only be distinguished under the regime of the functional differentiation of law; this applies regardless of the fact that performances of the functioning system are then also expected on the basis of the function and not, for example, on the basis of the status or ethos of a functionary in the system or with reference to general social morals.[48]

---

[47] Numerous references could be provided for support here. See as an extreme example Günter Frankenberg, 'Unordnung kann sein: Versuch über Systeme, Recht und Ungehorsam', in Axel Honneth et al. (ed.), *Zwischenbetrachtungen: Im Prozeß der Aufklärung: Jürgen Habermas zum 60. Geburtstag* (Frankfurt, 1989), 690–712.

[48] See for parallels in other cases of differentiation Niklas Luhmann, *Funktion der Religion* (Frankfurt, 1977), 54; Niklas Luhmann and Karl Eberhard Schorr, *Reflexionsprobleme im Erziehungssystem* (Frankfurt, 1979, reprint 1988), 34; Niklas Luhmann, *Politische Theorie im*

When we analysed the function of law, two aspects had to be held back which can now be discussed as possible performances of law, namely *behavioural control* and *conflict resolution*. It is not only the maintenance of normative expectations but also numerous other social functions and, last but not least, the coordination of behaviour in everyday life which depend on the fact that individuals actually behave in a way which is prescribed by law; for example, the fact that guests actually pay their hotel bill on checking out, that people actually observe the rules of the road, and above all, that people actually refrain from threatening others with physical violence. Even if one can be confident that one's expectations will be fulfilled, this alone will not bring about a somewhat more complex social normality of complementary behaviour. In this regard, the other interaction systems—or organizations—or functioning systems in society depend on support from the legal system.

That this support is only a performance of law, and not a function, is evident from the fact that other systems provide many functional equivalents for securing desired behaviour as a premiss for other behaviour.[49] For instance, the credit card system also serves to guarantee other payments not subject to legal control. Without a credit card many services (such as, for instance, renting a car) are no longer even provided. Or: the pumps at petrol stations in the United States are activated only after a certain payment has been entered. But these are forms that have developed only because the law can no longer guarantee certain behaviour or at least not guarantee it adequately. Since the discovery and recognition of the existence of primary group influences and informal organization,[50] the contribution of law to the control of individual behaviour has often been seen as very small. This applies, however, to only a few particular situations. It is inconceivable that law, under modern conditions, could be replaced to any considerable degree by other, equivalent sources of motivation.

Further, in order to understand the guidance of behaviour as a performance of law in support of other functioning systems, it is important to see that this does not only involve the setting of limits to 'natural freedoms', as assumed by Hobbes. More than that, in its own right law also produces freedoms, artificial freedoms, which can then be conditioned in other social systems, that is, fitted in, in a way that suits those systems. Such freedoms include, for example, the ability to resist offering social assistance and tax

---

Wohlfahrtsstaat (Munich, 1981), 81; id., *Die Wirtschaft der Gesellschaft* (Frankfurt, 1988), 63; id., Die *Wissenschaft der Gesellschaft* (Frankfurt, 1990), 635.

[49] This is an old topic in a new guise. It has been discussed previously in the form of the question whether the validity of law is premised purely on sanctions or on additional extralegal means of motivation; see, for example, Georg Jellinek, *Allgemeine Staatslehre*, 3rd edn. 6th reprint (Darmstadt, 1959), 332.

[50] See, for example, Richard T. LaPiere, *A Theory of Social Control* (New York, 1954), passim and esp. at 19 and 316.

demands and instead to accumulate capital; or to become a member of an organization or to opt out of an organization if the conditions are unfavourable. Such freedoms also include the freedom to reject an arranged marriage with a spouse found suitable by the family and instead to marry for 'love', or to express inconvenient opinions and to expose them to (then only retrospectively possible) criticisms. The 'media', which are used in other social systems for generating their own system-specific forms, depend in many respects on legally guaranteed options for rejection, that is, on the possibility of avoiding the pressures for conformity which are exercised under such headings as morals or reason. It was no accident, then, that one could hold the opinion in the eighteenth and nineteenth centuries—when the relationship between law and freedom became apparent—that the essential function of law was to guarantee freedom.

The performance of conflict-regulation is a similar case. Here too, society in many of its social systems depends on the legal system in the event of a conflict. This is especially true when unjustified expectations can be rejected and claimants can be directed to the legal processes. On the other hand, it is important to note that law does not necessarily solve the original conflicts but only those that it can construct on its own terms.[51] The deep structures of and motives for conflicts in everyday life, as well as the question of who commenced them, are largely ignored. This is one of the reasons why it is so difficult for the law to assess the effects which legal decisions, or legally enforced mediation, have on the situations that underlie conflicts. On top of that, the use of a legally organized conflict resolution has its own narrow limitations, especially when the parties have an interest in continuing their relations and are wary of the juridification of their conflicts. That is why one finds so much physical and mental violence in intimate relations, especially in families. That is why social dependence, for instance in a work situation, often does not permit communication about actionable rights. It is also why there will be a preference for finding another way of sorting out the conflict, that is to say, by establishing it as a permanent conflict in which all who are involved can take their chances.

Japan, especially, is famous for its extensive use of extra-legal mechanisms for conflict resolution. The limited use of courts in English common law countries has also been explained by extra-legal conflict resolution.[52] In England even such important matters as hunting and poaching do not appear to lead to litigation. With the increase in statute law and particularly with the increase in administrative regulations, however, there is also increased criticism of the narrow approach of and the difficult access to

---

[51] See here Johan Galtung, 'Institutionalised Conflict Resolution: A Theoretical Paradigm', *Journal of Peace Research 2* (1965), 348–97.

[52] See Richard Lempert and Joseph Sanders, *An Invitation to Law and Social Science* (New York, 1986), 133.

courts under the common law.[53] One can assume that this relief for the legal system through non-use is related to the fact that social classes and group loyalties continue to be experienced and accepted as the basis of social order. When this is no longer the case, the deficiencies of the courts will exacerbate the difference between the inclusion of small groups of people and the exclusion of large groups of people and will become a problem not only for the performance of law but also for its function.[54] We shall revisit this issue in the final chapter on society and its law.

Hence, it is largely the range of functional equivalents that instructs the difference between function and performance. There is hardly any alternative to law with respect to the stabilization of normative (and therefore not self-evident) expectations. But desirable behaviour can be achieved largely through positive incentives; here the legal form becomes relevant only in a few problem cases. Conflicts are made tolerable in a vast number of different ways, or are resolved. Here law is only one option, even if it is the one that assumes the function of a reserve currency and provides a kind of ultimate guarantee of freedom of choice. A differentiation between function and performance comes into being only as the consequence of the differentiation of a legal system. As far as the steering of conduct and conflict resolution are concerned, one must distinguish between society with and society without a differentiated legal system. The two situations are vastly different, even though one can of course compare diverse situations from the functional perspective of 'dispute settlement'.[55]

Legal matters in tribal societies and in the rural areas of 'peasant societies', which have to manage largely without formal law and courts, are usually handled by proceedings of conflict resolution that subject communicable issues to this goal. At stake here are practical arrangements, which are of vital importance, and not (or only as a secondary matter) the attribution of the values legal/illegal to entitlements.[56] The issue of local consensus has already been introduced into the procedure and the conflicting parties have to confront the question as to how they are going to organize their lives locally in future. In a modern context, however, mediation procedures are

---

[53] Cf. Brian Abel-Smith and Robert Stevens, *Lawyers and Courts: A Sociological Study of the English Legal System 1750–1965* (Cambridge, Mass., 1967).

[54] See Volkmar Gessner, *Recht und Konflikt: Eine soziologische Untersuchung privatrechtlicher Konflikte in Mexiko* (Tübingen, 1976).

[55] Nevertheless, it is questionable whether one can analyse ethnological material with empirical references to modern mediation procedures without accounting sufficiently for the highly different structural contexts.

[56] Cf. as a frequently quoted monograph Max Gluckman, *The Judicial Process among the Barotse of Northern Rhodesia* (Manchester, 1955), or Paul J. Bohannan, *Justice and Judgment among the Tiv* (London, 1957); see also Laura Nader, 'Styles of Court Procedure: To make the Balance', in id. (ed.), *Law in Culture and Society* (Chicago, 1969), 69–92; for the European situation before the differentiation of a separate legal system, see also Harold J. Berman, *Recht und Revolution: Die Bildung der westlichen Rechtstradition* (Frankfurt, 1991), 85.

conducted in the shadow of an imminent legal process. It is almost as if the parties are playing with fire—with the uncertainty of the outcome of proceedings, with costs and delays. But the option of legal protection is present at each instance, and the form of the possible agreement is a form of valid law, which in turn opens the way to litigation should the parties so choose. The mediation process thrives on the real function of law, which is to stabilize normative expectations; it can, however, extract from this form an added social value, which is a performance of law that in turn benefits the respective psychic and social systems.

If one wants to assess both the function and the performance of the legal system in context, one may usefully see law as a kind of immunization system of society.[57] With the increasing complexity of the social system, the discrepancies between the varied outcrop of norms increase and at the same time society has to find 'peaceful' solutions for conflicts more urgently. Otherwise the further development of means of communication and of functioning systems and, for example, the development of 'cities' would stagnate everywhere. The latter can, of course, still happen and has actually happened in most cases. There is, however, also the possibility of immunizing the system better against pathologies of this kind. It remains open, uncertain and unpredictable when and for what reason someone will opt for a conflicting course and will oppose a potential norm with another potential norm. And there is, as is generally the case in immunology, no concrete, ready answer for such incidents. The legal system makes no prognosis about when conflicts will happen, what the particular situation will be, who will be involved and how strong their involvement will be. The mechanisms of the legal system are geared to operate 'without fear or favour'. And they need time to prepare the immune response. The facts would be much too complex for a point-to-point correspondence between psychic dispositions and psychical-situational dispositions on the one hand, and proposed solutions to the problem that are acceptable to the social system, on the other. One can also talk of an immunization system with respect to the way in which solutions, once found, reduce the probability of new 'infections', particularly in view of the time it takes to find a solution.

It is evident, therefore, that even in the context of questions about the function of law, there are a number of arguments that demonstrate that the differentiation of a legal system, once set in motion, succeeds. We have established that the increase in uncoordinated flourishing of norms reaches a point at which a quasi-disorganized reflexivity of normative expectation of normative expectations can no longer provide solutions and must be replaced by the differentiation of an organized system for decision-making within the legal system. It is this system which attracts attention and which develops a network of officially valid norms for its own

[57] See Ch. 12 for a more detailed discussion.

orientation, provided there is sufficient support from the political system. We have also established that one can distinguish between the function of law and the performance of law as soon as there is a special, functioning system, and that there are a number of functional equivalents respecting the performance of law but that there is no functional equivalent (or practically none which could be realized) in relation to normative expectations. Finally, there are good reasons for arguing the case for the differentiation of law if one considers the advantages of an auxiliary immunization system, which operates at a lower level of complexity, referring back to its own history in the case of unforeseeable incidents.

With regard to the often discussed question why the development towards modern society took place in Europe and not, for instance, in China or India, all the issues mentioned above would have to be given more emphasis. If one focuses on a comparison of Europe and China in the twelfth and thirteenth centuries, the demographic facts, the technological developments, the spread of literacy, the standard of living would all speak against Europe. Europe, however, had a developed legal culture through the achievements of Roman civil law. A large number of clerics were in fact lawyers (of canon law). In England the independent development of the common law began on these same foundations. Municipal laws were collected, codified and used as models. The struggle for sovereignty in Italian cities was fought particularly with regard to legal self-regulation. Here justiciable law was incorporated into everyday relations much more fundamentally than anywhere else. When comparing these civilizations, one would find counterfactually stabilized expectations to a greater extent, even if it were still uncertain whether or not actual behaviour corresponded to these expectations. Thus it was possible to develop the social order in the face of a broader range of improbabilities if one could at least find out with what expectations one could approach the law and at what point conflicts would arise as legal conflicts which had to be decided, as a last resort, by the 'highest tribunal', namely war. In this context, monetary economy and regional diversification may seem just as important as religion, but it should not be overlooked that law gave development in Europe an important head-start, so Europe was legally prepared for higher complexity and for more improbability.

Even bearing all this in mind, it would not be correct to say that the advantages of functional specialization operate like an evolutionary mechanism. To explain historical events, a more complex evolutionary theory is required.[58] Furthermore, it does not follow from the function of law alone that law can execute its operative closure as an autopoietic system and reproduce itself. For this to happen, further structural conditions are required which will be discussed in the following chapter from the standpoint of (the difference between) coding and programming.

[58] See in this respect Ch. 6.

4 Coding and Programming

I

To maintain what the function of the legal system is, is not sufficient in itself to describe it adequately. As discussed in the previous chapter, the function alone cannot clarify what the legal system uses for its orientation when it reproduces itself and draws boundaries between itself and its environment. This is why sociological systems theory uses the concepts 'function' and 'structure' throughout. Structural fixtures are seen as indispensable because the description of function leaves too much open-ended.[1] This problem is also apparent in legal theory. Thus Jeremy Bentham, for example, ultimately saw the function of law as achieving security of expectations, but with law's orientation being provided by 'commands' from a politically authorized, powerful legislator. A command produces the differences between obedience and disobedience. In this respect, one can also refer to earlier sources, such as Cicero. When he asked himself what law is, the first thing that occurred to him (after consulting the experts) was: 'ratio summa insita in natura, quae iubet ea quae facienda sunt, prohibetque contraria'.[2] Obviously, the issue here is a distinction that is specific to law. In the following presentation the term 'coding' will take on this role, characterizing a distinction specific to law. This term 'coding', in contrast to the term 'command', leaves open the question of the source of validity of law. As has been shown, autopoietic systems theory sees the source of the validity of law as resting in the legal system itself. And the term 'coding' is more precise than the term 'structure' (even though codes most certainly are structures); it directs more attention to the development of structures by distinguishing between coding and programming.

As has been pointed out, the function of law produces a binary scheme in which normative expectations, whatever their origin, are fulfilled or disappointed as the case may be. Both of these things happen and the reaction of law is correspondingly different. It still remains open for consideration, however, how to treat those cases in which disappointing conduct, in its turn, envisages norms and insists that they are legal; not to mention those cases in which a violation of the law is only hypothesized, or in which the attribution of norm-violation to certain actors is contested. In these cases distinct normative propositions may find support in society, where one can resort to random mechanisms (for example, some sort of test by ordeal) in order to deal with disputes where there is social support for those distinct

---

[1] So for instance Talcott Parsons, *The Social System* (Glencoe, 1951), 19 and 202, where he introduces the trademark 'structural–functional analysis'.

[2] *De legibus* 1. VI. 18. In contemporary diction one should replace 'nature' with 'discourse'.

normative propositions, that is, for both sides.[3] To fulfil the function of law always depends on social structures which are not at the actual disposition of law, or—inevitably—on tricks through which one can eliminate such a dependence on social structures at a price, that of the consistency of law and possibly the density of its regulations.

The evolution of society has gone further than relying on the abstraction that superimposed the bifurcation between fulfilment and disappointment—which is so close at hand because it is linked to every expectation—but is a distinction of a different kind. As we have argued before, what matters remains whether normative expectations have been fulfilled or disappointed. This immediate observing of facts from this particular point of view invokes the function of law and cannot be eliminated. But it is complemented, and therefore we use the term 'superimposed', by a complementary second-order observing, which is oriented by legal coding differentiated for this purpose. It reserves the right to assess whether the expectation and the disappointing conduct are (or have been or will be) legal or illegal.

Even if the binary scheme of legal and illegal *logically* has a primary rank because identifying the legal system is based on it, it is *historically* a recent achievement and assumes that a repertoire of norms already exists.[4] It is by no means self-evident that this particular solution of a binary coding was chosen and eventually won out in the process of evolution. It could also have happened that such a binary scheme might have been avoided because it appeared to be too dangerous. There are indeed high cultures that suggest caution where the development of norms are concerned and, accordingly, see the insistence on law negatively.[5] Politically the preference here was for compromise, the unity of society being described as harmony

[3] See, for a contemporary example, see Salim Alafenish, 'Der Stellenwert der Feuerprobe im Gewohnheitsrecht der Beduinen der Negev', in Fred Scholz and Jörg Janzen (eds.), *Nomadismus—ein Entwicklungsproblem?* (Berlin, 1982), 143–58.

[4] See also David Hume, *A Treatise of Human Nature*, book III, part II, section II (quot. Everyman's Library (London, 1956), vol. 2, p. 203) for the distinction between justice and injustice. We will revisit this question in more detail with the discussion of the conditions under which an evolution of operative closure is possible. See below Ch. 6.I.

[5] See, for the Confucian tradition, Pyong-Cham Hahm, *The Korean Political Tradition and Law* (Seoul, 1967), esp. 29, 41, and 53; David J. Steinberg, 'Law, Development, and Korean Society', *Journal of Comparative Administration* 3 (1971), 215–56. For the discussion since then, see Kun Yang, 'Law and Society in Korea. Beyond the Hahm Thesis', *Law and Society Review* 23 (1989), 891–901. For the contemporary situation in Japan see the equally contested theses of Takeyoshi Kawashima, 'The Status of the Individual in the Notion of Law, Right, and Social Order in Japan', in Charles A. Moore (ed.), *The Status of the Individual in East and West* (Honolulu, 1968), 429–48. As for further research which supports restraint in relation to the harshness of the binary scheme, see also Zensuke Ishimura, 'Legal Systems and Social Systems in Japan', in Adam Podgórecki et al. (eds.), *Legal Systems and Social Systems* (London, 1985), 116–25.

and not as difference. From this perspective, law remains a technical last resort for hard cases but it is not further differentiated to become a functioning system in its own right. Its priorities are in the areas of criminal law and of the organizational and administrative law of the ruling bureaucracy. An ordinary member of society is well advised to avoid all contact with the legal system and to consider such contacts as bad luck.

Hence, the strict scheme of binary coding cannot be explained by the mere fact that normative conflicts arise or the fact that the harm created by their consequences prompts us to find a solution. On the contrary: every mediator will attempt to play down any differences and to avoid all definitions of the situation which suggest that only one *or* the other party is right. The authority of a mediator and his impartiality are expressed in the fact that, ultimately, a mediator is not obliged to support one party and decide against the other.[6] Thus, the occurrence of conflicts and the importance of independent third parties (usually of a higher status) that follows from them render, initially, a strict binary coding of law improbable. Evolution runs here, as it so often does, counter to probability, if it nevertheless perseveres with binary coding, which then prevails.

It is just this, however, which was significant for the European tradition: a level of secondary-order observations was established to deal with conflicting norms in law and, at that level, did not directly submit distinct norms to mediation but to a further distinction. This distinction formed the law into a coded system. This alone made the law ready to be applied under exclusively those conditions that it defined for itself.

The development that in fact became possible, namely the development of this distinction, can be described, logically and with hindsight, as an unfolding of the tautology or dissolution of the paradox of law. In a shortened form we shall call this the de-tautologization or de-paradoxication of law. One could almost say that the following steps occur.

That which has been created as law has always been there; that which has been defined as such and has been distinguished from something else (1), is amplified and emphatically transformed into the tautology 'legal is legal' (2). This tautology is turned into a paradox by introducing a negation 'legal is illegal' (3); in the social system this means above all that both legal and illegal exist in an unavoidable conjunction: the legal status for one party is the illegal status for the other party, while both are members of the same community. This form is turned into the form of a contradiction by a further negation: legal is not illegal (4); in order for the party who is right or wrong to rely on/must rely on this status, there must also be a temporal and social perspective. The finding that someone who is in a legal position is at the same time in an illegal position is a logically prohibited

---

[6] See also Vilhelm Aubert, *In Search of Law: Sociological Approaches to Law* (Oxford, 1983), 72.

contradiction. This contradiction is ultimately excluded by setting conditions (5) and only now can the tautology be unfolded, and the paradox dissolved. Legal is legal and legal is not illegal, if the conditions are met which are spelled out in the programmes of the legal system. On this level of programming (self-structuring), the system can confront temporal variation and through this become independent of the accidental events of conflicts. It can now determine in its own right what is to be treated as a conflict in which a decision can be reached, that is, what can operate as an evolutionary 'attractor' of cases. In a later chapter we shall assert that this results in an increase in the variety of the system and in a permanent problematization of the relationship between variety and redundancy.

The discussed sequence of unfolding steps can be summarized in a diagram:

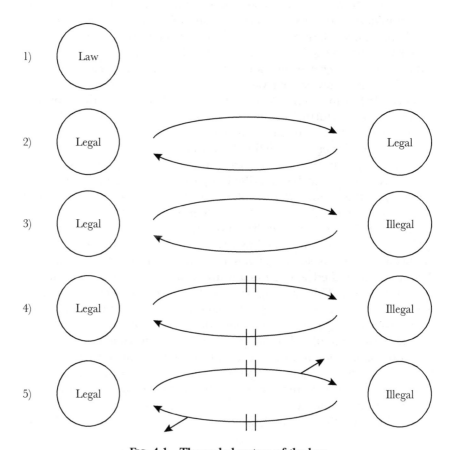

FIG. 4.1   **The coded system of the law**

It goes without saying that these are not empirical steps in the development of a system, not to mention historical stages of the legal system. At issue is a logical reconstruction of the autopoiesis of the system, which reconstruction should clarify why the development of the system cannot be logically deduced and why it is empirically improbable. A legal system does not come into being because it can be deduced from logical axioms,[7] but because the autopoiesis of the system is launched under highly exceptional historical conditions. And this leads to the constitution of a system that can describe itself with the help of the distinctions set out here.

It must be noted that the strict and unyielding distinction between legal and illegal is exceptional and not self-evident. This allows us to work out the extent to which the evolution of law is the result of a response to the provocations contained in this process. It appears, for instance, that one of the most important categories of Roman civil law, the *obligatio*, developed because someone was in an *illegal* position, either *ex delicto* or *ex contractu*, and this had to be turned into a legal form in order to be dealt with *lawfully*—as a link, as *vinculum*, as *adstrictio*, which specified the fault as a performance that was due.[8] Tort law and contract law with their typical forms develop as the forms of an unfolding of such an *obligatio* as expressed in the norms of contract law.

This does not mean that legal and illegal converge. On the contrary, with each obligation it has to be established anew which conduct is legal and which is illegal. One has to distinguish the values of the legal code, the positive and the negative, even though both are involved all the time and the distinction has to function as a mode for linking operations. One has to apply this distinction even though one can neither ask nor answer the question (because it would lead to a paradox) as to whether the distinction between legal and illegal itself is legal or illegal. The paradox itself turns unwittingly into a creative principle because one has to try so hard to avoid and to conceal it.[9] One is forced to implement the distinction between legal and illegal through further distinctions. There may for example be situations in which one is held liable for damage to goods belonging to

---

[7] This too is, incidentally, a foundational circle, as it is known in contemporary logic, because axioms are only formulated to facilitate deductions.

[8] It is a contentious issue whether or not one can explain the *obligatio* exclusively with the development of tort law and before the origin of an understanding of a contract, which is binding on conduct after the conclusion of the contract. See, for further information on this issue, Giovanni Puglieseor, *Actio e diritto subiettivo* (Milan, 1939), 73. What is above all remarkable is the abstraction of a category which embraces both original incidents, tort and contract, and through this the development of contract law from the perspective of the 'syllagmatical' obligations which arise *after the contract has been concluded* or as altogether new obligations.

[9] See George P. Fletcher, 'Paradoxes in Legal Thought', *Columbia Law Review* 85 (1985), 1263–92; Roberta Kevelson, *Peirce, Paradox, Praxis: The Image, the Conflict, and the Law* (Berlin, 1990).

someone else. This has to be explained by the fact that the person who has caused the damage acted unlawfully—as an exception, as it were, to the normal rules 'casum sentit dominus' or 'qui suo iure utitur neminem laedit'. Law, in other words, cannot prohibit or sanction its own use or impose liability in relation to the consequences of such use. One can only be made liable for a 'damnum iniuria datum'.[10] At first this may have appeared as self-evident as it is plausible. As legal policies made law more flexible, however, concerns arose that the maintenance of such clear distinctions would lead to the prohibition of too many forms of conduct, particularly if these had a bearing on the scope of possible liability for compensation. In other words: doctrinal law, which implements the scheme legal/illegal directly, is not compatible with the phenomenon of risk.[11] This problem was addressed by the development of the legal instrument of strict liability.[12] It allows the development of conditions, rules, and reasons for the distribution of harm from lawful conduct, that is, making someone liable for conduct that was otherwise permitted by law. The reasoning is that the permission for conduct with possibly harmful consequences must be paid for by the acceptance of liability for any damage.

Another example is the acquiescence of state agencies in unlawful conduct.[13] It is one of the persistently repeated doctrines behind the activities of state agencies that a sovereign has to turn a blind eye to illegality if to prosecute it would lead to uncontrollable unrest threatening both peace and authority.[14] In the nineteenth century one could still read that peace

---

[10] See the finding of the Faculty of Law, Jena in June 1879 (*Seufferts Archiv* 37 (1882), no. 224), 312–19) in relation to an exception: the public compensation for private disadvantages. A further exception for which compensation for the consequences of *lawful* conduct was conceded arose from emergency laws. See Rudolf Merkel, *Die Kollision rechtmäßiger Interessen und die Schadenersatzpflicht bei rechtmäßigen Handlungen* (Strasburg, 1895); this work is also remarkable in relation to its comprehensive and, compared with earlier discussions, unusual considerations about a 'weighing of interests', as if such interests were necessary as a substitute in cases in which a legal problem could not be solved with the code's law/non-law scheme.

[11] This finding came about parallel to the discussion on the *futura contingentia* which followed Aristotle's *De interpretatione* 9; the point here is that the truth or falsehood of statements on the contingent future cannot be decided in the present even if one has to take the future into account for conduct in the present.

[12] The classic monograph on this subject is Josef Esser, *Grundlagen und Entwicklung der Gefährdungshaftung, Beiträge zur Reform des Haftpflichtrechts und zu seiner Wiedereinordnung in die Gedanken des allgemeinen Privatrechts* (Munich, 1941).

[13] On an important aspect of this, see Georg Hermes and Joachim Wieland, *Die staatliche Duldung rechtswidrigen Verhaltens: Dogmatische Folgen behördlicher Untätigkeit im Umwelt- und Steuerrecht* (Heidelberg, 1988). See also Josef Isensee, 'Verwaltungsraison gegen Verwaltungsrecht', *Steuer und Wirtschaft* 50 (1973), 199–206.

[14] For further references, see Niklas Luhmann, 'Staat und Staatsräson im Übergang von traditionaler Herrschaft zu moderner Politik', in id., *Gesellschaftsstruktur und Semantik*, vol. 3 (Frankfurt, 1989), 65–148, at 89.

depended on a 'relaxation of the absolute demands of law'[15] and the Romantic Movement can be seen generally as the last well-directed opposition against the dominance of the binary code legal/illegal.[16] 'Altruistic crimes',[17] that is activities that attack the legal code in the name of certain ideas representing a particular binary value scheme, could be seen as a curiosity of that time, while today the lesser offence of 'civil disobedience' is promoted as a solution in similar situations. The problem of the rejection of the code is compounded when not only certain external ideas or instances reject the legal code but the law itself is also under pressure to do so. How can that be? Can someone who has acted illegally for a long time and with the collusion of the relevant authorities finally claim freedom from prosecution due to lapse of time or at least protection for their bona fide actions? Here too the problem has come to a head in a historical development that has increasingly led to situations in which the authorities do not know the law (or the facts) sufficiently, or cannot implement the law fully, or in which the turning of a blind eye provides a strategic advantage, which allowed the authorities to achieve something they could not achieve any other way.[18] In such a case of the blending (confusion) of legal and illegal one has to decide anew which mixture of legal/illegal is legal and which illegal. Then, however, law becomes dependent on points in time: only at the point of a decision by a court can it be known what the legal assessment of such conduct actually is.

Obviously, the legal system must take time if it wants to cross the boundary of its code legal and illegal, and sabotage the mutual exclusion of the values of the code. Through its own programmes law must be able to distinguish between earlier and later positions in law. From this perspective, the temporalization of the symbol of validity correlates with the implementation of a stringent validity of the binary code. The harshness of the code 'either—or' has to be compensated for by the use of time, that is, a difference

---

[15] Friedrich Schlegel, 'Signatur des Zeitalters', in *Dichtungen und Aufsätze*, ed. Wolfdietrich Rasch (Munich, 1984), 593–728, at 700, in the context of a general polemic against the reckless absolutism of opinions.

[16] See Regina Ogorek, 'Adam Müllers Gegensatzphilosophie und die Rechtsausschweifungen des Michael Kohlhaas', *Kleist-Jahrbuch* (1988/89), 96–125.

[17] Schlegel, 'Signatur', 598.

[18] See Keith Hawkins, *Environment and Enforcement: Regulation and the Social Definition of Pollution* (Oxford, 1984); Gerd Winter, 'Bartering Rationality in Regulation', *Law and Society Review* 19 (1985), 219–50. As evidence for the breadth of this phenomenon of the implementation of political goals in the form of a compact with legal arguments that are simply built in, see also Dieter Grimm, 'Die Zukunft der Verfassung', *Staatswissenschaften und Staatspraxis* 1 (1990), 5–33, at 17; Charles-Albert Morand, 'La contractualisation du droit dans l'état providence', in François Chazel and Jacques Commaille (eds.), *Normes juridiques et régulation sociale* (Paris, 1991), 139–58; Arthur Benz and Wolfgang Seibel (eds.), *Zwischen Kooperation und Korruption* (Baden-Baden, 1992).

in how the one follows the other, if the legal system is to be differentiated. The differentiation demands that the system be more dynamic.

There is no reason to conclude from circumstances like these, which have always accompanied the development of law, that the strict opposition of legal and illegal is of little importance.[19] To do so would be to conclude from the way in which law makes its own paradox invisible that it is non-existent. The evolutionary dynamics which are revealed under such circumstances can only be understood if one assumes that the risky distinction in the form of a binary code functions as a permanent irritation of the system brought on it by itself.

II

In practice binary codes are easily dealt with. Without this advantage they could not be institutionalized. With a limited attention to form it is possible to keep an eye on two values at the same time when the one excludes the other. All that is needed for the system to be closed is simply the further rule that all that is not legal is illegal, or vice versa. This advantage of the scheme, however, conceals complicated logical structures. We define them, using the logical-mathematical term of re-entry, as a double re-entry of the form into the form.

Normally, forms are constructed in such a way as to make re-entry possible on one side only (that is, on the inside of the form) because the other side is used only as an unmarked condition that serves the purpose of delineation. Prototypically, this applies to the distinction between system and environment, which can be made only in the system and not in the environment.[20] This asymmetry, however, is not logically compelling: the term re-entry assumes only that a space is divided into two halves by a gap (the delineation of the form) which, as a result, generates a specific space which represents the 'world' and which is, from then on, available for a re-entry of the distinction into that which has been distinguished.[21] In order to function as coding, re-entry on one side only is not sufficient. It would mean that the boundary of the form could not be crossed, or that in law one could only dream, so to speak, about illegality. Each crossing of the boundary would be irretrievably lost in the infinite space of otherness.

---

[19] See Niklas Luhmann, 'The Third Question: The Creative Use of Paradoxes in Law and Legal History', *Journal of Law and Society* 15 (1988), 153–65.

[20] The same applies to other important cases, for instance to the form of the sign which can only be copied into the signifier and not into the signified.

[21] See George Spencer Brown, *Laws of Form* (reprint New York, 1979), 56 and 69; Francisco Varela, 'A Calculus for Self-reference', *International Journal of General Systems* 2 (1975), 5–24; Louis H. Kauffman, 'Self-reference and Recursive Forms', *Journal of Social and Biological Structures* 10 (1987), 53–72, at 56.

Symmetry can only arise from self-reference if the option of re-entry is provided on both sides of the form. Then this symmetry can be returned to asymmetry in the system through conditioning.[22]

The asymmetry of the form of the system and the symmetry of the form of the code have to cooperate in the system. The asymmetry of the form of the system procures the closure of the system even when its operations are guided by references to the environment. The symmetry of the code procures the incessant crossing of the boundary that marks the code. If the system finds an incident illegal it cannot simply leave it to its own devices but must find ways of dealing with illegality legally. In other words, illegality is an indispensable trigger for legal operations. Not only the value 'legal' but also the value 'illegal' must be understood as a realization of the code as a whole in the coded area and as a counter-value to the counter-value. Such a structure has been called a structure of 'nested oppositions'.[23] This is, as will be shown in greater detail below, the basis for the ease and technical smoothness with which one can move from one value to the other and with which one can, at the same time, avoid any conflict between the values within the domain of the code. (In other words, conflicts between the code-values turn into conflicts between systems rather than within systems.)

All these findings assume that there exists a connection between self-reference and distinction. The one is only given by the other and vice versa. Only self-referential systems can distinguish (observe) because in order to do so they must distinguish between the distinction, or what has been defined with its help, by themselves; and, conversely, self-reference requires the distinction between self-reference and external reference. Kauffman writes: 'Therefore, self-reference and the idea of the distinction are inseparable (hence conceptually identical).'[24] No further complication can undo this elementary condition, or merge it 'dialectically'—all it can do is signify it. As a consequence, we end up facing a paradox with every attempt we make to observe the unity of the world in the world, that is, the unity of a distinction on which an observation is based. Therefore law can be explained only through the unfolding of a paradox, that is, through the introduction of identifying distinctions.[25]

---

[22] See especially Kauffman, 'Self-reference and Recursive Forms', on the issue of the conditions for self-reference, distinction, time-consuming operations, and re-entry needed for the generation of symmetry.

[23] See M. Balkin, 'Nested Oppositions', *Yale Law Journal* 99 (1990), 1669–1705 (in the context of a critique of the broad use of 'deconstruction' as a method for a rejection of distinctions, in the United States). Balkin notes: 'nested oppositions—that is oppositions which also involve a relation of dependence, similarity, or containment between the opposing concepts'.

[24] Kauffman, 'Self-reference and Recursive Forms', 53.

[25] For instance through a half-way measure such as the introduction of the norm of justice which is defined in the process as like treatment of like cases *and* as the different treatment of different cases.

The unity of a system operating a binary code can be described only as existing in the form of a paradox. Operatively, the unity of the system is continually being reproduced but one cannot observe it within the system—or, at best, only in the form of simplifying constructions, as will be discussed in Chapter 11. The paradox cannot be observed because to do so the code would have to be applied to itself. This would amount to the decision of whether the distinction between legal and illegal is made legally or not. The paradox of the system—in law as, in a different way, in logic—is its blind spot, one that renders the operation of observing possible in the first place.[26] One could say that the paradox of the system represents the world in the system—the latter is as unobservable as the former. It is the foundation that must be kept concealed, with the result that all further reasoning can only be doctrinal—including the thesis that the distinction between legal and illegal is obviously legal, because otherwise there could be no orderly administration of justice.

It follows that the introduction of the code itself is already the first step towards the resolution of the paradox, although the paradox exists only as a code-related problem of observation. It has to be practised as a distinction and not as the unity of what has been distinguished. By code we mean that law uses a binary scheme in order to structure its own operations and to distinguish them from other facts.[27] Codes are preconditioned structures which, when simplified radically, can be traced back to *bi-stability*. This refers to systems that can assume two states (positive/negative, 1/0, on/off, etc.) on which all further operations depend. These are systems with an inbuilt distinction, with an inbuilt form, and with the possibility of operations which can transfer the connecting point for further operations from one side to the other—'crossing' operations in the terminology of Spencer Brown. The achievement lies in the fact that only two connecting points are provided, and only these two connecting points can be used, one at a time. Bi-stability does not require the system to have the possibility of observation, of self-observation, of the distinction between self-reference and external reference (which are evidently all given in the case of the legal

[26] Or, put somewhat more poetically by Maurice Merleau-Ponty: 'une lumière qui, éclairant le reste, demeure à son origine dans l'obscurité' (*Le Visible et l'Invisible* (Paris, 1964), 172).

[27] It goes without saying that this usage of the term 'code' is not the same as in semantics. In semantics 'code' is a function or rule of attribution, which links a term with an intended content. See, for instance, with reference to the application of this concept to law, Thomas M. Seibert, 'Zur Einführung: "Kode", "Institution" und das Paradigma des Rechts', *Zeitschrift für Semantik* 2 (1980), 183–95. If, however, this is a matter of rules of attribution (and not of the contents themselves), the semiotic use of language is also based ultimately on a binary structure, and the suggestion of a definition here goes further only in so far as the code is seen as an artificial duplication of reality and through that changes the meaning of *both* sides of the coded relation. The question which then arises, is what can be achieved with the duplication as such (or: with the 'form' of the code).

system). Bi-stability already causes a system to respond to a highly complex environment with its own operations and in a fully predetermined manner *without the need to adjust* to that environment. This feature prevails in all further developments and never changes. Binary codes, such as the code legal and illegal, also come in the form of bi-stability and guarantee that the system can direct its further operations either towards a finding of what is legal or towards one of what is illegal—regardless of the difference between positive/negative which states that a position in the system can only be taken legally and not illegally.

Logically, bi-stability assumes the exclusion of third values (or definitions) that cannot be attributed to either of two values. Under these circumstances both values are convertible by mere negation without the need for an 'interpretation' of the values. The exclusion is achieved operatively by creating an environment that presumes this neither/nor. Contrary to a primary application of Spencer Brown's formula, the other side of the distinction is not the 'unmarked space' which cannot be specified. Rather, the system places its code, its guiding distinction, as a two-sided form into such an 'unmarked space'. The system is able to specify the two sides of the form of its code. This can only be done, however, in such a way as to produce a specific effect of exclusion that renders the world at large in the system as indistinguishable from its environment.[28]

Due to the binary code there is a positive value—we call it legal, and there is a negative value—we call it illegal. The positive value is applied if a fact conforms to the norms of the system. The negative value is applied if a fact violates a norm of the system. A 'fact' here is a construction of the system. The system does not acknowledge any external instance that could dictate to it what a fact is, even if the term 'fact' can apply to both internal and external phenomena. A 'jurisdiction' which administers justice by applying the values legal and illegal is an internal system arrangement. Outside, and apart from the legal system, there is no disposition of the values legal and illegal. This is, incidentally, a trivial statement (which, however, leads to non-trivial consequences in the context of its theoretical evaluation). It can be summarized in the observation that whenever an operation deals with legal and illegal, the system recognizes this as an internal operation and integrates it into the recursive network of its further operations. This leaves one last question unconsidered, namely the extent to which consistency (or informational redundancy) can be secured—in medieval times, for example, by the relationship between canon law, civil law, and local legal customs in the absence of any uniform administration of justice.

---

[28] As a precaution one should note that the terms 'world' and 'environment' are used here in a technically precise way and have to be distinguished from things and events in the world or in the environment. These can, of course, be specified by the system if its codes and programmes provide for this.

The ordering and distilling effects of coding are achieved by its binarity. This means first of all that the system cannot be a goal-oriented system, which works towards a purposeful end by teleological guidance and which stops operating once it has achieved this end. In other words, the *unity* of the system cannot be represented in the system *as a goal*, or as a final state that can be reached. Goal orientations can be given *in* the system but only for episodes, for instance individual processes that lead to a statute or a judicial decision, or contractual negotiations with the goal of finalizing a contract. Once they reach their goals, these interactionally operated procedures or dealings are at an end. The condition, however, for being able to operate with such goal-orientation and ending is that law itself does not end and that it does not stop operating. On the contrary, the creation of episodes, the marking of goals and temporal differentiations, require the legal system to continue operating and to integrate the results of these procedures or negotiations in the conditional matrix of its further operations.[29] If the law ended when proceedings reached their end, one would not even start with litigation. The law, therefore, is a never-ending story, an autopoietic system that produces elements only in order to be able to produce further elements; and binary coding is the structural form that underwrites its guarantee.

This guarantee also finds expression in the fact that each decision that confirms a legal or an illegal condition in turn goes on to produce more legal or illegal facts. It is illegal if someone who has obtained a judgment in his favour takes the law into his own hands; and someone who has been lawfully imprisoned still has the right to be provided with food and is entitled to be looked after humanely, even if he has committed an illegal act. Each operation, which opts for either value of the code, opens up the code again, making it possible to judge all following operations under the aspect of the one or the other value. This means that the system, in its temporal circumstance, is an open system as well, because of its closure. In this respect, the autopoietic reproduction in the system is the reproduction of the recyclability of the code. A differentiated system which is oriented by its own code is thus characterized by the way it subjects the ongoing connecting of legal conduct with illegality, and the ever-present possibility of acting illegally even while following the law, to *internal regulations* and *uses that for its self-confirmation*. The point here is no longer, as is the case of tribal legal regimes, to provide the plaintiff with satisfaction or to assist in the resolution of conflicts between groups.

Binarity is not only a minimal condition for keeping the operatively closed system open (in contrast to having only one code of value available).

---

[29] On the issue of linking episodes in the legal system see Gunther Teubner, 'Episodenverknüpfung: Zur Steigerung von Selbstreferenz im Recht', in Dirk Baecker et al. (eds.), *Theorie als Passion* (Frankfurt, 1987), 423–46.

Binarity is also a condition for the capacity for decision-making (in contrast to having multiple code values available) and is thus a condition for having courts (see Chapter 7). Each attempt to increase the list of code-values would immediately make decision-making so complicated that the system would not be able to operate in practice with sufficient security whatever supporters of the 'multiple-value logic' view might maintain. There were attempts to move in that direction, especially in the Middle Ages and in early modernity. For instance, it was accepted that the higher purpose not only of the Church but also of worldly authorities permitted a 'derogation' of the law—as if there were three values: legal, illegal, and the common good. It remained contentious as to whether or not this was a norm of natural law, and if it was, whether or not it justified violations of natural law.[30] Another example was the command of the *raisons d'état* which permitted non-prosecutions and ignored violations of the law if such a prosecution was thought to be politically too dangerous as it might lead to rebellion, civil war, or to resistance by powerful elites—as if there were three values: legal, illegal, and the maintenance of political authority.[31] These examples demonstrate, however, that the structure was not extended to a fully acceptable form consisting of three values, for that would evidently have led to a complete disorientation of legal practice. Instead the problem was contained and domesticated inside the legal system and with the background of a rather patchy implementation of law, that is, on the one hand toleration of the paradox of legality/illegality and on the other hand special laws, exceptional law, or dispensations of the type of a *ius eminens*. The candidate for the position of a third value could not simply be put on the list of values, alongside legal and illegal. The only possibility was to confront the binary code and to claim the position of a rejection-value[32] in the face of that code, that is, of a value which opens up the possibility of rejecting, in certain cases, the decision between legality and illegality or the validity of this option as the only one available. Here we find ourselves in the final stages of a debate in the classical and medieval periods as to whether or not law could dismiss itself from its own application. With the introduction and implementation of a prohibition on the denial of justice, this question has today been answered. The value of rejection no longer represents a higher value, as was the case in Roman rhetoric and in medieval theory of law.[33]

---

[30] See on this point, again Luhmann, 'The Third Question', 156.

[31] See above n. 14.

[32] See this concept in the framework of a logic of 'transjunctional' operations in Gotthard Günther, 'Das metaphysische Problem einer Formalisierung der transzendental-dialektischen Logik', and id., 'Cybernetic Ontology and Transjunctional Operations', in id., *Beiträge zu einer operationsfähigen Dialektik*, vol. 1 (Hamburg, 1976), 189–247 and 249–328.

[33] See the rich material in Alessandro Bonucci, *La derogabilità del diritto naturale nella scolastica* (Perugia, 1906), which is still unsurpassed.

One cannot impose higher standards on the code by rejecting it. At issue is only the logical form that has to be selected by the social system when it has to cope with a plurality of differently coded systems and it does not have a superior code at its disposal.[34]

Permission for the self-rejection of the code is constructed paradoxically because it is based on a claim of lawfulness for the rejection (not that it is contrary to the law). Therefore the paradox is unfolded by a distinction of levels for legal validity. This is different from a case where direct observation assumes the form of a tautology. Each functioning sub-system can reformulate its own binarity as excluding third values. In the context of society this means: it can reject the codes of *other* functioning systems on the condition that it accept its own code unconditionally. This, however, limits only the option and not the relevance of values, which have to be considered from case to case. The same applies, as far as the legal system is concerned and as will be discussed in greater detail below, to the differentiation between coding and programming, which allows the introduction of 'other values' at the programme level that have been excluded at the code level. This happens, however, only with the proviso that they are used exclusively to determine a decision between legal and illegal.

The unity of a code is expressed in the fact that there cannot be a decision on one value without having regard to the other. This undermines, one might say, an immediate sense of justice. One must always be prepared to replace the one value with the other, no matter how much one is convinced of their legality or illegality, as the case may be, in certain situations. Therefore, the coordination of values and facts requires an examination and refutation of the opposite possibility, just as in science a statement can only be held to be true if one declares at the same time that one has examined the possibility that it is not false. There is, of course, no absolute certainty in these matters nor a last instance that—one could almost say, independently of itself—could determine what applies for each possible position. But this lack of finality can be neutralized within the system— either by admitting the hypothetical state of all scientific statements, or by the legal institution of *legal force* that bars, by law, any re-examination of the same issues.

---

[34] Further to the logical form, it should be noted that the recognition of values of acceptance or rejection explodes the classical structure of binary logic. With it the connotation of an ontological and ethico-political world-view collapsed. This was built on a single guiding distinction, namely 'to be' versus 'not to be' and good versus bad, which did not on logical grounds alone provide the observer with structurally richer options. So one could not distinguish, as criticized by Heidegger for instance in ontological metaphysics, between truth (code-value) and correctness (conformity with programme). Right up to today, similar difficulties are the cause of the tenacity with which one searches for values of legitimacy above the law— or resents their absence.

Thus the code 'unfolds' the paradox which lies in the fact that the unity of the system is constituted by two incompatible values, that *one* distinction has *two* sides which, seen in a temporal aspect, can be *relevant at the same time* but *cannot be used at the same time.* The allocation of the second value prevents one from immediately following one's first intuition which wants to link further operations to what one considers to be legal (or if one does so, at one's own risk). Therefore the second value is a negative value, or a control value, which causes all legality, including illegality, to become contingent. Each attribution of values is a contingent result of contingent operations and, therefore, has to present itself as a decision which could as a matter of principle have gone the other way and *which has taken this alternative into account.*

This thesis can be reformulated in the statement that coding requires the possibility of second-order observation in the system. This does not exclude operations on the level of the first order, such as non-reflexive legal or illegal claims. These are also operations of the system within the system. The closure of the system, however, as noted in Chapter 2, is achieved only through subjecting all observations in the system to observations on a second-order level.

The closure of the code is achieved by making the transition from one value to the other, the 'crossing' of the border, easier. Legality, for instance, is more closely related to illegality than, say, to love. We can call the requirement of an effective coding its *technicalization.* This means that the crossing can be performed like a technical operation, the success of which depends on only a few conditions and not on either the sense that the world as a whole makes of it, or the particular characteristics of the 'subject' who performs the crossing.[35] As noted before, the values of the code do not require any interpretation. Even without being particularly knowledgeable about the world or people, one can know and anticipate under what conditions whether something is legal or illegal depends in a given case. One has to observe only those conditions and be able to mobilize only those facets of knowledge about the world and people that are defined in the legal system as relevant. One needs to look up a legal text first, and the only question that then remains is 'where'?

In spite, and indeed because of all of this, there is a very human side to the technicalization of the code legal/illegal. Most of those who are right and want to be right are not satisfied with that assurance alone. They want their opponents to be shown to be wrong, and it is often difficult to say which of the two is the primary motivation. The code helps this come about

[35] The concept relates positively to the independence of concrete and subjective creations of meaning which Husserl deplores in his criticism of the modern (and with regard to their technicity idealized) sciences; see Edmund Husserl, *Die Krisis der europäischen Wissenschaften und die Transzendentale Phänomenologie,* Husserliana VI (The Hague, 1954).

in a quasi-automatic way by the smooth (that is, technical) coupling of the positive value and the negative value, so that one does not need to be seen as the kind of person who is primarily concerned with having one's opponent proved wrong.

Technicalization can be understood as a condition and a request for rational decision-making. However, through this form of the code, demands on rationality become limited. One can speak of a specific 'juridical rationality'[36] but cannot deduce from this that there is a rationality that applies to the whole of society. In this context, the use of the term 'reason' also becomes problematic. What can be achieved, however, is the following: within a blurred margin of acceptance it can be established whether or not an error has been made in the attribution of the values, legal and illegal. This, in turn, is a precondition for considering the installation of a hierarchy of error checking as useful, that is, an organized sequence of specialized instances within the system. Only in this way can one assume that even though many proceedings take place at the same time they are all nevertheless decided in a similar manner—so that it does not matter, or matters very little, which court, which bench, and which judge have been involved in the decision. This issue has attracted considerable attention from practitioners and sociologists of law, and evidently it does matter. Even here, however, the technicalization of the code is successful in so far as this situation is treated as anomalous and one can specify, having regard to knowledge about the law and the facts, whether or not, and in precisely what respects, it matters who makes the decision.[37]

In contrast to immediate normative representations, the code enables highly varied qualities to be reduced to a form. This renders the legal assessment independent of the many assessments made by society and, at the same time, it provides a wide scope for the combination of properties that make it up. For example, there can now be people who are good but incompetent, and people who are competent but bad[38]—in contrast to the possibilities which are available in the harmony-conscious high cultures (and also in contrast to the concept of *areté* and *virtus* in the European tradition, which required a combination of good or bad properties).[39] This

[36] This is Schelsky's expression, cf. Helmut Schelsky, 'Die juridische Rationalität', in id. (ed.), *Die Soziologen und das Recht: Abhandlungen und Vorträge zur Soziologie von Recht, Institution und Planung* (Opladen, 1980), 34–76.

[37] Research on the assumed effects of the political bias of judges, especially in constitutional courts, shows that this possibility exists but is overestimated. The findings do not support such assumptions.

[38] See Siegfried Streufert and Susan C. Streufert, 'Effects of Conceptual Structure, Failure, and Success on Attribution of Causality and Interpersonal Attitudes', *Journal of Personality and Social Psychology* 11 (1969), 138–47, with regard to the effects of high system complexity.

[39] Seen from a formal aspect, the issues here are different models for dealing with variety and redundancy. We will revisit this issue in Ch. 8 under the heading of argumentation.

does not mean, of course, that one can no longer use society's values directly; but such a use has to be suitable for potential legitimation within the system, for being able to be linked to the reference structure in the system, and for autopoietic operation.

All this considered, there are still two possible interpretations of the code. One is to treat the code as a division of the world into two halves: legal and illegal. All that a case can be is either legal or illegal. In observing and describing the code in this way, one side of it is specified and the other side is taken on board as a residual category, that is, what remains an 'unmarked space' (Spencer Brown) with reference to the form of law. This leads to two further versions. One can treat either legal or illegal as the 'internal side' of the code and the other side as the 'external side', as a residual category. Any problems of the one or the other option can be corrected by formulating relatively vaguely the norms that permit or prohibit something. The 'programmes' of the system (we will return to this point in a moment) can direct their specification performances more towards the one or more towards the other side of the code. For instance, they may prefer to deal with a legal position under civil law or with an illegal position under criminal law.[40] The side that is under-defined serves as a 'variety pool', as it were, for the purposes of interpretation and argumentation. In spite of the mirroring of the situation, there remains a difference in presentation, a political difference, a semantic difference and also a difference when applied to the treatment of borderline cases, depending on whether one takes permission or prohibition as a premiss.

But this version of the code as a world-view, as a universal code, is not the only possible one. This is the one that the legal system itself practises and which structures its social operations (communications). The other version becomes available if one starts from the assumption that society is the system that encompasses and includes all communications. On the basis of such a reference to the system, there are many functioning systems with different codes, all of which claim a functional priority and a universal validity, but only from the perspective of that functioning system. For examples that can make this point clearer one can look at the property code of the economic system, the selection code of the education system, or the power code of the political system. These codes are valid in society only with reference to each special functioning system. Society demands only that it should be possible to distinguish between the different distinctions and their specific positive and negative values. Society itself does not need its

[40] It should be clear, after long discussions that reach back as far as Bentham, that this is only a rather superficial understanding of the difference between civil law and criminal law. In each case the other side of the code is taken into account as well, in criminal law, for instance, by an elaborate doctrine of weighting and the protection of legal values: see Knut Amelung, *Rechtsgüterschutz und Schutz der Gesellschaft* (Frankfurt, 1972).

own code because its operative closure and boundaries are secured and defined from case to case by a clear distinction between communication and non-communication. The problem for society today is to find a way to describe itself as a system that provides a number of different universal codes. Here the traditional means of description of a binary logic together with an ontology that structures observations according to the scheme to be/not to be, do not suffice. Nor is it appropriate to accept the code true/false of the science system as a form for the self-description of society (which nevertheless does not exclude science from describing society), because this code, too, is only the code of a functioning system. The resulting situation is often portrayed negatively, as the sheer impossibility of conceiving of a comprehensive account of any sort, as in Lyotard's concept of postmodernity. Following Gotthard Günther, however, one could also assume that society has to use transfunctional operations for self-description with the possibility of a design in which each functioning system has to adopt a rejection-value for the rejection of the relevance of the codes of other functioning systems.[41] This would constitute a second-order observation, namely the claim of the legal system to be entitled to use its own code and none other in the face of the availability of other codes provided in society. It could not be seen as an acceptance of a third value in the code, in contrast to systems that are strictly oriented towards multiple values. It would not be anything else but a reflection of the functional differentiation of the social system at the level of its functioning systems.

III

The legal code has properties that prevent the legal system from being oriented exclusively by the code itself. In other words, the concept of the code is not a successor to the old concept of principle. At the very most, it acts in this role only in some cases. We will discuss the deficiency of a pure coding from two vantage points: the temporal and the factual.

Seen from a temporal perspective, the code is and remains unchanged (invariant) even when specified transformation is applied to it. If it is replaced by other values—for example, the value of utility or the maintenance of political power—one is dealing with a different system. The addition of other values is also excluded (as has been argued), even if only for mere practical reasons. In this respect, the code represents the way in which the system produces and reproduces its unity. The code represents the autopoiesis of the system, which either happens or does not happen. As a result, there is a degree of harshness to the code. Or, to put it differently, the code does not allow the system to adapt to its environment. A coded

---

[41] See again the two studies by Günther, cited in n. 32.

system has already adapted—or it would not exist. A society can afford a differentiated legal system—or it cannot. In this area there are no interim solutions.

From a factual perspective the code is a tautology and is, if applied to itself, a paradox. This means that the code alone is not enough to produce information. The tautology results from the fact that the values of the code can be exchanged with the help of a negation that does not mean anything apart from being a negation. Legality is not illegal. Illegality is not legal. Negations are operations which demand, and which are not allowed to change, the identity of that which has been rejected. In this respect the code can be said to be a mere duplication of the preferred value. This value indicates that legal must not be illegal and illegal must not be legal. Only if this is assured—and the Greek tragedies still serve as the best counter-example, since they exactly mirrored this attainment in opposing cases—can one speak of technicalization in the sense used earlier. A paradox results from a situation in which the code is applied to itself; for instance, if one asks the question whether it is legal or illegal to distinguish between legal and illegal. The answer that it is legal—for lawyers (and logicians) a trivial answer—leaves open the issue of what can function as a possible counter-concept, as a possible negation of legality in this case. The other answer, that is, that it is illegal, creates a reversal of the same position. According to the first answer law is assumed to be lawfully legitimate, according to the second as lawfully illegitimate. But the question as to the *unity* of both assumptions, the unity of the code, has not even been asked. This question has been, as we put it, made invisible. This is yet another version of the much more general statement that the distinction which *is used* for the observation *cannot itself be defined* but serves the observation as a blind spot, that is, as a (non-rational) condition for its own possibility. Observers of this observer who do not want to accept this (and this can happen through theoretical reflection in the legal system itself) can see only tautologies and paradoxes.[42] They undercut their own possibilities for observation and manage to observe only this.

One long tradition, which still has its followers, has tried to move away from problems such as these by resorting to a 'higher' level of meaning, that is, by resorting to hierarchical ordering. The last instances or highest values referred to here would represent, on the one hand, unchanging ideas (eternity, fitness for survival) and on the other hand, would produce differences at the lower levels through a kind of emanation from those unchanging ideas. In logic and linguistics this same approach of applied

---

[42] See further on this, Niklas Luhmann, 'Sthenographie und Euryalistik', in Hans Ulrich Gumbrecht and K. Ludwig Pfeiffer (eds.), *Paradoxien, Dissonanzen, Zusammenbrüche: Situationen einer offenen Epistemologie* (Frankfurt, 1991), 58–82.

asymmetry is used and expressed with the prefix 'meta'. This approach, however, is not without its critics nowadays.[43] We will therefore look to a fundamentally different form for the solution of this problem.

We find it in the *internal distinction of the system* between *coding and programming*. Coding can be seen as a form of the unfolding of the tautology/paradox of law but it is a form that only reformulates the problem. Because of their binary nature, codes are conditions for further conditioning, that is, conditions for further possible conditions that regulate which of the two values applies.[44] Without them, programmes would not have an objective. But coding gives rise to the need for complementarity, something like the need for 'supplements' in Derrida's[45] use of the word, a need for sufficiently clear instructions. Since the values legal and illegal are not in themselves criteria for the decision between legal and illegal,[46] there must be further points of view that indicate whether or not and how the values of the code are to be allocated *rightly* or *wrongly*. We shall call these additional semantic elements (in law and in other coded systems) *programmes*.

It follows that codes cannot exist by themselves. If an operation is brought under a code and so subsumed to a system, the question inevitably arises of which of the two values has to be attributed. This means that a coded system produces the search for further aspects of coding. It either succeeds in this respect or it falters at the point of the tautology/paradox of its code, and disappears. Therefore, any features 'whatsoever' suffice to maintain the autopoiesis through de-tautologization and de-paradoxization; preferably these features are taken from tradition or can be reconstructed as tradition.[47] Only an elaborate programme structure allows for 'critical' discussion that permits the possibility of accepting or disproving criteria with the help of further criteria.[48]

---

[43] See, for instance, Douglas R. Hofstadter, *Gödel, Escher, Bach: An Eternal Golden Braid* (Hassocks, 1979), and his thesis that 'tangled hierarchies' are unavoidable.

[44] It should be noted that there are other forms of conditioning which are crucial for the generation of systems. These are, above all, conditions which couple independent possibilities for variations and synchronize them; and that means: make them independent of each other, *if* the conditions are met.

[45] For an introduction see Jacques Derrida, *Grammatologie* (Frankfurt, 1974), 244.

[46] The *reference* to a binary scheme was already accepted in the classical language of *kanon, kriterion, regula*, most of the time, however, with the tendency to justify the criteria with the preferred value of the scheme itself.

[47] We described the legal system in Ch. 2. III as a historical machine.

[48] This already happened in antiquity and long before a modern society discovered 'critique' as its speciality. See, with comprehensive documentation, Dieter Nörr, 'Rechtskritik in der römischen Antike', *Bayerische Akademie der Wissenschaften, Philosophisch-Historische Klasse, Abhandlungen* N.F. 77 (Munich, 1974). Much of the medieval and early modern legal criticism is to be found in objections to law's being *written* in a foreign language (Latin and, in the common law, French as well).

One could also say this in a condensed form: codes generate programmes.[49] Or better: codes are distinctions, which can only become autopoietically effective as distinctions with the help of a further distinction, namely the distinction between coding and programming. Codes are one side of the form and, on the other side, are the programmes of the system. What an observer could describe as the unfolding of the system's tautology/paradox can only happen and proceed along the lines of these complicated distinctions between distinctions within the system. Codes guarantee the autopoiesis of the system in so far as they counter every commitment of the system with the possibility of its opposite, but in doing so do not concede any finality, any perfection. In themselves codes do not provide any commitment of the system to finality or perfection, because they admit everything. The autopoietic self-determination of the system comes about only because of the *difference* between coding and programming.

This differentiation between coding and programming can already be found in pre-modern societies. It was used there, however, in a specific context. The binary scheme runs the risk of abstraction and the enforcement of a harsh either/or, which is hard to accept socially and which leads, even today (especially in East Asian countries), to the recommendation that it should not be applied in given situations. But this means that comprehensive juridification of the operations of the social system cannot take place. Since medieval times Europe has been on a different course. The risk of the coding legal/illegal was accepted[50] but the programming level was used to reintegrate law into society. The programming level thus functioned as a balancing level for any discrepancies that might arise between law and society. The corresponding product was called 'natural law'.[51] Truisms were transferred into law through the concept of nature, which in itself took on a normative form (permitting the distinction between perfection and corruption). Such concepts were above all related to social differentiation and to the advantages of the division of labour and the division of property. Both the aristocracy and property were indeed considered as institutions under positive law because they were very clearly subject to special rules, but the arguments used to justify this referred to the nature of the human community. Not until the social contract doctrines in the seventeenth

[49] We shall argue in Ch. 6 on the evolution of law that historically the process went the other way and the codes only came into being after a sufficient mass of programmed legal material was available. See also below at section IV on the remarkably long tradition of conditional programming.

[50] However, one must add: only in so far as concerns for political power relations do not stand in the way.

[51] Other forms of compensation are given by the concept of *iurisdictio*, which also includes the possibility of deviating from harsh law and applying equity with the possibility of linking to a secondary, more flexible legal order as practised above all in England.

century was there any indication of an approach that could abstract from particular historical formations of society and refer, instead, to inalienable human rights or to the limits of the rationality and self-preservation of legislative powers.

The transition to a social system with fully developed functional differentiation made it possible to dispense with natural law in this sense. The level of programming now serves the requirements that are projected in the code itself. As a supplement to coding, programming serves to orient the conditioning semantics by one code, and one code only. There remains only 'positive law', which is produced in the legal system itself. The demands for social integration are relaxed or delegated to decision-making processes. Moreover, a corrective mechanism exists in the fact that other functional sub-systems also become operatively closed under the direction of their own codes and specialized programmes.

Specific legal problems of correctness can arise only under the condition of binary coding because only under this condition is there a specific legal contingency. Only law's own programmes can then specify what is correct. Of course, there is also the option of rejecting the legal code as a whole and leaving the matter to judgement in other contextual structures—say, the codes of science or morals. From there, however, there is no access to law. Law would be more or less completely suspended if there were a need for a scientific or moral (or economic or aesthetic, etc.) re-evaluation. Therefore there is, for law, no problem of legitimacy which law itself is not obliged to solve. There is a host of problems as regards the compatibility of the different programmes. There is a rule that new law replaces old and there is an exception to the rule in the interests of the supremacy of constitutional law. This, however, only reinforces the reference to the components of the programme structure of law. Any question as to the correctness of this programme structure does not make much sense—or only, once again, in the context of a rejection of law's code.[52]

---

[52] Klaus Günther, *Der Sinn für Angemessenheit: Anwendungsdiskurse in Moral und Recht* (Frankfurt, 1988), 332, points out (and I may have overlooked this) that there is a chance for discourses of application which only admit what is appropriate. He asks: 'what can it mean that programmes decide on the proper coordination of facts and code value, if decisions such as this can no longer be programmed and conditioned unequivocally?' The answer can only be: this decision can be programmed and can be conditioned but not always unequivocally, and that means, achieved by purely logical means. The fact that programmes have to be sensitive to change, and must be changeable themselves, does not preclude that they do not fulfil their functions in the interpretation preferred at the time. It is a matter for juridical argumentation to find this interpretation and possibly its modification but not for an association of law with a regulative order of a superior kind. 'Appropriateness' is not a criterion of a superior kind but at best a formula for reasoning which can help to sum up the findings of juridical argumentation. Such findings only fulfil their functions (see Ch. 8) if they specify sufficiently what is deemed to be appropriate and why. Only in this way can they sustain their programming function and eventually vary their definitions.

The problems of the temporal invariance and yet the adaptability of the system can thus be solved by differentiating between coding and programming. Only in the structural form of its code is the system invariant and unchanging but always available to be adapted or transformed. Only on the level of its programmes, however, can it allow changes without fearing the risk of a loss of identity. This includes the decision not to change anything (for instance, constitutional norms). Just like the dimension 'true/false', the dimension 'changeable/non-changeable' is relevant only for consideration at the programming level. These distinctions lose their meaning at the level of the code, as the only relevant distinction here is between 'associated to the system/non-associated' to the system.

The non-ambiguity of the code—which is given only by its binarity—has to be relaxed for the purposes of programming. The values of the code have to be interpreted as *possibilities*, or in other words, as a *medium* which can assume various forms. It goes without saying that this cannot happen arbitrarily. Since the medium can only reproduce itself through its forms, there is always a historical context. Each fixing of a form, therefore, is a change of law and each change of a programme has to observe the limitations that are a result of the historically specified (pre-existing) affiliation to the system. The programmes must be suitable—but suitability is a broad concept here—to direct the allocation of the values legal and illegal. And, quite clearly, law's function is always involved at the level of programming as well, that is, that of keeping normative expectations stable. The issue is no longer a hierarchy of eternal law, natural law and positive (changeable) law, but, in a way, the theory outlined here offers an alternative to this: invariance and inalienability are represented by the code, changeability—and in this sense, positivity—is represented by the programmes of the system. In both cases, this is a matter of legal institutions within the system; they depend, however, on the comprehensive social system and its environment providing the conditions for their possible operations. As far as adaptation is concerned, one can suggest that the system in the fulfilment of its adaptability, achieved through variation in its programmes, has always been adapted.

Finally, the distinction between coding and programming allows one to distinguish between two different variants of the general problem of the *certainty of the law*. The certainty of the law must be given, first of all, by the certainty that, if requested, matters will be dealt with exclusively on the basis of the code of law and not, say, on the basis of the code of power or any other interests which are not recognized by law. This was an acute problem in all old societies and it is still acute in some developing countries, including countries that have already clearly passed the threshold of industrialization.[53] This

[53] See, for instance, for Brazil: Marcelo Neves, *Verfassung und Positivität des Rechts in der peripheren Moderne: Eine theorestische Betrachtung und eine Interpretation des Falls Brasilien* (Berlin, 1992).

issue has to be distinguished from the question as to whether or not court decisions, based on the programmes of the system, are predictable. Here one can cope with a considerable measure of uncertainty and, if necessary, prefer 'alternative' ways of conflict resolution—just as long as the possibility of having the case decided under the legal code is guaranteed.

IV

Contrary to the protests that I can be anticipate, and contrary to the way lawyers have grown accustomed to think since the 'social engineering' approach developed at the beginning of the twentieth century with its animated period of planning in the 1960s, one must insist: programmes of the legal system are always *conditional programmes.*[54] Only conditional programmes can instruct the continuous linking of self-reference and external reference;[55] only conditional programmes provide the system's orientation to and from its environment with a form which is cognitive and at the same time which can be evaluated deductively in the system. The formal Roman process began with the instruction: '*si paret* . . .' The converse model of programmes, which specify purposes, is suited to investment decisions, for example, or to a doctor's decisions or the planning decisions of an administration. Purpose-specific programmes, however, do not allow for the setting of adequate limits to the facts that must be considered in a legal process.[56] A purpose-specific programme is not a consideration for the legal system, or is to be found only—as will be shown below—nested in conditional programmes.[57]

---

[54] A good but little-known starting point for this discussion is Torstein Eckhoff and Knut Dahl Jacobsen, *Rationality and Responsibility in Administrative and Judicial Decision-Making* (Copenhagen, 1960). See also my much-criticized observations in Niklas Luhmann, *Rechtssystem und Rechtsdogmatik* (Stuttgart, 1974).   [55] See Ch. 2.VI.

[56] This is a problem that has been dealt with in economic decision-making theory by the concept of 'bounded rationality'. This, however, cannot be adopted in the legal system. It lacks the necessary control of the thresholds of attention that businesses have in their accounting figures.

[57] This has frequently been contested, especially in American legal theory. See typically Robert S. Summers, 'Pragmatic Instrumentalism in Twentieth Century American Legal Thought—a Synthesis and Critique of Dominant General Theory about Law and its Use', *Cornell Law Review* 66 (1981), 861–948. It is all the more remarkable because Summers distinguishes between two 'substantive reasons': 'goal reasons' and 'rightness reasons' and assumes that their relationship with each other is unresolved (p. 914). Apparently there is no formula for the unity or mediation of goal-specific programmes and condition-specific programmes. Incidentally, the rather confused discussion should remind us that there is no contesting the fact that purpose-specific programmes are subject to legal assessment like any other form of conduct. But then they have to be transformed into conditional programmes. For instance, if someone is entitled to pursue certain goals, he or she is entitled to act accordingly under the conditions a, b, c, etc.

Conditional programmes complement any perceived 'natural' causality. They provide more reasons for the generation of difference (an amplification of deviation) on the condition that the effects produced can be secured through the differentiation of corresponding systems. By programming itself in this way, the legal system constructs itself as a trivial machine,[58] even though—or exactly because—it must assume that the environment does not work that way, and that society itself operates like a historical machine which always reflects on its own state of being, that is, it does not operate like a trivial machine.[59]

The form of the conditional programme is one of the great evolutionary achievements of social development. It first appeared soon after the introduction of writing in Mesopotomia in divinatory texts of the doctrines of wisdom, in medical texts and in juridical texts.[60] In a world of rapid expansion they made it possible to think of order in terms of fixed links and to do this in areas in which knowledge and normative regulations (in today's terms) mattered. Guarantees of order in the form of sequences of 'if . . ., then . . .', which structure the realm of the possible and which are handled by experts, were established long before there was the opportunity to deduce logical and explanatory statements from rules or principles in this type of two-level thinking. So it became feasible to have an early form of jurisdiction, which related to an established order and which was legitimized by, one could say, an affinity of form in a general context of knowledge.

This form of the conditional programme survived all further differentiations in society through a change of context. The conditional programme made it possible to differentiate a binary coded legal system by assuming the function of regulating the coordination of code-values to cases in that system. Even then the formula of 'if—then' remained.[61] The conditional programme spells out the conditions on which it depends, whether something is legal or illegal. With these conditions it refers to past facts, which are stated in the present. This can include legal facts, for instance, by

---

[58] In the sense of Heinz von Foerster, *Observing Systems* (Seaside, Calif., 1981), 201; id., 'Principles of Self-organization—in a Socio-Managerial Context', in Hans Ulrich and Gilbert J. B. Probst (eds.), *Self-Organization and Management of Social Systems: Insights, Promises, Doubts, and Questions* (Berlin, 1984), 2–24, at 9.

[59] Complementing this there may be systems that attempt to translate their environments into trivial machines even though they do not perceive themselves in this way. The education system can be an example here: it operates on the basis of purpose-specific programmes in response to attainments, but in a way that the students can give the right answers and become ultimately reliable individuals.

[60] See here, above all, Jean Bottéro, 'Le "Code" de Hammu-rabi', *Annali della Scuola Normale Superiore di Pisa* 1 (1982), 409–44.

[61] For the meaning of this form of 'if—then' as a legal form see Neil McCormick, *Legal Reasoning and Legal Theory* (Oxford, 1978), 45 and 53. McCormick maintains that this form is indispensable, especially if juridical argumentation is directed at the consequences of decisions.

means of the question whether a statute has been passed validly and if so when. Here it is crucial that the attribution of the values legal and illegal depends on what can be treated as past at the moment of the decision. In this respect law always operates as an ex-post-facto, tandem-arranged system. That does not mean that the future cannot be kept in sight and it cannot mean this because time is, at least to our modern understanding, always the unit of difference between the past and the future. This leads to a prospective, prophylactic legal service when, for instance, statutes are formulated or contracts are designed. But here time is accounted for as *modo futuri exacti*. This means: one attempts to imagine how a legal dispute—which will be initiated with a reference to the text—will be decided and tries to ascertain the conditions for such a decision in advance.

Of course, the existence of a conditional programme does not mean that it is determined in advance that the specified conditions will necessarily be encountered. A large part of law consists of permissions, which leave it open whether people take advantage of them or not. Even these permissions, however, are conditional programmes because they establish that conduct will be legal or illegal depending on how the permission *will be used* in an applicable event (having regard or not to relevant restrictions). Therefore, conditional programmes are by no means fixated in tradition. Depending on the choice of conditions, they can be, to a large extent, future open programmes.

What the form of the conditional programme does is to prevent any future facts, not accounted for at the time of the decision, from being relevant to a decision concerning legal and illegal. That is exactly how the form of purpose-specific programmes is constituted. Modern subjectivization of the concept of purpose, however, has led to simplification, which is in dire need of correction, because it makes it hard to understand why there are reservations about the introduction of purpose-specific programmes into the legal system. This simplification consists of seeing purposes now as not much more than present ideas (intentions) in a polemical rejection of the old European (Aristotelian) tradition which thought of purpose (*tele*) as the final states of a movement and thus as the future seen from the perspective of that movement.[62] It is easy to see that this natural concept of purpose had to be replaced when social evolution opened the future to a greater variety of options. The form of the intentional concept of purpose which then became accepted, however, failed in its turn to do justice to the complexities of the temporal dimension. By defining purpose as the *present* state of a purpose-specific system, one grasps the temporal dimension only from one perspective. This had one principal advantage, among lesser

---

[62] See Niklas Luhmann, 'Selbstreferenz und Teleologie in gesellschaftlicher Perspektive', in id., *Gesellschaftsstruktur und Semantik*, vol. 2 (Frankfurt, 1981), 9–44.

ones, namely that one could define purpose, in contrast to tradition, as selectable. However, by intentionalizing (subjectivizing) the concept of purpose, that concept conceals the difference between the present future and future versions of the present; and this difference is increasingly becoming important while confidence in the future and, together with it, confidence in purpose-specific solutions are fading away. Purpose-specific programmes, therefore, mask the problem presented by the future: namely, that the future versions of the present will not be what they are projected to be in the present. The scepticism of Max Weber, for instance, or currently of Jürgen Habermas, concerning a purpose-specific rationality is fully justified, even if doubts are in order as to whether adding other types of rationality is a solution.

We do not want to come down (at this stage at least) against deciding on a contemporary concept of purpose, thus being able to call 'purpose-specific *programmes*' structures of systems that guide operations. If we did, however, we must acknowledge more clearly that the concept of purpose refers to a double difference, which can only be formulated with a double modality concept of time. This concept refers to the difference between attainable states and other states that will occur *and* (as far as attainable states are concerned) the difference between present future and future present. Perhaps one can say that the concept of purpose defines the unity of these differences. At all events, it masks these distinctions and permits rational decision-making (which is then relative to purpose). Thus purpose-specific programmes drag the risk of a divergence between the present future and future present into the present. They run the risk that the future present will not be what is assumed to be the present future. In order to deal with this risk, instruments are used such as the continuous calibrating of regulatory control, hedging (accumulation of reserves, liquid reserves) or the choice of the safe option when deciding between alternatives. Today this is called 'risk management'. Legal programmes are, however, constructed around a rather different approach. They have neither the function of realizing options, which can only be attained by accepting risk,[63] nor do they provide the instruments that guarantee an acceptable degree of system rationality.

The linkage of the legal system to the form of the conditional programme is a consequence of the function of law, namely the stabilization of contra-factual expectations. Expectations are turned into the form of norms in precisely those cases when they are not met. This substitution of certainty (of expectation) for uncertainty (of realization) requires structural compensations. What is more, one cannot make it contingent on the

[63] We have already discussed the fundamental difference between normative time-binding and risky time-binding and their very different social consequences above, in Ch. 3.

future whether the expectations to which one has to commit oneself now will be legitimate in the future. One needs to know now or at the moment of the decision, and this can only be achieved in the form of a conditional programme.

Despite all this, there are purpose-specific programmes in law, and so empirically oriented sociologists of law may see this as a 'refutation' of the theory that has been proposed here.[64] Before arriving at such a conclusion, however, one should conduct a more thorough analysis.

Evidently, no 'genuine' purpose-specific programmes are involved here, in the sense that only the future will decide what is legal and what is illegal. It would be a juridical disaster if measures had to be considered illegal if it turned out that their purpose could not be achieved in the intended way or that the expenditure of means would be unjustified if new information came to light, particularly in the case of ecologically oriented legislation which is characterized by an increasing lack of knowledge. One side of the problem is faded out, namely the question as to what the future present will be like. Judges can (and must) ignore this side of the future. They make their decisions according to the law, exclusively on the basis of what they see as the future at the moment of their decision, that is, on the basis of what appears to them—after careful examination of all the facts of a case— to be the present future. It was hoped that judges would be able to rely on empirical laws or at least on statistically supported probabilities indicating, for instance, that it was in a child's best interest after the divorce of the parents to be in the care of the parent with whom he had bonded most strongly. The moment this scientific theory is criticized a world of equivalents and certainty breaks down.[65] After repeated experience of this kind there is reason to doubt whether science can ever succeed in making sufficiently reliable assumptions about the relationship between past and future which judges could apply—like norms—in order not to make a wrong (that is, contestable) decision. If such a solution is not possible, what will the effect be on

---

[64] Helmut Willke, *Ironie des Staates* (Frankfurt, 1992), 177, holds, for example, that legal development has passed over these reservations and has firmly established purpose-specific programmes as legal institutions, even going so far as to formulate 'relational programmes'. He should, however, demonstrate more carefully how the juridical relevance of purpose or relations is effected. Political interpretations of this kind, which nobody would dispute, are not in themselves practical law.

[65] See, for instance, Jutta Limbach, 'Die Suche nach dem Kindeswohl—ein Lehrstück der soziologischen Jurisprudenz', *Zeitschrift für Rechtssoziologie* 9 (1988), 155–60. For the instruments of the decision-making of French judges in the same situation (parental consent, expressed wish of the child, given status quo, that is, all the facts which can be ascertained at the moment of decision), see Irène Théry, 'The Interest of the Child and the Regulation of the Post-divorce Family', *International Journal of the Sociology of Law* 14 (1986), 341–58. See also id., 'Divorce et psychologisme juridique: Quelques éléments de réflexion sur la médiation familiale', *Droit et société* 20–21 (1992), 211–28.

law in making a decision between legal and illegal—a decision which has to be made on the spot—contingent on the question as to how a certain purpose—in our case the child's best interest—can be optimally achieved?

Judges can become therapists and try to induce the partners in a failed marriage at least to care jointly for their child. The reforms of the juvenile courts in the twentieth century were undertaken with this moral-therapeutic purpose in mind.[66] Or judges can assume the roles of business consultants who attempt to prevent business firms which have received approval to merge from controlling a market. It is immediately obvious, however, that in this case judges would no longer be operating in the legal system.[67] Purpose-specific programmes, equipped with the cybernetics of a tandem-control, do not suit the legal system; with every decision such programmes would run into the same problem that the future gives no satisfactory answers to the question whether something is legal or illegal right now.

Political trends—especially towards the welfare state—have resulted in the public service and, to a much lesser degree the courts too, being confronted with purpose-specific formulations by legislators.[68] Orientation by purpose may well be a meaningful political perspective but as far as the legal system is concerned a lot speaks against it. On the one hand, the sensitivity of purpose-specific programmes to the conditions under which purposes can be achieved, cannot be used to its fullest. On the other hand, purpose-specific programmes are, as far as legal technicalities are concerned, too imprecise to be able to block effectively any abuse or resistance to the achievement of their purposes. This applies also and especially to laws, which are limited to the definition of purposes.[69] Seen from a juridical perspective, the definition of a purpose can only mean that measures are legal *only if* they satisfy purpose-specific criteria such as, for instance,

[66] For today's largely sceptical assessment, which can also be explained sociologically, see Richard Lempert and Jospeh Sanders, *Invitation to Law and Social Science: Desert, Dispute, and Distributions* (New York, 1986), 258. See especially the statement at p. 269 that the binary coding prevails contrary to all therapeutical goals and against the assessment of all the aspects of the personality of the child. See also Anthony Platt, *The Child Savers: The Invention of Delinquency* (Chicago, 1969).

[67] Charles W. Lidz and Andrew L. Walker, 'Therapeutic Control of Heroin: Dedifferentiating Legal and Psychiatric Controls', in Harry M. Johnson (ed.), *Social System and Legal Process* (San Francisco, 1978), 294–321, analyse cases of this kind in which the perspectives in a situation change from moment to moment under the aspect of de-differentiation.

[68] See for a view on the constitutional consequences Dieter Grimm, *Die Zukunft der Verfassung* (Frankfurt, 1991), esp. 197 and 411. According to Grimm, the constitution can only fulfil its function in the face of such changes if it adjusts to them.

[69] See, as a case study of the failure of such a statute and its subsequent reformulation, David Schoenbrod, 'Goal Statutes or Rules Statutes: The Case of the Clean Air Act', *UCLA Law Review* 30 (1983), 740–828. Schoenbrod underscores both the points made above: the non-use of the sensitivity of purpose-scientific programmes for achieving their purposes to their full effect and the difficulties in overcoming the resistance of stakeholders.

criteria for causal suitability or the justifiability of a choice of means. A legal or judicially established determination of a purpose can be no more than a guideline for the finding of conditions, which can support a decision between legal and illegal. The conditional programme has to be configured from case to case (more or less) and, to go by past experience, one can assume that judges then contemplate stereotypical 'measures' which they consider suitable. The purpose permits judges to abstract from incidental consequences. This evidently applies, for example, to corrective measures in juvenile law, which are a substitute for punishment. The more a decision is supported by such purpose-specific reasons, the higher the probability that it is wrong; for the future remains unknown—even to judges. Purpose-specific reasons expose judges to empirical criticism, which leaves only the authority of office and the necessity of decision-making to render judicial decisions valid.

The context of decisions in law, therefore, is never a purpose-specific programme which requires that a suitable means be found for certain ends—be they freely chosen or mandated—and does not require that restrictions imposed by such programmes, for example permissible costs or legal bars, be respected. Initially, a valid legal text is invariably made up of an if—then structure. And only if problems occur as to how to interpret this text can the legal system start to consider the purposes of the programme, as will be discussed in detail below. Here the conditional programme is particularly useful in allowing for a high degree of flexibility in imagining purposes, much higher than would be granted to anybody in the pursuit of purpose-specific programmes.[70]

At the extreme, then, conditioning is reduced to a norm of competence. Law is what a judge deems ultimately to be the appropriate means to an end. Even this, however, is still a conditional programme because it is only law if the judge acts according to the law, that is, if he is a judge. Then legal practice regresses to what an observer would describe as a tautology: legal is what legality deems to be legal. The programming function would tend towards zero. Even then the autopoiesis of the legal system would not be under threat because it would be clear whom one should observe if one wanted to find out what is legal and what is illegal. The autopoiesis is guaranteed by the code, not by the programmes of the system. The real issue, therefore, can only be what would be the structural consequences for the legal system, and for interpretations by other related systems in the social environment of the legal system, if the detailed conditioning of legal programmes were replaced by incorporated purpose-specific programmes.

The conditional programming of law does not preclude that the purpose-specific programmes of other systems use law. For instance,

---

[70] See below Ch. 8, n. 104.

the purpose-specific programmes of politics use constitutional law, those of the education system use laws on compulsory education, institutional regulations, parental rights and duties, and the purpose-specific programmes of economics use property law. This does not mean that the purposes themselves become juridified. The law offers only conditional certainties (and they would not be certainties, if they were not conditional) in order to provide a greater choice of purposes in other systems. For society as a whole, the combining of purpose-specific programmes and conditional programmes is particularly fruitful.[71] The interplay between them requires, however, that the systems and their types of programming remain separate. Only in this way can their interplay be productive.

V

Programming complements coding and fills it with content. The distinction between coding and programming makes it possible for the code itself to be made tautological, to be treated as a formal exchange relation of values and nevertheless to provide the system with the ability to be a decision-making system. The distinction combines the system's invariance (its non-changing character) with convertibility (its changing character), which also means that it combines invariance with possibilities for growth. Once the code as such is established (largely through the organization of courts), the process of producing rules picks up speed and assumes the autopoietic form that feeds on itself.

This can be seen as an unfolding of the original paradox of binary coding. Lawyers can try to stick with rules and forget that they are working in a system with binary coding, but not entirely. The problem here is that the unity of the difference of values returns within the system. This can occur in the form of matters that cannot be decided, such as those on which Athena had to help out at the Areopagus. However, this problem has become so much a part and parcel of the procedural principles of the courts, in the form of the prohibition against the denial of justice, that it functions, in its turn, as a principle for growth and generates judge-made law. We will return to this issue in Chapter 7. Apart from the above example— which belongs to procedural law—there is also an example from substantive law, which demonstrates that the excluded paradox returns to the legal system and how this occurs. Here I am talking about the problem of the *abuse* of law.

This is not, as the legal literature seems to suggest, a tiresome, ancillary problem in the form of indeterminacy, which could very well in practice be

---

[71] As will be followed up below, a development and normalization of this interplay with the help of 'structural coupling' also enhances productivity.

transformed into rules and so reduced to a matter of little importance. Rather, the simple fact that it occurs in relation to the problem of legal sovereignty points to reasons that go deeper.[72] And indeed, with the problem of the abuse of law the paradox of the identity of the difference in the system rears its head again and makes us aware that all exclusions, all unfolding, all dissolutions of the original paradox, have been only self-deception.

According to Spencer Brown and his 'Laws of Form', what we have here is the incalculable case of the 're-entry' of the form into the form. The distinction between legal/illegal enters into itself on the legal side. This means that it is activated twice over, not side by side or in tandem but *twice in one operation*. As indicated by the term 're-entry', Spencer Brown appears to be thinking of a temporal sequence of operations. This dilation of operations in a sequence, however, is already part of the solution, a part of the de-paradoxization of the problem. The re-entry quotes and uses the original distinction by copying it *back into itself.*

This 'retracing' of the same 'tracks' left by the excluded paradox also repeats the problem of the paradox—but now in a form that is easier to manage juridically.[73] Spencer Brown's 'cross' in the original distinction can occur without being observed (it merely occurs operatively), but the 'marker', as the distinction which enters into itself, cannot. Similarly, a lawyer does not have to reflect that *each* making of a new legality (law) produces a corresponding making of an illegality (law), but can nevertheless see that there are forms of the use of legality that are legally problematic and may have to be found to be illegal. In view of the unpredictability of the situations in which law will be used, law has to be equipped with a certain surplus of options, and that is all that can be done. Abused law is also law, which is recognized by law. Only certain applications of law have to be excluded. This can happen, for example, with the help of a rule/exception scheme or with the statement that law can serve certain purposes, including meaningful secondary purposes, just as long as the initial purposes are pursued. Thus, for instance, the use of taxes for economic and ecological regulatory purposes is permitted and is legal as long as the major purpose of taxes, to provide the state with money, is assured. (This example shows also that the secondary category of a purpose lends a high but not unlimited elasticity to interpretations.) Similarly, the audience at a theatre or the reader of a novel can observe and understand how the characters deceive

---

[72] Cf. to quote a long tradition in one sentence: 'Sovereignty provides its bearer not only with the monopoly to exercise force legally but also with the exclusive entitlement to define law and injustice, and that without sanctions in the case of abuse' (Ernst Forsthoff, *Der Staat der Industriegesellschaft: Dargestellt am Beispiel der Bundesrepublik Deutschland* (Munich, 1971), 12).

[73] It is debatable whether Derrida's terms 'itérabilité' and 'trace' are quoted properly here. At any rate they too are a reference to the paradox of the basic form of distinguishing. See, for instance, Jacques Derrida, *Limited Inc.* (Paris, 1990), 222 and 230.

themselves and others in the story; and they can even be aware that they are being deluded (in a detective story for instance). However, the audience or the reader can observe all this only if they do not, at the same time, take account of the fact that the story itself is a delusion and that it has no reality. The form in the form represents the form, and the paradox of this representation is that the distinction is both the same distinction and a different one.

<h2 style="text-align:center">VI</h2>

The paradox, which is produced by applying the code to itself, cannot be disposed of through programming alone. Programming that is initiated by coding complements the guiding distinction of the system with a second distinction, the distinction between the right and wrong application of criteria for the attribution of the values legal and illegal. In this way factual complexity is generated. The system can learn to learn, it can test criteria and it may possibly change them. It grows within the factual dimension of meaning (even if it also uses temporal concepts in secondary modes, for example in the form of a statute of limitations). One cannot, however, reach decisions by this means alone (and especially not in a logical-deductive way).[74] This brings us to the question whether the necessity for actually making a decision can be used—quite differently—to unfold the paradox.

This is in fact what happens. The legal system has been provided with possibilities to delay decisions and to operate with uncertainty for a while.[75] It uses the given time frame—since the future is always perceived as uncertain—in order to generate and maintain uncertainty with a view to arriving at a (not yet reachable) decision later. This is a matter of self-generated uncertainty, very much like the self-generated uncertainty in the cognitive realm of the science system, because there is no doubt about the world at large but only a lack of clarity as to the attribution of the values of the code (in science, what the truth about the world actually is). The legal system allows itself this uncertainty because it promises to clear the uncertainty up in due course. And it can, therefore, also establish legally unequivocal conditions, which regulate this approach on the basis of the assumption of a provisional uncertainty.

---

[74] For a more detailed discussion of what is meant here by 'decision' see below Ch. 7.III.

[75] Here see also the observations of John Rawls on the 'veil of ignorance' in relation to one's own position and one's own interests in relation to the future of society, in *A Theory of Justice* (Cambridge, 1971), quoted from the German edition: *Eine Theorie der Gerechtigkeit* (Frankfurt, 1975), 159. Rawls sees this as a mandatory condition for making decisions from general standpoints. This concept goes back to Aristotle but was initially restricted to the legislator only.

Clearly, we are talking here of legally regulated *proceedings*. Proceedings are organized in the form of an episode with a limited timeframe—they begin with a claim and end with a decision. A beginning and an end are thus the constitutive elements of every system of proceedings, which is individualized by them. The beginning and the end are markers that are produced by the proceedings, that is, which are identified recursively in the management of the proceedings. Of course, there are also observers (plaintiffs, defendants, judges, courts, court registrars, media, curious people of all sorts) who exist outside and beyond proceedings and who make observations before the proceedings begin and after they end. The only thing observers can observe, however, is the self-organization of the proceedings, which include the beginning and end of those proceedings. In other words, events in the world that are external to the proceedings—an accident, personal grievance, a crime—do not induce proceedings. There are external initiatives to proceedings themselves, but these initiatives succeed only in a form that can be identified in the proceedings as their beginning; and it is only in this form that they are the beginning of proceedings. The proceedings would not begin if it could not be established in them that they had already begun (that is, been initiated by events in the world).

We emphasize this artificiality because it highlights the beginning and the end of a conflict that is treated in legal proceedings. Generally in a legal dispute it does not matter who started it. All that matters is who is in what legal position. That is why the proceedings must produce their own autonomy in time. Filing a claim, in itself, should not be dragged into the proceedings as an indicator of fault or as any other indicator for a legal finding (even if such judgements are often made in the environment of the legal system).

Only if this operation is observed strictly is it possible to explain how the coding of the system and proceedings within it are related to each other. Only the code—which allows for the attribution of the values legal and illegal, but leaves their attribution open—can produce the uncertainty on which the proceedings feed. They, in turn, use this uncertainty as a medium for their own autopoiesis. They use it in order to call for contributions, encourage participation, offer opportunities (but not results) and thus invite participants to cooperate, that is, to acknowledge acceptance until they finally become prisoners of their own participation who have only the slightest prospects of contesting the legitimacy of the proceedings after they have run their course.[76] Irrespective of the actual context, the remaining uncertainty endures as assumed common ground for the duration of

---

[76] See on such an assessment of proceedings, Niklas Luhmann, *Legitimation durch Verfahren*, 2nd edn. (Frankfurt, 1983).

the proceedings. Apart from the beginning, the end and the file number are the only invariable factors.

The strict binary code of the legal system is augmented in this way with a third value, namely the value of the uncertainty of the value attribution.[77] Thus the paradox of the unity of the difference between legal and illegal is not solved either by a mere doubling of the positive value (the court is entitled to decide what is legal) or by a doubling of the negative value, as a kind of 'tragic choice' (whether it is legal or not—it is illegal in any event to decide in this way), but by defining the code as unity through the value of the uncertainty of the decision—a self-indication in the strict sense. This is exactly what happens through the inclusion of a time difference, through futurization. This does not occur as a determination of the validity of the legal system but only as an episode that is differentiated as individual proceedings, whose end is foreseeable.

Proceedings that have the function of generating uncertainty through the delay of decision-making are one of the most important evolutionary achievements. They leave the binary coding intact and do not introduce further values or super-values (such as religious doctrines, proof by ordeals, etc.) to the system. On the contrary, they allow the distinction between legal and illegal to be applied to *the proceedings themselves*. A special procedural law, which is carefully distinguished from substantive law, is created for the regulation of proceedings. This law applies its norms in the positive sense to support the management of the proceedings in order to bring about an appropriate judgment. Procedural injustice is therefore a violation of procedural norms. But the form of procedural norms has another side also, namely the maintenance of uncertainty. There may be written or unwritten laws for this, for instance in relation to the criteria for the impartiality of judges; however, all the norms and measures which assist the proceedings also serve the presentation of a 'not yet'. They make it clear that the proceedings are not yet over and that the result is still uncertain—until the proceedings finally declare themselves to be completed.

Here we have another distinction, namely that between substantive law and procedural law. The unity of law has to prove itself as a unity of this distinction as well. Usually this is achieved by a teleological, targeted-oriented concept of proceedings. In doing so, however, one inherits all the deficiencies of teleological concepts, which cannot give any meaning to their failure, that is, their other side. Uncertainty as to the outcome of proceedings then appears as a regrettable fact of life caused by the difficulties of rational

---

[77] In relation to the code of truth a similar discussion can be found following on from Aristotle, *De interpretatione* 9, under the heading *de futuris contingentibus*. Here, too, the solution is found in adding a self-indicative value of the indeterminacy of the present, and not in deviating from the binary logic.

decision-making. Here, the medium that carries the forms of the proceedings disappears from sight. A solely targeted-oriented, instrumental theory of legal proceedings is therefore far too narrow. Furthermore, idealized versions of legal theory, which maintain that proceedings are there to do justice or to establish the conditions for rational consensus, highlight only the presentable side of procedural systems. Each version of this type of theory is forced to confront the question as to whether proceedings which do not live up to such positive expectations are proceedings or not. If they are not proceedings, just what are they? Theories of this kind are only acceptable in the context of the self-descriptions of the legal system, which express their goodwill in the form of norms and then restrict themselves to highlighting deviations as violations of the norm or violations of the idea of proceedings. A sociological analysis cannot stop here. It must always ask about the other side of the form as well, about the distinction that is used by an observer to define something as proceedings. And this leads back to the form of a paradox—in this instance a paradox that serves to transform the paradox of the code into a smaller, episodic format. And then one sees something that one cannot see if one follows the formula of norm and deviance, or of the ideal and reality. One sees the peculiar diversity of perspectives, the litigation without consensus at the beginning or the end, even without any identical meaningful experience in the consciousness of observers. And one can see the irritability that stems from uncertainty; and with all that, the opportunities for creative transformation of its premisses, on which the legal system builds its future operations.

There is no other normative order that has developed a reflexivity that runs on proceedings. It can be found only in law and not, for instance, in morality. Perhaps we can find here the essential criterion for distinguishing between the two codes, the criterion that makes law an autopoietic system in contrast to morality.[78] Only law possesses the secondary rules, which have been the subject of much discussion ever since Hart. Only law can doubt itself lawfully. Only law gives its proceedings forms that permit a legal certification of a person's illegal position. And only law is aware of every threshold value of the temporal indeterminacy of the legal question and neither includes nor excludes such limiting values. Morality can deal with the problems which arise from the application of the code to itself only in the form of rationale discourses, that is, only in the form of ethics, in the form of semantic abstractions—where any gain in orientation remains uncertain.

---

[78] We assume that the criterion introduced in the eighteenth century, which distinguishes between internal and external coercions, does not work. On the one hand, morals also weigh in heavily with disciplinary measures that risk losing respectability along that path. On the other hand, many legal prescriptions serve to support conduct rather than to prescribe or prohibit conduct or omissions.

VII

To conclude this chapter, one aspect of the analysis that has already been mentioned several times must be stressed again. The autopoiesis of law is based on a uniform mode of operation in which the production and maintenance (or change) of structures may differ from each other but cannot be separated from each other.[79] Therefore codes and programmes (norms) are not facts that have their own unique quality—as if they were like ideas, leading a life of their own above the level of communication. Codes and programmes can be observed only as communication. Codes enable us to distinguish between belonging to the system and not belonging to the system, while programmes, which attribute the values legal/illegal, are the objects of judgements of valid/invalid. An observer can define and describe them as structures. Empirically, however, they occur only in the operations of the system. They are moments in the autopoiesis of the system and not states that exist in and for themselves. The opposing view owes its existence to the introduction of writing, as does Plato's doctrine of ideas. Written texts, on the material basis of being on paper, favour the perception that whatever has been written exists in its own right. The doctrine of ideas rightly observes the matching insight that one cannot simply define the essence of the world as paper and reduce it to that. In fact, writing is for social systems also merely a mode of production of communication—with considerable consequences for the form of the structures that are produced along the way. If one takes time into account, it becomes evident that the production and the formation of structures can only be performed as one and at once (because the system itself is their unity and makes their unity possible). The legal system establishes proceedings in order to have time (and thus a future, and thus uncertainty). The system operates in the form of a chain of individual events, creating its own time, which can be synchronized, more or less effectively, with its environment's times. This is the reason why the differentiation of the legal system has, through coding and programming, a strictly temporal side. This side subordinates everything that has happened and is being handled by the legal system to rules. They make the proceedings independent of when or how something has started and when or how it will end. For instance, it is irrelevant (or relevant only if stipulated by specific legal rules) when a dispute started or who started it. All that is relevant is who is acting within his right and who is not. Otherwise one would become embroiled in an endless story, which each participant would 'punctuate' differently, as psychoanalysts would say. It is a condition for differentiation in a temporal sense that the relevance of events and their sequence depend exclusively on what the programmes of

---

[79] See above Ch. 2.II.

the legal system include or exclude. The legal system itself constructs what has started and how it has started. (One needs only to think of institutions such as the land registry, or laws such as the statute of limitations, which make it easier to collect legal evidence and restrain within narrow margins the need to access historical events.[80])

The same applies in relation to the future. Past and future are related symmetrically to each other, or at least in so far as this relationship depends on margins set by the system. In relation to the future, we must consider above all the institution of legal validity. The much-debated unsuitability of teleological perspectives is also relevant here, for they, strictly speaking, would have to defer any binding finality until the desired teleological states had materialized. With its clearly established temporal self-rule, the legal system prevents unfathomable and uncontrollable interferences from external sources. Or, to formulate this differently, a legal order which wants to achieve differentiation and operative closure and which wants through this to constitute itself as a legal system can only do so if it gains control over the temporal references to its social interdependencies and severs them according to its own rules. This also means that one has to contend with a considerable degree of temporal disintegration in relation to the social environment. There are different pasts and different futures in the legal system compared with other spheres of society.

However, this is compensated for by other arrangements. One of them is *access to the legal system at any time* and detailed *specifications* on which legal issues can be taken up and dealt with. So, even in constantly changing situations it is still possible to make a fresh start with new perspectives on matters that, apparently, had already been settled.

---

[80] Comparative analyses could show that this is not a peculiarity of the legal system but in many ways a prerequisite for the differentiation of functional sub-systems in general. See Niklas Luhmann, 'Die Homogenisierung des Anfangs: Zur Ausdifferenzierung der Schulerziehung', in Niklas Luhmann and Karl Eberhard Schorr (eds.), *Zwischen Anfang und Ende: Fragen an die Pädagogik* (Frankfurt, 1990), 73–111.

5 Justice, a Formula for Contingency

I

The unity of the legal system is given first of all within the legal system by the form of its operative sequences, which reproduce the system autopoietically. These operations can observe their affiliation with the system, that is, distinguish between system and environment. This distinguishing is an instantaneous self-reference, that is, a designation of the system in an instant, which designates itself in contrast to everything else.

However, designating itself in this way, as a legal-system-in-an-environment, is too complex to be captured in a fully conscious way, not least because it is done by operations in a temporal sequence. The circle of self-reference, which exists with each operation, has to be repeated from moment to moment. It unfolds into a linear infinity of never-ending operations of the same system. In this way too the system refers to itself and appears as a self-referential system with operative self-references copied into it.[1]

The system has to be able to recognize, that is, to identify, operations as repeated ones in order to facilitate this form of self-reference through repetition. And it has to do this in ever-differing situations, that is to say, it must generalize. Spencer Brown describes this complex operation as the unity of condensing and confirming of the recursive operations of the system.[2] Condensing presupposes and produces identities. Confirming them achieves compatibility with ever-differing situations. In the medium of meaning, this facilitates the unity of experiencing identity and horizon, a meaningful core area of actuality with a host of references to other possibilities. This, in turn, leads to 'experience' in establishing meaning, which cannot be completely captured by concepts. As has repeatedly been established in the theory of consciousness, the system requires a relationship with itself, which is not fully covered by reflection, because the system has to reflect on itself and to do this must already be operative and stay operative. The solution to this problem lies in formulating only 'local' references in relation to particular texts, which function as 'valid law'. The formal symbol of legal validity provides the reference to the system, as pointed out above, without characterizing the contents of that system.[3]

---

[1] See Louis H. Kauffman, 'Self-Reference and Recursive Forms', *Journal of Social and Biological Structures* 10 (1987), 53–72, who deduces both the directed infinite linearity of the system process and the re-entry of the system form into itself from this basic self-reference of making observations.

[2] See George Spencer Brown, *Laws of Form* (reprint New York, 1979), 10.

[3] Ch. 2.VIII.

A further consideration leads to a similar result. Since every observation must be based on a distinction in order to designate its object, the unity of the observation itself eludes designation—unless another distinction, which applies in the same way, is introduced.[4] Observations, and even more observers, can only access themselves as a paradox, as the unity of something that must function as different.

The unity of the binary code, therefore, can only be understood as a paradox. This paradox can be unfolded, that is, translated into further distinctions in different ways. It can happen, for instance, in the form of a second-order observation, that is, by the distinction of a different observer and his/its apparatus for observing. One can say then (as we have done) that the legal system (and only the legal system) uses the code legal/illegal. This solution has important advantages. Above all, it makes it possible to clarify statements about the observer (the legal system) and its code (the distinction legal/illegal) as may be necessary so that one can ultimately forget that the final unit of distinction-making is always present only as a paradox. The paradox is rendered invisible through the process of its unfolding and determination.

A first step is the addition of the distinction between coding and programming. Conditional programmes can be added as 'supplements' (Derrida). As discussed in the previous chapter, this means that codes can become technical, and be reduced to the formal exchange relationship of two values (positive and negative). This is due to factual criteria in the realm of meaning which are an additional distinction and which can help decide the question as to whether the positive or the negative value applies. At this point the massed forces of legal theory appear on the scene to clarify which criteria apply to the distinction between the right and wrong allocations of legal values. In this way one arrives at a theoretically systematized positive law, which is based on rules and principles—and one can be satisfied with that. The traditional question of the justice of law thus loses all practical meaning. It cannot be added as a third value alongside legal and illegal, nor does it define any of the programmes of the system as if a just law were to exist alongside construction law, road traffic law, the law of succession, and the law of copyright. As a result, issues relating to the justice of law are treated purely as a question of ethics, as questions only about the foundations of law in the medium of morality. And one tries hard to find a place for ethics in law.[5]

---

[4] See also Niklas Luhmann, 'Wie lassen sich latente Strukturen beobachten?', in Paul Watzlawick and Peter Krieg (eds.), *Das Auge des Betrachters—Beiträge zum Konstruktivismus: Festschrift für Heinz von Foerster* (Munich, 1991), 61–74.

[5] The usual advice that one must discuss the issue of justice on a different 'level' from legal issues is unacceptable; because if one runs away from one paradox, one quickly and obviously ends up with another one, namely the question of the unity of the difference of 'levels', and thus returns to the problem of the self-observation of the system.

Alternatively, one takes justice to be a social principle, one that covers all areas of life and finds itself as a specific form in law.[6]

Even if there is clearly an ethical quality to the moral imperative of justice, this is no solution for legal theory. It hands over the idea of justice to ethics, as it were, only to find itself under pressure to reincorporate ethics in its turn. We wholly accept that moral norms are referred to in the legal system and through such references become juridified; but in order to show how this is so, this disposition must be backed up by evidence from specific legal texts. It does not merely follow from the fact that legal decisions have to have reasons. The difficulty lies, *horribile dictu*, in the same way as stating that technical standards or best possible expert knowledge should apply in individual rules and regulations of the legal system. But how should they apply?

This does not mean, however, that law has to abandon the concept of justice, rather that its position in legal theory must be reconsidered. What we are dealing with here—and this lies behind the long-winded introduction to this topic—is the issue of the representation of the unity of the system within the system. While 'validity' is a symbol that circulates in the system, links its operations to one another, and recalls the results of operations for further recursive use, justice has to do with the self-observations and self-descriptions of the system. Whereas a self-observation and self-description at the level of the binary code ends up faced with a paradox (because it ends up by reiterating that legal and illegal are the same), it is still to be decided whether or not there is a unitary projection, a programme of (all) programmes on the level of the programmes of the system. It seems likely that the meaning of the idea of justice is to be found here. And whereas self-descriptions are produced in the form of theories (and that also means that they are arguable) in other contexts, the idea of justice obviously assumes a normative quality.[7] In the old European tradition, this norm was understood as social harmony and was related to society as a whole which, in turn, was understood as a legally ordered communal life. This did not lead to any concrete directives, if only because the premiss of a legally constituted society is unrealistic. But even if one tailors the norm of justice to a differentiated legal system, any respecification of the norm of justice remains undetermined. The legal system wants to be just, regardless of the facts. Therefore, in raising the question of the form of a *genuinely* legal self-control of the legal system (which is induced neither by natural law nor by decisions which, therefore, can be revoked by other decisions), the topic 'justice' touches on the point which enables us to overcome the difference between natural law theories and positive law theories of the traditional

---

[6] See, for example, Heinrich Henkel, *Einführung in die Rechtsphilosophie*, 2nd edn. (Munich, 1977), 394.   [7] See Ch. 11.

kind.[8] If the system, however, describes itself with this norm, it cannot at the same time specify what it means by it—unless it defines its *own* operations as *not belonging to the system.*

Thus we have defined the problem of justice initially as being limited by distinctions. Justice is self-reference in the form of observation, but not in the form of an operation; not on the level of the code, but on the level of programmes; not in the form of theory, but in the form of a (disappointment-ridden) norm. All this means that there are unjust (or more or less just) legal systems. Neither the operative autopoiesis of the system nor the necessarily invariant code can be 'just'. These limitations are important in order to put the question more precisely. But what is really positively defined in this way? How can this self-confrontation with a self-referential norm be specified? How can the system express its own *unity* in a normative programme, which can be applied, at the same time, *in* the system and *everywhere within* the system?

II

In the search for an answer to these questions we start from the assumption that the idea of justice can be understood as a *formula for contingency* of the legal system. Thus, and without the need to talk about values, this formula can be put on a level at which it can be compared with the formulae for contingency of other functioning systems, such as the principle of limitation (via negations) in the science system,[9] the principle of scarcity in the economic system,[10] the idea of the existence of only one god in the system of religion,[11] or ideas on education or learning ability in the education system.[12] Hence the concept of a formula for contingency replaces numerous other central terms such as virtue, principle, idea, or value.[13] It does not, however, replace these terms completely. For only an external observer can talk of the formula for contingency, as we will show in the following analysis. The system itself has to define justice in such a way that makes it clear that justice must prevail and that the system identifies with it as an idea, principle, or value. The formula for contingency is stated within the system

---

[8] See also Arthur Kaufmann, *Theorie der Gerechtigkeit: Problemgeschichtliche Betrachtungen* (Frankfurt, 1984), esp. 31.

[9] See Niklas Luhmann, *Die Wissenschaft der Gesellschaft* (Frankfurt, 1990), 392.

[10] See Niklas Luhmann, *Die Wirtschaft der Gesellschaft* (Frankfurt, 1988), 177.

[11] See Niklas Luhmann, *Die Funktion der Religion* (Frankfurt, 1977), 200.

[12] See Niklas Luhmann and Karl Eberhard Schorr, *Reflexionsprobleme im Erziehungssystem*, 2nd edn. (Frankfurt, 1988), 58.

[13] See, for an overview that shows, at the same time, how the concept of justice can be abstracted from the concept of virtue only in modern times, Hans Nef, *Gleichheit und Gerechtigkeit* (Zurich, 1941), 58 ff.

non-contentiously. Following Aleida and Jan Assman one could say that the formula becomes 'canonized'.[14]

The concept of the formula for contingency is, primarily, a consequence of the insight that the conditions for an idea of justice based on natural law have vanished.[15] Nature itself is not just in any conceivable sense. In other words, there is no inference from 'natural' to 'just', as implicitly assumed by the tradition of natural law. There may be a kind of balance in the sense of compatibility in nature as a result of evolution. Applied to law this could mean, perhaps, that the administration of justice has adapted itself to a normal degree on the scale of quarrels and offences. But it does not follow from this that the corresponding norms and decisions are 'just'. Order is a factual result of evolution. Any normative idea needs to maintain a certain degree of independence, that is, it must ask for more than what happens by itself (i.e. naturally).[16] Otherwise the norm would be superfluous, especially as a norm.[17] Given this state of affairs, it would be disastrous if, as the proponents of natural law would have us believe, the reference to natural law were the only critical reference for valid positive law.[18] We need not be fooled by this trick, with which natural law has stealthily secured itself a certain measure of recognition. The concept of the formula for contingency points to a different approach.

The assumptions of nature are replaced by assumptions of the self-specification of the formula. Consequently, formulae for contingency take the form of circular statements—and this gives them their self-installing character, which cannot be resolved any further.[19] They refer to the difference

---

[14] See Aleida and Jan Assmann (eds.), *Kanon und Zensur* (Munich, 1987); Jan Assman, *Das kulturelle Gedächtnis: Schrift, Erinnerung und politische Identität in frühen Hochkulturen* (Munich, 1992), 1992.

[15] Utilitarian concepts of justice, which refer to natural properties of humans (Bentham), are subsumed under the natural law concept of justice as well. They differ from classical natural law only in so far as they move from acquired to achieved properties of humans.

[16] We revisit this issue in Ch. 11.III with a discussion of natural law as a form of the self-description of the legal system.

[17] It is obvious that this problem can be circumvented with a concept of nature which is specifically designed for the purposes of natural law, but this is even less satisfactory. In this case the concept of natural law does not express anything more than the determination to take something as right. If this is so, one could start better, and more precisely, from the direct assumption of self-reference.

[18] It is typically not *said* but *assumed* that this is the only possible critique. See on this Manuel Atienza, *Introducción al Derecho* (Barcelona, 1985), 121 and 122.

[19] Of course, the statement 'cannot be resolved any further' should not be taken to mean that a second-order observer is not able to describe such a circular reference in a different-iated way. See on this point, following Derrida's concept of 'supplément', Jean-Pierre Dupuy and Francesco Varela, 'Zirkelschlüsse: Zum Verständnis der Ursprünge', in Paul Wazlawick and Peter Krieg (eds.), *Das Auge des Betrachters—Beiträge zum Konstruktivismus: Festschrift für Heinz von Foerster* (Munich, 1991), 247–75.

between indeterminacy and determinacy. Their function is to cross this boundary and claim historically given plausibility for doing so. The same can be expressed with the logical concept of the unfolding of a paradox, namely unfolding its tautology. Or, with a concept of the theory of self-observing systems, as rendering observable what cannot be observed by the substitution of a distinction for a unity, but one which can only be described paradoxically or tautologically.

We do not refer to actually given (perceived, defined) facts when using the dimension indeterminacy/determinacy but to other possibilities of dealing with them. Therefore we use the term 'formula' for 'contingency'. A system which runs its internal operations on the basis of information always envisages other possibilities as well. In the case of the legal system, this orientation by contingency increases as the system moves along eluci-dating positive law. One could state that all legal norms and decisions, all reasons and arguments can take a different form, at the same time as recognizing or not contesting that what happens, happens the way it does.

Formulae for contingency cannot be legitimized through their function. The boundary between indeterminacy and determinacy must be crossed without attracting attention or remark. In other words, the function has to be performed latently. If it were otherwise, this would expose the initial paradox and also the paradox that both determinacy and indeter-minacy are bundled in the same formula, namely, treated as the same. The function of making such fundamental paradoxes invisible has to be made invisible in its own right, and this occurs when formulae of contin-gency install themselves and in so doing prove their own suitability for the system.

This applies to justice as well.[20] Since it is the function of the legal system to stabilize normative expectations, it is also appropriate to treat justice as a relevant norm. In so doing, one must avoid seeing this norm as a criterion for selection (or, in our language, a particular programme).[21] This would make the norm of justice appear alongside the system's other criteria for selection and thereby lose its function of representing the system within the system. It would also mean that the norm of justice had to be accepted without knowing in advance which decisions will follow from it and which interests it will support. And it would mean, finally, that the practice of legal decisions, from case law to legislative solutions of problems, is guided

---

[20] See also Edwin Norman Garlan, who talks about justice as a 'self-justifying ideal' in *Legal Realism and Justice* (New York, 1941), 124. But it does not necessarily follow is that a formula for contingency is only a nominal unification without an operative function. On the contrary, the unfolding of a paradox is only possible as an operation.

[21] John Rawls belongs to the group of currently most respected protagonists who see justice as a criterion of selection (or as a supercode just/unjust). See his *Theory of Justice* (Cambridge, Mass., 1971). This theory impresses above all by the precision it achieves.

by the impression of the injustice of particular regulations rather than by the application of the norm of justice.[22]

In the tradition of thinking about justice, this separation of the formula for contingency from the criterion of selection is frequently overlooked—particularly if justice is presented as a virtue, which makes it mandatory that everyone might reasonably be expected to be virtuous or is actually assumed to be virtuous. Equally, it is obvious that scarcity is not a criterion for assessing the rationality of economic decisions. And, finally, God, also, is a 'generator of diversity' (G.o.d.)[23] and not one factor of the diverse world amongst others—unless one is referring to the reverence of God in the world or to priestly advice to people to lead a life which is pleasing to God (that is, to act in a particular way).

Similarly, formulae for contingency cannot be understood as formulae for development or as an indication of the desired direction of a system's development—in the sense of more justice, more education, less scarcity. Such forms may have been plausible at given historical points in time, above all in the second half of the eighteenth century. They are, however, certain historical interpretations that can be valid only as long as one is prepared to ignore costs, negative effects, dysfunctions, risks, and amplifications of deviation in the system, which are the consequence of every forced advance of certain directions of selection.

Here, too, what is meant by norm is nothing but the contra-factual claim to validity, which can be maintained even in the face of disappointment. The special problem of the norm of justice is the relationship between generalization and re-specification. No individual operation of the system and, even less, no structure is exempt from the expectation that it be just; otherwise the norm's reference to the unity of the system would be lost. On the other hand, the norm of justice has to provide the individual case with some orientation, but it cannot follow directly from the operation's affiliation to the system alone that it is just.

Justice as a formula for contingency in its most general form has traditionally, and still today, has been identified with *equality*. Equality is seen as a general, formal element, which contains all concepts of justice but which means only something akin to regularity or consistency.[24] Equality is seen, and this applies to all formulae for contingency, as a 'principle' which legitimizes itself. Justice does not need to justify itself any further. Moreover, 'formula for contingency' means that justice is neither a statement about

---

[22] See Edmund N. Cahn, *The Sense of Injustice: An Anthropocentric View of Law* (New York, 1949), and his concept of the establishment of legal order through a sense of injustice.

[23] I owe this formulation to Perpaolo Donati, *Teoria relazionale della società* (Milan, 1991), 221.

[24] This is old doctrinal wisdom. See, for instance, P. A. Pfizer, *Gedanken über Recht, Staat und Kirche* (Stuttgart, 1842), vol. 1, p. 57: equality is a 'formal factor of all law'. Among the more recent literature, see Chaim Perelman, *Über die Gerechtigkeit* (Munich, 1967), 27 and 55.

the essence or nature of law, nor a principle for substantiating the validity of law, nor a value which could make law appear the preferred choice. In contrast to all these assumptions the concept of the formula for contingency achieves an abstraction—and this corresponds exactly to the formal principle of equality, which likewise does not define the essence of a matter, or its reason, or value. The formula for contingency is a scheme for the search for reasons or values, which can become legally valid only in the form of programmes. Every answer to whatever issue is addressed would then have to be found in the legal system by mobilizing its recursivity. It cannot be added from outside. Equality is first and foremost a term for a form that both refers to inequality and excludes it. In a further development, which began with Aristotle, the other side of this form, namely inequality, could be subjected to the principle of justice in terms of the postulate that different cases be treated differently. Only this made the system's formula complete by making it relevant to all decisions in the legal system.[25] However, the paradox which was to be disguised by the formula for contingency then emerged; for then the unity of the system required that the same be treated the same *and* the different be treated differently, so that the *unity* was expressed by the *difference* between same and different.

The principle of justice has overall responsibility for the system, if one may put it like that, both for the unfolding of the paradox of the unity of difference and as a concept for a form which enables one to define one side of a distinction by not defining the other. This formula, however, can find very different expressions depending on the historical circumstances. All the formulae for contingency have a core meaning which co-opts different re-specifications in their further socio-structural development and the same applies to the principle of equality contained in the concept of justice. The Aristotelian concept of distributive justice, for instance, assumes the existence of a stratified society in which there is no question that people differ from each other by birth, being either free or not free, and by rank.[26] If this can be assumed, clear rules follow as to what individuals are entitled to. In this case, formulations such as 'suum cuique' make sense,[27] because

[25] See on this point Ch. 2.IX. Today it is generally acknowledged that this second rule, to treat different cases differently, does not merely follow logically from the principle of equality. Moreover, the principle of equality itself is no reason for different treatment; see Albert Podlech, *Gehalt und Funktionen des allgemeinen verfassungsrechtlichen Gleichheitssatzes* (Berlin, 1971), 53. What matters here is the other side of equality as a form and that this other side cannot remain unmarked (in the sense of 'everything else') but has to be defined specifically in order to make it accessible. That is why we can say that the principle of justice is completed in relation to its function as formula for contingency by the second rule.

[26] See for support, for instance, Arlette Jouanna, *L'idée de race en France au XVIe siècle et au début du XVIIe*, 2nd edn. 2 vols. (Montpellier, 1981), esp. vol. 1, p. 275.

[27] See Wolfgang Waldstein, 'Ist das "suum cuique" eine Leerformel?', in *Ius Humanitatis: Festschrift für Alfred Verdross* (Berlin, 1980), 285–320, on the conditions for such a formula.

the entitlements for each individual are not the same. Once the structural conditions disappeared,[28] the formula for contingency had to be returned to a state of quasi meta-historical abstraction and new associations had to be found, for instance by replacing the reference to rank by a reference to functioning systems.[29]

This historical and socio-structural relativity of the requirement that consistent decisions be made means that it must be complemented with a further feature. If there were only a few types of decisions, consistency could be achieved by relatively simple means. This is not the case, however, in developed societies with a differentiated legal practice. Therefore, justice can only mean an *adequate complexity* of consistent decision-making.[30] What is adequate follows from the relationship between the legal system and the social system. This has also been called the 'responsiveness' of the legal system.[31] Within the theory of autopoietic systems the proper term would be 'irritability' (perturbability, sensitivity, resonance). The legal system cannot account for all social matters with its own complexity. It has to reduce complexity, like all systems in relation to their environments, and it has to protect the make-up of its own complexity by high thresholds of indifference.

[28] At the end of the eighteenth century this could be seen initially in the reduction of the stratification of property relations and the resulting quasi-illegal poverty. Jacques Necker remarked: 'Il ne suffit plus d'être juste, quand les lois de propriété réduisent à une étroit nécessaire le plus grand nombre des hommes' (*De l'importance des opinions religieuses* (1788), quoted from *Œuvres complètes*, vol. 12 (Paris, 1822), 80). But to prefer religious charity instead is even more anachronistic.

[29] Recent politico-logical and sociological research on the problem of justice has again taken up the assumption of a problem of distribution, and has, in this sense, remained true to the tradition of Aristotle. See for a typology with regard to spheres of goods: Michael Walzer, *Sphären der Gerechtigkeit: Ein Plädoyer für Pluralität und Gleichheit* (Frankfurt, 1992). This can be seen as an attempt to combine equality and inequality (of the spheres of goods). In relation to the recent literature, see also Volker H. Schmidt, 'Lokale Gerechtigkeit—Perspektiven soziologischer Gerechtigkeitsanalyse', *Zeitschrift für Soziologie* 21 (1992), 3–15; Bernd Wegener, 'Gerechtigkeitsforschung und Legitimationsnormen', *Zeitschrift für Soziologie* 21 (1992), 269–83; and since 1987 the journal *Social Justice Research* (New York). It is remarkable that the discussion so far arrives at solutions to the problem that differ from situation to situation without finding any recognizable principle. (One only wants to find out how the problem is solved locally.) That is hardly satisfactory and raises the question whether the concept of justice is being properly applied here. Therefore, we insist on the terminological distinction between the formula for contingency of scarcity and the formula for contingency of justice. Furthermore, the situational character of the different solutions raises the question whether there can be any justice at all without a (legal) system and without historical conditions for decisions from case to case (which allow one to identify what is the same and what is not).

[30] See in more detail Niklas Luhmann, 'Gerechtigkeit in den Rechtssystemen der modernen Gesellschaft', *Rechtstheorie* 41 (1973), 131–67, reprint in id., *Beiträge zur Rechtssoziologie und Rechtstheorie* (Frankfurt, 1981), 374–418.

[31] See Philippe Nonet and Philip Selznick, *Law and Society in Transition: Toward Responsive Law* (New York, 1978), and on this see Gunther Teubner, 'Substantive and Reflexive Elements in Modern Law', *Law and Society Review* 17 (1983), 239–83.

But then the internal reconstruction of its environment will become more or less complex. Such an internal reconstruction, however, will correspond to the requirement of justice only if it is still compatible with the consistency of its decisions. We shall revisit this question in the chapter on legal arguments using the twin terms variety/redundancy.

III

Seen from the perspective of historical development, the problem of justice seems to arise initially in the context of reciprocal performances. One cannot ask for more than one deserves by one's own actions or more than one is owed from someone who has done one a wrong. This can be deduced from the importance of the norm of reciprocity in segmental societies.[32] Aristotle used this principle as a special type of reciprocal obligation (synallagmatic, or since the Middle Ages, commutative) justice[33] and contemporary authors also adhere to this concept.[34] In feudal societies the maxim of reciprocity could be adjusted to their different social structures by putting a higher value on favours received from higher-ranked individuals, leading to the ultimate conclusion that God's favour cannot truly be earned by anyone.[35] In more complex societies, however, the assessment of the value of performances became difficult, unless it was fixed by market prices, and thus the norm of reciprocity lost its practical relevance. Moreover, numerous roles (especially professional ones including that of judge) had to be exempted from the domain of the maxim of reciprocity.[36] Nowadays their inclusion would be termed 'corruption'. Reciprocity is not able to represent the unity of the system in one maxim any more.

At the same time, legal practice geared to texts, concepts, and authorities made a different perception of the problem of justice possible. Now justice could be linked to equality in a different way, namely as the rule by which equal cases are decided equally (and consequently: unequal cases unequally). In short, justice came to be synonymous with consistency in decision-making.

Compared to commutative justice and, parallel to that, distributive justice, a degree of abstraction has been reached which depends on the existence of

[32] See, for example, Richard C. Thurnwald, *Gegenseitigkeit im Aufbau und Funktionieren der Gesellungen und deren Institutionen, Festgabe für Ferdinand Tönnies* (Leipzig, 1936), 275–97; or, for a more differentiated view, Marshall D. Sahlins, 'On the Sociology of Primitive Exchange', in *The Relevance of Models for Social Anthropology* (London, 1965), 139–265.

[33] See *Nichomachean Ethics*, vol. 5, chs. 5–7, with the well-known distinction between distributive and synallagmatic (retributive) justice.

[34] See, for example, Lon F. Fuller, *The Morality of Law* (New Haven, 1964), 19. There is also a wealth of socio-psychological research on the social relevance and perception of reciprocity.

[35] In the Middle Ages above all, this resulted in the devil, with his tendency to rebel, appearing as representative of justice.

[36] See Claude Buffier, *Traité de la societé civile* (Paris, 1726), vol. IV, p. 26.

a differentiated legal system constituting legal cases. At issue is no longer only whether what someone receives—either by exchange or grant—has been determined fairly but whether a concrete case before the legal system has been justly decided. The old call for fair measures and balance between extremes loses its meaning. The point of reference for the comparison shifts from the 'more or less' of performance to what is treated equally, or unequally, in the recursive network of the reproduction of decisions in the system. The point of reference for comparison has to be abstracted accordingly. A legal case derives its relative unity from references to certain texts, which have to be interpreted in relation to the two parties and the conflict requiring a decision. The decision in a case depends on delimiting one case from another and thus on rules for decision-making which can be treated as just in their own right if they can consistently arrange equal and unequal cases. This means that justice can no longer be perceived to be a 'virtue', or only if seen from a moral or ethical viewpoint.

The principle of consistency in decision-making is separate from other value judgements that circulate in society, for example, whether participants are rich or poor, or whether they lead morally impeccable lives, or whether they are in urgent need of help.[37] Such considerations are taken into account if they are represented in the programme structure of positive law, that is, if they must be taken into account as 'facts'. Otherwise they are ignored.[38] For as long as this programme structure was not sufficiently sensitive to values, nor sufficiently differentiated and complex enough, a compensatory concept of equity (*aequitas*) was included in the operation of law. This, however, required special competence within the common jurisdiction of the sovereign (or, in the parallel structure of religion, the motivational force of Mary).[39] The residual category of 'sovereign' decision-maker remained in the programme in the form of an unfolded paradox—justice *and* equity, or as virtues: 'iustitia' *and* 'clementia'. This could lead, as it did

[37] This separation is criticized by the majority of contemporary legal philosophers. Jurisdiction on the constitutional principle of equality justifies its discriminations through a democracy of words, that is, it refers to a putatively broad base of opinions. It remains, however, untested. It has the consequence that legal philosophy arrives at an ethical concept of justice that, in turn, is not the sum of the value judgements circulating in society. See, for example in relation to social and economic inequality, Rawls, *Theory of Justice*. We shall return to this issue with the discussion on legislation in Ch. 7.III.

[38] The break with tradition is to be found here and not in the scheme equal/unequal. Therefore, authors who are concerned with the continuation of tradition are using an empty formula in need of further substantiation when they talk of 'essentially equal' and 'essentially unequal'; see Ralf Dreier, *Recht—Moral—Ideologie: Studien, zur Rechtstheorie* (Frankfurt, 1981), 277, or Henkel, *Einführung*, 395, and a criticism of this approach by Nef, *Gleichheit und Gerechtigkeit*, 105.

[39] See Peter-Michael Spangenberg, *Maria ist immer und überall: Die Alltagswelten des spätmittelalterlichen Mirakels* (Frankfurt, 1987).

in England, to a dual jurisdiction, one branch of which, 'equity', became particularly fertile ground for legal development. This duality, however, became increasingly obsolete as legal development was directed more and more by legislation and, at the same time, courts started to claim greater freedom of interpretation.[40]

With the increase in legislation, thinking about justice has entered the modern-day phase. Legislation is necessarily adverse to the consistency of decision-making since it constantly changes the law. Legislation makes it possible to decide equal cases unequally and unequal cases equally, depending on whether a decision is made before or after the passing of a statute. There are provisions, such as transitional arrangements, for dealing with a disruption of consistency. In principle, however, legislation depends on the existence of a society in which structures change so rapidly that temporal divergences are no longer (or rarely) perceived as injustice. The reason for proceeding in that way is shifted onto the political system, which is trusted to make well-intentioned changes (for instance, under the heading of 'reform').

It may be that the contemporary tendency to perceive justice as a mere ethical or emotional-appeal principle, which must take second place in a conflict with other values, is a response to this temporal injustice in the legal system itself. Thus the demand for consistent and sufficiently complex decisions is not seen as an adequate characterization of the idea of justice,[41] but this would hardly justify totally ignoring this demand. Accordingly, we can understand attempts to come up with definitions of justice which encompass both the political and the legal systems. But in the semantics of 'values', justice can be understood as only one value among many, and that means that a decision must be made between these values in each individual case. The problem of the formula for contingency cannot be solved in this way.

One solution could be to assign the formula for contingency to the centre of the legal system, to the core area of judicial decision-making, because the paradox of deciding what cannot be decided is only relevant here.[42] Then all marginal forms of production of legal validity—from individual contracts to legislation—could be exempted because they are closely related

---

[40] See David Lieberman, 'The Legal Needs of a Commercial Society: The Jurisprudence of Lord Kames', in Istvan Hont and Michael Ignatieff (eds.), *Wealth and Virtue: The Shaping of Political Economy in the Scottish Enlightenment* (Cambridge, 1983), 203–31, in relation to the transitional situation in Scotland, which lends itself particularly well to a comparison with the legal development in England induced by equity; and also, including England, id., *The Province of Legislation Determined: Legal Theory in Eighteenth-Century Britain* (Cambridge, 1989).

[41] See Ralf Dreier, 'Zu Luhmanns systemtheoretischer Neuformulierung des Gerechtigkeitsproblems', *Rechtstheorie* 5 (1974), 189–200, reprinted in id., *Recht—Moral—Ideologie*, 270–85.   [42] See for more detail Ch. 7.

to the dynamics of other systems, such as economics and politics, even though they produce legal validity within the legal system. They are subject to the disciplinary operations in other systems and are generated without the controlling reference to justice, but that by no means implies arbitrarily. The legal speciality of communicating the right to legal protection and prohibition against the denial of justice could thus suffice as a practical, system-wide base for the principle of justice.

There is another reason for aligning the wheel of justice anew in order to guarantee it a smooth path under current conditions, namely the tendency of social welfare states to create purpose-specific programmes. Purpose-specific programmes legitimize the choice of means and thus generate injustice. Political legitimation is given via the principle of inclusion. Everyone who is favoured by the programme is favoured because of the programme. Disadvantage accrues for everyone—as taxpayers. One might be tempted to see this giant political machine for redistribution as an example of distributive justice. But the foundations of natural law are missing and the contingency of political decision-making has taken their place. This is not necessarily fair only because it goes hand in hand with the principle of redistribution. Without doubt, there is a widespread dichotomous belief—which is well reflected in socio-psychological research—that bad luck is either deserved or grounds for receiving support.[43] But to make a simple dichotomy out of complex and, above all, structure-related problems, evidently overtaxes the interventionist state. At any rate the dichotomy appears to flow from an individualistic orientation to this sort of political decision-making. This could explain why the welfare state has little problem in being accepted. This idea of justice, however, reminds one more of Leibniz's idea of the *ordo seu perfectio circa mentes* than anything one might expect the legal system to achieve.[44]

The problems that arise as a result of this dichotomy are a matter for the constitutional courts, or at least this is so in Germany.[45] They see themselves as reviewing the balancing of values, but in practice they only replace one arbitrary assessment with (possibly) another. The boundary between the political system and the legal system, which is the basis for the legitimacy

[43] See Melvin J. Lerner, 'The Desire for Justice and Reactions to Victims', in Jacqueline Macaulay and Leonard Berkowitz (eds.), *Altruism and Helping Behaviour: Social Psychological Studies of Some Antecedents and Consequences* (New York, 1970), 205–29.

[44] See C. J. Gerhardt (ed.), *Die philosophischen Schriften von Gottfried Wilhelm Leibniz*, vol. 7 (reprint Hildesheim, 1965), 290.

[45] See especially Dieter Grimm, *Die Zukunft der Verfassung* (Frankfurt, 1991). For an overview especially of legal opinions and decisions on the principle of justice see also Reinhold Zippelius, 'Der Gleichheitssatz', *Veröffentlichungen der Vereinigung der Deutschen Staatsrechtslehrer* 47 (1991), 8–33. There is evidently a tendency towards a material balancing of values, which depends on one's own assessment of what is important, and this is almost unavoidably political, even if one is convinced one is dealing with 'purposes of the norm'.

of the constitutional courts (both politically and legally[46]), becomes fuzzy. Therefore it is important to recall that the 'supplementation' of the code legal/illegal and the re-specification of justice as a formula for contingency require conditional programmes.[47] The abstraction of the conditions of legal relevance is a condition of differentiating between 'equal' and 'unequal' and attaching different consequences to them. Conditional programming is not only an instrument for decision-making in relation to 'equal' and 'unequal'. It is also the condition under which the idea of justice can be turned into the form of equality (i.e. equality in accordance with rules). Therefore, equality cannot be found under the circumstances to which the conditions refer[48]—either in the sense of the old principle of justice being exchange or revenge, or in the sense of its being a comparison between the facts of a case and its constituent facts.[49] Rather, equality is given by the form in which conditioned relations are related to each other, by the similarities or differences of the 'ifs' in the conditional programmes.

If all of this applies, it cannot be denied that purpose-specific programmes are also subject to a review in terms of justice. This, however, would not result in a balancing of values but in a reconditioning of them. Justice, then, would not present itself as a mere expediency of purpose-specific programmes or as the immanent limitation of these programmes, such as cost-effectiveness or proportionality of means would be. Justice would be achieved by a supplementary conditioning. It would stipulate, for instance, which facts are required to apply a purpose-specific programme, which are not found to be suitable as legal measures; it would determine the legal suitability of such policies.

In the light of the problems connected with a politically induced increase in both legislative interventions in law and purpose-specific programmes, we can understand how the principle of justice went through a crisis, which could no longer be redressed by natural law. This crisis, however, can be remedied neither by a retreat to ethics nor with a balancing of values. This would only move the problem into the area of the 'legitimacy' of positive law. Since, however, only positive law itself is valid, that is, able to use the

---

[46] For more detail see Ch. 10 on structural couplings.

[47] Kelsen saw a purely logical problem in the relationship between justice as equality and conditional programmes. See Hans Kelsen, 'Das Problem der Gerechtigkeit', in id., *Reine Rechtslehre*, 2nd edn. (Vienna, 1960), 357 and 393; Engl. translation: *Introduction to the Problems of Legal Theory* tr. B. L. Paulson and S. L. Paulson (Oxford 1992). We reject this argument with reference to Derrida's concept of 'supplément'. Kelsen simply did not register which problems were under discussion in relation to logic and paradoxes.

[48] The principle of equality is not a conditional programme; see also Podlech, *Gehalt und Funktionen*.

[49] See, for instance, Karl Engisch, *Logische Studien zur Gesetzesanwendung*, 3rd edn. (Heidelberg, 1963), 22.

symbol of legal validity, one cannot look for criteria of legitimacy outside law but must find them within law.[50] These criteria become relevant if the question arises as to how it is possible to continue making consistent decisions in the face of the increasing complexity of law, and that means distinguishing equal cases from unequal cases. It could be that a law, which is just in this sense, would be ethically preferable as well. But this is not self-evident, as we know from long tradition. A clear division between justice and moral judgement and ethical reflection is not only a matter of the autonomy of the legal system. It also guarantees that a moral judgement on law can be made independently from law, and last but not least, it allows for the possibility of moral dissent in the assessment of legal issues. And this is the precondition for understanding such issues when questions of the moral-ethical quality of justice arise.

IV

The problem of how to find a form for explicating the issue of equality/inequality has a long history, going back more than 2,000 years. As a form found in texts, it has appeared to remain the same. That makes it difficult to recognize the changes that have occurred with the historical transformation from old societies to very differently structured modern ones. To summarize our analysis so far, we once again return to the problem of natural law.

In the context of natural law it was possible to start from the assumption that objects differed because of their essences, that is, they were equal or unequal in themselves. These essences were not at one's disposal. They were considered recognizable—in the mode of a first-order observation. Anyone who found differently was thought to be wrong; and the problem then was only how to find out (by employing the dialectical method or the medieval technique of questioning (*quaestiones*), for example) who was wrong and who was right, as supported by expert opinion and authorities.

Early modern rational law, which still saw itself as operating within natural law, already deviated from this tradition. It generalized and parcelled out individual rights of freedom and equality as fundamental 'human rights' acquired at birth. In complete contrast to the concept of nature used in the natural sciences, what was assumed here to be 'nature' did not contain any information about the limitations imposed by nature. On the contrary, the idea of the natural superiority of certain individuals over others (which is, as we know from experience, an idea always close at hand) was rejected, based on the principles of the natural freedom and equality

[50] The old European tradition had a tendency, at least in one of its strands, to tailor the *ethical* concept of justice to fit the *substance* of law, for instance in the sense that justice related to external conduct (*operationes, actus*) with regard to other people (*ad alterum*) and to that which was owed by law (*sub ratione debiti legalis*), as it is known in the scholastic formulae.

of all people at birth. These principles did not help, however, with an interpretation of law.[51] On the contrary, they proved to be in conflict with the legal order as a whole because legal norms can only be formulated in terms of a limitation of freedom, if at all, and as a reason for unequal treatment.[52] Freedom negates necessity in order to give itself the possibility of being guided by chance, that is, by historical coincidence. This requires, however, that there should be ordered, namely closed, systems, which can guide themselves when the occasion arises. Total freedom would be the same as necessity and, as such, is a paradoxical concept. And equality in every respect would remove the identity that is needed to make decisions about what is equal or unequal. Again this is a paradoxical idea, which pronounces itself to be impossible.

The most important form for the unfolding of these paradoxes in modern times operates on the basis of a historical difference. This difference is expressed in the distinction between the state of nature and the state of civilization. As far as human rights are concerned, freedom is the exclusion of external limitations and equality is the exclusion of inequality. This is the only way in which these rights can be understood abstractly as distinctions and definitions. However, it only leads us back to the old paradox of natural law that law can exist only as a deviation from law. The dissolution of the paradox is achieved by a re-entry of the distinction into what has been distinguished. Freedom must accept legally accepted limitations, and equality must accept legally accepted inequalities. The 'other sides' of freedom and equality are internalized by law and the difference becomes the objective of legal regulation, which has at its disposal both sides of both distinctions. Once again, this confirms the differentiation of the legal system, because regulation has to take place within the legal system. This is a matter of legally valid limitations (and not a matter of reason). And it is a matter of

---

[51] The unquestioningly assumed compatibility of equality and slavery in the United States can serve here as an example. On this 'law at arm's length' in the form of the law on natural equality and its constitutional–political significance around 1800 see Ulrich Scheuner, 'Die Verwirklichung der bürgerlichen Gleichheit', in Günter Birtsch (ed.), *Grund- und Freiheitsrechte im Wandel von Gesellschaft und Geschichte: Beiträge zur Geschichte der Grund- und Freiheitsrechte vom Ausgang des Mittelalters bis zur Revolution von 1848* (Göttingen, 1981), 376–401.

[52] There are numerous variations on this theme and I name only one example: Emile Durkheim mentioned two independent variables in his theory of the constitution of social norms: desire (*désir*) and limitation (*sacré, sanction*). See his treatise 'Détermination du fait moral', in Emile Durkheim, *Sociologie et philosophie* (Paris, 1951), 49–90, and, on this, Francois-André Isambert, 'Durkheim et la sociologie des normes', in François Chazel and Jacques Commaille (eds.), *Normes juridiques et régulation sociale* (Paris, 1991), 51–64. This means (and this may be an overinterpretation because Durkheim does not define the concept of norm and hardly ever uses it): an appreciation of values cannot be established in the condition of unlimited freedom, while norms are the formulation to enhance the relationship between social conditioning and progress.

the difference between legal cases and not a matter of inequality between individuals. One consequence of the unfolding of the paradox is that law as a whole is maintained to be contingent, as is all positive law. The formulation of the starting points for decision-making as principles or rights only serves to camouflage this process.[53] The foundation of law is not an idea that functions as a principle, rather its foundation is a paradox.

If the camouflage is lifted, it becomes evident that the postulate of justice serves as a formula for contingency and it becomes clear how this happens. Contingency has to be accepted in each of its final formulations, since one can always resort to changing the law. Correspondingly, law exposes itself to a second-order observation, in order to be able to decide differently in the contexts of freedom/limitation, or equality/inequality. The same applies to modern society in general as a pervasive form of its operative self-determination. In a strict parallel to the differentiation of functioning systems as a prevailing form of differentiation, society has shifted to a mode of second-order observation. In order to find one's way in challenging, as it were, artificial situations, one must observe the observers. Presumably this is true for all functioning systems.[54] It also applies to what can be called the intellectual discourse of modernity. And it applies to the legal system too.

---

[53] This shrouding of the paradox by re-entry becomes even clearer if—in keeping with the style of moralizing rational law—freedom is not only distinguished from its opposite but a distinction is also made—within itself—between liberty and licentiousness. The distinction between *libertas* and *licentia* was the common property of natural law at the time, developed in the polemics against Hobbes, but it was also used to legitimize insistence on civilized rights of freedom and to disperse political concerns. See, for example, Christian Wolff, *Jus naturae methodo scientifica pertractatum*, pars I, para. 150 f. (Frankfurt, 1740; reprint Hildesheim, 1972), 90; id., *Grundsätze des Natur- und Völkerrechts*, para. 84 (here: freedom and impudence), (Halle, 1754; reprint Hildesheim, 1972), 52. As can be seen from these passages, the paradox of the re-entry, the repetition of the distinction in the distinction, can be used for both radically critical and for rather more conservative-analytical purposes (see on this point Richard Price, *Observations on the Nature of Civil Liberty, the Principles of Government, and the Justice and Policy of the War with America*, 2nd edn. (London, 1776), 12). Meanwhile the critical theorists have also turned conservative. Jürgen Habermas, *Faktizität und Geltung, Beiträge zur Diskurstheorie des Rechts und des demokratischen Rechtsstaats* (Frankfurt, 1992), 51, distinguishes between freedom from arbitrary rule and autonomy, following Kant (without reference to natural law).

[54] See, for instance, on the economic system, Dirk Baecker, *Information und Risiko in der Marktwirtschaft* (Frankfurt, 1988); on families, Niklas Luhmann, 'Sozialsystem Familie', in id., *Soziologische Aufklärung*, vol. 5 (Opladen, 1990), 196–217; on the political system, Niklas Luhmann, 'Gesellschaftliche Komplexität und öffentliche Meinung', in id., *Soziologische Aufklärung*, 170–82; on science, Luhmann, *Die Wissenschaft der Gesellschaft*, esp. 318 and 362. It is a matter of some contention whether the system of medical treatment represents an exception. Here the physician's observation is directed at the patient's body. The physician observes first of all how the patient's body responds to medicine. This means: how the patient's body discriminates, and this means, how the patient's body observes how it is observed. Psychosomatic processes must be taken into consideration but the social interaction with physicians is and remains decidedly difficult and quasi-insensitive.

Every decision on matters of law must put itself in the context of other decisions—we shall examine this in greater detail in Chapter 8 on argumentation. The decision must observe how other observers observe law. These other observers can be legislators, and then the central issue is their intention to change the law; or they can be judicial decision-makers and then the issue is how they defined the problem in a particular case and the reasons they used to support their decision. Common law, above all, has developed a careful, theoretically reflected culture of '*rationes decidendi*' as a consequence of its principle of binding precedent.

In this context the distinction between equal/unequal, that is, the issue of how to find a fair solution to a case assumes a new, contemporary function. There is good reason to believe that a system, which operates on the level of second-order observation, has the tendency to become conservative, that is, to decide in the same manner as the observed observers. For it is in the nature of things that no objection will then be raised. Furthermore, if everything is contingent, that is, if everything could be different, it is equally possible to do things the way they were done before. This applies even more to the legal system, which has differentiated the mechanism for change in the form of laws and contracts and which, in the hierarchy of the courts, has a mechanism which suggests, or even enforces, that the lower instances are guided by the decisions in the superior courts. This tendency to take cues from previous decisions, which is particularly well established in law, is corrected by the formula for contingency.

As decisions have to be made contingently, as is the way with decisions, there is something provocative about the question whether there is a relationship of equality or inequality in the relationship between precedents. The schema equal/unequal introduces a bifurcation into a system, which has good reasons (for instance, the certainty of law) for favouring repetition. A system which is operatively closed to the outside must, in particular, avoid closures inside. Obviously, this is achieved, above all, through those mechanisms that change the conditions of the validity for decisions—legislation and contracts. They are, however, mechanisms which rest on highly uncertain assumptions regarding a highly uncertain future. Therefore a second correction is needed—a subsidiary correction to create a new, open-ended situation—one in which decisions can be made about concrete cases that have already receded into the past. A comparison can be made with respect to the distinction equal/unequal, which distinction must be made over and over again, and which then seems to fulfil this subsidiary correction function. Testing the intentions of the legislator or the party to a contract is only a sensor that helps to establish whether or not an interpretation of the lawmakers' 'will' (regardless of the form it takes) is in line with their intentions (that is, is 'at one' with them). Further retrospective and prospective comparisons can be made in order to preserve the consistency of decisions and to expose decisions to further observation by others.

This understanding of justice is specifically adjusted to the mode of second-order observation. It is meaningful, then, to say that it is a formula for observation intended for the use of courts, for which legislators only supply new test material over and over again.

6   The Evolution of Law

I

The history of law from ancient times to the present is comparatively well known. The available sources, however, have not been evaluated from a theoretical perspective. According to contemporary understanding, only concepts of evolutionary theory are suited to this task. The concept of evolution, however, has been used very imprecisely in the literature (including in the legal literature, in so far as it is used there at all) and has, moreover, been presented in a distorted way in criticizing evolutionary approaches.[1] As far back as the eighteenth century accounts can be found of the evolution of law, by, in particular, Hume, Lord Kames, and Ferguson, who point out features which come close to modern evolutionary theories (such as the lack of a plan, retrospective acknowledgement of achievements, gradual development, accidental triggers, accumulation of wisdom through decisions on a case-by-case basis). However, all these accounts lack a clear structure from the point of view of the theory of difference. The same can be said for the works of the historical school of law in the first half of the nineteenth century.[2] As far as the contemporary literature is concerned, it is apparent that contributions that deal with relatively concrete legal issues or with the 'evolution' of individual legal institutions[3] use the concept of evolution without any theoretical precision, while, on the other hand, the application of Darwin's schema variation/selection/stabilization is not sufficiently well formulated in relation to the legal system.[4] We shall use the concept of evolution in accordance with Darwin's theory of evolution which, despite its need for further improvement, must be counted as

[1] For an overview which is historically far-ranging but limited in its language, see E. Donald Elliott, 'The Evolutionary Tradition in Jurisprudence', *Columbia Law Review* 85 (1985), 38–94. See also the heterogeneity in the more recent literature, as pointed out by Gunther Teubner, *Recht als autopoietisches System* (Frankfurt, 1989), 61, with a call for terminological clarification. There is not even a uniform answer to the question of which system reference could be used as a starting point, and even a socio-biological approach to the discussion is suggested by John H. Beckstrom, *Evolutionary Jurisprudence: Prospects and Limitations of Modern Darwinism throughout the Legal Process* (Urbana, 1989).

[2] See on the comparison between the evolution of language and the evolution of law in this school Alfred Dufour, 'Droit et langage dans l'École historique du Droit', *Archives de philosophie du droit* 19 (1974), 151–80.

[3] See, for example, Robert Charles Clark, 'The Morphogenesis of Subchapter C: An Essay in Statutory Evolution and Reform', *Yale Law Journal* 87 (1977), 90–162; Robert A. Kagan et al., 'The Evolution of State System Courts', *Michigan Law Review* 76 (1978), 961–1005; Ronald A. Heiner, 'Imperfect Decisions and the Law: On the Evolution of Precedent and Rules', *Journal of Legal Studies* 15 (1986), 227–61.

[4] As suggested, for example, by the sociologist Albert G. Keller, 'Law in Evolution', *Yale Law Journal* 28 (1919), 769–83.

among the most important achievements of modern thought.[5] Reference
to the origin of the theory, however, should not be taken as an argument by
analogy but as a pointer to a general evolutionary theory, which can have
many different applications.[6] We prefer this theoretical approach because
it starts out from the theory of difference. Its main theme is not the unity of
history as an evolution from a beginning up until the present day. It is concerned, far more specifically, with the conditions for possible unplanned
changes of structure and with the explanation of diversification or the
increase in complexity.

More recent developments of systems theory do not make it any easier to
express and solve this problem; on the contrary, they make it more difficult. For if one has to start from the assumption that systems are closed and
that their structures are determined, it is far more difficult to understand
(1) how structures can be changed at all, and (2) why it is possible at times
(but not necessarily, or is it?) to detect the direction of those changes, for
instance in the diversification of species or in the increased complexity of
societies. With the growing intensity of the problem, however, the demands
on the theoretical instruments used to solve the problem also increase, as
do the criteria for presenting something as evolutionary theory. Evidently
evolution happens only if both *difference* and *adaptation* are preserved in the
relationship between system and environment, for otherwise the object of
evolution would disappear. But this understanding does not in itself
explain how evolution is possible.

The form that explicates this problem is the distinction between variation and selection. If this distinction is established as a real distinction (for
example, as a distinction between, on the one hand, mutation or genetic
recombination and, on the other, the duration of survival), it necessarily
produces a multiplicity of forms which generates deviations—in relation
both to their points of departure and to differences between the species—
which, in turn, influence evolution itself in the shape of differentiated environmental conditions. Everything else, even the dogma of 'natural selection',
which was so important to Darwin, can be seen as secondary. The problem
of elaborating on these and other aspects of evolutionary theory is shifting
nowadays more and more onto the issue of the relationship between evolutionary theory and systems theory, or more precisely, onto the relationship
between variation/selection and system/environment as different forms of
a theory in need of further fine-tuning.[7] One can talk of 'natural selection'

---

[5] For emphatic support see Ernst Mayr, *Evolution und die Vielfalt des Lebens* (Berlin, 1979).

[6] See in agreement Kelle, *Law in Evolution*, 779.

[7] Evolutionary theory's recent flirtation with games theory is only one example of this state-
ment, beginning with R. C. Lewontin, 'Evolution and the Theory of Games', *Journal of
Theoretical Biology* 1 (1961), 382–403. For games within populations see also John Maynard
Smith, *Evolution and the Theory of Games* (Cambridge, 1982).

in the sense of a selection outside a system only if one defines which system is exposed to selection by the environment.

The question is thus: which features of a system make evolution possible? We want to answer this question by referring to the pressure of selection that arises from the operative closure of systems and their limited complexity in relation to the world. The concept of the autopoietic system will be our guideline and we shall leave aside the further question of whether one can also speak of evolution in relation to certain areas of physics, that is, in relation to the formation of atoms, suns, galaxies, chemical molecules, etc. It is easy to see that the maintenance of autopoiesis, as a *conditio sine qua non* of all evolution, can be equally well achieved with the help of a change of structure or that evolution is compatible with a change of structure. Accordingly evolution will occur if various conditions are met and are coupled conditionally (not necessarily) with each other, namely:

1. *variation* of one autopoietic *element* compared with the hitherto existing pattern of reproduction;
2. *selection* of the *structure* which is now possible as a condition for further reproduction; and
3. *maintenance of the stability* of the system in the sense of dynamic stability, that is, continuation of the autopoietic, structurally determined reproduction in this changed form.

This means, in a further abstraction: *variation* involves the *elements*, *selection* involves the *structures*, *stabilization* involves the *unity of the system*, which reproduces itself autopoietically. All three components form a necessary context (there are no systems without elements, no elements without systems, etc.), and the improbability of evolution is ultimately due to the circumstance that a differentiated leverage of these components is *nonetheless possible*. But how?

We cannot examine here whether the evolution of society can be portrayed with the help of this theory. We assume that this is the case.[8] However, the question then arises whether there are still further evolutions within an evolving society, for example the evolution of the legal system.[9] This problem is directly parallel to the question whether autopoietic systems can, strictly speaking, be found within autopoietic systems, or whether dependence on an environment, which is the internal environment of an autopoietic system, contradicts the concept of autopoiesis. Put more

[8] See Niklas Luhmann and Raffaele De Giorgi, *Teoria della società* (Milan, 1992), 169.

[9] Biologists encounter the same problem in tackling the question whether there is only one overall evolution which has led to the diversity of species on the basis of a strictly uniform procedure of reproduction in a chemical sense, or whether one can also speak of the evolution of individual species or populations when the conditions of bisexual reproduction exclude these systems.

concretely: society communicates and in so doing delineates itself from an external environment. The legal system also communicates and in so doing executes the autopoiesis of society. Society uses language. The legal system also uses language, with only minor variations of the conditions for understanding. Society depends on structural coupling with systems of consciousness. Law likewise. Do these dependencies exclude the existence of an independent evolution of the legal system?[10]

The thesis of an independent autopoiesis of the legal system leads us to affirm the finding of an independent evolution of the legal system.[11] At this point we repeat, once more, that the concept of operative closure does not exclude evolution. Evolution is not a gradual, continuous, seamless increase in complexity but a mode for structural change that is altogether compatible with erratic radical changes ('catastrophes') and with long periods of stagnation ('stasis').[12] Certainly, for a new formation to emerge suddenly, numerous conditions must be met and 'preadaptive advances' must be made.[13] This also applies to the possibilities that a legal system has to establish a level of secondary self-observation on the basis of its long experience in arbitrating normative conflicts with the code legal/illegal. Long before legal coding starts to act in a strictly binary manner, thus becoming logically technical, there is a wealth of legal material recorded in the form of conditional programmes.[14] One knows therefore what is meant (and what is not meant) when observers are instructed to turn to the legal system. The conditional programmes, which are already in practice, thus take on

---

[10] At this point objections are often raised (but why only in relation to these dependencies?) whether there could be an autopoiesis of functional sub-systems. See, for example, in relation to the economy, Josef Wieland, 'Die Wirtschaft als autopoietisches System—Einige eher kritische Überlegungen', *Delfin* X (1988), 18–29; for science, Wolfgang Krohn and Günther Küppers, *Die Selbstorganisation der Wissenschaft* (Frankfurt, 1989), 21; for the legal system, William M. Evan, *Social Structure and Law: Theoretical and Empirical Perspectives* (Newbury Park, 1990), 44. Here the (theoretically unconvincing) argument on 'empirical' evidence plays a part, namely in the shape of the assumption that action can only be observed in individuals. This assumption is doubtful even when applied to illiterate societies. However, to argue like this is to exclude every application of evolutionary theory, in the sense used here, to anything other than biological phenomena.

[11] See also Huntington Cairns, *The Theory of Legal Science* (Chapel Hill, 1941), 29; Richard D. Schwartz and James C. Miller, 'Legal Evolution and Societal Complexity', *American Journal of Sociology* 70 (1964), 159–69.

[12] Perhaps this is, indeed, the typical case. See Niles Eldredge and Stephan Jay Gould, 'Punctuated Equilibria: An Alternative to Phyletic Gradualism', in Thomas J. M. Schopf (ed.), *Models in Paleobiology* (San Francisco, 1972), 82–115.

[13] Hegel's analyses, which are related to the transitional problems dictated by his theory, can be understood in precisely this sense; as, for instance, the beginnings of symbolic aesthetics in his lectures on aesthetics, quoted in the Frankfurt edition 1970, vol. 1 (*Werke*, vol. 13), p. 418. For preadaptive advances of an autopoiesis of the system of fine arts see Hans Belting, *Bild und Kunst: Eine Geschichte des Bildes vor dem Zeitalter der Kunst* (Munich, 1990).

[14] See for the detailed account Ch. 4.IV above.

the function of regulating the allocation of legal and illegal, and mature with that function. A further evolutionary leap, which takes all this apparatus as its basis, occurs when the legal system is obliged to defend its autonomy in a new context, that of the functional differentiation of society.[15] Whenever an autopoietic system achieves operative closure for the first time or when it has to maintain its closure and restructure its closure in the face of radically changed social contexts, it does not happen as a planned reorganization but through an evolutionary restructuring of established installations.[16]

However, recognizing the compatibility of systems theory and evolutionary theory is not sufficient in itself. Further, one must be able to demonstrate *how* evolution occurs at the level of a system. If one succeeds with such an attempt, that success would be another argument for the assumption of an independent autopoiesis of the legal system.

II

Before we begin our study of how the evolutionary functions of variation, selection, and stabilization are differentiated in the case of the legal system, we must spell out just how the structures of legal systems were established so that they became subject to the impact of evolution. One obvious suggestion here concerns the existence of written records, but a closer look shows that this raises rather complex questions.[17]

Writing operates as a social memory with the advantage that it keeps knowledge readily available for unexpected, optional access. Of course, the advent of social memory existed in society before the invention of writing. The assumption is often made that these societies had to rely exclusively on the psychical memory of individuals. This, however, was not the case. Social

---

[15] Even in this difficult transitional period of turning the political system into statehood, the autopoiesis of law prevails in its evolution, see Rudolf Stichweh, 'Selbstorganisation and die Entstehung nationaler Rechtssysteme (17.–19. Jahrhundert)', *Rechtshistorisches Journal* 9 (1990), 254–72.

[16] There is a similar problem structurally in the jurisprudential discussion, namely the question whether one can talk of, or how one can detect, how customary law develops or changes even if a practice which deviates from law cannot, according to general opinion, form law and even if an error of law is excluded as a source of law (D.1.3.39: 'Quod non ratione introductum, sed errore primum. deinde consuetudine optentum est, in aliis similibus non optinet'). See also Friedrich Carl von Savigny, *System des heutigen Römischen Rechts*, vol. 1 (Berlin, 1840), 14: 'die unzweifelhafte Thatsache, daß überall, wo ein Rechtsverhältnis zur Frage und zum Bewußtsein kommt, eine Regel für dasselbe längst vorhanden, also jetzt erst zu erfinden weder nöthig noch möglich ist' ('the undeniable fact that whenever the question of a legal relationship is raised or is brought to attention, the rule for it has long since been established and it is neither necessary nor possible to invent it.').

[17] See for a first overview Jack Goody, *Die Logik der Schrift und die Organisation von Gesellschaft* (Frankfurt, 1990), 211.

memory was formed by handing on available knowledge, that is, by the *temporal delay* of performances of psychological memory in sequences of their activation. This sequencing achieves a gain in time and this makes it possible to sustain knowledge even as times passes.[18] This form of temporal memory, however, had distinct disadvantages, which were especially apparent in areas in which it was important to treat uncertainty or disputes with reference to complex bodies of non-contestable knowledge, i.e. divination and law. Here we find a relatively early move to other forms of knowledge storage, namely written records, which could be activated by a specific means of access when an unpredictable situation arose.

Writing is, like the ephemeral sounds of oral communication, a mechanism of the structural coupling of physics, consciousness, and the communication of physiological, psychological, and social realities. Seen from this perspective, writing achieves a great deal more than that which it expresses. It achieves, above all, a differentiation of texts, which can serve as the *identical* foundation for the formation of *different* opinions. In order to achieve this, writing presumes an 'espace blanc' as an 'infinité marqué et marquable',[19] that is, an unmarked space which can be crossed to reach a marked space, by at the same time producing and defining a marker.[20] Only in a medium of possible markers are markers possible which, in all their various possible combinations, provide a medium for the form which, in its turn, appears as text.

The physical form of medium/form–form gives writing its consistency— it exists quite regardless of whether it is used in communication—or it dissolves. In its physical features, writing belongs to the environment of the communication system. Judging by these features, writing cannot be a component of social communication. The communication system only 'assimilates' writing, in the words of Jean Piaget, by using it as information.[21] This assimilation only relates to the meaning of writing, not to its physics.[22] This is why writing can guarantee a consistency, which does not hinder the differentiated recall of information in the closed context of the communication of the system and which makes it possible for the system to condense

[18] See on 'transmission delay' as a form of 'temporal memory' Klaus Krippendorff, 'Some Principles of Information Storage and Retrieval in Society', *General Systems* 20 (1975), 15–35, at 19.

[19] This formulation is used by Julia Kristeva, *Semeiotikè: Recherche pour une sémanalyse* (Paris, 1969), 315.

[20] This is the terminology of George Spencer Brown, *Laws of Form* (reprint 1979).

[21] This applies even if the form of writing and its visual layout, etc. play an important role in communication, as has often been pointed out recently.

[22] There is a similar distinction in the membranes of cells. Here, too, physical objects are integrated in the closed context of metabolism and the reproduction of cells without being changed. See Jean-Claude Tabary, 'Interface et assimilation, état stationaire et accommodation', *Revue internationale de systémique* 3 (1989), 273–93.

its identities in the recursive use of meaning. Writing makes it easier to re-access meaningful subject matter and makes it harder to forget it (beneficial as that might sometimes be).[23]

Writing makes communication independent of the time at which a message was written and thus largely independent of the sender's intentions too. Whether these intentions matter or not, is open to interpretation. The situational and intentional evidence ceases to count and must be replaced by the clarity of the statement and the directives for its interpretation. All participants in this communication, including the one who authored it, must be treated as 'absent'.[24]

Long before writing was used for communication, it served to document information that was worth recording. Legal issues are among the earliest matters deemed appropriate for the development and use of writing.[25] As far as we know today, this did not apply so much to laws as such—because a concept for law had yet to be developed in a written culture—but rather to legally relevant transactions of all kinds, that is, to records of obligations of performance, contracts, wills—in brief, everything that was mentioned above under the heading of change in legal validity. Recent research indicates a close relationship between early scripts and divination practices[26] that tried to find answers to questions about the unknown in various situations in everyday life.[27] There are some indications that writing developed through the stabilization of forms used in divination.[28] Moreover, the use of writing in the context of divinatory practices became widespread, with the transition to phonetic writing in Mesopotamia being part of this

---

[23] We say 'harder' for it has to be added that written legal documents can be forgotten or became obsolete. This applies especially to the period before the invention of printing. See Mario Bretone, 'Le norme e il tempo fra tradizione classica e coscienza moderna', *Materiali per una storia della cultura giuridica* 19 (1989), 7–26.

[24] Derrida takes this idea as his point of departure in his radicalization of the concept 'écriture'. See especially Jacques Derrida, *De la grammatologie* (Paris, 1967); id., 'Signature, événement, contexte', in id., *Marges de la philosophie* (Paris, 1972), 365–93, at 376.

[25] As far as the registration of transactions is concerned, this presumably even holds true of a period which goes thousands of years back before the invention of writing, that is, to the beginnings of the neolithic age. See on this point Denise Schmandt-Besserat, 'An Archaic Recording System and the Origin of Writing', *Syro-Mesopotamian Studies* 1/2 (1977), 1–32.

[26] We are content to use the international term 'divination' rather than 'prophecy'.

[27] See above all Jean-Pierre Vernant et al., *Divination et rationalité* (Paris, 1974).

[28] See, in relation to China, Léon Vandermeersch, 'De la tortue à l'achillée: Chine', in Vernant et al., *Divination et rationalité*, 29–51. We also find here, incidentally, a good example of the evolution of writing. Characters were originally generated through the imitation of patterns found on bones and on tortoises if they were prepared in a certain way. They are read in great numbers, and enriched with meaning, as ideograms, and turned into independent writing. The suddenness of the generation of a rather complex writing cannot be explained any other way. Writing requires the 'preadaptive advance' of a rationalized divination practice, which extends to many situations in everyday life.

process.[29] In these early high cultures legal problems arose as divination problems, that is, as problems of finding out what had happened and how fault and innocence were to be distributed by relying on a close analogy to favourable and unfavourable circumstances.[30] In this way law participated in the increase in complexity and rationalization as well as in the increase in professional expertise which had been developed for the purposes of divination; and writing served as a record of the requisite knowledge in both these contexts. Thus the written records which have come to light, for instance the famous code of Hammurabi, were not laws in our sense, that is, they were not records of laws which had been enacted or authorized. In their form of if/then they corresponded exactly to the normal rules of divination and were used in this context to solve problems in cases, including in judicial practice.[31] The generalization of case law and the binary coding of favourable and unfavourable signs and symbols were created primarily for the purposes of divination, and law benefited from the associated push towards the increased complexity and sophistication of writing.

In other words, there existed a legal culture and associated expertise which developed with the help of writing, long before written records were recognized as a condition for legal validity. Even the Roman *stipulatio* was a unilaterally binding statement, which was made in an oral form but could also be written down for purposes of evidence. The written record did not dispense with the requirement that witnesses be present.[32] Written documentation, however, had the great advantage—and this may explain its early use in legal matters—of *highlighting deviations* that could easily get lost in the heat of contentious oral debate. In this respect writing also serves as a proactive and conflict-avoiding record. (On the other hand, as is pointed out time and again in antiquity, writing lends itself much more readily to deception and fraud than does communication between witnesses.) It is

---

[29] See Jean Bottéro, 'Symptômes, signes, écritures en Mésopotamie ancienne', in Vernant et al., *Divination et rationalité*, 70–197. See also further relevant references in Bottéro, Mésopotamie: *L'écriture, la raison et les dieux* (Paris, 1987), 133 and 157.

[30] See Bottéro, 'Symptômes', 142 who calls it 'identité formelle entre justice et divination'.

[31] See Jean Bottéro, 'Le "Code" Hammu-rabi', *Annali della Scuola Normale Superiore di Pisa* 12/1 (1988), 409–44, reprint in id., *Mésopotamie*, 191–223. Bottéro interprets the code as a self-aggrandizement of the king, as a kind of political will which indicates how legal decisions had guaranteed order.

[32] In commercially highly developed Athens, differently from in Rome, this stage seems to have been reached in the middle of the fourth century BC; Athens was engaged in long-distance commerce and depended on it and witnesses are, of course, only a locally useful legal institution. See, for instance, Fritz Pringsheim, 'The Transition from Witnesses to Written Transactions in Athens', in *Gesammelte Abhandlungen*, vol. 2 (Heidelberg, 1961), 401–09. See also William V. Harris, *Ancient Literacy* (Cambridge, 1989), esp. p. 68, and generally on the history of the increasing literacy in Greek law Michael Gagarin, *Early Greek Law* (Berkeley, 1986), 51, 81, and 121.

only relatively recently that writing has also assumed the function of 'publication' and 'revelation' of the law. A handful of expert scribes are sufficient to point out any concrete deviations from law; widespread literacy is necessary to make the law public.

While oral cultures depend on strict repetition (no matter how fictitious) to memorize things, for instance in ritual form, there is a greater degree of latitude with written documents because of their ability to be used in new or unforeseen situations, with the proviso, however, that the texts themselves have been carefully drafted. They have to be understandable in their own right and must set limits to how they can be interpreted. Above all, they have to eliminate contradictions and ensure sufficient consistency. Jan Assman has called this the 'transition from the dominance of repetition to the dominance of recall, from ritual to textual coherence'.[33] In very early times, as far back as the beginnings of written culture, the use of writing in legal matters served mainly, as mentioned above, to clarify and highlight possible deviations. And this was the extent of the development in those writing cultures. For their purposes it was sufficient to archive the documents only for the short period for which their context was topical. Originally the written form was not intended as a way of preserving a text for all foreseeable future applications, that is, for a free and active reinterpretation.[34] Only much later was writing given a further function, namely that of documenting a change of law or confirmation of law; and only then could writing become a *condition for the validity of law* because the written form could be identified relatively easily. It is only on this basis that *lex scripta* and *leges non scriptae* can be distinguished because there may also have been written records, speeches in courts, court records, collections of expert opinions, etc., behind such laws.[35] Long before an elaborate legal

---

[33] See Jan Assman, *Das kulturelle Gedächtnis: Schrift, Erinnerung und politische Identität in frühen Hochkulturen* (Munich, 1992), 17 and 18 (quoted at p. 18).

[34] On the slowness of this development, even when directed by literacy, and on the problems of archiving legal texts in Athens, see Rosalind Thomas, *Oral Tradition and Written Record in Classical Athens* (Cambridge, 1989), 34; Harris, *Ancient Literacy*.

[35] This distinction was a reason for the *criticism* of the literacy of law in Athens (among other things in relation to the possibilities of falsification and problems of interpretation). Thus unwritten law acquired an aura of 'superiority'. See John Walter Jones, *The Law and Legal Theory of the Greeks: An Introduction* (Oxford, 1956), 26; Jacqueline de Romilly, *La loi dans la pensée grecque des origines à Aristote* (Paris, 1971), 27. A related doctrine can be found even today in Jewish law. The law had been revealed for oral and written transmission on Mount Sinai. Jahwe, who was—according to his nature—supposed to be time and thus also the future, was supposed to have been aware of the need to create a flexible, adaptable law, that is, law which would leave room for interpretation at the expense of an incomplete and possibly controversial reproduction of law. See George Horowitz, *The Spirit of Jewish Law* (New York, 1953; reprint New York, 1973); Eliezer Berkowitz, *Not in Heaven: The Nature and Function of Halakha* (New York, 1983); Geza Vermes, 'Scripture and Tradition in Judaism: Written and Oral Torah', in Gerd Baumann (ed.), *The Written Word: Literacy in Transition* (Oxford, 1986),

culture existed, 'laws' were passed on verbally and in writing, one notable example being the Ten Commandments. New measures became necessary to stop people doubting these laws. This is difficult when written material is involved (for the simple reason that it gives people more time to think about it). To deal with this problem, an additional religious semantic was injected into the texts, mainly as a reference to a distant source of validity (or at any rate to a source which was in the past and thus no longer accessible) with corresponding myths concerning the origin of those texts. The semantics for all the divinatory practices which tried to find the unknown in the known were replaced by a new religion which measured, rejected, or accepted human practice in the light of God's will. Unlike in secular interaction, the written text became the familiar form of this religion, symbolizing the unfamiliar in the familiar, the secret in the revealed, and the transcendent in the immanent.[36]

The preservation of 'political' laws in writing, for instance Solon's Laws, is a comparatively recent product of evolution. It depends on legitimized proceedings. Because it does not cover all that can claim to be the law it causes all the problems of a written text that is unequivocal in its choice of words. After the Laws of Solon there developed the doctrine of *agraphoi nomoi*, to which a higher rank was attributed, starting the long tradition of the search for 'higher', 'extra-legal' foundations for law.[37] Obviously it is only after the introduction of writing that one can talk of an oral

79–95. There is an assumption here that the precept of oral doctrine and tradition does not exclude the recording of opinions in notes, glosses, and commentaries. Finally, for the common law see Sir Matthew Hale, *The History of the Common Law of England*, first published (posthumously) in 1713, quoted from the edition by Charles M. Gray, Chicago 1971, at 16: *Lex scripta* is defined as 'Statutes or Acts of Parliament which in their original Formation are reduced into Writing, and are so preserved in their Original Form and in the Same Stile and Words wherein they were first made'. There may well also be written material about the *leges scriptae* but it is not relevant to the identity and validity of the meaning of texts, and is only a form for the handing on of meaning.

[36] On this form of presentation of religious meaning see also Niklas Luhmann, 'Die Ausdifferenzierung der Religion', in id., *Gesellschaftsstruktur und Semantik*, vol. 3 (Frankfurt, 1989), 259–357. The Greek *symbólaion* has here the secularized meaning of a written contract (alongside the more common *syngraphé*) and this means the unity of something that is separated, or the possible proof of this unity.

[37] Possibly the best-known case of the claim to the higher ranking of unwritten law is that of Antigone. But it is directed typically against 'modern' tyranny. See explicitly on the topic of the old-fashioned use of language in written law which requires an interpretation, that is, a distinction between text and meaning: Lysias, *Against Theomnestus* I. 6–7, quoted from the edition of the Loeb Classical Library (London, 1957), 106. Incidentally, one can still find in Lysias' distinction between written and unwritten law the hint of a fundamental religious meaning (albeit for rhetorical reasons) when he stresses in *Against Androcines* 10, Loef edn., p. 121, that penance is also due to the gods for violating their law. Finally, it is evident that only a culture of literacy can speak of 'unwritten law'.

tradition—regardless of how one evaluates its importance—that is, after the distinction written/oral became available;[38] in this sense, every emphatic reminiscence, and every canonization of an oral tradition is the historical recall of a literate society (for instance, the oral part of the Torah is like a back-projection of the Talmud).

It must have been a 'catastrophe' for oral societies and their use of law when law became valid as a written text (and 'valid' is used here as discussed above in Chapter 2.VIII). It meant adjusting to a different principle of stability and to a radical change in the conceptual boundaries of everything that was meaningful to them, including a new attitude to religion, which excluded contingency and reconditioned its admission. Clearly the growing use of writing ran parallel to society's shift from a segmental to a stratifying differentiation, which, in its turn, encouraged the spread of literacy. This led to an unprecedented concentration of material and symbolic (rhetorical) resources in the upper classes, or, when the stratification was less pronounced, in a dominant bureaucracy.[39] However, this is a rather superficial explanation, which does not tell us much about the present day. For it goes almost without saying that all forms of communication are tightly linked to the forms of differentiation in their respective societies. As a study of the legal issues surrounding divination shows, the transition to urbanization and stratification, to the formation of empires and the endogamy of classes, was not enough to produce the differentiation of a special legal system, as happened in the form of the Roman civil law and then again with the medieval systematization of law. However, if writing is available in an easily understandable (phonetic, alphabetical) form, then—and then only—is a medium created in which legal texts can be distinguished from all other texts. Only then can law become autonomous in the sense that it not only uses writing but also depends on a kind of text which can be distinguished from other kinds of text. In view of this recent historical development, we must analyse the achievement of written law more thoroughly.

If meaning becomes set through writing, it is passed on in a process of repeated reading, of condensation and amplification of meaning. 'The original sign plus its reading constitutes an expanded structure. The expanded structure is composed of the sign and some form of response to it. This is the heart of cultural evolution.'[40] Owing to this expansion, the

---

[38] See Niklas Luhmann, 'The Form of Writing', *Stanford Literature Review* 9 (1992), 25–42.

[39] Peter Goodrich, *Reading the Law* (Oxford, 1986), deduces from this a *pervasive* connection between law, literacy, and the symbolic-repressive political use of power; but, of course, this tends to mystify the very concept of power.

[40] Dean MacCannell and Juliet F. MacCannell, *The Time of the Sign: A Semiotic Interpretation of Modern Culture* (Bloomington, 1982), 26. Further on, the authors call this the 'self-reading of culture'.

mechanisms of evolution are able to take hold and to select. There is hardly any research on the conditional relationship between an interpretation of texts (hermeneutics) and evolution (in a Darwinian sense);[41] but in both the circularity of the hermeneutical development of meaning and the autopoiesis of systems it is not hard to see the possibilities for responding relatively quickly to (equally sudden) changes in the environment.

At any rate, the access to law became both more open and more limited with writing, and the question since has been: access for whom? Law became enclosed in the written form and, through that, differentiated as a form. This made it easy to *distinguish* law but that does not necessarily mean that it became easier to find out what the valid law was. It was no longer readily available for the formulation of normative expectations, for which one could find support in social situations. Law could no longer be simply counted by the number of 'oath helpers' which a party could muster. 'The Code encodes the law, it secludes it in a new form and guards it with a new class of interpreters.'[42] On the other hand, the function of writing is premised on the fact that one knows that the written sign is not the law itself but only its expression. Like the evolution of language, the evolution of writing produces a difference. This evolution is dependent on the distinction working, the sign not being mistaken for its meaning and people being able to rely, in everyday life, on the fact that others can use this difference as well. Writing can too easily be copied and too easily destroyed for the artefact of the sign to matter much. But in that case, why have writing? Why have the duplication of the spoken word in signs? Or, more particularly: what is the eigenvalue [the function which under a given operation generates a multiple of itself] of the difference between written *and* oral communication?

It is worthwhile first to ask to which demands writing is a response. It then becomes clear that, together with an interest in representations of recall, it is *norm-typical* problems that have created this demand. This is linked with the *expectation of disappointment*, which is the core reason for communicating expectations in a normative style. This relates to a time difference, which needs to be bridged. The information, which says that a particular expectation conforms to the law, or not, must be able to serve twice (or more times) as information—at the time of its presentation and whenever disappointing conduct turns out to be the result. Deeds can be recorded, be it in the Quipu of the Incas or any other place, to remove any future doubt whether these deeds were really carried out. Similarly, laws serve as information that is used *over and over again*, whereas a piece of information usually loses its value if it is communicated time and time

---

[41] But see, for at least a few suggestions, L. L. Salvador, 'Evolution et herméneutique: vers une écosystémique de la cognition', *Revue internationale de systémique* 6 (1992), 185–203.

[42] Goodrich, *Reading the Law*, 27.

again. In other words, it is the precarious, contra-factual stability of normative expectations that is balanced by writing. As one never knows whether one's expectations will be met, and as one is reluctant to give in and learn from experience when they are not met, there is an advantage to be gained from being able, if necessary, to repeat the information about what is legal.

Thus it would be taking a rather simplistic view if one were to be satisfied with this reference to the stability of written signs. There is no interest in the stability of meaning in the dynamically stabilized, autopoietic social system. The issue here is the prospect of *repeated* interest in the *same information* and not simply the notion that the enduring is better than the transient. And this is why representations of norms were the first to create the acute need to couple the now with the later. The use of writing in the area of cognitive expectation (in the sense of *aletheia,* namely to save this information from oblivion) followed much later and required a high degree of adaptation of written signs to the diversity of expressions in the spoken language, for instance by phonetic character.

All this is not to say that writing brought the desired certainty to law. If it had, legal systems would not have evolved. It also did nothing to remove the uncertainty as to whether normative expectations might not be met at some point in the future or might not later be recognized as legitimate/ illegitimate. All writing did was to transform the uncertainty and substitute a new difference, namely the difference between sign and meaning. A written text, once it is taken into the context of meaningful communication, that is, when it is read, written, or quoted, etc., opens up and organizes references to possible meaning. Furthermore, this is a double process of reduction and creation of complexity, the creation of complexity through reduction. The difference between medium and form is doubled in the medium of meaning. New distinctions emerge in which the text occupies one side of the form and opens up the other: the distinction between text and interpretation, the distinction between text and context, the distinction between verbal and intended meaning. These are the largely overlapping distinctions which expose the written law to evolution, even and especially if the written body of law is passed on intact.

Written texts give us cause to review continuously the law in the light of new distinctions. With these distinctions, limits are set to the task of interpretation. This is the form in which the validity of law is accounted for. For instance, the form cannot be modified by an interpretation when there is a clear meaning (such as a statute of limitation). On the other hand, the question whether the meaning is absolutely clear is in itself open to interpretation.[43] Thus,

---

[43] See on this point Karl Clauss, 'Die Sens-clair-Doktrine als Grenze und Werkzeug', in Huber Hubien (ed.), *Le raisonnement juridique: Actes du Congrès Mondiale de Philosophie du Droit et de Philosophie Sociale, Brussels, 30.8.-3.9.1971* (Brussels, 1971), 251–5.

the interpretation remains sovereign even in its self-limitation. It applies to law as a whole and not only to those parts where the records are unclear.

It follows that all written law is law that requires interpretation. As soon as this was recognized, texts were expected to authorize their own interpretation, for instance to spell out who was in charge of the interpretation and how the interpretation had to be conducted. In selecting this 'who' and 'how', law, written law included, adapted to the evolutionary changes in society, even after legislation was introduced to change texts in their written form.[44] Every valid text is exposed to interpretation, and is indeed text only in the context of interpretation. In this sense the text constitutes a new medium, namely the totality of the interpretations which refer to it, and new forms can condense in this new medium, whether as intriguing, attention-hogging controversies (to take but one example, the 'original intent' controversy in the interpretation of the constitution of the United States), or as theories which are derived from the interpretation of texts and become accepted by 'dominant opinion'.

All legal evolution—above all, the unique evolution of Roman civil law over 2,000 years, but also the evolution towards law in modern society, in which legislation is beginning to drive evolution with consequences which are as yet difficult to ascertain—has been made possible by the difference between text and interpretation, and this has had a decisive impact on the form of outcomes.

III

As with autopoietic systems, the conditions for evolution are a product of evolution. This applies also to the difference between text and interpretation, which we have just discussed. But further amplification of the conditions of evolution, of the impact on elements (variation), the impact on structures (selection) and integration in the autopoiesis of the reproductive context of complex systems (restabilization), also comes about as a product of social evolution. The threshold for the autonomy of the evolution of law is given by the operative closure of the legal system. When we address individual evolutionary mechanisms, we have to keep the historicity of history in mind.

The decisive variation, as far as the evolution of law is concerned, relates to the communication of unexpected normative expectations. This probably happens retrospectively most of the time and is occasioned by conduct, which—with hindsight—turns out to be a disappointment. This

---

[44] Evidently, the problem culminates when legislation is insufficient or only barely sufficient, namely in the interpretation of *codifications* and, today increasingly, in the interpretation of *constitutions*.

disappointment brings to mind the norm, which did not exist as a structure for communication in society before this occurred.[45] *Ex facto ius orietur.* Such events happen as soon as there are normative expectations, that is, in all societies we can identify this in a historical retrospective. A variation of this kind does not even depend on a distinction being made in society between rules and conduct. It is sufficient for one to see a reason to reject certain conduct and to be successful in having this rejection accepted by others. The formation of structures and the change of structures are hard to separate if structural effects are to be discerned. Undifferentiated societies solve this problem by constructing a suitable story around such events. Variation and selection cannot be distinguished, and what is eventually passed on as expectation depends on a number of situational and socio-structural conditions. Even if orientation towards valid law is excluded, for whatever reason, one still finds exactly the same structure today, namely the tendency to create some form of ambivalence by accusation and counter-accusation, the introduction of further facts, and the realignment of the attribution of causes. Thus the tendency is to work against the assumption that only one party is right and consequently the other is wrong.[46] The reason underlying this is that accusations, on the other side of the form, are always at the same time self- justifications—and vice versa. This elementary mechanism undercuts the seemingly fixed and objective code of legal/illegal and creates ambivalence in the shape of the question of which norm can actually be applied to the case. The point of departure for an evolution that attempts to reduce the pressure for clarification may lie in this pressure-inducing tendency to make the reference to norms ambivalent.

In simple circumstances, one cannot really find out whether someone who offends against order—for whatever reason—simply goes ahead and does it, or actually does it in the belief that he is right. If caught, he will try to defend himself and will thus cooperate in the repair or the modification of the contemplated order.[47] However, in the absence of a differentiated

---

[45] We shall apply this observation to the evolution of 'human rights' in the modern global society in Ch. 12.V.

[46] See on this point Heinz Messmer, 'Unrecht und Rechtfertigung' (Doctoral thesis, Bielefeld 1993), which contains an overview of the relevant research. The study addresses attempts to avoid criminal proceedings in cases of juvenile delinquency by using perpetrator–victim conferences.

[47] Situations like these have been discussed in the sociological literature under the keyword 'neutralization'; the accused accepts the difference between law and non-law and thus defers to law; but he or she tries to find arguments (joint guilt, presentation of different causalities, etc.) that 'neutralize' this difference. See above all Gresham M. Sykes and David Matza, 'Techniques of Neutralization', *American Sociological Review* 22 (1957), 664–70; David Matza, *Delinquency and Drift* (New York, 1964), see especially on 'moral holiday' at p. 184. The reason for this form of presentation is that the accused always operates in other roles according to the norms and that he or she, most importantly, depends on the norm-conformist conduct of others.

legal structure, one laid down in a written text, legal conflicts are barely distinguishable from simple expectations, where the person who appears to offend against law and order has no legal claim. The multifunctional contexts of all social arrangements (especially, of course, family and religious arrangements) make it difficult to establish a stable set of rules, as the situations in which people have recourse to these arrangements differ widely from each other and thus appear not to be comparable or easily aligned.[48] This has nothing to do with inadequate procedural rules or the trend in proceedings towards opportunistic conflict-resolution, but is the consequence of the multifunctional embedding of all those points of view which could provide support. This is also the reason why contemporary observers of these societies might gain the impression that there was no law or only repressive, criminal law.[49] And it is the reason why the use of writing does not start 'from the top down' with the documentation of the most important rules and laws, but 'from the bottom up', with the evidentiary documentation of events, such as promises or performances. All the more remarkable, then, is the early development of a law of transactions in Asia Minor, which overcame such barriers, as did Roman civil law (apparently, largely independently from the former).

The departure point for the evolution of law is this initially barely marked distinction between uncontested and contested cases of disappointment. Only if conflicts can be verbalized and only if troublemakers defend themselves and try to achieve some recognition of their exceptional

---

[48] This has been captured accurately by Sally Falk Moore, 'Descent and Legal Position', in Laura Nader (ed.), *Law in Culture and Society* (Chicago, 1969), 374–400, at 276: 'the more multiplex the social relations, the more contingencies there are that may affect any particular act or transaction. This multiplicity not only makes it difficult to state norms precisely, but sometimes it may even make it impossible, since the assortment of contingencies can vary so much from one case to another.' Even in these societies there are rules with almost juridical quality, namely those that refer to the inclusion of persons in sub-systems of society. But these rules become evident as the acquired or achieved quality of persons and do not have any immediate legal consequences.

[49] Thus the research on law in undifferentiated societies was guided by the question whether one could even call it law if there were no fixed rules and frequently not even the possibility to distinguish between the quality of conduct and rules. Using this approach, social anthropologists have addressed the question of how conflicts are treated and resolved in disputes—with or without rules, which were evident from case to case. See, for instance, Max Gluckman, *The Judicial Process among the Barotse of Northern Rhodesia* (Manchester, 1955); Paul J. Bohannan, *Justice and Judgment among the Tiv* (London, 1957); Lloyd Fallers, *Law without Precedent: Legal Ideas in Action in the Courts of Colonial Busoga* (Chicago, 1969); Philip Gulliver, 'Structural Dichotomy and Jural Processes among the Aruscha of Northern Tanganyika', *Africa* 31 (1961), 19–35; id., 'Dispute Settlements without Courts: The Ndendeuli of Southern Tanzania', in Nader, *Law in Culture and Society* 24–68; Leopold Pospisil, *Kapauku Papuans and their Law* (1958; reprint New Haven, 1964). See also, for even more archaic conditions, Ronald M. Berndt, *Excess and Restraint: Social Control among a New Guinean Mountain People* (Chicago, 1962).

circumstances or even claim to have special rights, can a second-order observation arise, because only then is one obliged to decide who is in a legal position and who is in an illegal position. Only situations such as these lead to a gradual increase in critical confrontation with problems or to the development of the schema of rule/exception. In tribal societies proceedings relating to transactions and the ensuing demand for decision-making were created even when there was neither 'political' authority for collectively binding decisions nor a recursive network for argumentation based on written texts.

This point of departure can be put more abstractly. The evolutionary achievements of language and law not only adjust society as a collection of living beings to its environment *structurally* but also enable *transient* adjustments to deal with *transient* situations. As soon as conflicts explode, they have to be solved, or at least diffused, case by case. This does not necessarily require the rigid preservation of a set of decision-making rules which can be passed on from case to case, let alone a set of environmentally adjusted norms. However, the greater density of such problems leads to the demand for stable orientations, which can be formed in many ways, whether in the form of a situationally and pragmatically developed knowledge of divination, or in the form of normative principles. Both these scenarios result in the type of relationship with the evolution of writing discussed above. Evolutionary achievements, which are successful under these circumstances, must be able to provide transient problems with patterns of solutions that are available to be recorded, but also potentially to be redundant, and which thus combine both variability and stability.

Any further development depends, however, on the differentiation of interacting systems, which allow for the negotiation of solutions to conflicts of norms.[50] Then communication becomes possible, which first attempts just to mediate (not very differently from the negotiations that result in a contract),[51] but which—with the addition of further conditions—can also aim to find out who is in a legal position and who is in an illegal position. Then more is at stake than just pacifying the wrath of Achilles. Here procedures are at stake, which must lead to decisions on the issue of legal and illegal. With this task in mind an understanding of viewpoints develops

---

[50] Here and in what follows, we leave aside equivalent divination practices which were definitely functional but point out that societies which cultivated this orientation (for example, China) and developed their literacy on this basis had much less need of an elaborate legal culture.

[51] This is evident from a large number of studies on currently still existing tribal societies (see for references above n. 49) which, however, hardly bear the marks of their original conditions but are societies which live (especially in Africa) under the influence of high cultures and more recently under the influence of colonial regimes and are, therefore, really parts of global society.

which are situationally invariable and reusable, and they help to confirm the law when variations occur. In this respect, too, it all depends on how expectations can be maintained. Only in the case of deviation do expectations turn into norms and only in the case of variation does an interest develop in the choice of reusable viewpoints.

No 'natural' points of view for such a selection exist in the minds of people, as was assumed in older natural law theories. No society can found its law on consensus if one means by that that all of the people will agree to all of the norms all of the time. Such a fixation with such states of mind is not achievable and, even if it were achievable, it would not be ascertainable. Thus consensus cannot be a condition for the validity of law and would, incidentally, exclude any possibility for evolution. Evolution depends, *instead*, on how the problem of social reconciliation is solved. This is the aim of the development of norms of competence, and of the proceedings that limit the former. Before the advent of proceedings, one had to operate with the presumption of consensus and a successful disregard for those who dissent. Moreover, proceedings make it possible that *a few people* (judges, legislators) take the validity of norms as binding *for all of the people* and for those few to make the correspondingly relevant decisions. Compared with the mere presumption of consensus, this principle of 'a few for all people' allows for a higher specification of norms and thus a sophisticated awareness of legal problems and the inadequacies of a wide array of norms. Presumptions of consensus do not become dispensable in this way. There is only a clarification (and with that possibly also a question) as to who defines those presumptions and to what they ought to refer.

Obviously there are certain preconditions for the emergence of proceedings and with them the principle of 'a few for all people'. They require at least that there be societies based on rank with status roles, if not even stratification with status families and the possibility of different members of a leading social class (aristocracy, patricians in city-states) occupying these roles. Reading and competence in writing were added to this requirement in the further course of evolution. Only via the detour of the clerical structure of the Middle Ages did legal roles become increasingly independent of status at birth, and thus accessible to upwardly mobile individuals. And not until the functional differentiation of society is fully established can the principle of 'a few for all people' be replaced by the person-neutral principle: the legal system for society.

But perhaps we are moving on too quickly. Initially the evolution of proceedings, in the sense of goal-oriented, differentiated, decision-seeking episodes in the legal system, led to a clearer visibility of the processes of selection. Through this, the evolutionary functions of variation and selection were separated. Variation attended to the mutation of law (which is largely unsuccessful but occasionally can be confirmed). Without it, no evolutionary changes would be possible. Selection attends to the task of defining which opinion is in accordance with the legal system.

The decisive deviation from older social formations occurred when in the proceedings—which were differentiated for the purpose of selecting decisions—arguments were *no longer made exclusively ad hoc and ad hominem.* Such arguments, which are quite useful for conflict resolution and for an adjustment to changing situations, were discouraged, if not prohibited outright. They were perceived as not being in accordance with the law and were rejected. With this, the institution of confirming legal claims with oaths and oath-helpers lost its meaning. From then on—this must be noted and appreciated—people could manage without all the advantages of elasticity, which were only achieved by a transient adjustment to transient situations. The suppression of *ad hoc* and *ad hominem* arguments was initially improbable—and it is for that very reason that a decisive threshold of evolution lies here. The formulation of (and then, the memory of this formulation) law-specific concepts and rules for decision-making replaced the old arguments. The reference to old 'laws'—for instance, those of the reformer Solon or the people's laws in Rome—may have been helpful but they soon turned out as a more or less illusory reference in the daily business of legal decision-making. The decisive point was not the mode of legitimation but the unseating of the *ad hoc* and *ad hominem* arguments, which was achieved by one means or another. This prevented social structures outside the law—above all, of course, class-related status and familial relationships, friendships, and patronage—from having an excessively direct influence on the administration of justice. More than anywhere else, the forms of permissible argumentation and their limitations, however formalistic and traditionalist, reveal the differentiation of the legal system. The differentiation of legal proceedings is only a condition for the potential of evolution. The specification of the way in which arguments refer to legal materials in the legal system is the true carrier of the evolution of the legal system and the breakthrough to an autonomous legal culture, which can then even be differentiated from morals, common sense, and the everyday use of words.[52]

In sum, if *ad hoc* and *ad hominem* arguments are not permitted, a demand for justification arises which has to be satisfied in a different way, and that means that it must move, above all, in the direction of the identification of binding norms and the development of concepts and rules for

---

[52] There has been relatively little historical research on this process of differentiation, and ironically the adoption of social science approaches has led here to a move in the opposite direction, namely to an underscoring of what structures have in common and not what is different about them. See, however, on Roman law Antonio Carcatera, *Intorno ai bonae fidei iudicia* (Naples, 1964), and on the common law Oliver W. Holmes, 'The Path of the Law', *Harvard Law Review* 10 (1987), 457–78.

decision-making which can be assumed to apply to other cases as well. Not until this practice is established can a concept of justice be accepted which stipulates that equal cases are treated equally, and that unequal cases are treated unequally. This leaves it up to the legal system to establish what, based on what rules, can be seen as equal or unequal.[53] The long-term effect of all of this is a base of concepts, maxims, principles, and rules for decisions that forms the materials which are applied partly formally, partly critically, and which enable the judge to reject *ad hoc* and *ad hominem* arguments.[54]

Only in the case of Roman civil law did this result in abstractions, which rendered the law and its self-referential concepts independent of plain facts and made a law-centred evolution possible.[55] In conjunction with this there emerged a development, which is not found in the legal cultures of Asia Minor, or even of Athens: namely, the differentiation of special roles for legal experts, for lawyers. At first, this was restricted to the Roman aristocracy, and this restriction worked without the situation of members having specific offices or receiving role-specific forms of income.[56] A complete professionalization, equipped with the full range of economic and monopolistic offices, happened much later, especially in canon law and English common law of the Middle Ages, and in the early modern territorial states.

The decisive factor behind this non-standard development, which prepared the ground for a law-centred evolution, must have been the

[53] The reference to differentiation confirms indirectly that ethics never managed to solve *this* problem. The distinction between like and not like requires a lead from distinctions which were already successfully employed by the autopoiesis of law. A merely ethical and morally pure argumentation would lead to arbitrariness, and arbitrariness would lead to injustice. Obviously, this is contentious, but see David Lyons, 'Justification and Judicial Responsibility', *California Law Review* 72 (1984), 178–99; id., 'Derivability, Defensibility, and the Justification of Judicial Decisions', *The Monist* 68 (1985), 325–46, and on this point Neil MacCormick, 'Why Cases, have Rationes and what these Are', in Laurence Goldstein (ed.), *Precedent in Law* (Oxford, 1987), 155–82, at 166.

[54] This is not to deny that exceptions are possible. One of my first experiences as a legal trainee was the request of a judge in a local court that he noted in a draft of the judgment—on a motor vehicle accident—that the culpable driver had been awarded a war medal, an Iron Cross of the First Order. The amended draft gave, as a reason for the judgment, the fact that highly decorated persons presumably overestimate their driving competence and drive carelessly, if not aggressively. But this did not satisfy the judge either. He wanted the wartime decoration to be seen only as an aspect of the defendant's character, and it was not to be mentioned in relation to the (reviewable) juridical consequences.

[55] See Joseph C. Smith, 'The Theoretical Constructs of Western Contractual Law', in F. S. C. Northrop and Helen H. Livingston (eds.), *Cross-Cultural Understanding: Epistemology in Anthropology* (New York, 1964), 254–83.

[56] See Wolfgang Kunkel, *Herkunft und soziale Stellung des römischen Juristen*, 2nd edn. (Graz, 1967); Mario Bretone, *Storia del diritto romano* (Rome, 1987), 153. On the rhetorical and political handling of legal questions in Athens before this development see J. Walter Jones, *The Law and Legal Theory of the Greeks: An Introduction* (Oxford, 1956), 128; Hans Julius Wolff, *Rechtsexperten in der griechischen Antike, Festschrift für den 45. Deutschen Juristentag* (Karlsruhe, 1964), 1–22.

differentiation of Roman case law, especially the numerous instructions which office-holders passed on as premises for decision-making to judges whom they had appointed. Because this material was documented in the form of edicts, it could be edited or refined when new conditions so required. This gradually increasing complexity necessitated the existence of a corresponding expertise, which could be used by the participants (who, of course, were not lawyers in any modern sense of the word). Legal knowledge (jurisprudence), therefore, was initially no more than knowledge about what was happening and an attempt to order it with the help of classifications, and later epigrammatic forms (*regulae*). There was no need to assume that there was a self-evident order in the realm of helpful abstractions, and it was not until the Middle Ages that the accumulated texts began to be interpreted in this way and to be subjected in turn (i.e. independently of the demands of case law practice) to ever changing forms of tests for consistency. The idea of validity *qua* system was unknown to Roman civil law and so it remained. But at least the tendency to condense law in legal propositions (*brocardia*) was developed to provide a link to the Middle Ages; and only since then have legal dogmatics and doctrine become a stabilizing factor *which has begun to affect the evolution of law itself.*[57]

The development of Roman civil law into a more complex law, which refers concepts to cases and cases to concepts, certainly did not happen accidentally. It took place in conjunction with those legal concepts which lend themselves to a structural coupling of the legal system and the economic system, namely property and contract.[58] A specific concept for property was hardly necessary as long as all vital holdings could be subsumed under the concept of 'family': wife and children, slaves and cattle, house and land.[59] And for a long time it may have been sufficient to understand

---

[57] Harold J. Berman, *Recht und Revolution: Die Bildung der westlichen Rechtstradition* (Frankfurt, 1991), uses a similar argument when he refers to the confluence of social and organizational developments with the rediscovery of Roman texts in the eleventh and twelfth centuries as being the decisive turning point. Similarly, the motive here was the resistance of the Church to a possible theocracy of the emperor and a politico-religious despotism and not the still uncreated legal system.   [58] See for more detail, Ch. 10.III.

[59] Originally property in land did not belong to individuals but to the kinship. Only the movable, manipulable things were *res mancipi*. This, however, changed with the effects of the formation of cities. At first, even here a general concept of property and a distinction between law concerning persons and law of things were missing. For instance, distinctions here were between *res mancipi* (and consequently *mancipatio*, *emancipatio*) and *res nec mancipi* (for instance, cattle, *pecus*, *pecunia*). They reflect a clear reference to the prevalence of strongly segmental societies and what is important or unimportant to them. This also applied to the access to *mancipatio* for foreigners without *ius commercium*. Even the highly developed late republican jurisprudence sees law primarily under the perspective of the family household, *familia*. See on Quintus Mutius Scaevola, Aldo Schiavone, *Nascita della giurisprudenza: Cultura aristocratica e pensiero giuridico nella Roma tardorepubblicana* (Bari, 1976), 116.

property as possession and control over everything one owned. It may have been deemed adequate to protect it against interference from outsiders and, if necessary, to detect an offender and punish him, or to force him to surrender possessions or make up for loss. Only relatively recently do we find the decisive distinction between property and possession, that is, the purely juristic construction behind the visible property relations which also deserve protection in their own right. Not until recent times could property as a juristic construction be enforced, with the help of whatever protection could be given to factual possession; but such entitlements do not entitle the application of (putative) law coercively, but rather only and exclusively enforcement by legal procedure. Not until then did legal title become independent of the physical strength and fighting strength of the titleholder.[60] This alone led to the division between civil law and penal law and opened up property as a point of reference for quite different forms of contract, especially for the disposition of credits. Only then could possession be argued in legal proceedings, independent of the question of who was the owner of the things in possession.

One is an owner not only in relation to offenders but also in relation to everybody else, and in relation to any number of participants in the legal system who are bound to respect the property right and who have the option of eventually buying the property or obtaining other contractual rights over it, for example the rights of use. Thus the universality of property, and its reference to the legal system, is not related to the arbitrariness of the use or abuse of possessions. It is precisely this which was guaranteed or recognized as fact by *manus*, in terms of the control over things. The universality is, in fact, given by reference to the system, that is, by the fact that everybody has to respect the owner as the owner, unless the legal system provides otherwise. Universality is given by the fact that, in relation to all property, everybody else is a non-owner.

Similar specializations happen in contract law. Here the difficulty lies in seeing the contract as a reason for obligation and not simply as a transaction from hand to hand; one could say that the contract becomes synallagmatic (i.e. becomes a bilateral contract with binding reciprocal obligations), which is a regulatory principle for the relations between partners and, above all, in cases where performance may be disrupted. The transaction itself is irrelevant, or, at best, relevant only as a juridical condition for the development of special kinds of contracts (executed contracts). The contract itself takes the place of the exchange. It regulates its own execution.

---

[60] See on this point Robert C. Palmer, 'The Origins of Property in England', *Law and History Review* (1985), 1–50 for the period 1153–1215. Property in the modern sense is described here as a clear result of an evolutionary development, as 'part of the law developed by accident: by acts that had unintended consequences' (p. 47). The motive was originally the solution of political conflicts between vassals and between master and vassals in the context of feudal society.

There is little doubt that this is how it still works today, by and large, and that this working has been made easier by legislation that replaced the rules representing decisions that were developed and improved by legal practice. This sense of obviousness, however, diverts attention away from the forms of argumentation which are, once again, coming dangerously close to *ad hoc* and *ad hominem* arguments—take only, for example, the 'balancing of interests' as the Trojan horse of all juridical reasoning.

Neither variation nor selection amounts to an externally induced innovation of law. Evolution is not a planning scheme. Many different things can lead to a legal dispute, but they arise frequently (if not mostly) from an uncertain and unclear state of affairs. The legal system cannot control the factors that lead to a dispute and thus require a decision to be made. Neither do legal proceedings serve to change the law—they merely clarify it. Legal proceedings 'declare the law', as is said in the common law. Even if a court searches and finds rules for its decisions, which, according to the opinion of the judges are new, and even if there is a realization that an established legal practice is no longer satisfactory because circumstances have changed, this is merely an example of punctuated structural change and not evidence of a plan, or the control of the system as a system. It follows that the incremental transformation of law is not the result of purpose-oriented activities. It is a result of the ongoing reproduction of the difference between variation and selection and is a residue of effective evolutionary difference. Hence there is initially no need to find a place for the changeability of law in the self-description of law; this does not need to be reflected in law. Law's changeability comes by itself.

As such, dispute resolution is not always a decision between old law and new. For example, the myth of Antigone, which stylizes an exceptional situation, is not about this conflict. The idea that new law is better than old is a very recent reflection of a long-standing practice. When legal knowledge already exists, there is at first only room for cautious amendment, for arguments according to analogies,[61] for extending experience with cases to new cases. Evolution is here, like elsewhere, not a result of purposeful processes but an unintended by-product, a result that occurs for external rather than genetic reasons.[62] A society which can afford this kind of legal organization has already built in it a level of second-order observation that allows it to

---

[61] And one could add, in view of Jewish law, even allegories, see Louis Ginzberg, *On Jewish Law and Lore* (Philadelphia, 1956; reprint New York, 1977), 127–50.

[62] This applies as well to the evolution of organic systems, especially if one takes as the indication of its direction the sense of an 'increase of the systems' own complexity' as a feature of evolution. See on this point G. Ledyard Stebbins, 'Adaptive Shifts and Evolutionary Novelty: A Compositionist Approach', in Francisco Ayala and Theodosius Dobzhansky (eds.), *Studies in the Philosophy of Biology: Reduction and Related Problems* (London, 1974), 285–306, at 302. See also id., *The Basis of Progressive Evolution* (Chapel Hill, 1969).

differentiate the legal system. In the form of legal proceedings in courts, there is already a level on which normative expectations can be confirmed or rejected, depending on whether they are in accordance with the law or not. The code legal/illegal is already being used and the effect of this coding occurs as predicted: a residue of programmatic semantics builds up, which can be referenced if one needs criteria for the attribution of legal values.[63] The selection function, however, cannot, as yet, be distinguished from problems associated with the restabilization of the system. It operates in relation to law, which is assumed to be stable, with the justification of old law, or if that is not sufficient, with references to nature or to a divine order. Even if there exists, as in the later Roman Empire, a comprehensive practice of imperial edicts (*constitutiones*) which affect the law, the law gives such edicts—with every appearance of reluctance—only a special status.[64]

Independently of legislation with its poorly articulated concepts, the practice in courts and the doctrines, which paved the way for this practice, are also increasingly undermined by reference to the stability of the existing law. This began in the late republican epoch of Quintus Mutius Scaevola, after an earlier generation of lawyers had begun to record the products of their counselling activities in writing. First attempts at a conceptualization of a predominantly dialectical kind (that is, by abstraction of the '*genus*') appeared, together with a doctrine which was no longer interested exclusively in individual cases.[65] Because legal opinions (and not only laws) were recorded in writing, lawyers realized that traditional law was no longer suitable,[66] so they tried to preserve it by conceptual systematization—a typical example of the conservative tendency of evolutionary innovation.[67] With the rapid growth of textual material during the classical time of Roman jurisprudence, these attempts were extended to the establishment of legal concepts and rules for decision, which were supposed to assist in the application of law. In a society in which legal norms and opinions were recorded in writing but in which their diffusion was largely oral due to the

---

[63] See Ch. 4.

[64] This insight, formulated as a concession in the famous words of Ulpian 'Quod principi placuit, legis habet vigorem' (D.1.4.1.1), did not attain the status of a maxim of sovereignty until early modernity; and even then one could assume initially that a truly virtuous sovereign would not be pleased by just anything because if this were the case he would not be a sovereign but a tyrant who could be resisted legally.

[65] See on this point Schiavone, *Nascita della Giurisprudenza*, 69.

[66] Schiavone talks about jumps of quality in jurisprudence on the basis of an intensively nurtured bond with tradition, namely a 'nascita della giurisprudenza romana come pratica intellettuale definita, formemente portata all'autoriproduzione, dotata di un quadro concettuale e di meccanismi logici che le assicurano uno statuto teorico altamente specifico, autonomo rispetto ad ogni altra forma di sapere, e tendente a mantenersi costante' (ibid. 86).

[67] This is often called Romer's Principle following Alfred S. Romer, *The Vertebrate Story* (Chicago, 1959).

limited availability of books, that is, in a society before the invention of printing, legal knowledge often developed an idiomatic form for memorizing rules in cues or mnemonic devices which were listed and learnt for use as rhetoric in court.[68] In this way, idioms which had been borrowed partly from the *Corpus Iuris* and partly from other sources could be turned into legal maxims that could be learnt and used, as apparently old ideas, to implement innovative demands.[69]

Legal knowledge that gives stability to legal practice developed on the basis of the careful comparison of old, already decided cases with new ones. Relevant to this comparison were conceptual classifications, types of legal institutions, and tried and tested rules for making decisions. The method was basically the repeated testing of the scope of conclusions drawn by analogy—that is, neither a deduction from principles nor an inductive generalization—for the goal was not to find rules that could be generalized but to come to decisions that could be justified. In this process, the new and as yet unmade decision was not necessarily determined by what already existed in legal knowledge. It could very well be that the newness of the extant case was revealed by the existing repertoire of cases. As is typical of evolutionary contexts, the consolidated result was both the end of a phase

[68] It is widely acknowledged today that even 'literate' societies, which have achieved a high level of literacy, communicate almost exclusively orally and preserve requisite forms in written texts. See, for the case of law, especially Peter Goodrich, 'Literacy and Language of the Early Common Law', *Journal of Law and Society* 14 (1987), 422–44. The same can be said for the area of medicine and the study of medicine. See here above all the texts of the medical school of Salerno, in: *The School of Salernum: Regimen Sanitatis Salerni: The English Version by Sir John Harington, Salerno, Ente Provinciale per il Turismo* (n.d.). This English version was written in 1607 (!) to be printed (!).

[69] This can be seen very well from the juridical justifications which already proclaimed the legally sovereign domination of the ruling house before Bodin. In Jacobus Omphalius, *De officio et potestate Principis in Reipublica bene ac sancte gerenda libri duo* (Basle, 1550), the usual formulae can be found, such as 'Princeps legibus solutus est', 'Princeps lex animata in terris', 'Principis voluntas pro ratione habeatur', or the consistently applied formula quoted in n. 20, even though neither substantive law nor the texts themselves exempt the sovereign from being bound by law. As an example of maxims created out of context and thus given false meaning see also Adhémar Esmein, 'La maxime "Princeps legibus solutus est" dans l'ancien droit public français', in: Paul Vinogradoff (ed.), *Essays in Legal History* (London, 1913), 201–14, and on the history of this formula in more detail Dieter Wyduckel, *Princeps Legibus Solutus: Eine Untersuchung zur frühmodernen Rechts- und Staatslehre* (Berlin, 1979). Another example is the use of a formulation from D45.1.108, which deals with a complicated case of dowry. The text reads 'nulla promissio potest consistere, quae ex voluntate promittentis statum capit'. Jean Bodin, *Les six livres de la République* (Paris, 1583; reprint Aalen 1967), 132, quotes wrongly, namely instead of *promissio obligatio*, and deduces the momentous doctrine that a sovereign could not bind himself because of natural law. And a last example: the sentence 'quod omnes tangit omnibus tractari et approbari debet' referred originally to a case with a number of guardians but reappeared in the Middle Ages as an argument in discussion on the principle of representation in corporations.

of evolution and the condition for the recognition and specification of further variation.

If legal practice closes itself in a temporal continuity, if it is ready to be guided by self-produced rules and if the task in the individual case is to measure the case against the rules and the rules with the case, evolutionary selection achieves a very specific form. In each case one has to ask whether the case, when seen from the perspective of the rules, is equal to other cases or not. If it is equal to them, then and only then can one 'subsume' it, namely apply the rules to that particular case. If the case is not equal to other cases, then new rules have to be developed. It is this practice that provides the platform for understanding justice not as just the *idea* of equality but as the normative form of equality, that is, as the requirement to distinguish between equal and unequal, and to treat what is equal equally and what is unequal unequally.

Depending on the result of such (and exactly such) a decision, the evolution of law is within its own communication networks directed towards either negative or positive feedback. Either the legal system remains stable on the basis of existing rules, which are applied over and over again, and which may cause tensions outside the law, or it deviates from the existing point of departure and constructs a higher complexity by distinguishing and over-ruling (in the terminology of the common law) over and over again. Only in this last case is one faced with the problems of structural (and not only procedural) re-stabilization, namely the question whether and how the system can still function autopoietically in view of this ever increasing complexity and how it can remain, for instance, sufficiently attractive to users who rely on it, and keep on producing legal cases.

The guidance of effective legal knowledge by stereotypical formulae, initially delivered and implemented by oral transmission, disappeared with the increasing influence of printed literature. Increasingly, the medieval legal system with its glosses and commentaries, its privileges and contracted individual obligations, its procedural structure of writs and *actiones* by which the substantive law is guided, presented itself as tangled. Printing offered the opportunity for diffusion of legal material into other forms of texts. These texts were written directly for printing. Additionally, printing allowed for the collection, selective documentation, and further diffusion of this legal material, which until then had only been passed on orally.[70] Only printing provided the opportunity, and thus the demand, for simplification, systematization, and a methodical approach, which resulted in the

---

[70] Above all, the official editing of the French *coutumes* is famous in this context. It was begun in the fifteenth century, before the invention of printing, but was later improved, juridically worked through, and modernized with the help of printing. For a brief overview see Phillipe Sueur, *Histoire du droit public français XVe–XVIIIe siècle*, vol. 2 (Paris, 1989), 39.

shape of continental legal science.[71] At the same time, printing provided one opportunity which was used particularly by the common law: namely the opportunity to concentrate on the particularity and artificiality of case-law practice and on the context for the legitimation of historicity and rationality, that is, to move on to a phase of self-observation and an ideological and, in the eighteenth century, national self-aggrandizement.[72]

To sum up, we can now speak of legal dogmatics, which take note of historical consistency and the systematic use of concepts. This semantic material, which has been abstracted from legal practice (but which is by no means impervious to it), raises the opportunity to discuss issues of construction. This material can be used to reject decisions which cannot be so constructed; but it can also be used to justify decisions which comply with the long-standing use of concepts. The result is that in many cases the scope of legal institutions has gradually spread,[73] this being the typical evolutionary process of the 'amplification of deviance': institutions of considerable importance have developed from small but effective beginnings. Their significance can scarcely be described in the form of definitions because they sum up the experience of countless cases. Only practitioners 'understand' their relevance.

Not until the end of the nineteenth century did one begin to turn against this approach and to reject it as 'legal formalism'. Increasingly,

---

[71] In Italy a humanist (or better: rhetorical) criticism of the typical juridical working with texts began back in the early fifteenth century, namely before printing. Here, however, questions of style were in the foreground and long practice with the rhetorical tradition provided the means. See, for example, Domenico Maffei, *Gli inizi dell'umanesimo giuridico* (Milano, 1956; reprint 1968). On the consequences of printing, which did not turn out to be a problem until the sixteenth century, see Hans Erich Troje, 'Wissenschaftlichkeit und System in der Jurisprudenz des 16. Jahrhunderts', in Jürgen Blühdorn and Joachim Ritter (ed.), *Philosophie und Rechtswissenschaft: Zum Problem ihrer Beziehungen im 19. Jahrhundert* (Frankfurt, 1969), 63–88; id., 'Die Literatur des gemeinen Rechts unter dem Einfluß des Humanismus', in Helmut Coing (ed.), *Handbuch der Quellen und Literatur der neueren europäischen Privatrechtsgeschichte* II.1 (Munich, 1977), 615–795, at 741. In the area of the common law one can find initiatives in the same vein, which fall short of the rhetorical humanist trend on the continent. See Peter Goodrich, *Languages of Law: From Logics of Memory to Nomadic Masks* (London, 1990), esp. 70; further, there is also Francis Bacon's unsuccessful initiative to react by way of legislation through new compilations and a methodical and scientific approach to legislation. See *De augmentis scientiarum* 8. 3, aphorism at 59, quoted from the English translation in: *The Works of Francis Bacon* (London, 1857—), vol. V (1861), 10; id., A Proposition to His Majesty . . . Touching the Compilation and Amendment of the Laws of England, *Works*, vol. XIII (1872), 57–71, and on Bacon, Barbara Shapiro, 'Sir Francis Bacon and the Mid-seventeenth Century Movement for Law Reform', *American Journal of Legal History* 24 (1980), 33–360.

[72] See on this and counter-movements from Bacon via Hobbes and Blackstone to Bentham, Gerald J. Postema, *Bentham and the Common Law Tradition* (Oxford, 1986); David Lieberman, *The Province of Legislation Determined: Legal Theory in Eighteenth-Century Britain* (Cambridge, 1989).

[73] For examples, such as the law of liability and the due process clause in the United States, see Lawrence H. Friedman, *Total Justice* (New York, 1985).

innovations were justified directly as a result of the use of norms of competence, whether those of the legislators, or—increasingly—those of judges. The general instrument of making distinctions could then be used much more freely, even though it had considerable effects on what was produced as legal semantics with the requisite programme functions.

By differentiating legal dogmatics, which—with their unique features— belong to the legal system (and should not be confused with natural law as taught in Latin schools), the stabilizing function of law is also differentiated. Legal proceedings may adopt variations and give them structural significance for future decision-making. Even if this is successful, the question remains whether this has an impact on legal doctrine or is only part of the legal system, which can be changed or become a precedent for legal decisions at any future time. There is, in other words, a differentiation between the function of selection and the function of stabilization, and in this differentiation process everything that serves stabilization transmits its own impulses for innovation. As recently as the seventeenth century the political system was warned against reforms, which always brought the risk of resistance, rebellion, and civil war.[74] The legal system, however, had already achieved a dynamic stability, which gave rise to innovation with far-reaching consequences—for example, the concepts of property and of subjective rights, the latitude for litigation relating to informal contracts, and, last but not least, the innovative concept, compared with the Middle Ages, of a 'public law'.[75]

Only through complex legal dogmatics can the stabilization and restabilization of law be shifted from the simple (and most of the time religiously justified) validity of assigned norms to their *consistency*. Dogmatics guarantees that the legal system approves itself in its change as a *system*. That is why this dogmatic approach was called the 'systematic method'.[76]

---

[74] See, for example, Iustus Lipsius, *Politicorum sive civilis doctrinae libri sex* (Antwerp, 1604), 96; Jean de Marnix, *Résolutions politiques et maximes d'Estat* (Brussels, 1629), 286; Johann Hieronymus Im Hof, *Singularia Politica*, 2nd edn. (Nuremberg, 1657), 241; Estienne Pasquier, *Les Recherches de la France,* new edn. (Paris, 1665), 678 ('Il n'y a rien qu'il faille tant craindre en une Republique que la nouveauté').

[75] The finding that the conditions for a modern (capitalist) economic order are created in the legal system and not in the political system applies also to the United States at a later period. See Morton J. Horwitz, *The Transformation of American Law, 1780–1860* (Cambridge, Mass. 1977). But see criticism on this point by A. W. B. Simpson, 'The Horwitz Thesis and the History of Contracts', in id., *Legal Theory and Legal History* (London, 1987), 203–71. Simpson denies the independent achievement of common law and refers to receptions from European civil law. See also id., 'Innovation in the Nineteenth Century Contract Law', in *Legal Theory and Legal History,* 171–202.

[76] See, for example, following Nicolai Hartmann, Heino Garn, *Rechtsproblem und Rechtssystem* (Bielefeld, 1973), 28, in relation to the ongoing adjustment of system and solutions to problems.

However, consistency should not detract from the fact that such a dogmatic approach does not require a reflection on the unity of the system or orientation by a sense of the system as a whole.[77] It is only an attempt to solve 'similar' cases consistently. Like changed law, traditional law is valid if it can be upheld in the context of related legal ideas. The possibility of a dogmatic construction of a case solution can serve as proof of consistency. This, in its turn, makes it possible to identify situations where a construction is not possible, and to be aware that there is a problem if the result is at odds with a changed perception of justice or that which a trained legal mind would accept as a reasonable solution. Legal dogmatics, or a correspondingly broad knowledge of the *ratio decidendi* in a large number of legal decisions, makes it possible to identify defects and to look, not always successfully, for better possibilities of construction. The law gains the opportunity to mature through its own defects. An example of this would be the admission of strict liability in certain circumstances in spite of limited liability being acknowledged in principle and upheld by statute, either because the party not liable, by a subjective test, had created a dangerous situation or because this party alone controlled possibilities and alternatives which could have helped to avoid the risks altogether.[78] On the basis of dogmatic constructions, the idea was conceived in the late Middle Ages that the principle of *bona fides* could fill all the gaps in the traditional system of Roman contract types and corresponding litigation (*actiones*), so that each legal contract could be accepted as a title: *ex nudo pacto oritur obligatio.* Likewise, eighteenth-century interest in the accumulation of capital and limited liability searched for and found legal forms for juristic persons, forms which could not be accommodated in the old law on the privileges of corporations. This can be seen as an adjustment of law to changing conditions, but it does not mean that the environment determines the legal system. Rather, the legal system notices defects only in its own devices and fixes them with its own means.[79] The environment may irritate the legal system and it may cause disturbances for its sense of

---

[77] This is yet another version of the finding that the orientation by the function of law is not sufficient to determine the decisions of the system.

[78] See on this point and similar developments in the common law, Edward H. Levi, 'An Introduction to Legal Reasoning', *University of Chicago Law Review* 15 (1948), 501–74.

[79] See Alan Watson, *The Evolution of Law* (Baltimore, 1985), with good examples from the evolution of Roman contract law. Here the formation of types of contracts for non-pecuniary contracts (*mandatum, depositum*) is interesting because it cannot be explained by economic development, and the plausible (legally derived) explanation is that the law must especially protect acts of friendship where the insistence on a formal allocation of rights and obligations is felt to be an embarrassment. Moreover, the institution of contract is a good example of the fact that legal problems are not inherent in the balance of mutual performances—which can be left to the economic system—but in the persistence of the 'synallagmatic' connection and in the control of disturbances which can occur unexpectedly after the *conclusion of the contract.*

justice: already such irritations, however, are system-internal formulations of the problem and the solutions are of course tied to what is deemed to be within the reach of a construction made under valid law.

From the standpoint of law, legislation is included in this sort of innovation for the fixing of defects. When a deficiency is detected, it is a question of whether it can be overcome with or without changing the law. This kind of 'mischief rule' is still applied in the common law today, at least as a maxim for interpretation.[80] It postulates that law be seen as a system, as a totality of consistently practised problem- solving solutions, and that one of them be selected in a given case. Furthermore, it postulates in the case of the interpretation of legislation that it be seen that the legislator wanted to proceed in this particular way, or that a judge insert a suitable rule for generalization if no rule could be found. In this sense law itself is a motivator for innovation, but at the same time encourages the rejection of innovation for the sake of its stability, consistency, and justice. At any rate, legal evolution which advances in this manner cannot be thought of as blind, or wholly intentional or, least of all, as a point-by-point response to impulses from outside.[81] The evolution operates in a circular fashion by responding partly with variation to external impulses, and partly by reusing its stabilization as the motivation for innovation:

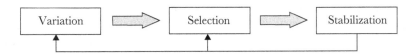

This circular and not sequential model of evolution allows us to pose the question of the evolutionary change of the conditions for legal evolution. First of all, it is important to note here that the arrangements for the stabilization and restabilization of law have become dynamic themselves and promote the variation of law in their own right. The legal system is no longer waiting in the wings for people to engage in a dispute in order that it can find a just solution that is in accordance with the law. Instead, law itself produces the situations, which trigger off conflicts, by regulatory manipulation of everyday life. Law promotes itself.

We can find the reasons for this changed form of evolution, above all, in the massive impact of legislation in the nineteenth and twentieth centuries.

[80] See Peter Goodrich, *Reading the Law* (Oxford, 1986), 55 and 117.

[81] See, for example, W. Jethro Brown, 'Law and Evolution', *Yale Law Journal* 29 (1920), 394–400, on the rejection of such a distinction. From a sociological perspective the assumption that the distinction between intention/non-intention amounted to a crucial distinction is related to the transition from the theory of social action to systems theory.

This is closely related to the democratization of the political system and the constitutional channelling of political influence through legislation. Politics has a massive impact on the legal system by issuing huge numbers of new directives, which need to be received, understood, and worked through. Of course, there exists in legislative procedure a professionally competent assessment whether political wishes can be fulfilled with existing valid law or whether they require a change of law. In this respect the legal system still operates as a system and, as before, a variation becomes effective only as something that is perceived by the system as an irritation and for which it can find a form. The mechanism of variation itself, however, has changed. The 'noise' of the political system turns into another incident for variation, but the one that is probably the most prevalent today. The law is no longer varied exclusively by disputes, which may precipitate a preference for new rules. Politics has its own goals and thereby creates the differences, which may result in other conflicts. If a country demands that certain forms be filled in at immigration control, and if—as in the United States—questions have to be answered regarding one's race, this does not provide a solution to a conflict but creates an unfavourable situation for someone for whom this question may create a conflict. Without the norm there would be no conflict. The mechanism of variation of law becomes circularly supercharged with self-produced conflicts, in which the norm stipulates how the conflict is going to be solved.

In situations like these, the evolution of law must resort to interpretation. Interpretation performs a consistency test by examining which meaning of a norm fits in the context of other norms. In contrast to the great codifications of the eighteenth and nineteenth centuries, statutes are no longer interested in consistency. In view of this, courts developed with much greater freedom for interpretation. But they cannot use this freedom to regain consistency in view of the mandated texts on which they must rely. There is now—and this is an indication of the crack that has opened up—a lively discussion about the methods of interpreting statutes, which, however, has little bearing on decision-making (why should courts lay down a certain method for their decisions?).[82] The solution rather lies in a higher tolerance of ambiguity, a softening of the traditional doctrinal positions, indeterminate legal concepts and forms for considering the facts and circumstances of a case, with which courts can find, *ad hoc*, a seemingly suitable solution, but which cannot establish a thoroughly consistent legal practice. Legislators, in turn, adopt these formulae because they, for their part, cannot make out the limitations through which consistency can be maintained in spite of adding new norms.

---

[82] See, from a comparative point of view and the resulting typification, D. Neil MacCormick and Robert S. Summers (ed.), *Interpreting Statutes: A Comparative Study* (Aldershot, 1991).

The fact that norms hardly represent their interest in consistency any longer indicates at the same time that they can easily be changed as individual norms. Legal change becomes normal. The average period of the validity of norms decreases. Often norms are put in force only temporarily or with the expectation of a better insight at a later point in time. Temporal inconsistency (which may be less painful or less unjust) compensates for what cannot be achieved through factual consistency.

Karl-Heinz Ladeur put forward the view that the unity of law can no longer be maintained under these circumstances and that it is replaced by a pluralist concept of law as far as values and interests are concerned.[83] What speaks against this concept, however, is the fact that the legal system continues to reproduce itself autopoietically, and that it is not interchangeable with other systems. Using a terminology which will be discussed in greater detail in Chapter 8, one can formulate the argument that the legal system increases its variety (its number of possible operations) while it decreases its redundancy (more economy of information, accessibility, and ability to recognize errors, etc.). In this way, law may become more robust and in this sense more 'amenable to errors'.[84] In turn, however, law loses its transparency and reliability for all the other systems in its environment that want to apply it. And that is exactly why the legitimacy of law is questioned time and again—acutely or hopelessly, out of frustration or anger, full of value-perspectives that are beside the point for law.

The consequence of this evolution for the legal system is that there is only positive law, although moral philosophers may want to express a different opinion. This means that there is only law which the legal system itself implements with the symbol of legal validity. And this applies independently of the actual historical form of legal tradition. This applies to continental civil law and it applies to English common law; and it also applies independently to our extensive legislation, which proactively creates new law or codifies old law. This can clearly be seen in the common law in the way, for instance, in which precedents reinforced decisions in the nineteenth century, when the legislative positivism recommended by Bentham and Austin could not take hold.[85] It is incontestable that valid law

---

[83] See K.-H. Ladeur, *Abwägung—Ein neues Paradigma des Verwaltungsrechts: Von der Einheit der Rechtsordnung zum Rechtspluralismus* (Frankfurt, 1984).

[84] The tendency discussed above in Ch. 4.IV to seek reasons for decisions in the *consequences* of decisions, which are not yet known at the moment of the decision but somehow have to be assessed, is clear evidence of this tendency to become more 'amenable to errors'. It makes no difference to the validity of law if the assessment of the consequences is faulty. See also the verdict on the apparently so precise 'economic analysis of law' by Anthony D'Amato, 'Can Any Legal Theory Constrain Any Judicial Decision', *University of Miami Law Review* 43 (1989), 513–39.

[85] On this development in England in the eighteenth and nineteenth centuries see the contributions of Gerald J. Postema and Jim Evans in Laurence Goldstein (ed.), *Precedent in Law* (Oxford, 1987).

cannot be understood as a logically closed system because no logical system can give reasons for the absence of contradictions in its own system. The answer to this problem of incompleteness, however, is not given by an external guarantee of validity but by the ongoing production of legal texts, which identify what is valid law and what is not. The 'rationality' of the system, then, is not given by a goodness which is secured by principles, but by the question, which arises anew in every situation, whether or not the valid law should be changed in relation to the references which have become a problem. Therefore, the validity of law is founded not on unity but on difference. It cannot be seen, it cannot be 'found'—it is the ongoing reproduction of law's difference.

IV

The previous comprehensive section, which discussed the evolution of law towards systemic operative closure, requires a correction in one important respect. The statement that law has evolved by itself and that society as its environment has provided accidental impulses, which have caused variations and occasional innovative selections, can still be upheld. Such responsiveness in relation to the environment is evident in individual legal institutions, for instance in the sensitivity to people's frailties gradually being recognized in criminal law or the forms of civil law with their preference for providing possibilities for litigation. Parallel to the development of the modern territorial state, such responsiveness is also evident in the development of public law (which at first sight is hardly distinguishable from civil law or natural law) and its culmination in modern constitutional law. However, are there not also social conditions—beyond the varied species of law—which determine that a legal system becomes operatively closed, specifying its own structures by its operations and changing them if events, internally identified, so warrant?

Our assumption is that Hobbes's problem—how to account for the ubiquity of physical force—represents such a condition. Formulated positively, the law has to start from the condition of peace already secured if it is to achieve more than just the conditioning of physical force. This, then, refers to the dependence of the evolution of law on the parallel evolution of the political system that, with a kind of primary expropriation of society, withdraws the means of power, of physical force, from society and consolidates its own powers on this basis.[86]

In a very basic sense, law has always had to deal with solutions to conflicts that might need to be resolved violently. This has to be seen in relation to

---

[86] See on this development in the context of a theory of symbolically generalized media of communication, Niklas Luhmann, *Macht* (Stuttgart, 1975).

the fact that law itself is a source of conflict in the first instance that often—and more frequently as law becomes more developed—leads to conflicts in which both of the parties refer to law. It is precisely this development that has led to the evolutionary achievement of proceedings in which law is, as it were, passing judgment on itself. This fact alone, however, did not facilitate the separation of civil law and criminal law even though it did make proceedings dependent in their decision-making on the question of which decision was enforceable. The sheer number of 'oath-helpers' which a party could muster and the obvious conspicuousness of being prepared to enforce the law could be taken as an indicator of that. Apart from some cities in ancient times and in the Roman Empire, which were islands of peace, the symptomatic incorporation of violence in law must be seen as normal until the high Middle Ages and as a barrier to the further development of juridical semantics and juridical self-reference.[87] In its readiness for violence, law was tied and remained tied to the structures of its societal environment, which it could not control, and it was tied, above all, to the kinship and clan formations of segmental societies. This necessarily impeded the refinement of juridical semantics, the condensation and confirmation of experience with new cases, and the juridical attention to conceptual and dogmatic consistency (and their impact on legal decisions).

It became possible to overcome this barrier to further evolution only when politics took control of physical force and promised peace (even though in the Middle Ages the prime political force was the organized Church, equipped with canon law). This implies that legal claims can be enforced once their legality is ascertained.[88] Then the problem of structural coupling can be restricted to the relationship between politics and law—either by taking these functioning systems as a unit, which converges at the top, or by coupling them with the special institution of the constitution.[89] One could say that evolution 'searches' for solutions to the problem of how the legal system can be structurally coupled which do not impede the evolution of the legal system—or, leading to the same result, solutions which facilitate the development of the internal complexity of law through the special evolution of the legal system.

If this starting point of the legal system has its critical moment in the problem of violence, it should be possible to observe that this dependence on violence takes on a different form after a new evolutionary push. This is, indeed, the case. Punishable offences were no longer understood as the

---

[87] See above all Berman, *Recht und Revolution.*

[88] Up to the seventeenth century, there were exemptions in a quasi-concentrated form, namely for the aristocracy; and they are still found today when police refuse to act on the grounds of 'public order and security', that is, in order to avoid further disorder.

[89] For a further discussion of these two concepts, which can, in their turn, be distinguished by the degree of freedom they leave to the coupled systems, see below Chs. 9 and 10.

violation of a victim, who could defend himself or demand satisfaction, but as a violation of criminal law. Because of this, there was an unprecedented rise in criminality in the seventeenth and above all in the eighteenth century—in the public interest, so to speak. It produced modern theories of crime (Beccaria, etc.), led to the establishment of penal colonies, and caused bourgeois society to sanitize itself with the help of work ethics and moral outrage. Only when mediated by legislation could legally protected interests find their way into law. Hence the rule: *nulla poena sine lege.* The archaic law of the repayment of violence with violence was broken, or transferred to the state as the only actor entitled to apply a violent response. Initially the state still claimed 'raisons des executions sans proces' with the quasi-medical advice 'le mal se guarist par le mal' [evil is healed by evil].[90] However, in the course of the developing pacification of various territories in the seventeenth century, even this right to adjudicate without proceedings turned out to be superfluous—at least as long as law and order prevailed.

Can one say that the law fractures its own peace with violence in the course of its differentiation as a self-evolving legal system? At any event, law's reliance on itself had thus become visible as a paradox—and was formulated in these terms.[91] An external reference—in this case, violence—had to be expunged and replaced with a self-reference which had to come to terms with the environment—and that now meant with the central will of the political sovereign—in a different way.

Since the eleventh century, a civil law has been developing in Europe on the basis of Roman law and separately from criminal law. Initially it was divided into canon law and secularized civil law.[92] The recourse to violence by an individual who felt his rights had been violated also had to be stopped in this area of law. Access to legal proceedings had to compensate for the removal of violence—legal culture could develop no other way. This compensation was, of course, only convincing if judgments by courts could be enforced and decision-making was not distorted by an anticipation of the particular power relations. If one wants to appreciate the evolutionary improbability of such a development, one has to note another remarkable fact: *law* itself had to determine and eliminate *violations of the law*. It had to

---

[90] See this justification by Pierre Ayrault, *Ordre, formalité et instruction judicaire* (1576; 2nd edn. Paris, 1598), 90 and 97. This text refers to criminal procedure.

[91] 'Qu'il n y a rien si iuste qui ne puisse avoir son opposite aussi iuste' [There is nothing so just that could not have an equally just opposite] says Ayrault, *Ordre,* 91. The example here is patricide or matricide in the case of Orestes. The solution to this paradox is executed straightforward juridically with the formula of rule/exception. One would also have to take into account that the cult of paradoxical formulations was quite fashionable in the late Renaissance and was not seen as an error in logic but as a challenge to think further. See for ample material on this point Rosalie L. Colie, *Paradoxia Epidemica: The Renaissance Tradition of Paradox* (Princeton, 1966).   [92] See in detail Berman, *Recht und Revolution.*

replace its test of power, which had secured its adjustment to the environment, with self-regulating proceedings—a paradox of determining illegality, which could be incorporated in the system according to legal rules. The paradox of the unity of the code legal/illegal was not to become 'gödelized'—was not to be solved by externalization—but had to be unfolded internally in the legal system.

The solutions are so familiar to us today that we can scarcely see the problem. However, as late as the early Middle Ages (for instance, in the context of the peasants' wars of 1525 and Luther's reaction to them), the connection between the functioning/non-functioning administration of justice and the violent approach of law was still very obvious.[93] Today the problem is evident in the anomaly of the self-defence/emergency law. There remain residual and borderline cases where the law permits the violation of law in legally defined terms and conditions. It is no accident that there are cases in which the use of physical force is permitted and the typical reference to legal procedure excluded. *Whenever violence is involved, the paradox of legal coding shows up—but in a form which is immediately unfolded within the legal system through setting conditions which make the paradox invisible.*

Translated back into the terminology of evolution, this analysis confirms the connection between autopoiesis and structural coupling as a precondition for evolution. Evolution can only use the autopoiesis of the systems that it requires. Therefore, circular formulations, such as variation/selection/re-stabilization, are unavoidable in the classical distinctions of evolutionary theory. Inputs from the environment appear as accidents in relation to an evolving system and these accidents are transformed by the system into a guided development. If one introduces the concept of structural coupling (to which we shall return more systematically in a later chapter), one can further describe how and through which forms these 'accidents' are domesticated, which accidents are felt as irritations in the system and which of them can be attended to, under the label of 'problem', with solutions which suit the system (that is, which function autopoietically). As far as the evolution of law is concerned, the problem of physical violence appears to perform this critical function of making evolution possible or blocking it.

V

The preceding discussion has not as yet produced a solution to the problem that has played a considerable role in the discussion on evolutionary theory. This problem concerns the question whether there are certain patterns in the formation and disintegration of structures throughout

---

[93] See, for example, Winfried Schulze, *Bäuerlicher Widerstand und feudale Herrschaft in der frühen Neuzeit* (Stuttgart, 1980).

evolution or whether all things happen arbitrarily. The concept of progress has been used to answer this question. It needs to be reformulated, however, if one does not see evolution as progress. In this case, either a new concept must be found, or evolutionary theory has to be detached completely from any description of an order which has come about through evolution.

Following Darwin, it has often been thought sufficient to use evolutionary theory to explain how society has achieved a highly developed and differentiated legal culture.[94] Institutions which have developed through evolution, such as property, contract, the juridical personality of corporations, subjective rights, court proceedings, etc., are taken as preconditioned and therefore need no further analysis. Evolutionary theory provides an explanation of how improbable achievements and far-reaching deviations from original states of affairs have become possible, and of how one can practise them as normal states of affairs. At the same time, this explanation implies that evolution is inevitable and that all intentions to plan and improve the law may contribute to its evolution but cannot have a decisive impact (or, if anything, a destructive impact) on the outcome.

Theories that attempt to say more noticeably seem to suggest that there is such a thing as progress. Frequently the argument of evolution serves to camouflage the fact that one has already opted for a preferred theory. Claiming that the structures, as stated by the theory, have been supported by evolution or have been created by it proves the theory. Ronald Heiner's writings can serve here as an example of the problem caused by incomplete information.[95] Similarly, Robert Clark states that evolution supports institutions that save transaction and other costs.[96] However, many old problems resurface (and that may be the reason why evolutionary theories of law and economics today resort to sociobiology). Above all, there is the problem that since participants do not calculate in a predictable way, one does not really know how quantitative conclusions are formed in their heads.[97] Then

---

[94] See for such an approach, even if it lacks a well-developed evolutionary theory, Watson, *The Evolution of Law*, in relation to the tradition of Roman civil law.   [95] Ibid.

[96] See Robert C. Clark, 'The Interdisciplinary Study of Legal Evolution', *Yale Law Journal* 90 (1981), 1238–1274. When studied in greater detail, a lot of things within this economic analysis of law are doubtful, and among them the exact formulation of the principle of selection. See also the contribution by Paul H. Rubin, 'Why Is the Common Law Efficient', *Journal of Legal Studies* 6 (1977), 65–83, and Jack Hirshleifer, 'Evolutionary Models in Economics and Law: Cooperative versus Conflict Strategies', *Research in Law and Economics* 4 (1982), 1–60. These approaches do not help us solve the question of the criterion of success, but they do take account of the advantages of litigation and economic cooperation with the view that the contesting of inefficient rules must make economic sense.

[97] See, for example, Jean Lave, *Cognition in Practice: Mind, Mathematics and Culture in Everyday Life* (Cambridge, 1988).

there are all the problems that are related to the unknown future and the inevitable social costs of all time-binding.[98]

Starting from the premiss of systems theory one is not gaining distance from one's own theory, but rather a more complex instrument for analysis.[99] We assume (and this is quite conventional) that evolution permits the formation and maintenance of highly complex systems, alongside which (or inside which) more simply structured systems also have a chance of survival. Evolution leads—without any particular purpose or *telos*—to the morphogenesis of systems, which can proceed with their autopoiesis, even when there is a high degree of structural complexity and requisite multiplicity and diversity of operations. Accordingly, such operations must be able to discriminate internally. Hence, what stands out, quite clearly, is that the development of higher complexity is triggered off unwittingly, and that the evolution of the legal system is a good example of this process. The main result is that people begin to complain of the complexity of the legal system and to look for relief from it. The evolution begins to react to its own result. But is there any 'higher meaning' involved in this—apart from the fact that it just happens? Is this the way in which 'civilization', or even 'spirit', is realized, as was assumed in the eighteenth century?

Today, hardly anyone still claims that complexity as such improves a system's chances of adaptation. If one entertained such a hypothesis, one would have to take into account the self-inflicted disadvantages of complexity as well. For us, the indisputable fact that evolution makes higher complexity possible suffices, and there can be no doubt that law in modern societies has become far more complex than the law of older social formations, regardless of all the new abstractions, generalizations, and simplifications.

It is simply another version of this state of affairs if one says that, as far as is possible, evolution normalizes improbabilities, improbabilities being understood here as the degree of deviation from an original state.[100] To put it this way, though, does little more than create new questions for further research, which would need to find out how a legal system adjusts its institutions to increasing complexity—or, in other words, how evolution

---

[98] These arguments are not meant to be a rebuttal; they are merely meant to draw attention to the fact that greater accuracy is needed in the application of empirical evidence and clearer argumentation in evolutionary theory.

[99] Another point that could be made in a comparison with the economic analysis of law is that systems theory analysis of law can produce references to itself (autologies) and can cope with them better.

[100] One can also define this as the improbability of the probable, and most likely incur a protest from statisticians. This merely means that, in language, it is highly improbable that a certain sentence is uttered and, at the same time, that this improbability is perfectly normal, that is, a characteristic of every sentence that is uttered. This is precisely the reason why the development of language can only be explained with evolutionary theory.

operates as pressure for selection and produces suitable structures—structures which allow for complexity, or obstruct further evolution.

Operative closure of the system and a coding that is indifferent towards the environment are the primary answers to these questions. The environment is excluded—unless the system itself considers it worth observing according to the system's own abilities for processing information. In order to achieve this, the system must develop the ability to distinguish between self-reference and external reference. We shall see later[101] that this takes place today in the form of distinguishing between concepts and interests,[102] provided that effective legal doctrines have been developed.

Further achievements, which correspond to higher complexity, are the dissociation of the symbol for legal validity from its historical origins (in the sense of *arche*, its ground) and from external references (in the sense of nature or reason given by nature). We have discussed the differentiation between property and ownership and the differentiation between transaction and contract above from the viewpoint of a loss of simplicity. The legal system renders itself autonomous in its self-description too. In this context, the system-internal distinction between legislation and jurisdiction has always made it difficult for the legislator, and impossible for the law-abiding judge, to be swayed by friendship, connections, attention to status, etc.[103] The dissolution of the uniform concept of the monarchical *iurisdictio* and the transition to doctrines of the separation of powers in the eighteenth century took this tendency further, restructured the system-internal feedback loop between legislation and jurisdiction, and permitted an increased use of undetermined legal concepts or political 'formula compromises' in laws, on the one hand, and the rejection of innovative judge-made law by reference to relevant legislation, on the other. As a result of these achievements the sum of all law can be described as self-made, as positive law. The doctrine of legal sources (whatever the term may now mean) was revised in the nineteenth and twentieth centuries to include, as legal sources, not only legislation but also jurisdiction, customary law—in so far as courts made decisions on it—and even legal dogmatics.[104]

The key concept here is 'temporalization of complexity' and it leads to further insights. The definitions in relation to persons and to space were in

---

[101] See below Ch. 8.VI and VII.

[102] At any rate it does not happen in the form of distinguishing between norms and facts. This is a distinction which runs across the distinction between concepts and interests. The reason for this is that the legal system can also receive external norms by having legal norms refer to them, and it can deem internal facts to be relevant (for instance, the formally correct publication of a law).

[103] This is at any rate the opinion of Aristotle, which was highly regarded in the Middle Ages, see *Rhetorics* 1354[b]. See also Aegidius Columnae Romanus, *De Regime Principum* (Rome, 1607; reprint Aalen 1967), 506.

[104] See on this point, as far as England and Scotland are concerned, Neil McCormick, *Legal Reasoning and Legal Theory* (Oxford, 1978), 61.

many respects replaced by definitions in relation to time.[105] New law annuls old law, and therefore even sharp temporal inconsistencies should not be seen as unjust *per se*.[106] Discussions which are triggered off by this circumstance become politicized.

Another mechanism which absorbs complexity can be described with the aid of the distinction between variety and redundancy. We shall discuss this in more detail in Chapter 8. For now it may suffice to mention that the legal system can deal with more and more varied cases if it relaxes strict requirements as to the consistency of legal decisions (redundancy) and instead finds new forms which are compatible with higher variety. In this context it has always been an important regulatory device to leave the decision to start legal proceedings in court to the concerned parties. Moreover, Roman law limited the number and types of legal actions which could be brought in courts. The litigation of all legal claims (a concept of the nineteenth century!), and the wide-ranging admission of the autonomy of the parties, adjusted the law to the requirements of modern society. In so far as the autonomy of the parties was accepted as a ground for the definition of rights, one proceeded on the assumption that the requirement of consistency (that is, justice as the equal application of all laws) could be relinquished. The protests which agitated against this development led to political pressures and a great amount of legislation that limited freedom. One could think here, for instance, of labour law or of socio-political legislation. As a result, however, the consistency of numerous laws has become a problem. Before one has come even faintly close to the end of experimenting with all the ways in which one might regain redundancy under these conditions, a new problem arises, namely the problem of public interest litigation undertaken by dedicated individuals, especially where it is undertaken in order to find an effective solution to ecological problems.

As a result of this evolution, which enables the differentiation and formation of complexity, and marks it, once achieved, for further evolution, we today find structures in the legal system that differ greatly from those which are found in tribal societies. The pivotal difference can be defined as the *personalization* of legal matters. It is connected to what is probably the most important achievement of the evolution of law in modern times: the concept of subjective rights.[107] Through them, an unfolding of the paradox

---

[105] This rules out the fixing of temporal limits in relation to persons, for instance, the linking of the validity of a law or the validity of a contract to the lifetime of a person who had agreed to certain conditions. This corresponds to a quasi-natural perspective that, as is well known, the Middle Ages relinquished only reluctantly.

[106] This has the remarkable consequence that constitutions must be exempted because otherwise new law would gradually undermine a constitution. It also has the consequence that changing the constitution must be largely achieved by interpretation.

[107] We note, however, that the modern form of the 'subjective law' represents only a part of this personalization. Essentially, one must also bear in mind that claims of the violation of

of freedom (that is, the necessity of the limitations of freedom as a condition for freedom) can be achieved, which is technically useful for law.[108] This paradox takes the form of an inclusion of the excluded and juridifies arbitrariness. In the framework of subjective rights, anybody can act arbitrarily; motives are not legally scrutinized. And if one wants to moderate this, one must (and can) do so by investigating the legal form of a limitation of subjective rights. Further achievements, which were available at the end of the eighteenth century, assumed this legal form and used it for related generalizations—for instance, a legal capacity which was independent of status and birth, and the positivization of law, which allowed the boundaries of the blank sheet of freedom to be reordered if there is a demand for it. The general access to law and legal proceedings (and through it the equal inclusion of all of the population in law) are premised on subjective rights too. For it is indispensable to the differentiation and combination of material law and procedural law that the material law indicates who appears as the plaintiff and who is sued. Also, the criminal law largely disregards collective liability and collective obligations of restitution or collective claims for compensation, which are customary in tribal societies. Organizations of any size are subject to this development. For such organizations, the legal form of the juridical 'person' has been developed in case they become a party in a legal action.

Since we are used to this form, considerable effort must be made to fathom the infrequency and the evolutionary improbability of its existence. First and foremost, law must provide social support for contra-factual expectations. A regulatory device for the solution of conflicts—which deprives the individual of all social support by possible allies, friends and relatives, or associations (for instance, guilds) to which he belongs and in which he can earn respect and merit—is likewise highly unlikely. In legal proceedings, the individual is at first isolated, confronted with the court, and then referred exclusively to the legal system for assistance. Corrective devices (in substantive law, for instance, trust funds which limit the control of the individual in order to protect family interests; and in procedural law, for instance, legal aid, legal insurance, or concepts of legal ethics and their implementation through professional bodies) require such a personalization and then build

rights or other forms of unlawful conduct can only be addressed to persons and not to groups or any other range of relations. See Brian Tierney, 'Religion and Rights: A Medieval Perspective', *Journal of Law and Religion* 5 (1987), 163–5, for the beginnings of this development, which are related to the dissolution of clan structures in the feudal system but also to the Church's resistance to a looming political theocracy, which already manifested itself in England as early as the twelfth century. See also in more detail, Tierney, *Religion, Law and the Growth of the Constitutional Thought 1150–1650* (Cambridge, 1982), and Palmer, 'The Origins of Property in England'.

[108] See also above at Ch. 5.IV.

on it. The differentiation of the legal system cannot be achieved without the decomposition of social ties, obligations, and expectations of help. And not until this pattern is successful in evolution can one see any direct social, influence on judges as a matter of corruption, and social influences on law as a general problem, which problem cannot be legalized, and as such having been found through the statistical methods of sociology.[109] Here, as in so many other functioning systems, the detour via the separation of 'persons', and the semantic correlates of modern individualism, prove to be a precondition for the formation of complex functioning systems and their ability to control decisions of inclusion and exclusion.

What has evolved in the legal system—and what is, by and large, successful if the harshness of the basic pattern is recognized—becomes more of a problem, the more the political system attempts to use law as a regulatory instrument. Comprehensive political goals, then, have to be detailed into a form which refers to justiciable persons. It becomes clear, however—above all by the transformation of ecological problems and regulatory aims in environmental law—how little the inevitable personalization suits the matters concerned. This relates primarily to the difficulties in the attribution of causes when socially conditioned conduct has an ecological impact. Here the ability to achieve significant results is precluded by the necessity to relate all arguments to individually motivating obligations and rights. This is why, for instance, there is so much discussion, with so little success, about litigation in the public interest without having corresponding positions defined in substantive law.[110] It is this, in particular, which makes it clear how much the form of personalization is a product of the evolution of law and not a dictate of the environment, whether internal to society or external to society. This example supports our theoretical assumption that the evolution of autopoietic systems is more a test of how much room autopoiesis frees up for the formation of complex orders, than of adjusting the system to a given environment.

This discussion must remain sketchy and should not anticipate the results of further detailed research. Hence it may suffice here just to introduce the hypothesis: it is not economic efficiency but complexity that is the intervening variable that translates evolutionary structural changes into adjustments within the system.

VI

In this chapter we have left to the last one of the most difficult questions for a historical discussion of law. Can we say that the social significance

---

[109] See also below Ch. 10.I.

[110] See, for example, in relation to constitutional law, Dieter Grimm, *Die Zukunft der Verfassung* (Frankfurt, 1991), esp. 190.

and above all the size of the legal system have increased because of the evolutionary internal dynamics of the legal system? If one relates this question to absolute numbers, this is evidently so. There are now more lawyers and more laws than ever before (even if there are considerable regional differences, as can readily be gleaned from a comparison of the United States and Japan).[111] There is, consequently, ever-growing weariness, more complaints about the excessive number of legal regulations oppressing every free individual, and demands for deregulation, alternative dispute resolution, and de-bureaucratization. The counter-argument would be that these kinds of enlargement developments could be found in all functioning systems, from the political system to the education system, from scientific research to the medium of money in the economy. Jürgen Habermas called this development, albeit in a slightly different context, the colonization of the lifeworld. In other words: the significance of the functioning systems in everyday life increases, and in many respects there are counter-movements of a 'back to nature' kind which, however, have little chance of succeeding. Generally, the result is the paradox that these counter-movements must use the structural means of the functioning systems, as if the production of organically grown plants were at issue. Simplifications of administration, however, require additional regulations of control and review procedures, which put more strain on that administration.

The impression of 'too much' can be confirmed superficially, but the problem is less one of absolute numbers and more one of relations. Since many resources, time of course above all, are finite, one would need to find out whether the increase of individual functioning systems takes up more time, more money, more natural resources, energy, motivations, etc., which are thus withdrawn from other usages. This leads empirical research to grapple with almost insurmountable problems. For, how can one find out which alternatives would have been used if the resources had not been taken up to such a large extent by the enlargements in the development of law? Above all, however, it is unrealistic to assume fixed sums in such a research design. Society at large has increased in size and complexity. With the increase in the means of communication the possibilities of satisfying demand have increased too.

Conventional empirical sociology may calculate the increase in the number of lawyers or of legal incidents (for example, laws, legal proceedings) per capita of the population.[112] But even this approach is fraught with

---

[111] See for regional case studies, for example, Vilhelm Aubert, *Continuity and Development in Law and Society* (Oslo, 1989).

[112] See, for example, Friedman, *Total Justice*, 6. But see also, contradicting his own earlier analysis, the important insight that the activity of just a few people can create the perception of considerable change (ibid. 97) and that this perception follows from the significance of communication.

difficulties because one can only define the correlated units (how large is the workload of a lawyer, how complex are legal proceedings) arbitrarily. Above all, the size of populations is not a relevant indicator with regard to the development of media and techniques of communication. What would be relevant is the number of communication units, and here it would also be meaningless to assess them regardless of quality and outcome. Indeed, there is hardly a methodology for operationalizing scientifically the strong impression that the legal system has grown explosively and is invading more and more areas of everyday life which used to be determined by customs, lack of alternatives, socialization, social control, etc.

This unsatisfactory state of knowledge should be one reason to avoid making statements on the unity of the legal system in the context of evolutionary change. One can certainly ascertain that structures change in the course of the evolution of the legal system, that new evolutionary achievements take shape, and even that expectations of the juridification of matters change, and that with the improvement of techniques of procedure and evidence, for instance, formalism can be reduced and 'internal' facts (motives etc.) can become legally relevant. In this sense one could follow Lawrence Friedman's thesis, which points out that expectations of justice have changed to assume the function of compensation for chance events.[113] More generally one could say that a full differentiation of the legal system leads to the universalization of its code and does not accept that there are any matters that are not by their nature juridifiable (for example, private family matters).[114] It is now a matter for the legal system itself to decide which matters are legally regulated and which are not, and which types of regulation are appropriate. The same applies, *mutatis mutandis*, to other differentiated functioning systems. Limitations can now be realized only as self-limitations. However, all these statements remain statements about the structures of the system and their variations. They do not permit us to make any inferences about the increase or decrease in the social significance of law. In the last chapter, we shall return to this discussion.[115] That chapter will not end with prognoses either. The concept of evolution itself prohibits such prognoses.

---

[113] Ibid.

[114] For curiosity's sake and as a comment on feminist jurisprudence, one can add that a society which used law to limit the *patria potestas* could be defined as a save society only 150 years ago, at least in Spain: 'El pueblo en que el jefe de familia no puede arreglar sus assuntos domesticos sin pedir permiso al juez, o sin consultar de continuo la ley, es un pueblo esclavo . . . Qué sacaremos de ser reyes en el Parlamento si no podemos reinar en nuestra casa?' (Felix M. de Falguera, 'Idea general del dérecho catalán: Su espiritu y principios que lo informan', in *Conferencia del dérecho catalán* (Barcelona, 1883), quoted in Juan B. Vallet de Goytisolo, *Estudios sobre fuentes del dérecho y método jurídico* (Madrid, 1982), 51.

[115] See Ch. 12, esp. section V.

7 The Position of Courts in the Legal System

I

General observations influenced by systems theory and empirical research both suggest that the differentiation of a system requires an internal differentiation, which is developing at the same time as the system itself develops.[1] The differentiation of a social system founded on communication could have been made possible only, and even in its most primitive beginnings (and before any segmental formation of families), if there was a possibility of distinguishing between the interactions of people who were present and society at large. This means that the social relevance of what happens with those who are absent has to be taken into account in the interaction, which can be done only selectively. Hence we have to assume that the legal system too can only become fully differentiated if it is an internally differentiated system. This, however, does not in itself specify the form of such an internal differentiation.

By the phrase 'form of internal differentiation' is meant the form through which the relations between sub-systems express the order of the whole system, for instance a hierarchical order of ranks. Internal differentiation means also, but not only, that everything is environment which, seen from the perspective of each sub-system, does not belong to that system. This is part and parcel of the concept of system, and hence is self-evident as far as systems theory is concerned. An internal order of a system requires furthermore that the relations between sub-systems be regulated either on the basis of equality (segmental order) or in various forms of inequality (a ranking order would be one of them). The overall order of the comprehensive system (for present purposes the legal system) is expressed by limiting the system/environment relation of sub-systems through an ordering design for system-to-system relations. The latter can provide different degrees of freedom, that is, differing degrees of density of integration depending on the complexity that has been achieved in the evolution of the comprehensive system, which has to be managed by the system. Segmental order suffices only on a low level of complexity. For instance, where there are a majority of courts that are similar, they have to respect each other as similar. Apart from this, however, forms of differentiation that have developed over a long time are based on inequality—for instance, courts and lawyers, courts and legislative parliaments, which have introduced more differences, and with them more degrees of freedom,

---

[1] See, for example Rudolf Stichweh, *Zur Entstehung des modernen Systems wissenschaftlicher Disziplinen: Physik in Deutschland 1740–1890* (Frankfurt, 1984).

into the system on the basis of inequality. This example shows that different forms of differentiation do not exclude each other.[2] Hence the dominant form of inequality must regulate where and how many other forms of differentiation are necessary and are allowed—for instance, in feudal societies, households which are stratified but equal within their class.

Using these guidelines as a basis, we want to explore the forms of the internal differentiation of the legal system. These forms cannot be established by reference to the different areas of law and to the corresponding historical change of distinctions. We are not talking about distinctions such as public law and private law, administrative law and constitutional law, law of property and law of obligations, nor are we talking about a principled division of legal matters, for instance with the formula *persona/res/actio* of Roman law. Semantic divisions of this kind cannot develop independently of the level of complexity of the system, and they do not give any information about the operative formations of the system within the legal system.

Neither should the conventional division of judicial law and statute law be followed. This division is determined, in its form, by the theory of positive law, which prompts the question whether one or several sources of law are to be assumed. This question is open to discussion but a definite answer without resorting to more abstract theoretical foundations is not available. And we must assume that a theoretical abstraction will make the question about the sources of law rather more doubtful in itself than is helpful for any discussion. Within the perspective of a theory of differentiation we are primarily interested in the position of the courts as a differentiated sub-system of the legal system. Hence the question for us will be which *form of differentiation* is propelled upon a legal system when it differentiates courts.

II

A first point of departure can be the distinction between legislation and jurisdiction, which figures prominently in the self-description of the system. This first distinction is particularly opportune because it is one that had been justified explicitly by differentiation in the old European tradition. Aristotle saw the problem as the independence of the judge from family relations, and from relations with friends, and his text on this was relied on again in the Middle Ages.[3] This referred to independence from the segmental differentiation in a society, which was already differentiated by

---

[2] Karl Otto Hondrich, 'Die andere Seite sozialer Differenzierung', stresses this in: Hans Haferkamp and Michael Schmid (eds.), *Sinn, Kommunikation und soziale Differenzierung: Beiträge zu Luhmanns Theorie sozialer Systeme* (Frankfurt, 1987), 275–303. However, a different opinion has never been voiced.

[3] *Rhetorics* I 1354[b]. See on this point Aegidius Columnae Romanus, *De regimine principum* (1277/79; Romè, 1607), 506.

classes and by the rural/urban divide. Aristotle's solution was to differentiate the administration of justice in order to separate legislation and jurisdiction. For the legislator was bound to issue general norms. Their impact
on friends and foes, on those in the vicinity and those far away was difficult
to assess because of the generality of the norms and their indeterminacy
with regard to future applications. Hence it would suffice to bind the
judges to the laws in order to prevent them from favouring friends and dis-
advantaging foes. Later, nothing else would be meant by the formula 'without fear or favour'.

As is well known, an additional differentiation developed in Roman law
in the form of distinguishing between legislation by the people and the
conditioning of the exercise of jurisdictional power by the relevant magistrate (the *praetor*). This was a legal regulation of the conditions under
which political power was granted in law. Hence, the influence of classes
became associated with legal knowledge to a considerable degree, namely
with the open counselling by legal experts (who initially belonged exclusively to the aristocracy). This led to the understanding—which was preserved until modern times—that legislation and jurisdiction were two
variants of a uniform task, namely the *iurisdictio* which pertained to political
power, that is, the sovereign in a territorial state.[4] In this respect the differentiation of law remained dependent on the precarious political autonomy
of the respective political systems, in contrast to the dominant order of
class and households.[5] Much depended on this situation as to whether or
not and against whom law could be enforced, and primarily the local
administration of justice was firmly controlled by the aristocracy (who were,
however, frequently absent) or the courts of the city.[6]

The signs of a changing order can be observed in the second half of the
sixteenth century and above all in the seventeenth century. The *potesta
legislatoria* was given more weight as a component of the early modern
concept of sovereignty and the corresponding competence to enforce the
ideas of order of the modern territorial state was used more comprehensively.[7] Almost imperceptibly the understanding of legislation shifted from

---

[4] See, for example, Pietro Costa, *Iurisdictio: Semantica del potere politico nella pubblicistica
medievale (1100–1433)* (Milan, 1969); Brian Tierney, *Religion, Law, and the Growth of
Constitutional Thought 1150–1650* (Cambridge, 1982); Edward Powell, *Kingship, Law and
Society: Criminal Justice in the Reign of Henry V* (Oxford, 1989).

[5] See on this point the global overview by Shmuel N. Eisenstadt, *The Political System of
Empires* (New York, 1963).

[6] Criticism does not arise until the formulation of a new concept of the sovereignty of the
state. See in this respect the incisive critique by C. L. P. [Charles Loyseau, Parisien], *Discours de
l'abus des iustices de village* (Paris, 1603).

[7] See Heinz Mohnhaupt, 'Potestas legislatoria und Gesetzesbegriff im Ancien Régime', *Ius
Commune* 4 (1972), 188–239; Michael Stolleis, 'Condere leges et interpretari: Gesetzgebungsmacht
und Staatsbildung in der frühen Neuzeit', in id., *Staat und Staatsräson in der frühen Neuzeit:*

the context of *iurisdictio* (legal statutes 'say' what is legal) to the context of *souveraineté*, and in this development the ideas of legal sovereignty and political sovereignty fused for centuries to come. The eminence of the concept of law required that sub-competences be included in the power of legislation—such as the competence of annulment or amendment, the competence of derogation in given cases, the granting of 'privileges' which waived the laws, and last but not least the competence of interpretation of laws in what one calls today 'hard cases'.[8] All of this leads to the necessity for a reform and unification of the administration of justice in the territorial states.

Initially only the unitary idea of responsibility for the law was defined anew. The changes on the way from the feudal state to the absolutist state created terminological variations and thereby contributed to a gradual undermining of ancient participatory rights. This did not change radically until the eighteenth century when the differentiation of legislation and jurisdiction reached its present-day level. Above all, Jeremy Bentham, in the context of an abiding interest in law reform, demanded a clear separation of legislation and jurisdiction without, however, having a noticeable practical impact on the common law tradition.[9] The concept of *iurisdictio* as a concept of authority was discarded. From that time onwards one reasoned strictly on the basis of positive law whatever reasons of nature or rationality may have implied. With hindsight one has the impression that the risk of legal decision-making had to be apportioned to two instances (jurisdiction and legislation) and was made more tolerable in this way. Not differentiation as such but the contingency of the already differentiated legal system was the problem to which the distinction between legislation and jurisdiction responded.

The distinction between legislation and jurisdiction depends on the differentiation of corresponding proceedings, that is, it depends on the evolution of norms of competence and their restrictive conditioning. It can be seen from both sides of the distinction and as such can be enacted as a doubly usable asymmetry. With this support from within, the legal system can relinquish external support—without having to leave society—and practise

Studien zur Geschichte des öffentlichen Rechts (Frankfurt, 1990), 167–96. For a contemporary reference see, for example, the combination of *promulgatio, interpretatio,* and *executio* of the laws as components of the *ius majestatis* in Johannes Althusius, *Politica methodice digesta* (1614), cap. X, reprinted in *Harvard Political Classics,* vol. II (Cambridge, 1932), 94.

[8] See for this *recourir au Prince,* also called *référé législatif* in the case in which no clear interpretation is possible, Jean Domat, *Les loix civiles dans leur ordre naturel,* 2 edn. (Paris, 1697), vol. 1, p. 25. See further the overview of European practice in the seventeenth and eighteenth centuries in Mohnhaupt, 'Potestas', 220.

[9] See, for example, Gerald J. Postema, *Bentham and the Common Law Tradition* (Oxford, 1986), esp. 191, who includes unpublished sources; David Lieberman, *The Province of Legislation Determined: Legal Theory in Eighteenth-Century Britain* (Cambridge, 1989).

its own autonomy. The judge applies the law according to the instructions of the legislation. And the legislator would embark on a 'trip into the blue' (Esser) if consideration were not given to the suitability of the new laws to the premisses on which decision-making is arranged in the courts. This difference between jurisdiction and legislation becomes a kind of cybernetic circle in which the law observes itself at the level of secondary observations. The judge must attempt to recognize the intentions of the legislator and how they observed the world. Accordingly, a methodology for the interpretation of the intentions behind legislation develops. However, the legislator must also anticipate in which forms cases are brought to the courts and how they are seen and managed there. Nevertheless, the eighteenth century chooses a different form of description whose basis is that of a 'civil society' concept of state, which is not yet fully differentiated from society. Here the hierarchical architecture of the old cosmological order still casts its shadow, and in this framework *lex* and *imperium* cannot yet be understood as separated. The relationship of legislation and jurisdiction was constructed in the fashion of a hierarchy, and hierarchy was understood as a hierarchy of command (rather than as a hierarchy of inclusion or a relationship between the parts and the whole). Courts were understood as agents charged with executing legislation and the methods of law were understood to be deductive. Integration was supposed to be guaranteed by logic and thus by the axiomatic application of norms. The resulting projects have been discussed since Leibniz. That reality did not reflect this presentation is a truism today.[10] Nevertheless, one can understand very well that the new harshness of the distinction between legislation and jurisdiction could only be recommended and managed with the help of such a corresponding concept of unity. Hence law became accentuated as a system in the sense of a diversity that could be constructed from one principle, and accompanied by the method of deduction, which did not allow for any deviation. Thus the requirement for the so-called *référé législatif* as an auxiliary device for cases in which (as an exception, or so it was believed) problems of interpretation arose. It was therefore not difficult to conceive of the legal system as being exactly parallel to (or even identical with) the political order.

Reality, however, contradicted this monistic concept of differentiation quickly.[11] At best, the after-effects of this hierarchical concept of the separation

---

[10] See Regina Ogorek, 'De l'Esprit des légendes, oder wie gewissermaßen aus dem Nichts eine Interpretationslehre wurde', *Rechtshistorisches Journal* 2 (1983), 277–96; ead., 'Zum politischen Selbstverständnis der Rechtsprechung am Vorabend des bürgerlichen Zeitalters—eine Fallstudie', *Ius Commune* 10 (1983), 69–95; ead., *Richterkönig oder Subsumtionsautomat: Zur Justiztheorie im 19. Jahrhundert* (Frankfurt, 1986), 13.

[11] See further Herman Conrad, *Richter und Gesetze im Übergang vom Absolutismus zum Verfassungsstaat* (Graz, 1971).

of powers can be found in the style of reasoning of the highest courts—especially in France.[12] The interpretation of laws and the self-determination of decision-making that, correspondingly, had to be granted to courts, could not be withdrawn from them. Constitutionality itself became an object of judicial interpretation. Courts had to decide how far they could demand change of laws by legislation if no satisfactory solution could be found. *And only this conception of the judicial task makes it possible to create norms about the prohibition of denial of justice and to demand that courts must decide all cases brought to them by themselves.*

Since the nineteenth century, the hierarchy model was weakened by changes but without being challenged, let alone being replaced by another model of differentiation. The powers of interpretation of the judge in relation to legislation increased—not least by the great codifications growing older. Increasingly, problems of interpretation of contracts (interpretation of the will of the contracting parties) keep courts busy. A plurality of methods is under consideration and strict deduction is less and less talked about. Judges face a double pressure: to decide every individual case and to decide it justly, and this means to treat individual cases, at least, equally and to apply the same rules. In this process, also, the interpretation of laws, with rules developed by the courts, must be just. The *obligation* to decide and the *freedom* to find reasons for a decision (however doubtful), which comes with that requirement and is produced by it, become *limited* by points of view on justice. And this triad of obligation, freedom, and limitation produces law. Together with ever more legislation-type law, there develops ever more judge-made law.

Initially, this development was explained in the nineteenth century with reference to the protective hypothesis that legislators had acted rationally and legislative texts had to be interpreted accordingly.[13] This made it possible to preserve the form of hierarchy in the relationship between legislation and jurisdiction and to include judges in the production of texts. Method is important as a guarantee for conformity to this up-and-down model. After this other constructions follow—above all the doctrine of the perfection of the legal order ('gaplessness'), in the form of a useful fiction and the distinction between the letter of the law and the spirit of the law with the function of releasing an, as yet covert, judge-made law. Finally, and after even rhetoric and themes had been accepted as methods, a critique developed which held that too much weight was being given to methods in

[12] See Michel Troper et al., 'Statutory Interpretations in France', in D. Neil MacCormick and Robert S. Summers (eds.), *Interpreting Statutes: A Comparative Study* (Aldershot, 1992), 171–212. See also the comparative accounts set at 487 and 496.

[13] Cf. François Ost and Michel van de Kerchove, *Jalons pour une théorie critique du droit* (Brussels, 1987), 355 (see also p. 97).

legal theories.[14] The opinion took hold (especially in American Realism) that law is ultimately only what courts take it to be. 'Judge-made law' became accepted as a source of law of its own kind.[15] This led gradually to the insight that the relationship between legislation and jurisdiction should be seen not as asymmetrical and linear, but as circular, and as mutual limitation of the ambit for decisions.[16] In spite of all that, the idea of a hierarchical superiority of legislation over the judge still appears to be dominant because the judge is bound by the laws—but should not one add, like everybody else, including the legislator? And how could one speak of 'democracy' if this were not the case?

How can this divergence between the facts and their description be explained? We assume that the special position of the courts in the legal system has not been understood properly, and so we address this question first.

III

The significance of the distinction between legislation and jurisdiction is demonstrated by the fact that the peculiarity of court operations is determined primarily if not exclusively within this distinction. In contrast to legislation, the matter at issue here is the 'application' of law by deciding in individual cases.[17] If one develops or confirms, following on from such decisions, general decisional rules, guidelines, guiding principles, and legal theories, this happens, as it were, at arm's length and only by following the statutes which demand that reasons must be given for decisions, for instance according to § 313 of the German Civil Procedure Act (ZPO). No court can begin proceedings by itself, even though calamities might have arisen. This

---

[14] See, for example, Martin Kriele, *Theorie der Rechtsgewinnung, entwickelt am Problem der Verfassungsinterpretation* (Berlin, 1967; 2nd edn. 1976), in which only vague ideas as to the separation between legislation and jurisdiction remain. Nevertheless, this is worth reading, especially the debate with Larenz and the attempt to replace awareness of methods with responsibility for decision-making.

[15] See, for example, on the debate whether or not judge-made law is a source of law, Josef Esser, *Richterrecht, Gerichtsgebrauch und Gewohnheitsrecht, Festschrift für Fritz von Hippel* (Tübingen, 1967), 95–130, who rejects the opinion, or Heinrich Wilhelm Krause, *Das Richterrecht als Rechtsquelle des innerstaatlichen Rechts* (Tübingen, 1971), who supports it. On the issue of the *factual* prevalence of the opinion that there is a special 'judge-made law' see also Eduard Picker, 'Richterrecht oder Rechtsdogmatik—Alternativen der Rechtsgewinnung?', *Juristenzeitung* 43 (1988), 1–12, 62–75.

[16] Cf. Torstein Eckhoff, 'Feedback in Legal Reasoning and Rule Systems', *Scandinavian Studies in Law* (1978), 39–51; van de Kerchove and Ost, *Jalons*, 205; van de Kerchove and Ost, *Le système juridique entre ordre et desordre* (Paris, 1988), 102.

[17] See on such a 'self-concept' of courts in contrast to a much more complex social reality which can be identified sociologically Klaus A. Ziegert, 'Courts and the Self-Concept of Law: The Mapping of the Environment by Courts of First Instance', *Sydney Law Review* 14 (1992), 196–229.

ensures that the decision-making of courts remains 'concrete' and that developing rules is a parallel operation. And this occurs even if it is obvious that judge-made law can be much more important in many areas than statute law!

By the arrangement of an asymmetric relationship between legislation and jurisdiction, and with the help of terminology that supports this, for example the doctrine of the sources of law, one tries to prevent a circularity, which would be the consequence of admitting that the court itself 'creates' the law that it 'applies'.[18] Presenting the decisions of courts as a 'finding' of law—and even the doctrine of the sources of law presents sources of law as sources for finding the law[19]—serves, above all, the purpose of rendering asymmetric a relationship which otherwise would have to be presented as a circle. However, the circle would not come about at all if courts could resort to a *non liquet* ('it is not clear') in cases in which they could not 'find' any law and then would not have to decide. But courts are not permitted to do that—that is, not permitted *by law*. The operative closure of the system and its detachment from any direct participation in the environment corresponds with the internal necessity to have to decide. The state of the system cannot be treated in the way in which it appears as a state of the world. The difference between the system and the environment is experienced in the system as an open problem. After long experience with this disjunction, and after the development of those legal institutions which make it possible to manage the disjunction, the system puts itself under the pressure of having to decide.

But what is it, really, that courts have to do: make decisions?

Because decision-making, as far as actual behaviour is concerned, is so familiar to everybody and because courts make their decisions explicitly, publicly, and, if one may add, with dignity, the particularity of this act is

[18] For an attempt to escape from this circle, see Josef Raz, *The Concept of a Legal System: An Introduction to the Theory of Legal System*, 2nd edn. (London, 1980), 187. See also Torstein Eckhoff and Nils Kristian Sundby, *Rechtssysteme: Eine systemtheoretische Einführung in die Rechtstheorie* (Berlin, 1988), esp. 134.

[19] For a position which has been influential in the history of legal theory, see Alf Ross, *Theorie der Rechtsquellen: Ein Beitrag zur Theorie des positiven Rechts auf Grundlage dogmenhistorischer Untersuchungen* (Copenhagen, Leipzig, Vienna, 1929), 290. That this serves the purpose of avoiding the circle becomes apparent when one reads that the dominant opinion—'which sees the statute as a source of law because it is seen as an expression of a particularly qualified will'—is rejected as 'controversial' (ibid. 294). For the school of thought which followed see, for example, Ronald Dubischar, *Grundbegriffe des Rechts: Eine Einführung in die Rechtstheorie* (Stuttgart, 1968), 58. According to Ralf Dreier, *Probleme der Rechtsquellenlehre: Zugleich Bemerkungen zur Rechtsphilosophie Leonhard Nelsons. Festschrift für Hans J. Wolff* (Munich, 1973), 3–36, the command of asymmetry can also be formulated in the following way: if judges are a source for finding the law *for others*, they cannot be such a source *for themselves*: the concept of source of law has to be used relative to the situation or role-specific (p. 8). However, the next question is then: why is the judge an exception and the same argument not applicable to the legislator?

usually not posed. The literature on the theory of decision-making does not lead very far either because it is mostly concerned with questions about the rationality of decision-making or with empirical research on the process of decision-making (in the sense of a sequence of micro-decisions). Furthermore, the literature on legal reasoning, one must not forget, assumes that what matters is the justification for, or the influencing of, decisions. The decision itself is not, however, a further (final?) argument. What is it, then?

An elaborate theory of decision-making would be out of place in an analysis of the legal system. However, since decision-making in courts commands a central position in the system, it is important to gain at least a basic understanding of the fact that the system becomes an enigma for itself at this point.

Certainly, a decision is always a matter of an alternative, which consists of two and frequently more paths that can be chosen. They may contain, in turn, further states and events, but also further decisions which are enabled by the decision, that is, which could not be realized without the decision, but which are foreseeable only to a limited degree, and which are, as far as further decisions are concerned, in principle unforeseeable. The decision itself, however, is not a component of the given alternative. It is not a further path. Hence one must assume that the decision is the third party, which is excluded by the alternative state of the two alternatives. It is the difference which constitutes this alternative. More precisely, the decision is the unity of this difference. This means it is a paradox. Decisions can only be made if undecidability is given as a matter of principle (and it is not merely something which is undecided!).[20] If this were not the case, the decision would already be decided and would only have to be 'realized'.[21]

This paradox is a consequence of the factual relationship between the alternative and the excluded third party, which constructs the paradox in order to be excluded (that is, in order to be able to decide). It is like an observer who cannot be the distinction with the help of which he defines something but who has to exclude himself as a blind spot of the observation. In addition, there is a problem with time.[22] One can say generally that

[20] See Heinz von Foerster, 'Ethics and Second-order Cybernetics', *Cybernetics and Human Knowing* 1 (1992), 9–19, at 14.

[21] The fact that courts choose this form and present 'findings' has to be taken as an evasion of the problem, perhaps also as an invisibilization and dissipation of the paradox. At any rate it should not lead to the mistaken view that legal disputes do not require a decision. If there is no alternative, the decision of courts has already been pre-empted by the legislator or a contract. However, even if this was the intention, frequently alternatives can still be found. There is no decision that could exclude, as a consequence of that decision, that further decisions are needed or become possible.

[22] See on this point and the following, G. L. S. Shackle, 'Imagination, Formalism, and Choice', in Mario J. Rizzo (ed.), *Time, Uncertainty, and Disequilibrium: Explorations in Austrian Themes* (Lexington, 1979), 19–31.

a system exists only at the point in time at which it operates and that it must assume a world which exists *simultaneously* at that point of time (and that means always—which is uncontrollable as well).[23] An extension of time is only possible by introducing the present as a distinction, as a unity of the difference between past and future. And so one makes the present the blind spot of time, which extends to what is not of immediate interest. Because this is possible, one can use the present as the point in time for decision-making, and make it what cannot be changed any more from the past and what can still be changed in the future, and thus turn the simultaneously existing world into the form of an alternative. One can be selective as far as the time horizons of past and future are concerned, *because they are necessarily not acute,* and one can construct an alternative with this selectivity which, in turn, enables one to understand the situation as a situation for decision-making. A decision can only occur if one temporizes in this way. For the rest, one is free to experience the world at any given moment as it presents itself.

An analysis of decision-making of this kind has serious consequences, which may be particularly unacceptable for lawyers. This analysis finds that the decision is *not determined by the past* (including, of course, laws which were passed, acts which were committed). The decision operates within its own construction, which is only possible in the present. Then it has consequences for the future present. It opens up or closes down possibilities, which would not exist without it. The decision assumes the past as immutable and the future as changeable and *it, therefore, turns around the relationship of determination.* It cannot be determined by the past but attempts to treat the future differently; this, however, has no determining effect because there will be more decisions lined up in the future. Hence, one can easily understand—even given all the problems which ensue—that courts are careful about the consequences of their decisions and try to legitimate decisions by an evaluation of their consequences. Unfortunately, courts are not able to know the consequences of their decisions in the strict sense (because further decisions will interfere with them and information about the future remains patchy). Perhaps this, more than anything else, fosters the illusion that a decision should and could be determined by the past, at least in the legal system with its capacity to capture the past in its proceedings.

Hence a decision is a paradox, which cannot make itself its own subject and which, at best, can only mystify itself. Authority, decorum, limitation of access to the mystery of law, texts to which one can refer, the pomp of entries and exits of judges—all that is a substitution at the moment at

---

[23] See also ibid. 20 on 'the notion of the *present,* the moment of which, alone, we have direct knowledge, the moment-in-being, the moment of actuality embracing all that is. All that is, is the present.'

which one must prevent the paradox of decision-making from appearing as a paradox, so as not to disclose that the assumption that one could *decide legally about what is legal and what is illegal,* is a paradox as well, and that *the unity of the system* can be observed only as a paradox.

This may be the reason why the system can translate its unity into operations only with the help of distinctions, and why distinctions such as legal and illegal, norms and facts, or validity (by decision) and reasons (by argument) cannot be reduced to a principle, to an origin, to reason within the system. This, then, means also as a consequence that the system can avail itself of its symbol for validity only in this mysterious form of decision-making. Thus the system can make available a great number of decisions, but it must also provide for the possibility of forcing itself to make decisions if the paradox of the distinction legal/illegal cannot be dissolved in any other way.

IV

This leads us to more depth in the discussion although, at the same time, perhaps undermining what has been said so far. Contracts need not be concluded and statutes need not be passed (unless specified otherwise in the constitution), but courts have to decide every case submitted to them. The corresponding norm is called—and the double negation of this formulation demonstrates its logic—the prohibition of the denial of justice.[24]

While Roman law, and even medieval law, provided legal protection only for a limited number of well-defined actions (*actio,* writ),[25] it has become a matter of course during the transition to modern times that each action which is brought must receive a decision in response even if this is not explicitly prescribed in statutes (as, for instance, in the famous art. 4 of the Code Civil[26]). Not until there was the requirement that judges *had to grant* decisions on the basis of their own responsibility, could judges be freed

---

[24] Seen in relation to the structural significance of this compulsory decision-making there is precious little literature on it in legal theory—as if the topic could be disposed of by neglect. See, however, Ottmar Ballweg, *Rechtswissenschaft und Jurisprudenz* (Basle, 1970), esp. 84 and 108.

[25] Accordingly the topic was limited in Roman law to the refusal of a judge to accept a permissible claim—'vel propter amicitias vel inimicitias vel turpissimi lucri gratis vel per aliud quicquam vitium' (either because of friendship or animosity or turpitude or because of any other vice)—as has been stated in a formula which is remarkable in respect to a theory of differentiation, a formula which can be found in the collection of *constitutiones* in the *Codex Juris Civilis* (C 3.1. de judiciis 13.8).

[26] The text is a follows: 'Le juge qui refusera de juger, sous prétexte du silence, de l'obscurité ou de l'insufficisance de la loi, pourra être poursuivi comme coupable de déni de justice' (A judge who refuses to make a decision under the pretext of silence, of obscurity or the deficiencies of the statutes will be prosecuted as culpable of denial of justice). The legal figure of the *déni de justice* is much older but earlier referred to an extraordinary remedy against delays of proceedings which could not be fixed in spite of repeated reprimands. (See, for example, Pierre Ayrault, *Ordre, formalité et instruction judiciaire* (1576; 2nd edn. Paris, 1598), 280.) These arrangements assumed the idea of an absolute supreme legal authority (*iurisdictio*) of a sovereign,

from the old imperial supervision and accede to their own political independence.[27] And only then could it become meaningful to transfer the competences of courts gradually to the activities of public life.[28] It has frequently been observed that courts are rarely approached for decisions in disputes compared with the frequency of legal problems in everyday life.[29] But this is not an objection to the *structural* significance of the *possibility* of filing a court action. For the possibility of being able to approach courts makes every waiver of this and each agreement outside the court appear as an anticipated solution of a problem—whatever one could say about the 'voluntariness' of such a solution.[30]

It may appear as a mere coincidence that the obligation of courts to have to decide was formulated at exactly the time in which the philosophy of Immanuel Kant announced the superiority of practice over knowledge, or at least that a causal link between these two events would be difficult to establish. It is no mere coincidence, however, that in conjunction with the appearance of modern social structures, awareness of complexity arises which eclipses the claim that the problems of the world can be worked out logically or even theoretically. The circumstances of human existence

and, therefore, had to be reformulated after the transition to a constitutional separation of powers. That one had to formulate so explicitly gave rise to the need to decide another question in connection with it, namely the question of the *référé legislatif* in cases in which a judge assumed that a decision was required which was not yet regulated in statutes. The rejection of the *référé legislatif* was then a consequence of the prohibition of the *déni de justice*. Hence art. 4 Code civil is the point of departure in positive law for a discussion of problems of legal sources and interpretation. See, for example, A. Bayart, 'L'article 4 du Code civil et la mission de la cour de cassation', *Journal des Tribunaux* 71 (1956), 353–5.

[27] Historical research has been almost exclusively dedicated to this political neutralization and the ensuing widening of competence, and has rarely dealt with the structural conditions that were set by the prohibition of the denial of justice.

[28] See, for example, as a recent overview of the development in the nineteenth century in Germany, Regina Ogorek, 'Individueller Rechtsschutz gegenüber der Staatsgewalt: Zur Entwicklung der Verwaltungsgerichtsbarkeit im 19. Jahrhundert', in Jürgen Kocka (ed.), *Bürgertum im 19. Jahrhundert: Deutschland im europäischen Vergleich* (Munich, 1988), vol. 1, pp. 372–405; ead., 'Richterliche Normenkontrolle im 19. Jahrhundert: Zur Rekonstruktion einer Streitfrage', *Zeitschrift für Neuere Rechtsgeschichte* 11 (1989), 12–38.

[29] See, for example, William L. S. Felstiner, 'Influence of Social Organization on Dispute Processing', *Law and Society Review* 9 (1974), 63–94, and for the significance of *partial* decisions in this context: Erhard Blankenburg, 'Mobilisierung von Recht: Über die Wahrscheinlichkeit des Gangs zum Gericht, über die Erfolgsaussichten der Kläger und über die daraus ableitbaren Funktionen der Justiz', *Zeitschrift für Rechtssoziologie* 1 (1980), 33–64; Marc Galanter, 'Justice in Many Rooms: Courts, Private Ordering, and Indigenous Law', *Journal of Legal Pluralism* 19 (1981), 1–47. For a wider overview which also takes into account preventive interests, see Barbara A. Curran, *The Legal Needs of the Public: A Final Report of a National Survey* (Chicago, 1977).

[30] See, for example, Richard Lempert and Joseph Sanders, *An Invitation to Law and Social Science* (New York, 1986), who state: 'There is good reason to believe that most settlements would not have been reached but for the possibility of a court-ordered resolution' (p. 138).

demand reductions. The interpretations of the world or of texts, endless as they are, must be aborted. Against better knowledge, it must be pretended that there was something which is reliable, or which—at least—justified a certain course of action. In view of this background to the description of the world, which tends toward pragmatism, the special form of the prohibition of the denial of justice no longer required any further reason. More than that: it resonates harmoniously with developing legal positivism. For, if the pressure for action cuts the search for knowledge short, no guarantee can be demanded for the enduring validity of a decision, and options must be kept open for new doubts, better insights, and a change in the rules.[31]

It should be uncontested today that a 'non liquet' cannot be excluded simply on logical grounds.[32] The world does not provide any guarantee for logical order and consistency of deductions. The prohibition of the denial of justice does not follow either from the fact that the binding force of statutes does not leave any other choice. For, as soon as there are problems of interpretation and application of statutes, a judge would be free to find 'gaps in the law' and to reject the need to make a decision. Hence there must be an institutional provision if the legal system is to be arranged as *universally* competent and *at the same time capable of making decisions.* This combinatorial problem of universality and a capacity for decision-making is expressed in the prohibition of the denial of justice appropriately, for the legal system, in the form of a norm. This, however, means also that the claim to validity may, if necessary, be maintained contra-factually.

There is a body of literature that deals with some of the practical difficulties that result from the prohibition of the denial of justice. Evidently, such a rule can only be practised if more or less formal decisions can be applied that do not go into the detail of the substantive matter, such as rules on the onus of proof, failures to observe time-limits, rules about standing, rules of procedure, more substantial rules of convenience (*de minimis non curat praetor* [the praetor is not concerned with minor matters]), or the famous doctrine of 'political questions' in the constitutional law of the United States.[33] This may lead the lawyer to ask when the use of such alternative options may reach the point of a violation of the prohibition of the denial of

---

[31] See for a study of how this logic of time accepts signs in a modern perspective, Josef Simon, *Philosophie des Zeichens* (Berlin, 1989).

[32] See on this point, Ilmar Tammelo, 'On the Logical Openness of Legal Orders', *American Journal of Comparative Law* 8 (1959), 187–203.

[33] See especially on this point, Fritz W. Scharpf, *Grenzen der richterlichen Verantwortung: Die Political Questions Doctrine in der Rechtsprechung des amerikanischen Supreme Court* (Karlsruhe, 1965); id., 'Judicial Review and the Political Question: A Functional Analysis', *Yale Law Journal* 75 (1966), 517–97. It should be noted also that this rule of conflicts is a rule that has been developed by the Supreme Court as a self-limitation within the legal system which is accepted by the courts, and is not a politically enforced limitation.

justice (a triple negation!).[34] More important, however, are analyses that link the tasks of judicial law-making with the prohibition of the denial of justice.[35] One can even go so far as to take the modern discourse on 'legal principles' (the Romans did not need that) as a by-product of the prohibition of the denial of justice.[36]

A similar problem is discussed in the common law under the key phrase of 'hard cases'.[37] As a sociologist one realizes immediately that, quantitatively, the courts decide only a small number of the total number of cases under consideration. However, for the development of law and for a legal theory which accompanies and justifies this development, these 'hard cases' have a crucial significance. For these are cases in which the existing, doubtlessly valid, legal norms applied with logically correct deductive methods do not lead to unequivocal decisions. These are cases, then, in which the knowledge of uncontested and valid law is not enough to state the facts of who is in a legal position and who is in an illegal position. *Nevertheless courts have to decide these cases as well.* This means: courts have to develop rules of decision-making for their decision and for its justification, which may be contested and may remain so contested. Courts cannot refer to uncontested and valid law but have to create, postulate, and assume such a law, without being in a position to guarantee that the programme for the decision-making in this case will be valid beyond deciding this particular case. This is exactly why the legal institution of making the *ratio decidendi* of a precedent in a case binding has been developed. But this solved the problems involved only to some degree by transferring them to the question as to what the *ratio decidendi* may be and how it could be found.[38] In this context, the influence of moral reasons on decision-making in 'hard cases' is discussed.[39] This may lead to some 'defensibility' for decisional rules but it cannot lead, under modern conditions, to the incontestability of their validity.[40] Apart from this, the reference to morals has the disadvantage

---

[34] See, for example, Louis Favoreu, *Du déni de justice en droit public français* (Paris, 1965).

[35] See Ekkehart Schumann, 'Das Rechtsverweigerungsverbot: Historische und methodologische Bemerkungen zur richterlichen Pflicht das Recht auszulegen, zu ergänzen und fortzubilden', *Zeitschrift für Zivilprozess* 81 (1968), 79–102.

[36] See ibid. on the idea of material justice.

[37] See, as a starting point, Ronald Dworkin, *Taking Rights Seriously* (Cambridge, 1977), 81 and 90. However, the concept of 'trouble cases' could already be found in the schools of realism.

[38] Contributions to the discussion of this problem can be found in Laurence Goldstein (ed.), *Precedent in Law* (Oxford, 1987).

[39] See, for example, David Lyons, 'Justification and Judicial Responsibility', *California Law Review* 72 (1984), 178–99.

[40] But see Dworkin, *Taking Rights Seriously*, against this argument using the distinction between rules and principles. See on the discussion of 'hard cases' and on the critique of Dworkin's assumption of a single correct decision for all cases Aharon Barak, *Judicial Discretion* (New Haven, 1989), with its further references.

(which is hard to accept) that legal positions which have to be rejected under the pressure of the compulsion for decision-making have to be disowned morally.[41]

The problem of 'hard cases' existed even before the onset of the differentiation of the legal system.[42] Then they were decided by ordeal. Today, the moral conviction of the judge or, better, his moral convictions of the people's moral convictions, seems to be a functional equivalent—in the same way unpredictable, but with far better possibilities for contributing to the making of law and, thus, for transforming unpredictability into predictability. Whatever legal theory may make of such a moral pretence, one cannot subject courts to the pressure of compulsory decision-making and, at the same time, subject the logic of the argumentation of courts to an infinite regression or logical circles. One has to understand that in practice they will follow principles.

In practice, courts will usually limit themselves to what is necessary for the justification of their findings. If there has to be a decision and a reason, it is done with the minimum of self-determination that is necessary for the decision in a concrete case. Useless verbiage is to be avoided. So-called *obiter dicta*, that is, occasional remarks, occur and can be useful in order to indicate the legal policy intentions of the court. This applies, above all, to superior courts, as a kind of practice for alerting future cases. However, in legal regimes that are bound by precedent, a clear distinction is made, if only by retrospective analysis, between *rationes decidendi* and *obiter dicta* in order to restrict the binding effect to what has in fact created legal validity. This self-discipline concerning what is 'essential' is also a result of the pressure for compulsory decision-making and the necessity of separating judge-made law, which is caused by it.

The discrepancy between compulsory decision-making and the possibilities of arriving at compelling decisions finds its expression in the legal institution of *legal force*. It occurs at a *certain point of time*. Contestable as a decision may be and remain, it is exonerated from protracted doubt by the fact that it can no longer be appealed against. This makes including the consequences of decisions in the making of decisions at the same time harmless and risky—harmless, because the consequences of the unappealable

---

[41] See on this argument (with the background in the Jewish tradition of a religious legitimation of dissent), Robert M. Cover, 'The Supreme Court, 1982 Term. Foreword: Norms and Narrative', *Harvard Law Review* 97 (1983), 4–68.

[42] 'Lorsque les éléments du dossier ne permettaient pas au juge de trancher, il remettait les parties au jugement des dieux' (If the elements of the case did not allow for a decision, the judge remitted the parties to the ordeal): Jean Bottéro, *Mésopotamie: L'écriture, la raison et les dieux* (Paris, 1987), 151, an account of the possibly earliest society with a highly developed interest in law and justice. See also for more detail, id., 'L'ordalie en Mésopotamie ancienne', *Annali della Scuola Normale Superiore di Pisa, Classe di Lettere e Filosofia*, ser III, vol. XI (1982), 1005–67.

decision lie, in the moment it is made, in the future, and risky for the same reason. Consequences which arise or do not arise and go against what was provided in the decision cannot change the decision any more. The decision, which may turn out to be a bad speculation *ex post facto*, is valid nonetheless and, unlike a statute, cannot be changed in the light of a new mix of consequences.

Nevertheless, the simple recognition of 'judge-made law' remains on the surface of the problem. The same applies to the dissolution of the classical hierarchy of legislature and courts into a circular relationship of influence on each other. Apparently the question here is how the legal system can absorb its own asking too much of itself, and that involves both how and where. This leads back, once again, to the logical and structural significance of the prohibition of the denial of justice. What is it about this prohibition which sets so much in motion? Is it only one norm among many others, only a rule of procedural law?

That a rule alone would not be sufficient is evident in the fact that what is involved here is an *autological* rule which includes itself in its application. A statement is autological when it applies to itself. If a compulsory decision is involved, non-decisions are excluded because they violate the rule—or, one would have to be able to enforce the application of the rule to itself by referring to the rule.[43] But by whom should the rule be enforced? By the courts themselves?

This autological property refers to a deeply situated paradox. Courts have to decide even when they cannot decide, or at least not within reasonable standards of rationality. And if they cannot decide, they must force themselves to be able to decide. If the law cannot be found, it must simply be invented. We shall see how a way out of this situation will involve arguments about consequences, which one cannot know yet because only the future will tell. The paradox of the undecidable decision has to be unfolded in one way or the other, and that means the decision must be translated into distinctions which can be managed, for example the distinction between decision and consequence or between legal principle and its application.

The fact that courts have to decide is the point of departure for the construction of the juridical universe, for legal reasoning, for juridical

---

[43] See on this point also Ludwig Häsemeyer, *Die Erzwingung richterlicher Entscheidungen: Mögliche Reaktionen auf Justizverweigerungen, Festschrift für Karl Michaelis* (Göttingen, 1972), 134–50. See also Art. 29 of the Vienna act of the German Federation of 15 May 1820 (quoted in Gustav Struve, *Das öffentliche Recht des deutschen Bundes* (Mannheim, 1846), 108 and 117), which provided a competence for the federal congress for cases of this kind, following the concept of quasi-sovereign law in the mould of the old empire. See Johann Ludwig Klüber, *Öffentliches Recht des Teutschen Bundes und der Bundesstaaten*, 3rd edn. (Frankfurt, 1831), 188 (which includes a collection of annotations which is also interesting from a historical point of view).

argumentation.[44] *Therefore*, 'legitimation', in the sense of a value relation, which transcends the law, ultimately cannot play any role in law. *Therefore*, everything depends on the fact that earlier decisions, which can be used for guidance, prevail if they are not changed. *Therefore, res judicata* is unappealable unless rules of exception, which are provided by law, can be applied. And *therefore*, law must be understood as a closed universe which refers to itself, in which 'pure juridical argumentation' can be practised even under extreme social tensions. And this argumentation decides for itself which scale of interpretation it can afford and when it has to reject a distortion that is asked of it.

The consequences of this compulsory decision-making can be seen in their fullest clarity in the forms in which legal proceedings are conducted, and—in its extreme—in the Anglo-Saxon institution of cross-examination. Two aspects dominate the scene: the high selectivity of the chosen points of view and the carefully maintained uncertainty of the outcome.[45] Guidance by rules of the decision-making in the system (programmes) drives the specification of the chosen points of view. The uncertainty of the outcome provides that only the code-values legal and illegal, which are yet to be determined, matter and that additional points of view, for example moral or political or utilitarian points of view, do not matter. The accused is innocent as long as there is no guilty verdict. Judges and counsel have to be careful to avoid any moral condemnation.[46] And counsel are expected to represent the interests of their clients in court—no matter what their personal opinion about them is. This provides for both conditions for the differentiation of the legal system and preparation for structuring the decision, which *has* to be made, and in which only the relationship between the code and the programmes should matter. Accordingly, the ultimate meaning of the constitutional guarantee for the legal system is found in the guarantee for procedures because, of course, it cannot guarantee that everybody receives justice in the way he expects.

---

[44] Vilhelm Aubert especially has followed up this relationship. See his 'The Structure of Legal Thinking', in *Legal Essays: Festskrift til Fred Castberg* (Copenhagen, 1963), 41–63; 'Legal Reasoning', in Vilhelm Aubert, *In Search of Law* (Oxford, 1983), 77–97; and also in id., *Continuity and Development in Law and Society* (Oslo, 1989), 11–135.

[45] See, for more detail, Niklas Luhmann, *Legitimation durch Verfahren* (1969; reprinted. Frankfurt, 1983), esp. 55.

[46] In the words of F. James David et al., *Society and the Law: New Meanings for an Old Profession* (New York, 1962), 98: 'There are no guilty clients until verdict has been rendered; guilty is a matter of moral judgment, not merely a question of whether conduct fits a statutory classification.' One can say, therefore, that the law creates its own cut-off points in time and its own time-horizons, and differentiates through these between itself and morals. At the same time the limits of a debate become obvious, which locates the problem of law and morals exclusively in the question whether or not legal rules require a moral justification.

Weaknesses of method, 'loss of certainty',[47] decomposition of doctrinal guidelines and their replacement by equity-schemes, and last but not least the increasing fuzziness in the demarcation between legislation and jurisdiction, and 'passing the buck' of regulatory problems, depending on whether or not and in which constellations they can be politicized—all these factors are late results of compulsory decision-making which have ever stronger effects in an increasingly more complex society and in the face of an acceleration of structural changes in nearly all social domains. From this perspective, many criticisms of courts, and the more recent focus of socio-legal research on the area of the administration of justice, gain increased weight. This applies to old criticisms such as the case overload of courts and the length of court proceedings, as well as to the most recent research on access to law (this means access to courts and not access to contracts or to legislation). It applies to the question of whether or not court proceedings are at all a suitable mechanism for the treatment of conflict if, as a direct consequence of compulsory decision-making, only a small section of the relevant subject matter are justiciable—in a normally broad band of conflict-inducing, conflict-compounding, or conflict-decreasing factors. And it applies, finally, to the profile of the role of the plaintiff and the defendant in terms of individual 'persons' (be those persons living or corporate) regardless of the fact that the parties are frequently representatives of a group of similar cases, yet capable of making their dispositions individually. A rich discussion on alternatives and possibilities for reform addresses these matters.[48] However, all this hardly touches the core of the matter—that is, compulsory decision-making, which distinguishes courts above all from other institutions of the legal system.

The paradox of undecidable decision-making searches and finds, as it were, acceptable forms of solution. The formulae that we have used to characterize this development sounded negative but were not meant in this way—as if there were better possibilities that had been missed. A far more important question is to ask how a legal system can be described in which the paradox of its self-constitution emerges more and more clearly and which also reveals the location in which the problem of unfolding the paradox has to be solved: in decision-making by courts.

V

Let us repeat: neither statutes nor contracts are the consequence of compulsory decision-making. The status of the validity of the legal system can

---

[47] Görg Haverkate, *Gewißheitsverluste im juristischen Denken: Zur politischen Funktion der juristischen Methode* (Berlin, 1977).

[48] See, for example, *Jahrbuch für Rechtstheorie und Rechtssoziologie* (1980) vol. 8 esp. 142. This volume is entirely dedicated to this topic.

be changed by choosing these forms—or not. In this respect, only courts are in an exceptional position. Laws or contracts may be forced to change for political or economic reasons, but these are pressures of a different kind and, when faced with them, the legal system is free to decide in which contexts such pressures are legally relevant—or not. Courts, however, have to decide each case that is submitted to them for legal reasons. Only courts are in charge of managing the paradox of the system, however one may define it. Only courts have to transform indeterminacy into determinacy where necessary, only courts have to construct fictitiously the availability or unavailability of principles, where necessary. Only courts are forced to decide and, consequently, to enjoy the privilege of being able to transform compulsion into freedom. No other legal institution commands a position of this kind.

The paradox, however, is the holy shrine of the system. It is a deity in many forms: as *unitas multiplex* and as re-entry of the form into the form, as the sameness of difference, as the determinacy of indeterminacy, as self-legitimation. The unity of the system can be expressed in the system as distinctions, which turn into guiding distinctions in this function because they hide from view what they reveal. This happens structurally through differentiation, through multiplication of the distinction between the system and its environment, in the system. Hence the issue of the unfolding of the paradox is the key to the problem of differentiation. And it is the form of differentiation that controls which semantics achieve plausibility and which do not and thus lose it.[49]

If this applies, that is, if courts are in charge of the task of unfolding the paradox of the legal system—as is required by and, at the same time, veiled by the prohibition of the denial of justice—it explodes the possibility of describing the differentiation of the legal system as a hierarchy in the form of a chain of commands. For the courts do not give orders to the legislator. At best courts formulate conditions for what courts can understand, accept, and practice. With that formulation, they do not insist on anything else but their own existence. Therefore it is necessary to replace the model of hierarchy with the concept of the differentiation between centre and periphery.[50]

---

[49] See for various case studies Niklas Luhmann, *Gesellschaftsstruktur und Semantik*, 3 vols. (Frankfurt, 1980–9).

[50] The use of this formula is firmly in the hands of geographers even when sociologists participate. See, for example, the reader by Jean Gottman (ed.), *Centre and Periphery* (London, 1980). The transfer to institutional contexts has been suggested in particular by Edward Shils, 'Centre and Periphery', in *The Logic of Personal Knowledge: Essays presented to Michael Polanyi* (London, 1986), 117–31. In our text, we abstract—as the reader can easily find out—from any materialization of space. For space is only one case of unfolding paradoxes through distinctions, which are tuned to the inconsistencies of the neurophysiological processing of information and therefore readily available for animals and humans.

Consequently, the organization of courts as a sub-system is at the centre of the legal system. Only here can one use the special feature of organization systems—to decide about the inclusion and exclusion of members—in order to create special ties for judges. For it is part and parcel of accepting the office of a judge that one accepts limitations on one's conduct which do not apply to everybody else, and that means above all producing new rules of law but subject to the applicable methodological and substantive standards.[51] Only organization can guarantee the universality of competence to decide all legal questions. All other areas of law belong to the periphery. This applies to activities which are usually described as 'private', namely contracts. But it also applies to legislation. The periphery is not subject to compulsory operation. Here interests of all kinds can be represented and enforced to the best of one's ability, notwithstanding a distinction between legal and non-legal interests. That is why the periphery is particularly suited as a zone of contact with the other functioning systems of society—be it economy, family life, or politics. In a frequent, quite direct connection with contract law, various new forms of privately produced law prosper. Above all, this can be seen in the internal law of organizations, and also in law created as a result of provisional collective agreements between interest groups and other big organizations, market-specific interpretations of general regulations, the law of general terms and conditions of trade, and others.[52] Similarly legislation proliferates, yielding to political pressure and seeping into previously unregulated areas in ever more increasing volume—such as the 'privacy' of the family home or schools, universities, and the relations between doctors and patients. It is in the periphery that irritations are translated into legal form—or not. Here the system demonstrates its autonomy by not having to decide. Here one can find safeguards against not being able to use law simply as a slavish extension of operations outside the law. The centre needs this protection—especially because it operates under the opposite premiss. Courts work under a much higher degree of cognitive self-isolation compared with legislators and contracting parties. One needs only to think of the formalities of evidence. Moreover, access to the courts must be free and organized in a highly selective manner. Only a

---

[51] It is striking how rarely this legitimation for judge-made law, which is exclusively based on organization, is used in the literature. Apparently legal theory is reluctant to surrender issues of vital social concern to a mechanism that can only work on the level of formally organized social systems. See, however, the quite casual comment of Melvin Aron Eisenberg, *The Nature of Common Law* (Cambridge, 1988), 3 'Like a conventional trustee, the judge is morally bound by his acceptance of office to obey the rules that govern the conduct of his office'. One may be excused for asking: only morally bound?

[52] See in relation to this proliferation, which is often called 'pluralist', Gunther Teubner, 'Steuerung durch plurales Recht. Oder: wie die Politik den normativen Mehrwert der Geldzirkulation abschöpft', in Wolfgang Zapf (ed.), *Die Modernisierung moderner Gesellschaften: Verhandlungen des 25. Soziologentags in Frankfurt/Main 1990* (Frankfurt, 1991), 528–51.

minute percentage of legal issues are submitted to courts for decision-making. However, if this happens and the parties are committed to it, a decision must be made, however easy or difficult this may be and however conservative or creative the result may be.

A further meaning of this form of differentiation of centre and periphery is given by achieving a socially necessary and sufficient consensus (or the maintenance of a fiction to that effect).[53] If courts are required to decide, to make decisions, they cannot, at the same time, depend on consensus. For courts have to decide all cases, including those in which the validity of law is not based on a secured consensus. The formulae used by courts for such a consensus (moral aspirations of the people, sense of decency of all fair-minded people) appear shallow and stale, and they are not tested in the proceedings but assumed in the form of legal fictions. Demands for consensus are directed to the periphery and introduced into the legal system in the form either of a contract or of laws, which have (in both cases) been created on the basis of political consensus. Then, in the interpretation of contracts and laws, the courts are required to exhibit a certain restraint, namely a restraint when creating new judge-made law relying on legal fictions and without clear-cut general criteria.

As a centre cannot operate without a periphery and a periphery cannot work without a centre, this distinction does not indicate a difference of rank or social relevance. Habermas fittingly calls court procedures 'the vanishing point of the analysis of the legal system'.[54] The matter is definitely not a reversal within the hierarchical structural pattern with the consequence that courts are seen as more important than the legislative body. It is exactly such a conclusion that needs to be avoided. For as with all forms of differentiation, the point at issue is simply to make it possible that opposites (compulsory decision-making or no compulsory decision-making) can happen at the same time and can complement each other. The form of differentiation guarantees the unfolding of the paradox—nothing more or less. However this is a condition for the operative closure of the legal system in order to achieve, with the help of a universal competence, a specific function for the social system as a whole.

Finally, it is significant for the higher level of the form of differentiation between centre and periphery that other forms of differentiation are only permitted in the centre—and here both segmentation and hierarchization arise. Only courts form a hierarchy. Only courts differentiate horizontally

---

[53] See on this point Gunther Teubner, 'Ist das Recht auf Konsens angewiesen? Zur sozialen Akzeptanz des modernen Richterrechts', in Hans-Joachim Giegel (ed.), *Kommunikation und Konsens in modernen Gesellschaften* (Frankfurt, 1992), 197–211, with similar serious doubts about the capacity of courts to secure consensus.

[54] See Jürgen Habermas, *Faktizität und Geltung: Beiträge zur Diskurstheorie des Rechts und des demokratischen Rechtsstaats* (Frankfurt, 1992), 241.

according to different regional or specialist competencies. This contributes to the asymmetry of the form of differentiation as well. For the periphery cannot be differentiated further, no matter how heavy caseloads may be. Even though, of course, there is delegated legislation, a hierarchical order within this sub-system, nevertheless delegated legislation is only the way in which commands are passed on, it does not produce any independent autopoietic sub-systems. In contrast, local courts can function without a district court. And superior courts have their own jurisdiction either because of their special competence, or because cases on appeal come up from the lower courts. In whatever way the internal differentiation of the centre is structured, it does not contradict the unity of the central competence but requires and reinforces it.

The main effect of such a transformation of the theory of differentiation from a schema of hierarchy (with circular feedback) to a schema of centre and periphery is probably a parallel processing and networking of the legislative and the contractual production of validity.[55] This is in stark contrast to the conventional doctrine of the sources of law, which is also accepted by the courts (with or without judge-made law). According to that convention, the contract (which includes other means of privately produced law such as wills and incorporated organizations) is only one among many legal institutions. It belongs, as it were, to the semantics and not to the syntax of the legal system. The reality, however, has been different for a long time. Already in the 1920s the law of the general or blanket clause was noticed and there was talk of 'self-produced law of the economy'.[56] Today, the great mass of relations within and between organizations, including those between large associations, and between such associations and local associations, has been put into a form that can, in a given case, be understood by the legal system as valid law. Moreover, a large part of legislation (for instance, relating to cartels) refers to this area of creation of law. Juridification of everyday life can no longer be understood without it. It would be quite old-fashioned to understand this as an area in which two individuals meet and make a contract according to, and solely in the context of, the typical programmes of private law.

Obviously, laws and contracts are still distinguished by their forms and effects. Otherwise it would not make sense to distinguish them. But equally important, if not more important, is the question of how the legal system adjusts itself with its peripheral sensitivity to other functioning systems.

---

[55] See on this point Charles-Albert Morand, 'La contractualisation du droit dans l'état providence', in François Chazel and Jacques Commaille (eds.), *Normes juridiques et régulation sociale* (Paris, 1991), 139–58; Arthur Benz, Fritz W. Scharpf, and, Reinhard Zintl, *Horizontale Politikverflechtung: Zur Theorie von Verhandlungssystemen* (Frankfurt, 1992).

[56] Hans Grossman-Doerth, *Selbstgeschaffenes Recht der Wirtschaft und staatliches Recht* (Freiburg, 1933), used this formulation in the 'nationalist' context.

Here, in the periphery of law, the higher tolerance of imbalances and the renunciation of compulsory decision-making are decisive factors.

VI

The relation between compulsory decision-making, court organization, and the central position of courts in the legal system should now be clear, and this leads to new insights into the operative closure of legal systems from both a temporal and factual point of view.

Decisions can be understood abstractly as a form, which allows disconnecting and reconnecting the link between past and future. Wherever a decision is made, the past does not automatically extrapolate to the future (qua essence or nature, or qua impossibility or necessity), but that link is disrupted and left to a decision which is only possible in the present and which always could be a different one. We must ask, then, how society can accept this risk of disruption. How is it possible to entrust this risk to the care of one of its sub-systems, here the legal system?

The answer is, as it were, the excuse for having a dispute at all. The meaning of winning or losing in a dispute is an open question. A dispute is an event that demands action. But this does not explain how an operatively closed system achieves reconnection between past and future.

Courts reconstruct the past in the context of the case at hand. What is necessary for deciding the case, and nothing more, will be taken into consideration. The valid law assists in reducing the demand for information. Valid law is assumed as a given and thus as the product of the past as well. The ideal of being able to deduce the decision from the law would mean in practice that the past is sufficient as input and that the future could be left to logical impossibility or necessity. One could calculate the future without the need to be decisive about it. However, it is well known that this is not the case. In fact, courts are forced to plot a future. This occurs in the form of designing rules for decision-making to which the court will adhere in future similar cases. These can be rules for the interpretation of statutes but also, particularly in the common law, rules which are derived directly by their abstraction from cases.[57] After all, what is at stake here is the creation of limitations, which have to be binding in the future as well. This means that the system is closed in regard to the temporal dimension by constructing the present (which passes anyway with the making a decision) as the

---

[57] There are extensive theoretical discussions about this point, for instance the 'juridical doctrine of methods' related to the techniques of statutory interpretation or the complicated discussion about the finding of decisional rules in previous decisions in relation to what could be binding in the case at hand. It is significant, however, that theoretical-methodological considerations are rarely to be found in the reasoning of judgments, as if one had to avoid extending the self-binding of the court to questions of this kind as well.

past of a future present. The decision is subject to rules *modo futuri exacti* and disciplined through those rules.

This form of mediation between past and future requires a second time frame, one which is centred and constructed in the present, and which changes with it. That does not change the fact that the scope, which has been projected fictitiously onto that time, does not exist in reality. For in reality, only that which happens, happens, and everything that actually happens, happens at the same time. This shows again that time, seen as difference, is always the construct of an observer. And this requires that society has to synchronize various observations of time. This occurs, determined by the reduction of further possible operations, by recursions. This is probably the reason why courts, apart from their problems with logical deductions, are required to produce, continuously, rules for future decisions. 'The function of resolving disputes faces toward the parties and the past. The function of enriching the supply of legal rules faces toward general society and the future.'[58]

In light of our actual experience it is apparent that only courts have the task of supervising the consistency of legal decisions.[59] This occurs in the mode of second-order observation, that is, in the mode of an observation of legal decisions (for example, those of statute, in contracts, or in judicial decisions) that in turn are observed in the law. The technical term for this is interpretation. Interpretation of valid law is also involved, of course, in the drafting of bills or contracts but only in order to assess the limits or latitude of their design. Courts interpret differently, namely argumentatively and in order to present the *ratio* of their own decisions. The level of second-order observation serves here the purpose of testing how far the consistency of the observation of law to date can be combined with the integration of new information or with a change of preferences. And when academic teaching and 'legal research' operate in a similar fashion, they do this with the reconstruction of correct legal decisions by courts in mind. In spite of unrelenting efforts it has been impossible to develop a convincing juridical doctrine for legislation—even though lawyers and non-lawyers (like Jürgen Habermas) maintain to this day that laws are the rational basis for all legal decisions.[60]

---

[58] Eisenberg, *Nature of Common Law*, 7.

[59] Lawyers in continental Europe will point to the codification of whole legal areas through legislation. Whether one wants to accept this as an exception or not, the point is that it does not happen any more and also the idea that courts can be reduced by codification to a mere 'application' of statutes and a mere routine decision-making is refuted by history.

[60] See for instance as a summary of a lifelong engagement with this topic, Peter Noll, *Gesetzgebungslehre* (Reinbek, 1973), with reasons for the deficit at p. 9. See also Hermann Hill, *Einführung in die Gesetzgebungslehre* (Heidelberg, 1982), and the shift of the problem area to a 'political science of law' (*Jahrbuch für Rechtspolitologie* [Yearbook for Legal Politics] since 1987).

VII

Apparently the goddess of evolution had courage—more than any person planning could have had after careful consideration. Evolution cuts out all societal guidelines for legal decision-making without providing any substitute. Nevertheless courts must decide. They cannot make their decisions contingent on whether or not they will be able to find a plausible solution, nor even on confidently knowing how to decide. How then could that work?

Formally courts operate in such a way that their decisions—which are, of course, made within the legal system (there cannot be any doubt about that)—are based strictly on valid law. The decision is deemed to be a finding of law or an application of law. And law contains sufficient rules (for instance rules of evidence) to guarantee that this can be done in all cases. Hence there cannot be any doubt *that* it can be done. One realizes this from reading the texts produced. But this does not answer the more demanding question of *how* it can be done.

A sociologist would have to ask more concretely: what can replace the societal guidelines for legal decision-making, such as concerns for the social status of the parties or for the social network of their relations? The usual answer here is, of course (and here we must think especially of the intonations of the critical legal studies movement or their neo-Marxist counterparts), that these guidelines are not replaced but continue to be effective. However, this statement is premature or at any rate produced without support from historical comparisons. Whatever can be found or stated with the help of a 'latent structure analysis' or with a simple new correlation of causes and effects, the question remains of which social institutions are required or are successful in securing the independence of courts and the prohibition on the denial of justice.[61]

The answer is: the organization and professionalization of juridical competence.

Established sociology of law holds to the view that the boundaries of the legal system are already to be found at this point. According to this view, the system is differentiated by organization and professionalization, and access to the system is access to organized procedures and to professional advice, which are effective in the system. However, if one relinquishes this concept and replaces it with a strictly operative understanding of the generation of systems and how they draw their boundaries, the phenomena of organization and profession can be seen in a different light and used in the context of a different theoretical approach.[62] The established view directs

---

[61] For example, the humanitarian movement to oppose child labour in the nineteenth century served in reality to strengthen big industry and eliminate competition from small businesses. The same could be said about the regulatory injunctions of ecological policies in the twentieth century.   [62] See above Ch. 2.V.

our search to latent, above all class-related, influences of society on its legal system. How could other sources of influence be conceived? If an extended concept of system, in the sense of the construct of autopoiesis, is applied, altogether different sources of limitations and the latitude of legal decision-making come into view: organization and profession.

The fact of organization has the effect, first of all, that the judges, as members of an organization, have to work. They are expected, partly by supervision, partly by collegiality, to deal with their caseloads.[63] This refers to a time-structure: one step after the other. The result is that dates for interaction are set down or 'appointed'. Membership in an organization also means that there are limitations on interaction, which, if breached, can result in a disciplinary complaint. Organization means that errors must be kept within the limits of what is 'juridically passable'. One can rebel against a dominant opinion and provoke the superior courts, but only with acceptable arguments. (In anticipation of what follows below, at this point a necessary cooperation of organization and profession can be seen.) Besides, the same dissenting opinion cannot be presented over and over again if the superior courts do not accept it, only to force the parties to appeal case by case to the higher court. A balloon can be sent up for trial but it must be envisaged that it can burst. Organization means, finally, that there are different positions, different salaries, and therefore different careers. With a career, much depends on where and how decisions are made about that career—each movement in a career always requires the cooperation of self-selection and external selection—such decisions invoke respect for opinions and even possibly motives towards work, opinions which exceed what can be demanded from any member of the organization.

On the other hand, organization is important because it filters out the consequences of decision-making for the income and status of the judge. He can survive media campaigns without loss of position or financial damage. Above all, and this is significant with regard to the great importance of an assessment of outcomes in the recent development of decision-making practice, *a judge cannot be held responsible for the outcomes of a decision.* The organization covers for the risks that are involved.[64] Hence, in a complicated way, decision-making can be made easier by irresponsibility, which is absorbed by the organization's guarantee for correct decision-making.

Organization and profession are functionally equivalent from the point of view of the question of how the limitations on the latitude of decision-making

---

[63] This also involves a high degree of self-regulation of the workload on the part of the courts even to the extent of the possibility of rejecting legally admissible problem solutions having regard to the consequences for the caseload of courts and for everybody involved in the proceedings. See, for example, with rich material on this point Lawrence M. Friedman, 'Legal Rules and Process of Social Change', *Stanford Law Review* 19 (1967), 768–840, at 797.

[64] We return to this issue in the final chapter.

are brought about by a combination of (1) independence, (2) dependence on legal texts (being bound by valid law), and (3) prohibition of the denial of justice. Therefore, a great number of different forms of organization and many different versions of the profession can be found in regional comparisons.[65] And this makes it plausible that the relative weight of organizational loyalty and professional solidarity can shift with time—today probably more in the direction of the dependence of the different branches of the legal profession on organization.[66]

The special significance of professions both as a form of ordering social life and as characterizing the professionality of juridical work has been frequently described, and described in great detail.[67] There is no need to repeat those descriptions here. But two features stand out if one looks at reality and the available research from the point of view of facilitating court work which is both independent and under the pressure of having to make decisions: on the one hand, the prestige of experts which allows lawyers to operate in the highly selective arena of what is legally relevant and to reject all further demands from clients or parties in a conflict;[68] and, on the other hand, the ability of lawyers to maintain friendly contacts with each other, even after the conflicts of their clients or parties have spun out of control.[69] The court-related function has two sides, the second of which becomes increasingly important. On the one hand, lawyers (not just legal practitioners but also judges) prepare for the formal decision on a legal conflict. On the other hand, lawyers are involved to a high degree in a preventive

---

[65] This is also an important area of comparative sociological research, especially in relation to the legal profession. See, for example, Dietrich Rueschemeyer, *Juristen in Deutschland and den USA* (Stuttgart, 1976); D. N. MacCormick (ed.), *Lawyers in their Social Setting* (Edinburgh, 1976); or, in respect of regional variety, Brian Abel-Smith and Robert Stevens, *Lawyers and the Courts: A Sociological Study of the English Legal System 1750–1965* (London, 1967); John P. Heinz, and Edward O. Laumann, *Chicago Lawyers: The Social Structure of the Bar* (New York, 1982); on Indian lawyers see *Law and Society Review* 3/2 (1968).

[66] Sufficient empirical research data or even hypotheses are not available. But it is worth considering whether opposition to political regimes strengthens professional solidarity or increased work of a preventive nature strengthens the ties with an organization, which one represents proactively and not only in open controversies. Also, the spectacular growth of the profession may lead to increased competition and dependence on organization.

[67] Especially since the pioneering public lecture of Talcott Parsons, 'The Professions and Social Structure', *Social Forces* 17 (1939), 457–67, reprinted in id., *Essays in Sociological Theories* (New York, 1949).

[68] Further special research is necessary to establish how far such expert knowledge as legal knowledge factually determines the practice (especially of legal practitioners), or whether it is not rather the local knowledge of organizations and milieux, the contacts that are available or the routines that does so. For some assumptions see Robert L. Kidder, *Connecting Law and Society: An Introduction to Research and Theory* (Englewood Cliffs, NJ, 1983), 240.

[69] That there is also a social side to it is shown by the yearly 'lawyers' balls' in provincial towns.

practice whose aim is to construct legal instruments in such a way that conflict can be avoided. This type of preventive work is by far the most important for lawyers in business organizations, public service, and many law firms.[70] Furthermore, it comes as no surprise for sociologists that the legal profession reflects the class structure of society (even if to a lesser extent), for instance in the form of differences of income or differences in the social rank of their typical clientele.[71] In other respects lawyers may also be politically connected, in spite of all subjective sentiments expressing independence.[72]

If one is more concerned with the operative side of the autopoiesis of the legal system and less with the institutional side, organizational and professional influences on what is actually communicated appear to be arranged as buffer zones around court work proper. Under their protection, courts can present their own decisions, which change the law as an interpretation and application of valid law.

Finally, legal proceedings also move in this direction.[73] They begin with the acceptance of, or even care for, the uncertainty of the decision, thereby inducing through that uncertainty the inclination for participation, specifying roles, encouraging contributions, positions of adversity, until finally the decision flows virtually as a logical consequence from the proceedings. By focusing communication through the cooperation of participants, protests can be absorbed at the same time. This has the consequence that after a decision has been made, it is only this decision that is open to attack, at least as far as appeals are concerned. Apart from that, one can only try to use political means to ask the legal system to change the law.

---

[70] The same seems to be the case as far as the demand for legal skills is concerned.

[71] This does not have to be expressed always in the form of a difference of ranks. There are also qualitative differences between the office buildings of law firms or single practitioners. I recall the smell of well-dubbed boots in a particular lawyer's office, which indicated the aristocratic background of the lawyer, who served mainly the local landed gentry.

[72] Studies in Washington, D.C., including more recent data show, however, that even here there is a tendency towards the specialization of contacts and to professional independence; see Robert L. Nelson and John P. Heinz, 'Lawyers and the Structure of Influence in Washington', *Law and Society Review* 22 (1988), 237–300, and references to further publications resulting from this study.

[73] See for more detail Luhmann, *Legitimation durch Verfahren*. It remains to be said that this critique has overestimated the range of the theses in this book. It is not on the widely discussed thesis of the 'proceduralization' of law, and hence not on the question whether or not, and then how, the 'finding of the truth' (as it was called earlier) or the acceptance of reasonable claims can be achieved with the help of the conditioning of proceedings. The book is not at all about the process of decision-making itself but only about the framework of conditions for bringing a social conflict (even conflicts with far-reaching economic, moral, or political implications) to a definite conclusion. And without such support, the legal system would not be in a position to implement the prohibition of the denial of justice.

VIII

If one is guided only by the social system as a whole, the differentiation between centre and periphery appears to be a rather old differentiation, certainly one that pre-dates modern forms of differentiation. One recalls the differentiation between city and country, and is sidetracked by geography.[74] This sidetracking rightly draws attention to the fact that the differentiation of the social system today no longer follows the scheme centre/periphery, except if one defines society in terms of economic and technological development.[75] Even then, a reference is made to the poor geographic stability of such centres.[76] Everything points to the fact that the classifications used of global society in terms of centres and peripheries are guided by, and follow, the primary form of functional differentiation.

This does not, however, preclude, but on the contrary, anticipates the possibility, that the form of differentiation of centre and periphery is experiencing a renaissance within functioning systems. Here, also, the form of hierarchy proves to be too restrictive. If this is the case, our finding in relation to the legal system may not be an isolated case and could be supported by comparative analysis of developments in other functioning systems.

To begin with, similar structures can be found in the economic system. The management of its paradox is here the task of the banks.[77] Only banks have the possibility of selling their own debts at a profit. Only banks have the problem of inciting the economy to save and spend money at the same time. Their function is based on the elementary fact that economic transactions operate with payments and that each payment produces, according to its monetary value, at the same time a capacity to pay and an inability to pay. The problems of timing that result from that are dealt with by a trade in promises to pay. This means that banks promise to pay out on deposits, give assurance to promises that credits will be paid back, and make a profit from the difference, hence maintaining themselves. The increase in the money supply is linked to that process, and hence the further paradox that money supply is treated in the economic system as a constant sum and a variable sum at the same time. And it works—under conditions that are closely observed, especially by the central banks.

---

[74] On the extension to empires and their self-description as the middle, centre, and navel of the world see, for example, Mircea Eliade, *Traité d'histoire de religion* (Paris, 1963); Hans Peter Duerr (ed.), *Die Mitte der Welt* (Frankfurt, 1984).

[75] This applies particularly to the widely known historical analyses of the capitalist global system by Immanuel Wallerstein.

[76] See, for example, Edward A. Tiryakian, 'The Changing Centers of Modernity', in Erik Cohen et al. (eds.), *Comparative Social Dynamics: Essays in Honor of S. N. Eisenstadt* (Boulder, 1985), 131–47.

[77] See Niklas Luhmann, *Die Wirtschaft der Gesellschaft* (Frankfurt, 1988), esp. 144; Dirk Baecker, *Womit handeln die Banken?* (Frankfurt, 1991).

As with legal theories, this state of affairs has not been sufficiently noted by economic theories. The centre of gravity of the economic system has been seen in commerce since time immemorial, and since the nineteenth century in market-oriented production. Monetary theories were largely neglected. In fact, deposit banks are a relatively new form of organization (and that distinguishes them from courts). Even in the eighteenth century, increase in the money supply was primarily a matter of state borrowing. And while the institutionalization of courts marks the beginning of the differentiation of the legal system, banks can be seen as the conclusion of the differentiation of the economic system, as the establishment of the autopoiesis of the economic system, including the financial markets, which can no longer be influenced (or can only be irritated and, of course, destroyed) from outside.

Given the degree to which rational calculation of investments (and, one should probably add, speculation) no longer depends on the owned capital but on the optimal mix of owned capital and credits, banks become the centre of the economic system. The economic system can correspond only in this way to the achieved levels of complexity of the system. Production, commerce, and consumption are located in the periphery of the system. This does not preclude but, on the contrary and like the legal system, requires a circular network. It is also comparable with the legal system that only the organization of banks is structured hierarchically by distinguishing between reserve or central banks, merchant banks and clients, while production and commerce form hierarchies only within individual organizations but not as functioning systems.

Corresponding conditions can be found in the political system as well. The centre of the system is here occupied by the state organization. It has the task of producing collectively binding decisions. Here the paradox of the sovereign has to be unfolded and this happens through the expectation (which is hidden in the word 'collectively') that the decisions also bind the decision-makers. They must be able to bind themselves but, at the same time, be able to free themselves from binding decisions in order to change their self-binding. Today this can be achieved by including a time-difference, by factual (above all procedural) conditioning, and by formulating minimal requirements for the political consensus necessary for changes.[78] That

---

[78] On the issue of the inconceivability of such a binding, before the creation of relevant institutions, see Stephen Holmes and Jean Bodin, 'The Paradox of Sovereignty and the Privatization of Religion', in J. Roland Pennock and John W. Chapman (eds.), *Religion, Morality and the Law*, Nomos XXX (New York, 1988), 5–45, at 17. Self-binding had been excluded with a reference to a misconception (see above Ch. VI, n. 69) of natural law, and so the only alternative were theories of contract which had their paradox in the fact that the binding effects of such contracts had to be based on the contracts themselves. The binding of the original social contract is still based on religion because it requires a sacrifice and a surrender of freedom, see Peter Goodrich, *Languages of Law: From Logics of Memory to Nomadic Masks* (London, 1990), 56.

is exactly why the state is no longer itself the civil society of the eighteenth century; nor is it the political system as in the nineteenth century. The state is merely the centre of the political system, which requires the peripheral processes of political grouping and disciplining in the form of parties, of acquiring consensus, and of everyday mediation of interests, which are relevant for politics. In order to perform its function of supply, the political periphery must have a freer position than the state. It cannot be that each voiced opinion, each attempt to exert political pressure, each political, strategic move is immediately turned into a collectively binding decision. Again, opposites have to be made possible and complementary at the same time, and again the form that has been found for that is the differentiation of centre and periphery.

The maintenance of the difference between centre and periphery is crucial for maintaining an order of this kind. Its internal boundary is marked by 'officeholdership' and it is reproduced by political power in its circuit, crossing the boundaries of the system. Otherwise there would no difference between state and political parties, no pressure groups, no difference between government and opposition, no competition for appointments to office—in short, no democracy. But this can also be seen the other way round: the democratization of the political process increases the complexity of the political system to such a degree that the system can afford to have a hierarchical order restricted to its state core area, necessarily taking the form of the differentiation of centre and periphery as far as the whole system is concerned.

Examples of this kind could be multiplied, but it suffices to recognize the form.[79] Problems of complexity can be solved, it seems, by regressing to a more 'primitive' form of differentiation: the acknowledgment of the difference between centre and periphery. It would not be appropriate to say that the centre 'represents' the unity of the system (as in the Greek city, which represented the potential for the good life and human perfection). What matters is not to represent the unity of the system but to unfold the paradox of the system. This is achieved with the help of forms, namely organization and hierarchy, which cannot be realized as forms of the system as a whole, and it involves the diversion of functions and processes which are not compatible with these forms—such as openings for variety and adjustments to pressures from the environment—to the periphery of the system. Not all functioning systems of modern society follow this pattern but its suitability is not only tried and tested in the legal system. Hence the suitability of this pattern cannot be explained by particularities that are only found in the legal system.

---

[79] Here is one more version of the differentiation pattern of note: in the system of mass media there are some prestige newspapers which are not only preferred by the 'elites' but which are also noted for their themes and news by the journalists and editors of the boulevard press or TV. However, this differentiation is rather fuzzy and fluctuating: *New York Times*—yes, *Der Spiegel*—yes, but *Le canard Enchaîné*(?).

8 Legal Argumentation

I

Argumentation is another form with two sides. The issue here, of course, is not the difference between good arguments and bad, between more convincing arguments and less convincing arguments, for they are already arguments. In order to understand argumentation it is important, first of all, to see what arguments *cannot* achieve and what they do *not* cause. And that is: to alter the symbol of validity of law. Unlike statutes or valid judicial decisions or contracts or wills, arguments cannot change the law, or implement new rights or duties and thereby create conditions, which in turn can be changed. The fact that arguments *cannot* change the law takes the burden off argumentation and frees it up to achieve a different kind of discipline. At the same time dependence on legal validity is also a precondition for limiting legal argumentation exclusively to law, which has been filtered by law, and for preventing legal arguments from being derailed by moral or other prejudices.[1]

Of course, changes in legal validity and argumentation do not operate independently of each other. Otherwise one would be unable to recognize that they are both operations of one and the same system. Structural coupling, that is, through legal texts, links them. Through texts, the system is able to coordinate itself by its own structures without being committed to indicate in advance how many and which operations, such as quoting certain texts, will trigger or change the reuse of certain structures. Only in this way can one posit and sustain the ideal postulate that equal cases must be decided equally (justice).

As texts represent this link between argumentation and legal validity, texts, and especially statutes, in their normal (or specifically technical) meaning carry an extraordinary weight in legal argumentation.[2] Texts enable simplified self-observation. In the normal process of decision-making, the system does not observe itself as a system (in an environment) but as an accumulation of legal texts that refer to each other. Lawyers, as we know, call this a 'system' as well. Recently there have also been references—more

---

[1] See Jürgen Habermas, *Faktizität und Geltung: Beiträge zur Diskurstheorie des Rechts und des demokratischen Rechtsstaats* (Frankfurt, 1992), esp. 250 and 286. Habermas formulates the important contention that we must ensure that juridical argumentation is able to respond to other than just moral premises.

[2] See Robert S. Summers and Michele Taruffo, 'Interpretation and Comparative Analysis', in D. Neil MacCormick and Robert S. Summers (eds.), *Interpreting Statutes: A Comparative Study* (Aldershot, 1992), 461–510, at 481. The authors give further, more practical reasons for this prevalence, namely the ready availability of texts compared with other media used for argumentation, and the difficulty of refuting texts.

informally—to 'intertextuality'. What is counted as a text is controlled by this function, namely the representation of the system in the system. This can be a statute or a commentary but may also be, of course, a decision or any other document relating to an established legal practice.[3] The crucial point is that the system can 'recall' internal contexts from the past and through that reduce the scope of possible operations in the present. Finding the relevant texts in decision-making requires professional competence and thus it represents a crucial (and frequently overlooked) instance of legal skill.[4] One cannot interpret and argue until one has found the relevant texts.

With the help of texts, the operations of the legal system—as first-order observations in the 'niches' of the legal system—arrive at their (relative) certainty in deciding cases correctly, or simply in giving the correct legal advice or in making legally sound (prudent) arrangements One lets oneself be guided by the understanding that one is applying the law correctly in the form of given text-based norms. The valid law is deemed to be sufficient grounds for deciding according to it. The verbal meaning of the text suffices. Interpretation is understood as an after-rationalization of the text, or as honouring the premiss that the legislator made a rational decision.[5] Older doctrines of interpretation assumed that texts remained identical during interpretation. And even today one can read: 'Interpretation must be understood as a clarification of "the same" by other signs.'[6] Admittedly the identity of the text itself is a matter of interpretation (if one is not simply content with a mere materialization). Hence interpretation is more likely to be understood today as the creation of new texts with the help of older texts, as the expansion of the basic text, with the original text serving merely as a reference. In any event interpretation is the creation of more text.

Both versions—the assumption that the text is invariant and the expansion and reconstruction of the text in other texts—can be endorsed at the level of first-order observation. Argumentation is an affair at the level of secondary observation and it happens when the question arises of *how* the

---

[3] The idea that precedents are texts has been questioned by Michael S. Moore, 'Precedent, Induction, and Ethical Generalization', in Laurence Goldstein (ed.), *Precedent in Law* (Oxford, 1987), 183–216. Then only free inductive generalization is left. That is what the author intends—see also his arguments against scepticism in moral theory in Michael Moore, 'Moral Reality', *Wisconsin Law Review* (1982), 1061–1156. His findings are, however, not convincing as far as legal practice is concerned but rather demonstrate the advantages to be derived from building all argumentation on the foundation of texts.

[4] It should be noted that the old *topics doctrine*, which stemmed from practice in predominantly oral cultures, accentuated this *inventio*—in contrast to what is recommended today as 'topics'.

[5] One could also say, using stronger wording, as a realization of the false premiss that the legislator made a rational decision.

[6] See Josef Simon, *Philosophie des Zeichens* (Berlin, 1989), 232.

text can be handled in communication.[7] Only at the level of secondary observation can rules be formulated such as: texts are not to be understood verbally but analogously.[8] Here one observes oneself (or others) reading a text and one has one's doubts. This is so because in most cases a decision that has been made solely with the help of a text leads to an unsatisfactory result. It may not give enough weight to one's interests or it may have consequences, which the author of the text could not have seriously intended. Faced with a number of possibilities one has to look for a convincing reason. One has to find the *ratio*, the rule in the decision on which the text is based, and justify it.[9]

When interpreting texts, the transition to a second-level observation can be made by asking the question: what was the text intended to mean (and then stopping there)?[10] Then the text must be deemed to be communication and the assumed rationality of the text must be deemed to be the rationality of the text-producing intention of the text creator (principally the legislator).[11] The theory of argumentation goes further than that. It evaluates arguments in relation to their persuasive powers in the process of communication and in relation to their impact on communication.[12]

---

[7] See for a similar approach Jürgen Habermas. In his view, which follows on from Max Weber, texts with the validity of positive law initially replace reasoning. 'The special achievement of the positivization of law consists of shifting *problems of stating reasons*, that is, largely relieving the technical operation of law of the problems of stating reasons, but it does not consist of the removal of these problems' (*Theorie des kommunikativen Handelns* (Frankfurt, 1981), vol. 1, p. 354). Habermas takes a different turn after that. A lawyer sees the deficiency of reasons as necessitating an *interpretation of texts*, which in turn requires further reasons. Habermas, however, sees the problem in the fact that the *'textuality' itself needs a reason*— neither a formal one nor a functional one (this is not possible without texts) but a substantial one in relation to postconventional criteria which are yet to be agreed upon. Clearly Habermas is demanding more than is and can be practised as law in view of the responsibility courts have to arrive at (quick) decisions.

[8] See typically Jean Domat, *Les loix civiles dans leur ordre naturel*, 2nd edn. (Paris, 1697), vol. 1, s. XCII and for the current discussion, for example, François Ost and Michel van de Kerchove, *Entre la lettre et l'esprit: Les directives d'interprétation en droit* (Brussels, 1989). Stanley Fish has become known for his fierce attacks on this rule; but ultimately this is only saying that working with texts happens in concrete situations with specific limitations, and it does not follow that there is no distinguishing between literal and analogous interpretations. See Stanley Fish, *Doing What Comes Naturally: Change, Rhetoric, and the Practice of Theory in Literary and Legal Studies* (Oxford, 1989).

[9] Neil MacCormick calls this accurately 'second-order justification' ('Why Cases Have Rationes and What These Are', in: Laurence Goldstein (ed.), *Precedent in Law* (Oxford, 1987), 155–82, at 161).

[10] In German legal theory this approach is called 'subjective doctrines of interpretations'.

[11] See François Ost and Michel van de Kerchove, *Jalons pour une théorie critique du droit* (Brussels, 1987), 97, 355, and esp. 405.

[12] It would be more common to say: convincing other participants in the communication. But how could that be tested other than by communication itself?

In many cases, these can be estimated easily. When, for instance, a municipal ordinance stipulates that dogs must be on a leash, there is no doubt
that the dog's master has also to be attached to that leash. Frequently,
however, doubts can only be ruled out during communication (and this
may be anticipated communication). This assumes communication to be a
process, one that observes itself and establishes second-order observation
in relation to that process. One must accept the premiss of an established
understanding of the text's existence and one must cope with the tasks con-
sequent on assuming rational meaning, but one is not otherwise bound by
what one deems to have been the author's intention (if one is not really
in a position to observe or interview him). Arguing over the legislator's
intention remains a possibility but becomes one form of argumentation
among many.

The primary distinctions, which are used by law both to observe argumentation and to evaluate its own propositions in relation to it, cannot be
put as a single formula because of the specific dependence of law on texts.
What we are dealing with here are, on the one hand, *errors* in reading texts
which represent valid law and, on the other hand, the *reasons* for a particular interpretation. That argumentation involves only the second case,
namely only matters of reasoning, is a foregone conclusion for lawyers
when the *term* argumentation is used, and it is in no need of further explanation.[13] But let us dwell for a moment on this perspective of observation,
because what is usually known as 'the theory of argumentation' goes
beyond this level of observation. Theories of this kind, at this level, are only
interested in a better quality of understanding of reasons.

At first sight it is apparent that there is a qualitative duality, similar to like
(reason) and dislike (error). This is not a symmetrical relation of substitution, in which one can produce one side by strict negation of the other
(avoiding errors is not in itself a good reason and good reasons can contain
logical errors, even if one is not readily willing to admit that).[14] Each component of this duality is in turn a further form of observation, that is, a distinction. As far as errors are concerned, this can easily be understood. Here
one can distinguish between erroneous and error-free argumentation, and
one can see errors either as breaching the rules of logic or in the consequences which flow from the assessment of facts, which prove to be untenable. As logic plays a role here (and only here) as an instrument for
checking errors, the description of the distinction between reasons and
errors as a qualitative (not further reducible) duality also says something
about the role of logic in legal argumentation. Logic can neither be used as

---

[13] See, for example, Gerhard Struck, *Zur Theorie juristischer Argumentation* (Berlin, 1977);
Robert Alexy, *Theorie der juristischen Argumentation* (Frankfurt, 1978).

[14] This finding also applies to the logical study of theoretically successful scientific arguments.

the justification of decisions, nor is it unimportant because of this; it has a different function and refers to a different form.

It is more difficult to arrive at statements about reasons if one looks here for a form with two sides. What could be the other side of a reason? A non-reason? The unfounded? Is it at all possible to cross the border of the form and descend into unfoundedness in order to dwell there? Or is the other side nothing but a 'reflexive value', which makes it possible for someone who defines it to reflect on the contingency of all reasons or even on the impossibility of all reasoning, that is, the paradox of giving reasons? And if this were the case, would this form of first-order observation in the shape of reasoning not have the disadvantage of confronting argumentation too quickly with its own paradox?

We can see, at any rate, that argumentation and, coming to its aid, the conventional theory of argumentation are content with a kind of *substituted distinction* which not only makes the paradox invisible but also produces further confusions by distinguishing between good and bad (or to put more politely, less good) reasons. This distinction gives rise to the question of the criteria for good and less good reasons. It is with the help of this question that the theory of argumentation itself enters the debate—on the good side, of course. However, criteria need reasons too. The construct of 'reason' fills that spot. Reason is attributed the quality of being able to justify itself.

These structures, together with their peculiar autologies (reason itself is reasonable, it is its own predicate), have become so transparent today that there is not much left to say. One can wallow in this—and enjoy it. This comes at the price, however, of ignoring a lot of what has today become the dense achievement of modern knowledge. As far as checking for logical errors is concerned, one would continue to believe that axioms of logic can still be held to be a priori reasonable rather than components of a certain calculus which can be replaced by another calculus. As far as checking for empirical errors is concerned, one would continue to believe in the classical natural sciences at the stage in which they relied on objectively determinable laws of nature and were unaware of the circular links of the scientific observing of the reality that it constructs.[15] As far as reasoning itself is concerned, one would have to ignore the erosion of all principles and their replacement by paradoxes and/or further distinctions. In order

---

[15] On the significance of this paradigm change for the concepts of norm-implementation in the legal system and on the necessity to have regard to 'epistemic risks' in juridical argumentation, see Karl-Heinz Ladeur, 'Alternativen zum Konzept der "Grenzwerte" im Umweltrecht—Zur Evolution des Verhältnisses von Norm und Wissen im Polizeirecht und im Umweltrecht', in Gerd Winter (ed.), *Grenzwerte: Interdisziplinäre Untersuchungen zu einer Rechtsfigur des Umwelts-, Arbeits- und Lebensmittelrechts* (Dusseldorf, 1986), 263–80. See also Ladeur, *Postmoderne Rechtstheorie: Selbstreferenz—Selbstorganisation—Prozeduralisierung* (Berlin, 1992).

to avoid these problems, theories of argumentation seem to be shifting more and more to principles of procedure.[16] What appears under the heading of 'the theory of argumentation' consists chiefly of commendations of one's own arguments for suitable approaches without much regard for how lawyers in concrete situations actually argue.[17] Meanwhile there is a broad discussion on 'proceduralization' which confesses openly to being part of this programme.[18] It does not involve a replacement of theory by method—at any rate not method in the sense that the certainty of (unproblematic) steps can be guaranteed and that the sequence of arguments needed to achieve a desired goal can be determined in advance. As with the old rhetoric, a lot is left to craftsmanship and thinking on one's feet, or simply to coincidence.

What really matters, however, is the inclusion of time and sequence, strategy and the possibilities for learning in the definition of the situation. Even those principles, which appear and reappear in time-honoured fashion, seem increasingly to take on the form of masked prescriptions for conduct. If, for instance, Klaus Günther recommends 'appropriateness' as a principle for testing norms in given applications, he combines it with the rule of impartiality and the rule requiring consideration of all (!) the facts and circumstances of a situation.[19] Both of these rules are, however, no longer factual criteria but are simply prescriptions for procedure or conduct for the creation of open-ended decisions, which have not yet been defined in respect of their subject matter. Further, it is telling that the plausibility of such rules correlates directly with their inapplicability. For how can it be possible to consider *all* the facts and circumstances of a situation (and of only that situation)?[20]

Legal argumentation itself, as it is factually conducted, shrugs off such theories and remains unaffected by them. It feeds off the variety of cases it is involved in, thus achieving a high degree of specificity, which cannot

---

[16] See, for example, Rudolf Wiethölter, 'Materialization and Proceduralization in Modern Law', in Gunther Teubner (ed.), *Dilemmas of Law in the Welfare State* (Berlin, 1986), 221–49; Klaus Eder, 'Prozedurale Rationalität: Moderne Rechtsentwicklung jenseits von formaler Rationalität', *Zeitschrift für Rechtssoziologie* 7 (1986), 1–30, and now Habermas, *Faktizität und Geltung*.

[17] Josef Esser comments on Alexy's theory (*Theorie der juristischen Argumentation*) that it proceeds 'without bothering about field work and empirical data' in *Juristisches Argumentieren im Wandel des Rechtsfindungszkonzepts unseres Jahrhunderts* (Heidelberg, 1979), 12.

[18] See, for example, the contributions of Klaus Eder and Karl-Heinz Ladeur, in Dieter Grimm (ed.), *Wachsende Staatsaufgaben—sinkende Steuerungsfähigkeit des Rechts* (Baden-Baden, 1990).

[19] See Klaus Günther, *Der Sinn für Angemessenheit: Anwendungsdiskurse in Moral und Recht* (Frankfurt, 1988).

[20] Of course this objection of impracticality applies only if one excludes circular arguments, which state—with reference to a contemplated decision—what, in this case, would be partial or impartial and what would be a criterion of the situation that needed to be considered.

be reduced to general principles (for instance, justice). It becomes highly sensitive towards individual problems and distinctions. In practice, however, it is not understood as an 'applied doctrine of methods' (for this would create unnecessary differences of opinion), but as an elaboration of differences in each specific case.[21] Likewise theories of ethics, of any kind, or the currently fashionable economic analyses are equally inadequate explanations of legal reasoning in practice.[22] Legal reasoning often uses relatively general terms such as fault, liability, contract, or unjust enrichment. But these terms feed off their repeated use in countless different contexts. Therefore it is possible to use them as the basis for a decision within a familiar meta-context, although they are not readily applicable without a concrete explanation. By doing so, conclusion by analogy builds a bridge between dissimilar cases.[23] Thus experiences from previous cases and expectations can be preserved, reconfirmed, and carefully extended to new facts and circumstances, or, if this is not satisfying, can be used to create rules for as yet unregulated situations.[24] Legal argumentation may deem its overall product to be 'reasonable' but that does not mean that it is derived from principles of reason. Nor does it refer to a universally equal capacity for thought. In a famous statement Coke rejected the authority that James I claimed to have over his own reasoning. Reasoning, in Coke's view, had to be 'artificial reason', that is, to be professionally induced through experience and competence.[25]

[21] Here I refer to a discussion with judges on the book by MacCormick and Summers, *Interpreting Statutes.* The comparative analysis operates on a level of secondary observation and therefore distinguishes *types* of methodical interpretation. It is difficult to apply these types to case-sensibility in legal practice, even if generalizing considerations and the inclusion of other similar cases guide it.

[22] See above all Charles Fried, 'The Artificial Reason of the Law, or: What Lawyers Know', *Texas Law Review* 60 (1981), 35–58.

[23] Melvin Aron Eisenberg, *The Nature of the Common Law* (Cambridge, 1988), 83 ff. (94) gives an important hint: it is equally valid to argue with an interpretation of a rule or with an analogy; the difference depends only on how far a decision rule is pre-formulated. On continental European doctrine see A. W. Heinrich Langhein, *Das Prinzip der Analogie als juristische Methode: Ein Beitrag zur Geschichte der methodologischen Grundlagenforschung vom ausgehenden 18. bis zum 20. Jahrhundert* (Berlin, 1992).

[24] It should be generally recognized that arguments by analogy cannot be justified logically and represent a conservative principle. 'The very process of reasoning by analogy facilitates relative stability in law', writes F. James Davis et al., *Society and the Law: New Meanings for an Old Profession* (New York, 1962), 122. With a different terminology, which will be explained below, one can also say that conclusion by analogy mediates between redundancy and variety, and can go—exactly because it is logically undetermined—more in one direction or the other, depending on how bold one is (or what goal one has in mind).

[25] See also the title of the lecture delivered by Charles Fried, 'The Artificial Reason of the Law', who picked up on this reference.

Someone who understands reasoning as a reference to reasons will feel the necessity to find reasons for the reasons as well. Someone who must find reasons for reasons needs tenable principles.[26] Someone who refers to principles ultimately refers to acknowledged principles in the environment of the system. This is especially the case when such principles carry the additional signature of 'moral', 'ethical', or 'reasonable' principles. If a theory of argumentation is constructed in this way, it cannot accept the thesis of operative closure of the legal system and will tend to make use of reasons which arise from the practice of argumentation itself, to contradict this thesis. Such an approach is reinforced both empirically and morally and that may explain the robustness of the discussion of the theory of operative closure.[27] Consider: can principles do away with the requirement of their having to distinguish themselves from each other? And if not: who does the distinguishing, if not the legal system itself? One can further assume that frequently, if not always, an opposing decision can also be justified by a principle (proportionality, appropriateness, appreciation of values, etc.). The nomination of a principle thus means the relegation of distinguishing back into the system. Finally, with its formulation the principle masks the time dimension of the operations of the system, the ongoing repetitions and modifications, confirmations and condensations, distinguishing and overruling in the daily practice of the system. This may serve to pretend that unity exists where rules have been changed over the course of time, that is, to present inconsistency as consistency.[28] Hence one can account for the use of principles in legal reasoning even if one accepts the theory of the operative closure of the legal system. Then, as will become clearer in the analysis below, one can understand principles as formulae for redundancy, which appear to be compatible with any degree of variety in the system.

As the anachronism of a belief in principles and the impracticality of flight into procedural directives reveal themselves as inadequate, there remains only the possibility of resolute resignation in the style of the Frankfurt School—or, the search for alternative possibilities for observation, which are richer in their structure. One could consider putting the question of the 'conditions for the possibility' of legal reasoning and, at the same time, replacing the auto-logic of reason with instruments that keep a safer distance from it. For this to succeed, however, one must be able to set out the details of how (that is, with which distinction) it can be done.

---

[26] Even proceduralists who try to circumvent such a commitment cannot avoid having to name principles of procedure or have to take reason itself as a principle to which one can refer irrefutably.

[27] See, for example, the contributions in of the *Cardozo Law Review* 13 (1992).

[28] I owe this observation to S. C. Smith.

II

If one is intent on improving theory and reviews what has been adopted and has posed under the title of a 'theory of argumentation' in the past decades, little can be found that is helpful.[29] We can find ideas, which are particularly well received in legal doctrine, of methods using decontextualized, classical, and early modern concepts such as rhetoric, dialectic and hermeneutics. The difficulty of making links to these doctrines of form and, primarily, oral culture are overlooked, even if this culture was already familiar with some written texts and the first reactions of doubt that came with writing. This is no longer the situation we are in. A second wave of normative theories about normative arguments, triggered by the 'linguistic turn' of philosophy, has not yet reached jurisprudence proper but is suspended at a 'critical' distance from legal practice. Even though there is little to be gained from a flat rejection of all these theories, it makes sense at least to look for alternatives.

First of all, we need a concept of argumentation, which does not by definition include the elements of a justification, but enables us to inquire into the conditions for the possibilities and the function of reasoning.[30] Let us stay for a moment with the self-presentation of argumentation as offering seemingly compelling reasons for decisions. Here it is useful to be aware that these reasons must be offered for repeated use. In each individual case they must relate to a recursive web of ancillary considerations at their inception. This can be done by analogy or by distinguishing. The problem here is different from what were thought to be earlier problems. Legal argumentation, which uses both analogy and distinguishing, is not concerned with the system (and that makes it different from reflexive theories). That approach to argumentation runs, in the old Aristotelian terms, not *de toto ad seipsum* but *de parte ad partem*.[31] This means that one employs—in classical terms—the effective and proven guidance given by *exempla*, as in rhetoric and pedagogics.[32] Such examples are sought in

[29] For an overview see Werner Krawietz, 'Juristische Argumentation in rechtstheoretischer, rechtsphilosophischer und rechtssoziologischer Perspektive', in Norbert Achterberg et al. (eds.), *Recht und Staat im sozialen Wandel: Festschrift für Hans Ulrich Scupin zum 80. Geburtstag* (Berlin, 1983), 347–90.

[30] Another reason for this revision of the concept is found in the typical deficiencies of teleological conceptualization; there is no room for failure, corruption, missing the goal. And even the normal solution of referring to the 'subjective' intentions of the individuals who give reasons leads to well-known difficulties, such as the distinction between purpose and motive.

[31] Thus the philosopher versus the theologian in Marius Salamonius de Alberteschis, *De Principatu* (1513), quoted from the reprint (Milan, 1955), 26. See on the earlier history of this presentation of an inference from one part to another (*hos méros pròs méros*) without reference to the whole, Aristotle's *Analytica priora* 69a, 13–15.

[32] See also one of the most impressive presentations of the methods of argumentation in common law, that by Edward H. Levi, 'An Introduction to Legal Reasoning', *University of Chicago Law Review* 15 (1948), 501–74.

relation to the case in hand, and are based if necessary on an original interpretation, but are not systematically deduced. The formulation of a rule is
the result of, and not the condition of, such a way of arguing.

But exactly because each individual case is understood within the framework of the recursive web of its own argumentation, it cannot lapse back
into a vacuum or anticipate a void. It must assume that cases have been
decided before and that others will follow after. In this sense (and this is different from referring to the *unity* of the system) even the technique that
uses individual cases as examples reasons quite systematically: on its own
level, it establishes itself as a contribution to the autopoiesis of the system.
As time passes, the situations themselves change with their recursivity,
which picks up selectively on the past and the future. Only with this in
mind can one talk about rules, which have to be applied again, and about
similar cases, which have to be decided again. On closer inspection it is
apparent that repetition is a rather complicated process and one that is
clearly different from mere copying.[33]

Repetitions happen again and again in entirely different circumstances.
Cases may be constructed as being comparable in view of the demand to
treat equal matters equally and only unequal matters unequally. However
the probing of equal/unequal is tested in a reality in which each concrete
situation is different, because of other earlier decisions and a different history. Repetitions, therefore, have a double set of demands placed upon
them (which reflects exactly what is required by justice): they have to identify rules and to confirm that they are identical in spite of the non-identity
of the case at hand. Repetition requires condensation and confirmation,
reduction to definable identities, and generalization. This is exactly how
legal practice works in courts, both in dealing with precedents and in
statutory interpretation.[34]

Hence one cannot expect the outcome of all this to be what is premised
by a theory which understands the practice of courts as an application of
fixed rules (even if they are rules of self-/judge-made law). On the contrary, argumentative orientation is constantly shifting because its recursive
support shifts from situation to situation.[35] This is exactly why the practice
of argumentation in courts is moving in the direction of special, juridical
semantics. It promotes the amplification of deviation in the cybernetical sense
of positive feedback loops or, in the linguistic sense, uses hypercorrection in

[33] See also the distinction between *itérabilité* and *répétabilité* used by Jacques Derrida, *Limited
Inc.* (Paris, 1990), e.g. at 230 and 234. In contrast to mere repeating, the process of repetition
accounts for the differences in situations that result merely from the passing of time.

[34] See on this point also Levi, *An Introduction to Legal Reasoning*, on some specific developments
of rules in the practice of US courts.

[35] Levi comments that: 'rules are never clear' (ibid. 501), 'rules are remade with each case'
(ibid. 502), and 'rules change as the rules are applied' (ibid. 503).

relation to language. Thus the process of operative closure exists not only at the level of deciding about legal validity but also on the level of argumentation. And evolution is also involved here.

From this position it is not a big leap to a description of legal argumentation with the help of concepts that are unsuitable as arguments and cannot enter into argumentative communication. Consequently, we can formulate the concept of argumentation quite distinctly from the question of how good arguments are. The distinctions we use are: (1) operation and observation, (2) external-observation and self-observation, (3) contested/ uncontested. Legal argumentation is a combination of one side of these distinctions, that is, the self-observation of the legal system, which reacts to past and/or anticipated differences of opinion about the attribution of the code-values legal and illegal in the recursive context of autopoiesis.[36] Observation is involved because cases or groups of cases have to be distinguished from each other. This is self-observation because the operation of observation takes place within the legal system. And contentious communication is involved because the mere disposition of the symbol of validity or the pure reading of statutes must be excluded from a concept of argumentation.

In spite of all the above-mentioned limitations, even this concept still comprises arguments which do not fulfil the function of argumentation—arguments such as: the landlord is always right, the political party is always right, the military is always right. Hence we must look for the conditions that make it possible for the function of argumentation in the system to be fulfilled.[37]

As always when 'conditions of possibility' or 'functions' are concerned, an observer on the level of secondary observation is involved.[38] It is on this level of second-order observation that we can pose the question of how a system can make its own autopoiesis possible, including its own self-observation (that is, how a system can make itself possible). The answer to this question is given by another set of instruments, which cannot be deployed meaningfully at the level of first-order observation.

[36] This concept can easily be extended to moral and scientific argumentation if one switches the codes accordingly.

[37] This is the point at which we definitely part company with theories that relate the concept of argumentation exclusively to the criteria of reasons, for instance the reasonableness of reasons. *In their place*, we look for the function of the system because we do not want to subject our analysis to the reasons that are mobilized in the system itself. This does not stop one, of course, from observing and appreciating that lawyers attempt to argue reasonably or well in other ways (elegantly, convincingly, etc.).

[38] Obviously, we are drawing from Kant's philosophy here without, however, taking up his distinction between the empirical and the transcendental. This is all the easier to do as the distinction between first-order observation and second-order observation provides us with a successor terminology.

Following ideas that originated in the technically oriented theory of information, we can distinguish between *information* and *redundancy*. Information is the surprise value of news, given a limited or unlimited number of other possibilities. Redundancy follows (in a circular fashion) from the fact that information is used when autopoietic systems operate. An operation reduces the selection potential from other contributions. A sentence, for instance, reduces the scope of contributions that fit into it. This results in the selection of connecting operations, being at one and the same time easy and difficult. It is easy if the scope for selection is small, and it is difficult because criteria for selection can now be introduced which are not easy to fulfil, or possibly only by a circumspective, renewed opening of the scope for selection by admitting further information. As a mechanism for the elimination of the demand for (or the interest in) further information, redundancy itself is *not information*. It enables *indifference*, both in respect of the relation between the operations of the system and, above all, in respect of the relation between the system and its environment.

Much has been written about the high degree of redundancy in legal language and its style (use of formulae, repetitiveness).[39] Basically these are only rhetorical-expressive means. In any event, one must not confuse the matter of style with conceptual accuracy or proper definitions, which are often missing from legal concepts. Rather, the form of language is the result of a system-internal use of language. It develops automatically when formulae are repeated and condensed to a core identity but are, at the same time, charged again and again with the new horizons of meaning taken from different situations. This has been expressed in the classical formulation: 'The science of jurisprudence [is] . . . the collected reason of ages, combining the principles of original justice with the infinite variety of human concerns.'[40]

Martin Shapiro has shown the importance of redundancy for the coordination of decisions in the legal system, which have been made independently (not coordinated by a hierarchically organized line of command), without distinguishing between first- and second-order observations.[41] This leads to a focus on the finding and avoiding of errors, which is an important aspect of operations on the level of first-order observations. Without redundancy, a loss of information (caused by the poor performance of the system of transmission) would remain unidentifiable and thus incorrigible. The more information a system has to process, the more it requires sufficient

---

[39] See, for example, Pierre Mimin, *Le style des jugements*, 2nd edn. (Paris, 1970), esp. 99.

[40] Edmund Burke, *Reflections on the Revolution in France, Works*, vol. III, p. 357, quoted by David Lieberman, *The Province of Legislation Determined: Legal Theory in Eighteenth-Century Britain* (Cambridge, 1989), 2.

[41] Martin Shapiro, 'Toward a Theory of *Stare Decisis*', *Journal of Legal Studies* 1 (1972), 125–34; see also Giorgio Lazzaro, *Entropia della legge* (Turin, 1985).

redundancy in order to avoid errors in the form of a loss of relevant information. But could one not equally well say: in order to legitimize errors? This alone shows that a system staves off an overload of information with established redundancy but precisely through this achieves new degrees of sensitivity for distinguishing and defining. Redundancies, therefore, not only exclude information but also produce it by indicating the sensitivity of the system. Thus there is information in the system which cannot be found in its environment, because it is not prepared for it. Accordingly the reduction of complexity serves to increase complexity.

Evidently such a development requires a high degree of indifference in relation to the environment of the system. Only a very limited number of communications in the environment have an information value for the legal system. Nevertheless, it would be too simple to interpret the demand for redundancy exclusively as a shield against noise from the environment, for the system requires that its individual operations be isolated from each other and then, however, connected selectively. Relatively small systems, let alone the legal system, can no longer connect all operations with all other operations. Structured complexity always requires selective links and also— this is the other side of the coin—a shield against internally produced noise. Information involves a difference; it makes a difference for the system by changing the system's state (Bateson). The selection of information with that ability is the function of redundancy. The operations of the system are intentionally dedicated to the processing of information: that is, the continuous transformation of information into different information for other operations. However, the reproduction of redundancy within the system follows this process like a shadow. Shapiro talks about a 'stream of reassurances' which can absorb only a very limited number of new differences.[42] In the terminology of evolution theory, and also neurophysiological theory and (constructivist) theories of perception, one could call redundancies 'attractors' which organize the processing of information.[43] Although this concept is not clearly defined, nevertheless two things are articulated clearly in the context of these theories: on the one hand, the ability to operate under circumstances which can be presupposed as 'chaos', and on the other, a local reference that makes priorities possible without being dependent on references to the unity or totality of the system. This means in the context of evolution theory that the formation of attractors cannot be traced back to some meaningful beginning or reason but that attractors spring up accidentally and are then preserved in their results. In this respect,

---

[42] See ibid. 131.

[43] See, for example, Michael Stadler and Peter Kruse, 'Visuelles Gedächtnis für Formen und das Problem der Bedeutungszuweisung in kognitiven Systemen', in Siegfried J. Schmidt, (ed.), *Gedächtnis: Probleme und Perspektiven der interdisziplinären Gedächtnisforschung* (Frankfurt, 1991), 250–66.

the system is a historical system without a final reason for its being as it is. In the context of theories of consciousness or communication, this means that attractors function as 'values'. One prefers to be guided by them because otherwise the loss of order, the 'chaos', would be unbearable.

From the viewpoint of coordination, redundancy is the 'invisible hand' of the system.[44] However, the visible hand, that is, the hierarchical line of command, would not be an example of the contrary case as the metaphor may suggest. It is a case of its application. Commands from a higher source are also supported by redundancy. They only turn the information which is circling in the system into a specific form (among others, the fact that one is not responsible for a selection of information that is covered by reference to a command). Hence the visible hand (for instance, the legislator's hand) too is at the disposition of the invisible hand. Thus, one must distinguish between the intended selection and the unintended reproduction of the redundancies of the system in each of its operations. An operation which does not exhibit this double feature would not be recognizable as an operation that belongs to the system and one which reproduces the recursive network of its interconnected operations. Other legal scholars use the term *institution*, in order to define the limitations of dealing with legal issues, which are imposed by the legal system itself.[45] This, however, does not distinguish clearly enough between limitation and reasoning. 'Custom' and 'practical reason' are attributed to the concept of institution, which defines the habit of practical argumentation guided by reason. Thus far the concept of self-interpretation of legal practice remains committed to the level of first-order observation. The use of the concept of redundancy has the advantage of replacing the fact of institutional reasoning with a variable, which reacts to other variables (as we will see later, this represents the variety of cases with which decision-making has to deal). Additionally, we can avoid combining 'custom' and 'practical reason' in one concept, but rather can look from greater distance at the performance of legal reasoning in its arguments. Then one can continue to say that the limitation of the scope of possible combinations (institution) is the condition for the possibility of reasons (institution), and consequently that redundancy is the condition for the possibility of legal argumentation.

Having clarified that, we need no longer treat the issue as if only the finding and eliminating of errors were involved, even if this may be the primary concern of lawyers. From the vantage point of a second-order observer who wants to assess the legal system in the way it operates (and not only assess the reasons, objectives, and conditions for the validity of operations), what

[44]   Shapiro, 'Toward a Theory of *Stare Decisis*,' 131.

[45]   See Neil MacCormick, 'Law as Institutional Fact', *Law Quarterly Review* 90 (1974), 102–29, reprinted in: Neil MacCormick and Ota Weinberger, *An Institutional Theory of Law: New Approaches to Legal Positivism* (Dordrecht, 1986), 49–76.

matters is to understand how it achieves sufficient consistency in the relations of a multiplicity of decisions related to each other. No single decision is able to define or determine the total sum of all the other decisions, let alone recognize their substance. Something has to happen 'in lieu', in order to stop a disintegration of the system into a group of single decisions, which have no relevance to each other and can only be recognized by an observer if he applies his own criteria to such a group (for example, criteria of genus or species). The creation of sufficient redundancies is the answer to this problem. If justice is given by the consistency of decisions,[46] we can also say: justice is redundancy.[47] And this distinguishes it from other ideals of decision-making, which aim, for instance, at the optimization of legal decisions by using as much information as possible.

Obviously, a systemic concept of justice cannot be realized in case-by-case decisions. Contrary to the opinion of almost every scholar who has dealt with this topic, this systemic concept eludes moral attribution and ethical evaluation; instead—once again 'in lieu'—the issue is how to avoid errors and that means how to avoid obvious inconsistencies.[48] Accordingly, errors are operative indicators for the possible injustice of the system. They serve at the same time as a form of knowledge, which enables one to distance oneself from the decisions of others that, one deems to be wrong, that is, to respond to the impossibility of the absolute consistency of all decisions.[49] As always, errors remain a schema of knowledge of first-order observation—one tries to avoid them or to blame others for them, but one does not query the conditions of their possibility or the constitution of redundancy. To a second-order observer, however, the question of the production and maintenance of redundancy is at the centre of interest. It is clear to a second-order observer that there are more imperatives for the system than just maintaining redundancy. Otherwise how can the growth of the system and society's tolerance of its law be explained (even if that tolerance is always modified by criticism)?

Are only the limitations on the processing of information the problem here? After all, each system has to cope with them. Is 'bounded rationality'

---

[46] See above Ch. 5.

[47] Or, to use the words coming from legal practice (that is, the judgemental view of a first-order observer), 'to keepe as neare as may be to the Certainty of the Law and to the Consonance of it to it Selfe', namely those of Sir Matthew Hale in an objection to Hobbes in the seventeenth century. See *Reflections by the Lrd Cheife Justice Hale in Mr. Hobbes His Dialogue of the Lawe*, in: William Holdsworth, *A History of the English Law*, 3rd edn. (London, 1945; reprint 1966), vol. V, Appendix III, pp. 500–13 at 506.

[48] Thus we find here the reason which has led many authors to the opinion that justice can only be explicated *ex negativo*, as a negative theology of the legal system, as it were.

[49] See on this point also the observations on 'mistakes' by Ronald Dworkin, *Taking Rights Seriously* (Cambridge, 1977), 118.

as defined by Herbert Simon[50] what is involved, or is the issue the necessity of a decentralized handling of complexity as defined by Hayek[51] and Lindblom?[52] Is consistency unachievable only because there is no central instance with adequate information (which must include all the information about all the possible resulting decisions and all the alternatives)? If it were only that simple, one solution would be to simplify radically the topics that are dealt with by the system.

It is apparent that this is not a viable approach if one accepts that redundancy is not the only condition on which the autopoiesis of the system depends. A second condition is variety and by that is meant the number and the diversity of the operations which a system can identify as its own and which it can execute.[53] At first sight, redundancy and variety seem to be opposing requirements: redundancy involves the information that is available for the processing of information, and variety is the information that is as yet missing.[54] The greater the variety of a system, the more difficult it becomes to use one operation about which there is little information to draw conclusions about other operations, and the more difficult it becomes to identify a system on the basis of knowledge of some of its operations, let alone describe it adequately; and the more surprises there are to be generated and processed; and the longer the linkages become, and the more time the system needs. This contrasting of redundancy and variety nonetheless falls short. Business economists have posited a relation of substitution between binding rules and variability.[55] We can go further than

---

[50] See, as the point of departure for wide-ranging further developments, Herbert A. Simon, *Models of Man: Social and Rational: Mathematical Essays on Rational Human Behavior in a Social Setting* (New York, 1957). See also the collection of essays *Models of Bounded Rationality* (Cambridge, 1982), esp. vol. 2, p. 401.

[51] See F. A. von Hayek, *Die Theorie komplexer Phänomene* (Tübingen, 1972).

[52] See Charles E. Lindblom, *The Intelligence of Democracy: Decision-Making through Mutual Adjustment* (New York, 1965); id., and David K. Cohen, *Usable Knowledge: Social Science and Social Problem Solving* (New Haven, 1979).

[53] The distinction between redundancy and variety has been elaborated on by Henri Atlan, who uses this distinction in his work to explain the conditions for the possibility of self-organization in living systems. For an overview see: 'Noise, Complexity and Meaning in Cognitive Systems', *Revue internationale de systémique* 3 (1989), 237–49, and before that above all *L'organisation biologique et la théorie de l'information* (Paris, 1972); 'On a Formal Definition of Organization', *Journal of Theoretical Biology* 45 (1974), 295–304; *Entre le cristal et la fumée* (Paris, 1979). Atlan, however, does not define variety in relation to the elementary operations of the systems which make surprises (processing of information) unavoidable only as a result of the complexity of the system, but as a concept in direct opposition to redundancy, namely as the quality of surprise of information.

[54] It is important to relate this availability or absence to the requirements of processing information in a system. Without that reference the difference has at best only a mathematical significance as, for instance, in Atlan's reciprocal relation of H (variety) and R (redundancy).

[55] See Erich Gutenberg, *Grundlagen der Betriebswirtschaftslehre*, vol. 1, 15th edn. (Berlin, 1969), 236.

that for there are several ways to generate redundancies, and it is possible that one form of redundancy is more compatible with greater variety than others. This applies, for instance, to sequential conditional programmes of the type: if x, y, z are given, a company can be validly formed with its own legal personality. On the basis of that legal status it can acquire rights (like anybody who has some legal status) if the necessary conditions are met. With those rights it can litigate and win or lose cases. As this example shows, sequential programmes lead to a partial, 'heterarchical' web of conditions, which can be applied to other combinations as well. (One does not, for example, form a company with legal status only to litigate in its name but also to accumulate capital or limit liability.)

Whether the legal system organizes its memory with the help of cases or with legal institutions or legal principles, all of which may happen concurrently, what it needs for producing all these references in any case is a restriction to a loose coupling.[56] Only in a few respects should decisions in one sub-complex affect another, just as, conversely, the necessary information on law must be kept in strict limits in all decisions because otherwise one cannot provide different decisions for different facts. However, this requirement is not an unchanging feature of the system—for example, in the sense of a negative justice. Rather, it varies with that much complexity of the system that is still compatible with its autopoiesis, and can remain so only with the help of loose coupling.

In other words, variety and redundancy are matters that can both increase in relation to each other. As mentioned earlier, the possibilities for increase are scanned by analogies, which lead either to a generalization of already existing rules or to the creation of new rules in situations which are deemed to be new and as such not yet documented. In the course of the evolution of law it happens from time to time that new legal forms are found which realize a higher potential for combinations.[57] Then the redundancies of the system, which adapt so successfully to great variety, may come to expect certain types of operation (for instance, particular forms of subjective rights), which are declining in importance or, conversely, cannot cope with

---

[56] See Robert B. Glassman, 'Persistence and Loose Coupling in Living Systems', *Behavioral Science* 18 (1973), 83–98; Herbert A. Simon, 'The Organization of Complex Systems', in Howard H. Pattee (ed.), *Hierarchy Theory: The Challenge of Complex Systems* (New York, 1973), 3–27, at 15; Karl F. Weick, *Der Prozeß des Organisierens* (Frankfurt, 1985), 163; J. Douglas Orton and Karl E. Weick, 'Loosely Coupled Systems: A Reconceptualization', *Academy of Management Review* 15 (1990), 203–23. Earlier on, one used to talk about partial functions and ultrastability in cybernetics, in order to define interruptions designed to enhance stability. See W. Ross Ashby, *Design for a Brain: The Origin of Adaptive Behavior*, 2nd edn. (London, 1954), esp. at 136 and 153.

[57] An argument along the same lines, but a questionable simplification, would be to say that evolution results in a reduction in the costs of transactions which otherwise would be incurred by adaptation to changes in the environment. See for this argument Robert C. Clark, 'The Interdisciplinary Study of Legal Evolution', *Yale Law Review* 90 (1981), 1238–74.

problems (such as 'public goods', or collective interests in acceptable environmental conditions) that have now acquired a great significance.[58] Or it may become useful to replace criteria for distinction, which result in too many doubtful cases under the pressure of variety, with others that can be generalized more accurately—for example, one might replace other forms of liability for dangerous objects with that of strict liability, itself a substitute for an outright prohibition.[59] Hence the relationship between variety and redundancy is one which is precarious and yet at the same time historically developed. It is more this relationship, and less the individual legal institution, that through its change reproduces the adaptation of the legal system to the environment.

The concepts of redundancy and variety fall outside the framework of legal argumentation. They formulate opposing requirements, which cannot be subsumed into contradictions between different reasons for decisions. They shed light on what is communicated within legal arguments from an incongruous perspective. Therefore they go further than the typical argument of the Critical Legal Studies movement: that the legal system presents the principles of its own reasons in a contradictory fashion in order to adjust better to the capitalist mode of production. What is more important is that a differentiated legal system has to provide both operative closure and high irritability and, on the level of its self-observation, both redundancy and variety. However, the explosiveness of this array of contradictory requirements does not take the form of a contradiction of reasons that is repeated over and over again. In the process of a translation into possible arguments, this issue becomes veiled and is reformulated with a web of principles and rules, to the effect that conflicts in decision-making are only felt locally and can thus be treated in individual cases or groups of cases. Legal theories, which are content with the internal observation and the self-description of the system, can do without concepts such as redundancy and variety. Then, however, they must also do without an understanding of the operative constructivism with which the legal system creates its own world. The risk of this is that terminologies of reasoning may become confused with terms that also have a currency outside the legal system. We shall revisit this issue below with the example of the term 'interest'.

III

Redundancy is not a quality that can be found with the means of logic. According to Hegel it does not belong to the realm of necessity but to the realm of chance, because the definition of one piece of information does

---

[58] See the illuminating discussion on the problems of the development of constitutional law in Dieter Grimm, 'Die Zukunft der Verfassung', *Staatswissenschaften und Staatspraxis* (1990), 5–33, reprinted in id., *Die Zukunft der Verfassung* (Frankfurt, 1991), 397–437.

[59] See this example in Levi, 'An Introduction to Legal Reasoning'.

not determine the definition of another. But this chance is a particularly prepared one, so we are dealing here with a highly defined commitment of the system that needs only a little bit of further information to sustain it. Similarly, writing alone is not fully determining of law, ready for decision-making. This prejudice (if it is a prejudice) was pointed out in the discussion of the concept of text.[60] Writing is only a form, which produces a difference between text and interpretation, between the letter and the spirit of the law. There is no written determination of the law without the need for interpretation. Both are produced in one move as a form with two sides. Hence, as soon as texts are written, the problem of interpretation arises.

In spite of an immense amount of literature on points of view and procedures for interpretation, reaching far back in history, we do not have to treat this topic under this heading. If one talks about interpretation, one thinks about the social behaviour of readers who concentrate on the text and obviously do not want to be disturbed. One cannot involve them in communication without forcing them to interrupt their reading. They can only read or communicate. Today reading is ordinarily done silently. And someone who reads out aloud to others does so as the mouthpiece of the text—and not as its interpreter.

It need not be of concern what a reader quietly thinks in the dark innermost of his own thoughts—if he finds time to digress from the text. Once the reader starts to interpret, argumentation is under way.[61] It can initially take the form of a simulation of communication, such as talking to oneself (and not talking to the text!) or in the form of articulated, verbalized thinking—in a trial run of communication as it were. But this talking to oneself is already dominated by the criteria of what can be said convincingly. It is no longer an issue of unclear 'lacunae' in the text but of questions of which texts one can refer to, in which contexts, while communicating.[62] Nothing is lost, then, if every piece of reasoning is understood as social

---

[60] See section I above, and also Ch. 6.II.

[61] This is not to say that all the authors who deal with argumentation share this approach or have to share this approach. In the context of theories on truth Donald Davidson, *Inquiries into Truth and Interpretation* (Oxford, 1984), starts at a much more basic level, namely within linguistic theory after the linguistic turn of analytical philosophy. Here the fact that all utterings need interpretation is seen as an indispensable condition for a non-circular theory of meaning, which does not accept (because it would result in a circle) that the task of the clarifying interpretation has to be done by communication itself or in anticipation of it. Such a theory, however, would have to postulate a non-socialized subject as a starting point, that is, a subject that only now and then engages in communication when it can imagine another subject. This demonstrates quite clearly how this variant of language-analytical philosophy argues in the tradition of transcendental theories.

[62] A similar turn in the traditional theory of argumentation is observed by Esser, *Juristisches Argumentieren*, 5: 'How differently must the task of argumentative discourse and argumentative justification be perceived if judicial opinions, and opinion about law altogether, have to be understood as the task of legal communication and the judicial assessment of a case, not as an argumentative dispute about the true content of a legal proposition, text or principle.'

behaviour, including the strictly logical evaluation of evidence.[63] Even theories of interpretation, which focus exclusively on the relationship between reader and text, try to find a second line of defence for the 'objectivity' of the interpretation in social relations.[64]

Thus the classic division between hermeneutics, dialectic (dialogic), and rhetoric leads us astray. It stresses distinctions that we can leave to one side.[65] One can plausibly assume that the interpretation can only read into a text or extract from a text that which can be used argumentatively in communication. If the text alone guarantees that all readers in all situations understand it in the same way, then we can do away with interpretation. One does not interpret in order to enlighten oneself but in order to engage in communication, no matter how selectively the outcomes, reasons, or arguments are presented and no matter how much the certainty of being able to add further arguments contributes to claims to and the acknowledgement of authority. The presupposition is that the other participants have their sight on the *same* text. Having a written form of the text does not necessarily guarantee that there are limits to the boldness of the interpretation. But it guarantees the *unity of the social context of a communicative episode*. It constitutes a social medium for the acquisition of new forms, namely good reasons for a certain interpretation of a text.[66] One can stray from the literal meaning of a text as long as one strays from the literal meaning. This alone is the difference between a literal understanding of a text and an analogous one, and is possible as long as the interpretation does not destroy the uniting function of the text.

There is a particularity of legal argumentation/interpretation that reinforces this relation. Legal argumentation must be able to propose a decision about legal and illegal and justify it. Decisions must be made within the legal system, and courts cannot refuse to make a decision (and this is, as has been argued, the reason for their central position in the legal system).

---

[63] This approach is shared by (sociological) theories of knowledge. See, for instance, David Bloor, 'The Sociology of Reasons: Or Why "Epistemic Factors" are really "Social Factors"', in James Robert Brown (ed.), *Scientific Rationality: The Sociological Turn* (Dordrecht, 1984), 295–324. This is contested in Germany. However, the reason for that is mainly that the 'social' that Bloor and other members of the Science Studies Unit in Edinburgh mean, is seen as too narrow (and tending to be tautological), namely in relation to interests.

[64] See, for example, Owen M. Fiss, 'Objectivity and Interpretation', *Stanford Law Review* 34 (1982), 739–63: 'Interpretation . . . is a dynamic interaction between reader and text'. Its limitation is supposedly given by the reality of an 'interpretative community'.

[65] It is well known that even the debate whether or not one has to be convinced by one's own arguments in order to be able to convince others has been conducted *inside* rhetoric.

[66] This has been formulated as an aside (but to the point) by Alexander Hamilton, *The Federalist Papers*, no. 78, quoted by Jacob E. Cooke (Middletown, 1961), 525: 'In such a case [when there are contradictions between statutes] it is the province of the courts *to liquidate and fix* their meaning and operation' (italics by N.L.).

Hence all legal argumentation that presents interpretations of texts has a reference to *decision-making*, and furthermore a reference to decisions in the matters of *other people*. Therefore legal argumentation *must* be guided by communication.[67]

This also explains why the theory of argumentation falls on particularly fertile ground in the common law. A lawyer in continental European law, who has to interpret legislation and who can find the 'dominant opinion' in commentaries, sees himself primarily as a reader and interpreter. In the common law, however, what matters above all is an assessment of precedents. One must find out, first of all, what the *ratio decidendi* of the precedent is, for—even as an interpreter—one is naturally not bound by the validity of the decision.[68] And one has to decide and reason argumentatively whether the case in hand is different from the precedent, and this is not done by studying the rule but by comparing the facts of cases to see how this particular case is different from the one before. Hence one cannot simply apply a rule, which may or may not require an interpretation, but *one has to decide* whether or not one wants to *distinguish between cases*. And one has to give reasons for the decision to distinguish or not.

However, the difference between the legal cultures of continental European law and the common law should not be overestimated. Obviously, in the common law world one also has to deal with problems of statutory interpretation, and in continental European law argumentation is required to present reasons for the ever new, ever different decisions in cases.[69] The legal institution of appeal alone imposes the necessity of an ongoing engagement with the decisions of other courts.[70] At issue always are reasons, which are at once *universally* and *specifically* applicable. Universally means here that the rule can be applied to all cases of a certain type, that it must be applied recursively to valid law, and that the number of cases to be decided according to this rule in the future remains indeterminable.[71]

---

[67] This, by the way, distinguishes dealing with legal texts from dealing with literary texts, and also sacred texts, which have this quality only for the believers with the same beliefs. A lawyer cannot choose for whom or against whom he or she argues.

[68] The legal institution itself needs a high degree interpretation and by defining it in all its details one can mediate between continuity and discontinuity, and between redundancy and variety. See for a remarkably measured account MacCormick, 'Legal Reasoning and Legal Theory' (Oxford, 1978).

[69] See, for example, for a theory of argumentation, which includes binding precedents, statutory interpretation, and the (specific freedoms of) judicial review in the United States, Levi, 'An Introduction to Legal Reasoning'. In all cases one is *inescapably* confronted with the problem of the repetition of rules in ever new, ever different case situations.

[70] Comparisons between the common law and continental European law often find differences that do not exist in practice. The orientation by precedents only surfaces in different contexts.

[71] This is nothing but a version of 'autopoiesis' that finds expression in this context. The system cannot envisage its own end and operates 'for the time being'.

Moreover, these rules can be highly specific and can become generalized only gradually or not at all.[72] However, neither interpretation nor argumentation in themselves change the law. They are not forms of a disposition that controls the symbol of the validity of law, but rather they are communications that clarify the conditions in which such a disposition can be made (and, of course, they exclude economic reasons which may advocate contracts, or political reasons which may advocate legislation). Because of its merely preparative function, argumentation has a greater degree of freedom. It only prepares for responsibility; it does not yet take it. Nevertheless, arguments are operations of the system, in so far as they serve to limit the range of decisions that ultimately have to be made. The dual structure of valid texts and argumentative reasons allows the normative ambivalence of argumentation to be translated into a distinction (and definitely not, in a Hegelian sense, to 'be merged'). Argumentation itself is not a normative process—it may disappoint and learn from disappointment. But what it produces can be distilled as rules or principles, with the effect that legal doctrine itself can be treated, with hindsight, as a 'source of law'.

Hence, according to the self-concept of argumentation, it proposes *reasons* for preferring one particular interpretation to another. Reasons are presented as good and reasonable reasons regardless of their success. They are also called traditionally '*rationes*' (*rationes decidendi*, reasons, etc.). As pointed out above, by bringing itself into play, it is ultimately only reason that can advise on how reasons can be justified. In effect, this practice of reasonable argumentation gives law itself the characteristics of a considered reasonableness, a condensation of tried and tested good reasons. Neil MacCormick calls this context an 'institution'.[73] This implies that there must be further criteria for the thoroughness of reasoning apart from the ones given in the reasons themselves—such as professionalism, elegance of expression, economy of expression, and last but not least the avoidance of absurdity.[74] The outcome of all these checks, which also serve to show what can go wrong, is a tradition of principles, rules, and doctrines but also of rejected alternative instructions which form the reservoir from which legislation and above all judicial lawmaking take their materials. Thus the result is again more texts, more interpretable texts. The reality of this structural

---

[72] According to MacCormick, 'Why cases have Rationes', 162 one has to distinguish in this sense between universability and generalizability.

[73] See especially his contributions in MacCormick and Weinberger, *An Institutional Theory of Law*.

[74] Not all but some of the terminological exercises collected by Rudolf von Jhering, *Scherz und Ernst in der Jurisprudenz*, 2nd edn. (Leipzig, 1885), could serve here as evidence. They are not examples of the errors of a 'terminological jurisprudence' [Begriffsjurisprudenz] (because they could just as well be collected in the domain of the 'jurisprudence of interests' which Jhering advocated), but examples of the violation of juridical taste.

framework is not a sphere of ideas existing in its own right. What are in fact real are only the actual operations of the system's communications that use this framework—or which can no longer recall it.

Such a web of points of view involved in decision-making—we call it legal doctrine—can be employed innovatively as well.[75] One may later realize that certain constellations were overlooked or that errors occurred in the argumentation when the earlier rules were determined. This may then call for a reconstruction of the intended meaning or for the introduction of new rules. Liability in tort is supplemented by strict liability, and if it is unable to award the responsibility for damage convincingly, it is supplemented by the liability of the party who is most likely to be able to prevent damage.[76] Initially, the quoting of proven principles and rules serves as a reason in itself and the consistency that is achieved by maintaining the tradition adds weight to it. But the character of a valid reason, and one that is claimable by law, is not a *character indelebilis*. It can be called into question by argumentation and especially by new distinctions, because the law is written law. Rules and reasons, which normally present themselves as a unity, can be dissociated if new problems or a social change in values irritate the legal system sufficiently. The new solution, if there is one, always appears as the better solution. Otherwise it would not be allowed to replace the older solution. And this always happens on the basis of an internal evaluation because the law can express its own superiority over itself only in this way.[77] It is not sufficient to refer to impulses from outside. Even statutes do not do this with arguments. They only state what will be valid law in the future. Untamed thinking outside the law cannot claim any relevance, simply because this kind of thinking is not obliged to make decisions about what is law and what is not and to bear the responsibility for those decisions.

While these observations are based on a broad discussion in legal theory, legal history, and methodology, there has been scant recognition of the fact that reasons produce differences and refer to themselves by what they exclude.[78] Bernard Rudden calls this an 'inbuilt consequence' but does not follow up this idea.[79] Perhaps the understanding of reasons as a point-by-point

[75] Cf. in the context of evolution, see above Ch. 6.III.

[76] See for the case of an abrupt change in Japanese environmental law, triggered by a legal decision, Helmut Weidner, 'Bausteine einer präventiven Umweltpolitik: Anregungen aus Japan', in Udo Ernst Simonis (ed.), *Präventive Umweltpolitik* (Frankfurt, 1988), 143–65.

[77] See also Peter Goodrich, *Reading the Law* (Oxford, 1986), 123: 'The view that a facet of a statutory text is absurd does not connote a critical evaluation of the text from outside the legal culture and professional competence but rather invokes the categories of legal doctrine, or the rationality and justice of the law, to secure an acceptable meaning for the text within the wider legal genre to which it belongs.'

[78] See fundamentally Jean-François Lyotard, *Le différend* (Paris, 1983).

[79] Bernard Rudden, 'Consequences', *Juridical Review* 24 (1979), 193–291, esp. 194 and 199. Inbuilt consequence is 'the effect of a rule upon itself'.

presentation has made broader recognition of this observation difficult. But reasons are not *points* of view, which can be defined simply. They are complex processes of thought, which justify both the inclusive and exclusive effects that they have.[80] Only with an eye to their reuse or the consequences of their reuse are they condensed into rules in order that their identity remain recognizable and referable. Simultaneously, reuse confirms the reason as being suitable for use in other decisions and gives it a generalized and enriched meaning.[81] The products of such a process of confirmation can, in turn, be condensed into *principles*, which say nothing about the original differences but which come to be treated as the definitive points of view for a decision.[82] It takes time and above all the experience of many cases to bring such principles to maturity. Their power to convince grows with a proven track record in a variety of cases. Once all of this has been put in place, it is no longer so easy to reject traditionally established reasons and to replace them with new ones. Tradition makes it only too apparent how much would have to be decided differently without it. Hence new points of view are added only as exceptions to rules, which continue to be valid, or as new principles in cases which have not yet been registered or registered wrongly. Essentially, existing law does not develop in respect of its principles but in respect of what its principles appear to exclude. Valid law is modified on its flip side. Argumentation increases the complexity of the system, with considerable consequences for the requisite terminological (doctrinal) systematizations.

The legal technique of the common law, with its high degree of attention to rules (and not only to statutes) that determine decisions, demonstrates the effect of exclusion particularly clearly. And the adversarial pleadings of barristers, who are conscious of this effect, contribute to the weighing up of

---

[80] It should be noted that, among other things, the *sequence* of arguments plays an important role, for instance for the question of which evidence is required, that is, in which respects the system is required to initiate contacts with the environment. See on this point Laurens Walter, John Thibaut, and Virginia Andreoli, 'Order of Presentation at Trial', *Yale Law Journal* 82 (1972), 216–26; Michael E. Levine and Charles R. Plott, 'Agenda Influence and its Implication', *Virginia Law Review* 63 (1977), 561–604; Charles R. Plott and Michael E. Levine, 'A Model of Agenda Influence on Committee Decisions', *American Economic Review* 68 (1978), 146–60. On a further aspect see Wolfgang Schild, 'Der Straftatbegriff als Argumentationsschema', in Winfried Hassemer et al. (eds.), *Argumentation und Recht*, Beiheft NF 14 of *Archiv für Rechts und Sozialphilosophie* (Wiesbaden, 1980), 213–29. One can accept the apt concept of an 'argumentation scheme' even if one does not agree that this has to be an 'image of the ontological structure of steps of reality' (p. 214).

[81] With the distinction of condensation and confirmation as two versions of a distinction in the process of its reuse I follow a suggestion of George Spencer Brown, *Laws of Form* (reprint New York, 1979), 10.

[82] The necessity of having to distinguish between rules and principles (which is conceptually difficult) is stressed above all in the literature on the common law, presumably because of the more important function of decisional rules in the common law.

the advantages and disadvantages of opposing rules in judicial reasoning. Dissenting opinions among judges are not glossed over but are made public in order to make the adversarial structure of reasons available for future reference.[83] Compared to that, legal argumentation in continental European legal orders has the features of a correctly carried out exegesis. However, the differences, especially in modern times, should not be exaggerated.[84] Further, it should be noted that an individual controversy by no means reveals the full exclusive effect of a well-reasoned rule.

The above analysis should make it clear that reasons have to keep silent on something, namely on their redundancy. They use distinctions with reference to their signified side and not their unsignified side. What cannot be signified cannot be used. Because it is concealed, redundancy cannot assume the function of a criterion. Or can it?[85] This leads to the question whether, and how, that which is concealed can be used for criticism, or even for the 'deconstruction' of legal argumentation.[86]

At any rate it cannot be used to say: 'I really don't know myself how it works'. Deconstruction does not lead to reconstruction but at best to the need for therapy according to the maxim 'hit the bottom'. One can reject the advice until one is at the end of one's wisdom. But who is to give therapy to the legal system? And who is to take over its function in the meantime?

If one observes that all signifying depends on distinctions, including the definition of 'deconstruction', one reaches firmer and more familiar ground.[87] Distinctions permit a 'crossing'. One can ask which decisions are excluded by which decisions and which reasons are excluded by which reasons. One can set up a definition on the other side of the distinction and thus distinguish the distinction itself as an instrument of observation, which is specified on both of its sides. However, this leads only to the definition of

[83] From a historical perspective, it should be noted that originally pleadings were published, while decisions were of minor importance. The formal binding of precedents, which required a different form of written records, developed only after a pervasive positivization of the law had taken place, that is, not until the middle of the eighteenth century, especially since the commentaries of Blackstone, and definitively not until a hundred years after that.

[84] See especially the strongly common-law-oriented interpretation of judge-made law by Josef Esser, *Grundsatz und Norm in der richterlichen Fortbildung des Privatrechts*, 2nd edn. (Tübingen, 1964); id., *Vorverständnis und Methodenwahl in der Rechtsfindung: Rationalitätsgarantien der richterlichen Entscheidungspraxis* (Frankfurt, 1970).

[85] See the chapter 'The Inscrutability of Silence and the Problem of Knowledge in the Human Sciences', in Steve Fuller, *Social Epistemology* (Bloomington, 1988), 139.

[86] Here the observation is in order that the Americans, with their sense for the practical, take 'deconstruction' as a method and try to apply it above all in literary science but also in some legal schools of thought. This, however, contradicts the original sense of the term, which Derrida left deliberately vague and which he keeps deconstructing with later self-commentaries.

[87] For a possible relation between 'deconstruction' and 'second-order observation' see J. M. Balkin, 'Nested Oppositions', *Yale Law Review* 99 (1990), 1669–1705. See also id., 'Deconstructive Practice and Legal Theory', *Yale Law Journal* 96 (1987), 743–86.

the distinction and conceals the other side of the distinction, which is required for this definition. A further question could be: what distinguishes the distinction between legislation and legal decision-making? Deconstructivists are, of course, never out of work. However, under their gaze the legal system can produce, step by step, an architecture of distinctions, with which it attempts to fulfil the task it sets itself each time of mediating between variety and redundancy. Further questions are always raised if distinctions can be specified on both sides of an argument, and proponents suggesting such distinctions thus signal that they have something to hide. This is only another version of the hypothesis that a system can only operate in the system and not in its environment.

IV

Reasons are distinctions made by an observer. In the context of legal argumentation the observer observes a text and, in interpreting it, must draft his own reasons, which take into account limitations on his points of view. The observer cannot merely present what he sees as the better reasons. Even an abstract value judgement requires a justification through the text; otherwise it loses all juridical meaning. And the value judgement can only achieve its scope for interpretation of the text if it attempts to restrict it anew within law. Good reasons alone do not suffice. One must also demonstrate that they are consistent with valid law—for instance, by splitting a norm into two different interpretations and then using one of them as a justification for the reason. Only if consistency with valid law is proven does it matter how good the good reasons are.

This, however, does not explain the functions of legal reasoning. The observers of the text present their case as if what mattered was that the better reasons lead on to their victory as interpretations. As participants in the legal system they are obliged to present issues as potentially decidable. They cannot merely draw attention to their preferences or interests. They are under the specific pressure of the system, which takes the form of binary coding and only recognizes the values legal and illegal as its code. This may apply to participants as insiders in the system but does not answer the question of the function of argumentation. To find an answer we observe the observers of texts, using the distinction between variety and redundancy introduced above. Through that distinction what is reached is the level of tertiary observation. We observe *how* the observers of a text understand it, when its meaning does not allow a first-order observer to come to a satisfactory decision. Reasons can then no longer be accepted, be they better or worse, but must ask the question: why reasoning at all? The distinction—which is necessary for dealing with this question and which cannot be applied at the system-internal level of secondary observation because it reveals too much—is provided by the system's distinction between variety and redundancy.

Reasons are symbols for redundancy.[88] Just as validity symbolizes the autopoiesis of the system, and through that makes the unity of, the system operable, good reasons operationalize the consistency of the system (or, expressed in terms of values, the justice of the system as a system). This statement is hardly contentious. But it needs further elaboration.

When the issue of reasoning is raised, the tautological self-reference of the symbol of validity is dissolved, unfolded, de-tautologized. In the first instance this indicates: what is valid is valid because it is valid. Next comes the assumption that there must be a sufficient reason for this. This assumption, however, can be followed up with the question whether what is valid has a good reason to be valid. From the semantic duplication of validity as the reason for the application of norms, the question arises of the reasons for validity—a question that is answered, for instance, in the doctrine on 'sources of law'. Nevertheless, what still applies is that anything that claims validity without a reason is simply not valid.

Such a self-description of reasoned argumentation is surpassed when one is aiming for the super-criterion of justice. This criterion, however, is of no help in reaching a decision on issues concerning the validity of law. Therefore it is understood as a criterion for ethics (only). The problem of validity dissolves in the distinction between law and ethics, with the consequence that postulates of justice can be treated as harmless in legal practice and as useless in its argumentation. However, if the postulate of justice is interpreted as a postulate for consistency in decision-making (equal cases must be treated equally and unequal cases must be treated unequally), consistency can be understood as redundancy.[89] It has been seen that redundancy is one side of a distinction, the other side being variety, which clearly prevents there from being justice [in some meta-ethical sense] in the world of law. The benefit gained so far from the distinction between variety and redundancy is the insight that there is another side to the matter. And this other side comprises not the lesser reasons or the unreasoned ('decisionist') decision-making, as an interpreter of texts is inclined to think, but the necessity of having a sufficient level (and under modern conditions a high level) of variety within the system.

---

[88] Hence the idea can be rejected that reasons serve the purpose of representing deference to law as a command of reason to legitimate the political power behind it. This is the tendency in the thinking of the Critical Legal Studies movement in the US. See also Goodrich, *Reading the Law* e.g. 122. People who think of themselves as 'critical' should develop a greater ability to make distinctions than is possible with the undifferentiated understanding of symbolic, political, and other sorts of power. One has to concede, however, that good reasons also have a social dimension and that they make it easier to assume that others will follow the well-reasoned rule from conviction. And that, in turn, is understandable if one considers that insight often comes coupled with a lack of interest.   [89] See above Ch. 5.

Cases that require a decision are concrete cases and that means they are different from each other. They provoke the system into acknowledging their differences. Argumentation picks up on this provocation and transforms it into redundancy—either with a simple reference to the programmes of decision-making which have to be applied or as a supplementation of such programmes with rules which are tested, condensed, and confirmed in relation to a great number of possible applications. Argumentation evidently opts for redundancy, for economy of information and surprises. However, it does so by tackling the special nature of the problems that come with the case. This can trigger an evolution towards forms that provide a higher level of variety with a sufficient amount of redundancy, and so approach Leibniz's formula of the best of all possible worlds.

A system that surrenders to its own criteria of redundancy loses the chance of responding to the irritations and surprises that the environment inflicts on it. In this respect, variety complements the system and prevents it from getting stuck in the rut of habit. However, the multitude and diversity of the communications that arise from cases, and their special problems, do not represent the environment of the system as such. Cases and the communications that refer to them exist only in the system for the system. Just like redundancy, variety is a variable of the system. The difference between variety and redundancy is a form with which the system operates as a system-in-an-environment. Other concepts must be used to answer the question of how the system constructs its environment semantically.[90]

The operations of the legal system require that the persuasive powers of the better reasons be communicated, no matter what the participants may experience psychologically and regardless of how insincerely it is done. The psychological motives of the judges are also irrelevant[91]—unless the law itself takes them seriously, for instance in the case of suspected bias (and even then, as is well known, not the bias itself but the mere possibility of a suspicion has to be proven). The professional ethics of lawyers, too, are stabilized by the fact that whenever communication takes place it has to appear as if the lawyer is convinced by the reasons which speak for his client. This cannot be done by referring to any reasons at random but has to be achieved within the limits set by legal argumentation. Observers of this style of communication (namely us) can, however, view it in a twofold way, as being both necessary and contingent—necessary for the system and

---

[90] See below section VIII.

[91] Neil MacCormick, *Legal Reasoning and Legal Theory* (Oxford, 1978), 17 comments on this point: 'The reasons they publicly state for their decisions must therefore be reasons which . . . make them appear to be what they are supposed to be'. One would have to refer here to a sociological version of the concept of motive, which dates back to Max Weber. See also Austin Sarat and William L. F. Felstiner, 'Law and Social Relations: Vocabulary of Motive in Lawyer/Client Interaction', *Law and Society Review* 22 (1988), 737–69.

contingent in so far as the variety of cases forces a continuous rethinking. The system cannot cope by relying on redundancy alone. Hence an understanding is gained of the necessity of the non-necessity of all reasoning and through that an understanding of why writing has such a paradoxical and yet fertile effect.

Those who see argumentation as the search for good reasons, while simultaneously avoiding errors, define a system that commits itself by argumentation. Only if the variety introduced by different cases is taken into account can the system, as a self-organizing and learning system, be understood.[92] In this respect early legal systems must be seen as highly redundant. They achieved the linking of everything with on the one hand, extremely formal terminology in respect of the admission or rejection of legal dispute resolutions, and, on the other, extremely ambivalent terminology.[93] As soon as—against all the odds—self-organization and learning gain momentum, the system begins to operate with the difference between redundancy and variety, and to build up complexity thereby. We will see below that this process is accelerated by structural coupling with other functioning systems leading, finally, to the internalization of the difference between self-reference (legal notions) and external reference (interests).

The transition from the search for reasons to the schema variety/redundancy, that is, the transition from second-order observation to third-order observation, precludes the retention of any of the premises of a theory of social action, such as are normally used in formulating theories of argumentation. Instead, the transition to systems theory is required. Argumentation then appears no longer as a more or less successful action (even if the concession has to be made that it can be described as such on the level of secondary observation). It appears rather as a massive and concurrent happening in a complex system—without clear lines and with cluster formations around certain texts, but without any hierarchies and without teleology in respect of the system as a whole. Like seeing a rippled sea from an aeroplane window, here a rippled sea of arguments can be seen. The overall meaning cannot be established from the goal of the individual operations or from the aggregate of individual goals, but only as a function of the fact that argumentation takes place. And it is precisely this that must be expressed in terms of variety and redundancy.

---

[92] The difficulty, which led Henri Atlan to understand systems as orders of the oppositional relation between redundancy and variety, was precisely the problem of self-organization and learning.

[93] This difference appears to be expressed in the distinction between *iustitia* and *aequitas*, which has only been abandoned in modern law. But this observation needs support from further historical research.

V

There is no doubt that one must find reasons for reasons because there are better and worse reasons. Besides, they exclude something, and a reason must also be given for that.[94] But this does not establish *how* reasons can be justified. There is no problem when the unequivocal verbal meaning of a text suffices (the speed limit is 100 km/h). However, with every interpretative argument going further than that, the question of 'how' arises.[95]

In old European law this problem was solved by turning back to the wisdom and will of God (that is, an observation of God reflected through the primary competence of priests). Or, if there was a disinclination to do that (and this disinclination increased in early modern times), the problem could be solved by a normative (hence corruptible) concept of nature that, as far as humans are concerned, refers them to their own reasonableness. It was self-evident to Grotius, Pufendorf, Locke, and their contemporaries—in clear contrast to modern ideas—that the nature of human beings was open to empirical (natural) insights. But at the same time it could serve as a source of knowledge about eternally and inter-regionally (*inter nationes*) valid law. The validity of law and legal knowledge had not been completely historicized, as was the case later with Lord Kames and David Hume. The nature of humans was, like all nature, a source of knowledge about God's will. And this was so, despite the concurrent development of national law, which referred to reason as the nature of humankind.[96]

Nature and reason are still an honorary title for the decoration of justifications after the event. However, seen from an empirical perspective, there can be no doubt that, in reality, argumentation justifies itself by an assessment of the *consequences* of legal decisions or, more precisely, by an assessment of the different consequences which would arise if different rules were applied. Natural law was geared to the social utility of legal norms,[97] even though it was based on the legal proposition that this utility, in case of doubt, had to

---

[94] The reader is reminded again that reasons are *sequences* of argumentation which are condensed into *points* of view for decision-making only in the process of their reuse or in anticipation of it.

[95] Focusing on the question of 'how' saves us from having to deal with two subject areas which keep legal theory, its literature, and its conferences occupied, namely the question of which lines of argumentation lead to reasonable results and the question whether juridical argumentation can be constructed completely logically.

[96] See on this point Rudolf Stichweh, 'Selbstorganisation und die Entstehung nationaler Rechtssysteme (17.–19. Jahrhundert)', *Rechtshistorisches Journal* 8 (1990), 254–72.

[97] See for example Thomas Aquinas, *Summa Theologiae* IIa IIae q. 57 a. 3 with the distinction between *secundum sui rationem* and *secundum aliquid quod ex ipso consequitur* using the example of the benefits of crop farming.

be assumed.[98] Utility has been the general formula for thinking about alternatives since time immemorial. It poses the simple question: what would be the case if not this rule but another one applied?[99] In the framework of the prince's *iurisdictio*, equity (*aequitas*) also served as a corrective for unacceptable outcomes of strictly administered justice.[100] But this hardly allowed any latitude in doctrinal formulations with respect to the consequences of legal constructions or rules. Rather it served as a correlate of the distinction between unchangeable and changeable law. In the meantime, the reviewing of law by reference to desirable or undesirable results has prevailed as the only convincing principle and is now generally supported by legal theory[101] and the careful analysis of decisions.[102] Nevertheless, the question remains: what are we observing when we observe this?

Frequently, when the arguments take possible consequences into account this is confused with the purpose-specific programming of legal decision-making. This conceptual mistake, however, can be, and often is,

---

[98] See Domat, *Les loix civiles dans leur ordre naturel*, vol. I, p. lxv; justice of the positive law amounts to its 'justice particuliere'; and further at xci for a 'presomption pour l'utilité de la loy, nonobstant les inconveniens'.

[99] See, for example, Alexandre Belleguise, *Traité de noblesse et de son origine* (Paris, 1700), 145. What would happen if one lost one's aristocratic title but then got it back by ceasing to do an activity which had been deemed unbefitting to one's status (trade) but one did not then have special *lettres de réhabilitation?* One could switch weekly between noble status and commoner status, the tax situation would be unclear, etc.

[100] This was simply a matter of interpretation. See Domat, *Les loix civiles*, vol. 1, p. 19: 'Les loix naturelles sont mal appliquées, lorsqu'on en tire des consequences contre l'équité'. Or, with the converse perspective against careless innovations ('qui ad pauca respicit facile pronunciat') Hale, *Reflections*, 504: 'The Expounder must look further than the present Instance, and whether such an Exposition may not introduce a greater inconvenience than it remedies'.

[101] See, for example, Adalbert Podlech, 'Wertungen und Werte im Recht', *Archiv des öffentlichen Rechts* 95 (1970), esp. 198; Wolfgang Kilian, *Juristische und elektronische Datenverarbeitung: Methodenorientierte Vorstudie* (Frankfurt, 1974), 211; Gunther Teubner, 'Folgenkontrolle und responsive Dogmatik', *Rechtstheorie* 6 (1975), 179–204; Thomas Sambuc, *Folgenabwägungen im Richterrecht: Die Berücksichtigung von Entscheidungsfolgen bei der Rechtsprechung, erörtert am Beispiel des Paragraphen 1 UWG* (Berlin, 1977); Thomas W. Wälde, *Juristische Folgenorientierung: 'Policy Analysis' und Sozialkybernetik: Methodische und organisatorische Überlegungen zur Bewältigung der Folgenorientierung im Rechtssystem* (Königstein, 1979); Hubert Rottleuthner, 'Zur Methode einer folgenorientierten Rechtsanwendung', in *Wissenschaften und Philosophie als Basis der Jurisprudenz, Beiheft 13 des Archivs für Rechts- und Sozialphilosophie* (Wiesbaden, 1981), 97–118; Hans-Joachim Koch and Helmut Rüßmann, *Juristische Begründungslehre: Eine Einführung in Grundprobleme der Rechtswissenschaft* (Munich, 1982), 227; for the special problems of criminal law see Winfried Hassemer, *Über die Berücksichtigung von Folgen bei der Auslegung der Strafgesetze, Festschrift Helmut Coing* (Munich, 1982), 493–524, and on the discussion about the reformalization of criminal law in the United States, Joachim J. Savelsberg, 'Law that does not fit Society: Sentencing Guidelines as a Neoclassical Reaction to the Dilemmas of Substantivized Law', *American Journal of Sociology* 97 (1992), 1346–81.

[102] See especially MacCormick, *Legal Reasoning and Legal Theory*.

easily avoided because a judge has neither the means nor the willingness to run risks, and both are required for a pursuit of purposes.[103] The same applies to the legislator as regards legal technique, even if legislators, to the extent that they participate in the political system, are free to pursue political goals with corresponding political risks.[104] A description guided by systems theory suggests that a distinction must be drawn, first of all, between system-internal and system-external consequences.[105]

System-internal consequences are legal consequences and there is of course a mandate to assess them. This is a normal element involving the recursive operations of all legal decisions which need a justification and which have to take into account both past and future decisions. When there is a discussion about reasons and the rules that generalize them, an essential part of the test is to check which conduct would be legal or illegal if a particular rule were adopted.[106] If, for instance, the question is whether putting goods on supermarket shelves is in itself an offer of a contract and, accordingly, the taking of goods from shelves amounts to acceptance of that offer, it follows that putting the goods back on the shelves would (in most respects) not be possible legally and taking goods from the shop without paying for them would not be theft but simply the failure to fulfil contractual obligations.[107] Even a lawyer will find the consequences of this construction unacceptable, regardless of the empirical question of how supermarket customers would behave empirically if one or the other legal construction applied. Such an assessment does not require an empirical

---

[103] More recently there has been awareness that a careful analysis of the ends–means structures has been neglected in the pragmatic-instrumental theory of law (for good reasons, one imagines!). See Robert Samuel Summers, *Instrumentalism and American Legal Theory* (Ithaca, 1982), 60, 240, and 255. Accordingly, criticism is growing and leading to a renewed interest in analytical jurisprudence.

[104] See on this point Robert Nagel, 'Purpose, Rationality and Equal Protection', *Yale Law Journal* 82 (1972), 123–54, who for good reason criticizes the tendency of courts to measure legislation with the yardstick of purpose-rationality and to charge the legislator with deficiencies in this respect (which may be the result of political compromises). In German law, where the argument of the 'will of the legislator' is much more frequently used, this warning is more necessary. Here judges often construct fictitiously, as a result of politics, a purpose-specific programme, which they need for a decision but would not be allowed to set up themselves.

[105] Of course, this can be done without explicit concepts of systems theory. See, for example, the distinction between behavioural and juridical consequences in Rudden, 'Consequences', and following him Neil MacCormick, 'Legal Decisions and their Consequences: From Dewey to Dworkin', *New York University Law Review* 58 (1983), 239–58. On the issue of the distinction between legal consequences and real consequences see also Niklas Luhmann, *Rechtssystem und Rechtsdogmatik* (Stuttgart, 1974), 41, and comprehensively Gertrude Lübbe-Wolff, *Rechtsfolgen und Realfolgen: Welche Rolle können Folgenerwägungen in der juristischen Regel- und Begriffsbildung spielen?* (Freiburg, 1981).

[106] This is also implied by MacCormick, 'Legal Decisions', when he interprets his earlier statements *Legal Reasoning and Legal Theory*, which were not yet fully elaborated on this point.

[107] This example is used by Rudden, 'Consequences'.

prognosis nor is it affected by corresponding uncertainties. It can be made with the legal knowledge available at the time and with the usual certainty of legal opinion. It is a matter purely and simply of the usual commitment to consistency, that is, the need to ensure sufficient redundancy.

But there is the question of whether the assessment could remain that way, or, seen from an empirical perspective, the legal system is satisfied with this. In most cases of reasoned argument this question is not put so succinctly. The fact that the distinction between internal/external consequences marks a significant threshold is simply overlooked. But even if this distinction were made explicit each time, the question would remain whether a choice between different legal constructions could always be made only with regard to the legal consequences—for how should these be assessed if the consequences do not clearly support one particular solution? The next question is: what would be the effect of actors conforming to a particular rule? In this regard the probability that actors would conform to one rule or the other cannot be completely ignored. In matters in which someone runs risks to save lives or other people's property, the question may arise whether or not a helper who suffers as a result should be compensated. It appears that it may be in the victim's interest that such a rule be introduced because if the helper does the saving at his own risk, he will think twice about it. Or, like the tugboat captain in the case of the stranded oil tanker, the helper will tend to negotiate the conditions of assistance until it is too late. However, who can guarantee that a judge's amateur theories about a helper's behaviour are right? One only has to think of the difficulty of relating consequences to causes even in past events (for instance, the statistics on traffic accidents after a change in the speed limit), in order to understand how a judge is skating on thin ice here. Even if scientific standards are applied, empirically supported prognoses are nearly always impossible,[108] or they lead to results with very little significance.[109] Hence it is hard to imagine that a judge could examine, let alone

---

[108] This is also demonstrated by socio-legal studies. They are, however, conspicuously rare, given the importance of the issue. But see James W. Marquart, Sheldon Eckland-Olsen, and Jonatan R. Sorensen, 'Gazing into the Crystal Ball: Can Jurors Predict Dangerousness in Capital Cases?' *Law and Society Review* 23 (1989), 459–68.

[109] From my own experience, the question whether a change of the public service law in Germany, which would mean abandoning the principle of tenure, would have consequences on recruitment and, if so, what consequences, can be tested empirically only with great difficulty or only with time-sensitive indicators (for instance, ones which depend on the labour market). See the study commissioned by the Committee for the Reform of the Public Service Law (1970–73) by Niklas Luhmann and Renate Mayntz, *Personal im öffentlichen Dienst: Eintritt und Karrieren* (Baden-Baden, 1973). This would have applied all the more if the authors had included further issues, which were publicly debated and relevant to political argumentation, such as the effects on professional ethics and the independence of public servants. The relevance of the social sciences for the administration of justice appears to be given less by the

interpret, a statute meaningfully from the viewpoint of finding it to be the means to a certain end. Nevertheless, courts have the tendency to do exactly that, and they have the uncontested competence to give their opinions legal validity. Orientation by the consequences of decisions is, measured by the standards of the empirical sciences, nothing but imagination with a legal effect.

From the perspective of legal theory it is tempting to describe if not to bemoan the use of law to perform the functions of social policy as the decay of a specific legal rationality.[110] Such a lack of concern for the consequences of being concerned with consequences is also referred to in legal literature.[111] Here the sociologist is in the fortunate position of being able to desist from making any recommendations. In this respect, the sociologist is different from a legal theoretician, who is committed to the legal system.[112] Sociologists can observe trends in reasoning at the level of second-order observation. And they are free to surmise that a trend towards an empirical prognosis of consequences serves the variety of the system rather than its redundancy and that it puts responsiveness to socially prevalent and changing preferences in the place of what is traditionally called justice.

To its long history of reflecting on reasoning the legal system reacts with perversity, as it were: the more necessities are sought, the more contingencies are discovered.[113] The more that confrontation with the paradox of reasoning must be avoided, admitting the impossibility of finding reasons for reasons, the more the argumentation shifts from the certain to the uncertain, from the past to the future, from what can be ascertained to

provision of prognoses and more by the expansion of the ambit of problems, that is, by increasing the variety of law, which does not make the regaining of redundancy easier but makes it more difficult. See on this issue, including comprehensive materials Paul L. Rosen, *The Supreme Court and Social Sciences* (Urbana, Ill., 1972).

[110] See for a study written from a broad historical perspective N. E. Simmonds, *The Decline of Judicial Reason: Doctrine and Theory in the Legal Order* (Manchester, 1984). See also Helmut Schelsky, 'Nutzen und Gefahren der sozialwissenschaftlichen Ausbildung von Juristen', *Juristenzeitung* 29 (1974), 410–16, reprinted in id., *Die Soziologen und das Recht* (Opladen, 1980), 196–214.

[111] See for the joint comments of a lawyer and a sociologist, those of Hans Joachim Böhlk and Lutz Unterseher, 'Die Folgen der Folgenberücksichtigung', *Juristische Schulung* 20 (1980), 323–7.

[112] MacCormick, 'Legal Decisions', 254, on the other hand, arrives at a different conclusion: 'So, in the main, what I shall call consequentialist reasoning law is focused not so much on estimating the probability of behavioural changes, as on possible conduct and its certain normative status in the light of the ruling under scrutiny'. However, he must then introduce the moral categories of 'rightness' or 'wrongness', which have their own problems and which 'the branch of law in question makes relevant' (p. 256), as a substitute for this risky 'conjectural answer'.

[113] See Raffaele De Giorgi, *Scienza del diritto e legittimazione: Critica dell'epistemologia giuridica tedesca da Kelsen a Luhmann* (Bari, 1979). German edition: *Wahrheit und Legitimation im Recht: Ein Beitrag zur Neubegründung der Rechtstheorie* (Berlin, 1980).

what is merely probable. If what is ultimately at issue is only the evaluation of consequences, everybody can be certain that others cannot be more certain in their decisions. Then the paradox of reasoning is changed to a paradox that is easier to accept, namely the paradox of time or of making the future present. However, what actually happens here—without this providing a better reason or a new reason—is that there is an increase in the variety of the system and the challenge goes out to reorganize the remaining redundancies.

It could be suspected that the future represents a third value, which binary coding should exclude. Recalling the discussion *de futuris contingentibus* that goes back well over 2,000 years, this applies to the schema true/false. First attempts to introduce the value 'indeterminable' as a third value have their roots there. In the context of law, the hypothetical 'what if' appears to be confronted by a similar problem (which cannot be brushed aside with a reference to science). Science finds a solution in prognoses (which can be corrected); law, however, finds them in decisions (which cannot be corrected). This can be neither avoided nor circumvented by shifting the problem. It is equally questionable whether time structure can be formulated as a problem of legitimation for law, thereby corking it like a genie in a bottle. What should be done is to keep the artificiality of every binary code thoroughly in mind. The world is not geared to that—neither by action, nor logic, nor the text of its creation. Whenever the world is observed with the help of distinctions, it withdraws from observation. Viewing it from this angle has at least one advantage: it allows contexts of variation to be seen where otherwise only misfortune threatens. The artificiality of the binary coding of law has to be paid for in the currency of the 'what if' and has to be reintroduced into the system in the form of the hypothetical. Here there is a form of management of the paradox: binary coding needs more than two values.

VI

We have said that good reasons must always be presented as possible interpretations of a text, which has an undisputed claim to legal validity. All argumentation must demonstrate consistency with valid law, and only on the basis of a suitable text (or a text made suitable by interpretation) can it bring the quality of its reasons into play and present its findings as a kind of logical subsumption. 'Deduction comes in only after the interesting part of the argument, settling on the ruling law, has been carried through.'[114] To say that lawyers deduce from legal notions would be a particularly abbreviated description of this complicated process.

[114] See MacCormick, *Legal Reasoning and Legal Theory*, 157.

Legal notions develop only during the processes of argumentation and, above all, in the course of manifold repetitions in situations of decision-making. Texts are not legal concepts but objects (even though there can, of course, be a concept for the text). Legal concepts develop in the process of working with texts, as the distinctions which define them are made more precise, that is, are distinguished themselves. This is what happens when argumentation takes place. What matters in certain circumstances is distinguished from what does not matter. And what does not matter is not just 'everything else' but a different understanding of the problem, a different interpretation, and a different rule that might lead to different legal consequences. Argumentation produces a sequence of reasons and inferences and, like all sequences, this one also conserves and reuses distinctions.[115] Concepts enable choice of access to already proven distinctions without having to go back to the sequence of their generation, and they also organize new emergent distinctions on that level. Thus one can come to the conclusion that it is possible to contest a contract under different conditions and that this has different consequences from the revocation of a contract, and that possession and property, intent and negligence, illegality and fault have to be distinguished, because only through that is it possible to couple the conditions and the consequences (the ifs and thens) differently.

With the help of concepts, distinctions can be stored and made available for a great number of decisions. In other words, concepts compound information, thereby producing the redundancy required in the system.[116] If a judge were to hear a case concerning damages for a broken vase, he would have little success if he looked up 'vase' in the statute.[117] The legal system applies a higher-ranking organization of redundancies and for that it requires a terminology that is particular to law. Where there is a developed culture of legal terminology, new texts also have to be formulated extremely accurately because otherwise there would inevitably be misunderstanding. And so legal language comes to deviate more and more from everyday language.

Hence concepts are genuinely historical artefacts, auxiliary tools for the retrieving of past experiences in dealing with legal cases. Accordingly, argumentation that uses concepts is historical argumentation (even if no old texts are used), and analytical jurisprudence is historical jurisprudence.

---

[115] See for a corresponding interpretation of causality Francis Heylighen, 'Causality as Distinction Conservation: A Theory of Predictability, Reversibility and Time Order', *Cybernetics and Systems* 20 (1989), 361–84.

[116] Gotthard Günther even claims that he can explain the evolution of consciousness as being a result of the demand for compounded information, see his 'Information als Informationsraffer', *Grundlagenstudien aus Kybernetik und Geisteswissenschaften* 10/1 (1969), 1–6.

[117] This example also tells us something about the connection between the prohibition of the denial of justice and terminological abstraction.

It is exactly that which gives it its function of boosting redundancy. The analysis of concepts, however, is motivated by innovation. It arises from doubts whether a case can be decided appropriately by subsuming it under the usual meaning of a concept.[118] This is more easily recognizable in the common law than in continental civil law, but it applies to both legal orders.[119]

Just as with rules, the creation of concepts follows the dual structure of condensation and confirmation as they go through the process of repeated use. Concepts have to be identifiable to be recognized again. They are given names: *ratio decidendi* and *obiter dictum*, delegation, felony, administrative action, direct liability, the effect of basic rights on third parties—and so on in their thousands. At the same time, the meaning of these concepts is enriched in the process of repeat-use—among other things by a great number of rules that are formulated with the help of these concepts, or by legal problems which arise through the use of the concept and which are solved in a particular way, which then co-characterizes the concept. For example, in relation to delegation it would be important to know whether a complete delegation of the full range of competence is possible without the transfer of such competence, whether and how far the specification of a delegated competence needs to have legal validity, and how one can prescribe generally (!) such a requirement with sufficient certainty; whether delegated competences can be delegated further, etc. Decisions and rules then become components of the concept, and if one does not want to refer to them as well, one had better choose another word or, if possible, another concept. In this sense, concepts store experiences and keep them on call, even though the concept does not formulate these experiences (otherwise it would become a text) but only re-actualizes them in a given instance.

The discussion of legal concepts has suffered considerably from the fact that concepts were mainly understood as being defined by certain attributes. Accordingly, the reason for the validity of concepts was seen in the 'system' of their contexts or in the principle that defines the unity of the system. This led to the impression that concepts were valid by themselves, an impression which was reinforced by the idea emerging in the nineteenth century that legal dogmatics was a source of law. Since legal theory has given up the concept of a source of law, the relation between legal concepts and legal dogmatics requires clarification.

---

[118] This is not to deny that explanations of terms also fulfil didactical functions and belong more to legal education (where cases are used only as illustrations) than to legal practice. But what we are concerned with here is a theory of the legal system and not a theory of the education system.

[119] See Oliver W. Holmes, 'The Path of the Law', *Harvard Law Review* 10 (1987), 457–78. He observes in an address dedicated to the prognosis of legal decisions: 'The rational study of law is still to a large extent the study of history' (p. 469).

Legal doctrine is certainly not a 'system'—neither in the sociological sense nor in the juridical sense of something being constructed from a principle. Rather, one can define it as a summative expression for the necessity of legal argumentation, or as a shield for legal terminology against a constant and ultimately limitless political 'questioning', that is, as a rule of limitation for reasoning in its quest for reasons.[120] It is apparent that such a striving for consistency can easily lead to a 'mirage of impolitic practice' and that it carries the risk of 'dangerously falsifying facts and interests juridically'.[121] That does not speak against legal concepts. It just speaks of the need for an exclusively conceptual, that is to say, exclusively self-referential, orientation to be sufficiently balanced.

Concepts in themselves are not instructions for decisions. They are building blocks for legal constructions, which in turn become part of conditional programmes, and their practical relevance feeds back into the profiles of concepts. The formulation of concepts ('illegal action', 'unjust enrichment') may express displeasure and call for action. However, anything that goes further than that depends on the conditions that control the use of concepts. In this respect, not only does legal doctrine maintain its dogmatism and refer not only to itself, its historical track record and its sensitivity to criticism. Legal doctrine is also maintained by a context of usages, which would be difficult to formulate repeatedly if there were not conceptual specifications, which had already been laid down. Hence a critique of conceptions requires the return to the problem to be solved, and this leads to the question of functionally equivalent constructions.

It becomes clear that legal concepts do not have the direct, and above all, not the only function of making logical reasoning possible. They are nothing but distinctions, and such a characterization can be formulated in this way ever since the linguistics of Saussure. They draw attention to differences and, through that, guide argumentation by limiting what could be similar and hence suitable for analogy. The classic monograph, which has contributed more than any other text to the establishment of a 'conceptual' jurisprudence ('Begriffsjurisprudenz') as it was later called, Savigny's *Recht des Besitzes* [Property Law, 1803[122]] has the merit of elaborating upon the meaning and function of the distinction between ownership and possession. Thus legal notions make precise what is problematic in the *quaestio iuris* but do not establish an automatic device that leads to a decision without any further deliberation. This has nothing to do with logic. A conceptually

---

[120] For a brilliant discussion of this point, see Esser *Juristisches Argumentieren*, esp., 20—brilliant in respect of his masterly use of language, sensitive terminological presentation of terms, and exactness in his focus on problems.

[121] Formulations used by Esser, ibid. 21 and 22.

[122] Quoted from Friedrich Carl von Savigny, *Das Recht des Besitzes: Eine civilistische Abhandlung*, 5th edn. (Stuttgart, 1837).

elaborate network makes errors detectable. These are not logical errors but deviations from the meaning of one of the concepts that have been laid down. Hence concepts make checks on errors possible. More importantly, however, they put limitations on the conditions for the success of operations, which go beyond the literal sense. They have to be used uniformly, that is, consistently and with the distinctions that are marked out by them (just like the words in a language). They form a second, meta-textually supplied security net for redundancy in the system. Once they are worked out and legal texts make use of them, argumentation without legal concepts is well-nigh impossible. One can introduce new distinctions, refine and break up notions or—as in the case of *de facto* marriages—look for a new generic term. But to rebel against legal concepts is just as meaningless as an attempt to make do exclusively with an assessment of values and interests.

VII

Perhaps the concern to consolidate law conceptually in the process of the positivization of law in modern society was exaggerated, like the reaction of an immune system to an external intrusion. Perhaps the problems of decision-making in the system made the demand for more variability more acutely felt. In any case, a new legal theory burst onto the scene around 1900, buoyed up by a dynamic intellectual movement. It placed more importance on pragmatism than on conceptual clarity and more on utility than on rules. In Germany it appeared, with reference to Jhering's analysis, as a 'jurisprudence of interests'.[123] This was soon copied in the United States[124] and combined with concepts such as social engineering, social policy, instrumentalism, and later 'legal realism'.[125] The function of law (the 'purpose' of law) was formulated as the protection of interests—evidently legally entitled interests—and thus formulated tautologically.[126] The

---

[123] For a selection of important texts see: Günter Ellscheid and Winfried Hassemer (eds.), *Interessenjurisprudenz* (Darmstadt, 1974); see also Paul Oertmann, *Interesse und Begriff in der Rechtswissenschaft* (Leipzig, 1931). An early attempt from the point of view of combining legal terminology and evaluated perspectives of interests with goal-orientation is Gustav Rümelin, *Juristische Begriffsbildung* (Leipzig, 1878). For the wider context of the discussion of methods since the late eighteenth century see also Johann Edelmann, *Die Entwicklung der Interessenjurisprudenz: Eine historisch-kritische Studie über die deutsche Rechtsmethodologie vom 18. Jahrhundert bis zur Gegenwart* (Bad Homburg, 1967).

[124] See, for example, Roscoe Pound, 'Mechanical Jurisprudence', *Columbia Law Review* 8 (1908), 605–23.

[125] By now there are many biographical studies and much research on the history of these ideas. For an overview with an accent on a critical review of the theoretical concept, see Summers, *Instrumentalism and American Legal Theory*.

[126] An elaboration on the concept, which repeats and summarizes many earlier statements, can be found in Roscoe Pound, *Jurisprudence* (St. Paul, 1959), vol. III, pp. 3–373.

validity of law was seen as a kind of self-prognosis in relation to the judge-made law of the United States, which allows the experienced repeat players to predict which interests can be infused into law and where and how. This in turn denotes attentiveness to sufficient redundancy. In Germany, however, it was—in the light of the recently introduced code of civil law—more like a new version of civil law doctrine, which soon found good reason to insist on the supremacy of statute law in the face of some rather liberal doctrines of interpretation.

This movement led to new distinctions and to a corresponding understanding of the legal theory that was currently dominant. In Germany this legal theory was dubbed 'Begriffsjurisprudenz' (jurisprudence of concepts); it involved a massive simplification of the polemical debate,[127] as we now know.[128] In the United States, the movement was also directed against analytical constructivism and additionally—with strong 'social policy' connotations—against social Darwinism and against the thesis that the function of law was to guarantee the greatest possible individual liberties.[129] In view of the simplified contrasting of a jurisprudence of interests and a jurisprudence of concepts it is important to keep these polemics of freedom in mind. One can see, then, how the change of theory replaces one formula of the external determinacy of law with another—namely freedom with interests.

The fact that the concept of interests was introduced in the form of a theoretical debate and that the history of legal theory is still described today in this form, even though its approach is now more balanced, disguises an important issue. Obviously interests are not the only things that matter,

---

[127] See particularly Horst Jakobs, *Wissenschaft und Gesetzgebung nach der Rechtsquellenlehre des 19. Jahrhunderts* (Paderborn, 1983); Regina Ogorek, *Richterkönig oder Subsumtionsautomat? Zur Justiztheorie des 19. Jahrhunderts* (Frankfurt, 1988); Joachim Rückert, *Autonomie des Rechts in rechtshistorischer Perspektive* (Hanover, 1988); Ulrich Falk, *Ein Gelehrter wie Windscheid: Erkundungen auf den Feldern der sogenannten Begriffsjurisprudenz* (Frankfurt, 1989); id., 'Ein Gegensatz principieller Art', *Rechtshistorisches Journal* 9 (1990), 221–40.

[128] But polemics against polemics should not be exaggerated. Jhering's concept of 'Begriffsjurisprudenz' was quite clearly *not* aimed at the indispensable use of concepts in law but 'at those misconceptions of our modern jurisprudence which, ignoring the practical ultimate purpose and the conditions of the applicability of law, see in it only an object for testing a self-serving logical reasoning which finds its attraction and purpose in itself'. Further Jhering's 'Begriffs juris prudenz' suggested that 'each jurisprudence operates with concepts—no matter whether it is juridical or conceptual reasoning—and in this sense every jurisprudence is a jurisprudence of concepts, the Roman one first of all. That is why the attribute does not need to be added'. (Rudolf von Jhering, *Scherz und Ernst in der Jurisprudenz: Eine Weihnachtsgabe für das juristische Publikum* (1884), quoted from the 13th edn. (Leipzig, 1924; reprint Darmstadt, 1964), 347). The exaggeration in the use of the label 'Begriffsjurisprudenz' is explained by Jhering (ibid. 363) as the result of the modern separation of (university) legal *doctrine* and legal *practice*.

[129] Roscoe Pound, *An Introduction to the Philosophy of Law* (1922; 2nd edn. 1954; reprint New Haven, 1959), holds that this idea of the 'maximum of free individual self-assertions' was overtaken by social change (p. 40). And indeed, even in North America, no further frontier space could be found for that.

especially if, it should be stressed, the law does not create interests but only acknowledges them.[130] The question, then, is which interests are deemed worthy of protection by law and how law decides any conflicts of interest. To know the answer, the law itself must be observed (legal realists would say: judicial behaviour must be predicted) *rather than the interests themselves*. The relevant redundancies must be identified. Reluctantly it must be admitted that evasive formulations turn out to be correspondingly vague. 'If you ask how he [the judge] is to know when one interest outweighs another, I can only answer that he must get his knowledge just as the legislator gets it, from experience and study and reflection, in brief from life itself', muses a judge.[131] We have already seen that even though the prediction of consequences makes the problem more complex it does not in principle solve it. The formula of interests tips legal practice in the direction of conditioning by the environment. According to that formula, the best law should be that which realizes the maximum number of interests. Such a law would not have any intrinsic value ('eigenvalue').[132] But it is exactly this notion of intrinsic value which makes it unclear what law can offer as a counter-concept to interests, as the other side of the form, if one does not merely concern oneself with vague appeals to 'the life experience of the judge' (and who wants to be at the mercy of that!).

Of course, one can say that the public interest, the common good, and the sum of these 'public goods', are themselves interests too. But what, then, is not an interest? Ultimately the law itself becomes an interest. To use Cardozo's words again: 'One of the most fundamental social interests is that the law shall be uniform and impartial'.[133] The law, then, mirrors itself in its environment as the interests of that environment. It observes how parties with interests observe it. It has to be available for the weighing up of interests. How can the life experiences and the common sense of the judge assist in this—and assist in such a way that the interests of the environment are satisfied and justice is done to other interest-bearing, interested parties? On balance, much dogmatic rigour and conceptual control are going overboard as the demands on the flexibility and responsiveness of legal practice are increased. With regard to judicial practice in the highest appeal courts, Esser states 'there is an increase in decisions which use situational and notational deliberations about the responsibility and duties required for legal reasoning without a large amount of doctrinal

[130] See Pound, *Jurisprudence*, vol. III, pp. 17 and 21.

[131] See Benjamin N. Cardozo, *The Nature of the Judicial Process* (New Haven, 1921), 113.

[132] For a critique, which takes this view as its point of departure, see Julius Stone, 'A Critique of Pound's Theory of Justice', *Iowa Law Review* 20 (1935), 531–50. Pound, who quoted it frequently, obviously took it seriously.

[133] See Cardozo, op. cit. at 112. See also Philipp Heck, *Gesetzesauslegung und Interessenjurisprudenz* (Tübingen, 1914), 180, on the 'interest in the maintenance of an order once it has achieved validity'.

effort'.[134] Or in a different context: 'Apparently one does not get beyond the stage of verbalising valuations.'[135]

VIII

Once the problem has been recognized, it is not difficult to reconstruct it with the help of systems theory. In a very general sense one can distinguish between formal and substantive arguments.[136] Formal arguments are limited by reference to the system, to texts, to procedural precepts (for example, the need for an affidavit by a notary), which are designed to prevent the drift into arguments about facts. In contrast, substantive arguments include considerations, which are also accepted outside the legal system (at least this is the assumption inside the legal system).[137] Accordingly the system practises *self-reference* with *formal* argumentation and *external reference* with *substantive* argumentation. Formal argumentation is ultimately predicated on the necessity at all levels to come to a decision and to avoid submersion in the full complexity of the factual world. Substantive argumentation prevents the system from isolating itself in formal argumentation. If one looks at this distinction from the perspective of a second-order observer, one can see that substantive reasons for formal argumentation, which are not included in legal reasoning, certainly do exist; and that substantive argumentation also provides rules of limitation and enables recourse to be given to an immediate comprehensibility and the power of persuasion, that is, to conditions which can have doubt (argument) thrown at them at any moment.

With the help of this distinction we can describe reference to concepts as formal argumentation and the reference to interests, in contrast, as substantive argumentation. Concepts are stored experiences taken from cases, which are no longer perceived or critically discussed as experiences. Interests,

[134] Esser, *Juristisches Argumentieren*, 22.

[135] See Josef Esser, 'Argumentations-und Stilwandel in höchstrichterlichen Zivilentscheidungen', *Etudes de Logique Juridique 6* (1976), 53–77, at 61.

[136] This distinction is usually introduced with a reference to Max Weber. See, for example, Richard Lempert and Josef Sanders, *An Invitation to Law and Social Science* (White Plains, 1986), 9 and 444. It should not be confused with the distinction between procedural law and material law, even if procedural law exhibits more formal elements than material law because of its function of organizing decision-making. See, for example, Patrick S. Atiyah and Robert S. Summers, *Form and Substances in Anglo-American Law: A Comparative Study of Legal Reasoning, Legal Theory, and Legal Institutions* (Oxford, 1987), who use the distinction between formal and substantive law for a comparison of the more formal English with the more substantive American orientation of the common law. This distinction is also used in a comparison of different interpretations of last-instance courts in various countries. See MacCormick and Summers, *Interpreting Statutes*, with France (more formal) and the United States (more substantive) as the extreme cases.

[137] Atiyah and Summers, *Form and Substance*, 65, formulate: 'A substantive reason may be defined as a moral, economic, political, institutional, or other social consideration'.

however, refer to catalysts for the self-organization of references to the relevant environment. In spite of this double reference, argumentation is and remains an internal operation—be it a formal or a conceptual one, be it a substantive or an interest-related one. Hence interests have to be prepared and presented for the legal system and its operations in such a way that they make reasoned decisions possible—particularly where there is a conflict. Those who communicate their interests in a different form, for instance as mere wishes or preferences, do not present themselves as participants in the legal system. Seen from the perspective of the system, interests are equal in their natural states. The system homogenizes, as it were, what it recognizes as information on interests and, while steering towards a decision, is concerned only whether the interests are legally protected or not and which interests have to give way to others in the case of a conflict. That, and that alone, must be demonstrated by argument.

With the concept of interest, the system constructs an external reference for its internal purposes. The concept refers to something that must be assumed to be the environment, however, with a compact access, which corresponds to the capacities of information management within the system. The unit of an interest could be decomposed further and further (for instance for therapeutic reasons), but it is and remains an internal product of the system.[138] This applies to the reflexive version as well as to cases where the legal system constructs its version of the interest of its environment in law, that is, an interest in the reliability, uniformity, predictability, and impartiality of the administration of justice.

However, the self-reference of the operations of the system can also be a point of departure. This self-reference is expressed in the form of legal concepts which restrict the constructions that are suitable for linking in the system and can be associated with the existing symbols of validity. This does not mean that every time one refers to a legal concept one argues in a circle.[139] Ultimately, legal concepts are based on a tautology and the general recursivity of the operations of the system. But legal concepts help to unfold this tautology and to break it down into distinguishable identities, which can be used as a reference to distinguish legal problems.

If each concept which is used in the system is a legal concept and fulfils the function of de-tautologizing the self-reference, it is apparent that the concept of interest is also a legal concept for the legal system, which forces the system (and only this system) to distinguish between legally justified

---

[138] To emphasize this point we repeat, the *unit* of interest. In other words: the communicative conservation of the interest as a reference in further communication. We do not dispute that there is a reality behind everything, which cannot be changed in the system at will.

[139] Circular argumentation is, indeed, a special case, which Julius Stone lists under the general title of 'illusory reference'. See Stone, *Legal System and Lawyers' Reasonings* (Stanford, 1964), 235 ff., 258 and the examples there.

and unjustified interests. The system can, if it commands sufficient forms for its observations (distinctions), observe itself from the point of view of its environment or observe the environment from its own point of view. It can assume one of these references or the other. And it can reduce these possibilities, if not by reference to the one and only quasi-'objective' one, but to an oscillation between the two,[140] in order to extract, from the other one, limiting points of view, which lead towards a reasoned decision.

The debate between a jurisprudence of interests and a jurisprudence of concepts has a number of similarities with the much older debate in the theory of science between rationalism (*à la* Descartes) and empiricism (*à la* Bacon). It is not easy to let go of 'controversies', but after some endeavour the theory of science arrived at the finding that the factual operation of the science system uses both. The legal system operates in the same vein.

Jhering made it clear that emphasizing the protection of interests must by no means be understood as a recommendation for judicial decision-making without legal concepts. The criticism of the 'jurisprudence of concepts' is directed more against its idea of the system than the use of legal concepts as lawyers' tools of trade. In this respect the perspective is changed from deduction as a system to juridical technique, but at the same time as detracting from it, it also affirms it.[141] It is well known—or at least it used to be—that a decision cannot be inferred from interests alone.[142] However, in the controversy too little attention was paid to the meaning of the distinction between interests and concepts. The issue here is the distinction between distinctions. Legal concepts are distinguished differently from interests. However, in both cases the distinctions are made within the system and are meaningful only for the operations of the legal system. Concepts are directed at the refinement of the *quaestio juris* and at the limitation of using analogies. Interests are referred to, however, if the distinction between legally preferred interests and legally disallowed interests is involved. This distinction has the merit of letting disallowed interests be stored in the system's memory as well. One can test whether there are new facts and whether in consequence it is still justified that these interests be disallowed.[143] In the words of Yves Barel, one could talk here of a

---

[140] See Stein Bråten, 'The Third Position: Beyond Artificial and Autopoietic Reduction', in Felix Geyer and Johannes van der Zouwen (eds.), *Sociocybernetic Paradoxes* (London, 1986), 193–205.

[141] See above all François Gény, *Science et technique en droit positif: Nouvelle contribution à la critique de la méthode juridique*, 4 vols. (Paris, 1913–30).

[142] See Edelman, *Entwicklung der Interessenjurisprudenz*, 89 in quoting Heinrich Stoll.

[143] Günter Ellscheid, 'Einleitung', in Ellscheid and Hassemer, *Interessenprudenz*, 5 talks about the 'hermeneutical significance of the disallowed interests' and remarks: 'The jurisprudence of interests obviously translates more than only a formal idea of justice into juridical method if it advises against losing sight of the disallowed interests when interpreting'. Here one should also remind the reader of the wise arrangement of Jewish law: to preserve dissent in legal tradition and so keep it available for further decision-making; see above Ch. 2.X, n. 153.

'potentialization' of interests.[144] This gives the entire decision a paradoxical twist. The conflict of interests is decided on one level and treated as non-decidable on another by recalling the disallowed interest as possibly preferable, and by this recall itself being generated through the very fact of the interest being disallowed. Even when, and especially when, the jurisprudence of interests interprets decisions by the legislator as a decision for and against interests, with the formula of interests it reserves to itself a re-evaluation of new constellations not taken into account by the legislator. In this sense the jurisprudence of interests is distinct from a strictly teleological interpretation of law, which tries only to establish the purposes that the legislator had in mind in order to apply them in cases of conflict. It is exactly this reservation of the option of a reassessment, however, which presupposes that the legal system first presents interests as preferences which are motivated by the legal system itself and which can be distinguished only in a legal assessment as either preferred or disallowed.

As far as legal doctrine and methods are concerned, it follows above all from these observations that the formula of 'weighing of interests' has to be abandoned as a legal principle.[145] With the wisdom of a Latin proverb one could say *in hac verbi copula stupet omnis regula*. Methodologically the formula is unsuccessful, anyway, because the eagerly awaited operable instructions have not materialized. In practice, the formula serves as a defence for what Weber called 'Kadi-Justiz'.[146] In constitutional law it is also problematic, if not plainly unconstitutional. From the values expressed in articles 1–3 of the (German) constitutional law it follows that the judge must see all interests as equal unless the law (not the judge) provides for a different valuation in cases of conflict. In other words, the formula 'weighing of interests' is not valid law. It refers to problems with the establishment of facts, but not to the legal reasoning in the decision.[147] In other words, it lies squarely in the realm of the external reference of the system and does not achieve what must be demanded from every decision: the mediation of external reference by self-reference. The transition from the jurisprudence of interests to the jurisprudence of valuation[148] and from the appreciation of interests to the appreciation of values goes some way to meeting this

---

[144] See Yves Barel, *Le paradoxe et le système: Essay sur le fantastique social*, 2nd edn. (Grenoble, 1989), 71 (1985 edn., p. 392).

[145] See particularly the criticism in Gerhard Struck, 'Interessenabwägung als Methods', in *Dogmatik und Methode: Festgabe für Josef Esser* (Kronberg/Taunus, 1975), 171–91. And also: Heinrich Hubmann, 'Die Methode der Abwägung', in id., *Wertung and Abwägung im Recht* (Cologne, 1977), 145–69, who demonstrates that legal practice leaves a lot to be desired in methodological clarity when it practises a weighing of interests.

[146] So also Hans-Martin Pawlowski, *Methodenlehre für Juristen: Theorie der Norm und des Gesetzes*, 2nd edn. (Heidelberg, 1991), 24.

[147] See Struck, 'Interessenabwägung als Methode', 183 and 185.

[148] See, for example, Pawlowski, *Methodenlehre*, 381; on weighing up of goods see also at 351, Karl Larenz, *Methodenlehre der Rechtswissenschaft*, 5th edn. (Berlin, 1983), 117.

criticism, in so far as the appreciation must not be based on interests but on legal regulations which the judge must find himself, or, perhaps one should say, which the judge ought to find.[149] For legal practice is—as any theorist of decision-making would attest—completely out of its depth when it comes to assessing the values of law in cases of value conflicts and is then dependent on guidance by interests. On the other hand, formalistic expressions can now be found for valuations which cannot be tested, the use of deterrent terms ('social harm' for instance) without further reasoning, and the very rapid abandoning of system-related arguments, especially of laboured attempts to adjust concepts provided by legal doctrine to the desired result of an innovative decision. Further, 'substantive' rationality is usually defined in relation to socially accepted values.[150] The rhetorical component in legal reasoning increases. Trying to please (which is exactly what one finds here) fits the 'democratic' style of politics.

It is for more detailed studies to explore whether there are marked historical imbalances in the swings between the preference of legal practice for external-referential concepts (e.g. instrumental, substantive, interest-related ones) or for self-referential concepts (e.g. formal, analytical, conceptual ones).[151] At any rate, no system can totally lose sight of the two sides of the form external/self. That would obliterate the form altogether. If reference is made to the possible latitude for argumentation using this form, that is, to the distinction between self-reference (= formal) and external reference (= substantive), it becomes apparent that there is no 'natural' (natural law?) preference for self-reference. The old doctrine of the *conservatio sui*, which was directed against doctrines of nature of the Aristotelian kind, has been taken on board by systems theory in the concept of autopoiesis (which defines the existence of the system, rather than a preference of the system). This allows the issue of self-reference/external reference to be

---

[149] Another modification would be to consider the weighing of interests right from the start only as a supplement to the classical repertoire of methods of interpretation. This, for instance, is the suggestion of Reinhold Zippelius, *Einführung in die juristische Methodenlehre*, 2nd edn. (Munich, 1974), 58. However, this assumes that one specifies which valid legal proposition is interpreted this way in a concrete case, or that a weighing is applied only if the situation leads to a collision of norms or duties. See on appreciation of values, Larenz, *Methodenlehre*, 388. However, this assumes that one can specify which legal propositions will collide in a concrete case.

[150] See above, n. 137.

[151] William E. Nelson, 'The Impact of the Antislavery Movement upon Styles of Judicial Reasoning in Nineteenth Century America', *Harvard Law Review* 87 (1974), 513–66, proposed a change from instrumental to formal argumentation as a consequence of the antislavery movement. There are, however, criticisms with reference to counterexamples in Harry N. Schreiber, 'Instrumentalism and Property Rights: A Reconsideration of American 'Styles of Judicial Reasoning' in the Nineteenth Century', *Wisconsin Law Review* (1975), 1–18. See also the study of Marc Tushnett, *The American Law of Slavery 1810–1860: Consideration of Humanity and Interest* (Princeton, 1981) and critical reviews.

understood as a chronic problem of the system, which permits weighting in various ways. What matters is the distinction. Then one can explore, in relation to certain historical conditions of the legal system (or of other systems), whether changes can be expected, like the change from a formal to a substantive rationality predicted by Weber, or one in the opposite direction, as is frequently called for nowadays, in the return to formal criteria for decisions which are oriented by law and justice (equality/inequality).[152] The relation between external reference and self-reference is a fundamental problem in highly developed systems which operate in the medium of meaning, as is demonstrated by the famous test case of individual consciousness. This problem is not identical with the problem of the relation between variety and redundancy. Nevertheless, it can be assumed that with the external reference term 'interest'—with which the system can even 'alienate' itself by reducing itself to an interest—more variety can be imported into the system than by the ultimately hollow conceptual technique of distinction. If this applies and socially, religiously, or politically promoted censure does not give a different twist to the communication of interests, it is easy to understand that the growing importance of the semantics of interest signals the demand for an order of a higher variety. This happened in economic theory a long time ago, in political theory in the seventeenth century and in aesthetics in the eighteenth century, but it did not happen until much later in legal theory when the positivization of law started to bite.

IX

If interpretation, argumentation, and reasoning are regarded as operations in the legal system, then logical deduction is also covered by this concept. Logical deduction is distinguished by a special kind of certainty, or more precisely, by the form logically cogent/logically wrong. Logical deduction manipulates the operation in such a way that an unequivocal attribution can be made to the one or the other side respectively. However, insufficient control of its premises prevents logical deduction from giving reasons. This has been known since Gödel's findings. Nevertheless, it would be wrong to infer—to infer!—from that problem a criticism of logical deduction or even the irrelevance of logical deduction for legal decision-making. What must be done, though, is to formulate the task of logic differently.

Logic has a special function in the context of systems theory, or more specifically, in the context of organizing redundancy. Formulated negatively,

---

[152] That there is little prospect of success in the United States seen from an *institutional* perspective (and the same can be argued for Germany), is demonstrated by Joachim J. Savelsberg, 'Law that Does Not Fit Society: Sentencing Guidelines as a Neoclassical Reaction to the Dilemma of Substantivized Law', *American Journal of Sociology* 97 (1992), 1346–81.

it makes the *proof* of errors possible (on the other side of its form). It is sensitive to errors and heightens awareness of them. The logical reconstruction of a legal argument, therefore, is a technique of refutation, of redirecting of reasons, primarily in favour of a different decision. Above and beyond that, logical deduction also has a positive function. It serves, like the prediction of the consequences of decisions, to *channel irritations.* Whenever and for whatever reasons normative expectations are upset and subjected to doubt, logic can demonstrate what else would have to be changed if expectations were changed. The translation from cognitive to normative expectations, as is well known, cannot be imposed. An inference about norms cannot be made from facts. However, if norms are sufficiently irritated by facts, one can recognize with the help of logic what consequences would flow from a change of norms, from an 'overruling' in the system. Logic provides the network, which frequently goes beyond what can be understood intuitively, and through this produces the arguments against a change of law with reference to concrete cases.

This too has another side to it, for one can also see with the help of logic what is not involved. It may be that the extension of the householder's agency to the husband of a wealthy woman has consequences for marriage law, but also for the law relating to the sale of goods. In other words, logic protects the system against the extremely complex consequences of change. This makes the introduction of changes easier. It makes the system 'ultra-stable' in Ashby's term.[153]

Together with the classic idea of a 'logocentric' argumentation, the assumption that rational argumentation could be projected onto the unity of the system and guarantee 'right law', also fails. In its dependence on cases and texts, argumentation can achieve, at best, only a 'local' rationality. In this sense, political rationality is also only a strategic rationality. And likewise, economic rationality is tied to balance sheets and budgets with their extreme limitations on what can be achieved and what is meaningful in relation to the information required. Argumentation cannot guarantee, even when applied with the sharpest mind, that a certain solution will always pass the test as clearly the best, leading to the one and only correct solution. The practice of legal counsel demonstrates that different decisions can often be made on the basis of equally good reasoning. Then there arises a situation which is not determined unequivocally by argumentation but which, in the terminology of Herbert Simon, allows for several variants of 'satisfying behaviour'.[154] Here the decision can, or rather must, be made on the basis of second-rate criteria (or, in the case of a majority

---

[153] See W. Ross Ashby, *Design for a Brain: The Origin of Adaptive Behaviour*, 2nd edn. (London, 1960), 98.

[154] See Herbert A. Simon, *Models of Man—Social and Rational: Mathematical Essays on Rational Human Behavior in a Social Setting* (New York, 1957), 204 and 252.

vote, without uniform criteria). To put it differently, even with the best possible criteria the system cannot guarantee, either in whole or in detail, a rational state—and this applies even with high expectations of good, judicious, professionally skilled argumentation. Any theory of discourse (such as Jürgen Habermas's) that ignores this neither does justice to the highly developed peculiarity of the legal methods of persuasion nor achieves its goal. It cannot reintroduce into the system the demand for information caused by arguments, but is forced to work with the legal fiction that reason will ultimately prevail as long as certain procedural conditions are met.

Our reluctance to accept the assumption of an operatively achievable rationality, as some sort of totality, is consistent with the thesis provided by evolutionary theory that complexity is not a natural or rational goal of evolution but a by-product that occurs together with it.[155] Hence argumentation is not a matter of the instrumental exploitation of resource complexity but a matter of how the system can cope in spite of increasing complexity, or, how the system can continue to reproduce itself in an operatively closed way in a competent and continual relation to its environment.

X

Finally, we return to a point of view that has been mentioned several times before. We have said that argumentation always sees itself in the context of a second-order observation. What matters is always the elaboration of an argument—for other observers. By being attuned to argumentation (however abbreviated in legal practice), the legal system exhibits criteria that are, generally, typical of all functioning systems.[156] The economy orients its operations around prices because this makes it possible to observe how observers observe the market. Politics steers its operations towards public opinion in order to observe, in the mirror of public opinion, the resonance of its actions in the perception of other observers. The artist arranges a piece of art by selecting its defining forms in a way that observers can observe how he observed the piece of art. An educator is assumed to

---

[155] See above, Ch. 6.V.

[156] See for details of the examples used in the following discussion, Dirk Baecker, *Information und Risiko in der Marktwirtschaft* (Frankfurt, 1988); Niklas Luhmann, *Die Wirtschaft der Gesellschaft* (Frankfurt, 1988), esp. 93; Niklas Luhmann, 'Gesellschaftliche Komplexität und öffentliche Meinung', in id., *Soziologische Aufklärung*, vol. 5 (Opladen, 1990), 170–82; Niklas Luhmann, Frederick D. Bunsen, and Dirk Baecker, *Unbeobachtbare Welt: Über Kunst und Architektur* (Bielefeld, 1990), 7–45, at 23; Niklas Luhmann, 'Das Kind als Medium der Erziehung', *Zeitschrift für Pädagogik* 37 (1991), 19–40; id., 'System und Absicht der Erziehung', in Niklas Luhmann and Karl Eberhard Schorr (eds.), *Zwischen Absicht und Person: Fragen an die Pädagogik* (Frankfurt, 1992), 102–124; Niklas Luhmann, 'Sozialsystem Familie', in id., *Soziologische Aufklärung*, vol. 5 (Opladen, 1990), 196–217; id., *Die Wissenschaft der Gesellschaft* (Frankfurt, 1990), esp. 362.

have the intention of educating, for otherwise one could not observe, with specific reference to the education system, how he observes his pupils. And, in turn, these pupils are presented as students, so that a medium can be assumed in which one can observe how the educator selects the forms according to which he is going to educate. Many more examples could be given. It therefore no longer appears a coincidence that, parallel to the ascendancy of a growing number of functioning systems in the eighteenth century, interaction theory—for instance in the form of prescriptions for conversation—switches to observing the observers. When this shift of the core operations to a second-order level correlates with the differentiation of functioning systems, one can presume that, seen from the point of view of social theory, this is part and parcel of the structural criteria of modernity.[157] Then the peculiarities of individual functioning systems recede. The question of *how* this is achieved is answered differently (but comparably), system by system. However, *that* it is achieved (or at least pursued) in every case appears to be one of the conditions for the differentiation of the system. *That is why* there must be argumentation in the legal system. For under the condition of differentiation, the system must try to find support in itself (and not in the world) and that requires this recursive closure on the level of second-order observation.

These insights lead to questions concerning the way in which the reflexive theories of the respective systems describe this state of affairs, or, to be more precise, how reflexive theories make sure that they observe meaningfully even if they only observe their own observing. Such a coordination of self-description with making sense of self requires emphases which cannot be doubted any more; that means that 'inviolate levels' must be set (Hofstadter). Thus the economy (or economic theory, if we rely on Hayek) associates market-qualified prices with the rationality of information processing; or politics associates public opinion with democracy; or education systems associate educational intentions with good intentions. The culture of argumentation within the legal system is also based on such stop-rules. They take the form of asymmetries, which cannot be questioned any further. What matters is the 'application of a norm' and, in so far as argumentation is necessary, the 'interpretation of a text'. These are very specific distinctions. After careful scrutiny of how this works in practice, circles have been detected. The norm is not created until it is applied, or at any rate it is only then that it is attributed with a meaning that can be identified. The interpretation produces a hermeneutical circle by first defining what is to be interpreted and then adjusting it so that reasons can be found why an interpretation is necessary.

In all of that we remain on the familiar terrain of a modern discussion of methods. However, what if all of this—circles and all—is arranged in order

---

[157] See for more detail Niklas Luhmann, *Beobachtungen der Moderne* (Opladen, 1992).

only to make a second-order observation possible? If this assumption could be shown to be true, what we are talking about here is ultimately the production of normative texts in order to organize relations of observation. In this case, one would have to deal with texts which are 'abstracted from time' and which, even if they could not guarantee a uniform way of observing by all observers, would be capable of providing sufficient guidance through the use of specific forms (distinctions), and thus through that use exclude arbitrariness (that is, dissolution, and so entropy). Such normative texts, similar to complex computer programs, would no longer allow us to understand how operations actually run and they would no longer guarantee a uniform meaning to be given to the results of observation. They could, though, become so specific that it would become obvious when there was a reason to consider changing the text itself. They would make it possible for the system to react to irritations without the need for a full review of all its operations.

With these considerations in mind, we can see that the discussion of legal methods has taken a similar direction in recent years. This applies to older notions of judicial review, which use interpretation to circumvent the arduous route of repealing legislation and reformulating statutes.[158] It applies to work that follows the structuring legal doctrine of Friedrich Müller.[159] It applies especially to the multi-contextual, relativist discourse, and organization-specific ideas about the use of law, developed by Karl-Heinz Ladeur.[160] Extending into sociology, Giddens's concept of 'structuration' comes to mind; or in philosophy one could think of Wittgenstein's concept of a language-game (in so far as a language-game can be understood as an arrangement of observers for observers). There is no lack of indications as far as this tendency is concerned. However, it is important to see more than just the phenomena accompanying the dissolution of the classical canons of norm, text, and method. Perhaps we can see a new form of order in its development, which has shifted entirely onto the level of second-order observation and, from there, defines what is useful for a recursive procedure and therefore what counts as reality.

To this we must add that the legal profession overestimates the importance of interpretation and argumentation precisely because lawyers see the system as belonging on the second-order observation level. It should again be borne in mind that we are talking here about a system which is coded with

---

[158] See, for example, F. James Davis et al., *Society and the Law: New Meanings for an Old Profession* (New York, 1962), 163: 'The result has been that judicial construction has become as much a part of statutes as the text itself.'

[159] See Friedrich Müller, *Strukturierende Rechtslehre* (Berlin, 1984).

[160] See, for example, Karl-Heinz Ladeur, 'Gesetzesinterpretation, 'Richterrecht' und Konventionsbildung in kognitivistischer Perspektive: Handeln unter Ungewißheitsbedingungen und richterliches Entscheiden', *Archiv für Rechts- und Sozialphilosophie* 77 (1991), 176–94.

a binary code and that the decisions regarding validity/non-validity are ultimately the crucial operations. On the one hand, the masterly achievement of legal craft is constituted by the production of texts from texts, by interpretation and by argumentation, and this is also the case where facts and questions of evidence, etc. are concerned. On the other hand, lawyers lose half their cases after argumentation from both sides. Just as there are always some patients who die in the health system while others survive, and in this lies the risk for the medical profession, lawyers must live with the fact that their argumentation, even if it has been most carefully thought through, does not always determine the final, all-deciding decision. Therefore there can, at times, be observed in lawyers' attitudes a certain ironic distance from legal ideas and means of argumentation, coupled with an alertness to what ultimately carries the decision (for example, court conventions and tradition). The ultimate reasons are always only penultimate reasons.

9   Politics and Law

I

Systems theorists generally assume that a distinction must be made between the legal system and the political system.[1] These systems are seen as different sub-systems of society. This is especially true if we embrace the concept of autopoiesis and insist upon the autonomy and historical individuality of all social systems. However, most other social theorists reject this viewpoint because of the close and obvious relationship between politics and law.

A theory of the autopoietic, operatively closed legal system envisages that this system is able to draw a distinction between itself and other functioning systems. Hence if any external observer of the system wants to observe and describe it appropriately, he will eventually confront this distinction, which is produced in the system itself. Even if this is plausible on the whole, it creates a problem regarding the relationship between politics and law. A long tradition, going back to early modern times, makes us inclined to see only a unified politico-legal system. This is evoked to a large extent by the concept of the state, which is at the same time legal and political.[2] Since the writings of Francisco Suárez, Thomas Hobbes, and Samuel Pufendorf, this view has also been adopted by the theory of natural law. On the other hand, as we have seen in the chapter on the function of law, we must distinguish between the functions of politics and law as well as their modes of actualization.

One peculiar feature of European development is the emphasis given to the legal preconditions of social life derived from Roman civil law and its basis in natural law. In medieval times, this excluded the idea of a unity of law and politics. Without these foundations the revolution of the church, organized around the pope against the empire, with its tendency towards theocracy, could not have happened and the binding legal character of a 'constitutional state' could not have been invented.[3] The law was already

---

[1] See, for example, Jay A. Sigler, *An Introduction to the Legal System* (Homewood, Ill., 1968), 42 (but in contradiction at p. 150: 'The legal system, which is a subsystem of the political system is typically used as an output channel for the political system'). See also, following Parsons, William M. Evan, *Social Structure and Law: Theoretical and Empirical Perspectives* (Newbury Park, 1990), 219. However, see a different view in several publications—for example, Glendon Schubert, in *Judicial Policy Making*, 2nd edn. (Glenview, 1974).

[2] For more recent literature on the history of the idea and reality of the 'state' see, for example, Perry Anderson, *Die Entstehung des absolutistischen Staates* (Frankfurt, 1979); Gianfranco Poggi, *The State: Its Nature, Development and Prospects* (Cambridge, 1990); Michael Stolleis, *Staat und Staatsräson in der frühen Neuzeit: Studien zur Geschichte des öffentlichen Rechts* (Frankfurt, 1990). However, this literature does not see a problem in the unity, which is promoted in this way by the concept of 'state'.

[3] See on this point, for example, Brian M. Downing, 'Medieval Origins of Constitutional Government in the West', *Theory and Society* 18 (1989), 212–47.

there when the modern state began to consolidate itself politically, partly in the form of local customs and partly as a formally elaborated law which was differentiated into many legal institutions, laid down in writing, and capable of being taught and learned. There was feudal, urban, and regal law, and, since the High Middle Ages, the separation of canon law and secular civil law, which was reflected in differentiated jurisdictions. From a juridical point of view, there was no 'public law' until the sixteenth century and no unifying legal concept (*dominium, imperium, iurisdictio*) that could represent the intended unity of territorial authority. On the other hand, one could not separate *iurisdictio* and *imperium*, for that would have meant, in the concrete way of thinking of those times, an *imperium* in a space devoid of law and a *iurisdictio* without the capability of enforcement. At the same time, the extensive penetration of social issues by law reduced the importance of this distinction. The concept of *potestas* bridged the divide further without, however, being able to permeate legal instruments in detail. The same applies to the new understanding of 'sovereignty'.

Then, and later to a far greater extent, legal regimes in different parts of Europe differed depending on whether legal development was primarily linked to legal practice in courts, to the erudition of legal academics, or to the legal advice given to legislators; that is, whether it was judge-made law or the law of law professors or codified law. There may have been more or less direct reasons for these different options in an otherwise similar simultaneous political evolution. But law's own dynamics and the specificity of the set of problems with which it has to deal, prevent political ideas of order from being copied directly into law.[4] Of course politics influences individual decisions but it appears that it has its structural effect in the preference for certain types of legal roles with the help of which the legal system stimulates itself.

In the face of rapidly increasing complexity and ensuing legal uncertainty, the early modern territorial state initially saw its mission in the unification of valid law within its territorial boundaries. Accordingly, the organization of the administration of justice and the centralization of control serve the purpose of its own unity.[5] This constituted the state's understanding of

---

[4] See for more detail on this point, R. C. van Caenegem, *Judges, Legislators, and Professors, Chapters in European Legal History* (Cambridge, 1987).

[5] On the issue of the territorial states of the (German) empire see Dietmar Willoweit, *Rechtsgrundlagen der Territorialgewalt: Landesobrigkeit, Herrschaftsrecht und Territorium in der Rechtswissenschaft* (Vienna, 1975). There were functional equivalents for territorial consolidation but they too depended considerably on law. This applies above all to political promotions to aristocracy and thence to the juridification of a recognition of the aristocracy in the context of exemptions from tax: see, for instance (using the example of Savoy), Claudio Donati, *L'idea di nobilità in Italia: Secoli XIV–XVIII* (Rome and Bari, 1988), 177. This procedure is particularly interesting because it allowed for a temporary compromise with the still existing stratified differentiation and for a downward inclusion of aristocracy, a new aristocratization of the aristocracy as

sovereignty (in contrast to the understanding in early medieval times) and its political consolidation. The concepts of sovereignty and of sovereign power (*potestas*) concealed two rather different ideas of political power that were in play: first, the idea of a *generalized* capacity to secure obedience to commands; secondly, the idea of legal force, which reflected the fact that power presented itself and was enforced in the form of law, that is, in a form which was always already *specified*. The combination of both aspects of power was indispensable because courts operated principally at the level of local administration. Hence since the second half of the sixteenth century, sovereignty meant in practical terms the centralized political control of the courts and the removal of feudal rights, church law, other corporative laws, or, at any rate, of all courts based on any particularistic rights. Sovereignty meant the recording and unification of special regional laws aided by publication; it meant reception of the language and the conceptual achievements of Roman civil law—at least as a basis for legal erudition, if not as a basis for valid law. And it meant an increasing legal competence to enact laws.[6] Hence one can talk, in Franz Neumann's words, of a 'political concept of law',[7] and see in that idea a kind of relay between political reason and legal validity. From the second half of the sixteenth century onwards at the latest, with Bodin, Suárez, Pufendorf, and others, theorists assumed there was a unity of politics and law in natural law.[8] This belief was based on the assumption that only through this unity could the individual be constituted as a subject of law, and as such it was a precondition for the development of an economy based on contract and the division of labour. Hobbes provided arguably the strongest formulation of this belief. Individuals, until then only bodies which could kill and be killed and act in that way with fore-thought because they were equipped with reason, became individuals in the sense of a second, artificial nature, by 'authorizing' the sovereign to

---

it were. But how would that have been possible without a realistic-practical motive of a clarification of the status of aristocrats: the tax privilege?

[6] See in this context the impressive implementation of political sovereignty as legal sovereignty in France and Philippe Sueur, *Histoire du droit public français XVe–XVIIIe siècle*, vol. 2 (Paris, 1989), 29 (in relation to the editing of *coutumes*), 164 (in relation to the control of the legal authority of landlords), and 56 (in relation to legislation).

[7] See in: *Die Herrschaft des Gesetzes* (1936; Frankfurt 1980), in relation to Bodin and Pufendorf.

[8] There are also many authors who are no longer known who supported this idea of the unity of politics and law on the basis of religious law (intended by God) and natural law (the logic of facts, as it were). For examples see François Grimaudet, *Les opuscules politiques* (Paris, 1580), esp. opuscule I: De la Loy. Laws are the 'souveraine raison, empreinte par Dieu, qui command les choses qui sont à faire, & deffend le contraire faicte, & publiee pa celuy qui a puissance de commander'; 'Car la Loy est l'oeuvre du Prince'; and 'La fin de la loy es le bien public & salut des hommes en general'. This has to be clearly distinguished from the good of individuals, including the prince himself. All quotes from fol. I.

enact law at will. Only through this could the link between rights and duties be established. Accordingly, the individual owes his civil identity to the unity of law and politics, and this unity is, therefore, irretrievably tied to the individuality of individuals. At the end of this organizational and semantic movement, which integrated politics and law, we find the great codifications of the eighteenth and nineteenth centuries and finally the idea that the function of the state is to guarantee freedom in terms of, that is, within the boundaries of, the law.

The crucial motive for the union of politics and law was the problem of the right *of resistance*, which flung Europe into a century of civil war. No one portrayed this more clearly than Hobbes.[9] His insight was that peace could not be secured just by law itself, deploying the resources of an unwritten tradition, of the 'artificial reason' of lawyers and the justification of what individuals put forward as their rights. If everybody could refer to their natural reason and find justifications in legal materials that were widely disseminated in print, law would destroy the precondition for its own existence, namely peace. This observation gained added force given the decline of the structural and social ability of the aristocracy to make its own decisions about what was lawful or not on the basis of its (armed) households. And this observation applied all the more as religion, law, and morals were not rigidly separated in late medieval thought but were integrated in one context of meaning, so that issues of religion and morality could immediately become issues of law and be fought over in the legal domain.[10] A fortiori, a right of resistance was implied if the available theoretical concepts could be deployed—that is, if it could be said that the prince was only a *civis* too and as such subject to law, or if a distinction could be made between *rex* and *tyrannus* and it could be left to the balance of power among the aristocracy to decide which of the two applied. Was there a solution to these obvious problems other than the unity of politics and law, other than the founding of the validity of law on politically implemented force, which then adopted the name of 'auctoritas' for legal purposes?[11] And how else could law have

---

[9] Apart from *Leviathan* see also: *A Dialogue between a Philosopher and a Student of the Common Law* (quoted from the, edition Chicago, 1971); and *Behemoth, or the Long Parliament* (quoted from the edition by Ferdinand Tönnies, London, 1889; new edition by Stephen Holmes, Chicago, 1990).

[10] See Quentin Skinner, *The Foundations of Modern Political Thought*, vol. 2: *The Age of Reformation* (Cambridge, 1978); Richard Saage, *Herrschaft, Toleranz, Widerstand: Studien zur politischen Theorie der niederländischen und englischen Revolution* (Frankfurt, 1981); Diethelm Böttcher, *Ungehorsam oder Widerstand? Zum Fortleben des mittelalterlichen Widerstandsrechts in der Reformationszeit (1529–1530)* (Berlin, 1991).

[11] However, authority—and this is new in Hobbes's argument—is not a natural superior ability or even less an aristocratic competence. It is based on 'authorization'. In the text of the Covenant in *Leviathan* II at 17, Everyman's Library (London, 1953), 89, one can read: 'I Authorise . . .' . However, the argument based on authorization replaces the reference to nature with a circle; authorization assumes a validity of law, which has yet to be justified by authorization itself.

worked through these conflicts if not with self-controlled action backed by the politically assured validity of law?

Even later criticism of the circular argumentation for the construction of a social contract could not avoid reviving the right of resistance. David Hume, for instance, based the commitment of governments on promises which were valid by convention but which, for their own part, were based on human nature.[12] The argument shifted into the domain of economic property interests. But a government that does not represent and protect these interests, which are the foundation of society itself, can expect resistance. As before, the argument is based on the old formula of virtue and corruption, but it no longer drew conclusions in terms of positive law but in terms of political consequences.[13] At the same time, there emerged a tendency to describe 'corrupt' practices as 'unconstitutional', albeit initially without foundation in a text.[14]

As long as there is no constitution in the modern sense of the term, the problem of resistance remains the core problem of the modern state, the point where law is in conflict with politics. Here lies the hidden motif of all theories built on the unity of politics and law. In other words, the difference between the legal system and the political system can be understood, under the prevailing premises, as legitimate resistance to the political exercise of power.

Apart from the practical, political purpose of eliminating the right of resistance, the unity of politics and law also met the demand for the self-correction of law, either through the old distinction between law and equity,[15] or through its general capacity for legitimizing deviations from the law in the form of dispensations, privileges, and even self-tolerated breaches of the law.[16]

---

[12] See David Hume, *A Treatise of Human Nature*, Book III, Part II, Sect. IX, Everyman's Library (London, 1956), vol. 2, p. 250.

[13] On this point see David Lieberman (following Pocock), *The Province of Legislation Determined: Legal Theory in Eighteenth-Century Britain* (Cambridge, 1989), 7.

[14] See Niklas Luhmann, 'Verfassung als evolutionäre Errungenschaft', *Rechtshistorisches Journal* 9 (1990), 176–220, at 188.

[15] Here the English jurisdiction of equity in the Court of Chancery is famous and influential. For originally parallel-running considerations in France see Grimaudet, *Opuscules politiques*, opuscule II, fol. I IV ff. or François de Lalouette (L'Alouette), *Des affaires d'Etat, des Finances, du Prince et de la Noblesse* (Mets, 1597), 88. This developed in France more in the direction of the competence of interpretation of the legislator (*référé législatif*), whenever cases occurred in decision-making, which had not yet been decided by the legislator.

[16] See with its comprehensive material Francisco Suárez, *Tractatus de legibus ac Deo legislatore* (Lyons, 1619), vol. II, cap. XIV and XV, p. 91, for dispensations from natural law and vol. VI, p. 368 for dispensations from positive law, or Scipio Ammirato, *Discorsi Sopra Cornelio Tacito* (Florence, 1598), 223, in the context of a very circumspect treatment of the topic of the reason of state. Frequently the possibility to derogate from natural law was contested. However, whenever this is the case one can typically find the opposite opinion in the same

Formulated more generally, one can say that the paradox of the self-constituting difference between legal and illegal was not simply externalized with respect to the given power relations but shifted to a superior unity of law and politics, embodied in the 'person' of the sovereign. This, however, remained a precarious solution. Its success depended on the sovereign being what he was supposed to be: pious, reasonable, and open to what law itself inspired in him.

The operative differences between political and legal communication could not really be integrated in this way. Seen from the perspective of the right of resistance, the modern political system of the territorial state could not accept that subjects intervene in politics through recourse to law, and thereby disturb the peace. The political system had to claim closure, that is, closure in relation to everything that had to be defined as political in relation to the code and the function of politics. Exactly the same applies also to the legal system. The legal system cannot tolerate any exceptions either. This was the issue in the dispute between the parliament in London, as articulated by Coke, and the Stuarts. If there were only one tribunal or authority, which decided upon life and limb and property independently of the law, there would be no law because all legal certainty would be destroyed. This is the argument which lies at the genesis of the origins of civil rights under the common law and is yet another instance of the operative closure of a functioning system.

Thus one demand for, or attempt at, closure opposes another. At the same time, crucial points of view are exposed by this confrontation. The understanding of the relationship between politics and law attained in this way was consolidated and apparently overcome with the schema of the *Rechtsstaat* (rule of law). In this schema the context of conditions for the relationship between law and freedom, and thus also the strengthening of both, was preserved and so made available for communication.[17] With

text. See, for example, Jeremy Taylor, *Ductor Dubitantium, or, the Rule of Conscience in all her General Measures* (1660), quoted from *The Whole Works*, vols. IX and X (London, 1851/52; reprint Hildesheim, 1970), vol. II. I, Vol IX at 333 and especially at 347 as to dispensations from natural law only by God and not 'by any human power'. See, however: 'The exactness of natural law is capable of interpretation, and may be allayed by equity, and piety, and necessity'. The problem could be avoided if one understood the maintenance of authority itself that is the *ratio status* as the only binding natural law, which made all other laws possible in the first instance. For then one could argue that any deviation from that would be self-destructive. See, for example, Ciro Spontone, *Dodici libri del Governo di Stato* (Verona, 1599), 122.

[17] The concept of 'schema' can be used here quite explicitly as a form for the preservation of a higher-order arrangement of contingency, or, in the words of Novalis, as a self-referential reciprocal action. Novalis talks about the 'all-inclusive unity of the schema. Free can only be determined, that is, necessary, and necessary can only be determined, that is, free.' Or: 'The schema is related to itself by reciprocal action. Each thing in its place is only what is determined by other things'. Both quotations from Philosophische Studien 1795/96, quoted from *Werke, Tagebücher und Briefe Friedrich von Hardenbergs*, ed. Hans-Joachim Mähl and Richard Samuel (Darmstadt, 1978), vol. 2, p. 14.

it came a reaction against the historical situation of the social system (specifically: the time after the French Revolution), in which it had become abundantly clear that there was no consensus over the criteria of reason and morality. In their place we find a difference between necessity and freedom and various resulting combinatory possibilities—partly in the schema education (as the task of the state) and partly in the schema *Rechtsstaat*.[18] As a *Rechtsstaat* the state was, at the same time, an institution of the law and an example of the political accountability of law, that is, of the implementation and development of law as it adjusted to changing social conditions and goals which could be implemented politically.

This model for describing a legal and political system became democratic in hardly noticeable transitions, marked only by the 'constitutional question'. The forms of inclusion of 'the citizen' in legal and political contexts started to diverge—precisely because system-specific terms such as juristic capacity, citizenship, and the right to vote became available.[19] Political and juridical controversies relating to this process recurred throughout the nineteenth century. They referred to the legal forms for political influence on law, but also to the legal protection of the citizen against state authority no matter how it was politically practised. Initially these controversies did not deal with the premiss of state characteristics of law and politics but rather they were derived from it. Since the nineteenth century, the concept of the political has been understood almost exclusively as referring to the state. This has made possible the development of organized parties which, delineated by membership, have provided access to state offices for the implementation of political goals. At the same time, the law has offered an area for political creativity. Together with the budget, financed by taxes and stamp duties, the law has become the principal instrument for the implementation of political goals. This has been reflected in the idea of a hierarchical order of legislation and dispensation of justice.[20] The result has been a massive increase in normative material. Legal norms have become the sediment of past politics and it has become increasingly difficult to reactivate them for new political ambitions. Valid law is now no longer the result of conflicts for which generalizable rules must be found in order to

---

[18] This parallel problem will not be dealt with further here. See instead Heinrich Stephani, *Grundriß der Staatserziehungswissenschaft* (Weißenfels and Leipzig, 1797); id., *System der öffentlichen Erziehung* (Berlin, 1805); Christian Daniel Voß, *Versuch über die Erziehung für den Staat, als Bedürfnis unserer Zeit, zur Beförderung des Bürgerwohls und der Regenten-Sicherheit* (Halle, 1799); Karl Salomo Zachariae, *Über die Erziehung des Menschengeschlechts durch den Staat* (Leipzig, 1802). It is evident that these were attempts at reform were triggered off by the French Revolution.

[19] See in this context, especially in relation to the problem of legal protection against state actions, Regina Ogorek, 'Individueller Rechtsschutz gegenüber der Staatsgewalt: Zur Entwicklung der Verwaltungsgerichtsbarkeit im 19. Jahrhundert', in Jürgen Kocka (ed.), *Bürgertum im 19. Jahrhundert: Deutschland im europäischen Vergleich* (Munich, 1988), 372–405.

[20] We already discussed and rejected this model in Ch. 7.

come to a decision. Rather, by its attempts to realize political goals, law creates the conflicts that it is then called upon to solve. Since the capacity for activating politics in order to change law is continuously reproduced by communication in society and since law legitimizes itself by legalizing parliamentary democracy, legal practice must keep distinguishing between introducing legal change through an 'activist' interpretation of law and waiting for change in political and public opinion. Overall, the positivization of law and the democratization of politics support each other reciprocally and they have left a significant mark on both the political system and the legal system of today. Therefore, it is difficult to imagine two different systems, and in particular two systems that are operatively closed and non-congruent with these movements. But it is precisely the democratization of politics which calls for much more legal protection for the individual, especially in regard to his constitutional rights.

As a matter of fact, the thesis of the unity of the two systems has never been pushed to the point where it has been postulated that what is legally permissible in politics is decided by politics on exclusively political terms. Nor has there been any serious suggestion that law is merely the inbuilt inertia in politics, which prevents it from giving in too easily to all sorts of whims. In view of the traditions of the common law and Roman law and the awareness that their historical structures were built on the testing of legal ideas, the proposition that all those legal ideas were just the politics of yesteryear would have been misconceived. However, how should the legal restraint of politics in a single system be understood if not in this way? The *Rechtsstaat* formula has obviously concealed the problem. And this ambiguity may also have contributed more than anything else to keeping the idea of natural law alive, at least to impress on those who could no longer subscribe to this idea the demand for legitimacy of the political regime. Nevertheless, these kinds of ideas can no longer be supported by any convincing arguments. They can be discarded or reformulated, if politics and law are seen as two separate functioning systems.

Hence our point of departure in this chapter and the following one goes against the plausibility of those arguments, which come from a long tradition. Our proposition will be that there is not one system under the heading of the concept of the state but that there are two different systems, both being operatively closed, having different functions, different codes, and different code-dependent programmes. The unitary view, which is based on the concept of the state and especially on the schema of the *Rechtsstaat*, is understandable in a historical perspective. It is more or less adequate for a phase in which the positivization of law had to be implemented in the legal system with the help of a doctrine of the sources of law which referred to the (political) state and in which the political system had to stake out a domain and enforce it against the established structures (above all, class structures), so that politics could become a practice of continuously processing collectively binding decisions. The more this is achieved, however, the more the concept of unity loses its plausibility. The legal system can do without a sovereign, even in the form of the *Rechtsstaat*. It does not have a place for nor does it need a sovereign, because it dissolves its paradoxes in a different way.[21] But it has to make decisions on demand. The paradoxes of the political system culminate in the formula of the sovereign, or, finally, of the sovereignty of the people. This concept, however, implies that the sovereign does not need to decide: the sovereign is sovereign even when it comes to the question of deciding or not deciding. The concept of the sovereignty of the people shifts the paradox onto a sovereign who cannot decide at all. Whether or not and how decisions are made are political issues. The concept of the state becomes an artificial device for holding together what has emerged as the self-reinforcing dynamics in the political system and the legal system. It is wholly impossible to see politics as an ongoing interpretation of the legally fixed constitution, no matter how much political goals may aim at, among other things, producing 'talk' and making topics available for further 'talk'[22] in the form of sections of the constitution (for instance, the protection of the environment as a task for the state). Similarly, an adequate theory of the legal system cannot be constructed if its factual operations are defined as the implementation of political programmes, no matter how much legal decision may be guided by politically desirable consequences. Even when it comes to the political appointment or election of judges, only suitable candidates are considered. All efforts to steer courts onto a politically desirable course must confront the internal workings of courts. Most of the time they founder on the internal culture, the mode of argument operating within the legal system.[23] Even if we find here too a relatively conservative approach, which is oriented by redundancies, and a relatively progressive approach, which is

[21] For instance, in the form of procedures, or in the form of subjective law, see above Ch. 4.VI and Ch. 6.V.

[22] In the sense of Nils Brunsson, *The Organization of Hypocrisy: Talk, Decisions and Actions in Organizations* (Chichester, 1989).

[23] See, for example, Jessie Bernard, 'Dimensions and Axes of Supreme Court Decisions: A Study in the Sociology of Conflict', *Social Forces* 34 (1955), 19–27; Eloise C. Snyder, 'The Supreme Court as a Small Group', *Social Forces* 36 (1958), 232–8. The famous example to the contrary is in fact only a single case, in which Roosevelt's judicial appointment stopped the frequent use of judicial review by the Supreme Court against social legislation and forced the court back to the conservatism of the nineteenth century. See on this case, from the perspective of political science, C. Hermann Pritchett, *The Roosevelt Court: A Study in Judicial Politics and Values 1937–1947* (New York, 1948). On the methodological problems and ambiguities in relation to empirical findings in the 'Bermuda Triangle' of ideological controversies (political and economic 'liberalism'), psychological variables ('attitudes'), and juridical categorizations of respective decisions, see Glendon Schubert, *The Judicial Mind: The Attitudes and Ideologies of Supreme Court Judges 1946–1963* (Evanston, 1965).

guided by variety, this has very little to do with ongoing politics and the spectrum of parties and pressure groups.

At any event it is completely impossible to put political questions—for instance, the timing and conditions for the reunification of Germany, the homogenization of living conditions in different areas, etc.—to the legal system and expect a decision. The same applies for marital conflict, academic or religious controversies, economic investments, etc. To quote from article III of the American Constitution, the legal system accepts only 'cases and controversies' for decision-making. Problems must be turned into a justiciable form to have access to law. This means that they can be defined recursively in relation to the historical condition of the legal system and the validity of law. The law cannot be used as a machine for the investigation of truths, or for the discovery of intelligent solutions to problems. If, for example, the spelling of one particular dictionary is to apply throughout the texts of a country, this must be stipulated in the publisher's contract. Another typical restriction is that a request for a legal decision must be articulated in the form of the violation of a subjective right.[24] It is undeniable that state administration is programmed in the form of law, for instance in the legislation of the state budget, but here, too, law is actively involved only if 'cases and controversies' arise from this.

The idea has long been abandoned that the legally sovereign state constitutes the individual's legal subjectivity, so creating the foundations for division of labour and the market-orientation of the economy. Following the ideas of Hayek and Simon, one can see the problem of the economy as lying in the processing of information or the analysis of the contingency and transaction costs within an organization. It is, at any rate, a problem specific to the economy and cannot be deduced from constituting the legal capacity of individuals, even if this evidently remains a condition which must be met by the performance of another functioning system.

It was precisely the implementation of 'legislative positivism' in the nineteenth century and the rapid growth of new legislation—at first sight, indicators of the political system's increasing domination of the legal system—which led to developments which raised awareness that the legal and political systems were, in fact, separate. Parallel to this, there grew up awareness, both in the common law with respect to statutes, and in Europe, that the freedom of a judge to interpret and even make law cannot be avoided. It became evident that, even if only in relation to the interpretation of statutes, it is not just a matter of re-engaging in political controversies in court after they have been resolved in parliament by a decision resulting in a legislative text. Nor

---

[24] At least possibilities to overcome such restrictions while keeping within constitutional law are the subject of discussion; see, for example, Dieter Grimm, *Die Zukunft der Verfassung* (Frankfurt, 1991), esp. 408. It is, then, particularly impressive how circumspect lawyers are when it comes to the connectivity of law.

is it a matter of having judges investigate and clarify political motives in doubtful cases.[25] The nature of compromise and the 'contractualization'[26] of political opinion on the one hand, and the political conditions of neo-corporatism on the other, make it impossible to look for a juridically useful 'intention of the legislator'.[27] Instead, the legal system develops its own internal theories of interpretation, in which legislative intent plays only a minor role but one that is constructed strictly on the basis of a text.

The separation of the two functioning systems is particularly evident in their different coding. Even if the implementation of law is still believed to depend on a political-hierarchical coding of power through the organization of state facilities, and both law and politics find their freedom in the form of the state, it is evident today that, in the legal system, there is no equivalent to the democratic coding of power in the form of government and opposition.[28] In the political system, ideas arise about alternative decisions as soon as the system observes itself in relation to collectively binding decisions, which become condensed in the form of opposition as soon as such counter-positions can be carried over from decision to decision. This can be easily observed in the highly personal-interactive factions of regal court politics in the period of the absolutist state and particularly clearly in the seating arrangements of a parliamentary democracy. Once the organization of political parties is consolidated, there is an organizational guarantee that no matter what the issue to be decided is, there will always be an opposition. The opposition is no longer disciplined by different alternative decisions but by the prospect of taking over government and of having to present a programme (which is feasible or, at least, acceptable and which could find sufficient political support). The schema government/opposition becomes the 'form', the 'code' of the political system in the sense that the form has an internal side and the code has a positive, connective side, 'where the action is'. But the inner side of the form is only what it is because there is the other side where alternatives are available. The legal system handles alternatives quite differently. They are and they remain scattered and dependent on individual cases and rules, and there is not the slightest hint of any 'consolidated opposition'. And even if it did exist, it would not be recognized as a form of law but as a form of politics.

---

[25] There are, however, grey areas and new controversies; see, for example, F. James Davis et al., *Society and the Law: New Meanings for an Old Profession* (New York, 1962), 162.

[26] In the sense of Charles-Albert Morand, 'La contractualisation du droit dans l'état providence', in François Chazel and Jacques Commaille (eds.), *Normes juridiques et régulation sociale* (Paris, 1991), 139–58.

[27] If there is anything at all like such an intention, most of the time it will consist of trying to save what can be saved after much argument.

[28] See on this point Niklas Luhmann, 'Theorie der politischen Opposition', *Zeitschrift für Politik* 36 (1989), 13–26.

It goes without saying that the separation of the systems does not mean that intensive causal links between them do not exist. In fact, such causal links can be found only if distinctions can be made between the systems (and, let us add, this is possible in reality only if the systems can distinguish themselves). The hypothesis of the separation of the systems provides a better explanation for the finding that systems are dependent on each other in their 'structural drift' and structural development. This will be discussed under the heading of structural coupling in the next chapter.

II

Now we must take a closer look at the connecting concept of the *Rechtsstaat*.[29] This concept functions as a schema which makes it possible to define two *reverse* perspectives as a *unity* and to celebrate it as an achievement of civilization: the juridical shackling of political force and the political exploitation of law.

Seen from the perspective of law and its function, there can be no areas without law, no forms of conduct that cannot be subject to legal regulation, no enclaves of unregulated arbitrariness and violence. The common law calls this the 'rule of law';[30] as Herman Finer puts it, 'the law and the rule [of law, N.L.] cover the same ground'.[31] If legal indeterminacy is to be at all acceptable, it must be legally qualified. This is done by declaring such indeterminacy to be the freedom given by law—be this the freedom of economic enterprise (the right of property use, freedom of contract), or the freedom of political decision, for instance in the form of the 'political questions' doctrine,[32] or, finally, the freedom of the law to deal with itself, namely with the decision whether to litigate or not. Seen from the perspective of law, the *Rechtsstaat* is the consequence of the universal relevance of law for society (or to put it another way: of the autonomy of law, of the differentiation of the legal system). Accordingly, there is a juridical 'framing' of state-issued decisions and finally a juridical concept of the state as a point of reference for all decisions that are supposed to be collectively binding from the perspective of the political system. Seen from the perspective of

---

[29] See also Niklas Luhmann, 'Zwei Seiten des Rechtsstaates', in *Conflict and Integration—Comparative Law in the World Today: the 40th Anniversary of The Institute of Comparative Law in Japan Chuo University 1988* (Tokyo, 1989), 493–506.

[30] See most importantly A. V. Dicey, *Introduction to the Study of the Law of the Constitution*, 10th edn. (London, 1968), 182, with a rather more national interpretation 'peculiar to England, or to some countries which like the United States of America have inherited English traditions'.

[31] See *The Theory and Practice of Modern Government*, rev. edn. (New York, 1949), 922.

[32] First quoted in Marbury vs. Madison I. Cranch (1803), Supreme Court (USA), pp. 137–80. See also Fritz W. Scharpf, *Grenzen der richterlichen Verantwortung. Die Political Questions Doktrin in der Rechtsprechung des amerikanischen Supreme Court* (Karlsruhe, 1965); 'Judicial Review and the Political Question: A Functional Analysis', *Yale Law Review* 75 (1966), 517–97.

the legal system, decisions have this effect only if they are lawful and not in contravention of law.

The German doctrine of *Rechtsstaat*, especially, has rarely dealt with politics in the original meaning of the word or with the problems associated with the constitutional democratization of politics. Instead, it has stressed the protection of individual rights and the legal binding of the executive. Hence we find in one leading textbook (and this is the only place where the topic is discussed according to the index): 'A state in which the competences of the executive are legally bound and can only be exercised according to statute is defined as a *Rechtsstaat*.'[33] Consequently, the German understanding of the *Rechtsstaat* has been said to be academic and out of touch with political power, to think in narrow confines, and even to show little concern for the democratization of the political system.[34] This may be related to the necessity in the nineteenth century of making the idea of the *Rechtsstaat* acceptable to conservative circles.[35] With hindsight this remarkable political abstinence in dealing with the concept of the state could also be interpreted as the legal system simply elaborating further its own point of view.

The political system operates on an altogether different terrain. It tries to bring together opinions in such a way that collectively binding decisions can be made. It searches in the medium of the politically possible for political criteria of a form through which politics can solve problems, and that means, get the problems out of the system. Thanks to its equation of positivity with changeability, law provides a possibility for legal form-fixing and depoliticizing problems. It ensures that matters continue to be handled under specific legal criteria, even if politics has in the meantime moved on to other issues. According to accepted opinion, this shift takes place in parliament. However, it also takes place with local government ordinances and, increasingly importantly, in international public law which binds domestic law. In all these cases, it does not follow from the political function of collectively binding decision-making that the decisions are lawful and not illegal. This can be tested in advance and, in fact, this is increasingly being done. Such a test is, however, an internal operation of the legal

---

[33] See Georg Meyer, *Lehrbuch des deutschen Staatsrechts*, 6th edn., ed. Gerhard Anschütz (Leipzig, 1905), 27. In a note we find the comment with references: 'This is the meaning of the word as it is used in modern times'. It appears that the great debate on the rule of law in the nineteenth century was only concerned with the question whether the review of the activities of the executive should be delegated to the ordinary courts or to special administrative courts.

[34] See Ulrich Scheuner, 'Begriff und Entwicklung des Rechtsstaates', in Hans Dombois and Erwin Wilkens (eds.), *Macht und Recht: Beiträge zur lutherischen Staatslehre der Gegenwart* (Berlin, 1956), 76–88, esp. p. 80, in contrast to the legal traditions of England, France, and Switzerland.

[35] See Dieter Grimm, *Recht und Staat in der bürgerlichen Gesellschaft* (Frankfurt, 1987), 298.

system, no matter in which institutional or organizational framework it is executed. And it is fair to assume that the political system mistakenly makes illegal decisions or that it—as is frequently the case—takes legal risks. Risk-taking is, however, a good indicator of the fact that system boundaries are being crossed.

Seen from the perspective of the legal system, the *Rechtsstaat* formula is a grandiose tautology (to quote again: 'the law and the rule cover the same ground'), albeit a tautology defiantly directed at political transgressions. Seen from the perspective of the political system, law is an instrument for the facilitation and realization of political goals.[36] The terms 'facilitation' and 'realization' indicate that the political system would not exist in its known form, if the legal system did not offer a difference between medium and form, in which prevailing legal forms can be established and changed on the basis of political initiative. Even though law functions autonomously in this respect and does what it does by itself, it is still the most important imaginable precondition for the making of politics, apart from money coming from the economy. Making politics means deciding politically which law is to be valid law (or, parallel to this, how to spend politically allocated funds). Without this, politics as a system would collapse. It would not be worth building up a massive apparatus of political parties and pressure groups if the only decisions that mattered were how and for what purpose to use physical force. Politics owes the vast expansion of its field of possibilities to law and money. Even the self-representation of politics, political rhetoric, the portrayal of good intentions and the opposition's bad deeds, are all born of the same source.

The *Rechtsstaat* formula is used by the legal system to describe only itself. Therefore it is a fitting description. The reference to the state in the concept of *Rechtsstaat* indicates that the law (especially private law), can develop only if peace is secured politically, that is, if violence can be prevented. There is a good reason to point this out now in view of the situation in many parts of the world and especially in the big cities of the American continent. There is also another, contradictory context in which breaches of law and political corruption can maintain social order, albeit at a reduced level.

For the political system, which defines itself as the state, the *Rechtsstaat* formula expresses a further precondition for increasing complexity. Law, as the enforcement of politics, is only available if and in so far as the political

---

[36] This is, on the one hand, the subject of so-called implementation research and, on the other hand, with a somewhat broader perspective, the subject of a discipline which calls itself 'legal politology'. See, for example, Rüdiger Voigt (ed.), *Recht als Instrument der Politik* (Opladen, 1986), and the Yearbook of Legal Politology since 1987 (Jahresschrift für Rechtspolitologie). Currently the discussion seems to be bogged down in conceptual ambiguities, which relate to the concept of 'steering' (political guidance).

system lets law be law and defers to it, and does not apply force illegally. Consequently, the *Rechtsstaat* formula means different things, depending on which system is using it. However, it expresses these different aspects in one formula, or—as it can then be said—in one schema and by that it enables its definition. Hence it is possible to assert that the political and the legal systems would not be what they are without each other.

To sum up, one might say that the *Rechtsstaat* formula expresses a reciprocal and parasitical relationship between law and politics. The political system benefits from the difference between legal and illegal being coded and administered elsewhere, namely in the legal system. Conversely the legal system benefits from having peace, a clear differentiation of authority, and with it the enforceability of decisions, secured elsewhere, namely in the political system. In this context parasitical, then, merely means the possibility of growing out of an external difference.[37]

III

Functional differentiation frees up functioning systems to determine their own conditions and structures. This also means that system-specific time frames develop. The question of what is recalled or anticipated and in what time period varies from system to system. The same applies to the expected speed of linking communication to communication and to the corresponding distinction of urgent and less urgent. These differences are identifiable where communications are organized. They occur as well, rather drastically, in time frames that cross organizations. The speed with which the economy reacts to price changes with more price changes is in remarkable contrast to the slowness with which science puts forward new research findings—the latter being an area in which interplay between the long-term and the surprise event tend to dominate the orientation.

This general problem of temporal disharmony in modern society is of particular significance for the relationship between law and politics. In the modern political system politics are under considerable time pressure— and this applies to an almost unlimited range of objective topics (but limited by politics itself). Politics reacts with acceleration and delay, by managing this difference with the insider knowledge of it and its dependence on power. In contrast, the legal system is very slow, as far as its jurisdiction is concerned, being held back by the need to demonstrate accuracy and substantiation. This applies not only to decision-making but also, above all, to structural consequences, to the changing of law through judicial activity. Building up through experience concepts and rules that are available for transmission takes centuries. The range of topics here is

---

[37] See Michael Serres, *Der Parasit* (Frankfurt, 1981).

equally broad, and the repetition of similar cases decreases with increasing complexity. If a comparison had to be made between the self-inspiration of politics, accelerated by the mass media, and the development of judge-made law, the time discrepancies would be huge. Contact between the systems would cease for reasons of time alone.

This is, of course, not permitted when the law is one of the most important, formative elements of politics and, at the same time, other functioning systems constantly confront the political system with new situations, which require speedy decisions. This is the situation in which legislation comes to the rescue as an important mechanism for balancing societal time-differences. Given sufficient political pressure, legislation can be initiated and completed relatively quickly. As far as the political system is concerned, the passing of a statute (that is, the activation of the legal system in a politically desired direction) is a symbol of the success of one or other dominating faction. The legal system can mobilize little resistance to new statutes. They are new law and it is not a question of dealing with law's own experiences or of transforming law that has proven the test of time. The acceleration device of using legislation (that is, its use or non-use) obviously depends on not knowing and not being in a position to know what will happen to the statute in legal practice.[38] The legislature has its own ideas about the 'outcomes' of a statute; but these are ideas and not information. The basic condition behind all acceleration applies here too, namely that the future cannot be known.[39]

The factor of time guides and falsifies the observation and description of systems to a high degree. There is, especially in the age of mass media, a preference for attention to be focused on novelty. Everyday life is not being reported. Hence we do not know anything about the effects of statutes after they have been passed (unless special studies have been carried out or we have some specific knowledge of local milieux). Nor do we know who does not use the creative potential of a new statute. We are constantly hearing of new statutes. Therefore we cannot be blamed for perceiving the legal system

---

[38] The same applies *mutatis mutandis* to leading decisions in higher courts. These decisions, too, are mobilized by the lack of information about what the actual outcomes will be—and become the object of 'impact studies'. See Stephen Wasby, *The Impact of the United States Supreme Court: Some Perspectives* (Homewood, 1970), and also the examples discussed by Robert L. Kidder, *Connecting Law and Society: An Introduction to Research and Theory* (Englewood Cliffs, 1983), 112. For a case study see Gordon Partic, 'The Impact of a Court Decision: Aftermath of the McCollin Case', *Journal of Public Law* 6 (1957), 455–64 (concerning scripture classes in public schools), or James Croyle, 'The Impact of Judge-Made Policies: An Analysis of Research Strategies and an Application to Products Liability Doctrine', *Law and Society Review* 13 (1979), 949–67.

[39] This observation leads to the assumption, which can only be noted here, that modern society's relationship with its future has a lot to do with the increase and acceleration of structural changes that are visible to this society itself.

principally from the viewpoint of legislation or even assuming a hierarchical relation between legislation and judicial decision-making.[40] This in turn has led to there still being 'optical' difficulties in seeing the political system and the legal system as separate systems. It could be one of the tasks of the sociology of law to correct this optical illusion. This would not mean denying the interdependence between the systems or dismissing them as unimportant. On the contrary, more specific forms of a description must be found, which express much more clearly how and why politics and law are so well attuned to each other in modern society, therefore triggering structural drifts in both systems (although in very different forms). Here it may be helpful to put forward the thesis that legislation, as the place for the transformation of politics into law and for the control of politics by law, has assumed the important function of balancing the different time frames for society.

This view from the top down can be complemented by a view from the bottom up.[41] Even what is perceived from a juridical perspective as the application of statutes is practised by the administration more as goal-oriented, problem-solving behaviour.[42] Especially since the massive expansion of public administration to cover social welfare tasks and, more recently, ecological tasks, it is decreasingly a question of legal problems occurring from case to case, and increasingly one of conditions which are the subject of attempted influence or change. Such conditions include the cleanliness of water and air, industrial development, truancy and alcoholism, traffic control or its reduction. If we observe these conditions from a legal perspective, the issue is not individual breaches of law but a permanent deviance, as it were, or conditions under which breaches of law are repeated on a daily basis. Time is relevant here, too, and in a way for which the legal system has no equivalent categories.

Hence public administration's contacts with persons who are concerned, whose behaviour is supposed to be influenced, develop their own criteria for measuring success or failure. Such contacts are established in order to be repeated. In the process, moral criteria emerge for what can be demanded and for mutual respect, for the conditions and limits of cooperation, and for the extent of mutual understanding. Only when tensions or cracks occur in the network of this reasonable cooperation is resort had to law, to explicit instructions concerning what can be legally enforced or not. Here, like everywhere else, law serves as a safety net in the event of the

---

[40] We pre-empted the criticism of such an assumption above in Ch. 7.

[41] This is a demand made by studies in the sociology of organizations which are oriented towards the processes of decision-making; see, for example, Colin S. Diver, 'A Theory of Regulatory Enforcement', *Public Policy* (1980), 247–99.

[42] See, for excellent socio-legal analyses Keith Hawkins, *Environment and Enforcement: Regulation and the Social Definition of Pollution* (Oxford, 1984).

breakdown of primary relations. The transformation may occur for reasons that appear to be quite irrelevant juridically, and often with motives that cannot be revealed—for instance, because of a lack of mutual respect (the status differences between bureaucrats and their clients can especially aggravate sensibilities). But motives are not arguments. They remain latent before and after juridification and can be understood, at best, by a sociological analysis.

Moreover, bureaucracies are largely aware of the fact that law enforcement can have far-reaching political repercussions if it is directed at interests that can be represented politically. Local industry or farmers, wine-producers or fishermen, can demand consideration for their equally demonstrable interests even after the legislator has made a decision, the consequences of which are unpredictable. And government is well advised to develop sensitivity for such situations, especially in cases in which the connection between a violation of the law and harm cannot be ascertained immediately or only with the help of artificial tests. Hence there exists a kind of secondary chain of command for the lowest tiers of bureaucracy, 'street level bureaucracy'. This operates through the media or influential stakeholders, and protective strategies must be developed in the form, above all, of written reports or paperwork, which may ensure that nothing happens if something happens.[43] While juridically a tight connection, dealing only with issues of evidence and interpretation, is forged between legislation and law enforcement, politically the horizons between these two levels of decision-making are wide open.

In view of this state of affairs it would obviously be missing the point if the essence of administration were thought to reside in the application of laws. We no longer live in early modern times when all administrative matters were in the hands of local courts. The binding of government by law, the result of nineteenth-century developments, is not at issue, even though it could only offer the possibility of resorting to law if difficulties arose. Even modern analyses which research the 'implementation' of formally enacted programmes and lament their deficiencies or find typically flawed, bureaucratic behaviour are often guided by the prejudice that statutes must be 'implemented'. Government and public administration, however, is from top to bottom an organization of the political system. It realizes politics, not law—even though the question may be asked at any time whether

---

[43] This is documented particularly well by police studies, see, for example, Jonathan Rubinstein, *City Police* (New York, 1974); Michael S. Brown, *Working the Street: Police Discretion and the Dilemmas of Reform* (New York, 1981); David E. Aaronson, C. Thomas Dienes, and Michael C. Musheno, *Public Policy and Police Discretion: Processes of Decriminalization* (New York, 1984). See for other areas also Richard McClary, *Dangerous Men: The Sociology of Parole* (Beverly Hills, 1978), esp. 145, or Jeffrey M. Prottas, *People-Processing: The Street-Level Bureaucrats in Public Service Bureaucracies* (Lexington, 1978).

this is lawful or unlawful. With this question, however, communication changes its system reference.

IV

We could test theses on the separation, on the one hand, and intensification, on the other, of contacts between the political system and the legal system empirically by examining the political influence of lawyers. Any such studies would, however, have to be carefully guided by theory and would, above all, have to be advanced on the operative level and not only on the personal level. There is a difference between whether lawyers are particularly suited to political careers by virtue of their legal education and legal practice, and whether they can then actually operate as lawyers in political contexts, that is, observe the attribution of decisions to the values of legal and illegal.

There is a widespread assumption, but not much hard evidence, that politics is practically the domain of lawyers. People point to the so called 'lawyers' monopoly' in careers in government administration or to the fact that influential lobbyists in Washington are represented by (influential) legal firms.[44] This still does not explain, however, on which type of skills this influence is based and on which functioning system it impacts. It is recognizable that lawyers, who are used to adversarial negotiations based on (professional) recognition of the opposite party, have a more open relationship with politics than other professionals.[45] Still, that does not necessarily mean that their possible influence on politics is based on a legal leverage over political issues. It may be that, as in other management positions or in the preference of certain businesses for certain lawyers or law firms, social skills, the capacity to stand one's ground in face-to-face interaction or on the phone, local knowledge, organizational skills—including being known in the right places—are more important than legal knowledge itself. It may be and certainly often is the case that legal issues project the claims of the politically possible and that one needs legal expertise for argumentation and decision-making if one ventures across its boundaries. However, even then it is still a political question what legal risks one is prepared to take.[46] We should note that lawyers can use their ability to talk and

[44] See, for example, the report of one such lawyer, Charles Horsky, *The Washington Lawyer* (Boston, 1952). See also Heinz Eulau and John D. Sprague, *Lawyers in Politics: A Study in Professional Convergence* (Indianapolis, 1964).

[45] See Elmar Lange and Niklas Luhmann, 'Juristen—Berufswahl und Karrieren', *Verwaltungsarchiv* 65 (1974), 113–63, at 156.

[46] The report of the German commission for the reform of public service law (*Studienkommission für die Reform des öffentlichen Dienstrechts* (Baden-Baden, 1973), with 11 volumes of appendices) could provide good material for a case study. In keeping with the name of the commission, it was concerned with legal issues and, indeed, a great number of reports by legal

communicate about legal and political issues in a succinct and competent manner and that they can prevent politics from getting bogged down needlessly in such issues. But we should also note that something entirely different is actually involved here.

Research into legal firms in Washington shows that their influence on politics is overestimated.[47] Wealthy clients can undoubtedly seek the services of 'better' law firms, but it remains to be seen whether their influence is based on their legal argumentational skills (if the case proceeds that far) or to the political importance of the client.[48] This also indicates that the use of lawyers for political contacts is connected to the political system rather than to the legal system and does not, at any event, require any particular legal expertise. Empirical studies demonstrate a considerable discrepancy between professional self-description and the actual operation of networks of contacts.[49] This should not, however, lead us to conclude that lawyers cannot distinguish between political and legal issues. With analyses of networks of contacts, obvious political one-sidedness can also be seen, which cannot be the result of pursuing legal matters but demonstrates non-juridical self-selection, so contradicting the image of the impartial lawyer.[50] Hence the mere status of a lawyer is not a reliable indicator of whether a communication is operating more in the political system than in the legal system. In any event, no lawyer could operate successfully in this domain if she were not able to distinguish between legal and political issues or if she relied on the misconception that political problems could be solved as legal problems.

Another possible way to test the hypothesis of the separation of the systems empirically would be to analyse important doctrinal inventions and to ask whether and in what circumstances they could have even appeared on the political agenda in the party-political system. Take, for instance, agency by estoppel, which is based on someone giving the appearance, or tolerating,

experts were commissioned in order to explore the constitutional scope for reforms (institutional guarantees for career public servants, etc.). However, the appointment of the commissioners was politically pre-selected, and the commission's recommendations were almost exclusively concerned with structural and organizational issues.

[47] See Robert L. Nelson and John P. Heinz, 'Lawyers and the Structure of Influence in Washington', *Law and Society Review* 22 (1988), 237–300. The summary notes: 'the findings indicate that lawyers occupy a relatively specialized niche in the system of interest representation, one that allows them to command substantial economic rewards and to maintain a measure of independence and autonomy in their work, but that limits their influence in policy formation.'

[48] See Robert L. Nelson et al., 'Private Representation in Washington: Surveying the Structure of Influence', *American Bar Foundation Research Journal* 1 (1987), 141–200.

[49] See Edward O. Laumann and John P. Heinz et al., 'Washington Lawyers and Others: The Structure of Washington Representation', *Stanford Law Review* 37 (1985), 465–502.

[50] See Nelson and Heinz, 'Lawyers', 290.

or not recognizing (three variants!), that someone else is authorized. Or take *culpa in contrahendo*, which makes litigation possible even when the agreed contents of a contract rule this out. It is highly unlikely that problems of this kind can be successfully turned into political problems at the moment of their discovery. It is likewise highly unlikely that the courts will desist from making their own law in these cases and refer them to the politically inspired legislator.

Despite everything that may be assumed by the image of a common state, there are so many differences on the operative level that the assumption of the operative closure of two separate systems is the better option. If one finds individual connections, one can explain them as coincidences of the internal modes of selection of two systems and, as such, as coincidental ones (regardless of how frequently they occur). However, this explanation must be factually supported by an internal analysis of the system; it cannot be included without being tested. Otherwise the theoretical concept would involve the counter-indicated case, namely its self-refutation.

V

After all, the irrefutable density of the contacts between politics and law does not allow us to talk of only one system. On the contrary, it can be assumed that any appropriate description requires references to two different systems.

This does not (and cannot) exclude individual operations from having both a political and a legal meaning for an observer. Passing a law in parliament can be counted as a political success, as it marks the end to lengthy efforts to achieve a consensus. At the same time it changes the state of validity of the law and serves as an instruction to courts and, beyond that, to everyone who wants to know what is legal and what is illegal in the appropriate context. The fact that an observer might recognize such an event as a unity says nothing about the unity of systems. As soon as one considers the recursive networking of operations with other operations, the unity of the individual act disappears. It is only a fictitious unity which disregards time, for the political history of the statute is entirely different from the legal situation on which the statute impacts and which has anticipated the possibility of such a change of law. Politically this is a history of 'talk',[51] of strategic positioning, of operations under the schema of government and opposition, of negotiations, of public declarations of intention and the secondary intention of testing public opinion, etc. Politically the matter comes to rest with a symbolic act of legislation and the possibility of a mention in the success stories of the party or government. This occurs, however,

[51] Again, as used by Brunsson, *The Organization of Hypocrisy*.

quite independently of the legal or actual effects of the legislation medi-ated by law.[52] Moreover, one has to consider the political relevance of the failure of a planned or proposed change of law, for which there is no equiv-alent in the legal system.

This non-identity of systems cannot be affected by the legal regulation of legislative procedure, even if it is carried out in a most detailed manner by either the legislators themselves or constitutional courts.[53] As legal regula-tion, it remains a structure of the legal system. It may stimulate or irritate political communication and be referred to as legal advice. But the possible exploitation of ambiguities in the law for political reasons remains a polit-ical risk, and a potential illegality is not relevant in itself, but is relevant only if it is, at the same time, an indication of political failure and point-scoring for the political opposition. The reason for the difference between the sys-tems is their autopoiesis, that is, the fact that each system defines the ele-ments that are allowed to operate within a network of operations, by the network of its *own* operations. If the classic doctrine of the state and its sovereignty takes a different form in law from the corresponding form expressed as a theory of politically based legislative positivism, each view must be observed as itself by observers of the systems and those views questioned—historically, for instance, in relation to the social system which lent at that specific time plausibility to such compact descriptions. The separation of systems is, however, irrefutable, if the description of systems theory as a theory of operatively closed systems is accepted.

System operations are identified separately because systems reproduce themselves and in so doing decide on their own boundaries. This occurs with the help of their own codes. In the political system, this is achieved by the distinction between superior power (authority) and those subordinate (the governing/the governed) and by the coding of authority by the schema government/opposition. In the legal system, coding is based on the quite different kind of distinction between legal and illegal. Accordingly,

---

[52] See, for example, the case study by Vilhelm Aubert, 'Einige soziale Funktionen der Gesetzgebung', in Ernst E. Hirsch and Manfred Rehbinder (eds.), *Studien und Materialien zur Rechtssoziologie*, Special Issue 11 of *Kölner Zeitschrift für Soziologie und Sozialpsychologie* (Cologne, 1967), 284–309. The study concerns the Norwegian legislation on housemaids, which brought political controversies to an end by its enactment, without having ascertained beforehand whether housemaids were indeed still employed in sizeable numbers and how, if there were any, they could be informed of their rights. For another case with politically in-built self-blocking of new law see Leon H. Mayhew, *Law and Equal Opportunity: A Study of the Massachusetts Commission Against Discrimination* (Cambridge, 1968). See also Niklas Luhmann, *Reform des öffentlichen Dienstes: Ein Beispiel für Schwierigkeiten der Verwaltungsreform* (1974), quoted from the reprint in: Andreas Renner (ed.), *Verwaltungsführung* (Berlin, 1982), 319–39.

[53] See Charles-Albert Morand, 'Les exigences de la méthode législative et du droit constitu-tionel portant sur la formation de la législation', *Droit et Société* 10 (1988), 391–406, with further references to literature on this topic.

the programmes which regulate the attribution of negative and positive values diverge. Correspondingly, the conditions for the recognition of belonging to the system within each system diverge as well, as do the connectivity within the same system and the identification of what is system and what is environment. If this ability to distinguish and refer to systems in this way did not exist, chaos and extreme simplification would result. Each legal decision, each conclusion of a contract would be a political action, just as, conversely, a politician could interpret and change the law by his communications alone and would therefore have to conduct himself with corresponding care.

The internal use of symbols for the unity of the system, within each system, differs as well. If belonging to the legal system is to be symbolized— even if, and especially if, changes to the law are concerned—reference is made to 'valid' law. We discussed this above (Chapter 2.VIII). Where the political system is concerned, the formula for identification is called the 'state'.[54] This also becomes particularly relevant if one wants to channel concerns for change in the direction of systems. This does not mean that the concept of state is not also a concept of valid law. However, if judges and police officers, teachers and medical officers are considered public servants, reference is made not only to the statutes which regulate the circumstances of their existence but also to the fact that their conduct can be made a political topic—in contrast to private medical practitioners or private 'bodyguards' scandals can only, if at all, lead to the political call for legal regulation, which has to be addressed, of course, to the state as well.

Looking back from this position to the traditional semantics of the state, the respective fissures between politics and law can be recognized, especially in the case of avoiding public unrest and turbulence, in which the internal peace of the country consists. Already the older doctrines of the state conceded to the prince that he could break the law or ignore breaches of the law in the interest of maintaining his power (and so the existing peace), and that meant breaking the law but without incrimination.[55] The doctrine was embedded in a context of ethical-natural law, in which the maintenance of peace (under the given circumstances) ranked highly, and even higher than occasional violations of the law. Even after the breakdown of such comprehensively legitimating semantics at the end of the eighteenth century the problem resurfaced. Already David Hume had commented: 'A single act of justice is frequently contrary to public interest; and were it to stand alone, without being followed by other acts, may, in itself,

---

[54] See Niklas Luhmann, 'Staat und Politik: Zur Semantik der Selbstbeschreibung politischer Systeme', in id., *Soziologische Aufklärung*, vol. 4 (Opladen, 1987), 74–103.

[55] See on this point Niklas Luhmann, 'Staat und Staatsräson im Übergang von traditionaler Herrschaft zu moderner Politik', in id., *Gesellschaftsstruktur und Semantik*, vol. 3 (Frankfurt, 1990), 65–148.

be very prejudicial to society.'[56] The absolute insistence on one's own rights is seen, if not as injustice, yet as a disturbance of the peace with horrible consequences—for instance, as demonstrated in the Kleist novella *Michael Kohlhaas*.[57] And in Friedrich Schlegel's 'Signatur des Zeitalters' (Signature of the Era) one can read: 'no form of peace which is based on continuous independence . . . can be imagined without a mutual give and take in the absolute demand of law.'[58] What was combined in the old moderate concept of justice had already fallen apart in the medieval early modern formula of *pax et iustitia*. Any remaining reference to unity was lost with the collapse of ethical-natural law argumentation and the development of monarchical autocracy to which it was addressed. The 'contradictions' established themselves as such, no matter how much the romantic period tried to avert this. The abduction of Erich Honecker in a Soviet military plane, in order to remove him from German justice, and the understandable protest from the German side (in March 1991) show that the problem has lost nothing of its relevance.[59]

This need not mean that the existence of contradictions is necessarily the last word on this issue. Switching from goals such as peace and justice to systems analysis, a far richer range of combined possibilities can be attained. The separation of systems can be seen as the precondition for the increase of interdependence, and society itself as a system as the precondition for the possibility of this. The democratization of the political system and the positivization of the legal system have only been able to develop by conditioning and stimulating each other. We will see in the next chapter that this cannot happen without both the separation of systems and a mechanism for their structural coupling.

[56] *A Treatise*, vol. 2, p. 201. One can easily understand this as a contradiction on the level of individual results while being compatible with recursively operating systems. For Hume, however, this meant only that the use of property had to be secured even if it contravened the public interest in individual cases.

[57] Kleist describes the hero of his novella in its first sentence as 'the most righteous and at the same time the most awful human being of his time'. On the romantic context and its relation with a forced new European schema law/non-law see Regina Ogorek, 'Adam Müllers Gegensatzphilosophie und die Rechtsausschweifungen des Michael Kohlhaas', *Kleist-Jahrbuch 1988/89*, 96–125.

[58] Quoted from the edition Friedrich Schlegel, *Dichtungen und Aufsätze* (Munich, 1984), 593–728, at 700. And ibid.: 'if there was an absolute insistence on law, each war would necessarily be a war of life and death'.

[59] Honecker was the last General Secretary of the (East German) Communist Party (Sozialistische Einheitspartei [SED]) before reforms were initiated under pressure of the Soviet Union in 1989, leading to German unification (note by the translator).

10   Structural Couplings

I

The more systems theory stresses the operative closure of autopoietic systems, the greater the need to establish how the relations between the system and its environment are shaped. Neither reality nor the causal relevance of the environment is denied (otherwise one could not even talk about difference, differentiation, etc.). Operative closure means only that the autopoiesis of the system can be performed only with its own operations. Hence the unity of the system can be reproduced only with the system's own operations. Conversely, the system cannot operate in its environment and hence cannot communicate with the environment by using the system's operations.

The advantage of this starting-point for theory construction is that it demands an unusual, as yet underdeveloped, amount of precision in propositions about the 'relations between system and environment'.[1] The response to this demand lies in the concept of structural coupling.[2] It is called this in contrast to operative couplings (couplings of operations with operations) and in order to distinguish it from the ongoing causalities that (and it can be put like this) ignore or disregard the boundaries of the system.

There are two variants for operative couplings. One is called autopoiesis. It involves the production of operations of the system by the operations of the system. The other is based on a synchronicity of the system and the environment, which must be presumed at all times. It allows an instantaneous coupling of the operations of the system with operations that the system attributes to the environment, for instance, with the possibility of fulfilling a legal obligation by making a payment or symbolizing political dissent or consensus by passing a law. However, operative couplings between the system and the environment brought about by such identifications are possible only for the duration of the event. They do not last and they depend on a certain ambiguity in their identification. The identity of such individual events is, in fact, always created in the recursive network of the individual system. The economic aspect of a payment, which relates to the reuse of money, is quite different from the legal aspect, which relates to the change in the legal situation induced by the payment.

---

[1] This is meant in a conceptual sense. What can be achieved by mathematics is an entirely different issue and presupposes the conceptual clarifications attempted here.

[2] See for this concept at the level of organic systems (cells and organisms) Humberto R. Maturana, *Erkennen: Die Organisation und Verkörperung von Wirklichkeit: Ausgewählte Arbeiten zur biologischen Epistemologie* (Braunschweig, 1982), 150 and 251; id. and Francisco J. Varela, *Der Baum der Erkenntnis: Die biologischen Wurzeln des menschlichen Erkennens* (Munich, 1987), esp. 85 and 251.

By contrast, coupling mechanisms are called structural couplings if a system presupposes certain features of its environment on an ongoing basis and relies on them structurally—for example, the fact that money is accepted, or that it could be anticipated, that people can find out what time it is. Hence structural coupling is a form, too, and a two-sided form at that, and that means it is a distinction. What it includes (couples with) is as important as what it excludes. Accordingly the forms of a structural coupling *reduce* and *so facilitate* influences of the environment on the system. Cells receive only a certain kind of ion through their membranes (for instance, natrium and calcium) and not others (such as caesium or lithium).[3] Brains with their eyes and ears are coupled with the environment only in a very narrow physical range of frequencies within a given band (and at any rate not by their own neurophysiological operations). And that is exactly why they sensitize the human organism to the environment to an improbably high degree. Reduction is a necessary condition for the ability to resonate; reduction of complexity is a necessary condition for building complexity.

How structural couplings separate and link systems at the same time can be understood by pointing to the distinction between *analog* and *digital* processing, which refers to the time dimension.[4] Systems grow older together in the same time frame without having to measure time and in this sense they age analogously. At the same time, however, they process their own temporal contexts digitally and correspondingly quickly or slowly, with longer or shorter references to the past or the future and with longer or shorter periods of what is constituted in the system as an individual event. Time passes for everyone in the same way, and that is a guarantee of the operative maintenance of structural couplings. At the same time, different distinctions can be brought to bear on this time with the consequence that legal proceedings, for instance, are often far too slow for the purposes of the economy (or politics) and can be in this respect nearly useless as a mechanism for decision-making.

Since the system is determined by its own structures and can digitalize— namely, particularize itself only by its own operations' events in its environment—regardless of which system they belong to—those events cannot intervene in the system in the form of 'inputs' for the purposes of their structural coupling. To put this differently, the system is not a transformation function, which always transforms inputs into outputs in the same way; nor does it do so when the system structures itself with the help of conditional

---

[3] See Maturana and Varela, *Baum der Erkenntnis*, 86.

[4] See for this distinction, for example, Anthony Wilden, *System and Structure: Essays in Communication and Exchange*, 2nd edn. (London, 1980), 155 and *passim*.

programmes.[5] As far as the system itself is concerned, structural couplings can only trigger irritations, surprises, and disturbances. The terms 'structural coupling' and 'irritation' are mutually inclusive.[6]

Irritation is also a form of perception within the system, but one that *does not have a correlate in the environment*. The environment is not irritated and only an observer can formulate the statement that 'the environment irritates the system'. The system itself registers the irritation—for instance, in the form of the problem of who is right if there is a conflict—only on the video screen of its own structures. Anomalies, surprises, and disappointments all presuppose expectations in which they can be reflected, and these are structures that result from the history of the system. The concept of irritation does not contradict the hypothesis of operative closure or deny that the system is determined by its own structures. Rather the concept presupposes the theory.

This then leads to the question of how a system can develop its ability to be irritated, how it can realize that there is something wrong. An internal preparedness is indispensable, for even irritations could not be recognized as such if they were not expected. Expectations, however, presuppose in turn that, in the case of a disturbance, there is the possibility of finding sufficiently quick solutions, which do not block out further operations, but rather suggest them.

The concept of irritation highlights the fact that coupled systems react to irritations *at different speeds* in spite of and especially because of structural coupling. The speed of the response depends on the structures of the system and therefore on the respective histories of the different systems. Hence structural coupling guarantees only the synchronicity of the system and the environment in a given event and not *synchronization*.[7] Similarly, waves of resonance can be of different lengths in coupled systems and of different complexity. Thus, even if, as we will demonstrate in the following discussion, the legal system is coupled with the political and the economic systems by highly specific devices (constitution, property, contract), there is no guarantee of time-invariant coordination. There is only the guarantee of sufficient specificity for the systems to surprise each other.

---

[5] This is a correction of my own earlier findings, see Niklas Luhmann, *Zweckbegriff und Systemrationalität* (reprint Frankfurt, 1973), 88; id., *Rechtssystem und Rechtsdogmatik* (Stuttgart, 1974), 25. However, there is no doubt that an *observer* can use the input/output model as a crudely simplified causal model in order to sort out facts. In the present text, however, a more complex theory is preferred.

[6] Competing conceptual pairs, which also attempt an explanation of the phenomenon of self-organization and learning of operatively closed systems, are assimilation/accommodation (Jean Piaget) or the above terms variety/redundancy (Henri Atlan). We cannot follow up on a more detailed comparison of the different theoretical approaches here.

[7] See for more detail: Niklas Luhmann, 'Gleichzeitigkeit und Synchronisation', in id., *Soziologische Aufklärung*, vol. 5 (Opladen, 1990), 95–130.

Structural coupling with its double effects of exclusion and inclusion makes it easier to focus irritability and to prepare, in the ambit of its possibilities, for what may happen. Only on such a basis can the system develop sensibilities, which nevertheless keep within the framework of manageable operations. As far as the brain and its derivative systems (personal systems, social systems) are concerned, even endogenously agitated systems develop, which are constantly irritated, above all when irritations fail to materialize. This too (indeed especially this) presupposes an indifferent coding in the system and seclusion from all the stimuli in the environment that are not delivered to the system by structural coupling.

In this sense the communication system that is society depends on a structural coupling with systems of consciousness.[8] Only when consciousness is involved (and not just chemical, biochemical, or neurophysiological processes) can society be affected by its environment. Only in this way is it possible to develop a high level of complexity in the operatively closed system of society, on the basis of communication. The operation of communication even contains a component which can only be realized in the form of surprise, namely information. The physical ending of life and consciousness would not irritate communication—it would terminate it.

The normative form of expectations is explicitly designed for surprises. It requires structural coupling of systems of consciousness and communication (but not their congruency) and is prepared for an incessant stream of disappointments of expectations flowing from it. In the form of law it provides immunity structures, which prevent ongoing disappointment from resulting in the annulment of the structures. This repeats and confirms what has been said about the function of law above. The development of law is a function of the social system in relation to a problem, which arises with the structural coupling of this system with its environment.

The situation changes with the differentiation of a specialized legal system to fulfil this function. Societal communication is still coupled with systems of consciousness and societal communication is still irritated by what may be going on in these systems. However, with the development of the legal system, an additional and new relation of system/environment arises within the social system, namely the relationship of the legal system with its environment within the social system. Communication also takes place within the legal system and the legal system, too, is irritated by systems of consciousness. But, in addition to all that, there arise opportunities for the legal system to develop new forms of structural coupling in relation to the social systems in its environment within the social system of society.

---

[8] See Niklas Luhmann, 'Wie ist Bewußtsein an Kommunikation beteiligt?', in Hans Ulrich Gumbrecht and K. Ludwig Pfeiffer (eds.), *Materialität der Kommunikation* (Frankfurt, 1988), 884–905; id., *Die Wissenschaft der Gesellschaft* (Frankfurt, 1990), 11.

No matter which way complexity can be increased, the norms of the environment are never delivered to the legal system by structural coupling. They only irritate. The form 'structural coupling' is not a normative topic; it is not something that can be prescribed. Even if those institutions which, seen from the perspective of law, perform such a prescriptive task—and we will discuss here property, contract, and constitution—and adopt a legal form, *they cannot do this in their function of structural coupling*. This function must be presupposed as given. Its design is at right angles to the operations that the system-internal structures (norms) develop and which are guided by those structures.

The general rule applies here as everywhere: as long as the legal system is directly exposed to the pressures of its environment within society, it cannot focus on particular disturbances. Then all possible pressures deform the law, either by ignoring it or by bypassing it, or they make the system declare legality illegal or illegality legal, as the case may be. Without structural coupling in the relations of the functioning systems of society with each other, law is corrupt in the modern sense of that term.

Corruption clearly has a pejorative meaning. One must, however, acknowledge that the issue is not simply the fight against corruption, the formulation of norms against corruption and their enforcement. The deeper-lying question is, rather, which structural couplings in relation to other sub-systems can replace corruption and can make it possible to reduce and at the same time increase, with the help of structural coupling, the influence of the environment on the legal system.

II

It is the form of differentiation that clearly determines which structural couplings are established by a society for linking its functioning systems and, at the same time, limiting such links. That is why structural couplings, which link the legal system with other functioning systems of society, do not develop until the functional differentiation of the social system is so far advanced that the separation and the cohesion of the functioning systems are one and the same problem and the paradox of the unity of a whole, which consists of parts, can be off-loaded on to structural couplings and thus be provided with a form. This theory can be tested empirically, if it can be shown that, in the course of functional differentiation, new mechanisms of structural coupling do in fact emerge.[9]

---

[9] Whether or not and how the newness of contemporary differentiations is seen or hidden is a second question. Especially in the eighteenth century the figure of 'natural law' was also used to conceal innovation, in constitutional law as well as in contract law. We shall analyse this in more detail in the following discussion.

As long as societies are differentiated segmentally (e.g. tribally), there seems to exist only the general mechanism of structural coupling of law and violence, which we described in the chapter on the evolution of law.[10] Normative expectations cannot be practised without a side-glance at their enforceability, and enforceability varies depending on who the groups of participants are. Compurgators (i.e. witnesses attesting to good or bad character) can testify to group membership (and only that). Property must be defended and law is one of the means by which this can be done. Hence one cannot see any specific problems as regards the structural coupling of law and economy. Property cannot be distinguished from family relations,[11] and contracts, if one can call them that, are embedded in general obligations within a framework of balanced reciprocal relations.[12] Even early Greek and Roman law showed signs of this. A special concept of property was largely dispensable because the concepts *oikos/familia* sufficed. And, apart from some highly formalized exceptions, contracts consisted of the transactions themselves and no legal problems were expected after the transactions had been executed, since social conventions evidently played a role here.[13]

Once societies have made the transition to a primarily stratified differentiation, structural couplings of this kind are found in the differentiation pattern itself, but they are limited in their effects. They provide the upper class with privileges—as in all things, also in access to law. The only question can then be how far real estate and accordingly 'old wealth', as a basis for political power on the one hand, can coexist with commercially, that is, quickly, acquired wealth, on the other. Law cannot decide this question, and consequently the one exceptional case, namely Roman civil law, in which legal development took place independently of this question, is quite remarkable.[14] The regulation of interaction between social classes was primarily a question of household economy (including farming), and accordingly this institution of the 'whole household' carried the main weight

---

[10] See above Ch. 6.IV.

[11] See Max Gluckman, 'African Land Tenure', *Scientific American* 22 (1947), 157–68; id., *The Ideas in Barotse Jurisprudence*, 2nd edn. (Manchester, 1972).

[12] See for an example T. Selwyn, 'The Order of Men and the Order of Things: An Examination of Food transactions in an Indian Village', *International Journal of the Sociology of Law* 8 (1980), 297–317.

[13] On the point of obligation without any formal, legally enforceable liability in the early Greek law see Fritz Pringsheim, *The Greek Law of Sale* (Weimar, 1950), 17. Pringsheim stresses, however, that the inference cannot necessarily be drawn that the recognition of informally consented contracts amounted to a legal institution.

[14] One can glean that from the development of the types of contracts which provided not only commercially relevant contracts but also non-monetary 'good offices' (for instance, *depositum, mandatum*) with plenty of possibilities for litigation and which only reluctantly incorporated foreign trade through a *ius gentium*.

of the structural coupling in this type of society.[15] Only the transition to functional differentiation created conditions for a structural coupling of the different functioning systems.

The premiss for this development appears to have been the differentiation of economic systems and the political system, which was not compatible with stratification. Until the Middle Ages, politics and economy both depended on the resource of real estate. Land represented a number of important features, such as (1) artificial and changeable partitioning; (2) permanency of holdings; (3) self-regeneration of income and income surpluses; (4) foundation for an intergenerational continuity of families; (5) vulnerability as far as violence is concerned but not as regards theft or fraud. The fusion of all these structural advantages in one institution explains the remarkable stability of the 'political economy' which depended on it. In the Middle Ages, however, the rapid process of erosion of this unity began with the fast development of the money economy. Land was now required as a security for credits, and this changed the legal forms of property and brought about the transferability of property.[16] The *conceptual* development of the legal institution of property was hampered, however, by the fact that in the economy of donations and grants in the Middle Ages the Church, but also secular rulers, had a vital interest in land and they accordingly built up competing jurisdictions and legal regimes. Nevertheless economic development, which cut across this conflict, circumvented it by shifting the economic interest from land to money and by valuing land purely economically, as a source of income and as a basis for credits.

Since the late Middle Ages, the problems of economic development (the money economy) have no longer been soluble at the level of territorial states.[17] Until the eighteenth century, phenomena were described on the basis of assumptions about the nature of mankind and were responded to with a 'mercantilist' policy of increased wealth of individual states. The autonomy of economic systems first became noticeable in (international)

---

[15] See the influential work of Otto Brunner, *Adeliges Landleben und europäischer Geist: Leben und Werk Wolf Helmhards von Hohberg 1612–1688* (Salzburg, 1949); id., 'Das ganze Haus und die alteuropäische Ökonomik', in id., *Neue Wege der Verfassungs- und Sozialgeschichte*, 2nd edn. (Göttingen, 1968), 103–27. For the preceding history see also Sabine Krüger, 'Zum Verständnis der Oeconomica Konrads von Megenberg: Griechische Ursprünge der spätmittelalterlichen Lehre vom Hause', *Deutsches Archiv für Erforschung des Mittelalters* 20 (1964), 475–561.

[16] See Robert C. Palmer, 'The Economic and Cultural Impact of the Origins of Property 1180–1220', *Law and History Review* 3 (1985), 375–96, at 386; see also id., 'The Origins of Property in England', *Law and History Review* 3 (1985), 1–50. See also Emily Zack Tabuteau, *Transfers of Property in Eleventh-Century Norman Law* (Chapel Hill, 1988), 80, for a transitional situation with the dominant motive of taking over land from insolvent debtors.

[17] See Immanuel Wallerstein, *The Modern World System*, vol. 1 (New York, 1974), on the development of an international division of labour.

trade. The flow of money, the procurement of work, the quality of products and wealth were subsequently seen as dependent variables. In so far as these variables had an effect on the finances of the king, which in turn provided him with political freedom of action, commerce could consequently be described as a 'politique exchange'.[18] However, the 'corruption' of the parliament in London by Walpole, which attracted widespread attention, made it clear that the influence of money on politics had to be ruled out and, instead, the influence of economic interests on law through property, corporatization, and freedom of contract had to be given more weight.[19] Everything depended on establishing and using proper channels. Only when this was more or less achieved, in the second half of the eighteenth century, was the essential non-identity of the economic and political systems recognized and accepted. And it is only in this context that institutions find a form, which makes a structural coupling of sub-systems possible.

Until the second half of the eighteenth century, when a specific economic perspective took hold, property and contract were still based on references to nature.[20] On closer inspection it is clear that the schema equal/unequal was used in both cases as the distinction which, as it were, operationalizes what nature requires. It was said of property that even if human beings were all created equally without any 'belongings', the development of society would lead to *inequality* for the sake of the greater good.[21] This inequality was explained partly economically (division of labour, reward for strength of motivation) and partly politically (necessity of the differentiation between government and governed). As far as the concept of a contract was concerned, the idea of the *equality* of the contracting parties was maintained, whereby this referred to the parties' equal freedom to make a deliberate decision (and not of course to the equal value of the assets they owned).[22] Not until the nineteenth century did questions arise in

[18] Edward Misselden, *The Circle of Commerce, Or, The Balance of Trade, in Defence of Free Trade* (London, 1623; reprint Amsterdam, 1969), uses this term at p. 98.

[19] Bolingbroke's 'Dissertation upon Parties' (quoted from *Works*, vol. II (Philadelphia, 1841; reprint Farnborough 1969), 5–172) shows that until then the British constitution had managed to deal with the medium of power (in the form of crown prerogatives and the exclusion of all rights to resistance) rather well, but had not dealt so successfully with the political use of the medium of money, which, according to Bolingbroke, had a more subtle and more deleterious long-term effect, because it cannot be fought openly with a revolution.

[20] For the evolution of these concepts in civil law see Ch. 6.III above on Roman law.

[21] See for references Niklas Luhmann, 'Am Anfang war kein Unrecht', in id., *Gesellschaftsstruktur und Semantik*, vol. 3 (Frankfurt, 1989), 11–64.

[22] See for instance Hugo Grotius, *De jure belli ac pacis libri tres*, 1.II. C.XII, § VIII (Amsterdam, 1720), 373: 'In contractibus natura aequalitatem imperat'. See also, but restricting this to onerous contracts, Samuel Pufendorf, *De officio hominis & civis juxta Legem Naturalem libri duo*, 1. I cXV, § III (Cambridge, 1735), 226. Natural equality most certainly had to be presupposed in theories on state and social contracts which tried to explain how it was possible to arrive at the institutionalization of inequality.

the socialist movement about how such freedom could be possible in view of the organization of manufacturing industries and the absolute dependence of the non-propertied classes on work. In the tradition of natural law and the economic theory following on from it, however, people were full of praise for a society that could combine the inequality of property and the equality of contracting parties. It was precisely this combination that was seen, in terms of old European semantics, as a sign of the justice of the social order.

However, there are a few other factors to be taken into account. Until the end of the eighteenth century, the free exploitation of market opportunities was not implied in the concept of property.[23] In the context of a 'civil society', the political connotations of the concept were still too strong. Even if property was no longer seen as an indispensable condition for winning political power, it was nevertheless assumed to be a citizen's only legitimate interest, as a justification for political participation by representation. As we will show in the following discussion, until around 1800 the legal institutions of property and contract were not regulated in such a way that they were able to couple with the economic system. But around that time a new concept of the constitution emerged, which impacted on the relation between the political system and the legal system. As long as the old class structures prevailed, no structural couplings were possible in the relation between the legal system and the political system. There existed only the recognition in law of the differences between the different social estates and the rule that in proceedings in which aristocrats clashed with burghers, the aristocrats won the case if the law or the facts were unclear.[24] Conflicts between the legal order and the already differentiated political authority were regulated in the legal form of a contract (or were in some cases interpreted as if they had been regulated long ago). The constitution replaced the semantic figure of the social or state contract, including the whole tradition of contractual arrangements of the 'Magna Carta' type.[25] Only then was one free to see that the old doctrines of social contracts had performed a grandiose tautological act, namely the creation of legal liability on the basis of the legal liability of contracts.[26]

---

[23] See for example, for the United States, Forrest McDonald, *Novus Ordo Seclorum: The Intellectual Origins of the Constitution* (Lawrence, 1985), 14.

[24] See Estienne Pasquier, *Les Recherches de la France*, new edn. (Paris, 1665), 577, for his report of a case in which the emperor solved the problem by ennobling a bourgeois and thus helped him win the case.

[25] Seen from this perspective the historical account of a movement 'from status to contract' (Maine) applies only, if at all, to private law but not to public law. It should be noted, however, that this distinction itself takes on its modern features only as a result of the development discussed here. See on this point Gerhard Dilcher, 'Vom ständischen Herrschaftsvertrag zum Verfassungsrecht', *Der Staat* 27 (1988), 161–93.

[26] See John Stuart Mill, *A System of Logic, Ratiocinative and Inductive*, 9th edn. (London, 1875), vol. II, p. 408 (Book V, ch. VII, § 2).

It is striking that both couplings, the one with property or contract, the other with the constitution, refer to the legal system, which is thus itself contributing to the differentiation of the economic and political systems. It was not clear until the twentieth century that there was also a structural coupling between the economic system and the political system. It can be seen in the institution of the reserve bank (which around 1800 was still hidden behind funding through credits taken up by states) and in taxes which make it possible to condition parts of the circulation of money with economic consequences politically (and that means unprofitably). But this topic lies beyond the present context of our analysis. We shall restrict the discussion to a presentation of the structural coupling between economy and law (III) and politics and law (IV).

III

When the law responds to economic demands and interests, it is already dealing with the economy at a secondary level. Law has its own concept of 'interests'—as we saw when we discussed the so-called jurisprudence of interests[27]—but this applies exclusively to the network of the law's own operations. Economic interests become 'homogenized' by those operations. They are divorced from their specific economic context (for example, from their monetary value) and abstracted in the form of pure interests. As such they are, then, sorted into legally protected/unprotected interests according to the legal code. This presupposes that the legal system and the economic system are structurally coupled in the sense expounded above but it does not explain how. The concept of interest, even more so than the concept of subjective rights,[28] points to the fact that the legal system has built up a highly sensitive reception and transmission station for economic news, but it does not say anything about the mechanisms which guarantee that a high level of mutual irritations in both systems can be absorbed. Sociology of law, which does its research only on this level in order to study the influence of economic interests on law or, conversely, the straitjacketing of economic interests by law, is missing the point of the constitutive relation between economy and law. Above all, it overlooks the social conditions that are necessary to make differentiation possible.[29]

[27] See above Ch. 8.VII and VIII.

[28] See for this comparison D. Neil MacCormick, 'Rights in Legislation', in P. M. S. Hacker and J. Raz (eds.), *Law, Morality and Society: Essays in Honour of H. L. A. Hart* (Oxford, 1977), 189–209.

[29] For research of this kind, the potential and successes of which should not be denied, the diffuse concept of 'relative autonomy' suffices, which then cuts off all further theoretical inquiry. See Richard Lempert, 'The Autonomy of Law: Two Visions Compared', in Gunther Teubner (ed.), *Autopoietic Law: A New Approach to Law and Society* (Berlin, 1988), 152–90; and above at Ch. 2.IV. If this were really to be an indispensable precondition for empirical research, its theoretical underpinning would be implied too. Any level of dependency or autonomy can be called 'relative'. The term does not exclude anything.

The problem lies in the differentiation and coupling of the autopoiesis of different functioning systems. The symbolically generalized medium of communication of money is the crucial precondition for the differentiation of a self-contained autopoietic economic system.[30] As soon as transactions can be balanced in terms of money and whenever this then happens, the complete and consistent repeat usability of money (in contrast to the poor or inconsistent or patchy repeat usability of goods or services) makes possible an autopoietic network, in which the possibility of paying can either be relinquished by making payments or, in the hands of others, be reproduced by payments. Whatever the reason why money was originally invented, it has its communicative meaning only in this nexus of payments. There must be a sufficiently broad range of opportunities for repeat use, that is, a large number of goods and services and, last but not least, markets, so that accepting money is worthwhile. Thereafter money payments are a clearly identifiable indicator of an operation of the economic system, irrespective of the milieu of the transactions that are paid for with money. What can be done without money is, accordingly, not part of the economic system—whether it is arduous digging in one's own garden or washing dishes in one's own kitchen, unless these are done to save the expense of personnel or machinery.

A differentiated money economy makes high but (and this is crucial!) *unpayable* demands on the law. In order to make the economy possible in the form of its own autopoiesis, law has to fulfil its own function, not that of the economy, effectively. Law must not belong to the type of goods or services that can be bought in the economic system. Otherwise there would be a vicious circle in the use of money, and the conditions which make money transactions possible would have to be transacted and paid for in their own right. This negative (and hence improbable) condition is met by mechanisms of structural coupling, which must be compatible with the separation of these systems and their respective operative closures. The formulae that were created to enable this to happen, are property and contract.

As with the legal system, there are minimal requirements for the autopoiesis of the economic system. These requirements must be able to survive changes of structure (for instance prices), if their autopoietic reproduction is to be continued. These are factual, not normative conditions. In the legal system, legal and illegal must be distinguishable and exclude each other. In the economic system, there must be scope to distinguish between who has and who does not have the disposition over certain goods (in the broadest sense, including money and services). Just as the legal code transcends all programmes as a precondition for the possibility of the conditioning of the system, the coding of the economy is a requirement, which must be compatible with every kind of distribution of goods, because otherwise goods would lose their character as goods.

---

[30] See for more detail Niklas Luhmann, *Die Wirtschaft der Gesellschaft* (Frankfurt, 1988).

Commonly this precondition for the possibility of economic conditioning is called 'property'. Property is a form of observation of objects based on a specific distinction, namely the distinction of various owners, regardless of whether this refers to ownership, or being in possession of something, or whatever. The meaning of property, therefore, lies in the *disjunction of the requirements for consensus*. In order to be successful in certain communications, the owner's consent matters, and *not somebody else's*. The substance of property law defines the area of communication, which is specified in this way, again by reference to certain things or in other ways. What is crucial is the disjunction of symmetry, to express this in the terms of systems theory.

It is a requirement of the *distinction* of owners that any form of violent expropriation be ruled out and possibly sanctioned by law.[31] This does not necessarily demonstrate a commitment to a definite legal concept. Rather, the observation scheme of property makes various forms possible in both the legal and economic systems. That is the reason why property is suited to the structural coupling of the economic and legal systems. The coding of the economic system constitutes the intrinsic values of that system and keeps the system running. It does that regardless of the question of which limitations of the concept of property are identified in the legal system, for example, whether it uses the classic concept of *persona/res/actio* (Digests 1.5.1), or, as in the present day, distinguishes between property law and the law of obligations. The economic system consolidates its code simply by using it and by the fact of the impossibility of matching distinctions, which would lead to the end of the economic system.

Hence property can only be properly understood as a mechanism of structural coupling with regard to its double significance in its position within the legal and economic systems, respectively. And, understanding it properly means seeing it from the perspective of society as the encompassing social system. The coupling turns operations of the economic system into irritations of the legal system and operations of the legal system into irritations of the economic system. But that does not affect the operative closure of each system. It does not alter the fact that the economic system is looking for profits or profitable investments under conditions which have been made more difficult by the legal system, and that the legal system is

---

[31] This has also applied since early modern times to expropriation in the public interest, which is legally permitted but differently constructed, for instance by reference to *dominium eminens*. The construction makes different demands here (closer to the paradox!) because a *legal* invasion is permitted, which is nevertheless a reason for compensation. Lawyers sorted this case out in the course of the seventeenth century (including the legal *obligation* for compensation). See Christoph Link, 'Naturrechtliche Grundlagen des Grundrechtsdenkens in der deutschen Staatsrechtslehre des 17. und 18. Jahrhunderts', in Günter Birtsch (ed.), *Grund- und Freiheitsrechte von der ständischen zur spätbürgerlichen Gesellschaft* (Göttingen, 1987), 25–233, at 221, for further references.

looking for just or, at any rate, sufficiently consistent decisions under conditions which have been made more difficult by the economic system. Classical theories of natural law, such as Locke's, have already shown quite clearly how property renders every legal order unfair but nevertheless gives economic advantages.

The mere guarantee of property alone is not in itself a mechanism that prepares the transition to a market ('capitalist') economy.[32] And, the economy must transform itself in order to deliver the material in terms of problems and cases, which can confront and irritate the legal system.

Leaving that aside, property still remains only as an initial distinction. Further, the status of a unit of property has to be distinguishable in its state before and after a transaction. Transactions require a distinction of distinctions (and not just a movement of objects). This distinction of distinctions must be capable of being stabilized over time, although (or precisely because) it is a temporal distinction itself. To put it more simply, it must be possible to ascertain and, over the course of time, remain able to ascertain, who the owner is before and after the transaction, and who is not. This form also has a legal name, namely 'contract'. In the economy it is called exchange. There is no term that is neutral, rather each use is partial, with respect to the system in which it is used. Here we have another mechanism of structural coupling, because the economic and legal systems would largely collapse (that is, would be reduced to dealing with residual property without the possibility of disposition over it), if the possibility of distinguishing distinctions did not work.

Autopoiesis is operations-based system dynamics and, in the context of structural coupling, dynamic stability. The differentiation of the economic system is not simply a matter of the shoring up of property—the prevailing interest in stratified societies—but is only possible through the recursive network of transactions, and this means only through money. This has the consequence that property, which is to be assumed as the basis in all transactions, must be measurable in money. Hence the secondary code of money dominated the primary code of property during the course of the differentiation of the economic system. As a capital investment, property increasingly became used as an asset in transactions or to offset a momentary lack of liquidity. This development removed the political relevance from land ownership as a form of political power based on local, municipal, or mayoral (oiketic) power, and brought about the shift to state taxes, which emerged at around the same time.[33]

---

[32] See on this point the contribution 'Capitalism and the Constitution', in Forrest McDonald and Ellen Shapiro McDonald, *Requiem: Variations on Eighteenth-Century Themes* (Lawrence, 1988), 183–94.

[33] See Joseph A. Schumpeter, *Die Krise des Steuerstaates* (1918), reprint in: *Aufsätze zur Soziologie* (Tübingen, 1953), 1–71. We can, at this point, only note again that taxes constitute one decisive element in the structural coupling of the political and economic systems.

These considerations take us on to a historical-dynamic analysis of the structural couplings of the economic and legal systems and thus to some research in legal history. The law responded slowly, with its own concepts and programmes, to the differentiation of an economic system based on money. One of the principal reasons for this slowness was the fact that until the full development of the modern state, law had to fulfil the political functions of property as well as other functions.[34] Landed property served above all to supply a class-based society with goods, which were required to satisfy demand as determined by birth. This led to different legal situations in relation to one and the same piece of land.[35] In the late eleventh century there was a special development in England which—whilst still within the framework of feudal law and legitimated by the supreme property of the king—attributed property individually, registered it in writing, and put it up for sale in a legal package.[36] It appears that it was exactly a strong regal authority, with its stake in raising revenue and controlling the administration of justice, which was the prerequisite for such a development. But similar, albeit more drawn-out, developments can be found on the Continent—even without the direct influence of Roman law![37] Conceptual adaptations did not occur until later—and then elsewhere than in law. Not until the late Middle Ages did the criterion of '*dispositio*', as used by Bartolus, penetrate the concept of property like a Trojan horse steered by the money economy,

---

[34] It did this, of course, with its own means and not by implementing political instructions. Thus *dominium* and *imperium* are distinguished, both being understood as hierarchically organized (and thus having an effect only from the top down and not supporting claims against the master). They are contrasted with the concept of *ius*, which is kept free of hierarchical asymmetries and expresses a reciprocal relation of rights and obligations. If *dominium* is called *ius* this is, on the one hand, a subsumption under the more general concept but also, on the other hand, a reference to limitations within the law. Political dispositions can only (and, in fact, must) bypass these legal barriers with special laws and derogation competences, that is, on the basis of a *ratio status* (reason of state).

[35] And this applied until early modern times. See principally Renate Blickle, 'Hausnotdurft: Ein Fundamentalrecht in der altstädtischen Ordnung Bayerns', in Günter, Birtsch (ed.), *Grund- und Freiheitsrechte von der ständischen zur spätbürgerlichen Gesellschaft* (Göttingen, 1987), 42–64; ead., 'Nahrung und Eigentum als Kategorien der ständischen Gesellschaft', in Winfried Schulze (ed.), *Ständische Gesellschaft und soziale Mobilität* (Munich, 1988), 73–93. At the same time, however, a demand also for the legal protection of the interests of disposition gained ground.

[36] See for a brief, recent summary of the latest research Carlo Rosetti, 'Diritto e mercato: Le origini del capitalismo moderno', *Rasegna italiana di sociologia* 33 (1992), 33–60. For more detail see Alan MacFarlane, *The Origins of English Individualism* (Oxford, 1978), Palmer, 'Economic and Cultural Impact'. See, for the onset of interest in a better *conceptual* precision, but not until the seventeenth century (because of print? as a result of the differentiation of interests of disposition?), G. E. Aylmer, 'The Meaning and the Definition of 'Property' in Seventeenth Century England', *Past and Present* 86 (1980), 87–97.

[37] See Hans Hattenhauer, *Die Entdeckung der Verfügungsmacht: Studien zur Geschichte der Grundstücksverfügung im deutschen Recht des Mittelalters* (Hamburg, 1969).

and change the concept from within. As absurd as this may seem at first glance, enjoyment and use (in the sense of *fruitio* and *usus*) of property may come precisely from the ability to relinquish it. This can only be understood through acquisition of the freedom to negotiate the conditions of a transaction. *Dispositio* refers to the structures of contract law, which, as juridical structures, are much more difficult to adjust.

While it took nearly 2,000 years for the concept of property to change in civil law and move towards distinguishing property and defining the disposition over property of individual owners, including their disposition of land, the dynamics of this process are much more pronounced in the hundred years of colonial history in the nineteenth and twentieth centuries. The often widespread forms of land use which were legitimated by custom and squatting became de-legitimated by the requirement that owners be named in writing in cases where the issues at stake concerned disposition, taxes, or loans.[38] This happened frequently even when owners had no particular use in mind and it resulted in land users of the old and the new order becoming squatters without any legal protection—which meant without access to the money economy. Structural couplings, as they were required, were then inclusive—but they were also exclusive.[39]

Similar observations can be made in relation to a development which could be called the juridification of contract. In contrast to the usual forms of reciprocity—from primitive societies to modern clientele arrangements—the inequality of the parties is not involved in the assessment of performance.[40] The legal validity of a contract does not depend on inequality, which is exactly why the contract is suitable as a mechanism for structural coupling.

The contract is one of the most important evolutionary achievements in social history. Without contracts, for instance, there would be no differentiated business organizations in the economic system. Thus one could hardly act rationally/economically.[41] But what is this all about—what is its achievement?

---

[38] See on the issue of writing (even if this is only a superficial phenomenon here) Jack Goody, *Die Logik der Schrift und die Organisation von Gesellschaft* (Frankfurt, 1990), esp. 252.

[39] Whether or not new legal orders arise from this uncoupling, which is not linked to state law, is a frequently discussed topic, especially with regard to the *favelas* in the big cities in Brazil. The supporting view appears to be too positive, especially in view of the current situation. See Boaventura de Sousa Santos, 'The Law of the Oppressed: The Construction and Reproduction of Legality in Pasargada', *Law and Society Review* 12 (1977), 5–126; Joaquim A. Falcão, *Justiça Social e Justiça Legal* (Florianopolis, 1982); also id. (ed.), *Conflito de Direito de Propriedade: Invasões Urbana* (Rio de Janeiro, 1984). For the reality, see the report of Amnesty International 1990 (Brazil).

[40] See, for example, Luigi Graziano, *Clientilismo e sistema politico: Il caso d'Italia* (Milan, 1984); Shmuel N. Eisenstadt and Luis Roniger, *Patrons, Clients and Friends: Interpersonal Relations and the Structure of Trust in Society* (Cambridge, 1984).

[41] See Dirk Baecker, *Die Form des Unternehmens* (Habilitation dissertation Bielefeld 1992), 193.

Contracts stabilize a *specific difference* over time while being *indifferent* to everything else, including the consequences of the contract for individuals and businesses not party to it. Indifference for difference's sake—that is the gain in form that is made by a contract. Its specific point of reference for observation is the difference which makes a difference, namely information.[42] Courts supervise this device for generating indifference, which is the main reason why the legal system was so reluctant to accede to the contract as long as there were no other instruments of control (namely the market).

No matter how little we know about old oriental commercial law, or think of it, synallagmatic (reciprocally obligating) contracts, as they are known today, are the result of 2,000 years of evolution of Roman civil law and, as is evident from the past, one of the most complicated ideas which lawyers have ever had to think through. It is especially remarkable that the problems relating to contracts of sale in the context of the law of property (transfer of property with protection against access of third parties) have been shifted to the framework of the law of obligations. At issue here is how disruptions and their consequences can be cushioned and defrayed with the help of a legal construction that can, eventually and with hindsight, be seen as a contract. In this way the concept of contract became relevant in relation to the cause (*causa*) of obligations and this situation, in the system, was diagnosed and observed by fully developed legal theories on contract.[43] The essential point was to deal fairly with deficiencies in the performance of reciprocal relations and in keeping with standard expectations of the conduct of parties in such situations.[44] So, initially, there was no general concept of contract; there only existed the question of which deficiencies of performance would yield the grounds for a claim in a particular contract, that is, how a liability in substantive law should be constructed as a basis for a decision. There was no general legal recognition of agreements without a legal form (*nudum pactum*)[45] in either ancient Greek or Roman law.[46] Moreover, there was no litigation over unperformed contracts of sale

---

[42] Experienced lawyers might add: in the hope that courts take note of this.

[43] See for example formulations in the treatise by Robert-Joseph Pothier, *Traité des Obligations* (1761), quoted from *Œuvres*, vol. 2, 3rd edn. (Paris, 1890), ch. 1, sect. I.I, which were crucial to the Code Civil and the common law.

[44] See for the common law, even in the eighteenth century, Peter Gabel and Jay M. Feinman, 'Contract Law', in David Kairys, *The Politics of Law: A Progressive Critique* (New York, 1982), 172–84, at 173. The authors point out how poorly the law corresponded to the requirements of economic development.

[45] See detail on this point, and contrary to a widely held older opinion, Pringsheim, *The Greek Law of Sale*, 13. There is, however, no doubt about the evolution towards forms which were easier to manage and towards a slowly spreading tendency to replace witnesses with written documents as a prerequisite for validity.

[46] Or more precisely: agreements without a legal form can *modify* existing contracts but not *cause* legal obligations.

before the invention of the civil law contract of sale in Roman law.[47] Until long after the Middle Ages, contract law remained a collective term for different forms of claim and types of contract, which all had their own names and special conditions. 'Causa' is, however, just another prospective expression for that. Contract is a 'conventio nomen habens a iure civili vel causa'.[48] Hence the modern-day adjustment of contract law to changing economic conditions has taken the form of a change in the understanding of cause. It is now seen as relating to the purpose of a contract and to the corresponding intention of the contracting parties to the extent that, in German common law for instance, only an expression of intent and the motives of the contracting parties matter, without there being any reference to a separate doctrine of cause. Now a contract is defined with extreme formality and is just a consensus between the contracting parties' expressions of intent.[49]

This development did not reach its conclusion until the nineteenth century. Obviously courts were extremely reluctant to surrender their legal, technical instruments, which they used to implement their decisions on how to deal fairly with defaulting performance after the signing of a contract. These instruments were eventually replaced with an interpretation of the contracting parties' expression of intent based on their presumed interests. The legal basis for this general development, which started in canon law and, eventually, made the purely consensual contract enforceable (but never the mere *nudum pactum* as a formally consensual expression of intent), eventually became the general rule of 'natural law' that one had to keep one's word (*fides*).

The corresponding development in the common law was less consistent. It is remarkable proof of the autonomy of the evolution of law that an economically less developed territory such as the German empire drew more radical conclusions than the commercially more progressive England with its market economy. This can be explained, above all, by the fact that crucial limitations on freedom of contract were not the result of a lack of private

---

[47] See on this point Fritz Pringsheim, 'Gegen die Annahme von "Vorstufen" des konsensuellen Kaufes im hellenistischen Recht', in: id., *Gesammelte Abhandlungen*, vol. 2 (Heidelberg, 1961), 373–81; id., *L'origine des contrats consensuels*, 179–93. The reason for this delayed development may have been the fact that alternatives were available. One could transform a not immediately paid sales price into a loan (with possible interest).

[48] Thus Pothier, *Traité des Obligations*, rejecting this meaning of *causa*.

[49] It should be noted, however, that Roman law (and presumably rather early, namely in late republican times) defined the contract extremely formally, but basing it on a quite different distinction, namely the distinction between *contrahere* and *solvere*. The digests quote Pomponius from the *Libro quarto ad Quintum Mucium*: 'Pro ut quidque contractum est, ita et solvi debet' (D 46.3.80). The 'quidque' should be noted. Nevertheless, this abstraction was compatible with limitation on the admitted types of contracts and with uncertainty about the contracting parties' expressed intentions.

law instruments but of regulation by the authorities of land transactions, manufacturing, commerce, and service obligations. The solution in Germany, initially, was a cautious generalization of privilege.[50] In England limitations were removed earlier than in continental Europe.[51] So differences in the law of contract could not have had a great impact at first. In the common law, they may have been the result of the stronger position of the courts, which tried to maintain their traditional instruments of control, but they are also certainly related to the lesser importance of academic legal education and doctrinal texts. The development of the legal institution of contract began in the Middle Ages, in parallel with commercial development. Issues relating to a violation of law were moved from tort law to contract law, which had avenues for litigation.[52] At the end of the sixteenth century, the doctrine of consideration introduced a factor of motivation into contract law, namely the binding promise in view of a fulfilled or expected mutual performance.[53] Even Hume, who distanced himself from the concepts of jurisprudence with a progressive concept of contract in the context of his theory of the historical development of society, still postulated 'that *delivery,* or a sensible transference of objects is commonly required by civil laws, and also by the laws of nature'.[54] Not until the

---

[50] See Diethelm Klippel, ' "Libertas commerciourum" und "Vermögens-Gesellschaft": Zur Geschichte ökonomischer Freiheitsrechte in Deutschland im 18. Jahrhundert', in Günter Birtsch (ed.), *Grund- und Freiheitsrechte im Wandel von Gesellschaft und Geschichte: Beiträge zur Geschichte der Grund- und Freiheitsrechte im Wandel von Gesellschaft und Geschichte vom Ausgang des Mittelalters bis zur Revolution von 1848* (Göttingen, 1981), 313–35.

[51] See Gerald Stourzh, *Wege zur Grundrechtsdemokratie: Studien zur Begriffs- und Institutionsgeschichte des liberalen Verfassungsstaates* (Vienna, 1989), 31. He describes this development with the fitting term 'fundamentalization' (in contrast to the legal term of 'constitutionalization') of individual rights in the common law with the consequence that invasions were not only against the law but also raised public and political concerns. See also Dieter Grimm, 'Soziale, wirtschaftliche und politische Voraussetzungen der Vertragsfreiheit: Eine vergleichende Skizze', in id., *Recht und Staat der bürgerlichen Gesellschaft* (Frankfurt, 1987), 165–91.

[52] This can be gleaned from the history of the action of *assumpsit.* See, for a discussion of the starting point of this development and its duration, William M. McGovern, 'The Enforcement of Informal Contracts in the Later Middle Ages', *California Law Review* 59 (1971), 1145–93.

[53] See for detail A. W. B. Simpson, *A History of the Common Law of Contract: The Rise of the Action of Assumpsit* (Oxford, 1975; new edn. 1987), esp. 316. In contemporary law, consideration is understood to comprise all conditions that make a promise enforceable. The concept, therefore, is open to its extension by new, case-related insights. See Melvin Aron Eisenberg, 'The Principles of Consideration', *Cornell Law Review* 67 (1982), 640–65. For comparisons with the development in continental European law, especially the doctrine of *causa,* see above all Max Reibstein, *Die Struktur des vertraglichen Schuldverhältnisses im anglo-amerikanischen Recht* (Berlin, 1932); also Eike von Hippel, *Die Kontrolle der Vertragsfreiheit nach anglo-amerikanischem Recht: Ein Beitrag zur Considerationenlehre* (Frankfurt, 1963). The reason for this doctrine was most probably the suspicion of lawyers about donations.

[54] See David Hume, *A Treatise of Human Nature,* Book III, Part II, Sect. IV, quoted from the Everyman's Library edition (London, 1956), vol. II, p. 218.

beginning of the nineteenth century did English law recognize contracts as completely oriented to the future, that is, not prejudiced by any created or assumed facts but exclusively based on the intent of the contracting parties.[55] It was not until then that English law recognized the legally constructed substitute for the old contract doctrines of legal action, namely that a contract is created by the accord of two expressions of intent, by offer and acceptance.[56] Only then were there *time-binding* contracts, *which were enforceable even if neither of the contracting parties had made any dispositions out of reliance on the contract.* And only then did the law of contract become a sizeable topic fit for presentation in a textbook.[57]

The structural coupling of economy and law achieved its modern (if not perfect) form with the institutionalization of freedom of contract. The economy can arrange transactions without having to consider a tight net of types of contract.[58] Concerning legal issues it can focus on the respecting or circumventing of prohibitions. Conversely, the legal system gains the freedom to interpret the intentions of the contracting parties *ex post facto*, to infer something not expressly considered in the contract,[59] to add more contractual elements through 'supplementary interpretation' or to disqualify them with reference to 'contra bonos mores' (§§ 157, 138 BGB), and to codify the results of such case-law regulation, for example, in the annotations to § 242 of the German civil code (BGB). In this way, control can largely be regained which was surrendered with the concession to 'freedom of contract'. This solution passed its crucial test in the economic crises following the First World War. The courts adapted contracts to economic conditions on a large scale—for instance by equating the concept of 'economic impossibility' with 'impossibility of performance'.[60] Seen from the perspective of the legal system, the contract is and remains a form for obligations,

---

[55] See Philip A. Hamburger, 'The Development of the Nineteenth-Century Consensus Theory of Contract', *Law and History Review* 7 (1989), 241–329. This is also a good analysis of an evolution that is conditioned by its own internal problems, rather than by external expectations of adaptation.

[56] See Patrick S. Atiyah, *The Rise and Fall of Freedom of Contract* (Oxford, 1979), esp. 419.

[57] See for the United States see Lawrence M. Friedman, *Contract Law in America: A Social and Economic Case Study* (Madison, 1965), 17.

[58] Sociologists of law love to dwell on this aspect of ignoring the law; see, for example, Stewart Macauley, 'Non-contractual Relations in Business: A Preliminary Study', *American Sociological Review* 28 (1963), 55–67.

[59] See Jay A. Sigler, *An Introduction to the Legal System* (Homewood, 1968), 35. The author adduces the example that risk control, in relation to harm inflicted by workers on each other during work, is an obligation of the employer in the sense of the work contract, even though this is not expressly stated in the contract (in the development of the common law in England and the United States in the nineteenth century).

[60] See Josef Esser, 'Argumentations- und Stilwandel in höchstrichterlichen Zivilentscheidungen', *Etudes de Logique Juridique* 6 (1976), 53–77, at 68, in the context of general trends towards the development of incalculable formulae of judicial reasoning.

which have to be assessed retrospectively if there is a dispute, while the economic system changes its state through the mode of its transactions, with consequences that can hardly be controlled, let alone 'steered', by law.

Among the most remarkable forms of structural coupling between the legal and economic systems, which have developed well nigh unnoticed as a consequence of the institutionalization of property and freedom of contract, is one important exception in the area of the law of liability regarding deliberately caused economic harm. This is a legal privilege with far-reaching consequences, which permits deliberate harm to others in the context of economic competition. One can start a business or open a shop, even if one knows and accepts that others will suffer a loss or may even go out of business as a consequence. This is the case in spite of legal protection (§ 823 BGB) for a legally established and conducted business. This privilege to harm others is granted because the economic system is built on competition and without it, or so the assumption goes, it would not produce sufficiently good results. This illustration also demonstrates the difference in the forms in which this example presents itself in the legal system and in the economic system. Lawyers have difficulty in seeing that competition is a principle, a fundamental structure in the economic system, which is just as important as property and contract is to them.

The fact that structural coupling is a mechanism that both separates and joins can be demonstrated further if one looks at how the context of property and contract is treated differently in the legal and economic systems. In the economic system, the value of property comes largely (for economic theory almost exclusively) from its use in transactions in an existing money economy. Value is the value of exchange. Lawyers, in contrast, are used to treating legal claims arising from property separately from legal claims arising from contract. It would amount to a revolution in civil law if one were to give up this separation. It is not clear, however, whether constitutional law, when interpreting the protection of property, must apply the same separate treatment or should not rather advocate a readier opening up to economic reality (regardless of the juridical consequences).[61] At any rate the separation of the systems prevents the automatic reception of the economic approach into the legal system (despite all the theories of 'economic analysis of law'). At best, it is questionable whether the clear separation of property and contract in the legal system is only a tradition which is kept up

---

[61] For example, the German Bundesverfassungsgericht (Federal Constitutional Court) decision (18.12.1985—*Arbeit und Recht* 24 (1986), 157) and the German Bundesverfassungsgericht (Federal Constitutional Court) refused to protect the right of the employer to determine working hours according to article 14 GG (Basic Law) because this was based on contract not property. See critical comments in Rupert Scholz, 'Verdeckt Verfassung neues zur Mitbestimmung?', *Neue Juristische Wochenschrift* 39 (1986), 1587–91; Dieter Suhr, 'Organisierte Ausübung mediatisierter Grundrechte im Unternehmen', *Arbeit und Recht* 26 (1988), 65–77.

for fear of the unforeseeable consequences of change or whether sound legal reasons still continue to support it.

One reason for this separation could be that the contract, as a source of legal claims, provides the private sector with power over the implementation of political power. Political power has to be available for the implementation of contractual claims even though it is not a party to the contract. The audacity of this form does not reveal itself until it is realized that through it the legal system and, as far as the use of physical force is concerned, the political system, can be conditioned by the private sector, that is, the economic system. The symbol 'legal validity', the use of which changes the condition of the legal system and then forces the political system to deal with that change, becomes partly open to conditioning which is, as far as its motivation is concerned, not controlled by law. The consequence is a massive increase in the variety of the system and, accordingly, a statistically measurable higher volume of litigation.[62] Still the courts have the last say when it comes to determining whether a contract has been drawn up legally or not. The opening up of the system rests on its operative closure. It is brought about by a structural coupling between the economic and the legal systems, and proceeds—as this brief history has shown—at an extremely cautious pace, which does not immediately give in to pressure from problems, but first gains experience and tries minute variations in its own system. Nevertheless, the consequences of this restructuring of the concept of property and contract are immense. One of the most important consequences is perhaps that the regulatory state—in response to democratic developments—must proceed with interventions in the problematic (because indirect) form of curbing the use of property and freedom of contract.

Extending this analysis to the political system as a further functioning system, it becomes fully apparent that this system is affected to a high degree by the form of the structural coupling between the economic and the legal systems. The reason is that the political conditioning of a vast transfer of money (keyword: taxes) and of legislation are the most important, indeed the only, political instruments which have an impact on a myriad of unforeseeable details.[63] This was not an acute problem in the Middle Ages because

---

[62] See Christian Wollschläger, 'Zivilprozeß-Statistik und Wirtschaftswachstum im Rheinland von 1822–1915', in: Klaus Luig and Detlef Liebs (eds.), *Das Profil der Juristen in der europäischen Tradition: Symposion aus Anlaß des 70. Geburtstags von Franz Wieacker* (Ebelsbach, 1980), 371–97. In the meantime the situation has changed as far as long-term perspectives are concerned, and there are now other intervening variables such as ADR (alternative dispute resolution), see, for example, the country reports in *Law and Society Review* 24 (1990), 257–352.

[63] This can be gleaned empirically and comparatively from cases where such conditions do not apply or do not apply to the same degree—for instance China; see, for example, Li Hanlin, *Die Grundstrukturen der chinesischen Gesellschaft* (Opladen, 1991).

dominium meant as much as political authority and could not be distinguished from *iurisdictio*. The eighteenth century produced two concepts in
response to the political release of property, which were intended to deal
with the new circumstances. These concepts were (1) the substantive definition of 'despotic' political force as a national and thus limited administration over property by government according to the natural order, and
(2) the theory of the political representation of the people linked to property
in Britain and, even more clearly, in North America.[64] For a brief moment
in history—and this is the moment that produced the concept of the
constitution—it seemed as if politics would restrict itself to an observation
and a possible correction of the relations between law and economy.
However, the irritations of the legal system and the economic system upon
each other then began to exercise an irresistible attraction for the political
system. Not until the middle of the nineteenth century did the catch
phrase 'freedom (or liberty) of contract' arise,[65] whereas earlier only the
binding effects (obligations) of contractual intentions had been generally
discussed. This new concept appeared to be primed for resistance against
state intervention, especially in industrial law and the law of cartels.[66] The
structural coupling between the legal system and the economic system
became the medium for the medium of political power. This meant that a
loose coupling of possibilities was turned into politically acceptable forms
by collectively binding decisions. In order to achieve the desired economic
gains, the use of property and freedom of contract became more and more
restricted. For some time now, the political system has been experimenting
on the borderline of this possibility. The question is how far the political
system can go with intervention without putting the autopoiesis of the
respective systems at risk, that is, the self-regenerating forces of money and
law. The lesson of it all, which is now quite clear, is that outcomes achieved
in this way never meet political expectations because they are always determined by the self-referential mode of operations and the established structures of the affected systems. This does not seem to matter much, however,
for the autopoiesis of the political system. All that matters for the autopoiesis
of the political system is the collectively binding communication about
intentions to intervene, and not the actual effects of intervention—which
occur much later, or not at all.

---

[64] Despite all the emphasis on the promotion of the representation of the people, it is clear
that 'people' really only means adult male owners of property with considerable income.
'Representation of the property of the people' is an almost inadvertent admission of the truth,
according to James Burgh, *Political Disquisitions*, 3 vols. (London, 1974–5), vol. 3, p. 272.

[65] Somewhat earlier in England, peaking around 1870 (see Atiyah *The Rise and Fall of
Freedom of Contract*, esp. 383) and in the United States not until the end of the century.

[66] See, as a remarkable historical document, the essay of Roscoe Pound, 'Liberty of
Contract', *Yale Law Review* 18 (1909), 454–87.

IV

The development of property rights and freedom of contract could only deal with some of the problems posed by society as it became modernized. It could only provide irritations for a branch of the law, which was then called private law. In the relations between political and legal systems totally different problems cropped up and consequently, after the modern territorial state rose to prominence, there was a much clearer division between private law and public law.[67] The different situation for the political system in relation to the legal system may have been caused by the circumstance that the stratified differentiation of landed estates, in spite of their loss of dominance to the territorial state, slowed down political development much more than it did economic development. As long as the economic system was dominated by agricultural conditions, the nobility remained politically indispensable for the organization of labour and the production of values in the countryside. The management of landed estates and, hand in hand with that, the local administration of justice, spread all over Europe, with the exception of Scandinavia, after the eleventh century. For the money economy it was not so important which class fulfilled the political function. However, politically the status of the nobility could not be disregarded, irrespective of whether its political function was fulfilled personally or by its representatives. The situation in the different European countries varied considerably depending on the degree of commercialization, capitalization, and public debt. With further development it was possible to think of representative constitutions, which provided proprietors in general with political influence. As far as Germany is concerned, mutual respect between the sovereign and landed estates was unavoidable.[68]

After the sixteenth century, developments took place that not only put financial pressure on the nobility (and as a result made it dependent on politics) but also subverted the whole stratified order with the parallel establishment of a 'state'. These developments were based on the semantic unity of politics, law, and society (as discussed in the previous chapter) but did not prevent the spread of new forms of differentiation into various

---

[67] Morton J. Horwitz, 'The History of the Public/Private Distinction', *University of Pennsylvania Law Review* 130 (1982), 1423–8, shows that this distinction had a lot to do with the difference between the legal system and the political system, but it is not adequate for a categorization of the different branches of law. For the older German development, see Rudolf Hoke, 'Die Emanzipation der deutschen Staatsrechtswissenschaft von der Zivilistik im 17. Jahrhundert', *Der Staat* 15 (1976), 211–30; Dieter Wyduckel, *Ius publicum: Grundlagen und Entwicklung des öffentlichen Rechts und der deutschen Staatsrechtswissenschaft* (Berlin, 1984), esp. 131; Michael Stolleis, *Geschichte des öffentlichen Rechts*, vol. 1 (Munich, 1988).

[68] See on this point Gerhard Dilcher, 'Vom ständischen Herrschaftsvertrag zum Verfassungsgesetz', *Der Staat* 27 (1988), 161–93.

functional areas. As a result, the 'state' eventually emerged as the carrier of the structural coupling between the political system and the legal system—however, only under the special condition that the state was given a constitution which made positive law the instrument of choice for political organization and, at the same time, made constitutional law a legal instrument for the disciplining of politics. This form of coupling by the constitutional state made possible *higher degrees of freedom* and a remarkable *acceleration of the dynamics within both systems*, that is, for the legal system as well as for the political system.

Not until the end of the eighteenth century—and at the periphery of Europe at that, namely in the states of North America—was the form invented which guaranteed the structural coupling between the legal and political systems. It was and still is called 'constitution'.[69] Constitutions are real achievements (in contrast to mere texts) if there is success, on the one hand, in restricting the influences of law and politics on each other to the channels provided by the constitution of a state and, on the other hand, in increasing possibilities in the framework of this coupling. It can be seen, nevertheless, that other possibilities are effectively excluded with this kind of coupling. Other possibilities mean, for example, the exploitation of legal positions in the economic system (wealth, legal control of politically important options) in order to achieve political power,[70] or political terrorism, or political corruption. As long as the political system on the one hand and the legal system on the other are linked by the power of 'private' pressure, terrorism, or corruption, neither of the systems can achieve high complexity—not would it even be possible to distinguish one from the other. Rather, an *immense increase* in mutual irritability can be achieved through constitutions by limiting the corridors of contact—more possibilities are created for the legal system to register political decisions in a legal form, and also more possibilities for the political system to use the law for the implementation of politics. The problem on both sides is, then, how to cope structurally with such an increase in variety. It is perhaps not too far-fetched to say that democracy is a consequence of the positivization of law and the ensuing possibilities of changing the law at any time.

However, that was of course not the motive for the invention of the mechanism, which has been called 'constitution' since the last third of the eighteenth century. That outcome could neither have been planned nor

---

[69] See for more detail, Niklas Luhmann, 'Verfassung als evolutionäre Errungenschaft', *Rechtshistorisches Journal* 9 (1990), 176–220.

[70] With such a controversial topic the reader is asked to read carefully. Of course, the possibility that legal positions are a factor in political strategy is not and should not be excluded. An example would be the legally protected possibility of moving production sites and labour offshore. What is excluded by the constitution as a form of structural coupling is only that this possibility be used to build up pressure in the pursuit of other goals, or generally, that it be used for politics.

intended. This evolutionary invention, which bears the name constitution and took on the function of coupling, is due to a specific historical situation and, by no accident, to the geopolitically peripheral position of North America.[71] In post-revolutionary North America there was not even a predominant concern with a radically new law or juridical innovation. The fabric of legal norms existed and the reference to natural law was taken for granted. The concern was rather with filling the vacuum, which derived from independence from the United Kingdom. First of all, sovereign states had to be formed at the level of individual states and at the national level, and a written constitution was a suitable, sufficiently unequivocal, and instantly effective instrument for this. Compared with the development of civil law over 2,000 years, this mutation was sudden and came in the form of a conceptual innovation. The concept '*constitutio*' itself had historical roots. Partly it defined the (healthy or sick) condition of an individual or political body; partly imperial edicts, princely decrees, statutes, ordinances, etc., which were understood as laws. However, the political and the legal uses of language ran parallel to each other, but only in England had it become accepted to talk of the 'constitution' as the supporting principle of legal and political order in the country.[72] The fusion of these two conceptual traditions did not occur until political changes, revolutions in North America and Paris and the abolition of superior judicial control by the Empire in Germany, had taken place. From that time, constitution has been understood as positive statute law, which constitutes positive law itself and through that regulates how political power can be organized and implemented in a legal form with legally mandated restrictions.[73]

---

[71] The important semantic and structural conditions of colonial charters can also be explained by the difference between centre and periphery.

[72] On the development of the relevant language use see Gerald Stourzh, 'Constitution: Changing Meanings of the Term from the Early Seventeenth to the Late Eighteenth Century', in Terence Ball and John G. A. Pocock (eds.), *Conceptual Change and the Constitution* (Lawrence, 1988), 35–54; id., 'Vom aristotelischen zum liberalen Verfassungsbegriff', in id., *Wege zur Grundrechtsdemokratie: Studien zur Begriffs- und Institutionengeschichte des liberalen Verfassungsstaates* (Vienna, 1989), 1–35; Heinz Mohnhaupt, 'Verfassung I', in *Geschichtliche Grundbegriffe: Historisches Lexikon zur politisch-sozialen Sprache in Deutschland*, vol. 6 (Stuttgart, 1990), 831–62. There is no doubt that the concept acquired a new meaning conditioned by the politics of the time during the American and French revolutions. However, it is unclear *what* actually constituted the innovation. The problem arises in part because political concepts, postulates, and organizational suggestions took on quite a different meaning in France compared with the United States, where there was no problem of estates but one of a tradition of colonial charters which could be adapted, and where there was no uniform central state and a nation had yet to be formed on the basis of the constitution, etc.

[73] See, for this switch from a juridical perspective, Dieter Grimm, *Entstehungs- und Wirkungsbedingungen des modernen Konstitutionalismus*, Akten des 26. Deutschen Rechtshistorikertages (Frankfurt, 1987), 46–67; id., 'Verfassung', *Staatslexikon*, ed. Görres Association, 7th edn. (Freiburg, 1989), vol. 5, pp. 634–43; id., 'Verfassung II', in *Geschichtliche Grundbegriffe*, vol. 6, pp. 863–99, both reprinted in id., *Die Zukunft der Verfassung* (Frankfurt, 1991).

From a juridical perspective, a text with such a status can only be an auto-logical text, that is, a text that prescribes itself as being part of the law.[74] This can take the form, for instance, of a collision rule, but occurs above all in the form in which the constitution exempts itself from the rule that new law breaks old. In other forms of this the constitution regulates whether and by whom there is a review of how law conforms to the constitution, and finally that the constitution itself contains the proclamation of the consti-tution and externalizes this symbolically by a reference to the will of God or the will of the people. The historical reasons and intentions behind the issue of the constitution refer back to the constitution, if at all, only via rules of interpretation.[75]

Such peculiarities of constitutional law were unfamiliar to Americans, who were the first to practise them.[76] There were no traditional examples of this kind of autology. Moreover, the constitution also ended the old law's openness to the past and replaced it with openness to the future. This meant that arguments based on historical claims also had to be measured against the constitution, and conversely that the constitution normalized the procedure of the ongoing change of law.[77] To achieve this, constitu-tions prescribe legislation, which is to be negotiated by parliament and to be formed juridically.[78]

Quite rightly, the legal system treats the constitution as a statute, which needs to be interpreted and applied. From a juridical perspective the inno-vation lies in the positivity of this statute, in the inclusion of the difference between constitutional and other law in positive law. This applies as well and most particularly to the rules about collision between rules and about possible prohibitions on changing rules. Thus positive law can even perpet-uate itself—for the Middle Ages a quite unheard of and at any rate dubious idea. The traditional legal hierarchy of divine law, eternal law or variable

[74] Old theological models come to mind, for instance, of religious explanations of a uni-versal order containing a component that explains that order, namely God, in order to cut off an infinite regress.

[75] See the contentious doctrine of 'original intent' of US constitutional law.

[76] See, on judicial review, Commonwealth v Caton, 8 Virginia (4 Call) at 5; Cases of the Judges of the Court of Appeals, 8 Virginia (4 Call) at 135; Barnard v Singleton, 1 North Carolina (1 Martin) at 5; and at the federal level the famous decision Marbury v Madison, 1 Cranch (1803) at 137 and especially at 176.

[77] See, on the already untenable claims of legitimacy of any purely historical reasoning, Henry, Viscount Bolingbroke, *A Dissertation upon Parties*, letter IX, quoted from *Works*, vol. II (Philadelphia; reprint Farnborough, 1969), 79.

[78] One does not have to stop there if one can assume the separation of the political and the legal systems, that is, that the legal system is not corrupted by political expectations of change. Especially in the United States, quite successful social movements have formed which have requested a change of law without addressing Congress for that reason. See, for numerous examples, Joel F. Handler, *Social Movements and the Legal System: A Theory of Law Reform and Social Change* (New York, 1978).

natural law, and positivistic law vanished. Its cosmological and religious fundamentals had dissipated anyway. Instead, the constitution proclaimed that the responsibility for all law lies with the legal system. At first there was a belief, especially in the area of private law, that reliance could be placed on the stable forms and traditions of the common law and continental Europe's civil law and especially, of course, on the legal institution of property. Hence private law had close links with constitutional law, especially in the eighteenth century. Step by step, however, constitutional law, including its concepts, emancipated itself from these conditions. From here on it had only itself to refer to, and it began to develop counter-principles in constitutional law proper—for instance, unchangeability of otherwise changeable law, or the direct reference to 'values' or 'moral' principles, which otherwise could be entertained only in the context of valid legal norms and on the basis of their authorization.[79] In the eighteenth century, the term 'unconstitutional' appeared.[80] As soon, however, as the distinction emerged between constitutional/unconstitutional and legal/illegal, the constitution gathered momentum. Now every legal norm could be unconstitutional— old law, new law, decrees and laws—but not the constitution itself. Now the law mustered a mechanism, which was secured by self-exemption, to pronounce itself illegal. It is not surprising, then, that Thomas Jefferson initially held that the mandate of the people to pronounce a constitution did

[79] Of course, one could say that this applied to the constitution itself where it refers to the dignity of humans, etc. However, the present-tense construction of 'is inviolable' immediately makes one think. And a glance at the highly controversial literature on constitutional interpretation shows that here values, morality, etc. in various versions (constitutional morality, aspirational morality, civil religion) are recommended not only as the substance of certain norms but as general points of interpretative reference, or more clearly, as rules for the closure of an otherwise open horizon for argumentation. See for an especially clear account of this, Ronald Dworkin, *Taking Rights Seriously* (Oxford, 1977); and also, for example, Michael Perry, *Morality, Politics and Law* (London, 1988), esp. 121. However, most of this literature lacks the sharp distinction—drawn in the text above—between constitutional interpretation and statutory interpretation at large. (This lack of such a sharp distinction is particularly evident in Neil MacCormick, 'Institutional Morality and the Constitution', in Neil MacCormick and Ota Weinberger, *An Institutional Theory of Law: New Approaches to Legal Positivism* (Dordrecht, 1986), 171–88). This distinction is, at any rate, a distinction of the *legal system.*

[80] The first reference can be found in the Oxford English Dictionary in 1734 (2nd edn. Oxford, 1989), vol. XVIII, p. 925). See also Bolingbroke, 'Dissertation upon Parties', 11 ('unconstitutional expedients'), but here, as can be inferred from the context, in the framework of a distinction between constitution and government and not in the sense of a distinction between constitutional law and law at large. A wider diffusion of the term occurred only after the American polemics against the practice of the parliament in London to assume itself to be sovereign and hence to believe that it could never act unconstitutionally. Not until the pronouncement of written constitutions did the term infiltrate legal decision-making too as a legitimation for judicial review. Probably the first case was Commonwealth v Caton, 8 Virginia (4 Call) at 5, November 1782.

not go that far and that the normal change of law by normal laws should be maintained.[81]

It is worth mentioning that the underestimation of the law-specific substance of this achievement helped it to prevail. The constitution was discussed as a problem of sovereignty, as a problem of the supreme political power. Then it could be argued successfully that the courts, which can declare individual statutes to be unconstitutional, do not claim to be the government or even the legislators.[82] The courts stay within the framework of their specific judicial function. The transfer of the problem to the political system, which has its own difficulties with problems of self-reference under the heading of sovereignty and its paradoxical foundation, made the logical revolution of the legal system—the shift to self-referential closure—go unnoticed. At any rate it reduced the pressure, from this reflection of the unity of the system, to respond to this 'catastrophe' before there were any specifically juridical instruments to apply to the new situation.

This problem had surfaced in the political system about 200 years earlier; usually Bodin is quoted as the source. Sovereignty was no longer understood as mere independence from emperor and pope in political affairs, as was the case in the Middle Ages, but as the unity of state power within territorial borders, that is, as sovereign in internal affairs as well. The political situation of the religious civil wars had made it necessary that issues of religion, morality, and law were no longer left to the nobility's own judgement. Now this judgement was seen as arbitrary, with the consequence that arbitrariness was positioned against arbitrariness, and with the further consequence that arbitrariness became acceptable as sovereign arbitrariness in one place only, namely in the state. This, however, touched upon the problem, which has occupied the theory of the state since then, namely how one could take away arbitrariness from the unfettered arbitrariness at the top ('*quod principi placuit . . .*' was no longer understood in relation to the virtues of the prince but as a carte blanche for arbitrariness) and how one could bind the sovereign to rational rules and, above all, to his own promises. The theory of the state was thus left stranded with the paradox of the binding of necessarily unbound authority.[83] Perhaps the most acceptable formulation of the concept of paradox, which captures this

---

[81] See his polemic against the constitution of Virginia, which went against his ideas of a constitution (1776): Thomas Jefferson, *Notes on the State of Virginia* (1787), quoted from the edition of William Peden (reprint New York, 1982), 110.

[82] See the arguments of Alexander Hamilton, in: *The Federalist Papers*, no. 78 (Middletown, 1961); or the arguments by John Marshall in Marbury v Madison, 1 Cranch (1803), pp. 137–80.

[83] See on this point Stephen Holmes, 'Jean Bodin: The Paradox of Sovereignty and the Privatization of Religion', in J. Roland Pennock and John W. Chapman (eds.), *Religion, Morality and the Law* (New York, 1988), 5–45.

achievement of dynamic stability with increasing irritability between systems, is that of Friedrich Schlegel. He claimed that the representative constitution is 'nothing . . . but fixed unrest, arrested revolution, the bound [but at the same time] absolute state'.[84]

We cannot go any further here into the historical details of this critical development.[85] But we can note that every supreme position—God's as well as that of the sovereign state—is premised on an *unformulable* rule. So much for that. However, that does not mean, as was thought at the time of the absolute state, that decisions could be made arbitrarily in any given situation. It is this interpretation of sovereignty as arbitrariness that was discarded with the modern constitutional state and transferred to a number of positions with various identities. Initially it occurred with the principle of the separation of powers, and then factually with the differentiation of the legal system and the political system and their different ways of handling the paradox. The fixed form of hierarchical differentiation of levels had to be discarded here (as well as in logic). It could only be replaced by making the difference inside/outside more ambiguous. The constitution has its highlight in points where it becomes unformulable whether it owes its validity to the system or to the environment. But even this is and remains a system-internal ambiguity, which has a different sense in the legal system and the political system respectively, depending on how these systems normalize this interface when irritations occur. Seen from the perspective of sociological distance, a mechanism of structural coupling is established which is accessible to the participating systems but only in their internal interpretations. From the perspective of modern semantics, this develops into a shift from distinctions between top and bottom to distinctions between inside and outside. This makes all 'principles' dependent on the system, that is, contingent. Their ultimate formulation must be replaced with the rule of the unformulability of the rule, which constitutes the unity of the system.

What matters in our analysis is the insight that problems of self-reference and paradox present themselves in different ways in each system, in the political system differently than in the legal system. This is the crucial reason why the unfolding of the respective self-references and the dissolution of the respective paradoxes has to be mediated by mechanisms of structural coupling and not by meta-rules or logical solutions that are found in the systems themselves. This also means that the invisibility of the problem and its solution, its incommunicability, and the impossibility of making it

---

[84] In: 'Signatur des Zeitalters', quoted from Friedrich Schlegel, *Dichtungen und Aufsätze*, ed. Wolfdietrich Rasch (Munich, 1984), 593–728, at 713.

[85] See, for the social theory context, Niklas Luhmann, 'Staat und Staatsräson im Übergang von traditionaler Herrschaft zu moderner Politik', in id., *Gesellschaftsstruktur und Semantik*, vol. 3 (Frankfurt, 1989), 65–148.

a topic have been taken care of in the system itself. This is precisely what happens, representing what could be called the meta-constitutional meaning of the constitution.

In sum, we can say that the constitution provides political solutions for the problem of the self-reference of the legal system and legal solutions for the problem of the self-reference of the political system. The constitution is a constitution of the 'state' and presupposes that the state is a real object, which needs to be constituted. Not the text but the constitutional state fulfils the function of coupling—regardless of whether it is understood as a people-in-a-form, as an institution, as an organization, or just as 'government'.[86] The constitution, which constitutes and defines the state, has a correspondingly different meaning in both systems. For the legal system it is a supreme statute, a basic law. For the political system it is an instrument of politics, in the double sense of both instrumental politics (which changes states of affairs) and symbolic politics (which does not). Moreover, in spite of their seemingly contradictory semantics, both versions are compatible because of the operative closure of the different systems. Only in their version of their own system can conditions be altered through the operations of their system. It may be that the political and the legal meanings of the constitution drift apart in this way, and will be fed back via an increase in irritations of each other. It may also be—as can be observed in many developing countries—that constitutions serve exclusively as an instrument of symbolic politics because the legal system has not yet become operatively closed and thus shielded from the direct influences of politics or other social powers. But even there the modern pattern of structural coupling can be seen, if only as true (that is, functioning) make-believe. The mere symbolic use of constitutions enables politics to pretend to be limited and irritated by law, while leaving the real power relations to insider communication.[87] However, the full meaning of the evolutionary achievement of 'constitution' is developed only under the conditions of functional differentiation and operative closure of the political system and the legal system. And it is precisely because this condition was latent and could be ignored that the evolution of this achievement became possible. Constitutions in the modern sense of the concept were invented under the protective umbrella of the persisting (medieval) illusion that politics could be constituted as a legal order. And this practice continues in order to make invisible the fact that the real limitations on the sovereignty of

---

[86] Semantic imprecision is another indicator that we are dealing here with a mechanism of structural coupling (with different perspectives).

[87] See, for example, with a somewhat different understanding in the sense of unrealised modernity, Marcelo Neves, *Verfassung und Positivität des Rechts in der peripheren Moderne: Eine theoretische Betrachtung und eine Interpretation des Falles Brasilien* (Berlin, 1992). See also above at Ch. 2.IV for the discussion of autonomy.

political systems are power struggles and the strategic calculations of political elites.

What was in practice set in train is the story of the effects of mutual irritations, which in the long term affect the direction in which the coupled systems develop by building and removing structures. The political system is subject to self-irritation by the possibility of stimulating a change in law. The positivization of law provides an immense potential for political action, and politics is continuously engaged in the selection of such possibilities. It is politics if a change of law is suggested. The political system can respond in various ways to such initiatives but not by disowning them as system-internal operations. Hence positive law means an overburdening of politics, especially when a structural decision has been made in favour of democracy.

The legal system is likewise exposed to political initiatives with which it has to deal in legislative procedures, administrative regulations, and legal decision-making (including the decision-making of constitutional courts) on an ongoing basis. It is undeniably evident that this deforms traditional forms of consistency-test through decision-making in courts with their indifferent development of legal doctrine. This traditional order is subject to and is mediated by constitutional interpretation which uses 'basic values' or moral intuitions (as in the United States) and thus keeps a change in the weighing of values open from case to case. The seemingly firm order of legal propositions is guided by fluid, provisional decision-making on the basis of an appreciation of values, and thus by unstable guides for the relatively stable system.[88] This means, using the terminology introduced above, that the variety of the system increases and that the maintenance of redundancy becomes a problem. New forms must then be introduced—perhaps as a consequence of the systems' mutual appreciation.

What matters—and is made visible by the concept of structural coupling—is that the reinforcement of mutual irritations depends on and remains dependent on the exclusion effect of the same mechanism. Only indifference to each other makes it possible that a specific dependence on each other is increased.[89] Under these conditions, which can be understood as functional differentiation in relation to the social system of society, the systems dissolve the circular structure of their self-references by externalization.

---

[88] See also the accent on 'the experimental, projecting character of "values" (in the interpretation of the constitution) which is aimed at self-fulfilment but the real currency of which is decided provisionally by the constitutional court and always brought into play afresh' in Karl-Heinz Ladeur, *Postmoderne Rechtstheorie: Selbstreferenz—Selbstorganisation—Prozeduralisierung* (Berlin, 1992), 166.

[89] This argument can already be found in the eighteenth century in the context of the first discussions on the checks and balances of the separation of powers. See Henry, Viscount Bolingbroke, *Remarks on the History of England* (1730), quoted from *Works*, vol. I (Philadelphia, 1841; reprint Farnborough 1969), 292–455, at 333.

The legal system exposes itself to political influences by providing the possibilities for legislation. In democratizing, the political system exposes itself to the appeal of bringing the initiatives for a change in law to a head. The self-reference of the system thus takes a detour via the inclusion of the environment in the system. This makes hierarchical asymmetry dispensable, especially since the glance heavenwards [to natural law] has lost all meaning.

There is discussion today—as a consequence of this development—on whether and how the apparatus of classical constitutionalism can be adapted to the developments of the welfare state.[90] The clarity of civil law forms, which could be presumed to exist in the common law as well as in continental European law around 1800, is no longer given. Notions about the meaning and the function of basic rights are changing more and more in the direction of general programmes of values, which must be understood as guidelines for politics. The problems for decision-making no longer occur when barriers are overcome politically but every time new value-conflicts have to be resolved. Constitutional courts are intervening more and more frequently in politics with instructions on how conflicts ought to be resolved and are dictating spending, for instance, where thrift is advisable. This development confirms the political power of persuasion of the welfare state and, in particular, the idea that undeserved misfortune ought to be compensated by the community.[91] The original function of the constitution—to limit politics—disappears from view. It is easy to see that the welfare state is a fast-selling item, but it is not recognized that the function of the constitution should be to *oppose* such trends.[92] Thus the adjustment of the constitution to the conditions of the welfare state should be sought in a guarantee of independence for the central bank and by mandating firm limits on government spending.

V

The transition to a primarily functional differentiation of the social system requires structural couplings of a new kind in the relations between the different functioning systems. These are couplings that are capable of taking the autonomy and the operative closure of the functional systems into account. Functional systems are kept within society through these mechanisms. However, since the functional sub-systems have to operate as systems of communication anyway, they cannot operate outside of society. Thus the

---

[90] See above all Grimm, *Die Zukunft der Verfassung*.

[91] Lawrence Friedman, *Total Justice* (New York, 1985), shows that private law also follows such ideas and adjusts to changes in the social climate.

[92] See Grimm *Die Zukunft der Verfassung*, 325, with further references, and the finding that the welfare state could cope more easily with the loss of constitutional guarantees than with the loss of other goals of the state.

mechanisms of structural coupling develop in line with new functional autonomies. The one could not be possible without the other.

In the discussion so far we have not taken into account the fact that there are always structural couplings for the external relations of the social system (society), for instance psychological systems that, by constituting consciousness, are a necessary environment for communication. Of course the legal system, because it has to communicate, has direct relations with the psychological environment of society. It is internalized in the consciousness of participants directly (and not via any other societal occurrences). Hence the psychological environment must be able to motivate perceptions and actions if the corresponding internal communication is not to come to a standstill owing to a lack of resources. For example, that environment might determine that to be able to be right, to be confirmed in one's sense of justice or not, can decide one's fate, or at least that this is no small matter. In this respect, then, the reorganization of social structures in the direction of functional differentiation requires changes in the mechanisms of coupling, because now each functioning system has to define the conditions for the inclusion of consciousness and/or conduct by itself (such as actual presence, disciplining, restricted movement, paying attention—for example, during legal proceedings). There are no longer any reliable general mechanisms for social ordering, apart from language. If the legal system has to deal with differentiated sub-systems such as money economy, privatized families, politically programmed state organizations, etc. and has to rely on corresponding structural couplings to do that, it must also reformulate its relations with systems of consciousness.[93]

Modern legal development has done that by abstracting general, socially based norms of reciprocity from the legal figure of subjective rights.[94] Thus legal validity has become formally independent of mutual, local obligations, which permeate all the different functional contexts. Legal validity has also gained independence from the localized influence of the nobility and the social pressure of neighbours against whom one can now be defended with law. Now, legal validity only allows conditioning by the history of legal validity of the legal system itself. The old reciprocal duties have receded into a much-discussed morality of gratefulness.[95] Actual mixes of

[93] Talcott Parsons uses a similar argument (*The System of Modern Societies* (Englewood Cliffs, 1971), esp. 18 and 82) in relation to the increased demands which are made on the integrative function (that means inclusive in relation to individuals) of the 'societal community' and which are translated into the usual human rights with the help of legal systems.

[94] See for more detail Niklas Luhmann, 'Subjektive Rechte: Zum Umbau des Rechtsbewußtseins für die moderne Gesellschaft', in id., *Gesellschaftsstruktur und Semantik*, vol. 2 (Frankfurt, 1981), 45–104.

[95] And are keenly maintained here. See, for example (Charles de) Saint-Evremond, *Sur les ingrats*, quoted from *Œuvres*, Vol. 1 (Paris, 1927), 153–8; Claude Buffier, *Traité de la société civile: Et du moyen de se rendre heureux, en contribuant au bonheur des personnes avec qui l'on vit* (Paris, 1726), 177 ff. (note the restriction in the subtitle to 'avec qui l'on vit'!).

rights and duties have been dissolved. Rights which A can invoke against B, do not have to correspond to rights which B can invoke against A. The symmetries of complementarity were dissolved into tautological relations of corresponding rights and duties—on the condition (which was put in place socially on rather unequal terms) that everyone has access to such rights and can perform such duties independently of the requirements of social status. This evidently required a differentiation of private law and public law in areas in which one had previously talked about a law that was dependent on a citizenship status (civil law). And it required the dissolution of the old Roman term of a *ius*, which presupposed the existence of ties which corresponded to rights in concrete legal relations.[96] It is evident how strongly the transition to a legal conceptualization of 'subjective rights' since the middle of the seventeenth century has influenced the mechanisms of structural coupling which we discussed earlier—property law and the expectations held of a constitution.[97] As soon as it was possible to formulate subjective rights in terms of natural law, human rights (or at any rate civil rights) could be seen as preconditions, which every legal order had to respect if it wanted to qualify as law. It is understandable that people thought that there could be no law without recognition of the individual rights of natural law. To a certain extent, this concept took over the function of the old distinction *rex/tyrannus*, which legitimized resistance for

---

[96] See on this point the widely discussed hypotheses of Michel Villey, *Leçons d'histoire de la Philosophie du droit* (Paris, 1957), 249 ff. and, as an overview of the subsequent discussion, Karl-Heinz Fezer, *Teilhabe und Verantwortung: Die personale Funktionsweise des subjektiven Privatrechts* (Munich, 1986), 111. Romanists also find little evidence for an abstract subject-related interpretation of *ius* in old Roman law; see, for example, Max Kaser, *Das altrömische ius: Studien zur Rechtsvorstellung und Rechtsgeschichte der Römer* (Göttingen, 1949), esp. 96. One should note above all the breadth of the meaning of the concept, which has hardly any exclusive effect (for instance in distinguishing between *ius* and *lex*). In a certain sense, the concept is a declaration of the autonomy of jurisprudence, which then has to decide the legal matter in a dispute. The only thing that is certain is that the distinction between subjective and objective was clearly not the form in which *ius* was conceived of initially.

[97] Hobbes is usually seen as the leading writer in this respect. However, he did not influence the jurisprudence of his time very much. The reinterpretation of *ius* in the sense of *facultas* or *potentia* already started in the sixteenth century, if not even earlier. See Hans Erich Troje, 'Wissenschaftlichkeit und System in der Jurisprudenz des 16. Jahrhunderts', in Jürgen Blühdorn and Joachim Ritter (eds.), *Philosophie und Rechtswissenschaft: Zum Problem ihrer Beziehungen im 19. Jahrhundert* (Frankfurt, 1969), 63–88, at 81; Fernando N. Arturo Cuveillas, ' "Luis de Molina": el creador de la idea del derecho como faculdad', *Revista de Estudios Politicos* 75 (1954), 103–16; see also Richard Tuck, *Natural Rights Theories: Their Origin and Development* (Cambridge, 1979); Fezer, *Teilhafe and Verantwortung*, at 140. For what happened *c.*1200 (replacement of the feudal reciprocal relations with a *state* guarantee of the owner's individual disposition as a consequence of the first major inflation) see Robert C. Palmer, 'The Origins of Property in England', *Law and History Review* 3 (1985), 1–50; id., 'The Economic and Cultural Impact of the Origins of Property 1180–1220', *Law and History Review* 3 (1985), 375–96.

the revolutionary movements in the eighteenth century. In this context the natural law of property rights as the basis for the development of individuality reached a position which simultaneously fulfilled the demands of political economy. The concrete obligations of the use of property were replaced with the assumption that the individualist-rational use of property in itself increased welfare, because rationality now meant being guided by the conditions of the economic system. However, what is left of such a construction when the reference to 'nature' begins to fade or can only be maintained in an ambiguous, specifically juridical use of language?

Even Kant and Savigny still used the old rule of reciprocity, although they no longer formulated it as a command of gratitude (because ingratitude towards business partners or the state in questions of truth or love had become a command of appropriate, system-adequate behaviour) but abstracted it as a general, ethical rule. Every subject could thus ascertain its validity personally (and without having to accept external authorities).[98] The old form only became generalized in order to cope with the more complex conditions. However, this solution did not last long and had already broken down in the middle of the nineteenth century under the impact of the question of the relation of validity between subjective and objective rights, that is, the question of the unity of the legal system.

For the idea of an *objective* validity of *subjective* rights is nothing but a hidden, unfolded paradox—at any rate as long as the distinction between objective and subjective was considered relevant. The basic paradox of the sameness of legality and illegality could be diverted to a different distinction, a more harmless paradox, and one that worked well as long as it functioned as a legal technique and as long as its main issue, in the context of legitimation, was the question whether and how society could concede individuals' freedom for self-development. The difficulties legal theory had in reflecting this paradox in its constructions were less important. For legal theory it was only a matter of finding the right construction.

Not until the courts had to reconstruct subjective rights in matters of public law and the social welfare state was developed, and not until reciprocity became a political slogan under the new name of 'solidarity' and a legal principle with practically no shape, did cracks appear in legal doctrine and maxims of reciprocity were voiced more and more strongly solely

---

[98] Among relevant contemporary authors, Jürgen Habermas gives this principle a further abstraction, which switches the a priori of the system conditions from analyses with a theory of consciousness to linguistic foundations. His thesis is that, used appropriately, language itself presupposes a symmetry of relations of mutual recognition and thus forms the basis for *normative* demands on social rationality; see for detail Jürgen Habermas, *Faktizität und Geltung: Beiträge zur Diskurstheorie des Rechts und des demokratischen Rechtsstaates* (Frankfurt, 1992).

as ethical principles.[99] One can understand why the idea of reciprocity was retained for such a long time in legal reasoning if one looks at how well it reflected the social conditions of the time. This can be seen, for example, in the suitability of the contractual model for understanding the economy or modern marriage and for the rise in the demands for civil participation in the governance of the 'state'. But this equivalence was outside the semantics that could be mobilized for the purposes of a juridical doctrine. The doctrine could really only report on its own difficulties—by attempting to explain the concept of nature which was presupposed in the talk about natural law[100] and by trying to define subjective rights by the difference between them and objective law.[101] We can clarify what was meant but could not be said, using the distinction between system references and different corresponding structural couplings.

The general coupling between consciousness and communication with all its consequences, such as socialization, individual expectations, focal points of irritability, etc., refers to the system of society in all its different branches. Without communication and without the participation of consciousness in communication, nothing works. In this respect the transformations of this relation lie on a deeper, more fundamental level of the development of modern individualism than those institutions that regulate and limit the irritations of the functioning systems on each other. Irritations come together in the consciousness of the individual and have socializing effects, which come from different functional areas of society. They irritate these functioning systems in return and the individual is not able to relate to society as a whole, let alone identify with it as a member of a community of solidarity, which could take care of all the aspects of everyday life. At best, and seen from the viewpoint of the individual, the relation to society as a whole can only be defined negatively—which also includes the advantages of distance and freedom. As far as the law is concerned, the legal institution of subjective rights reflects such a state of affairs, as does contract as a legal form. They make a highly selective, transient satisfaction of transient needs possible without affecting the individual's social status. In the form in which subjective rights are provided, namely as objective

---

[99] See especially on this point Dieter Grimm, *Solidarität als Rechtsprinzip: Die Rechts- und Staatslehre Léon Duguits in ihrer Zeit* (Frankfurt, 1973). See also J. E. S. Hayward, 'Solidarity: The Social History of an Idea in 19th Century France', *International Review of Social History* 4 (1959), 261–84; Jan Milic Lochman et al., *Solidarität in der Welt der 80er Jahre: Leistungsgesellschaft und Sozialstaat* (Basle, 1984).

[100] Such attempts have since been abandoned and natural law is understood as the presupposition that moral problems can be decided independently of fluctuating opinions—for which arguments have to be found. See, for example, Michael S. Moore, 'Moral Reality', *Wisconsin Law Review* (1982), 1061–1156.

[101] See, for example, Alf Ross, *On Law and Justice* (London, 1958), 170.

rights, the legal system alerts itself to the problematic nature of the inclusion of individual human beings in the legal system. This problem results from the very fact that the fusion of psychological operations and social operations in one system is impossible.

If this applies, it can explain—independently of the historical terminologies which were used to engineer the change—that the yet to be developed forms of coupling which connect the separate functional systems also need to be coordinated with the legal institution of individual rights. The constitution, apart from its function as an 'instrument of government', was introduced explicitly in order to implement a 'Bill of Rights'. It has also been widely observed that property law was reconstructed individualistically in the eighteenth century. Last but not least, the new individualism and the juridical disentangling of rights and duties affect the justification for taxation, that is, the coupling of the economic system and the political system.[102] Accordingly, the legal system functions largely, or at least initially, to cushion the consequences that the restructuring of society towards functional differentiation has on the individual. The individual is provided with subjective rights as a compensation for the loss of all that was certain before. In this line of development, social welfare law complements mere rights of freedom, and participatory rights complement merely protective forms of law, as if using the same form of law with just a few additions thrown in could solve all these problems.

But is it reasonable to assume that individuals experience their society positively and are satisfied when they are given rights and are protected in their rights? Until recently it was only the (on the whole) unfair distribution of goods which gave rise to this question. Nowadays growing anxiety about the future and concern about the risky behaviour of others, against which rights only provide limited protection, joins this background problem. The technical difficulties faced by law are well known—for instance, in the case of ecologically mediated, indirect, and long-term causality or in the case of an interest in prevention, which cannot yet be voiced because the injury has not yet materialized or is not immediately threatening. So far, legal solutions have been offered, above all, by the paradoxical instrument of strict liability, which permits action but provides liability in the case of legally (!) committed harm. This, too, is an indication of how law is losing its relevance and information value for individuals coping with everyday life. The law no longer specifies what one ought to do or not do. All that is left for law to say is: 'If things work out, they work out. If they don't, they don't'. And subjective rights come into play only by defining those who can claim damages, but not in the form of protective rights which allow people to access the courts if they only fear injury.

---

[102] See, for example, William Kennedy, *English Taxation 1640–1799: An Essay on Policy and Opinion* (London, 1913), esp. 82.

All this increases the importance of what could be called 'the flip side' of subjective rights: the fact that they are limited in their allocation, their use, and above all their access to courts, and the fact that it was exactly these limitations which protected people against the only too efficient intervention of third parties. As a marker of a form with two sides, a subjective right offers a guarantee of freedom in a double sense: for the holder and for those against whom those rights are ineffective.

This delicate balance could be dislodged under the massive pressure of ecological threats. It is more probable that it will be diminished in its importance and replaced with, or at least complemented by, increased regulatory activity on the part of states to which the constitution increasingly yields by way of amendments or supplements.[103] However, the consequence of this would be that law would lose its importance for the structural coupling of individual consciousness and social communication. And then law would lose the certainty of being able to mobilize consciousness for legal purposes when it needed to, for instance if there were a political need. Then the legal system would require scandals, which attract high levels of publicity or huge 'Amnesty International'-type reports, in order to maintain its rule of law, in which individually nobody any longer has an interest.

In this context one aspect of subjective rights will come to gain importance, which has so far been almost completely neglected by legal doctrine and which cannot be grasped either by complementing social welfare law with more rights of freedom. Concerns about the legitimacy of the law that, according to Habermas, should be the figure into which subjective rights should be transferred do not adequately reflect this increasingly important problem.[104] Subjective rights guarantee that it is up to individuals whether they decide to make use of their rights or not.[105] Purely psychological factors may play a part in this decision, but it may also be influenced by differences in support of social networks, for instance, opinions of family and friends, the extent of financial risk, or the question of how much time they are willing to sacrifice for this kind of stressful activity. The realization of human rights cannot progress beyond this point as long as there are ways of influencing the decision actually to invoke these rights politically. Legal proceedings are a nuisance of the highest order for the individual, and

---

[103] See, for example, Dieter Grimm, 'Die Zukunft der Verfassung', *Staatswissenschaften und Staatspraxis* 3 (1990), 5–33; also id, in Grimm, *Die Zukunft der Verfassung* 397–437.

[104] See for detail Habermas, *Faktizität und Geltung*, 109.

[105] A similar discussion can be found in relation to the system of religion under the heading 'secularization'. According to it, religion has become a private matter in modern society and is as such a matter for individual decision. Without doubt such decisions are also subject to social influences. However, under the conditions of an 'institutionalized individualism' (Parsons), these influences clearly no longer support particular religious ties.

from the perspective of everyday life it will rarely be meaningful to get caught up in them. 'Litigate' or 'exit', that is the question.[106]

When a violation of subjective rights is the reason for litigation, a structural coupling of individual consciousness and irritations in the legal system is put into practice. In other words, the legal system depends on stimuli which appear as coincidences to the law. And it would be an illusion to assume that the law itself could control the dependency on stimuli in view of the extent to which outcomes of legal proceedings depend on matters of fact (evidence). The legal system is autonomous as far as operative closure is concerned. But as long as it is working, it is not a cybernetic machine, which uses its own output as input.

Having subjective rights allows one to have a lethargic attitude towards the law and encourages the non-participation of those whom they are meant to empower. Subjective rights do not only guarantee freedom under law but also freedom from law. The more frequently other functioning systems, above all the political regulatory machine of state governance, use the law and seek certainty of success in it, the more disturbing those effects will be on the subjective rights form of coupling with its unstable, inscrutable, and subjective environment.

VI

In the old European tradition based on Roman law's concept of *societas*, society itself was seen as a contract, albeit a contract which corresponded to the nature of humans as social beings. Perhaps this can be interpreted in the following way: conduct in the context of inescapable sociality had to be understood as a contract, the consequences of which could only be evaded in the form of that which is illegal *venire contra factum proprium*. However, if the unity of society was based on its legal form, law could not be properly understood as a sub-system of society. Rather, the legal order was constructed, parallel to the hierarchical stratification of society, as a hierarchy of *legis actiones* with the steps of divine law, natural law, and positive law.

After the High Middle Ages an alternative interpretation developed using the metaphor of an organism. It described society as a political body and assumed not an artificial, but a natural constitution. However, the concept of nature contained the dual possibility of a natural (perfect) and a corrupt state of affairs, as reflected, for instance, by the variants *rex* and *tyrannus* in the governance of society. The normative option for perfection, which is immanent in the concept of nature, was understood as law, namely natural law. The basis for that view was the assumption of the unity of the divine origin and reasonableness of law, which was pervasive in the Middle

---

[106] In the terminology of Albert O. Hirschmann, *Exit, Voice and Loyalty: Responses to Decline in Firms, Organizations, and States* (Cambridge, Mass., 1970).

Ages, combined with the widespread perception of corruption.[107] Thus both constructions, the artificial one (contract) and the natural one (organism), albeit in opposition to each other, shared the presumption that society was a legal order.

Not until the eighteenth century did it become clear that this concept no longer reflected the state of affairs in a modern society, and David Hume is possibly the most impressive author in this respect. As before, a society without law was unthinkable; however, society was now seen as a product of its history, and law as a corresponding matter representing the resulting changes. Law developed in society and with society. If the sheer size of modern commercial society no longer permitted social control by proximity, law had to adapt to that and declare promises, including those made to unknown persons, as legally binding.[108] The binding nature of promises is not a result of nature or of morals. It is a convention of recent history. Property was made disposable on the single condition that the proprietor gave his consent. Compared with brute force, but also with local arrangements regarding property, a better, more flexible distribution of goods became possible.[109] Securing property was now seen as the main function of law because this (and through it the economy) was seen as a precondition for the possibility of society.[110] What we have defined as forms of the structural coupling of law, property, contract, and in a different respect the constitution, were seen as necessary forms of civil society proper in the transition period of the eighteenth century, and it appears that overestimating them was a condition of their implementation.

However, compared with the precision of the classical-juridical concept of *societas*, it was now unclear what society meant. In spite of establishing all the internal structures in society, a concept for the unity of the system was lacking. Even if the historical approach of societal analysis made descriptions possible, it did nothing to address the lack of theory. Hence one continued to talk about civil society. Accommodating greater differentiation required a corresponding generalization of the symbols that could represent the unity behind differentiation. In these terms theory seemed to lag behind. Its relevance was based on how it marked the historical distance from ancestral societies and defined it as a result of social development.

---

[107] See on this point the study of Edward Powell, *Kingship, Law and Society: Criminal Justice in the Reign of Henry V* (Oxford, 1989), esp. 38, which even looks at popular poetry.

[108] See Hume, *Treatise*, Book III, Part II, Sect. V at 219. See also Annette Baier, 'Promises, Promises, Promises', in ead., *Posture of the Mind: Essays on Mind and Morals* (Minneapolis, 1985), 174–206, esp. 181.

[109] See Hume, *Treatise*, Book III, Part II, Sect. IV, p. 217.

[110] Hume is very clear on this. Nevertheless, it is a view that was widely held in his time. See on this issue, and for further references, Niklas Luhmann, 'Am Anfang war kein Unrecht', in id., *Gesellschaftsstruktur und Semantik*, vol. 3 (Frankfurt, 1989), 11–64.

Similarly, the spread of class-society terminology in the nineteenth century did not achieve any satisfactory results and remained controversial. It postulated that the ideas of the ruling classes were the dominant ideas and that the legal system could not develop independently of them. This view of domination theory can be presented using the following quotation:

General value judgments of the dominant class, which *contradict* existing legal value judgements, are rare. As a rule the legal value judgement will at least be partly accepted in society. Opinions will differ. Even in those cases in which there is no legal value judgement, the notorious general consensus is not particularly frequent. The rule is a diversity of judgements.[111]

If one reads the whole text, one gets the impression that the reason why the contradiction, mentioned in the first sentence, is rare is the fact that 'general value judgements of the dominant class' do not exist or only rarely. 'The rule is a diversity of judgements'. Law does not use its autonomy in order to create and establish its own counter-culture.[112] Rather, the problem is that a generally accepted value judgement includes individual values and founders when value conflicts arise. And that happens in the majority of cases the law has to deal with. The autonomy of the law develops—and this can best be seen in the example of Roman law—by asking the *quaestio juris* in cases of conflict and superimposing it on hopeless attempts at finding a consensus on social values. The conceptual and organizational apparatus, which grows with the task of applying the leverage of the *quaestio juris* effectively and of proceeding as consistently as possible in answering this question, leads to the differentiation of the legal system. Its eigenvalues can then only be reached through structural couplings. This means: the system can now be irritated only by its own eigenvalues [those values that function to, and generate, a multiple of themselves].

Evidently this is not the way in which the legal system can insulate itself against generally accepted value judgements. A deviation from such value judgements in the internal working of the law—for instance, in the area of sexual offences, *de facto* relationships, homosexuality, abortion, etc.—will cause irritations and thus trigger the search for other solutions to the problem, which may appear 'better' in a particular situation. On the other hand, the equally necessary redundancies—that is, that which the legal system considers to be an equal treatment of cases, justice, etc.—slow down such a development. When abortion is legal, that legal/illegal communication limits

---

[111] Phillip Heck, *Gesetzesauslegung und Interessenjurisprudenz* (Tübingen, 1914), 292. A more recent sociological account of this view in relation to the systems of science is G. Nigel Gilbert and Michael Mulkay, *Opening Pandora's Box: A Sociological Analysis of Scientists' Discourse* (Cambridge, 1984).

[112] We do not contest that this might be possible, for instance to a limited degree in South Africa or Israel.

the arguments that can be used in disputes over experiments with genetic material. This is not necessarily a political limitation but it is a juridical one.

These considerations must lead us to abandon crude concepts of the 'power' of the ruling classes, implementing their values with the help of law, but also to abandon Gramsci's more flexible concepts of hegemony and relative autonomy. Hence, even if this perception is controversial, it is questionable whether it can be maintained that a structural coupling exists between class, society, and law. In all events, one must make do without the simple dual terminology of up and down, or purpose and means, in these areas of theory, and must shift analyses of social development into the more open-ended context of evolution theory.

Evidently the social system materializes through the difference between autopoietic functional systems and structural couplings, and through that difference draws a line between itself and an environment, which has entirely different types of structural coupling (namely couplings with consciousness systems).[113] Therefore, one can neither say that society reproduces itself as a sum of its functioning systems nor assert that those forms through which structural coupling is realized are representative of the social order (in our discussion these forms were constitution or property and contract, or in the terminology of the nineteenth century, state and society). Rather it is crucial to understand that the realization of autopoietic functioning systems and the putting in place of structural couplings—which at the same time increase, direct, and exclude irritations—can only evolve together.

In this way there evolves what Maturana calls 'structural drift', namely, coordinated structural developments, trends in the developments discussed here, for instance towards the welfare state, positive law, and a decentralized economic development controlled by budgets and balances. The functioning systems of politics, law, and the economy (others have not been discussed here) exhaust the limits of their possibilities, and their intensive reciprocal irritation ensures the maintenance of sufficient compatibility. With all the attempts today to transform socialist economies into market economies, one-party systems into multi-party systems, and planning law into a regime of subjective rights (especially property), it is clear how difficult it is to catch up with structural drift through belated planning.

---

[113] Here also a formal similarity with living systems is apparent without having to fall back on an 'organism theory of society'. Certainly the ways of operating of life and communication are rather different, but nevertheless the living organism is dependent on internal autopoietically living cells and massive, and at the same time highly selective, structural couplings as well.

11 The Self-description of the Legal System

All efforts to know and understand the law are made in society. They are tied and remain tied to communication, and thus also to language. This was the presupposition of the preceding chapters, for they also had to use language. This reference to language addresses an issue that has not always been taken seriously enough in legal theory. It implies that all communication in legal theory is historically conditioned. Legal theory must make itself understood under its given social conditions. It is legal theory's object, law, but also legal theory itself, that varies with the structures to which societies subject their communication about law. Nowadays, for instance, we cannot ignore the fact that we look back on a long legal history. This means that any contemporary legal theory which tries to explain the nature of law must demonstrate a remarkable abstraction encompassing epochs and societies and at the same time an understanding of historical variety, including the relatively recent requirement of abstraction itself.

This does not prevent us from observing the legal system, once it is fully differentiated in society, and at the same time avoiding all commitment to the function, coding, and norms of the system. However, if that is done, a different system must be chosen for one's point of reference with different commitments. Thus the legal system can be described from the perspective of the political system as an instrument of politics; or from the perspective of the education system as a didactic instrument of time saving and effective teaching; or from the perspective of the system of science as an object of research. None of these descriptions of law works without a commitment to the system, which operates as the describing one, and thus without a commitment to the distinctions used by that system. But also, in each case the external observation and description of the legal system is owed to the society reproducing the communication, in other words, a society that differentiates sub-systems, in our case the legal system. So, we cannot ignore the fact that these systems can be described from inside and from outside. Both self- and external descriptions are possible. The structure of social differentiation makes distinguishing between them both possible and meaningful. At the same time, this structure allows internal descriptions to influence external ones and vice versa, because all-embracing communication is, as carrying out operations in society, always possible, even when there are system boundaries within society.

Insight into this state of affairs makes our task more difficult. An external, scientific description of the legal system does justice to its subject only if it describes the system as a system that describes itself and constructs theory about itself.[1] Therefore a sociological description must include legal theory's efforts at clarifying the basic issues of law, for instance the concept of justice. But the character of legal theory itself is also at issue. Either it must opt for a law-external mode of description and in doing so must answer the question of its own theoretical foundations, or it must see itself as a self-description of the legal system, which raises its own normative claims—otherwise legal theory could not be attributed to the system. Then the question arises how such claims to validity can be enforced if they are just like any other arguments in the system, that is, that they are also observable.

To be able to give an account of such a complex situation, we must make the concept of self-description more precise and capable of drawing distinctions. First of all, we must distinguish between observing and describing. Self-observation is merely the coordination of individual operations with the structures and operations of the legal system and is thus primarily the implication or explication of the fact that a communication involves legal or illegal communication. This is not particularly problematic but is a matter of everyday communication. However, quite different problems arise if it is a matter of self-description, that is, the presentation of the unity of the system in the system. This is not just the ongoing maintenance of connectivity with the help of selected references but the reflection of the unity of the system in the system, which reflects itself.

As specified by the term of description in general, this operation is designed to create texts, that is, reusable premises for further communication. A self-description ('Vertextung') makes the system, in which the operation of self-description takes place, into a topic. This is not just any operation of the system, but an operation with the intention of self-description. Hence we can define it with the classic term of reflexion [reflection]. And it is a description which in addition to reflexion reflects that it is part of the system which it describes, and which must respect and accept the system if it wants to be seen as belonging to the system. We can also say, using a term from linguistic semantics, that self-description is the creation of an autological text, that is, a text that includes itself in what it means.

Self-descriptions respect the limitations that stem from being part of the system that they describe. For instance, a self-description of the legal system

---

[1] See also, in the context of a broad discussion of the problems of internal and external descriptions of the legal system, François Ost and Michel van der Kerchove, *Jalons pour une théorie critique du droit* (Brussels, 1987), 27, 30, and 251. For Gunther Teubner this is also a condition of the applicability of the concept of autopoiesis. See G. Teubner, 'Hyperzyklus in Recht und Organisation: Zum Verhältnis von Selbstbeobachtung, Selbstkonstitution und Autopoiese', in Hans Haferkamp and Michael Schmid (eds.), *Sinn, Kommunikation und soziale Differenzierung: Beiträge zu Luhmanns Theorie sozialer Systeme* (Frankfurt, 1987), 89–128. As far as I am concerned, it would suffice to see here only the requirement of an adequate description of autopoietic systems in cases in which self-descriptions at the operative level can indeed be found.

cannot deny that the system is entitled to distinguish between legal and illegal or that one has to adhere to 'valid' norms. This does not mean necessarily that the texts of self-description guide the everyday practice of the system, as statutes do. This is rather unlikely 'and indeed it is hard to imagine many JPs [Justices of the Peace, N.L.] thumbing through the *Summa Theologiae* after a hard day at the sessions'.[2] But it can be assumed that legal practice presupposes that the fundamental questions of the meaning of the system can be answered and it bases its decision-making on that in the form of a presupposition (rather than on information).

These requirements, namely the reference to the identity of the system that describes itself and the autological inclusion of the description in what is described, distinguish reflexive theories from normal juridical theories, for instance, on the irrelevance of motive in contract with a possible exception in the case of a mistake, which can be detected by the contracting party. Such distinctions were made traditionally, including orthodox ones between the general principles of the doctrine of natural law and what lawyers adduce in their reasons for decisions. Today this difference is marked by the distinction between legal philosophy (or more recently also 'legal theory') and jurisprudence. We will not discuss such academic distinctions any further but maintain that the special task of the self-description of the legal system is not highly differentiated reasoning in decision-making but the presentation of the unity, function, and autonomy, and also the indifference of the legal system. There are only relatively few points, which make the transition from one context to the other possible, such as the connections between freedom/subjective rights/right to take legal action in person.

The above distinction notwithstanding, self-descriptions are, like all descriptions, concretely performed operations, which depend on the system and on a context. They do not present what 'there is' but construct what follows from their presuppositions. In this regard we follow Stanley Fish's widely known neo-pragmatic theory of interpretation.[3] Hence self-descriptions operate invariably within accepted limitations, which another observer can observe as particular to them. Further they have to install a boundary within the system, which they describe and thus perform, and across which they can observe something else and, from there, themselves.

---

[2] Edward Powell, *Kingship, Law, and Society: Criminal Justice in the Reign of Henry V* (Oxford, 1989), 29.

[3] See, with respect to both literary and juridical interpretations, Stanley Fish, *Doing What Comes Naturally: Change, Rhetoric, and the Practice of Theory in Literary and Legal Studies* (Oxford, 1989). This is, however, quite a different perspective in so far as Fish, without giving any further thought to the matter, talks about describing, interpreting, etc. individuals, whereas for us the basic operation is communication and accordingly the respective reference is to the social system, be it the social system, society, or the legal system.

The problem that arises in this way has been known since Fichte's writings. It has to do with the embedding of difference in a system, which not only has to be identified but also has to be performed. The result is always a paradox, which can be unfolded.[4] It requires that the paradox be hidden during the process, that there is a partial invisibilization, and that the invisibilities that are the result of the operation be accepted. In the case of the legal system this means, above all, that a stop must be placed somewhere in the system where the quest for finding the final reason of law must end. In performing its self-description the system must presuppose and accept itself.[5]

It is self-evident that self-descriptions presuppose writing as a form for texts. As long as books were relatively rare and not easily accessible, the possibilities for differentiation were limited. The postulate of justice referred to society as a whole, to keeping one's station and to the conduct of the political regime. It applied to any kind of body, in medicine as well as in law. Not until the advent of printing was a sufficiently large volume of text created which made further differentiations possible. There were specific legal texts before the invention of printing. But only printing made reflexion possible, which was differentiated in the legal system itself—initially under the traditional name of philosophy, that is, legal philosophy. The operation of self-description is accordingly related to printed publication. And what cannot be printed for one reason or another (which does not need to be related to law) has no chance of impacting on the self-description of the system.

II

To describe the self-description of the legal system from the outside, it is tempting to use identification with legal norms. Participants can be expected to conduct themselves loyally to the demands of the system, regardless of whatever their subjective motives, their own thoughts, their ambitions, or their interests may be. Likewise, various other forms of communication, which are possible and can be expected in society, must be ignored, if they cannot be attributed to the legal system. Even within the

---

[4] There is supporting literature on this point, but most of it is on the sidelines of the dominant discussion in legal theory. See, for example, Benjamin N. Cardozo, *The Paradoxes of Legal Science* (New York, 1928); George P. Fletcher, 'Paradoxes in Legal Thought', *Columbia Law Review* 85 (1985), 1263–92; Roberta Kevelson, *Peirce, Paradox, Praxis: The Image, the Conflict, and the La* (Berlin, 1990); Michel van de Kerchove and François Ost, *Le droit ou les paradoxes du jeu* (Paris, 1992).

[5] Pierre Bourdieu formulates a similar situation somewhat more strongly as a connection of description and prescription in: *Ce que parler veut dire: l'économie des échanges linguistiques* (Paris, 1982), 149.

legal system, quite clearly not every communication is a contribution to the self-description of the system.

No description can afford to miss its object, but the internal ties of self-description go further than that. For the self-description must integrate *itself* in the system that it describes and this can happen only when system-specific ties are adopted and made into a topic. If it were otherwise, the self-description could not present itself as such or distinguish itself from external descriptions. In other words, a self-description cannot contest that it is in principle right to follow norms and do what the legal system pre-scribes.[6] The function of stabilizing expectations is interpreted as an instruction on how to conduct oneself. And this is the point: the function is interpreted. What is involved is neither simply more norms nor 'higher' norms but just reasons—not recipes for legal conduct, but an account of reasons for such conduct. Above all the distinction between norms and facts, which is of central importance to the system, is not marked in its rela-tion to facts but in its relation to normativity. That means that it is unac-ceptable for the system to see mere facts when it encounters norms (for instance, factual normative expectations). Instead it prefers a tautological symbolization of normativity (against the uncontested background that norms are indispensable if society is to continue): norms signify what ought to be. And sociology of law, when it insists on the simple facticity of norms, is accused of misunderstanding the special characteristics of norms.[7] Because the distinction between norms and facts is crucial to the system itself (because it closes itself through norms), every 'reduction' of norms to facts is unacceptable.[8]

This description needs further explanation. It fits the normative pro-grammes of the legal system but not its binary coding, which is the crucial feature for maintaining the identity of the legal system. Without coding there would be no compulsory decision-making in the legal system and hence no full responsibility for the function conferred on it by society. Without the reduction to two values, which can be converted into each other, there would be no practicable logic in the system.[9] The conventional

---

[6] This is the core issue of the so-called neutralization thesis, which is presented as a socio-logical theory of deviance. See the references above (Ch. 6.III, n. 47). The difference between external and internal description is also evident here. Obviously, 'neutralization' is not an argument that can be used in the legal system itself, and is even less a form for the description of the unity of the system.

[7] See, for example, Werner Krawietz, 'Staatliches oder gesellschaftliches Recht? Systemabhängigkeiten normativer Strukturbildung im Funktionssystem Recht', in Michael Welker and Werner Krawietz (eds.), *Kritik der Theorie sozialer Systeme* (Frankfurt, 1992), 247–301.

[8] This, by the way, has nothing to do with the undisputed, frequently quoted insight that logic does not permit us to draw inferences about norms from facts.

[9] I say 'practicable' with regard to the possibility of developing multiple-values logic, which would, however, create insurmountable difficulties in the everyday administration of justice.

technique of argumentation depends on coding as well. It posits tacitly that there are no other values apart from legal and illegal, and that in pleading for the legality of one's position one can show that an opposing position is illegal. This technique presupposes, for instance, that for certain facts there is only one correct decision, which must be repeated in a repeat case. Hence this technique would not be able to deal with the experience of equal cases being decided unequally (or it would have to construct them as unequal cases). The self-description of the system would not be able to instruct insiders in any other way than what is expected of them by the system.

In other words, self-description must presuppose that controversial communication is being dealt with in the legal system and that this is not the result of an unfortunately unavoidable defect but the consequence of the function and the coding of the system. This leads to a further compulsory element of the description, which all self-description has to accept. All communication in the system must be styled as leading to a decision and a decision is that which can claim to be based on good reasons, even if they only mention valid law. It does not suffice simply to present personal wishes, interests, and preferences, as with transactions in the economic system.[10] Rather, forms of presentation must be sought and found which suggest that a solution which conforms to the system is possible—whether labelled as rational, reasonable, or just.[11] The system must be addressed as a decision-maker, however controversial the ensuing facts, rules and principles may be and may remain. Communication can be critical about every norm but if it is critical, it must offer a substitute suggestion. It cannot simply suggest anarchy, free choice, or nothing. It must respect the necessity of arriving at a decision in the centre of the system, that is, in the courts. Therefore, the self-description of the system has also to fulfil the requirement of styling controversies argumentatively, otherwise it would not be a self-description. Regardless of the attempted achievement, this must be tested in the system and with reference to the means of argumentation available in the system. It is not necessarily a matter of ultimately finding the right answer to every question but rather of communicating as if there were one, *etsi non daretur Deus.*

In contrast to normal communication in the legal system, which needs reasons for the request for legal decisions and reasons for the decisions themselves, the self-description of the system can avoid partiality. It is not involved in deciding whether a manufacturer is liable for faulty goods and any resulting damage, or whether the purchaser must accept the risk. It is comparatively easy to support the one or the other solution in such cases

---

[10] See the discussion above at Ch. 7.IV and Ch. 8.VII and VIII.

[11] See on this point of 'taking its postulate seriously', Ronald M. Dworkin, 'No Right Answer?', in P. M. S. Hacker and Joseph Raz (eds.), *Law, Morality, and Society: Essays in Honour of H.L.A. Hart* (Oxford, 1977), 58–84.

(especially since in the above-mentioned case the purchaser will in any event incur the costs of the insurance). Only the giving up of partiality in controversies leads to the *real* problem of self-description, namely of finding out *what is implied when a system promises to give an answer to every question and forces all the operations of the system to presuppose that there is such an answer.*

Means of argumentation may change, but compulsory decision-making stays. One must describe the system in such a way that the search for the right answer remains meaningful—even if there is increasing doubt that there is *one* right answer. Again and again, attempts are made to suggest principled answers—if no longer the *will of God*, then the *maximization of welfare*. It may be no accident that these descriptions recur to an Archimedean point outside the legal system, to *religion* and *economy* in our examples. The same applies to Jeremy Bentham's or John Austin's suggestions of usurping the sovereign authority of the *political* ruler as a source of law. Kelsen's Pure Theory of Law ultimately falls into this pattern, too, by formulating the problem as a problem of legal knowledge, therefore trying to solve it in the *scientific* style of a proposition being introduced as a hypothesis. This dominant reference to the science system shows up quite differently in the type of reflexions which have been called 'legal theory' for the past decades.[12] Here the self-description of the legal system has tried to find support from interdisciplinary approaches, such as linguistics, semiology, hermeneutics, sociology, and anthropology. There are evidently four suggestions to describe the unity of the system by reference to religion,[13] economy, politics, and science as a precondition for the possibility of controversies, and at the same time as a precondition for the possibility of deciding them. All of these four suggestions make use of plausible arguments that are provided by modern, functionally differentiated society, namely recurrence to a differentiated functioning system.

It is easy to see how the functional differentiation of society is used here to explain the unity of the legal system with the help of external references. Logic also tells us, according to Gödel, that a system of logic is unable to explain its status of being without contradictions (as a symbol of its unity) by reference to itself and must find the conditions for that outside and apart from itself. In this respect, the self-description of the legal system is confronted with a plurality of possible reference points in its environment. We have mentioned religion, economy, politics, and science as being the reference points used up until now in reflexive theories of law. This leads

---

[12] See also Ch. 1.I.

[13] Even in strictly religious legal regimes based on the will of God, this factor is recognized and dissent cannot be condemned only because it is dissent. See, for example, David Daube, 'Dissent in Bible and Talmud', *California Law Review* 55 (1971), 784–94. Or even more clearly, see the myth of the oven of Akhnai, which serves as an introduction to Gunther Teubner's book on *Law as an Autopoietic System* (Oxford, 1983).

on to the question of how to decide between these different options on the basis of the legal system itself, or whether they can be tested historically, one after the other, and thus exhausted. It would seem reasonable to replace this kind of externalization with a reference to the social system of society as a whole. However, this would mean designing reflexive theory in far more complex way. For the legal system is, after all, a sub-system of the social system and, in referring to society, it thus refers both to its environment inside society and to itself. In this form, which is guided by systems theory, we can perhaps find a convincing solution to the problem. However, this has not yet been attempted, at least not in a form that could demonstrate its benefits to the legal system's own operations.

Whatever principle is chosen, the insider perspective tells us that there are no longer any alternatives to it. The principle can be realized with more or less success, but for example it may be that the maximization of welfare is as impossible as a life without sin, assuming the existence of God. Taken as a principle, however, the principle does not differ from other formulae with the same function. It has to be followed 'blindly'. However, what happens when one person observes that another person follows a principle?

A critique based on systems theory has little trouble here. Once the difference between system and environment is presupposed (and this is not done by the above-mentioned theories), it is easy to see that the unity of the system cannot be found in this distinction. Neither can it be found in the system or in the environment. The search for the Archimedean point[14] reacts to the impossibility of representing the unity of the system compellingly and meta-controversially in the system. Hence to seek to locate it in the environment is equally misconceived.[15] Seen from outside, the system is a web of operatively used distinctions, 'polyvalence sans unité possible' in the words of Julia Kristeva.[16] And this is the problem to which one can apply only the distinction between operation and observation/description and see the unity of the system as a result of operations, which are unobservable while being performed. The self-description of the system, then, is one among many operations in the system. If one wants to know how the system describes itself, one must observe this operation and expose oneself to being observed while observing the observations of the system.

[14] In the context of a self-referential explanation of his utilitarian theory of law, Jeremy Bentham, *An Introduction to The Principle of Morals and Legislation* (1789; New York, 1948), 5, writes: 'Is it possible for a man to move the earth? Yes; but he must find out another earth to stand upon'.

[15] The theological solution has at least the advantage that it can refer to God as an observer of the system. Unfortunately this is not very helpful if one has to concede in the same move that this observer cannot be observed in turn. This is the reason why Pufendorf, Locke, and many of their contemporaries could not but specify the will of God with a kind of calculus of utility, with the presupposition that the welfare of humans was in God's interest. Then, however, one cannot avoid having to concede considerable deficiencies in creation.

[16] Julia Kristeva, *Semiotikè: Recherches pour une sémanalyse* (Paris, 1969), 11.

This includes having to give up the idea of a unitary solution. Instead, attention is drawn to the way in which the system limits validity and its means of argumentation. This is exactly what the contemporary 'institutional' theory of law does.[17] It explains our presuppositions that the self-description of the system must identify with its conditions, to which there must be agreement when looking for problem-solving in the system. This makes it tolerable for us to accept that we must live with an 'open texture'[18] and that there are some controversies that cannot be decided by argumentation.[19] The crucial point is that the system itself limits the latitude with which it must recur to its norms of competency, and factually makes dispositions over the symbols of validity that then provide points of departure for further operations.[20] Reference to the unity of the system is replaced with reference to the operative closure of the system.

III

The natural law of old Europe is so far back in the past and is so removed from us today that not even the full extent of this distance registers properly with us. On the other hand, the reflexive theories in current legal thought can be understood only if we see both that distance and how they developed from natural law and, in doing so, encountered the problems that define the current discussion. This also applies to those cases in which argumentation even nowadays still refers to traditional natural law (or refers to it afresh).

Seen from the perspective of social structures, the important starting-point for natural law was the discrepancy between legal-political units, especially city-states or small territorial states, and trade, which went far beyond their borders. Out of that there continually arose issues of the legal status of strangers, to whom the law, reserved as it was for citizens, could not be applied—or to put it in Roman terms: issues associated with *ius gentium.* Some important legal propositions in the Digests in medieval times go further than that by including animals, thus distinguishing between natural law and the law of nations (law of all human beings).[21] This detour via the

---

[17] See, for example, as a representative work, Neil MacCormick and Ota Weinberger, *Grundlagen des institutionalistischen Rechtspositivismus* (Berlin, 1985).

[18] H. L. A. Hart, *The Concept of Law* (Oxford, 1961).

[19] See for arguments against Dworkin, Neil MacCormick, *Legal Reasoning and Legal Theory* (Oxford, 1978), 229.

[20] I have tried to show that this procedure also has a factual side of gaining acceptance and of isolating or politicizing protests, in: Niklas Luhmann, *Legitimation durch Verfahren* (Neuwied 1969; reprint Frankfurt, 1983).

[21] See D.1.1.1.3: 'Ius naturale est, quod natura omnia animalia docuit', distinguished from D.1.1.1.4: 'Ius gentium est, quo gentes humanae utuntur'. Perhaps the most famous example is the right to procreate, which is constituted as a natural instinct but can be *limited as natural*

animal world is significant in relation to the practice of argumentation, because it started a tradition that was maintained well into modern times of justifying deviations from the quasi-animalistic natural law: marriage as a deviation from the natural drive to reproduction, slavery as a deviation from natural freedom, property as a deviation from natural collective ownership, in short: culture as a deviation from natural law. In no way, however, can natural law be seen—in this strand of argumentation (there are of course other strands![22])—as a higher order of law, not to mention a legal form of moral principles. When moral legal principles were referred to in medieval times, the term *aequitas* was preferred.[23]

Interwoven in this argumentation is another idea. Following on from Aristotle, but above all since the High Middle Ages, natural law has assumed that in nature there natures (beings) which are conscious of themselves. Reason (*ratio*) is thus allocated its place and develops as nature in nature. When self-knowledge was referred to in the Middle Ages, it did not mean the recognition of one's own individual special status, let alone subjectivity. Rather it meant recognition of one's own nature, which was understood in *analogia entis* as the individual case of the soul of the world, as *imago Dei*, as a creature of creation.[24] In particular, the idea of the human being as a 'microcosm' suggested that the whole world was accessible through introspection.[25] Even the Aristotelianism of the German Protestants kept alive the idea that theological, moral, and political norms of natural law could be recognized by introspection.[26] Pufendorf demanded that human beings *know* their natural rights by association in a civil society, even if only through a secularized and thus diffuse concept of nature which could only be used polemically. However, interestingly enough, he was no

---

law by international law and to an even greater extent by civil law. On the discussions in the glosses see in considerable detail Rudolf Weigand, *Die Naturrechtslehre der Legisten und Dekretisten von Irnerius bis Accursius and von Gratian bis Johannes Teutonicus* (Munich, 1967), esp. 12 and 78.

[22] For instance, *aequitas* which was used in law rather more innovatively (D.1.1.11, Paulus), or the *ius suum cuique tribuendi* (D.1.1.10 pr and 1. Ulpian) which was used more for definitions of justice and with direct reference to stratification.

[23] Thus Johannes of Salisbury, for example, in the book of Policraticus IV, ch. II, often quoted from the edition *Ioannis Saresberiensis . . . Policratici . . . libri VIII* (London, 1909; reprint Frankfurt, 1965), vol. I, p. 237, with reference to *aequitas* and the *tribuens unicuique quod suum est: lex vero eius interpres est, utpote cui aequitatis et iustitiae voluntas innotuit.*

[24] The mirror metaphor used in the Middle Ages can only be understood in this way. The mirror does not just double the pure facticity of individual specialness but it reflects what one ought to be according to nature (including social status).

[25] See on this point Marian Kurdziak, 'Der Mensch als Abbild des Kosmos', in Albert Zimmermann (ed.), *Der Begriff der Repraesentatio im Mittelalter: Stellvertretung, Symbol, Zeichen, Bild* (Berlin, 1971), 35–71.

[26] See Horst Dreitzel, 'Grundrechtskonzeptionen in der protestantischen Rechts- und Staatslehre im Zeitalter der Glaubenskämpfe', in Günter Birtsch (ed.), *Grund- und Freiheitsrechte von der ständischen zur spätbürgerlichen Gesellschaft* (Göttingen, 1987), 180–214.

longer concerned with knowledge about the *nature* of the individual but with knowledge about the rights of the individual.[27] Other authors of early modern times also distinguished between natural instincts and natural rights, following on from Melanchthon.[28] Their reasoning led people to the insight that they were made for a life in society and one dependent on cooperation. This led to law as a precondition for the possibility of society. However, it is easy to see at the same time that this did not solve all legal issues. On the one hand, nature gives different preferences to individuals or to various groups of individuals—also and especially in relation to the goal of living together. This follows from the rationality of pursuing one's own goals. Consequently, issues that are important for the common good must be regulated.[29] Moreover knowledge of nature does not provide an answer to some questions. These *adiaphora* require regulation.[30] This in turn follows from knowledge about nature, whereby action is oriented by goals and must adjust to very different natural and social conditions. In this respect the demand for positive law and authoritative legislation follows from nature itself.[31] *Natural law itself creates the difference between natural law and positive law.* Accordingly, the problem of the validity of law is solved by a re-entry: the distinction between natural law and positive law is copied into natural law. Only under these conditions can one talk in any seriousness about a foundation of law in natural law. One often finds the formulation that the legal quality of positive law presupposes the indifference of natural law to the corresponding issue of regulation. Hence natural law was understood as a higher order of law in the cosmological world-view of the Middle Ages. At the same time, however, the 'animalist' concept of natural law was maintained in the discussion, according to which human society develops as a deviation from a natural (legal) state, that is, against natural law. Thus the relation between natural law and positive law remained ambivalent in the self-description of law of the Middle Ages and early modern times. In this tradition, which still took natural law seriously, one cannot find what contemporary philosophers of law would expect: namely that natural law provides the foundation for positive law.[32] Natural law was seen as either

---

[27] See Samuel Pufendorf, *De jure naturae et gentium libri octo* 8.I.II. quoted from the edition Frankfurt-Leipzig 1744, vol. II at 287: 'Enimvero heic preasupponi debet, homines in civitatem coituros iam tum iuris naturalis fuisse intelligentes.'

[28] See Horst Dreitzel, *Protestantischer Aristotelismus und absoluter Staat: Die 'Politica' des Henning Arnisaeus (ca. 1575–1636),* (Wiesbaden, 1970), 197.

[29] Thomas Aquinas, *Summa Theologiae* Ia IIae q. 96 a.3. See also IIa IIae q. 57 a.2.

[30] See Aristotle, *Nicomachean Ethics,* vol. v, ch. 10 1134^{b}18–24. See also Thomas, *Summa Theologiae,* Ia IIae q. 95 a.2.

[31] The argument is: 'Natura autem hominis est mutabilis. Et ideo id quod naturale est homini potest aliquando deficere' (IIa IIae q. 57 a.2 ad primum).

[32] Perhaps one can be so bold as to assume that such a proposition is completely meaningless until there is not only civil law but also public law, that is, at the earliest, after the seventeenth century.

indifferent about civil law or prepared to accept deviation. And the idea that both kinds of law corresponded to God's creation-plan served as a unifying perspective.

Even though it was apparent that the law was not natural law in every detail and that in different countries and at different times there were different legal regimes all based on natural law, natural law was seen as the foundation for the validity of law proper, because the nature of the world order and of humankind required that there be law. It followed that the positive statute was a part of reason, in so far as it was deduced from natural law. Vice versa, it followed that in the case of the violation of natural law, there was no statute but only a corruption of the statute.[33] If such a corruption *is* not a law (just as a tyrant is not a king), no one will have to obey it and resistance will be permitted, or maybe even commanded.

As will be evident, this theory concluded from the schema of natural perfection/corruption that there is a schema of validity/invalidity of all derivatives of natural law. Depending on whether one opted for one side or the other, it legitimized obedience or resistance—but only on the condition that there was no ill will or intractably conflicting values, but always only the question of true knowledge or error.

This theory became unacceptable in the modern territorial state. On the one hand, the hope lingered on that God might influence the sovereign sufficiently, and this expectation was used as the concluding formula for the validity of law. But on the other hand, for all practical purposes it was already clear in the sixteenth century that the authoritative declaration of law was all that mattered.[34] The contribution of religion to the development of law and the constitution was now mainly their form, associated with the reaction to civil wars. Further, a binding to nature was now claimed only for the rational nature of human beings, which could be connected to the increasing legislative activities of the modern territorial state and the need to find reasons for the claim that they were binding. Natural law became rational law almost seamlessly while knowledge of the nature of

---

[33] 'Unde omnis lex humanitus posita intantum habet de ratione legis, inquantum a lege naturae derivatur. Si vero in aliquo, a lege naturali discordet, iam non erit lex sed legis corruptio' (Thomas, *Summa Theologiae*, Ia IIae q. 95 a.2).

[34] See, apart from the frequently quoted Bodin, for example, François Grimaudet, *Opuscules politiques* (Paris, 1580), fol. II: the laws are the 'souverain raison, empreinte par Dieu, qui commande les choses qui sont à faire & deffend les contraires, faicte et publiée par céluy qui a puissance de commander'. And: 'Car la loy est l'Œuvre du Prince'. The transitional character of such strong words reveals itself in the fact that, although justice is required from the prince, the author keeps the distinction *rex/tyrannus* (fol. 3–4ʳ) and advises that orders which violated natural law (unlike violations of civil law) do not have to be carried out (fol. 5ᵛ ff.). However the initial statement is reminiscent of John Austin or other legal positivists of the nineteenth century who, of course, no longer referred to God but to politics guided by public opinion before legal process.

reason was gradually replaced with a discussion of the rational principles of legal reasoning.[35] The law of reason, however, had always been associated with revolutionary law and thus could be made into positive law after the revolution, or at least that is what was believed. It was taken over by constitutional law. Hence this breakaway did not manifest itself in the harsh way in which it was actually carried out. And the circumstances were favourable in that the special social conditions in the British colonies in America permitted a greater mix of natural law and positive law.[36] Moreover, in a seemingly conspicuous display of consent, reason appeared to accept the different national contexts of the different legal orders of territorial states, as if even their differences were reasonable. Nevertheless, it still remained uncontested that natural law was not only the foundation of validity of all law but also its *knowledge* foundation.[37] This changed, as law became positive law. There was a dramatic increase in legislative activity. This was noticed, but it was not seen as being a problem of the new foundation of law.[38] From now on the law *recognized a demand for change measured exclusively on its own terms* (triggered by external demand, of course); and a theory which tried to reflect that could, at best, look at concepts of values, or raise issues of legitimation. This called for new attempts at a synthesis. Hence around 1800, the new philosophy of positive law tried to establish a connection between legislative decisions and the principles associated with the experience of legal practice (probably under the influence of Hume, who was preferred to Kant) and here rationality was inferred, at best, only secondarily, namely on the basis of proven historical practice.[39] The contemporary codifications may have served as evidence and at the same time as a

---

[35] A comparison with the preceding tradition can help to show what was happening. Matthew Hale argued in his work directed against Hobbes on the following basis: Reason (reasonableness) pervades the context of things, 'Congruity, Connexion and fitt Dependence' and precedes all exercise of human faculties. A judge has to acknowledge this reason, in spite of compelling 'Inevidence of Laws' and unavoidable disadvantages ('mischiefs') of all solutions. The judge should trust 400–500 years of tradition more than his own theories. See *Reflections by the Lord Cheife Justice Hale on Mr. Hobbes His Dialogue of the Lawe*, printed in: William Holdsworth, *A History of English Law*, 3rd edn. (London, 1945, reprint 1966), vol. V, Appendix III, pp. 500–513.

[36] See *Gerhard Oestreich, Geschichte der Menschenrechte und der Grundfreiheiten im Umruß* (Berlin, 1968), 58.

[37] See, for example, Jean Domat, *Les loix civiles dans leur ordre naturel*, 2nd edn. (Paris, 1697), vol. I, p. lxxiii.

[38] See, with quantitative data for England, David Liebermann, *The Province of Legislation Determined: Legal Theory in Eighteenth-Century Britain* (Cambridge, 1989), 13.

[39] See on terminological aspects, Jürgen Blühdorn, 'Zum Zusammenhang von "Positivität" und "Empirie" im Verständnis der deutschen Rechtswissenschaft zu Beginn des 19. Jahrhunderts', in Jürgen Blühdorn and Joachim Ritter (eds.), *Positivismus im 19. Jahrhundert: Beiträge zu seiner geschichtlichen und systematischen Bedeutung* (Frankfurt, 1971), 123–59, especially on the connection between Hume, Pütter, und Hugo; see also for greater detail Giuliano Marini, *L'opera di Gustav Hugo nelle cisi del giusnaturalismo tedesco* (Milan, 1969).

guarantee of the possibility of such a synthesis. In this context one can understand the controversy between Savigny and Thibaut.[40] These were developments which in modern times have become irreversible. Consequently, the argumentational practice of today no longer talks about what the reasonableness of the nature of humankind predicates as right, but rather about reasonable and expected behaviour in situations that are already fully regulated by positive law—as in traffic regulation or in relation to consumer consciousness.[41] All in all, the breakaway from the traditional foundations appears not to have been so abrupt as to bring about special epistemological reflections, as occurred in the parallel context of knowledge.[42]

The new natural law of the seventeenth and eighteenth centuries turned against the traditional order by stressing the individuals' right to have their own interests and proclaiming self-determination, liberty, and equality as natural human rights. This is understandable in the historical context, considering that the aristocracy could no longer be seen as an emanation of natural law, due to the many political elevations to the rank of nobility and the many privileges and dispensations for nobles (as exemptions from valid general law). The aristocracy, rather, had to be seen as a mere state institution (even if 'birth', 'race', etc. were still stressed and even more so than before).[43] With the natural right to individuality, it became possible to formulate a principle that was neutral in relation to class. It no longer referred to natural law in the old sense but to limitations under positive law and to their guarantees in constitutional law. The constitution became necessary as a limitation of the limitations of natural ('wild') freedom and of natural equality (which could not be realized in society).[44]

The old question of the legitimacy of the deviations from natural law also reacted to this change—which can easily be defined with the keywords of

---

[40] See for a new edition: Jacques Stern (ed.), *Thibaut und Savigny: Ein programmatischer Rechtsstreit auf Grund ihrer Schriften* (Darmstadt, 1959). See also Franz Wieacker, 'Die Ausbildung einer allgemeinen Theorie des positiven Rechts in Deutschland im 19. Jahrhundert', in *Festschrift für Karl Michaelis* (Göttingen, 1972), 354–62.

[41] See Jutta Limbach, *Der verständige Rechtsgenosse* (Berlin, 1977).

[42] This is the thesis of Christian Atias, *Epistémologie juridique* (Paris, 1985), 45.

[43] See for a concise overview of the diversity of the criteria for aristocracy in France, Arlette Jouanna, 'Die Legitimierung des Adels und die Erhebung in den Adelsstand in Frankreich (16.–18. Jahrhundert)', in Winfried Schulze (ed.), *Ständische Gesellschaft und Mobilität* (Munich, 1988), 165–77. Even if natural law, in the strict sense, was eliminated by this, *ius gentium* as well as the civil law could still be conceived of as representing the undoubted historical and international general pervasiveness of the distinction between the aristocracy and the people. However, *ius gentium* was then still interpreted according to Roman law sources. See Klaus Bleeck and Jörn Garber, 'Nobilitas: Standes- und Privilegienlegitimation in deutschen Adelstheorien des 16. und 17. Jahrhunderts', *Daphnis* 11 (1982), 49–114, at 90.

[44] See Benjamin N. Cardozo, *The Paradoxes of Legal Science* (New York, 1928), 94: 'Liberty as a legal concept contains an underlying paradox. Liberty in the most literal sense is the negation of law, for law is a restraint, and the absence of restraint is anarchy'. This applies correspondingly to equality. Thus the contested compatibility of both these human rights depends

absolutism and individualism. This question was then answered by reference to the constructions of contracts. Natural freedom was limited, if not altogether sacrificed, by the social contract, the state contract and individual contracts. The emphasis on freedom, which includes a free, that is contractual, renunciation of freedom, at the same time legitimates the renunciation of a right to resistance and of the subjection of the subject to the absolute state.[45] Here, too, the achievements of civilization in the form of individual freedom and a (peaceful) society organized by state order were presented as deviations from natural law, that is, as paradoxes.

A further change involved the rationality of the individual's attitude towards law. Under a regime of natural law, it was considered rational to observe the law and follow its commandments. The individual could not win against the law. This applied to everybody equally without regard to character or circumstances. A respect for individuality could be expressed only within the law itself and, of course, through a differentiation of status, roles, and contractual obligations. This premiss was changed with the development of positive law, because the law itself no longer expressed any rationality which was binding for the individual. According to Bentham's calculus of utility, the overriding benefit to an individual could be achieved by violating legal norms. At any rate it was no longer possible to deduce the rationality for the individual from the rationality for all. In contemporary theories on rational choice, or the 'new political economy', or the economic analysis of law, we are thus able to draw the conclusion that the rationality of law has to be calculated on the level of a second-order observation. Law is only rational to the extent that it is designed in a way that makes it rational for individuals to follow legal norms.

These considerations show that the positivization of law is tightly linked to semantic and structural innovations, which attempted to adjust society to the individuality of individuals to a greater degree, abstaining from the implementation of the rationality of cosmic or religious or communal conditions in individual behaviour. The new formation of freedom rights as human rights was set against the background of the positivization of law by the territorial state.[46] This applied particularly to the extravagant claim that the individual was the subject. It also applied in literature, especially the

---

in both cases on dissolving a paradox. However, this happens in different ways, leading to contradictions. Using in a different formulation, one could say that the paradoxical, basic structure of these two human rights has the function of keeping the future open for the preservation of limitations and for their substitution by such limitations. If this is still called 'natural law', the concept loses any connection with its conventional use.

[45] See for great detail, Diethelm Klippel, *Politische Freiheit and Freiheitsrechte im deutschen Naturrecht des 18. Jahrhunderts* (Paderborn, 1976).

[46] See ibid., and also Winfried Schulze, 'Ständische Gesellschaft und Individualrechte', in Günter Birtsch (ed.), *Grund- und Freiheitsrechte von der ständischen zur spätbürgerlichen Gesellschaft* (Göttingen, 1987), 161–79.

modern novel that puts the individual centre stage. And it applied to the new demography and the concept of population, which, from the second half of the eighteenth century, started to replace the old thinking in natural categories with a generative isolation that had to be explained by evolution. It also applied, in the same context of social transformation and for the same reasons, to the positivization of law.[47]

As a result of all this, the positivity of law became the theme of the self-presentation of law in modern society. The reflexion was considerably hampered by the fact that 'positivity' was a traditional term. The pejorative connotation and the expectation of a 'higher' meaning could not be entirely suppressed. The humanist-anthropological foundation of positive law in the 'human will' (in contrast to the nature of things) lost its unequivocal reference. Who or what was meant? The formula of a *volonté générale* expressed this dilemma. And yet it was difficult to give up the traditional voluntarism. After all, what was at stake was making decisions which constitute or remove legal validity, while all social theory still referred to the individual human being. Thus the problem of the arbitrariness of the will remained unsolved or was shifted to the political postulate of representative democracy. Nevertheless, the semantics of 'positivity' had the advantage of being at the crossroads of various distinctions and of thus being able to juggle the swapping of opposites. Positive is *not natural* but is posited and hence can be observed as a decision. Positive is *not speculative* but is founded demonstrably on facts and statutes. And positive is *not negative*. In the nineteenth century, these distinctions, which left the definition of positivity open, merged, and this is where the secret of the success of 'positivism' can be found.[48] However, it became clear in principle that the differentiation of a special system of legally protected expectations out of the full range of socially habituated norms could be achieved only by positivization, that is, by a recursive closure of the system. The only choice left was to see this as ethical or as unsatisfactory in other respects. However, one was then obliged to accept the onus of proof and demonstrate how one could come to an unequivocal definition of certain norms in a different, super-legal way, and declare that as binding.

When there is talk nowadays of natural law regardless of all these developments, there is no support for it from the concept of nature and the natural sciences. The need to explain things, which is expected of this concept, certainly cannot be filled by the mindless continuation of one of the great labels in the history of ideas. This applies, a fortiori, to a transcendental

---

[47] See, for more detail, Niklas Luhmann, 'Individual, Individualität, Individualismus', in id., *Gesellschaftsstruktur und Semantik*, vol. 3 (Frankfurt, 1989), 149–258.

[48] See on this point the erudite discussion in Jürgen Blühdorn and Joachim Ritter (eds.), *Positivismus im 19. Jahrhundert: Beiträge zu seiner geschichtlichen und systematischen Bedeutung* (Frankfurt, 1971), 27.

concept of reason in the Kantian tradition, which was removed from nature and which could only go as far as Kant himself took it, having already involved a certain amount of impartial, supposedly judicial, competence.[49] It is staggering how freely and how out of context these labels are dished out today and used as a stop to reflexion or how they are misused as a reinforcement of mere postulates.[50] The concept of natural law, in particular, has shown its powers of political adaptability by staying the course of the development of the medieval legal order, the transition to the 'sovereign' territorial state, absolutism, enlightened absolutism, and finally the constitutionally legal positivization of human rights. If one today hopes to derive from that an insurance against the possible return of National Socialism, or a similar regime of terror, one can only say that the history of this formula for the self-description of the legal system shows exactly the opposite. Even if we share Jürgen Habermas's view that there is a need for a reasonable legitimation of law, even in our 'post-conventional' age, and some attempt is made to find it in a theory of discourse, this is incompatible with a legitimation of law based on natural law (and therefore rigid legitimation).[51]

Quite apart from the obsolescence of the semantics, the social-structural foundations, which once made the coupling of natural law, common good, and justice plausible, are also gone. In the old world of aristocratic societies, the foundations of legal order could be found in justice. Justice was, on the one hand, an appropriate, virtuous attitude towards living sociably with others and was, on the other hand, what was owed to the individual in view of his station in society, and such stations were regarded as immutable. Thus justice was the rational perfection of the (urban, political, civil) social nature of humans and, as such, the object of a knowledge base in which one could be wrong but could not express value in any other way. The social structure took for granted that even if there were social conflicts, it was possible to discern and distinguish with the existing law how, and possibly with which rules, neutral third parties would assess those conflicts. This was even the case when professional juridical knowledge was required for the formulation of a decision. Given such conditions, it was also possible to find fictitious reasons for the validity of law, for instance myths or assumptions about the ancient origins of a law which had since proved itself in practice.[52]

---

[49] See Joachim Lege, 'Wie juridisch ist die Vernunft? Kants "Kritik der reinen Vernunft" und die richterliche Methode', *Archiv für Rechts- und Sozialphilosophie* 76 (1990), 203–26.

[50] See the overview and critique by Noberto Bobbio, *Giusnaturalismo e positivismo giuridico*, 2nd edn. (Milan, 1972), esp. 159. Bobbio concludes from the constant rebirth of natural law doctrine that it does not manage to grow up (p. 190).

[51] See, for one of his many repeated arguments, Jürgen Habermas, *Faktizität und Geltung: Beiträge zu einer Diskurstheorie des Rechts und des demokratischen Rechtsstaats* (Frankfurt, 1992).

[52] A formulation that survived in English common law until far into the eighteenth century.

This concept of the world lost its structural conditions in the transition to modern society. In spite of all the efforts to preserve or even revive it, the original sound can no longer be reproduced.[53] When in doubt, social reflexivity does not lead back to consensus but to dissent. As Giddens's terse comment suggests: 'Reflexivity subverts reason'.[54] Even the early modern debate, triggered by Hobbes, whether reason can be found in the rules and principles of law itself or only by following authoritative statute law, did not survive the nineteenth century.[55] The legal theory of modern society instead offers two different models of the self-description of law, to which it must be added immediately that there is no agreement about either of them. Each side to the controversy, which we can also call the 'debate on positivism' in legal theory, takes its direction from the defects of the other side, but cannot, it appears, see its own defects.

IV

The need to find a new concept of law, which would reflect social change, had already become apparent in the sixteenth century, in connection with the reconstruction of the political order of states after the breakdown of religious unity, and the political realization of this new order in the idea of empire. Now more than ever before, law itself became the guarantor of national and international order—or at least this was what innovators like Vitoria and Suárez intended. The desired unity of political and legal order could be legitimized theologically only with the old means of voluntarism.[56] The frequently used theories of social contract were marred by their not being able to remove entirely the people's right to resistance in the case of a (putative) breach of contract on the part of the sovereign. Hence a frequently used alternative was found in the theologically contended theories of immediacy: God had appointed the sovereign immediately to exercise authority immediately. The double 'immediately' is important: this was neither a delegated authority depending on the inauguration of the sovereign by the people; nor was this exercise of authority limited in any way by the consent or even just the participation of the estates. But this alternative solution had, in its turn, the flaw of being fully

---

[53] See for example Otfried Höffe, *Politische Gerechtigkeit: Grundlegung einer kritischen Philosophie von Recht und Staat* (Frankfurt, 1987).

[54] See Anthony Giddens, *The Consequences of Modernity* (Stanford, 1990), 39.

[55] See Gerald J. Postema, *Bentham and the Common Law Tradition* (Oxford, 1986).

[56] This story has often been told. See only I. André-Vincent, 'La notion moderne de droit et le voluntarisme (de Vitoria et Suárez à Rousseau)', *Archives de Philosophie du Droit* 7 (1963), 238–59; Michel Villey, *La formation de la pensée juridique moderne*, Cours d'histoire de la philosophie du Droit (Paris, 1968); Juan B. Vallet de Goytisolo, *Estudios sobre fuentes de derecho y método jurídico* (Madrid, 1982), 939.

contingent on the cooperation of theologian-jurists, and left itself open to the question of what God was up to when installing rulers who were more often than not stupid, warmongering, unjust, or simply ineffective.

One important variant with far-reaching consequences was found in the common law reflexions, which have been celebrated in Britain as a national achievement since the seventeenth century (regardless of how much they owe to canon law and civil law influences). These reflexions began with Edward Coke and the deflection of regal demands for control. This already took the form of a theory of positive law, even in the guise of natural law and history.[57] For the first time we find explicit historical reasoning for the validity of law. In view of a very long, uninterrupted legal tradition, the validity of law cannot easily be attributed to a fixed historical origin. It must be found in a historical succession of decisions, made after careful consideration of established rules brought about by ever changing cases.[58] Whatever the original sources of law were, the permanent testing of the law by the courts turn law into 'common law'.

Since the second half of the eighteenth century, positivism has forged ahead both semantically and structurally.[59] Except in Britain, it was based on the presupposition of the unity of state and law.[60] Natural law and the law of reason were relegated to second rank and fed off all the objections that can

---

[57] This interpretation as an early positivism may seem misconceived. However, the central argument is that a practice of decision-making is at issue, the reasonableness of which has been confirmed in history time and again. With all the talk about expounding, declaring, and publishing the law, this could only be convincing, if the judges had, in principle, the possibility of deciding otherwise and had tested that possibility over and over again but had rejected any alternatives. See, on the difficulties of understanding the common law as positive law in the nineteenth-century sense of the word (that is, a law which is enacted by decisions), A. W. B. Simpson, 'The Common Law and Legal Theory', in id. (ed.), *Oxford Essays in Jurisprudence (Second Series)* (Oxford, 1973), 77–99.

[58] This argument is made particularly clearly in ch. IV: 'Touching the Original of the Common Law of England' of Sir Matthew Hale's posthumously published work *'The History of the Common Law of England'*, quoted from the new edition by Charles M. Gray (Chicago, 1971), 39. Similarly, also in his work directed against Hobbes (*Reflections*). At the same time, the argument disarms the question of a possible foreign origin of common law (pp. 42 and 47). The temporalization of the argument is also remarkable in a further respect. On the one hand the conquest of a country gives legitimacy to the conqueror ('War is the highest tribunal that can be'). On the other hand the next question is *from when on* is the conquest legitimate, that is, *when* is the conquest *final*. And the answer is: not until the conquered begin to accept and use the conqueror's legal order (p. 48).

[59] For the current situation see, for example, Werner Krawietz, *Recht als Regelsystem* (Wiesbaden, 1984), esp. 166.

[60] This, by the way, explains the ease with which Protestants accepted earlier theories of Spanish Catholicism. See, for example, Ernst Reibstein, *Johannes Althusius als Fortsetzer der Schule von Salamanace: Untersuchungen zur Ideengeschichte des Rechtsstaates und zur altprotestantischen Naturrechtslehre* (Karlsruhe, 1955); Dreitzel, *Protestantischer Aristotelianismus und absoluter Staat*, 188.

be rightly made against the positivist solution to the problem of order. Legal theory shifted to positivism *c.*1800.[61] This did not mean (and still does not mean) that self-control of law is not considered necessary in view of the legislator's all too erratic actions, for instance in the case of unjust laws.[62]

After the erosion of their cosmological foundations, the advocates of reason today distil the self-description of the legal system from the arguments produced within the system and maintain, on the basis of those arguments and supported within the system, that there are indeed things like good reasons (and less good reasons), reasonable principles, or ultimate values as the nominal values of the system.[63] Currently the discussion is centred on Ronald Dworkin's works.[64] The problem here is that the hope for decision-making based on reason collides with the highly developed social reflexivity of modern society.[65] To the same degree that understanding for the views of others increases and becomes a requirement of civilized behaviour, so hope in the persuasive power of a common creed diminishes. Hence all that is left to the theory of reason is to justify its statements in an increasingly polemical way and to warn that doing away with all common grounds or values subjects everything to arbitrariness. All those who reject this are called destructive, nihilists, anarchists, decisionists, opportunists, positivists. From there it is only a short step to insinuating or arguing openly that theories of this kind are disposed to or, in a given context, can be used to legitimize any crime in society and, above all, any political crime.

Parties associated with positivism see these statements as nothing but a strategy of deception applied by the devotees of principles. The latter are said deliberately to ignore exactly those issues that are of interest to positivists. They just do not want to acknowledge the difficulties they will get into if they have to respecify the principles that they abstract from the practice of the system. Here the *reductio ad unum* falters and results in a great number of conflicting good reasons and values, making it necessary to proceed, *horribile dictu,* opportunistically. The devotees of reason can

[61] The historical situation is difficult to assess, especially because not even Kant uses his critical potential to the full in his legal doctrine on the metaphysics of morals. One must read Kant's legal doctrine with Kant's critique in mind.

[62] Both in the historical school and in the philosophy of positive law, there was suspicion of the legislator from the onset, which was reinforced in Germany by the fact that there was no national legislator. See, apart from Savigny, also the inaugural lecture of Paul Johann Anselm von Feuerbach 1817 on the high office of the judiciary (*Die hohe Würde des Richteramtes*).

[63] See, for instance, Ralf Dreier, *Recht—Moral—Ideologie: Studien zur Rechtstheorie* (Frankfurt, 1981).

[64] See Ronald Dworkin, *Taking Rights Seriously* (Cambridge, 1978); id., *The Law's Empire* (Cambridge, 1986). See also the critical discussion by Habermas, *Faktizitat und Geltung,* 248.

[65] See, for example, Giddens, The Consequences of Modernity, 39: 'the reflexivity of modernity actually subverts reason, at any rate where reason is understood as the gaining of certain knowledge'.

respond neither to the failing of reason when it comes to constituting unity nor to the impossibility of closing the system logically. They do not have a ready answer to the question of how to decide between more than one principle (for instance, between liability in contract or liability in tort) and between several values. The positivist knows how to decide, namely by reference to valid law.

Nevertheless, this does not lead much further than to the next question. What is valid as law and what is not? We have already answered this question in our way by pointing to the theory of the symbol of validity circulating within the closed system. But this was an external description, not a justiciable self-description of the system. Therefore a distinction must be made between the positivity of law and the legal theory of positivism as a self-description that operates within the system.[66] The legal theory of positivism answers the question of the validity of law with the help of the concept of sources of law.[67] The metaphor of sources was used, in fact, in antiquity, even in its application to law, and was also applied to matters of natural law.[68] It appears, however, that this was understood as relating merely to the creation of just solutions to cases.[69] In Roman law and later medieval law, a rule was only a *brevis rerum narratio*.[70] What was important was the *ius* in the matter itself, the law that was found to be just. Therefore the issue was not that the rule, as a precondition for a decision that could be deduced from it, needed a legitimizing source of law. Not until modern theories of contract (Grotius, Hobbes) and the legislative authority of the state based on them were developed, and not until the importance of state codifications and regulations increased, did the reference, and hence the meaning, of the metaphor of sources of law change.[71] It became the concept for the validity of abstract legal norms based on reason.

---

[66] See Hendrik Philip Visser't Hooft, 'Pour une mise en valeur non positiviste de la positivité du droit', *Droits* 10 (1989), 105–8.

[67] See for detail Alf Ross, *Theorie der Rechtsquelle: Ein Beitrag zur Theorie des positiven Rechts auf Grundlage dogmenhistorischer Untersuchungen* (Copenhagen and Leipzig, 1929). An older, more conventional discussion can be found in: *Le Problème des Sources du Droit Positif*, Annuaire de l'Institut de Philosophie du Droit et de Sociologie Juridique, Paris 1934.

[68] Later authors often quote Cicero, *De legibus* I.VI.20. But one finds there only a rather cursory and obviously metaphorical use of '*fons*' and also synonymously '*caput*' (I.VI.18). See also René Sève, 'Brèves réflexions sur le Droit et ses métaphores', *Archives de philosophie du droit* 27 (1982), 259–62, on the equivalent use of metaphors of source and metaphors of the body until early modernity. Apart from that there are few thorough explorations of the history of legal concepts. There are many references in the collection of essays of Vallet de Goytisolo, *Estudios*. See also Enrico Zuleta Puceiro, *Teoria del derecho: Un Introducción crítica* (Buenos Aires, 1987), 107.

[69] See Vallet de Goytisolo, *Estudios*, 60.

[70] See Paulus, *Digests* 50.17.1. And therefore: *non ex regula ius summatur, sed ex iure quod est regula fiat*.

[71] See Sève, 'Brèves réflexions', who observes the increasing importance of this metaphor in the sixteenth century in connection with the interests of the territorial states in making the

The theoretical benefit of this change is clear. The concept of sources of law made a simple identification of valid law possible and saved any further questioning of the nature of law, the essence of law, or the criteria for the delineation of law from customs and morals.[72] It made it possible to identify the law as valid, no matter what the concrete situation of the case in which the law was applied, and no matter which individuals were involved.[73] (Even though it was still not applied to the highest-ranking persons as a matter of course, this did not relate to the validity of law but to its enforceability.[74]) The metaphor of a source, however, suggests a distancing from the origins of the source.[75] It worked then as long as people *did not* ask what lay before the source and what was produced by the difference between 'before the source' and 'after the source'. It worked only for a while, for a transitional period, but could not provide a lasting, satisfying solution. The deficiencies were soon apparent in the fact that a very similar distinction was introduced, with a conspicuously similar metaphor, and it took over the onus of reasoning, namely the distinction between reason and argument. This seemingly offered greater possibilities for refinement than the rule of reason and did not exclude, but rather included, a culture of argumentation, as the positivists in the common law have shown.

The further development of law, particularly the development of the idea of binding precedent in the common law of the nineteenth century[76] as a reaction to the full positivization of law, required a widening of the concept of sources of law.[77] Not only legislation with all its delegated competences

---

law simpler, more uniform, and more transparent. See also Hans Erich Troje, 'Die Literatur des gemeinen Rechts unter dem Einfluß des Humanismus', in Helmut Coing (ed.), *Handbuch der Quellen und Literatur der neueren europäischen Privatrechtsgeschichte II* (Munich, 1971), 615–795, esp. 700.

[72] See also Atias, *Epistémologie juridique*, 80.

[73] See, for example, Pierre Ayrault, *Ordre, formalité et instruction judicaire* (1576; 2nd edn. Paris, 1598), 10: 'Car il est des Lois, comme des fleuves. Pour considerer quels ils sont, on ne regarde pas les contrées par où ils passent mais leur sources & origine' (Laws are like rivers. To find out what they are, one does not look at the countryside through which they pass but at their source and origin).

[74] This is not only apparent in the literature on the reason of state but also in legal literature written by jurists like Ayrault (*Ordre*, 111).

[75] This is the reason why Jacques Derrida distinguishes between source and origin, following on from Valéry. But Derrida sees more clearly that the problem of making a distinction is repeated with respect to origin, see 'Qual Quelle', in: *Marges de la philosophie* (Paris, 1972), 325–63.

[76] On the earlier development in the eighteenth century, see Jim Evans, 'Change in the Doctrine of Precedent during the Nineteenth Century', in Laurence Goldstein (ed.), *Precedent in Law* (Oxford, 1987), 35–72.

[77] Or, from a different perspective: a narrowing of the concept, especially in rejecting the opinion that customary law was an effective legal source on its own and valid even without being recognized by decisions in courts.

but also jurisdiction were now seen as sources of law. Now statute law and judge-made law could be distinguished. This meant above all that legal positivism gave up its link with a source of law which was external to law, namely enforceable political power, and instead included a new source of law which could be used as a source of law only if it was 'reasoned'—whatever that may mean.[78] From here it was a small step to accepting legal doctrine as a source of law, too, because it dealt with reasoning and assessed it critically. For the courts referred to—in some countries more so than in others—scholarly writings, textbooks and other publications of respected legal academics, and permitted their involvement as expert witnesses under certain circumstances.

The doctrine of sources of law makes it possible to dodge the question of the nature of law. However, a substitute to cover the full scope of this question must then be supplied and the concept of sources of law then becomes unclear. As in the case of the principles of reason, one is here confronted with the problem of the unity of a plurality. In contrast to the theory of the principles of reason, the positivist theory can respond to this problem by formulating rules of collision with clear priorities. In the case of a contradiction, which can often be solved by interpretation, that is, reasonable argumentation (!), statute is valid, not the judicial decision, and case law is valid, not legal doctrine. The problem can be solved. Only the concept of sources of the law defines a point at which the self-description of law stops and further questions are ruled out. The applicability of this concept has been widened so considerably that the threshold has been reached at which it could well be said: the legal system is the source of law. But only an external observer can say this. The legal system itself depends on the asymmetry, on the stop rule, on the disjunction of the symmetry which is intended by the metaphor of the 'source', but this intention (or 'function') cannot be called the reason or 'proto-source' for law. One is not allowed to argue tautologically, that is, fruitlessly. Hence the metaphor of sources of law has, as far as validity is concerned, the function of a formula of contingency—just like the concept of substantive justice from the perspective of a rule of reason. The concept transforms a tautology into a sequence of arguments and makes something that is seen as highly artificial and contingent from the outside appear quite natural and necessary from the inside.

As long as constitutions are valid and not contested in principle, positivism can refer to the constitution and avoid references to the sources of law, which go further than that. This may seem to be a solution once the

---

[78] This is precisely what is criticized by the proponents of critical legal studies and similar groups who claim to argue sociologically and to have incisive insights. Their argument is that the positivists conceal their true (whatever that may mean) political dependencies with their positivist concepts.

external references to religion (God), economy (maximization of welfare), politics (enforceable state power), or science (conditions for the possibility of legal knowledge) have run their course. The constitution is, as we have seen in the previous chapter, an autological text. The self-description is an autological operation. Both text and description concur that self-placement within their objects, the legal system, is unavoidable. What can be observed as a consequence of this alliance appears to be like a kind of bilingualism in the interpretation of the constitution. We speak of basic rights when we refer to the technical legal apparatus of subjective rights, access to law, limited liability, etc.; in short, we refer to justiciability. In addition, we speak of basic values when we use that lofty language which seems to be required for the self-legitimation of the legal system. Reference to justiciability corresponds with the central position of the courts in the legal system. The semantics of values makes it clear that the meaning of the validity of law is not exhausted but can claim to have a higher level of meaning which lies beyond fluctuating validities—in modern terms, civil society—in which the necessary foundations can be found. In order to communicate at this level and incorporate that communication in the legal system, there are those who have even gone so far as to elevate the constitution above itself and call it 'supraconstitutionalité'.[79] But that has not achieved much more than the self-confirmation of the opinion that there has to be something unconditional over and above everything that is conditional, something necessary beyond everything that is contingent.

The theory of reason and positivist theory can be identified as self-descriptions of the legal system by the fact that they do not shy away from accepting responsibility for results but get involved in the system 'practically', as it were. From the dizzy heights of reason, pointers to what constitutes proper law are dropped, as if on a parachute, or at least this is what one thinks one sees if one is on the ground looking through binoculars. With the appeal to reason, to the reasonableness of all reasonable people, the impression is given that law is a procedure for bringing about consensus. Obviously this cannot be taken too far. Hence the fixed points of legal positivism invariably come into play. However, on which texts are they based, and on which foundations, which have, after all, yet to be found? Positivists believe in sources of law in the sense of a concept that makes distinctions possible and allows us to distinguish between valid law and law that is not valid. Only in the individual concrete case can it be found out just how far such points of departure in the system lead to different constructions and how far different constructions lead to different results. We know nowadays that a text is only the result of an interpretation which

---

[79] See, for example, Stéphane Rials, 'Supraconstitutionalité et systémacité du droit', *Archives de Philosophie du Droit* 31 (1986), 57–76.

must, however, in its turn, be shown to be necessary on the basis of the text. In any event these are neither external descriptions nor sociological theories.

Finally, we notice a remarkable shift in the point of reference of the discussion, which has occurred in the last two decades. As before, two parties confront each other because this is indispensable for a dispute, but the topic has moved away from the question of the reason for legal validity. What was a positivist position before is now taken by those who insist that decisions must ultimately be justified by weighing up the consequences. This is often called balancing of goods or balancing of interests. This is positivist in so far as the decision, regardless of whether it is made by the judge or enacted by the legislator, is valid even if interests have been misjudged or consequences have materialized differently from what was assumed in the decision. The opposition argues that there is law which does not have to be subjected to such weighing up but must be implemented in any case. Winfried Hassemer provides the example of the prohibition of torture, which would still have to be followed even in a case in which the torturing of a witness might prevent worse harm.[80] He argues that there is something like 'non-disposable' legal principles of a—no matter how historical and therefore contingent—legal culture. This is no longer the positivism of legal sources or of a reason based on nature or reasonableness. It appears that the argument here is almost one for the necessity of redundancies in law, or at any rate of eigenvalues which express the reference of law to persons and which are no longer available as formulae for the balance of internal and external references.

In order to assess these reflexive theories (which assessments are invariably conducted in the course of controversy) from outside, it is useful to relate positivist theory and theories of reason or those of weighing up consequences, or the moniqlic theory insisting on non-disposable principles underlying the reason for the validity of *rules*.[81] This makes it possible to use a limited concept of system as the model for observation of the system in the system. In contrast to that, the external observer of the system, in which he does not participate, can define the system by its particular way of

---

[80] See Winfried Hassemer, 'Unverfügbares im Strafprozeß', in *Festschrift Werner Maihofer* (Frankfurt, 1988), 183–204.

[81] In this case even the generalization of the concept of the sources of law discussed above becomes acceptable. For example, MacCormick, *Legal Reasoning and Legal Theory*, writes, following on from Hart: 'It is useful to take it as a defining characteristic of legal positivism that every genuine positivist holds that all rules which are rules of law are so because they belong to a particular legal system, and that they belong to the system because they satisfy formal criteria of recognition operative within that system as an effective working order' (p. 61). Also Hart insists on 'rules of recognition', even though the given explanation makes one think of practices of recognition. See, for a critique of this limitation by reference to rules, N. E. Simmonds, *The Decline of Juridical Reason: Doctrine and Theory in the Legal Order* (Manchester, 1984), 99.

operating (including self-observation/self-description). What should not be excluded in principle is the truism that the system receives the concept of operative autopoiesis in its self-description, perhaps as a substitute for all other formulae for the externalization of the interruptions of symmetry. However, this would make it more difficult to identify—in the system—with the way in which the system resolves its paradox/tautology in the validity of norms. The relation of reflexive theories of law with other operations of the system would have to be redefined. At any rate, it is not the proper goal of such external descriptions to trigger such repercussions. The external description as a scientific description has its premisses and goals in the scientific system.

Regardless of such as yet untested possibilities of bridging the difference between internal and external descriptions, it is worth noting that there are apparently two different reflexive theories in the modern legal system, namely the theory of reason and the theory of positive law, and the difference between them cannot be bridged. This is a difference between principles (even if they have only recently become procedural principles) and sources of law. The defect of one approach is the absence of a reason for validity in a decision between conflicting principles. The defect of the other is the absence of an ultimate justification for what is practised as valid law. Neither of these approaches to the self-description of the system can account for the unity of the system in the system. Validity and justifying reasoning cannot be reconciled and hence one must opt for one version or the other.

This, however, is only a problem for the self-description of the system. The external description is happy with the statement: this is how it is!

V

Leaving the debate undecided may be an appropriate reflection of the current state of affairs. But it need not be the final answer to the question of how the legal system reflects on its own unity. Positivity and reason are (or were) traditional formulae, which were used in the eighteenth century to come to grips with a new situation (in the knowledge of that newness). This was 200 years ago. Traditional formulae for self-description appear to us today as 'obstacles épistémologiques', in Bachelard's sense of the word.[82] They have too little complexity, and overvalue and homogenize the points of view that guide them. Besides, there may be other theoretical perspectives to be gained, leaving aside the issue for the present of whether they can be used for a self-description or as an external description of a self-description (as is the case here).

---

[82] See also Ost and van de Kerchove, *Jalons*, 121, on the thesis of a rational and sovereign legislator.

In view of the track record of the two formulae for self-description, positivity and reason, the external observer must first find an explanation for this. Generally, it can be said that legal knowledge in the era of positivism is turned into the form of observation of observers. In the case of continental European law this means the interpretation of the legislator's will. The form of legislation, the form of *a change* from previous law, in itself implies that there is an intention. Legislators do not just happen to pass a statute—they want to achieve something specific and hence observe the world with the help of one or several distinctions. This leads to a methodological problem: how can the observation of this observation be assessed, and above all, how can it be transferred onto changed circumstances as statutes get older? This is never an issue of the factual (sociological) researching of motives but always only a matter of reasons, which make juridical sense and can be presented as reasonable.

In the nineteenth century, the transition to fully positive law in Anglo-Saxon common law was completed with the recognition of the binding power of precedent. A purely mechanical compulsion to accept premises for decisions was not intended. The decisions, which can be considered as precedents, are observed in later cases in relation to the 'ratio decidendi', and that determines whether or not and to what extent they can be followed.[83] In the American version of the common law, the dominant idea is that attorneys have to observe judges in order to know how they observe and decide cases.[84] That is the message of legal realism (represented in a number of variants). None of these versions of the positivity of law excludes an orientation by legal principles. However, legal principles can now be understood to be only that which remains stable during the observing of the observing. Legal principles, then, are the 'eigenvalues' of a system, which secures its autopoiesis on the level of observing the observers. And how could it be otherwise? If one no longer knows how law guides others, all knowledge of law ceases. A widened time horizon—be it old statutes, be it future court decisions—can be perceived only by second-order observation at that particular moment. Alternatively, one can merely continue to do what one normally does, that is, rely on interaction with those present and hope for the best.

The materialization of such a divergence in observers' perspectives is found in the differentiation of the system—above all, the differentiation of

---

[83] See Evans, 'Change in the Doctrine of Precedent', 71, where he notes that the flexibility thus achieved to a large extent cushioned the break with tradition, which occurred with the transition to the binding by precedent, that is, the positivization of the common law.

[84] The lead for this came from American pragmatism at the turn of the twentieth century. See for example Oliver W. Holmes, 'The Path of the Law', *Harvard Law Review* 10 (1897), 457–78. For the high point of this school of thought see especially Jerome Frank, *Law and the Modern Mind* (New York, 1930).

lawyers, law firms, in-house law departments in organizations and legislative bodies with different boundaries, and with society as their environment. A common legal education and corresponding professional socialization maintain the standards of observation and the possibilities of communication between the different strands of the system. However, it would be too simple to explain the gain in structure merely as 'professionalization'.[85] The formation of professions appears to be a solution, which was generated in older social structures and is no longer particularly constructive. The problem of the legal system today lies in its operative closure, in the resulting unavoidable autonomy, and in the shift of the autopoiesis of the system to the level of second-order observation (which is self-sufficient). A further observer can, then, observe conventionalism or constructivism, but that does not mean that he can see arbitrariness.

Hence the current conditions for the self-description of the system can be described structurally as the differentiation of a closed functioning system, which is, operatively, exclusively self-referential and which has integrated a consistent approach to second-order observations. Both of these things correlate with each other. Because the system is closed, it must subject all of its operations, with which legal matters are constituted and observed, to its own observations.

Reason thus becomes the symbol for the self-referentiality of the system. Positivity becomes the formula which assists observers of the observers to concur that they observe the same thing, namely the corresponding valid law. Conversely, positivity holds that all law is based on decisions, which can be observed as decisions and can be recalled as decisions (that is, in relation to other possibilities). Reason includes, then, the reference to the circumstance that—given the onus of selecting—there must be reasons, which justify themselves as reasonable. In order to serve the purpose of self-description, both formulae conceal the fact that the system operates without transcendental support, without cosmic *periechon*, and without interventions from God. At the same time, they also conceal the fact that the system depends instead on countless direct and indirect structural couplings that are not suitable as reasons for legal validity. The exceptions which have been tested—the subject and his awareness of reason and the constitution for the positivity of law—both obscure the societal and, in a broader sense, ecological dependencies of the legal system. In order to provide a foundation for reflexion, they have to condense the problem of the unity of self-reference

---

[85] Tendencies of this kind were prevalent in the 1940s and 1950s following Talcott Parsons, 'The Professions and Social Structure', *Social Forces* 17 (1959), 457–67. But the argument then was about filling the gap that had been left by the utilitarian theories of social behaviour (nowadays we might call them theories of rational choice). In our text, we replace the then prevailing view of how value-relations could be enacted (Rickert, Weber) with the question for the preconditions for the possibility of second-order observations.

and external reference to an extreme degree. However, as soon as it is realized that this problem, too, can be observed and described, the formulae lose their support from within themselves and turn against each other, as if polemics could be a substitute for reasoning.

Reason becomes a quotation, which disguises the fact that one is at one's wits' end but nevertheless wants it to be known that one thinks certain opinions are the right ones. By referring to general reasonableness (instead of, for example, to one's own experience) one exposes oneself to observation. One says, 'My argument is open to scrutiny'. And that may well be so. The positivity of valid law has the same function. As long as one refers to valid law, one exposes oneself to observation. We can distinguish between observations, which are *de lege lata* and *de lege ferenda*, and all observers who diverge too widely or are too 'critical' can be referred to the possibility of a change in law. In this sense the positivity of law can also be understood as a permission for the changing of law. The old form of the binding to 'something higher' is replaced with a combination of binding and change, which must be constantly negotiated anew. The distinction between *de lege lata* and *de lege ferenda* unfolds the paradox that law is valid for the very reason that it can be changed.

As soon as the system becomes self-referentially closed at the level of second-order observation, these formulae can also be recognized as directives for the observing of observers. The ultimate questions have to be translated from the form of 'what' to the form of 'how'. One no longer asks: what is valid law based on the corresponding sources of law? Instead the question is now: how does the system do what it does? How does it link operation to operation under the impact of permanent irritation by the environment?

Thus closure of the legal system becomes the departure point for a new understanding of the relations between the system and its environment. Legal theory must deal with the social conditions of the legal system's functional autonomy—on its own terms, of course, and guided by the unity of its own system. At any rate it can see the unity of the system within the system only from the perspective of the environment.[86] However, this can be achieved neither with the end-formula of 'reason' nor with the end-formula

---

[86] Spencer Brown, to quote him one more time, hides the problem in the hazy formulation: 'We may also note that the sides of each distinction experimentally drawn have two kinds of reference. The first, or explicit, reference is to the value of one side, according to how it is marked. The second, or implicit, reference is to an outside observer. That is to say, the outside is the side from which a distinction is supposed to be seen' (69). However, the system about which we are talking here is at the same time the system which produces the distinction, marks itself and is, having created its own outside, the only environment from which unity can be observed. Hence the system must observe itself with its own operations of self-observation and self-description *as if it were an observation from outside.*

of 'positive law' if it is to compare favourably with what has already been achieved by traditional philosophy of law.

<h1 style="text-align:center">VI</h1>

The preceding discussion dealt with a problem that has traditionally been seen as a problem of the sources of law. The theory of sources of law makes it possible to distinguish between valid and invalid law and to focus on valid law with the help of this distinction—as if this were 'the law'. Another fundamental distinction, which is equally important today, if not more important, is the distinction between substantive law and procedural law. Especially when there is only positive law, the old distinction between the different sources of law loses its meaning. As far as the self-description of the system is concerned, the question that then becomes more important is how substantive law and procedural law relate to each other in order to achieve the unity of the legal order.[87] It is no coincidence that the category of the legal claim[88] was invented at a time when legislative positivism was blossoming. It replaced the distinction between *ius* and *actio* with a uniform concept and a dual function in relation to substantive law and procedural law.

This is also a consequence of the prohibition of the denial of justice discussed previously.[89] If every legal issue can be submitted to a court for a decision, there must be a corresponding general link between substantive and procedural law. This is established by connecting concepts like legal claim, subjective law, and legal subject. In attempting to define the meaning of these concepts more precisely, it was recognized in the second half of the nineteenth century that what was implicated was only the subjective disposition over the use of legal protection.[90] Someone whose rights have been violated cannot be forced to lodge a claim and go to court because he may have good reasons unrelated to law for preferring not to do so. In other words, the concept of (subjective) rights refers to the difference between external and internal conditions for the juridification of communication, that is, the boundary of the legal system. And in the second half of the nineteenth century they knew full well how to distinguish between this legal-technical problem and an 'individualistic' philosophy.

---

[87] This means important for self-description. It goes without saying that from a legal-technical point of view (for instance in systems based on legal actions) it always was important.

[88] See Bernhard Windscheid, *Die Actio des römischen Zivilrechts vom Standpunkt des heutigen Rechts* (Düsseldorf, 1856).   [89] See Ch. 7.III and IV.

[90] See, for example, August Thon, *Rechtsnorm und subjektives Recht: Untersuchungen zur allgemeinen Rechtslehre* (Weimar, 1878). This applied particularly to the yet to be created new public law regime for legal protection where the matter of legal material became an issue for decision-making only once legal protection had been provided.

Nevertheless, enthusiastic descriptions with an emphasis on values addressed the topic of subjective rights. In the nineteenth century it was proclaimed that the law protected human beings against social oppression, and that it empowered individuals to make their own decisions. In the twentieth century it was said that the law realized 'values' which were a precondition for law as a condensation of a long humanist tradition, made positive in the form of basic rights. Basic human rights became overvalued in this interpretation of their constitutional function. They were seen as documents of a general value orientation, which commits the law to serve humanity. This made it possible to make statements about the purpose of law in a way that fulfilled legal-technical demands at the same time. The difference between substantive and procedural law was seen as evidence for the purpose of the unity of the system, as were the combination of these components of the legal system and the importance of the legal concepts that achieved this and at the same time guaranteed that the human being was included in the legal system.

Only in the past two decades what has become more clearly visible and, about which there is now more scepticism, is what this approach has excluded. If every plaintiff has to appear as a 'subject', albeit as a corporate subject (a legal personality), then interests that are presented legally have to be individualized. That requires organization if one cannot find the necessary individuals. However, by no means every collective interest can be organized, particularly not those of the 'concerned parties', and particularly not if they live in an environment which is meant to be protected from the impact of technology.[91] Hence the form which has as its inner side the legal subject, as both plaintiff and defendant, has as an outer side all the situations and interests which, in the regime of the subject, cannot become relevant in the legal system unless they are components of subjective rights or duties. This bias may lead to an increased use of organizations for articulating legally relevant interests and to a tendency to declare organizations as having a legal standing, even if in a technical-legal sense one cannot speak of their 'rights'. But in this way the clamp that kept substantive and procedural law together is slackening, prompting the question why an organization as a legal person can claim rights over which it has no disposition. And above all: why should such a legal person have the same freedom as the individual who has to make claims or not to make claims according to his wishes?

Seen from a sociological perspective, this would only be a matter of providing agents with authority. They could threaten legal action, procure adjournments, and induce their opponents to come to an agreement even

---

[91] See Christian Sailer, 'Subjektives Recht und Umweltschutz', *Deutsches Verwaltungsblatt* 91 (1976), 521–32.

though their own rights are not at stake. This may be appropriate as a matter of legal policy (but this is not the place to assess that). However, the focus of the self-description of the system is then no longer on the legal subject. According to Karl-Heinz Ladeur, there should be a refocusing on a plurality of organizations.[92] But then the human being would become only a leftover item for interests that are not, as such, worthwhile for bundling up in an organization. The self-description of the legal system could still relate to values and hence to externalities. However, values would be provided with intrinsic dynamics by organizations and the *human being* would no longer appear empirically as a living individual but only as a vanishing point in which all values converge diffusely.

Whether it is dealing with individual humans or organizations, the legal system has to adjust its self-description to an environment in which self-referential systems create turbulences that cannot be controlled from anywhere else and which, most certainly, cannot be fixed hierarchically. This is precisely the reason why expectations have to be reproduced in the mode of contra-factual normativity—and if this was already the case in the past, it applies even more so today. The legal system has responded to this in different ways: through the positivization of the validity of law; through the doctrine of subjective rights filtered from reciprocal relations; through the replacement of a principled, uniform guarantee with a list of values (one could almost say: waiting list), which require a weighing up in all decisions; and by shifting the centre of gravity of operations to due process, to guarantees for proceedings which require that the decision not yet be final. From an institutional perspective, such guarantees are based on the self-produced uncertainty of an open future and yet nevertheless fulfil their function.

Whether or not one wants to keep the concept of the 'positivity' of law and positivist legal theory in this situation is more or less a matter of semantic tactics. If one does, the idea of authoritative legislation and a source of law behind it (which transcends the law) have to be abandoned. Neither the state nor reason nor history can legitimize law. There may be theories that propose this, and they are still around today. However, if they are described as self-descriptions, they are required to adjust to the mode of second-order observation. They must learn to reflect on themselves as a self-description of a system, which describes itself. Otherwise they become an anachronism (and it is one of the most significant achievements of Jürgen Habermas's legal theory that it demonstrates how all the approaches in the

---

[92] See Karl-Heinz Ladeur, 'Gesetzesinterpretation, "Richterrecht" und Konventionsbildung in kognitivistischer Perspektive: Handeln unter Ungewißheitsbedingungen und richterliches Entscheiden', *Archiv für Rechts- und Sozialphilosophie* 77 (1991), 176–94. See also id., *Postmoderne Rechtstheorie: Selbstreferenz—Selbstorganisation—Prozeduralisierung* (Berlin, 1992), especially the discussion on basic human rights at p. 176.

past have reverted to natural history, morality, principles, or practical reason). What remains, then, is the recognition of the unavoidable diversity of observers and their perspectives—in one and the same system. What remains is the replacement of the known past with the unknown future as a constant, continuously operating premiss. What remains is the ongoing creation of contingencies as stable eigenvalues, as recursively renewed values of the legal system. Under these circumstances and in these terms self-descriptions have to be found which can still deliver.

VII

It is definitely too early to arrive at a final verdict on the possibilities for a self-reflexion of the law of modern society. This also applies to the contribution that a sociological theory could make in this context. For the time being, there are increased signs of uncertainty, which come from many different sources. The problem discussed above—that the attribution of rights to subjects is no longer satisfactory but is nevertheless indispensable—is only one of the reasons. Another is the fact that one turns increasingly to the prognosis of consequences and to the justification of decisions by reference to their consequences without being able to deal doctrinally with the problems that arise from such prognoses and justifications. Instead, doctrinal resources are depleted and replaced with the flexible, if not empty, paradigm of the weighing up of interests or balancing of values. Legal theory, for which people had such high hopes, has not been able to contribute to any sufficient consolidation. The various 'approaches' and the different interdisciplinary imports take pride of place. All this makes one accept the existing state of affairs as a fact for the time being and declare the situation 'post-modern'.[93] However, this only confirms the obvious, namely that the legal system currently produces a number of self-descriptions and hence problems of inconsistency about which the different strands of legal theory can no longer communicate.

In any event, the term 'post-modern' is misleading. It underestimates the structural continuity of modern society and above all the unrelenting impact of the form of differentiation based on functions. The past and especially the past of the currently existing self-descriptions of the legal system of

---

[93] See, for example, the special issue on post-modernism of *Droit et Société* 13 (1989). Since then see also Boaventura de Sousa Santos, 'Toward a Post-Modern Understanding of Law', *Oñati Proceedings* 1 (1990), 113–23; André-Jean Arnaud, 'Legal Interpretation and Sociology of Law at the Beginning of the Post-Modern Era', *Oñati Proceedings* 2 (1990), 173–92. Similarly also Karl-Heinz Ladeur, ' "Abwägung"—ein neues Rechtsparadigma? Von der Einheit der Rechtsordnung zur Pluralität der Rechtsdiskurse', *Archiv für Rechts- und Sozialphilosophie* 69 (1983), 463–83; id., *'Abwägung'—ein neues Paradigma des Verwaltungsrechts? Von der Einheit der Rechtsordnung zum Rechtspluralismus* (Frankfurt, 1984); and explicitly id., *Postmoderne Rechtstheone*.

modern society appears more unitary than they actually were.[94] As the double perspective of positivity and reason (or legality and legitimacy) alone indicates, there has not been a uniform, harmonious description since the hierarchical model of sources of law was abandoned. Obviously, according to this version, the only difference between the semantics of post-modernity and the semantics of modernity is that the former sees the unity in the future and the latter sees the unity in the past, which must be rejected as being traditional. And one would have to concede by way of conclusion that the unity can now be found only in hazy points of reference to time and certainly not as the actual present.

Currently not much can be said to support the expectation that sociological theory in general and the theory of society in particular will be able to help and contribute anything remarkable to the self-description of the legal system. Compared with the situation *c*.1900, there has been a process of shrinking on both sides, a process of pegging back hopes of a 'grand theory'. Our reflections above make that understandable but do not compel us to accept it as the last word.

As we established in section II, the self-description of the legal system starts from the presupposition of its code. Totally different, even diametrically opposed approaches (which must appear to lawyers as outright subversive) have been developed by the general sociological description of legal practice. Sociology is mainly interested in the differences in legal practice, which are *not* accounted for by law and, therefore, cannot be legitimized legally. But *that does not mean that the differences observed can be shown to be illegal only because of that.* The sociological description explodes the condition of the binary code or even turns a blind eye to it and thus to the schema of the totality of the operations of the legal system in the form of legal and illegal. This is done mainly with the help of statistical methods which leave the individual case alone but overall show quite a different picture than that which would emerge from a generalization of individual case decisions or from the rules which are applied in decision-making. Donald Black provides a good overview (see Table 11.1 opposite).

Thus sociology finds, for instance, that by far the most legal disputes are not decided in formal proceedings but 'in other ways'; or, that social status has an effect in different ways, depending on whether participants in a dispute face each other as equals or with different social ranking; or, that legal problems are treated differently, depending on whether they arise in face-to-face and continued (intimate) relations or at a greater social distance; or, that it is significant whether the plaintiff or the defendant is an individual or an organization; and so on. While lawyers refer to norms in making predictions of possible decisions, sociologists look for the social indicators of the case.

---

[94] See above all Arnaud, 'Legal Interpretation'.

Table 11.1 *Black's summary*

	Jurisprudential model	Sociological model
Focus	Rules	Social Structure
Process	Logic	Behaviour
Scope	Universal	Variable
Perspective	Participant	Observer
Purpose	Practical	Scientific
Goal	Decision	Explanation

It should be noted that here social structure means only the relations between the social attributes of persons.

Source: Donald Black, *Sociological Justice* (New York and Oxford, 1989), 3. I present the summary table (at 21) because it makes the discrepancies particularly clear.

While lawyers, encouraged by the self-description of the system, aim at ensuring that equal cases are decided equally and mobilize juridically useful reasons for differences, sociologists find that statistical differences occur which cannot be explained juridically and for which sociological explanations must be found. And while lawyers are interested in prognosis and the influence of argumentation on decision-making in individual cases, statistically robust predictions suffice for sociologists. Sociologists are neither interested nor irritated when they learn that individual cases are decided according to the law.

As is clear to lawyers, these differences in the descriptions are related to a different sensitivity to differences. Sociologists need broad categories for their statistical analyses, which can cover a large number of equal cases. They have to neglect the fine detail. Lawyers in contrast make subtle distinctions to arrive at the results, which appear just to them. To lawyers, murder does not equal murder and rape does not equal rape. Therefore lawyers have no problem in assessing the rape of a black woman by a white man differently from the rape of a white woman by a black man and they can find distinctive criteria other than race for arriving at a decision. One could say that they are able to hide their prejudices behind other categories. Fair enough. But likewise it is prejudice when sociologists select criteria that can produce sufficient numbers of equal cases and lend themselves to a critical analysis.

At any rate, even if one does not contest the scientific merit of the sociological analyses of law (and this could be done only by evaluating individual studies), their assessment remains inadequate in relation to the point at issue here. Sociology does not account for the fact that the legal system is an operatively closed, autopoietic, and self-descriptive system. The legal system cannot utilize sociological analyses. It cannot, in turn, treat statistical relations as rules that must be considered in decision-making. There is no need for further explanations or 'critiques' (in the vein of the critical legal studies movement) if law does not 'apply' sociological findings.[95] Each set of distinctions is founded on a specific blindness. If this applies generally, there is little to be gained from accusing the opposition of bias and evading the autological inference to oneself.

Thus the conventional empirical analysis of sociology of law does not describe the legal system as a legal system. Sociology of law is recording its subject matter incompletely. The gap between internal and external descriptions may thus appear wider than need be. At any rate, a more complex sociological theory which sees this gap as the consequence of the differentiation of systems could bring about an understanding of why this is so and come up with mediating concepts on the part of the external (sociological) description. The conceptual analysis of terms like reflexion or self-description makes it clear that one must abandon the idea of an absolutely correct and fitting description of an object if the description itself is part of that object and, consequently, that a description changes its object by describing it. The system itself changes if a theory of the system is constructed within the system and the object of the description changes through that description. As a result, other descriptions become possible and are perhaps even called for. This applies to both the sociological execution of the self-description of society and the legal theory's execution of a self-description of the legal system. In both cases the mere conditions for operating in this way result in an irretrievable plurality of possible identifications or a 'fragmenting into versions', as Jonathan Potter calls it.[96] This, at least, should be something capable of fostering agreement and it means in fact that there is no authority of superior and exclusively correct knowledge. Instead, sophisticated communication shifts to the level of observing of observations, namely the level of second-order observation. This allows for rather large (too large?) degrees of freedom by allowing everybody to use a convenient schema in order to observe what is remarkable about others. In this way sociological curiosity can develop about the class background of judges, which may lead to important insights but cannot be used in legal reasoning.[97] The insight is of interest only to the sociologists involved, and if

[95] We agree with Donald Black's demand (*Sociological Justice* (New York and Oxford, 1989), 3) that the sociological analysis of law—as a consequence of its specific claim to be a science—should not indulge itself in the criticism of legal practice and should restrict itself to the expounding and further refining of its research findings.

[96] See Jonathan Potter, 'What is Reflexion about Discourse Analysis? The Case of Readings', in Steve Woolgar (ed.), *Knowledge and Reflexivity: New Frontiers in the Sociology of Knowledge* (London, 1988), 37–53, at 43, in relation to the sociology of knowledge. See also the chapters on plural versions of the world and plural versions of relations in Gregory Bateson, *Geist und Natur: Eine notwendige Einheit* (Frankfurt, 1982).

[97] The problem of the two truths was, consequently, the point at which the classic sociology of knowledge came to a halt. See for an overview of the discussion Volker Meja and Nico Stehr (eds.), *Der Streit um die Wissenssoziologie*, 2 vols. (Frankfurt, 1982).

the attempt were made to translate it into policies (then it would be called 'reform'), it would most probably conflict with the principle of the independence of courts and the formally equal access to judicial office.

However, more recent developments in theory suggest going a step further. One could think of establishing *theory* itself as a *form of structural coupling of the science system with the reflexive theories of the functioning systems*. This would mean realizing the mechanism of structural coupling as a form, that is, channelling of irritations by the exclusion/inclusion of possibilities, at this interface. Evidently this would be an autological operation. For the concept of structural coupling is a theoretical concept, which theory applies to itself. The separation, the operative closure, and the functional autonomy of the individual systems, in this case the legal system and the science system, could be maintained. As before, the legal system would be concerned with taking care of normative expectations and the science system with conducting research. And as before, it would still be true that facts cannot be used to draw conclusions about norms, and any underhand deception relating to this issue could be cut short. Nevertheless, a mechanism of structural coupling could be established with a corresponding selection of terminology. The science system would be faced with the ongoing question of how to cope with systems, which describe themselves, as its research objects. The legal system, on the other hand, could equip its self-reflexion with the conceptual achievements provided by the theory of self-referential systems, as applied in science at large. Even then, though, the actual selection must be left to the receiving system. Sociologists may advertise their theories. But lawyers know only too well that advertising a product does not mean admitting liability for the product's possible defects.

In sum, we can note the suggestion that theory is a mechanism of structural coupling between the science system and the reflexive theories of the functional sub-systems, although this does not commit anyone to accepting a certain version of theory. There are, to be sure, certain conditions for suitability in the concept of structural coupling. Indeed, the concept targets a problem that cannot be solved indiscriminately. However, if one can demonstrate at all that there are theoretical instruments that are fit for such tasks, one indicates at the same time that there are also other possibilities. For whatever is possible is also possible in other ways.

VIII

Neither the forms of self-description of the legal system discussed above, nor their allocation by sociological observation from outside, lead back to the problem that we have touched upon in various contexts—the problem of paradox. Self-description itself is a paradoxical enterprise, because it deals with the internal description as if it were an external description, capable of reporting objective matters. But this version of the basic problem is only one of many. We have found that the code of the system turns into a paradox if it is applied to itself. We have found that the efforts of the legal system to come to terms with justice as a formula for contingency hide the fact that it is concerned with unfolding a paradox. These analyses do not aspire to be understood as a 'deconstruction' of all legal principles. However, they draw attention to the basic circumstance that every question concerning the unity of a distinction, or, put differently, each attempt to observe the schema of the observation, leads to a paradox, that is, to an oscillation between two opposite positions (legal/illegal, internal/external, equal/unequal), which can neither establish memory, nor produce structural complexity, nor secure connectivity. In that way, in other words, the legal system is not able to operate.

On the other hand, if the legal system seeks to guarantee its autonomy then it must include the negation of this very autonomy and the negation of all the conventions that support it. It must not exclude them.[98] Or to put it differently: the legal system must include what is excluded and, in doing so, subvert the requirements of logic, such as the axiom of the excluded third question, the prohibition of contradiction, or the presupposition of identities free of oscillation. A reconstruction of what is happening here (if it happens) requires either trans-classical logic, for instance in the sense of Gotthard Günther, or a sufficiently exact analysis of the way in which the system deals with what it has to keep latent. It requires either a disposition towards rejected values, which allow the suspension of primary distinctions (such as true and false with reference to logic or, in the terms of systems theory, system and environment), or it requires the admission that, in every operation of observation, there is an unavoidable blind spot which can be shifted to a different apparatus of observation but not erased.[99]

This also provides a basis for the analysis of the reductions that are indispensable if the unity of the system is to be presented within the system. Texts are used only when they are valid. Justifications are based ultimately on doctrine. Justice is not adduced in its function as a formula for contingency but as a value. All this breaks the cycle of self-assertion and self-rejection in the system itself. Self-rejection is excluded. It makes sense in the system, for instance, that orientation by the distinction between legal and illegal is legal and not illegal. That is its premiss.

As Jacques Derrida has demonstrated with the relation between philosophy and writing, everything that is indispensable is not carried along as

---

[98] See on this point Jean-Pierre Dupuy, 'Zur Selbst-Dekonstruktion von Konventionen', in Paul Watzlaweck and Peter Krieg (eds.), *Das Auge des Betrachters—Beiträge zum Konstruktivismus: Festschrift für Heinz von Foerster* (Munich, 1991), 85–100.

[99] See Gotthard Günther, 'Cybernetic Ontology and Transjunctional Operations', in id., *Beiträge zur Grundlegung einer operationsfähigen Dialektik*, vol. 1 (Hamburg, 1976), 249–328, at 287.

co-equal but as subordinate, as 'supplément'.[100] A symmetrical relation is turned into a hierarchy of superior and subordinate. Of course, one can— on detecting the secret of such arbitrariness—'deconstruct' this solution. However, one can then also deconstruct the deconstruction itself, by demonstrating that this step only leads to the paradox of the beginning or the paradox of the origin, which every system has dealt with in its past.[101] Therefore we prefer to present the forms of the unfolding of the paradox as forms of invisibilization of the paradox, well aware that the system itself cannot operate them like that. We remain in the position of a third-order observer who observes the self-observation and self-description of the system. Thus one finds that the illogical turn of this foundational cut (or foundational step)—this 'différences/différance' in the sense of Derrida— is the point at which one can see the historical capacity for adjustment or the contemporariness of semantics.[102]

A system can only found itself on a paradox and cannot found itself on a paradox. However, it then recovers itself by using the re-entry of the difference between system and environment as a distinction. Thus it can re-establish the *tertium non datur* with the help of its own distinction and leave the problems of a multi-valued logic—which would be necessary to reflect on the unity of the system and its boundaries—to the third-order observer. However, everything that results from such observations applies only to the system itself.

We cannot pursue this problem any further at the level of *theories* and *texts* of self-descriptions, on which we have been focusing almost exclusively. The paradox can neither be named nor can it be celebrated as the solution to all problems. However, the selectivity and the inconsistency of all self-description return to the system as a problem of everyday behaviour. The reality, especially of legal proceedings in courts and parliaments, differs widely from what is said, desired, and intended. For instance, the courts call what they are doing the application of law. The reality is quite different.[103] The daily workload appears to be approached with the goal of clearing the desk. Dates and deadlines, files and distractions absorb the attention. There is always something to be done in order that something

[100] See Jacques Derrida, *De la grammatologie* (Paris, 1967); id., 'Le supplément de copule: La philosophie devant la linguistique', in Jacques Derrida, *Marges de la philosophie* (Paris, 1972), 209–46.

[101] See Niklas Luhmann, 'Sthenographie und Euryalistik', in Hans Gumbrecht and K. Ludwig Pfeiffer (eds.), *Paradoxien, Dissonanzen, Zusammenbrüche: Situationen offener Epistemologie* (Frankfurt, 1991), 58–82.

[102] See also Niklas Luhmann, 'The Third Question: The Creative Use of Paradoxes in Law and Legal History', *Journal of Law and Society* 15 (1988), 153–65.

[103] See on this point and for the following analysis, Klaus A. Ziegert, 'Courts and the Self-Concept of Law: The Mapping of the Environment by Courts of First Instance', *Sydney Law Review* 14 (1992), 196–229.

can be done. What the participants see is quite different from what is stipulated by the self-description. Thus the sociological analysis of how the system deals with its basic paradox finds other mechanisms, which are quite different from the mere logical and methodical ironing out of inconsistencies.

Lay participants will be frustrated, not only when they lose their cases but also by the way in which this happens. On this side of the divide between lawyers and clients, the system is helped by the fact that no consequences follow from frustration. Even though a considerable number of clients are 'recycled' by the system, it treats every instance as an individual case. The people who deal with legal work occupationally or professionally develop different ways of handling this pressure. On the one hand, they are better positioned to make comparisons, including amongst themselves, and therefore feel less personally involved. Thus the communication on this side of the divide is different, as is the expectation of understanding. An important frame of reference is the issue of working hours and working conditions. On the other hand, the focus of what is important can be shifted onto formalities, because errors are most noticeable here. A considerable measure of cynicism, irony, and humour is part of the typical profile of a profession. They are forms for testing understanding. And last but not least, on this level the system produces the constantly repeated demand for better equipment and reforms. On the flip side of this demand are the scapegoats who are responsible for the fact that nothing ever changes.

The discrepancy between text forms and theoretical forms of unfolding the paradox of the system, and the rather more orally or behaviourally communicated forms of everyday life, is so significant that no improvement (according to sociology) can be expected to be derived from advances at the level of reflexive theories. The adjustment to irritations of the system at this level will always take the form of idealizations, which cannot immediately be declared as not being 'meant that way'. Reforms cannot be justified by declaring them to be the self-appointed task of the juridical establishment, a mental exercise for the profession's cognitive dissonance, or a demonstration of its 'critical' attitude towards the 'system'. More likely, what is expressed in the discrepancy and divide between different levels of communication is the fact that the system must operate 'acratically', which means that it does not have sufficient means to control itself.[104]

---

[104] See for parallel observations of the education system and the communication of pedagogues, Niklas Luhmann and Karl Eberhard Schorr, 'Strukturelle Bedingungen von Reformpädagogik: Soziologische Analysen zur Pädagogik der Moderne', *Zeitschrift für Pädagogik* 34 (1988), 463–88.

IX

Whichever semantics are preferred for the self-description of the system and whichever distinctions have to be refreshed in the process, one negative basic condition appears to be inescapable: the system cannot allocate positions which are or will be legal *in any case*—that is, without regard to the conditions set by the system. The allocation of a special position to the Great Leader, the Party, etc. would remove the distinction between coding and programming. There can be conditional special rights, emergency laws, exceptional laws, etc. What is not possible, however, is an unconditional law for self-exemption. For in the case of such a 'law', whether a decision ought to be made within the legal system or outside it could not be decided.

In other words, autonomy cannot be understood as arbitrariness. It contains the prohibition of self-exemption, which prevents capriciousness and forces it to conform to the law of historical self-specification.

The contrary opinion can often be found in the context of polemical theory, under the heading of 'decisionism'. However, this polemic can easily be refuted as insufficiently thought through.

12   Society and its Law

The relationship between the legal system and the social system is the theme of this book. The reflexion (self-observation) and the non-reflexion of this relation in society's legal system was the topic of a chapter in its own right. If we devote yet another chapter to this question, at the end of our considerations, it is not with the intention of repeating the same arguments, but because in the discussion so far we have left open the question of which concept of society we propose and what follows from it for the analysis of the relation between society and law. We know that the law operates in society, performs society, fulfils a social function, and has been differentiated to fulfil this function by its autopoietic reproduction. At any rate that is what the theory says, and thus what has been proposed here. However, it should also be asked how a society in which all that happens can be understood.

A theory of society suitable to this task does not exist. So-called critical theory and especially the critical legal studies movement have contributed a number of insights but have ultimately worked with simplifications which are untenable in order to sustain a vision of an alternative society. Here we will not comment on these approaches any further because, after all, the really important issue is which theory can be used to describe modern society, in a manner which will also be acceptable to those who want to change a little or a lot of it.

We shall simplify this task by proposing a change to the guiding paradigm of systems theory. If society is understood as the comprehensive system of all social operations (however one understands them), the theory of open systems, nowadays already a classical theory, has understood society, too, as an open, adaptive system with internal (for instance, cybernetic) self-regulation.[1] The findings of evolutionary theory led to the assumption that society was adapting increasingly well to its environment, as demonstrated in the increasingly thorough exploitation of natural resources in order to improve the standard of living (but not the moral perfection) of humankind. Compelling arguments for this, complemented by planning, were given by progress in science, technology, and market-oriented production, but also by the adaptation of democratic politics to individual opinions. Thus one can read even today: 'Clearly, society is an open system

---

[1] See, for example, with perspectives towards the future and the demand for better adaptation (active adaptation, adaptive planning) Fred Emery, *Futures We Are In* (Leiden, 1977).

that seeks to achieve a steady state by means of a progressive process of adaptation to its environment.'[2]

If this concept of society is accepted, then law appears to be a regulatory mechanism, serving the adaptation of society to its environment. It does this, however, in a secondary position, as society itself always achieves its own adaptation to its environment (via market prices, democratic elections, and 'empirical' research). Reference can then be made to the cybernetic notion of a system in tandem, which steadies society in the case of disturbances,[3] or to anthropology, which sees law as a secondary institutionalization of existing institutions, as a 're-institutionalization at another level'.[4] The law can then be seen outright as a cybernetic machine in a cybernetic machine, which is programmed to maintain a steady state.[5] Whatever the differences are with regard to the concrete details, law supports and confirms its society. Society is described as adjusted externally, while law deals internally with conflicts, which conflicts can be played down with a moralist-conformist attitude or simply postulated to be social structures from a critical class theory perspective.

A different concept of society leads to entirely different conclusions—different concepts, different distinctions, different perspectives, different problems. On the basis of the general concept of autopoietic systems, we assume that society is an operatively closed system, which reproduces itself with its own and exclusively its own operations. This means that society cannot communicate with its environment through its own operations. Social operations—that is, communication—are not designed to make possible contacts between the system and its environment. They only prepare the conditions for the continuation of system operations. Conversely, the environment cannot insert operations of any other kind in the network of the autopoiesis of the system—just as a chemical transformation or the

---

[2] And this from the pen or word processor of a sociologist, who criticizes the theory of the autopoietic reproduction of social systems for a lack of interest in empirical research, but 'clearly' contradicts obvious empirical facts. The quote is taken from William M. Evan, *Social Structure and Law: Theoretical and Empirical Perspectives* (Newbury Park, 1990), 219.

[3] See for example Ottmar Ballweg, *Rechtswissenschaft und Jurisprudenz* (Basle, 1970).

[4] See Paul Bohannan, 'Law and Legal Institutions', *International Encyclopedia of the Social Sciences*, vol. 9 (Chicago, 1968), 73–8, at 75. Further on in the text he talks about double institutionalization. See also id., 'The Differing Realms of the Law', *American Anthropologist* 67/6 (1965), 33–42. But for criticism of this concept see Stanley Diamond, 'The Rule of Law Versus the Order of Custom', in Robert P. Wolff (ed.), *The Rule of Law* (New York, 1971), 115–44, who views law rather more as an instrument of oppression.

[5] See Jay A. Sigler, *An Introduction to the Legal System* (Homewood, Ill., 1968), and id., 'A Cybernetic Model of the Judicial System', *Temple Law Quarterly* 41 (1968), 398–428. If one considers additionally, following Sigler, that the output of the system can become the input of the same system, one can see the transition to a theory of operatively closed systems.

replication of a cell cannot work as a sentence in the context of language communication. Hence cognition is no longer being understood as a representation of the system and evolution no longer being understood as an improvement of the adaptability (or even adaptation) of systems.[6]

With this in mind, society can no longer be described as an adaptable system in the terms of older systems theory.[7] Society may well communicate *about* its environment but not *with* it. In doing so, society is, as always, restricted to its own operations and can be guided only by their reality for the creation of further connecting operations. Society does that as long as it works and with the degree of complexity that society derives from its own operations.[8] Its environment may irritate or destroy society but it cannot control how communication ought to be conducted. Ernst von Glasersfeld formulated the idea: 'We can do everything that is not against the world',[9] and that includes not knowing what is, in fact, against the world. All we know is the result of communication about the world.

But that also forces us to correct what we understand so far of the future. Autopoiesis is no guarantee for survival, let alone a formula for progress. The concept belongs to the wider context of chaos theory or the theory of catastrophe. The evolutionary one-off invention of life has proved remarkably stable over many billions of years and under a variety of environmental conditions. Whether this will also apply to the evolutionary one-off invention of meaningful communication cannot be established. At any rate, the theoretical concept does not exclude severe forms of destruction, catastrophic regressions, and losses of complexity; indeed there is already talk about a catastrophe that could extinguish all life on planet earth.[10] But at the same time the internal dynamics and the capacity of quick structural

[6] See on this point concerning a parallel criticism of representation and adaptation as the behavioural modes of systems, Francisco J. Varela, 'Living Ways of Sense-Making: A Middle Path for Neuro-Science', in Paisley Livingston (ed.), *Disorder and Order: Proceedings of the Stanford International Symposium, Sept. 14–16, 1981* (Stanford, 1984), 208–24.

[7] There are many more (but no more radical) reasons why one should be sceptical towards adaptionism—including in biology. See, for example, Stephen J. Gould, 'Darwinism and the Expansion of Evolutionary Theory', *Science* 216 (1982), 380–7; Richard M. Burian, 'Adaptation', in Marjorie Green (ed.), *Dimensions of Darwinism* (Cambridge, 1984), 287–314. Whether or not Darwin was 'originally' an adaptionist can safely be left to specialist historical research. There are also criticisms in sociology which however, are directed against systems theory at large. See, for example, Anthony Giddens, *The Constitution of Society: Outline of the Theory of Structuration* (Berkeley, 1984), 233.

[8] This means also that the increase in complexity (just as in biology the polymorphous reproduction of life and biodiversity) cannot be understood as a better adaptation to the environment.

[9] In 'Siegener Gespräche über Radikalen Konstruktivismus', in Siegfried J. Schmidt (ed.), *Der Diskurs des Radikalen Konstruktivismus* (Frankfurt, 1987), 401–40, at 410.

[10] See on these theoretical concepts Walter Bühl, *Sozialer Wandel im Ungleichgewicht* (Stuttgart, 1990).

variation are stressed. All in all, this theory is more open than older systems theory to experiences that result from recognizable ecological threats, their unpredictability, and the specific time structures of modern society. From this perspective the future appears in the present as a risk.

What does all this mean for understanding the role of law in modern society?

As stressed many times now,[11] we have to presuppose that it is possible to form further autopoietic systems within autopoietic systems.[12] Evidently the legal system operates within the social system. It performs society with each of its operations by reproducing communication and delineating it against everything else. But it instantiates its own autopoiesis, the autopoiesis of the legal system, by following the legal coding rather than any other coding or even no coding at all. It thus delineates the legal system from the environment within society. Differentiations become conditions for further differentiations and systems become, if further differentiations are evolutionarily successful, environments for further systems. All this is achievable—and this is what autopoiesis tells us—only through the system's own operatively closed efforts and not through a decomposition of a whole into parts.[13]

One could say that society tolerates such differentiations if they maintain a functional relation to the problems of society. What we have said about the function of law as a systemic stabilization of normative (=counterfactual) expectations does not need to be rephrased.[14] On the contrary, it can serve as the constant, with the help of which we can demonstrate what it means to understand society as an operatively closed social system. When

---

[11] See, for instance, Ch. 1.V.

[12] This is criticized by Jürgen Habermas, *Faktizität und Geltung: Beiträge zur Diskurstheorie des Rechts und des demokratischen Rechtsstaats* (Frankfurt, 1992), 73. But Habermas appears to ignore that autopoiesis is concerned with the reproduction of the *difference* between system and environment. If that is taken seriously, it is not theoretically impossible that communicative operations at the same time reproduce the outer boundary (with non-communication) and the internal boundary between legally coded and other communication. Apart from that, I do not know of any other theory construction that has attempted at all to deal with both the autonomy of law and its position in society. The usual solution being the concept of 'relative autonomy', which is neither theoretically nor empirically satisfactory because it does not draw distinctions.

[13] And not, as Parsons says, as the unfolding of the concept (!) of social action in components which make themselves independent.

[14] Karl-Heinz Ladeur appears to accept that as well. He formulates: 'Die Funktion des Rechts besteht in der Ermöglichung der Bildung von Erwartungen in einer sich mehr und mehr selbst zum Problem werdenden Welt' (The function of law is to make the formation of expectations possible in a society which is becoming more and more a problem for itself), in: 'Gesetzesinterpretation, "Richterrecht" und Konventionsbildung in kognivistischer Perspektive: Handeln unter Ungewißheitsbedingungen und richterliches Entscheiden', *Archiv für Rechts- und Sozialphilosophie* 77 (1981), 176–94, at 176. However, further on in the text Ladeur no longer talks only about the change in the context of the function but about a change in the function itself.

we discussed the distinction between cognitive and normative expectations, the question was whether and how far society is capable of learning and is able to adjust its expectations to a constant stream of disappointments. The question was, in other words, how far structural stability is found only in the framework of what can be recognized as the results of learning, or to what extent normative expectations—which explicitly refuse to learn—must be established in addition. To a theory of operatively closed systems this appears to be a purely internal problem. There is no transfer of information from the environment to the system. The system reacts only to its own internal states but does this with an internally used distinction between system and environment, that is, by means of a bifurcation of the attribution to causes. The issue, then, is which structural arrangements strengthen or weaken the irritability of the system, whereby irritability is to be understood here, as always, as the internal state of the system depending on its structures.

At first sight, the inclination is to prefer cognitive expectations, expectations that are capable of learning. And indeed, such expectations have led the trend in consolidation of global society.[15] National legal systems can still be afforded today (even if only in the terms of international associations, in which they recognize each other on the condition of intra-state order and through public international law, but with the proviso of the possibility of a violation of law). In contrast, national sciences and even national economic systems are hardly imaginable any longer. As soon as expectations are sensitized to learning, society finds it hard to escape the internal pressure and, increasingly, the ecological pressure to learn. Does this mean that law loses its importance?

If the question is put in such a general form, there are presumably no unequivocal answers. There are some indications that an important support mechanism for law, the normative expectation of normative expectations, is losing importance. There are no longer unconditional demands (if there ever were[16]) that someone stands up for his rights. On the other hand, 'human rights' have, as a kind of programme for catching up, a market as never before. Value commitments are no longer presented as the mere preference for values or a 'dispreferencing' of negative values, but are largely insisted upon normatively. It is not merely that one has values; rather, that one must have them and impress them on others. The normative institutionalization of value commitments extends to morally motivated programmes of demands. Hence one not only has to extend one's own values to include the values of others (in the interests of the poor, the

---

[15] See Niklas Luhmann, 'Die Weltgesellschaft', in id., *Soziologische Aufklärung*, vol. 2 (Opladen, 1975), 51–71.

[16] This would be the place for a history of opinions. The mere collection of data on 'opinions about law', or on 'the prestige of law' etc., can at best only address the current situation.

disadvantaged, the hungry, the 'third world'), but one must also join in these demands in order that others commit themselves to these values as well. However, this form of the normative expectation of normative expectations lies largely beyond the established juridical world of forms and is also directed against the law. Legal or illegal—what counts is humanity.

If these impressions and assumptions were to be supported by empirical research, one could demonstrate that the law as practised in the legal system deviates once more from 'living law'. But here 'living law' does not mean the customary law of local ethnic groups. It would have to be sought not in Bukovina but rather in particular youth sub-cultures or the attitudes of by now ageing youngsters who, with their insistence on their right to wear jeans, attempt to prevail against established conventions.

II

The legal system itself appears to react in different ways to what superficially seems to be a change in values but what is in reality a far more sustained trend, not just related to a difference between generations. Taking the constancy of the normative function—without which law would not be law—as a benchmark, a tendency can be detected which could be called the *temporalization of the validity of norms*. Norms, and the validity that supports them, are no longer based on the constants of religion or nature or an unchallenged social structure, but are now experienced and dealt with as time projections. They are valid 'until further notice'. This not only makes them felt as contingent but also as cognitively sensitized. However, that does not mean, as is maintained by critics of the distinction cognitive/normative, that this distinction is itself collapsing or is not supported by empirical research.[17] It cannot be said that the law reacts to the pure fact and frequency of deviant behaviour with a change of norms. There is no example of an entitlement to make such decisions to change and organize corresponding processes. What is meant is only that norms are equipped with assumptions of reality, which turn out to be errors in the *legal system itself* or become inadequate in the course of changed circumstances. This is particularly evident in relation to the dynamics of technological and scientific developments in the pharmaceutical and medical industries, the spread of computerization and information technology, the increasing discrepancies between education and the lifelong use of occupational know-how in jobs protected by law from 'unfair' dismissal, and the many changes

---

[17] For example, Richard Lempert, 'The Autonomy of Law: Two Visions Compared', in Gunther Teubner (ed.), *Autopoietic Law: A New Approach to Law and Society* (Berlin, 1988), 152–90, esp. 178; Arthur J. Jacobson, 'Autopoietic Law: The New Science of Niklas Luhmann', *Michigan Law Review* 87 (1989), 1647–89; Evan, *Social Structure and Law*, 41.

in the science system but also in 'private' areas such as the dependency of career options on an individual's social status.

In such a dynamic society, expectations addressed to law are changing. As society increasingly comes to be seen as the cause of what was previously accepted as fate and was dealt with by religion, if at all, society is now expected to come up with ways of preventing, solving, and compensating for disadvantages which affect individuals differently. This function, besides being carried out by the political system, is primarily the responsibility of law.[18] On the other hand, for the same reason, it becomes increasingly difficult to ask for 'legitimacy' in the sense of guidance by undoubted and hence constant values and principles. And even those who try to adhere to the term legitimacy and with it the trans-positive foundations of the validity of law, have come to narrow down their expectations to proceedings, that is, they have proceduralized the problem of legitimacy.[19] And that means that they have temporalized it! Like all positivists, the rational positivists must guarantee the future in the present and they therefore use the presupposition that as long as certain procedural criteria are maintained, a reasonable consensus about the outcome will eventuate somewhere along the line. One can easily assume that this, too, is only a temporal position which will see itself being subjected to the test of time, namely the question whether proceedings, if they are really instituted and carried out, will live up to expectations or whether one has also been operating here only with presuppositions about real possibilities. Such assumptions may well work under 'laboratory' conditions, as Habermas has sketched them, but not in the real world, which is determined by social organization and the human factor. This foreshadows a return to an earlier, forcefully rejected legalism in which, in a kind of legal fiction, the holding of proceedings under the rule of law is seen as the basis of legitimacy.

In all the dynamism of modern society, the law of modern society must *make do without a certain future*[20] and that shows how dependent on society it is. Natural parameters in relation to society cannot be taken as constant (even if it can be assumed that the sun will still shine for a long while), nor can values where they inform decisions—that is, where they function as rules of conflict—be projected onto the future. All future presents itself in the medium of the (more or less) probable and the (more or less) improbable.

---

[18] See Lawrence M. Friedman, *Total Justice* (New York, 1985), esp. 45.

[19] See, for example, the contributions of Klaus Eder and Karl-Heinz Ladeur, in Dieter Grimm (ed.), *Wachsende Staatsaufgaben—sinkende Steuerungsfähigkeit des Rechts* (Baden-Baden, 1990); Karl-Heinz Ladeur, *Postmoderne Rechtstheorie: Selbstreferenz—Selbstorganisation—Prozeduralisierung* (Berlin 1992); and now also Habermas, *Faktizität und Geltung*.

[20] This applies by the way to all systems of signs generally and hence to all that is directly understood or practically accepted as a sign. See Josef Simon, *Philosophie des Zeichens* (Berlin, 1989).

This means that predictions about the future can differ[21]—and there is no general faith in 'salvation', 'progress', or 'apocalypse', which can give some sense of stability.

Nevertheless, because this is so and because it is becoming increasingly irrefutable, normative expectations and their stabilization through law retain their importance. The fact has not changed that current communication must be guided by and is dependent on the ability to ascertain which expectations are covered by law and which are not. The fact has not changed that law is concerned with the protection of specially designated expectations, that is, with the contra-factual stabilization of projections of the future. There is still, too, the general principle of the protection of trust for cases in which people rely on valid law. There is no change in relation to the highly specific requirements for having access to the use of the symbolism of validity if one wants to change the law, whether in the form of contracts, or in the form of legislation. But there is an intensification of the problem that can be defined as the distinction between the present's future and the future's present. Law cannot be stable over time in the sense that what is valid once is valid forever. If one wants to rely on law, one can count on support against resistance and disappointments but one cannot expect that the law will not change. In this sense we arrive at a broader *ius vigilantibus scriptum*. If one marries, one has to expect that divorce law and the legal regulation of the consequences of divorce will be changed. If one wants to invest for the long term, one cannot expect that—during the period of amortization—tax law, environmental law, etc. will remain the same as they were when the decision was made to invest. Consequently, one always has to check in case the law relied upon changes. Legal change itself must not only avoid formal repercussions but must also increasingly protect those who are particularly hard hit by having already made their dispositions.

This, by the way, is not an entirely new problem. There has already been some discussion, for example, from the viewpoint of the law of expropriation, whether someone who has built a petrol station on a well-used road should be entitled to demand compensation if the traffic on that road is re-routed. Problems of this kind can only become more frequent, especially in cases in which not only the different points of view about facts but also points of view about law are challenged. The problem becomes even more acute when the legal change is not the result of legislation, which can take

---

[21] Here reference could be made to a host of empirical studies on attitudes to probabilities, estimates of risks, etc., but the knowledge about this problem is almost as old as the probability calculus itself. Jean Paul already knew that 'das Menschenherz . . . in Sachen des Zufalls gegen die Wahrscheinlichkeitsrechnung kalkuliert (the human heart . . . calculates against the probability calculus where chance is concerned), *Siebenkäs*, ch. 7, quoted from Jean Paul, *Works*, vol. 2 (Munich, 1959), 226. Hopes and fears prove to be stronger.

into account new facts, but is due to superior court decisions, which provide little or at best sibylline possibilities to integrate these issues through their individual case decisions.

Hence communication in the legal system—to sum up all these considerations—has to pay more attention to the *law's own risk*. Issues of risk do not only turn up in the form of law which declares risky behaviour to be legal or illegal, although this certainly is a problem which has already led to legal change in many areas and will continue to do so in the future. But more and more, what matters is to tie responsibility and liability to the possibilities for controlling risk, and thus to counteract the 'illusion of control', which is so typical of decision-makers. Another question that goes beyond the issue of risk control, however, is whether or not and how capable law is of recognizing its own risk. This question is part and parcel of the differentiation, operative closure, and functional specification of the legal system. In this respect the legal system is a mirror image of the social system. Law itself is risky because society is risky. Or, to put it more precisely, law has to observe and describe itself as risky because that is what applies to society at large.

The formula of risk replaces the formula of adaptation in the design of systems theory, and this applies at the level of society as a whole and at the level of its functioning systems. The consequences of welfare state policies over decades have determined the structural drift of the legal system. They remain inscribed in the legal system. They become evident in the indeterminacy of legislative mission statements as well as in judicial activism (especially in constitutional law) using social values that are thought of as plausible. Overall, the reference to presumptive consequences as a criterion of decision-making has increased. This did not, however, result in the adaptation of the system to its environment, let alone the adaptation of the social system to its environment—which might have suggested that individuals were now more satisfied with society. Rather, what has developed is, on the one hand, a greater discrepancy between demands and realizations and, on the other hand, disappointments with politically fuelled hopes.[22] With its market-oriented mass production, the economic system presumably contributes more to the equalization of inequalities than any law, which is being pushed politically to produce more equality.

---

[22] There is broad-ranging reflection at present on disappointments. See, for one example among many, Marc Galanter, 'Why the "Haves" Come out Ahead: Speculations on the Limits of Legal Change', *Law and Society Review* 9 (1974), 95–160. It is remarkable in this context that sociology of law is interested only in the law of the poor but not in the law of the rich—as if the inequality of the legal positions could be compensated for by research (which is a particularly unrealistic idea for sociologists). See on this point Maureen Cain, 'Rich Man's Law or Poor Man's Law?', *British Journal for Law and Society* 2 (1975), 61–6.

However, there is now, additionally, a high temporal instability in norm structures. Law cannot guarantee security if society itself sees its future as a risk which is contingent on decision-making. Law gives a specific legal form to risk. From the perspective of external-references—that is, interests—the risk of decision-making and the danger to others posed by that become the outstanding legal problem. In its self-referential mode—that is, with the help of legal concepts—law must reflect on its own riskiness. That does not mean simply accepting one's own unreliability. The issue is finding legal forms which are compatible with the autopoiesis of law, with its specific function and the peculiarity of its coding from the perspective of risk and danger.

If one is realistic, one can soon see that such a development cannot be set in motion by comprehensive planning on the basis of newly found principles, or by the codification of approved law. What appears to be happening is a concern with individual issues, an incremental approach which depends largely on incidental events and tries to solve problems unsystematically as they occur in the course of political lobbying or legal decision-making. If there are ever to be legal concepts which are socially adequate, they will have to be found through a testing and re-testing of solutions to establish potential eigenvalues of the legal system in modern society.[23]

Notwithstanding this general abstinence from principles, it might make sense to use legal theory and its discussions to draw greater attention to the dimension of time in the self-descriptions of the legal system. The most important findings of the preceding study can be summarized once more from this perspective:

1. The function of law as the normative stabilization of expectations can be related to the general problem of the social costs of time-binding. This relation does not need to appear in normative texts and thus does not have to interfere with their interpretation. However, one can only come close to the roots of the problem of legitimation and reasoning which is discussed in normative texts, if one sees that every temporal extension of expectations puts a burden on those who will suffer if their future becomes restrained. Is it, then, not a general risk underlying all law that one tries to brand all those who violate the law to be criminals once and for all, even though it is generally impossible to know and predict situations and motivations?

2. We have switched the concept of the validity of law from the static with relative invariance, to the dynamic. Legal validity serves as a circulating symbol helping to mark the actual state of the legal system, which has to be taken unavoidably as its point of departure, if validity is to be changed in

---

[23] See on this perspective Niklas Luhmann, *Rechtssystem und Rechtsdogmatik* (Stuttgart, 1974), 49.

one or other respect. The concept of positive law gets carried away with this. It defines the opposite value to the specifics of the change of law. One can presuppose that law is valid law as long as it is not changed. One can do that with full justification, because the law could have been changed but obviously there was no reason to do so. Prohibitions on changing law can create excessive pressure that is ultimately released violently. Learning from revolutions tends to promote positive law and democracy.

3. Further, the decision criterion of the estimation of consequences relocates the validity of law to time, and again, to the future. This applies with a double meaning—on the one hand, with respect to the presupposition of the constancy of assessments, and on the other hand, with reference to the probability/improbability that these consequences will actually materialize. In this respect, at present legal systems lack risk awareness. This may be so because time problems are generally underestimated, but also because lawyers' decision-making texts do not provide opportunities for expressions of insecurity or risk awareness, as lawyers have learnt to produce only the information which is needed to justify a decision. Therefore it would be all the more advisable not to overdo the prognosis of consequences on the level of decision-making programmes. This is because here the legal system is taking risks, when it lacks both the methods and procedures to assess them.

4. All this, finally, has consequences for the understanding of law's own peculiar rationality. In the legal system itself, rationality was seen traditionally as the rationality of the legislator,[24] but today it is seen rather as the reasonableness and reasoning in decision-making[25]—either in relation to principles (Dworkin), or in relation to what is culturally intelligible (Parsons), or, finally, in relation to consensus without coercion (Habermas). This, however, leaves unanswered the question of what happens after the (however convincing/plausible) reasoning has been delivered. Taking the dimension of time into consideration, the advantages of the temporalization of complexity[26] become apparent and rationality can then be understood as meaning an increase in the possibilities, which are liable to restrictions, and as a broadening of the latitude for decision-making with an increase in the limitations on decisions, which depend on time.

[24] See the discussion of this premiss with references to the literature in François Ost and Michel van de Kerchove, *Jalons pour une théorie critique du droit* (Brussels, 1987), 116. Ost and van de Kerchove treat this premiss as an 'obstacle épistémologique' (Bachelard) for further critical studies of law.

[25] As representative of such accepted opinion, see Heino Garrn, *Zur Rationalität rechtlicher Entscheidungen* (Stuttgart, 1986). Then in view of the 'unresolved' problems of interpretation only the insufficiency of mere logical, axiomatic-deductive theories of justification remains to be discussed.

[26] On this see Niklas Luhmann, 'Temporalisierung von Komplexität: Zur Semantik neuzeitlicher Zeitbegriffe', in id., *Gesellschaftsstruktur und Semantik*, vol. 1 (Frankfurt, 1991), 235–313.

These findings make it clear why the legal system is hampered in expressing its own risk appropriately in its normative texts. The pretence of the security of decision-making corresponds to its normative function. The normative texts have to be hermeneutically useful and interpretatively valuable in accordance with the normative function of law. And all the reflexive efforts of the legal system tie in with its normative texts. Its risk becomes externalized in this fashion. Again, this is observable by an external description—but a description cannot blame law.

Nevertheless, the level of abstraction of 'theory' can be imagined as a mechanism of structural coupling which connects the reflexive skills of the legal system, which are called 'legal theory' here, with the theory skills of the science system. This results in the irritating experience for the science system that the legal system operates with its own dynamics and not in the sense of 'applied science' (regardless of how one may rate science in the specific German intellectual tradition of 'legal science' [*Rechtswissenschaft*]). This problem is addressed in the science system by the theory of autopoietic systems, or to be more exact, the description of the functional differentiation of modern society as a release of the functioning systems for autonomous, autopoietic self-reproduction. The fact that there are systems, which observe and describe themselves, restricts (if one cannot contest and refute this fact on the basis of empirical research) the possibilities of theory construction in the science system. That is why a sociological theory, which has set its sights on a theory of modern society, cannot expect to have its findings acknowledged as legally relevant and as a basis for valid law. Likewise, sociological theory and its approaches derived from a specific functionally differentiated system do not contribute any useful knowledge to the self-descriptions of the legal system, which must be based on the norms of valid law. Sociological theory, however, may well contribute irritations instead. For one might expect the legal system to be interested in looking for some guidance from sociological theory after the collapse of natural law, transcendental foundations, and logical-axiomatic principles.

III

If the legal system is seen as a way to take an open future into society and bind it there, law can also be seen as the 'immune system' of society. Like 'autopoiesis' (and closely connected to it), this phenomenon was first detected by biologists but has a wider significance. Consequently, we are not arguing by analogy and are not using the concept of immune system purely metaphorically. Rather, we are dealing here with a very general problem, which is typical of systems that organize the construction of their own complexity on the reduction of the complexity in their environment, in the form of operative closure and structural coupling. Whenever this occurs, a system cannot rely on its prediction of possible disturbances to defend itself against them. It cannot hold countermeasures ready for a point-to-point defence. This would amount to an intolerably high degree of external complexity being deflected into the system. Point-to-point relations between the system and its environment are feasible in neither a positive sense nor a negative sense, because this would reduce the difference between system and environment to that of being a mirror image of each other. In sum, the immune system compensates for the lack of 'requisite variety'.[27]

An immune system gets along without knowledge of its environment. It only registers internal conflicts and develops for them case-by-case solutions which can be generalized, that is, providing surplus capacity for future conflicts. Instead of researching its environment, the immune system generalizes experiences with itself. These generalizations serve as symptoms of the unknown causes of disturbances—and they remain unknown. In doing so, the immune system is supported by specific, highly selective structural couplings, which make it possible to ignore everything else, including the possibility that disturbances may bring destruction—an apocalypse. An independent immune system for intercepting and neutralizing unpredicted disturbances develops only in the area of structural couplings (which is on the whole a very narrow field). The communication system of society depends on the cooperation of individuals' consciousnesses. Normally, consciousness accompanies communication, registers it, stimulates the corresponding sense-motor cooperations of the organism, and recalls, in sufficient detail, what has been communicated, or assumes that others remember enough for the purposes of communication. It is likewise perfectly normal that utterances occur which contradict assumed expectations or—and this is more problematic—expressed expectations. These trivial incidents become disturbances of communication only if a 'no' is answered with an opposing 'no'. In this event it is tempting to insist on the no and to reinforce the no on both sides with further communication. We can call this a conflict.[28] (Another fitting word would be 'dispute'.) Accordingly, conflicts are always systems in society, parasitical systems, which depend on society establishing structures (expectations) and continuing its autopoiesis in conformity with these structures, or innovatively with new structures or, finally, too, in the form of conflicts. There are, however, no conflicts in opposition to society and no disputes with society.[29]

---

[27] As used by W. Ross Ashby, *An Introduction to Cybernetics* (London, 1956). See also id., 'Requisite Variety and its Implications for the Control of Complex Systems', *Cybernetica* 1 (1958), 83–99.

[28] See for more detail Niklas Luhmann, 'Konflikt und Recht', in id., *Ausdifferenzierung des Rechts, Beiträge zur Rechtssoziologie und Rechtstheorie* (Frankfurt, 1981), 92–112; id., *Soziale Systeme*, 488.

[29] The point that is at issue (to mention the counter-theory again) is not a description of participating individuals' state of mind, just as biology does not develop immunology by describing the states of participating cells. See N. M. Vaz and F. J. Varela, 'Sense and Nonsense: An Organism-centered Approach to Immunology', *Medical Hypotheses* 4 (1978), 231–67.

The immune system does not correct errors but cushions structural risks. It is not directed by the ideal of a rational practice that is free of troubles. Its function is not to eliminate misconceptions about what is right because in that case any problems would be easily solved (whatever the criteria may be). The immune system enables society to cope with the structural risk of the continuous production of conflicts. The demand for an immune system is not the result of poor adaptation to the environment but is a result of giving adaptation a miss, in other words avoiding it.

And it fits in with the theory of the immune system to say that law learns from conflicts. Without conflicts law would not develop, would not be reproduced, and would then be forgotten. This includes conflicts that the law itself provokes, for instance conflicts arising from state regulations. At any rate, law does not spring up from the nature of matter or from human nature, as assumed earlier, but it emerges and develops during the search for solutions to conflicts as soon as these solutions are not just *ad hoc* (like and including the use of violence), but are intended to apply to more than just the case in hand. The immunity answer uses the time-binding effect of normative rules. Accordingly, the formulation of rules is like the generation of antibodies for specific cases. If no demands are made on the immune system of society, it cannot learn and consequently cannot generate disturbance-related defence mechanisms. In other words, the immune system stores its own system history. But it does not adapt to its environment. There is no 'similarity' between trigger and defence. On the contrary, the legal rule is not a conflict. When it is a trigger for further conflicts—which is typical in the legal system—new rules develop or at the very least new interpretations of the rule to be preserved in a text.

A mature juridical immunology requires the closure and autopoietic reproduction of the immune system of law. Only in this way can it be understood how the development of the system is always historical, self-regulatory, and at the same time cascading.[30] The differentiation between law and politics is vital as a setting of necessary closure and to stop excessive auto-aggression in the system. Other theoretical premises would lead to the conclusion that the immunity answer is lost in the surrounding environment. This would mean that the system is not able to learn from itself. It scarcely needs to be repeated that the closure and autopoietic reproduction of the legal system does not exclude causal relations between system and environment (law and society and their environment) but requires them.

IV

Under modern conditions in the societal context of society and law tensions arise that have as yet been little analysed, and understood even less. Possibly the most important problem is the growing demand for individual

---

[30] See again for the biological parallels, Vaz and Varela 1978, 'Sense and Non-Sense'.

self-determination, on which the classic liberal (form-giving) instruments appear to founder. It becomes increasingly clear that one can abide by every statute but not by all. Breaking the law becomes vital if living means existing according to principles of self-determination. This is no longer the classic problem of the unavoidable lack of legal knowledge. Crimes like tax evasion and moonlighting are indicators of the fact that nothing works without violation of law—if not for all individuals then at least for quite a few (simply because not all people work or have to pay taxes). Considerable parts of the economy would collapse if the law were to be enforced. Above all, numerous possibilities for individuals to give their lives a meaning would be cut off if the bureaucracy succeeded with in implementing its programmes. Without the possibility of moonlighting, house-owners could not fulfil their commitments to tenants. Without smuggling, many thousands of unemployed could not survive in Italian coastal towns. Without 'vote buying', there would be no electoral participation in the rural and slum areas of Thailand.[31] It is well known that 'work to rule' serves just as well as a strike programme for trade unions and often breaking the law is the only meaningful work practice in organizations.[32] More effective administration of criminal justice would cause problems for prisons.[33] The police and many people in caring professions are faced with the problem that the strict observation of law can reduce the effectiveness of their work drastically and can ultimately be used as an excuse for doing nothing. Accordingly, 'pardons' are not granted in practice by heads of states but by the police. Law can slow down important operations to such a degree that they can hardly be distinguished from inactivity. But, above all, the individualism that is so highly valued in modern society (emancipation, self-realization, and all that) cannot be lived out if total obedience to law is expected. We have not even mentioned the destructive side-effects for individuals, particularly the frustrations and the self-exclusion from the domain of activities requiring high motivation, which are all a consequence of abiding by the law.

Certainly this argument should not be overdrawn. It does not mean, of course, that only criminals have chances in life today. Often an 'active interpretation' helps, or identification with defensible legal opinions even if they are not the dominant ones. However, it is a fact, which deserves more attention that socially, widely appealing goals of perfection are no longer

---

[31] See on this especially Ananya Bhuchongkul, 'Vote-Buying: More than a Sale', *Bangkok Post*, 23 Feb. 1992, 8.

[32] See, as the best-known case study, Joseph Bensman and Israel Gerver, 'Crime and Punishment in the Factory: The Function of Deviance in Maintaining the Social Systems', *American Sociological Review* 28 (1963), 588–93.

[33] See Heinrich Popitz, *Über die Präventivwirkung des Nichtwissens: Dunkelziffer, Norm und Strafe* (Tübingen, 1968).

attainable without violation of the law, for individuals as well as at the level of functioning systems. In other words, society also uses law to contradict itself.

We have already mentioned that this problem cannot be solved or even understood adequately with the means of classical liberal legal theory. The legal form of 'subjective rights' as an instrument for releasing arbitrariness in the legal system does not suffice as a corrective, not even when considering that the law permits the holder of a legal title to tolerate the violation of his rights. To define the function of law as an instrument for securing freedom has, as do all definitions of function, hardly any interpretative value. This applies also to human rights, which we will discuss further below and which are hardly at the disposition of individuals. Accordingly, they cannot be understood as subjective rights. Human rights are definitely a result of modern individualism, but disobedience of the law is an equally important result as well.

If more attention were paid to this problem, an important reason for the regional differentiation of law would come to light. The positive side of law, that is, differences between different 'legal cultures' in relation to norms and styles of interpretation, is not sufficient for a comparative sociology of law. The issue of structurally induced violations of law provides much better information, at least for sociology. Violations of law have their own logic, especially in modern society, and can serve as indicators of different social conditions—the problems of the welfare state, problems connected with dependency on organizations, the problems of inflation in regional economies, or the apparently increasing lack of motivation in individuals.

This shift of orientation towards including self-induced violations of law in the observation is already contained in the idea that law must be identified by its binary coding (and not by its state of perfection). However, in view of the phenomenal spread of, and regional variety in, the violations of law, this idea is also meaningful because a uniform global legal system could not otherwise be spoken of as the functioning system of a global society. I will say more on this in the following, final section.

V

Whatever concept of society is applied—whether the traditional concept of autarky (economic self-sufficiency), that is, autarky with the conditions for a perfect human life (happiness), or the closure of communicative operations—there cannot be any doubt that under current conditions there is only one single society: global society. As long as no sufficiently refined theory of society is available, this concept may have unclear contours.[34] However,

---

[34] This is pointed out, for example, by Kurt Tudyka, ' "Weltgesellschaft"—Unbegriff und Phantom', *Politische Vierteljahresschrift* 30 (1989), 503–8.

that is no reason to prefer the even less clear term 'international system', which leaves open what is meant by 'nation' and by 'inter'. Even if most sociologists refuse to bestow the label of society on this global system,[35] it is even more impossible to call national 'systems' (if the term system is at all appropriate here) social systems.[36] This definition has no criterion for delineation whatsoever, apart from territorial borders—and they are singularly unsuited to deal with this issue.

Neither in the regional framework nor in the global framework is similarity of living conditions an issue because then not even Manhattan would be a society. For our purposes the recursive network of communication is crucial—given: that languages can be translated and that there is a world-wide communication of media and 'private' communication networks; the unity of the cognitive efforts in the science system, despite any local or regional-cultural points of interests which may have arisen; the global economy based on credits with global markets for their most successful products; but also given the global political system, which makes states enter into indissoluble dependencies on each other and do this in view of the ecological consequences of modern warfare with the compelling logic of prevention and intervention.[37]

The frequently raised complaint about the post-colonial exploitation of peripheral countries by the industrial nations under the headings of dependency or marginality is, whatever one thinks of its substance, an argument for and not against global society. The worldwide interweaving of all functioning systems can hardly be disputed. Global society is defined by a primacy of functional differentiation in the context of system differentiation. Its economy cannot be controlled politically;[38] its science can be sponsored

---

[35] See particularly Talcott Parsons, *The System of Modern Societies* (Englewood Cliffs, 1971). Others speak about response to globalities or about trends towards globalization on the level of regional societies, as if global society was in the making but not yet achieved. See, for example, Roland Robertson and Frank Lechner, 'Modernization, Globalization and the Problem of Culture in World-Systems Theory', *Theory, Culture and Society* 11 (1985), 105–18; Margaret S. Archer, 'Foreword', in Martin Albrow and Elisabeth King (eds.), *Globalization, Knowledge and Society* (London, 1990), 1; Roland Robertson, 'Globality, Global Culture, and Images of the World Order', in Hans Haferkamp and Neil J. Smelser (eds.), *Social Change and Modernity* (Berkeley, 1992), 395–411; id., *Globalization* (London, 1992).

[36] Which is what, however, Anthony Giddens adamantly maintains with his departure point in political analysis, *The Nation-State and Violence* (Cambridge, 1985); id., *The Consequences of Modernity* (Stanford, 1990), 12.

[37] Only here would it be meaningful to view global society from the perspective of 'international relations', see for example John W. Burton, *World Society* (Cambridge, 1972).

[38] This is not only demonstrated by the implosion of the political reality of a 'socialist economy', but also by the economic failure of isolated national economies because of their political self-preference (for example, Brazil and Mexico), the loss of creditworthiness of nearly all the states in the international financial system (with considerable consequences for this system), or the gross underestimation of the economic consequences of the politically desirable

by the economy but not thereby made to produce results that are scientifically credible. The remarkable religious revivals of the last decades can be used politically (as happened during the Protestant Reformation), but not practised as politics. Functional differentiation, though, does not hold that there must be regional parity of development, let alone a convergent evolution. Especially if functioning systems are presupposed to be operatively closed autopoietic systems, their interdependent effects can be expected to result in quite different outcomes, depending on the global situation and the conditions they start from. Here, too, the insights of systems theory are valid (including its mathematical variants). They tell us that disturbances and fractures of the system can have very different consequences depending on the historical path of the development, positive or negative feedback, and regional particularities. A functionally differentiated society is anything but a harmonious society with inbuilt guarantees of stability.

The legal system of global society is in many respects a special case. It too is, of course, a worldwide functional system,[39] in which one can distinguish legal issues from all other issues in the regions, in which rules can be translated from one legal order to another, above all in international private law, and into which one can usually enter without having to worry that one will be treated as a lawless stranger.[40] Nor does one have to fear, in contrast to merchants in the High Middle Ages, that one will be held to ransom for the debts incurred by one's countrymen in a foreign country. A strong 'equal-finality' of legal institutions has also contributed to conditions where the institutions of different legal orders are more similar than might first be assumed. There is legislation, there is the difference between penal law and private law, there is property, there are contracts, there are legal proceedings, etc. However, in spite of these rather more formal similarities, enormous differences in the different regions of the globe cannot be overlooked and sociologists of law could well be asked how to describe and understand them. There cannot be any doubt that the global society has a legal order, even if it does not have central legislation and decision-making.[41]

German reunification. Politics can make decisions for valid political reasons but the consequences are decided in the economy.

[39] The majority of lawyers are of a different, 'dominant' opinion. See, for example, Werner Krawietz, *Recht als Rechtssystem* (Wiesbaden, 1984), esp. 51. But of course lawyers also have the courage to travel and to leave the territory in which their legal order is valid.

[40] There are exceptions—places where one cannot enter without special protection, for instance the favelas of the big Brazilian cities. And it cannot be ruled out that in the near future there may be states in which whites will be practically without legal protection.

[41] Occasionally this legal order is compared to the legal situation in tribal societies. See Michael Barkun, *Law without Sanction: Order in Primitive Societies and the World Community* (New Haven, 1968). But this hardly does justice to the instruments of modern legal relations. It is more appropriate to think of a society of economic citizens without a corresponding state, as for instance suggested in Gerhart Niemeyer, *Law without Force: The Function of Politics in*

Among the most important indicators of a global legal system is the increasing attention paid to the violation of human rights.[42] The idea of human rights (in the modern sense) developed with the demise of the old European natural law and in close connection with the construction of social contracts.[43] Until well into the eighteenth century, 'contract' was the form for the unfolding of the paradox of natural rights, namely, that they did not contain an exemption from themselves, thus making themselves absurd.[44] This only shifted the paradox and made it resurface in the construction of the contract. For now the validity of the contract, which is the basis of the rule that contracts are binding, can be justified only with a paradox. But it is precisely that paradox which provides this construction with its superiority compared with older natural law. For now the *validity* of the contract is based on the fact that one *renounces* one's natural rights in it.[45] With doctrines of social contracts providing the solution to the problem of the foundation of social order (in the sense of *pactum unionis* and not just *pactum subiectionis*), it became possible quasi-retrospectively to equip individuals who were required to make these contracts with natural rights, and then there remained only the problem of how to define the form of these

International Law (Princeton, 1941). Experiences with a stateless legal culture (supported by the law in foreign states) could also be gleaned from the 2,000 years of Judaic law. It can be seen how legal terms can be constructed (for instance based on the concept of duty and not on the concept of individual rights) and how political 'anarchy' cannot be considered to equal a lack of legal organization. See, for example, Robert M. Cover, 'The Folktales of Justice: Tales of Jurisdiction', *The Capital University Law Review* 14 (1985), 179–203. Evidently the foundations of this law in a religious and ethnic unity and with a common tradition of texts cannot be institutionalized worldwide.

[42] There is no lack of broad, descriptive studies of the development of this idea. See, for example, Günther Birtsch (ed.), *Grund- und Freiheitsrechte im Wandel von Gesellschaft und Geschichte: Beiträge zur Geschichte der Grund- und Freiheitsrechte vom Ausgang des Mittelalters bis zur Revolution von 1848* (Göttingen, 1981); id., *Grund- und Freiheitsrechte von der ständischen zur spätbürgerlichen Gesellschaft* (Göttingen, 1987), or, focusing more on contemporary issues, Ludger Kühnhardt, *Die Universalität der Menschenrechte: Studie zur ideengeschichtlichen Bestimmung eines politischen Schlüsselbegriffs* (Munich, 1987). The theoretical context, however, is left unclear. The use of the concept '*Mensch*' (human being) in the formulation of this legal idea would require a special analysis, which would be too far-ranging for our purposes. It must suffice here to recall with Foucault the semantic invention of the individual human being at the end of the eighteenth century and possibly the 'return of the human being' which appears so irresistible to philosophers—for instance in the re-anthropologization of the subject *c.*1800 or in the re-anthropologization of Heidegger's '*Dasein*' (being) in France. From a juridical point of view it is clear that this also includes foreigners.

[43] This is the generally accepted doctrine nowadays. See, for example, Gregorio Peces-Barba Martinez, *Tránsito a la modernidad y derechos fundamentales* (Madrid, 1982), esp. 159.

[44] In modern constitutions this function of the contract is taken up by the constitutional requirement of a specific enactment.

[45] For the reference of this idea to religious ideas of a sacrifice which was demanded and practised by God, see Peter Goodrich, *Languages of Law: From Logics of Memory to Nomadic Masks* (London, 1990), 56.

rights in their civil state. Pufendorf's attempt to combine very disparate ideas about the original natural state (Grotius, Hobbes, Spinoza) into one theory led to formulations which gave rise to the idea of human (but not necessarily anti-social) rights by birth. This made it possible to undercut traditional distinctions or to present them as mere products of private law. For instance, there were no longer human beings with and human beings without *dignitas*, as in the tradition of aristocratic societies, but human dignity was now seen as a characteristic of every human being and thus became a barrier for the differentiated performance of private law.[46]

When these contractual constructs were criticized and rejected as a result of the deepening historical consciousness in the second half of the eighteenth century, it was thought that a solution to the problem could be found in the textualization and positivization of individual rights as required by state law—either in the form of special Bills of Rights, or in declarations of recognition or, finally, in constitutional laws proper.[47] This solution is no longer a convincing one. Its problem is that it enacts supposed meta-positive law as positive law, which cannot be adequately explained by the advantages it offers of having texts available for interpretation. Its great disadvantage is that the whole apparatus of text-based validity can be translated onto the level of a global legal system only with great difficulty and with many inadequacies. The legal system remains state law or law based on treaties between states. Accordingly, states are expected to be responsible for their compliance with human rights on their territories and the rights themselves appear as a requirement of state legislation and state law enforcement.

There is no lack of texts, conventions, resolutions, or of positive expressions of opinion in the literature.[48] The extensive debate on the controversy between Universalists and Relativists led no one to contest the point of having some ultimate legal protection against the arbitrariness of states.[49] Indeed, that idea arose in Europe in parallel with the formation of

[46] Samuel Pufendorf formulates 'in ipso hominis vocabulo iudicatur inesse aliqua dignatio', *De jure naturae et gentium libri octo* 3.II.I. quoted from the 1744 Frankfurt-Leipzig edition, Vol. I at 313. See also with the same words id., *De officio hominis & civis iuxta legem naturalem libri duo* I.VII. (Cambridge, 1735), 143. It is striking, and indicates a conscious attempt at differentiation, that the word used is '*dignatio*' and not '*dignitas*'.

[47] For the German version, which picked up these ideas after the French Revolution and again expected a solution from 'natural law' because there was no prospect of a revolution and a constitution, see Diethelm Klippel, *Politische Freiheit und Freiheitsrechte im deutschen Naturrecht des 18. Jahrhunderts* (Paderborn, 1976), 178.

[48] See for an overview, for example, Wolfgang Heidelmeyer (ed.), *Die Menschenrechte: Erklärungen, Verfassungsartikel, Internationale Abkommen*, 2nd edn. (Paderborn, 1977).

[49] See Louis Henkin, *The Rights of Man Today* (Boulder, 1978), 129: 'Cultural differences . . . cannot explain or justify barbarism and repression', quoted from Kühnhardt, *Die Universalität der Menschenrechte*, 140.

the modern territorial state and it is this *difference*, not necessarily the historical argumentation based on natural law, which has become more pressing as the global extension of the form of statehood in political systems has spread worldwide rather than being confined to the relatively uniform cultural conditions in pre-constitutional Europe. Particularly in the global perspective it is evident how meaningful it is to differentiate the political system by region in order to relate it more effectively to local conditions and to utilize the chances for consensus better. It is also evident how unbearable it would be to leave the legal system in the control of arbitrary, regional, political processes. The discrepancy between politics and law, which first appeared in Europe with the formation of the modern state, is spreading and takes a vastly different form.

In this situation, human rights law hardly appears to benefit from the clarity of its basic principles and the precision of the relevant texts, but from the evidence of human rights violations. In view of all sorts of horrific scenes, no further discussion is necessary.[50] Exactly which norms and, above all, which texts should be referred to in this context cannot be said with any certainty.[51] To a considerable degree the liberal tradition of bourgeois society and its constitutional law continues. Basic rights such as freedom and equality are still recognized—but with full knowledge of how much they can be modified by legislation and how little they reflect real situations.[52] As we mentioned before,[53] basic laws serve the purpose of creating and unfolding a paradox in the system by introducing a self-reference into it, thus acquiring practical significance only as positive law. Where this liberal tradition is transgressed—and nowadays this happens dramatically in the area of 'collective rights', especially the right to independence and self-determination of nations, ethnic groups, and ethnic groups in the territory of other ethnic groups—one ventures into uncharted terrain and here, once more, violence is the ultimate arbiter.

One reason for this highly unsatisfactory situation is the development of the welfare state after the Second World War, which affected the formulation of human rights. Today, human rights are understood increasingly not only as protective rights but also as supportive rights, especially in particularly

---

[50] It may appear cynical today, but if one considers Kant's theory and his critique on sound judgement in the context of his three critiques, one could also appeal to the effectiveness of sound judgement in relation to 'legal taste', in order to make it clear that this is neither a merely cognitive issue nor one of the application of practical postulates in the form of moral law.

[51] And this does not change simply by the UN passing resolutions.

[52] Following Hasso Hofman, 'Menschenrechtliche Autonomieansprüche: Zum politischen Gehalt der Menschenrechtserklärungen', *Juristenzeitung* 47 (1992), 165–73, at 171, one can detect in these modifications and in the links of human rights with the rule of law the crucial meaning of their positivization, which goes beyond natural law.

[53] See above Ch. 5.IV.

crass situations of undersupply. The basis for this development is an anthropological concept that attributes to human beings in general (independent of regional and cultural differentiations) a composite of material and spiritual needs and interests, even interests in personal development and self-realization.[54] In relation to them, crass discrepancies in supply chances and life chances can be marked as 'exemplary experiences of social injustice' and made the point of departure for the question of the criteria for delineation.[55] Broadening the issue in such a way, however, entails the danger of inflating the discussion and making it an ideological one.[56] Furthermore, the problem arises that the addressees of law are no longer people who break the law *stricto sensu* but the people who can provide help. The problem of human rights fuses with an immense expansion in the demand for social work and development aid. The difference between the economy (provision) and social help (care) can no longer be translated into clear, enforceable legal claims in view of the great variety of regional differences. The inflation of this symbolic medium ruins its value, and any really crass, shocking, active incursions into the sphere of the unconditional need for protection—the key term here is human dignity—no longer stand out if it begins to appear normal that human rights will not be taken seriously.[57]

In view of this problem, attention appears to shift to the global *violation* of human rights *when these violations are particularly severe*, such as officially condoned disappearances, deportations and expulsions by force, illegal killings, arrests and tortures with the knowledge of or under the protection of state bodies. The guarantee of a functioning rule of law is, then, the functional equivalent of the recognition of human rights and, at the same time, makes them almost superfluous in a technical, legal sense.[58] Only where the rule of law is not secured and states are unable or unwilling to deal with offences against human rights by normal legal means are such

---

[54] The (juridical) inadequacy of such anthropological reasons has not gone unnoticed. See, for example, Eibe H. Riedel, *Theorie der Menschenrechtsstandards* (Berlin, 1986), 205 and 346.

[55] See Winfried Brugger, 'Menschenrechte im modernen Staat', *Archiv des öffentlichen Rechts* 114 (1989), 537–88; id., 'Stufen der Begründung von Menschenrechten', *Der Staat* 31 (1992), 19–38. [56] See Brugger, 'Stufen', 30.

[57] For similar reasons Heiner Bielefeldt recommends that the discussion concentrates on the issue of the violations of human dignity, see 'Die Menschenrechte als Chance in der pluralistischen Weltgesellschaft', *Zeitschrift für Rechtspolitik* 21 (1988), 423–31.

[58] This is vaguely reminiscent of the thesis in Kant's work on eternal peace ('*Zum ewigen Frieden*') that international peace can only be expected from a federation of republican states, that is, states that are based on the rule of law. Because this argument refers to the rights of individuals, it runs counter to the widely held opinion that world peace is to be achieved as an 'international' order by treaties between states. On the relevance of this concept for the present, see Fernando R. Tesón, 'The Kantian Theory of International Law', *Columbia Law Review* 92 (1991), 53–102.

offences actually perceived as being violations of *human rights*. Because such violations are widespread—if not to say normal in the majority of countries—the problem is not related, primarily, to the unequivocal nature of the texts which could make a decision between legal and illegal possible. For the time being it is enough to draw attention to the worst cases. At the same time, the problem is shifting away from classic, modern legal thought. On the one hand, it is no longer enough to refer to the positive law of states (for instance, in the form of constitutions) because positive law can also be used to cover up violations of human rights or to make kidnapping and breaches of international law possible, as for instance in the decision of the US Supreme Court in the case of Álvarez Marchain (1992).[59] On the other hand, it is not enough to see human rights as subjective rights, thus leaving them to the individual to invoke, or not, because under particular political circumstances this decision cannot be made freely.[60] This would suggest that the system of global law should not be constructed on the basis of rights but of duties. Finally, sanctions remain a problem. It will become unacceptable that an individual state, even if it is the United States, conducts itself as judge and sanctioning power (when it has itself refused to be subjected to the Inter-American Court of Human Rights[61]). On the contrary, there is likely to be an increasingly international focus on this problem, probably also in connection with development aid. With the end of the Cold War, new perspectives have developed regarding this.

One can only talk about extremely severe human rights violations with respect to human dignity. Limitations of people's right to freedom and equality are so normal and so indispensable that the legal order of states must be given a large degree of latitude (through special enactment). The issue here is not principally the unity of a norm (idea, value) but the paradox of forms for the distinctions between freedom/restriction and equality/inequality, which can be unfolded quite differently in different legal regimes. Or, in other words: at issue are the perspectives of the future that converge in the unknown. Nevertheless, there appears to be a specific sensitivity that is taking root globally. It can be recognized in cases in which *asymmetries of roles become fixed and are treated as irreversible by a reference*

[59] It should be added: because there is no basis in positive law that allows the illegality of kidnapping to be adduced as an objection in domestic state courts. This case demonstrates more than clearly that the rule of law is no protection against 'outrageous' results. The turbulent state of global law is particularly clear in this case: the translation of international law into domestic law is rejected, that is, violations of law are treated as legal because otherwise the implementation of law itself could not be achieved.

[60] Also Hofman, 'Menschenrechtliche Autonomieansprüche', 166 doubts that the characteristics of human rights equal those of subjective rights, but he uses other arguments to present this view.

[61] See the first *Annual Report of the Inter-American Court of Human Rights 1989* (Washington, 1989).

to outside.[62] This applies particularly to cases in which race is used as a criterion for the allocation of roles (especially with reference to the allocation of life or death, hunger or proper food). Religiously or ideologically inspired systems also have this tendency to make the allocation of role-specific opportunities dependent on a factor that cannot be controlled in the roles themselves. Role-asymmetries, which to modern understanding are acceptable only in functioning systems (physician and patient, producer and consumer, plaintiff and defendant in relation to the judge, etc.), are generalized by a reference to outside, so generating structural disadvantages which pervade transversally very different functioning systems. The offensive nature of these disadvantages to our modern understanding is more related to structure than to individual cases. Therefore the grounds for outrage and intervention are hard to pinpoint and it is difficult to distinguish them from what is acceptable. However, it appears that at least the standpoint of race is clearly seen as a violation of human rights.

In a brief summary of the development of the doctrine of human rights, what is at issue, it can be said, is always the unfolding of a fundamental paradox, which was defined historically by the relation between individuals and law. The doctrine of social contract presented a circular argument: the fact that the contracting individuals were bound by the contract could only be explained by the contract. The doctrines of natural law also remained circular because the nature of the human being was referred to only in cases in which a violation was claimed and a corresponding norm sought. That meta-positive law is in dire need of positivization is an open paradox, which is barely disguised by purely pragmatic considerations about the usefulness of written texts. And, of course, it is also a paradox to say that rights are implemented only by their violation and the corresponding outrage (Durkheim's *colère publique*). But perhaps it is exactly *this* paradox that is the *appropriate* one for the turbulent, global conditions of our times, particularly in view of the loss of relevance of the old state orders of the classical type. However, when *every* notion of reasons founders on a paradox, this also marks the end of the discussion concerning the relevance of the specific European tradition. A global society, which is scandalized sufficiently by gross failures could be expected to establish a structure of legal norms, independent of regional traditions and the political interests of regional states.

Considered in the round, the establishment of global law will not do away with different regional developments in law. One of its most important triggers is the segmental, secondary differentiation of the global political system into 'states', that is, into political systems specializing in the state organization of collectively binding decisions. The result is that the structural coupling of the political system and the legal system through

---

[62] I am indebted to Vessela Misheva who expressed this idea in a manuscript.

constitutions does not have an equivalent at the level of global society. This alone, however, does not explain why there are so many divergent developments that can go so far as to throw doubt on the functionality and the differentiation of orientation by law.

One has a suspicion that the initial problem is that large parts of the population are not included in the communication of functioning systems, or, to put it another way, that there is a stark difference between inclusion and exclusion that, while it is produced by functional differentiation, is incompatible with it and ultimately undermines it.[63] Owing to a lack of other terminology, sociologists tend to present this situation as a pronounced form of social stratification, or even as an internationally operating 'class society'. However, these concepts refer to a social order which is recognized or accepted and which serves inclusion (even if it is extremely uneven) because it is order.[64] The ranking of families and their households (including dependants) or the organisation of manufacturing in the nineteenth century can be viewed as a model for class society. The pronounced difference between inclusion and exclusion has far graver consequences, for under the regime of functional differentiation each functioning system controls social inclusion by itself and what is left of the old stratified order can only be differentiated according to the schema of inclusion/exclusion. The problem is compounded with rampant urbanization and the demolition of all certainties that were provided by a largely non-monetary self-sufficient economy. Everyone affected by this problem is now dependent on the money economy, without being able to participate in it to any appreciable degree. Criminality and/or participation in criminal organizations must take the place of self-sufficiency economics.

Undoubtedly one cannot say that under such circumstances there is no longer any law (there never have been societies without law). It would also

---

[63] Inclusion is defined by Talcot Parsons thus: 'This refers to the pattern of action in question, or complex of such patterns, and the individuals and/or groups who act in accord with that pattern coming to be accepted in a status of more or less full membership in a wider solitary social system', in 'Commentary on Clark', in Andrew Effart (ed.), *Perspectives in Political Sociology* (Indianapolis, n.d.) 299–308, at 306.

[64] The traditional reflexion of this stratification-specific inclusion was conducted partly following the criteria of the anthropological characteristics of the human being (above all reason) which are shared by all human beings, regardless of their social position, and partly in line with a philosophy of happiness which was available to all human beings through God's will. The latter was particularly the case in the eighteenth century in a situation of transition to other principles of inclusion, which were then circumscribed with freedom and equality. See, for example, on the happiness of the peasant and on the reflexion of the upper classes on the limits of their happiness, the chapter 'Conversation avec un laboureur' in Jean Blondel, *Des hommes tels qu'ils sont et doivent être: Ouvrage de sentiment* (London and Paris, 1758), 119. However, stratification was always presupposed as a schema for inclusion in all of this, while exclusion was determined by membership/non-membership in a family or family household.

be wrong to assume that positive law could not be applied or that international relations, traffic, trade, etc., lack a basis in law. A description of the phenomena must start from a much more differentiated approach. What is probably the best approach is to use the hypothesis that the difference between inclusion and exclusion functions as a kind of meta-code, which mediates between all other codes. The difference between legal and illegal certainly exists and there are legislative programmes (statutes) that regulate how the values of legal or illegal are attributed to facts. But this question is of little importance to the excluded groups of the population compared with what is imposed on them by this exclusion. They are treated legally or illegally and accordingly conduct themselves legally or illegally, depending on their situation and opportunities. The same applies to those who are included and, in particular, to the politicians and the staff of bureaucracies. And again: this is not a question of social stratification, which would provide ordering substitutes for law, but is directed at undermining the legal order proper. Whether law is applied or not cannot be known *and even the attribution of communication to the schema inclusion/exclusion does not change that* because legal or illegal behaviour can be chosen regardless of the 'label' on both sides of this schema (even if in a very different, 'fatal' way).[65] In other words, the difference between coding and programming does not function or functions only at a reduced rate because other preferences come first. The dominance of the distinction inclusion/exclusion changes the expectations that sociologists usually associate with the concept of integration (and thus often with law).[66] If integration is defined as the limitation of the degrees of freedom of the integrated parts, it is immediately obvious that the area of exclusion, in particular, functions in a *highly integrated* way. Negative integration in society is nearly perfect. Those who have no address cannot send their children to school. Those who have no registration certificates cannot marry or apply for social aid. Illiterate persons, whether formally excluded or not, are prevented from participating in politics. Exclusion from one functional area prevents inclusion in others. In contrast, inclusion makes a *lesser* integration possible, which means more freedom, *thus* corresponding to the logic of functional differentiation. Functional differentiation requires a loose coupling of the functional systems, and a curb on inferring the role of one from that of another. In this lie opportunities for the violation of law and for corruption. The opportunities that are provided by inclusion can be turned into personal advantages, upward mobility, and careers.

---

[65] For support from the relationship of Brazilian politics with its constitutional law, see Marcelo Neves, *Verfassung und Positivität des Rechts in der peripheren Moderne: Eine theoretische Betrachtung und eine Interpretation des Falles Brasilien* (Berlin, 1992).

[66] We have already dealt with these expectations of the function of law in Ch. 3.I.

To a certain extent this is normal. If, however, the inclusion of some depends on the exclusion of others, this difference undermines the normal functioning of functioning systems. This affects law, especially, for the legal system is based not only on the sanctions of the system, on sentencing and punishment, but also on the society-wide resonance of breaches of law, which is an additional motivation for obeying the law. There is nothing to lose in the highly integrated area of exclusion, apart from control over one's own body. In the poorly integrated areas of inclusion, the consequences of legality or illegality are non-transferable and there is nothing to be gained from paying attention to decisions on such values under the direction of law-specific programmes. In (the not so rare) extreme cases it is even irrelevant to politics and politicians' reputations whether they act legally or illegally. The organization of the administration of force, that is, the police, is also guided primarily by status, which is provided by inclusion or exclusion and not by law. To deduce from that the irrelevance or stalling of the legal system would be an exaggeration (apart from dealing with the case of acute civil war). However, whether or not and for which reasons legal coding is used depends on another difference, namely the difference between inclusion and exclusion.

Seen from the perspective of policies for developing countries, it might appear as if the exclusion of large parts of the population from participation in the advantages of development is only a transient condition of development. It could be said that not all can share the advantages of modern societies instantly and at the same time. The question remains, however, whether the worldwide realization of the currently high level of welfare found in some industrial countries is at all possible—for ecological reasons alone.

The high dependence of all autopoietic systems on history also has to be considered. Autopoietic systems always lever their operations on conditions that already exist as a structure. Hence they can work equally well towards an amplification of deviance (positive feedback) or curbing of deviation (with negative feedback). After all, the currently dominant system of the structural weighting of functioning systems cannot be assumed to remain the same in the long run. In contrast to Parsons's theory of a general system of action, we find functional differentiation to be a product of evolution and not a logical consequence of the analysis of the concept of action. Therefore it may well be that the current prominence of the legal system and the dependence of society itself and of most of its functional systems on a functioning legal coding are nothing but a European anomaly, which might well level off with the evolution of global society.

Index